**Bibliotheca Persica**

Columbia Lectures
on Iranian Studies
Number 3

# Persian Literature

***Bibliotheca Persica*** consists of:

*Persian Heritage Series,* devoted to translations of Persian
    classics
*Persian Studies Series,* monographs on Iranian studies
*Modern Persian Literature Series,* devoted to translations of
    modern Persian writings
*Columbia Lectures on Iranian Studies*
*Tabarī Translation,* an annotated translation of
    al-Tabarī's *History*
*Persian Texts Series,* critical editions of Persian texts

### Columbia Lecture Series

The Columbia Lectures on Iranian Studies are intended to
serve as a vehicle for the presentation of original research or
synthesis in Iranian history and culture by distinguished
scholars.

Columbia Lectures on Iranian Studies

Edited by Ehsan Yarshater

Number 3

# Persian Literature

edited by
**Ehsan Yarshater**
Columbia University

Bibliotheca Persica

Published by

The Persian Heritage Foundation under
the imprint of Bibliotheca Persica

© 1988 The Persian Heritage Foundation

Printed in the United States of America

**For information, address State University of New York
Press, State University Plaza, Albany, N.Y., 12246**

**Library of Congress Cataloging-in-Publication Data**

Persian literature / edited by Ehsan Yarshater.
  (Columbia lectures on Iranian studies: no. 3)
  "Select bibliography of translations from Persian literature"; p. 499
Includes index.
  ISBN 0–88706–263–6.  ISBN 0–88706–264–4 (pbk.)
  1. Persian literature—History and criticism.  I. Yar-Shater,
Ehsan.  II. Series.
PK6097.P47  1987
891'.55'09—dc19                                             87–16613
                                                              CIP


10  9  8  7  6  5  4  3  2  1

# Contents

# Contents

# Editorial Note

The present volume, which follows in the wake of *Highlights of Persian Art*,[1] grew out of a series of lectures delivered between 1974 and 1976 at Columbia University's Center for Iranian Studies. A number of contributors were invited later to complete the original design.

The focus of inquiry in this volume is imaginative literature; the treatment of the subject is thematic rather than chronological, generic rather than biographical. The historical development of Persian literature can be seen, however, through the discussion of the various genres and styles. Moreover, the introductory essay seeks to place the various phases of the literatures of Iran in perspective and to expand upon some areas of interest not fully treated in the ensuing chapters, notably Old and Middle Persian literatures. Furthermore, the chapter on Indian style attempts to explain the progression of the classical tradition from a robust start to an effete old age before a new beginning is made. Occasionally the reader may find that a work has been discussed or a point elaborated by more than one author. It is hoped that the difference of outlook will be found of interest, rather than redundant.

A number of significant writers have been highlighted in separate chapters: Ferdowsi, Khayyām, Nezāmi, Rumi, Sa'di and Hāfez, Iqbāl, Hedāyat, and Farrokhzād. In such chapters an effort has been made to bring out the formative elements and the essential qualities of the works of the writers, rather than to linger on the minute details of their lives. A chapter on Nimā may appear to be missing, but despite his unmistakable importance as the founder of the modernist school of Persian poetry, he is hardly comparable in readability and attractiveness to Farrokhzād, nor can he match Nāderpur in poetic imagination, linguistic aptitude, and verbal and musical elegance. Nimā's significance, however, as well as the impact of Shāmlu's innovative spirit and experiments, have been made clear in the chapter on modern poetry. Sepehri receives ample treatment in the same chapter.

Traditional prose literature has received only brief treatment, chiefly in the introductory chapter, for reasons that are explained there. If the aim had been to treat Persian "writing" rather than creative "literature" in a narrow sense, then classical Persian prose would have required fuller treatment.

[1]Richard Ettinghausen and Ehsan Yarshater, eds. (Bibliotheca Persica, 1982; this book bears the imprint of its originally intended distributor, Westview Press, 1979.)

The word "Persian" in the title of the volume has been used in a broad sense to denote all literatures produced in Iran and Iranian-speaking lands, including Avestan and Parthian, which are not, linguistically speaking, Persian. A more accurate title would have been the less familiar and perhaps not so felicitous "Iranian Literatures."

Four chapters have been devoted to the Persian literature of the Indian subcontinent, Afghanistan, and Tajikistan in order to do justice to the literatures produced outside of the political boundaries of Iran. The subcontinent was for many centuries a second home to Persian literature; indeed, it would not be much of an exaggeration to call it the primary home of Persian letters during the seventeenth and eighteenth centuries. And many of the major writers and poets of the Persian language rose from Afghanistan and what is today Soviet Central Asia. It may be noted that the most significant poet in Persian in modern times was Iqbāl of Lahore (d. 1938), and the ablest living Persian poet in the traditional style is Khalili of Kabul. Thus classical Persian letters are the product of many lands and ethnic groups which shared a common tradition. In the twentieth century, however, differing political circumstances and outlooks have made for considerable variety in the literature of these lands. The chapters on the Persian literature of Afghanistan and Tajikistan seek to place the literary products of these areas in the context of their political and intellectual history.

The chapter on Persian literature in translation is designed to help students and other interested readers who want a taste of Persian literature but do not know Persian. Bibliographical references are generally given in the footnotes; in the case of only a few chapters did the authors deem it necessary to provide separate bibliographies.

In the transliteration of Persian and Arabic words, a simple scheme indicating only long *a* (*ā*), *ʿayn*, and *hamza* by diacritical marks has been used, but rigorous transliterations of all proper names and foreign words have been furnished in the index for the benefit of those interested.

A volume composed of contributions by many experts does not have the same degree of evenness and unified organization as can be expected in a book written by a single author. On the other hand, this volume condenses in its chapters the scholarship and expertise of many specialists, thus offering a more authoritative presentation of various aspects of Persian literature than can be expected from a single scholar. The Editor, while observing a strict editorial policy in the overall design of the chapters, has considered the application of too restrictive a policy on outlook and expression counterproductive. The introductory essay, however, attempts to take up the themes expanded in the various chapters and to construct a cohesive view of the development of Persian literature from earliest times to the present.

In the last section of the book will be found an annotated selection of translations from Persian literature for the benefit of those who would like to gain familiarity with the subject but do not know Persian.

Most of the chapters were written in the mid- to late-1970s, and some as late as 1984. I am grateful to the early contributors for their forbearance with the slow process of publication.

Ehsan Yarshater
Editor

# Abbreviations and Short Titles

| | |
|---|---|
| *ADAW* | *Abhandlungen der Deutschen Akademie der Wissenschaften* |
| *AMI* | *Archäologische Mitteilungen aus Iran* |
| *AO* | *Acta Orientalia* |
| E. G. Browne, *Lit. Hist.* | Edward G. Browne, *A Literary History of Persia* (Cambridge, 1929) |
| *BSOAS* | *Bulletin of the School of Oriental and African Studies* |
| Cam. Hist. of Iran | *The Cambridge History of Iran* (Cambridge, 1968– ) |
| Gibb, *Ott. Poetry* | E. J. W. Gibb, *A History of Ottoman Poetry* (London, 1900) |
| *HO* | *Handbuch der Orientalistik* (Leiden and Cologne) |
| *JA* | *Journal Asiatique* |
| Rypka, *Iran. Lit.* | J. Rypka, *History of Iranian Literature* (Dordrecht, 1968) |
| *SI* | *Studia Islamica* |
| *TPS* | *Transactions of the Philological Society* |
| *SPAW* | *Sitzungsberichte der Preussischen Akademie der Wissenschaften* |
| *ZDMG* | *Zeitschrift der Deutschen Morgenländischen Gesellschaft* |

# I. INTRODUCTORY SURVEY

# 1. The Development of Iranian Literatures

## Historical Perspective

In the course of the seventh century Persia was overrun by victorious Muslim armies, and the Sasanian Empire (A.D. 226–652), fabled for the splendor of its court, crumbled. The conquest proved to be far more than military, for it introduced a new religion into Persia and opened an entirely new chapter in Iranian history. The country whose soldiers had subdued faraway Yemen, captured Jerusalem, and marched to the gates of Constantinople only a few decades earlier, now came under the aegis of the caliphs and was ruled by Arab governors for some two hundred years before it could assert its identity again. In the meantime the majority of the Persians, particularly in urban centers, converted to Islam. With conversion came a new spirit and a new social order. As the unity of the overwhelming and transcendent Allah was impressed upon the converts, the characteristic belief in the dualism of the Iranian religion disappeared. Gone, too, were the class distinctions which had been the backbone of Sasanian social and political organization. The powerful Zoroastrian church was reduced to a marginal institution catering to the spiritual needs of a declining community. The remaining Zoroastrians watched in amazement and despair as their erstwhile brethren buried their dead, desecrated fire, offended dogs, and faced Mecca for their prayers.

The Islamization of Persia brought about such deep and enduring transformations in the life and culture of the country that some Persians began to regard their pre-Islamic past as a pagan era which had ended with the fall of the Sasanian Empire. The advent of Islam indeed marked a unique turning point in the life of the Persian people; however, it would be an error to view the change as too drastic. There were powerful links between the pre- and post-Islamic eras of Persian history. Changes which appeared radical at first, proved to be less trenchant as the old habits and traditional modes of thought returned in a new guise. Many of the old religious beliefs and practices found a home within "Iranian Islam," to borrow Henry Corbin's phrase. Popular religion, in particular, preserved many aspects of old religious thought and practice, albeit with different terminology. People continued to expect a savior who would rise one day, punish the wicked, and fill the world with justice. They continued traditional practices: visited sacred shrines, revered the spirit of the dead, and knotted pieces of rags to the branches of sacred trees for boons. They avoided scattering their fallen teeth and pared nails for fear of contaminating the good earth, took great care in ritual purification, and uttered a benediction when candles or lamps were lighted. But now they called the Soshyant, their expected messiah, "Mahdi," named the Chinvat Bridge to be crossed by the dead on the Day of Judgment "Pol-e Serāt," and replaced Mashya and Mashyāna with Adam and Eve.

The most effective link between the two periods of Persian history, however, was a linguistic one. Most of the countries that were conquered by the Arab armies in the first century of Islam, when the new religion was at the height of its drive, lost their language to Arabic and eventually shed their previous identities, becoming "Arab." Such was the case with Iraq, Syria, Egypt, and much of North Africa. Persia was a notable exception: although conquered completely and absorbed inextricably into the Muslim world, it nonetheless retained its language and its identity.

The Sasanians had strongly promoted the language of their homeland Persis (Fārs), making it the official tongue of their empire. This language, called Middle Persian in modern scholarship, continued to be used in Iran after the Islamic conquest; it underwent some gradual changes and emerged in the ninth century as the language of a "renaissance" in Persian literature. In the process, its grammar had become simpler, it had borrowed some vocabulary from Arabic, and it had shed a number of words with Zoroastrian connotations or else adapted such words to the prevailing Islamic environment. It is through this later language, called New Persian (or simply Persian) that the literary gifts of the Iranians found their major channel of expression.

The term "renaissance" implies an earlier period of literary activity, and indeed the early Persian poets and writers owed much to the literature which had flourished in pre-Islamic Iran. The greatest monument of Persian language and literature, the *Shāh-nāma* (Book of kings) of Ferdowsi (completed ca. A.D. 1000), although the work of a literary genius, is in substance the reworking of the national saga compiled and committed to writing in Middle Persian toward the end of the Sasanian period.

Middle Persian was itself an outgrowth of Old Persian, which was the language of the Achaemenians (559–330 B.C.) and which was spoken in the southern province of Persis (Fārs). Together with a number of cognate Iranian tongues, like Median and Avestan, it belonged to the Indo-Iranian branch of the Indo-European family of languages. Iranian languages were introduced into the Iranian plateau by waves of invading Aryans from the Eurasian steppes in the late second millennium B.C. The vigor and energy of the Aryan tribes who had occupied northern Iran led to the formation of the Median kingdom (ca. 670–559 B.C.); soon after, the Achaemenian Empire rose from the south and became the largest and most powerful empire that the world had yet experienced. In its heyday it stretched from India to the Sudan and Libya in North Africa, and from the southern shores of the Persian Gulf to the Eurasian steppes.

In the northeast lived other Iranian peoples, identified generally by the languages they spoke. Among one such people, possibly centered in the vicinity of the city of Marv (now in Soviet Turkmenistan) or Herat (in Afghanistan), rose Zoroaster, a prophet inspired to reform the ancient Iranian religion with a fresh and strong moral direction. The dates of his life are disputed, the best estimates ranging between 1100 and 600 B.C. Since their exact habitat is not certain, Zoroaster's people are called Avestan, after Avesta, the holy scripture of the Zoroastrians. However, the tales of adventure and heroism that were to evolve into the Iranian national epic first emerged among the Avestan people and their related tribes long before Zoroaster.

## Old Iranian Literature*

We have few literary remains from the ancient Persians. Most of these consist of the royal inscriptions of the Achaemenian kings, notably Darius I (522–486 B.C.) and his son Xerxes. Old Persian, the language of these inscriptions, is an inflected tongue like Greek and Latin and shares many linguistic features with its close relatives, Avestan and Sanskrit. Old Persian inscriptions were engaged chiefly to record the deeds of the "king of kings" or to commemorate the foundation of a building. They have a declaratory, direct and unadorned style, and are laced with repetitive set-phrases, a style common to the genre in the entire ancient Middle East. A typical opening statement of longer Achaemenian inscriptions can be seen in the inscription of Darius I at Naqsh-e Rostam (DNa, 1–15) in Persis. It tells us something about this monarch's faith, as well as his pride in his ancestry and race:

A great god is Ahura Mazda, who created the earth, who created

---

*In this introductory chapter Old and Middle Persian literatures are treated more fully, since they are not discussed separately in later chapters.

the sky, who created man, who created happiness for man, who made Darius king . . . I am Darius, the Great King, the King of Kings, king of countries containing all kinds of men, king of this great earth far and wide, son of Hystaspes, an Achaemenian, a Persian, son of a Persian, and Aryan, having Aryan lineage.

In another inscription (DNb, 5–21) we have an instance of Darius's comments on his rule, his temper, and his moral objectives:

Says Darius the King: by the favor of Ahura Mazda I am such a man who is friend to right; I am not a friend to wrong. It is not my wish that the weak man should have wrong done to him by the mighty; nor is it my wish that the mighty man should have wrong done to him by the weak. What is right, that is my wish. I am not a friend to the man who follows the lie;[1] I am not quick-tempered; things which develop in my anger I hold firmly under control by my thinking power. I am firmly in control of my own [impulses]. The man who cooperates, I reward him according to his cooperation. He who does harm, him I punish according to the damage. It is not my wish that a man should do harm; nor is it my wish that he who does harm should go unpunished.

The same theme is expressed toward the end of Darius's Great Inscription at Bistun (DB IV, 61–67).

The most interesting story that Darius tells concerns the episodes which led to his killing the pretender Gaumāta and assuming royal powers—events which, in effect, transferred the line of kingship from Cyrus to a parallel Achaemenian line. The story is related in greater detail by Herodotus (i. 61–79), who essentially agrees with Darius's presentation. We hear it from the mouth of Darius himself (DB I, 26–71) as a specimen of the Achaemenian recording of history:

Says Darius the King: This is what was done by me after I had become king. Cyrus's son, Cambyses by name, of our family, was king here. Cambyses had a co-parental brother by the name of Smerdis. Cambyses slew Smerdis. When Cambyses slew Smerdis it did not become known to the people that Smerdis had been slain. Then Cambyses went to Egypt. When Cambyses had gone off to Egypt, the people became evil. Then the lie waxed great

[1]In Iranian religion hypostatized as an archdemon.

6

in the country, both in Persia and in Media and in the other provinces.

Says Darius the King: Then there was a man, a Magian, Gaumāta by name, who rose up from Paishiyāuvādā. . . . He lied to the people thus: "I am Smerdis the son of Cyrus, brother of Cambyses." Then all the people rebelled against Cambyses and went over to him, both Persia and Media and the other provinces. He seized the kingdom. . . . After that Cambyses died by his own hand. Says Darius the King: This kingdom which Gaumāta the Magian took away from Cambyses from long ago belonged to our family. . . . Then Gaumāta the Magian took it from Cambyses, he took to himself both Persia and Media and the other provinces. . . . He became king.

Says Darius the King: There was not a man, neither a Persian nor a Mede nor anyone of our family, who might deprive Gaumāta the Magian of the kingdom. The people feared him greatly, [thinking that] he would slay in numbers the people who had previously known Smerdis. He would slay people "lest they know me, that I am not Smerdis son of Cyrus."[2] No one dared say anything about Gaumāta the Magian until I arrived. Then I besought help of Ahura Mazda; Ahura Mazda bore me aid; of the month of Bagayādi ten days were past when I, with a few men, slew Gaumāta the Magian and those who were his foremost followers. A fortress by name of Sikayauvati [in] the district of Nisāya in Media—there I slew him. I took the kingdom from him. By the favor of Ahura Mazda I became king; Ahura Mazda bestowed the kingdom upon me.[3]

We have no direct record of the myths, legends, and stories of the ancient Persians, or of their poetry, since this literature was orally transmitted and was eventually lost or absorbed by the oral literature of eastern Iran (see below). So, too, was the literature of the Medians, the erstwhile masters of the Persians. The case is different with the Avestan people, who produced the most notable religious and literary monument that we have in writing from ancient Iran, namely the Avesta. This book contains not only a number of hymns by Zoroaster himself (the Gathas), but also hymns (Yashts) inherited from the pre-

---

[2]The use of the first person rather than the third in such quotations is common to Old and Middle Persian style.

[3]The translations of Darius's inscription are taken, with some modifications, from R. G. Kent, *Old Persian*, 2nd ed. (New Haven, 1953), 119, 120–21, 132, 140.

Zoroastrian past and addressed to various Iranian deities. Frequently displaying a remarkable poetic quality, the Yashts describe with moving eloquence lofty mountains, rolling rivers, refreshing rains, and green pastures, as well as radiant, all-powerful deities (yazatas, izads) and virtuous, brave heroes.

## Epic Literature of Ancient Iran

The most significant literary heritage of ancient Iran, however, is the heroic poetry which eventually evolved into the Iranian national epic. The core of this poetry belongs to a heroic age of remote antiquity, that of the Kayanians. Under this dynasty, whose history is wrapped in legend, the ancestors of the Avestan people offered worship and sacrifice to a broad range of deities who often symbolized the forces of nature. Grappling with the hazards of a cold, frost-stricken climate, beset by demons of drought, and harassed by marauding neighbors, they struggled to overcome the physical and social challenges of their environment. The institution of kingship had already developed among them; the worship of tribal gods and ancestral spirits had given way to a common worship of universal gods and the spirits of protective, departed heroes.

The first adumbration of the major legends of the Iranian epic are found in the Yashts of the Avesta, where Kayanian kings offer sacrifice to the gods in order to earn their support and gain strength in the perpetual struggle against their enemies, the Turanians. As the major concern of the Kayanians, this bitter, never-ending feud with the Turanians constitutes the main theme of the Iranian epic. Zoroastrianism adopted these legends of the past and extended its blessing to their protagonists.

Transmitted by professional minstrels, the legends were inherited in turn by the Parthians, who lived close to the Avestan regions and had become Zoroastrian. During the long reign of the Arsacids (247 B.C.–A.D. 226) these legends spread to the rest of Iran and overshadowed the local ones. In the process, the memory of the Medes and the Persians, who did not figure in the eastern epics or in Zoroastrian literature, faded into oblivion; when the Sasanian scribes (*dabirs*) eventually attempted the compilation and systemization of an Iranian history, all they could find for the ancient periods were the cycles of legends and stories that had come down from Parthian times, reaching back into Kayanian memories.

The Parthian period itself saw the resurgence of a second heroic age, and the Arsacid princes and some of their vassal lords became the focus of a number of adventure tales; in the hands of the minstrels (*gosāns*) these tales eventually became legend. The *gosān* was a poet-musician, "privileged at court and popular with the people; present at the graveside and at the feast, eulogist, satirist, storyteller, musician; recorder of the past achievements, and commentator of his own times,"[4] who performed at courts and among the people, entertaining them with his repertoire of tales of heroism, love, and adventure to the accompaniment of musical instruments.

As time went by and the history of the Arsacids was also lost to the people, their legends, together with other myths and legends of eastern Iran (notably those of the house of Rostam of Seistan), were mingled with Kayanian legends and woven into the fabric of the national saga. Parthian figures, such as Gōdarz, Giv, Bizhan, Milād (Mehrdād), and Farhād generally appear as warrior nobles at the court of the Kayanians. It is hard to say to what extent the linear systematization of the heroic cycles was created by the *gosāns*, guided by their narrative instincts, and to what extent created through a conscious effort of the Sasanian compilers. The compilation toward the end of the reign of Khosrow II (590–628) in the form of the *Khwadāy-nāmag* (Book of lords) may have been subconsciously prompted by a perception of the deteriorating national spirit and a need for boosting national pride by recalling past glories. The result, in any event, was a long history of the Iranian nation from the first world-king, Gayōmart, to the reign of Khosrow II, with events arranged according to the perceived sequence of kings and queens, fifty in number. Although the legends have been skillfully reconciled and read as a progressive history, some incongruities traceable to the independence of different cycles remain.[5]

The fierce struggle with the Turanians, symbolic of the recurrent menace and destructive invasions of the Central Asian nomads, runs through the mythical and legendary parts of the epic almost as a connecting thread. Naturally the heroic legends of the past did not reach the compilers in their original purity. With each major social and religious reform the legends had to be adjusted to comply with new sensibilities. Heroic ages, in which the warrior class stands out, are generally succeeded by periods of predominantly moral and spiritual concerns, when the seer, the saint, and the prophet outshine the

---

[4]M. Boyce, "The Parthian *gosān* and the Iranian Minstrel Tradition," *JRAS* (1957): 10f.

[5]See E. Yarshater, *The Cambridge History of Iran* (Cambridge, 1983), vol. 3, 429ff.

warrior, and the literature reflects the change. Such literature, be it magical, didactic, or apocalyptic, is often superimposed on or mixed with the heroic tales, as is most noticeable in the Indian epic *Mahābhārata*. The Iranian legends, too, were augmented by a considerable number of religious postulates and moral and moralizing comments. Accordingly, the Middle Persian *Khwadāy-nāmag*, as seen through the pages of the *Shāh–nāma*, was studded with royal words of wisdom, priestly discourse, moral precepts, philosophical observations, and testaments and enthronement speeches extolling justice, religiosity, and honesty. Thus the *Khwadāy-nāmag*, rather than being the work of a single genius, was a compendium of Iranian epics and morals, elaborated and refined throughout the ages. As such it constitutes the most important literary heritage of ancient Iran.

Admittedly, the *Khwadāy-nāmag* was regarded primarily as a book of history, but we must remember that "history" did not mean the factual, dispassionate investigation and recording of events as expected from modern scholarship. Rhetorical in style and edifying in effect, history was an instrument of literary entertainment and social education. It was meant to promote the moral and social ideals on which Sasanian society was built; the life stories of kings and heroes provided a suitable frame within which to expound these ideals. In the face of this social and recreational function, critical objectivity weighed little; a distinction between myth, legend, and fact was irrelevant, and indeed the *Khwadāy-nāmag* combined all three indistinguishably. If the subject was historical, the method was literary, and ample use was made of metaphors, hyperboles, and other rhetorical devices to enhance the effect of the narrative. Action, pageantry, scenes of battles, hunting, banquets, and drinking bouts were depicted with relish, but logistics, dates, and circumstantial details were mostly ignored. The emotional force of the narrative, moreover, was kept at a high level: warriors' conceits were cited with dramatic impact, and the miraculous was conjured up without reservation. Thus the *Khwadāy-nāmag* was indeed also a work of artistic merit and literary effect.

It is sometimes suggested that Middle Iranian did not produce great works of imaginative literature. This judgment ignores two basic facts: that the secular literature of Iran prior to Islam was essentially oral, and that much of the early New Persian literature was in fact only a new recension or direct rendering of Middle Persian and Parthian creations.

## Parthian and Middle Persian Written Literatures

The remains of Parthian writings, mostly inscriptions from the early Sasanian period and Manichaean hymns, are few, but renderings into other languages from Parthian testify to the existence of genres other than epic. One such work is the love story of *Vis and Rāmin*[6] of which there exists a versified Persian version by the eleventh-century poet, Fakhr al-Din Gorgāni (based on a Persian prose translation of a Middle Persian model), as well as a thirteenth-century Georgian translation. It describes the ardent love between Rāmin and the bride of his brother, King Mōbad. Its remarkable resemblance to the story of Tristan and Isolde has often been pointed out. The story, set in a feudal society, is embroidered with various episodes, tender love scenes, subterfuges, intrigues, escapades, wars, sieges, chivalrous deeds, and feminine resourcefulness, all blended in a meandering series of events framed by a loose plot.[7]

An example of a different genre is afforded by *Draxt ī asūrīg* (The Babylonian tree), extant in a Middle Persian verse rendition. It concerns a contest of merit between a palm tree and a goat, and provides a precursor of the *monāzara* or contest poems in Persian. The Manichaean hymns in the Parthian language are valuable remains from pre-Islamic Iran and give us an idea of the religious poetry of this Middle Iranian language.[8]

More works are preserved in Middle Persian than in Parthian; these include inscriptions, books, tracts, and epistles. The bulk of the material, however, consists of religious books which were revised and edited in the ninth and tenth centuries, when the *mōbad*s of the diminished and enfeebled Zoroastrian community made an effort to defend their religion and instruct the faithful in the face of Islamic inroads.

A few poems also survive; in fact, the *Ayādgār ī Zarērān* (The memorial of Zarēr) and the *Draxt ī asūrīg* are both metrical, if somewhat corrupt in the extant manuscripts. From the little written poetry that remains it is clear that Middle Persian meter, like the Parthian, was

---

[6]Translated by G. Morrison, Persian Heritage Series no. 14 (New York, 1972).

[7]See V. Minorsky, "Vis o Ramin, a Parthian Romance," *Iranica* (Tehran, 1964), 151ff.; M. Boyce, "Parthian Writings and Literatures," *Cam. Hist. of Iran*, vol. 3, chap. 31, 1151ff.

[8]See chap. 3. For a discussion of Parthian metrics, see G. Lazard, "La Métrique de la Poésie Parthe," *Papers in Honor of Prof. Mary Boyce* (Leiden, 1985), 371–99.

governed by stress, the quantity of syllables being flexible within limits. Poems were generally sung or chanted, with instrumental accompaniment. The Sasanian court extended generous patronage to its poet-musicians, and Bahrām V is said to have promoted their rank to one of the highest in the court.[9] Minstrel poetry continued into Islamic times, particularly in the countryside, which was less susceptible to Arabic influence and court formality. Shams-e Qays, the famous thirteenth-century prosodist who knew nothing but the quantitative prosody of the *'aruz*, expressed bewilderment that some cultivated Persian poets of high literary standing could not see the flaw in the meter of their dialect poems, the *fahlaviyyāt*. Elsewhere, however, he concedes[10] that no poems could move even the literary elite as these *fahlaviyyāt* did.[11] Among the varieties of Sasanian poems one may count the *sorud* (ode), used for celebration and panegyrics; the *chakāma*, for narration; and the *tarāna*, for light poetry, generally in quatrains.[12]

Unfortunately, few original Sasanian works have survived. Many were lost in the course of the Muslim invasion and other foreign conquests, and others were lost because of the religious zeal of the Muslim Persians themselves; but, mostly, their loss is due to the neglect of these works after the change of script from Aramaic to Arabic. Judging by their Arabic and Persian translations and adaptations, and by bibliographical notices, Middle Persian literature (apart from clerical writing) included historical, geographical, didactic, and astronomical works; books on land survey and travel; rules of conduct and etiquette; law books, historical novels, romances, folktales, and fables.[13]

## The Rise and Development of Persian Literature

When (New) Persian literature finally found royal patronage, and social and political circumstances made possible the tenth-century renaissance, Persian society had undergone far-reaching transforma-

---

[9]Jāhiz, *K. al-Tāj*, ed. Ahmad Zaki (Cairo, 1914), 28.

[10]*Al-Mo'jam*, ed. M. Rezavi (Tehran, 1957), 88–101, 165ff.

[11]This kind of poetry, written in native meters measured by stress within a limited range of the number of syllables, survives to this day in some villages and among dialect speakers. See E. Yarshater, "The Affinities between Persian Poetry and Music," *Studies in Art and Literature of the Near East in Honor of Richard Ettinghausen*, ed. P. Chelkowski (Utah and New York, 1974), 62ff.

[12]See M. T. Bahār, "She'r dar Iran," *Majalla-ye tufān* (January 1928), repr. in *Bahār o adab-e fārsi*, ed. M. Golbon (Tehran, 1972), 78ff.

[13]For a detailed account of Middle Persian writings see M. Boyce, "Middle Persian Literature," *Iranistik II, Literature, HO* (Leiden and Cologne, 1968), 33ff. and J. de Menasce, *Cam. Hist. of Iran*, vol. 3, chap. 32(a), 1166ff.

tions. Persia was now part of the Muslim world, a world in which Arabic was the lingua franca. Middle Persian script had been given up for the Arabic alphabet and a number of Arabic words had entered the language. It was now fashionable to write poetry, like the Arabs, in quantitative meters (based on the number and length of the syllables) and the adaptable Persians proceeded to apply the rules of Arabic prosody to their favorite meters, making them even more strictly quantitative than Arabic ones.[14] Blossoming first in Greater Khorasan (an area which is now part of Iran, Afghanistan, and the Central Asian Soviet Republics of Turkmenistan, Uzbekistan, and Tajikistan), Persian poetry soon evolved into a pervasive literary force. Far exceeding the geographical boundaries of the Iranian plateau in its dominance, it provided a literary model for the entire eastern half of the caliphate.

This penetration was accelerated, and became particularly widespread after 1258, when the Mongol armies occupied Baghdad and put an end to the long-lived Abbasid caliphate. For some five centuries the caliphate in Baghdad had provided a focal point of religious and cultural unity in the Islamic world. With its disappearance, Muslim countries were left practically free to go their separate ways and cultivate their own idiosyncrasies. In the western half of the Islamic world, namely Arabia, the Levant, Egypt, and North Africa, Arabic continued as the cultural and administrative language. In the eastern half, however, including Iran, Afghanistan, Central Asia, and India (as well as Anatolia), Persian performed the same function, and its literature benefited from a great many talents nurtured in these countries. In the same way that Islamic culture, although Arabic in origin, was developed by a variety of peoples who accepted Islam,[15] Persian literature was likewise reinforced and expanded by the valuable patronage of many non-Persian dynasties as well as by the poetic gifts, sensibilities, and contributions of numerous non-Persian poets and writers. Farrokhi, son of a Turkish slave, Khosrow of Delhi, Fayzi of Agra, Fozuli of Iraq, Ghāleb of Delhi, and Iqbāl of Lahore are only a few of the non-Persian luminaries of Persian literature.

Persian was introduced into India in the tenth century by Mahmud of Ghazna, who led many raids into the subcontinent and occupied the Punjab. His descendants continued to rule in northwestern India until 1168. They were followed by other Muslim houses, mostly of

---

[14]On the continuation of Middle Persian meters within the frameworks of the *'aruz*, see L. P. Elwell-Sutton, *The Persian Meters* (Cambridge, 1976), 169ff., and G. Lazard, op. cit., 390–91.

[15]See R. A. Nicholson, *A Literary History of the Arabs* (Cambridge, 1965), 290.

Turkish or Afghan origin: the Ghorids, the sultans of Delhi, Kashmir, Gujarat, and Bengal; the Bahmanids of North Deccan, and others. They extended Muslim rule, and with it Persian language and culture, to most parts of the subcontinent, as far east as Bengal and as far south as Hyderabad. Although for the most part these dynasties were not ethnically Persian, they were so culturally and therefore became propagators of Persian language, literature, and way of life.

In the meantime a large number of dedicated Muslim missionaries from Persia and Central Asia, as well as other Islamic lands, were active in India. Most notable among these were Persian or Persian-speaking Sufi mystics, whose saintly bearing and passionate preaching were important elements in the conversion of many Indians to Islam and in the spread of Persian language and culture. They also laid the foundation for a number of Sufi orders. Persian lyric poetry has always been popular with the Sufis as a symbolic expression of their love of the divine and their longing for union with God. Therefore the Sufi brotherhoods and their hospices also became instruments for cultivating Persian poetry among the Muslim Indians.

The patronage of Persian literature in India reached its culmination with the Moghul emperors (1526–1858), whose reign constituted a golden age of Indo-Persian literature. Some of the emperors, like Homāyun and Jahāngir, as well as many Moghul princes and princesses, governors, nobles, and high officials, were not only enthusiastic sponsors and promoters of Persian letters but they wrote Persian poetry themselves. The court of Akbar (1556–1605) was studded with a large number of poets who wrote in Persian. An indication of the extent and popularity of Persian poetry in India may be seen in the notices of poets by Qāne' Tatavi and Khalil Tatavi, who mention 719 Persian poets in Sind province alone.[16] Indeed, under the Moghuls, India (rather than Persia) became the center of Persian literature. A large body of Persian poetry, historical works, mystical treatises, literary criticism, biographies of poets, works of theology and Koranic literature, and numerous Persian grammars and lexicons were produced in India during this period, many of these works still unpublished.

In Turkey, Persian was first sponsored by the Seljuks of Rum (1077–1307), who introduced Persian culture into Anatolia. When the Ottoman Turks penetrated Asia Minor in the thirteenth century, they found that "Persian literature and Persian culture ruled supreme."[17]

---

[16]Qāne' Tatavi, *Maqālat al-sho'arā'*, and Khalil Tatavi, *Takmela-ye maqālat al-sho'arā'*, ed. and annot. Rashedi, 2 vols. (Karachi, 1956–57). See also chaps. 13 and 14.

[17]E. J. W. Gibb, *A History of Ottoman Poetry* (London, 1900), vol. 1, 10.

The Ottomans soon absorbed the Seljuks into their ranks and readily embraced this culture; they even took Persian models as their guides when they encouraged the creation and growth of Turkish poetry. Thus, in the words of E. J. W. Gibb, they "forthwith appropriated the entire Persian literary system down to its minute detail."[18] For five and a half centuries the Ottoman sultans, like the Ghaznavids, the Seljuks, and many other ruling Turkish houses before them, were patrons of Persian letters.

Between the fifth and the nineteenth centuries, Persian was the literary and cultural language of most of the Islamic countries east of the Tigris and north of the Fertile Crescent. More important, its influence was such that poems written in the native languages of these regions—Turkish, Urdu, Azeri Turkish, and Chagatai—were modeled after Persian poetry in form, outlook, and imagery. Such poems are similar to their Persian counterparts in sentiment, concepts, and content, and differ in language only; even so, they are replete with words and phrases borrowed from Persian and, by extension, from Arabic.

Thus in the vast regions where Persian literature was patronized, it was a mere ethnic or linguistic accident whether the poet wrote in Urdu, Sindi, Turkish, Chagatai, Pashto, or Persian; the poetic ideas and images were the same, and the characteristics of the poetry of any of these languages, except the folk idioms, are the same. In other words, Persian poetry was written not only in Persian, but in Turkish, Urdu, and Chagatai as well. Therefore, in a discussion of Persian letters our scope extends beyond what was written in the Persian language to encompass works by those who thought in Persian when it came to literature, irrespective of their native tongues and ethnic origins.

## General Features of Persian Literature

At this point we may consider some of the general characteristics of this literature.

i. *Preponderance of Poetry.* A fairly extensive prose literature, mainly of a narrative, anecdotal, and moralizing kind also flourished, but it is overshadowed by poetry in terms of quality and quantity alike. In fact, poetry is the art *par excellence* of Persia, and her salient cultural achievement. Despite their considerable accomplishments in painting,

[18]Ibid., 7.

pottery, textiles, and architecture, in no other field have the Persians succeeded in achieving the same degree of eminence. Whereas the scope of the other arts remained limited, poetry developed into a vehicle for the most refined thoughts and the deepest sentiments. Contemplative and passionate at the same time, poetry speaks the language of the Persian heart, mind, and soul, fully reflecting the Persian world view and life experience.

ii. *"Tangential" Structure and Organization.* The literatures of Persia generally tend to be descriptive rather than dramatic, expressionistic rather than naturalistic, organic rather than architectural. This does not mean that Iranian literatures lack dramatic or well-constructed stories. The *Shāh-nāma* contains some powerful stories with considerable dramatic effect. The episodes of Rostam and Sohrāb, Siyāvosh and Sudāba, and Rostam and Esfandiyār, are not only effective in themselves, but are also told with commendable structural cohesion—as are a number of events reported by the eleventh-century historian Bayhaqi. From their Persian renditions, it is clear that the Middle Persian historical novels based on the lives of Mazdak and Bahrām Chobin were dramatic and well-constructed.[18a] One need only refer to the epigrammatic quatrains of 'Omar Khayyām and his imitators to show that dramatic technique was not alien to Persian literary taste. Many writers and poets excelled in driving a point home effectively by the judicious use of contrast, emphasis, paradox, and irony, but most of all by a fitting illustration (which is frequently used in Persian didactic literature to dramatize an abstract point or dictum).

And yet it is the creation of moods and effects and the description of scenes and sentiments that have remained the chief concerns of the writers and poets of Persia. Literary constructions of an architectural nature, where all details are subordinated to the requirements of an overriding theme or idea, have seldom been the compelling aim of Iranian literary works. Structural frames as they are understood in the West, with dramatic tension resulting from the development of characters and their contrived interaction do not preoccupy the Persian literary mind. Rather than following a planned development from initial premises to climax and resolution, the Persian writers allow

---

[18a]The fullest version of the fictionalized account of Bahrām Chobin occurs in Bal'ami, ed. M. T. Bahār, 1077–89. For the story on Mazdak, of which a goodly portion has been retained by Nezām al-Molk, *Siyar al-Moluk,* ed. H. Darke, 254ff., see A. Christensen, *Le Regne du roi Kawadh I et le communisme mazdakite* (Copenhagen, 1925), 65ff.; O. Klima, *Beitrage zur Geschichte des Mazdakismus* (Prague, 1977), 55ff.; E. Yarshater, *Cam. Hist. of Iran,* vol. 3, 994f.

themselves to explore, often at a leisurely pace, the scenes and details that excite their own imaginations, and to share these with the reader. This unfocused, meandering type of literary construction finds its supreme example in Rumi's *Mathnavi,* where mystical ideas and preachings are illustrated by stories within stories, with no clear structure between rambling sermons and philosophical comments. Gorgāni's *Vis and Rāmin,* the first major romance, with its circuitous episodes, divergent descriptions, and wandering plot, sets the example for later narratives—an example followed by numerous popular prose epics.

In light of this tendency, it ought not surprise us that Persian lyrics usually lack a controlling theme, each line expressing, as a rule, an independent thought; nor should we find it unusual to see in Persian histories of literary bent prolix excursions meant to display the author's rhetorical dexterity. In this context we may recall that whereas Persian literature abounds in contemplative ideas and flashes of speculative thought, whole philosophical systems have hardly ever developed in Iran. Nor were tightly organized dramatic plots favored in premodern Iran. Even in recent decades, with the adoption of drama as a new literary genre, Bayzā'i's plays—dramas of mood and poetic feeling—are more representative of Persian literary taste than the plays of Sā'edi, who employs Western technical concepts.

It is also revealing that in the present century, when fiction writing has become popular, it is the short story (mostly descriptive) and not the novel that has attracted the best talents. And in Afghāni's *Showhar-e Āhu Khānom* and Dowlatābādi's *Kelidar,* two significant post-World War II novels, frequent peregrinations, delight in exploiting the ramifications of their subjects, and branching off into side alleys are typical of the same centrifugal tendency that we notice in the works of Nezāmi or 'Attār.

On the other hand, Persian poets and writers are proven masters of vignettes, aphorisms, pithy remarks, proverbial sayings, felicitous formulations, pregnant allusions, illustrative anecdotes, and imaginative short descriptions; almost all of these techniques are exemplified in the pages of the most celebrated Persian prose work, Sa'di's *Golestān* (The rose garden), composed in the thirteenth century. Persian and Middle Persian possess a rich store of wisdom literature, consisting mainly of detached or loosely connected moral maxims and ethical observations from which one can hardly deduce a coherent system of ethical philosophy. It is symptomatic of the Persian mode of thinking and literary predilection that the true unit of Persian poetry is the line (distich or *bayt*). The best Persian poets often succeed in expressing profound thoughts or impassioned sentiments within the confines of a single couplet.

iii. **Decorative Tendency.** A third feature of Persian literature is its taste for the use of rhetorical devices and ornament. It has often been observed that Persian art has a marked decorative tendency. This is clearly seen in the visual arts: architecture, book illustration, wall painting, bookbinding, calligraphy, and textiles, as well as in music.[19] In modern Persian criticism this tendency, an integral part of artistic expression in Persian letters, has been somewhat deprecated, partly as a result of changes in literary values and partly because the critics have usually focused on excessive examples. Such a view, however, ignores the standards of taste prevailing in medieval Persia and its spheres of cultural influence, and it misses, as well, the true nature and function of ornament in Persian literature. Far from being a mere addition or embellishment, ornament is a vital element of literary expression. It is one of the major devices writers or poets use to display their ingenuity, imparting elegance and sophistication to their products, and rousing the reader's admiration. If in treatises on rhetoric the embellishing devices occupy such a conspicuous place, it is because they were seen not as marginal but rather as essential parts of the craft.

In early Persian poetry, ornament is minimal, partly as a result of the poetry's youth and partly because it was modeled on Sasanian poetry. In pre-Islamic Persia, as we have seen, poetry and music went hand in hand, and the minstrels usually sang their poems to the accompaniment of instruments. Poetry, to judge by our few remaining examples, was fairly simple in composition since the music was there to help deliver its emotional impact. Many early Persian poems were, in fact, conceived as songs and were sung by the poet or a *rāvi* (Arabic *rāwi*, reciter) as instanced by Rudaki's famous poem on Bukhara, which reportedly made his patron king abandon Herat and rush to his capital without even taking time to put on his riding boots.[20]

It was not long, however, before poetry achieved a totally separate existence from music and its own tradition was established with a repertory of conventional themes, motifs, and imagery. Since the free play of imagination was somewhat limited by the restraints of this tradition, embellishment and decoration became a primary means of

[19]See E. Yarshater, "The Affinities," 74–76.
[20]Nezāmi 'Aruzi, *Chahār maqāla*, ed. M. Qazvini, revised by M. Mo'in (Tehran, 1952), 49f.

exhibiting literary dexterity and of impressing one's audience. Stylistic mastery and rhetorical craftsmanship gradually became a hallmark of good writing. Even the writers of informative prose who mastered the craft were considered practitioners of literary art.

Embellishments enjoy a wide scope and variety in Persian letters. Sometimes they have to do with the sound and the music of the word and include such devices as alliteration, homophony (*jenās*), internal rhyming, double rhyming, and the addition of a *radif* (refrain)[21] to the rhyme. At other times the embellishment takes place at the semantic level and plays on the associative meanings of words or metaphors and their connotations; these devices include amphibology (*ihām*), antithesis (*tazādd*), congruence (*morā'āt-e nazir*), and various types of allusion. Again, it may concern the arrangement of words and their messages in some pleasing or impressive pattern such as *laff o nashr* (involution and revolution), in which a number of words in a hemistich or line find correspondances normally in the next hemistich or line.[22] Embellishment also results, though less frequently, from playing on the shape of the letters or the presence or absence of dots. And finally, ornament may be brought to bear on the metaphorical plane by means of statements, similes, and tropes that enhance and elaborate the effect of the basic metaphor or expression.

In the hands of masters like Hāfez, who use ornament aptly and with discretion, poems become contrapunctal designs in which the substance and ornament interact with considerable aesthetic effect. In the hands of less-endowed writers, however, meaning often becomes overshadowed or obscured by excessive ornamentation. Some writers of a turgid inclination have produced florid prose and stilted poetry that are almost nothing but extravaganzas of ornamental bombast and pedantic *tours de force*, giving embellishment a bad name. Like some notorious histories such as *Tārikh-e Vassāf* (fourteenth century) and *Dorra-ye nādera* (eighteenth century), these are mostly the products of periods of literary decline, when indigence of thought led to a surfeit of ornament.

iv. *Conventionality.* A fourth feature of Persian literary tradition is the conventionality of its themes and imagery. The major themes and forms of Persian poetry were set in the first century of its appearance; they are seen as early as the works of Rudaki (d. 940–41). Further-

---

[21] A word or phrase which follows the rhyme and is repeated without change after a given rhyme.

[22] Among other examples are *taqsīm* and *radd al-'ajoz*; see Edward G. Browne, *A Literary History of Persia* (Cambridge, 1929), vol. 2, 60–61, 72.

more, the different genres of Persian poetry generally correspond to specific forms: the *qasida* (ode), a long monorhyme, for panegyrics; the *ghazal,* a shorter monorhyme of about seven to fourteen lines, for lyrics; the *mathnavi* or couplet, for narrative themes; the *robā'i* or quatrain for epigrammatic poems; and the *qet'a* (piece or fragment) for casual themes. These forms and their corresponding genres have remained fairly constant for nearly a thousand years.

Traditional poets have always composed their works within the requirements of formal canons and thematic and imagistic conventions. If this framework has made the poet's task of achieving originality more difficult, it has also made it more impressive once accomplished. Such originality is often achieved not by deviating from the norm but by improving upon it: development in Persian literature consists mostly of the refinement of existing techniques, not bold or unsettling innovation.[23]

Since the merit of Persian literature rests largely on its poetry, we shall address ourselves to it in more detail. We may begin with a brief sketch of the periods and styles of Persian poetry and then consider its development.

## The Development of Persian Poetry

Basing a chronological division of Persian poetry on radical changes, we can distinguish no more than two periods of Persian poetry: one traditional, from the tenth to nearly mid-twentieth century; the other modernist, from about World War II to the present. Within the long period of traditional poetry, however, four periods can be traced, each marked by a distinct stylistic development.

The first of these, comprising roughly the tenth to the twelfth century, is characterized by strong court patronage, a profusion of panegyrics, and an exalted style (*sabk-e fākher*). One may define this style (generally known as Khorasani, from the association of most of its earlier representatives with Greater Khorāsān) by its lofty diction, dignified tone, and highly literate language. The second, from the thirteenth to the fifteenth century, is marked by the prominence of lyric poetry, the consequent development of the *ghazal* into the most significant verse form, and the diffusion of mystical thought. Its style is generally dubbed Eraqi because of the association of some of its earlier exponents with central and western Persia (even though its two

[23]See below under lyric poetry for some of the Persian conventions.

major representatives, Sa'di and Hāfez, were from the southern province of Fārs); it is known by its lyric quality, tenderness of feeling, mellifluous meters, and the relative simplicity of its language.

The third period, which extends from the fifteenth well into the eighteenth century, is associated with the Indian style of Persian poetry (sometimes called Isfahani or Safavi). It has its beginning in the Timurid period and is marked by an even greater prominence of lyric poetry, although it is somewhat devoid of the linguistic elegance and musicality of the preceeding period. The poets of this period often busied themselves with exploring subtle thoughts and farfetched images and elaborating upon worn-out traditional ideas and metaphors.

The fourth period, from approximately the eighteenth to the mid-twentieth century, is known as the Literary Revival (*bāzgasht-e adabi*). It features a reaction against the poetic stagnation and linguistic foibles of the late Safavid style, and a return to the Eraqi style of lyric poetry and the Khorasani style of panegyrics. One can certainly make a case for dividing this period into two parts: before and after the Revolution for the Constitution (1906–11). The latter part saw many attempts at modernizing Persian poetry by the introduction of new themes, colloquial language, patriotic subjects, and political and social satire; nevertheless, the formal aspect of Persian poetry resisted change, and major poets continued writing in the traditional styles.

The current phase of Persian poetry, which dates from World War II, is characterized by a radical break with the literary tradition of the past and by the introduction of fresh imagery and poetic forms.

i. **Court Poetry.** Recorded Persian poetry began under court patronage, a continuation of the Sasanian and Abbasid practice. As a result, much of the earliest classical poetry is court poetry. The poets were to compose for formal occasions: major festivals, the birth of a son, deaths, conquests, and the like. Eulogy constituted the principal part of the panegyrics, but the poet was also expected to be entertaining. Therefore great attention was paid to the lyrical or descriptive preludes of the panegyrics. (Today, when euologies have fallen low in the estimation of modern readers, these introductory sections are the best-appreciated parts of this poetry.) The favorite form of panegyrics was the *qasida*, but occasionally narrative or didactic works in couplet form contained praise of the patron in their introductions, particularly when such works were commissioned by or dedicated to a ruler or grandee.

The ambiance of the court imposed a certain formality on its poetry. Diction was lofty, language elegant, and grammar impeccable. Much

21

of its imagery, taken from battle scenes, banquets, palaces, gardens, flower beds, hunting scenes, polo, chess, drinking parties, and weaponry, mirrors the milieu of the court. The earliest poets also show a remarkable love of nature and acquaintance with flowers, trees, and birds, and their descriptions of nature are refreshing.

The earliest period of Persian poetry is marked by a hopeful and resilient spirit, and although its contemplative pieces betray age and experience, its lyric lines display a youthful and joyous mood. The deep-seated sense of melancholy that characterizes later lyrics is absent. The poet sings of his rather mundane love in a light-hearted manner, seeking pleasure where beauty lies. The chief representatives of this happy lyricism are Rudaki, Farrokhi (d. 1037–38), and Manuchehri (d. 1040–41); their lyrics appear generally as introductory preludes (*tashbib* or *taghazzol*) to their panegyrics.

Rudaki, attached to the court of Nasr b. Ahmad (913–43) of the Samanid dynasty, was (like the Sasanian minstrels) a poet-musician who wrote songs as well as *qasida*s. The first major Persian poet, he is generally considered the father of Persian poetry. Farrokhi, for his part, is the most readable of the court poets. His poems are lively and abound in descriptions of nature, be it the arrival of spring or the onset of autumn, garden flowers, clouds, or rain. He wrote his lyrics, one imagines, with a twinkle in his eye. Manuchehri, too, excels in descriptive poems. His fertile imagination, which poured out original images and metaphors, has given us some of the most attractive poems on vineyards, wine, and wine-making.

ii. *Epic Poetry.* With Ferdowsi's immortal poem, the *Shāh-nāma,* epic poetry rose to the height of its achievement almost at its beginning. Hailed as the greatest monument of Persian language and one of the major world epics, it consists of some fifty thousand couplets relating the history of the Iranian nation in myth, legend, and fact, from the beginning of the world to the fall of the Sasanian Empire. The genesis and character of the Iranian epic as it took shape in the late Sasanian period has been already noted. Ferdowsi, who belonged to the landed gentry (*dehqān*) and was well versed in Iranian cultural heritage and lore, fully understood the sense and direction of the work he was versifying. His approximately thirty years of labor produced a magnificent epic of tremendous impact. By glorifying the Persian past in heroic and high-minded poetry he presented the Persian nation with a source of pride and inspiration that has helped to preserve its sense of identity over the centuries. Ferdowsi set the model for a host of other poets who followed his meter and style, but whose works never reached similar heights.[24]

iii. *Lyric Poetry.* Important as epics are, the heart of Persian poetry is its lyrics. In the poems of the tenth and eleventh centuries, lyrics appeared mostly in the introductory parts of panegyrics, as we have noted. But lyric poetry can be found in several forms; many romances, for instance, contain numerous lyric sections or lines, and quatrains have been frequently used to express the pains and passions of love. There are even *qasidas*, most notably by Sa'di, given to lyrical themes. But the form *par excellence* of Persian lyric poetry became the *ghazal*, which in some ways resembles the sonnet. In the twelfth century a number of poets, notably Sanā'i (d. 1130–31), Khāqāni (d. 1199), Nezāmi (d. 1209), and 'Attār (d. ca. 1220), were writing independent *ghazals*. By the thirteenth century, with major lyricists like Rumi (d. 1273), 'Erāqi (d. 1289), and Sa'di (d. 1292), the *ghazal* had become indisputably the most favored form of Persian poetry.

With the passage of time, the spirited and youthful poetry of the earlier lyrics gained in tenderness and depth of sentiment. It was poets such as Anvari, Nezāmi, Khāqāni and 'Attār who, although better known for other genres of poetry, contributed to this development of the *ghazal* into a heartfelt, intimate poem of love and its afflictions.

From about the twelfth century, lyric poetry was enriched with a spirituality and devotional depth not to be found in earlier works. This development was due to the pervasive spread of mystical experience. Sufism (Islamic mysticism) developed in all Muslim lands, but its literary expression reached its zenith in the countries located within the sphere of Persian cultural influence. As a counterpoise to the rigidity of formal Islamic theology and law, mysticism sought to approach the divine through acts of devotion and love rather than through mere rituals and observance. Love of God being the focus of the Sufis' religious sentiments, it was only natural for them to express it in lyrical terms, and Persian mystics, often of exceptional sensibility and endowed with poetic verve, did not hesitate to do so. The famous eleventh-century Sufi, Abu Sa'id of Mehna, for example, frequently used his own love quatrains (as well as others') to express his spiritual yearnings, and with the appearance of avowed mystic poets like 'Attār and 'Erāqi, mysticism became a legitimate, even fashionable subject of lyric poems. Furthermore, as Sufi orders and hospices (*khānaqāhs*)

---

[24]See chap. 5 for further discussion.

23

spread, mystical thought gradually became so much a part of common culture that even poets who did not share Sufi experiences ventured to express mystical ideas and imagery in their poems.

Mystical lyrics culminated in the *ghazal*s of Rumi. Fired by an irresistible love of the divine and endowed with unusual poetic gifts, he wrote lyrics of extraordinary passion and musicality. The ecstatic fervor, explosive spontaneity, and rich but unconventional language of Rumi's lyrics place him in a class all his own. His *Mathnavi*, generally considered the greatest literary monument of Islamic mysticism, is a long poem of twenty-seven thousand couplets designed primarily to expound and preach his dynamic mysticism. His method is anecdotal, his tone frequently lyrical. The complexity of Rumi's mystical thought, wedded to a loose, "centrifugal" treatment, and his indifference to polishing his language do not make the *Mathnavi* easy reading, but the work contains many charming stories, moving passionate lines, and well-expressed profound thoughts that account for its great popularity.

As time went by, a set of poetic conventions began to crystallize, and the world of Persian lyrics became recognizable by a repertory of conventional themes, motifs and images. We meet stock characters and types such as the Lover, the Beloved, the Wine-Seller, the Shaikh, the Sufi, the Judge, the *Mohtaseb* (supervisor of religious observances), the Blamer, and the Rival; their behavior is predictable to a certain extent. The beloved, for example, becomes more disdainful and inaccessible than before, and the joys of union rarer than ever. Songs of love become mostly fervent laments of a spurned but dedicated lover who, afflicted by the pains of love and tormented by a fickle fate, has to endure interminable nights of separation. He sees his plight in the candle's silent and tearful burning, in the moth's perishing in the consuming flame of the candle, and in the nightingale's outpouring of love to the inconstant rose. The sorrow of love becomes his constant companion; he flouts the counsel of the wise, who advise him to abandon his unavailing passion. He is ready to give up his faith and sell out the two worlds for a fleeting sign of favor from the beloved; wandering aimlessly and suffering the heartless blame of both friend and foe, his best solace is wine and his favorite refuge the tavern. He abhors the tedious company of the self-righteous and those who pretend to virtue as much as he treasures the society of carefree drinkers, the *rend*s, and those who flout social decorum. In today's terms he would be called an anti-establishment advocate of a counterculture, who prefers the free and sincere atmosphere of the tavern to the cant-ridden precincts of the madrasa and mosque. To exult in the liberating effects of wine and the virtues of wine-sellers and tavern buffs becomes as much a theme of the lyrics as love and beauty. The major representative of this poetry is Hāfez (d. 1390), who perfected the paradigm of themes and imagery and provided the model for all the lyric poets who followed him.

It must be pointed out that the subject of Persian love poems, from the period of court poetry through later lyrics, is not always the woman but often a young man. Since the Persian language does not distinguish between genders, even in pronouns, this goes mostly unnoticed, but much of the imagery and many of the conventions of Persian lyrics become understandable only by appreciating this point. Young slaves, bought at markets or captured in wars, were often the subject of amorous feelings. They were trained for a variety of courtly professions, including playing musical instruments, serving wine at banquets as *sāqi,* and of course also serving as pages, bodyguards, and soldiers. Some grew into accomplished companions (*nadims*), and others rose to high ranks. Ayāz, a favorite of Sultan Mahmud of Ghazna, ended as one of his major generals. It is not surprising, therefore, if the beloved is sometimes pictured carrying a sword, commanding a company, serving wine at an all-male party, being himself drunk or obstreperous, or surrounded by a host of eyeing admirers. Many of the metaphors and similes that describe the beloved in terms of weapons and soldiery is derived from this situation; so too is the fact that *sāqi* passes practically as a synonym for *ma'shuq* or the beloved. The typical image of the beloved that emerges is an epitome of beauty beset by a host of lovers to whom he is indifferent; when importuned by them he flies into a rage, abuses them, and is liable to draw his sword or bend his bow. On the other hand, we see him occasionally as a sweet companion reciting poetry and playing music for his lover.

In order to better appreciate Persian lyrics one should take into account some of their other features. While a *ghazal* has a stringent formal frame, using the same strict meter and rhyme throughout, its content need not observe any thematic unity. In fact a *ghazal* often consists of a set of distinct themes or ideas, each expressed in a distich (*bayt*). Sometimes a common mood governs the lines of a *ghazal,* and less frequently a theme is pursued in several lines or throughout the poem, but the norm tends toward disparity. This situation also explains the fact that a number of traditional anthologies consist mostly of single lines.

It is this thematic disunity that has made it possible for the poet to

25

juxtapose amatory, satirical, mystical, and didactic themes in the same *ghazal*. Of course, there is an ultimate connection among the ideas of a *ghazal*; it derives from the conventional repertory of themes and basic images that are already known to the reader, in the same way that the episodes and themes of passion plays are known to the audience in advance. Thus, although the ideas in a *ghazal* may appear disparate, the reader can always recognize them as belonging to a familiar "master design" that, in its totality, displays the unity of a coherent outlook. The poet, one might say, uses fragments of a mosaic; the reader, already familiar with the whole picture, is capable of recognizing its pieces from the total context.

With such a basic set of conventions and images, there is little personal detail in Persian lyrics; the poet hardly reveals any information about his personal circumstances. The beloved invariably shines as a manifestation of unsurpassed beauty, and the lover as a symbol of devoted suffering. This abstract quality imparts a welcome sense of universality to the lyrics, inviting the readers to see a description in them of their own situation. What keeps the poems from losing their emotional impact in the face of this universality is the brimming passion which infuses their tone and imagery.

A new height in Persian lyric poetry is reached in the thirteenth century with Sa'di, a versatile poet and writer of rare passion and eloquence. He holds a position in Persian literature, in terms of the power of expression and the depth and breadth of his sensibilities, comparable to that of Shakespeare in English letters. His sparkling *ghazal*s display a youthful love of life and passion for beauty, be it natural, human, or divine. Sa'di's dexterous use of rhetorical devices is often disguised by the beguiling ease of his locution and the effortless flow of his style; his masterly language has been a model of elegant and graceful writing.

Sa'di is also the author of the best known work of Persian prose, the *Golestān*,[25] a collection of moralizing and entertaining anecdotes and aphorisms written in elegant rhymed prose and interspersed with fitting lines of verse. Sa'di's ideas, observations, moral convictions, and social comments, which appear in the *Golestān* in a lively, world-wise, and witty fashion, find a fuller expression, in a more sober and mature vein, in his *Bustān* (The orchard).[26] Didactic in content, lyrical in tone, and anecdotal in composition, this poem is one of the masterpieces of

[25]Repeatedly translated into English. See chap. 26.
[26]Latest translation, *Morals Pointed and Tales Adorned*, by G. M. Wickens, Persian Heritage Series no. 17 (Toronto, 1974).

Persian literature. It is probably the best expression of the humanitarian outlook on life and its moral dimensions that evolved in Islamic Persia among enlightened preachers as a result of the interaction between religious precepts and Sufi teachings; it embodies an ethical philosophy emphasizing moderation, justice, contentment, humility, detachment, and compassion for the weak and needy. An admirer of the ethics and the tolerant attitude of the venerable Sufis, Sa'di often draws on the lives and sayings of Islamic mystics to illustrate moral virtue. His humanitarianism, however, avoids the pantheistic and ecstatic excesses of some of the extreme Sufis. His approach remains one of the applications of ethical and devotional principles to common circumstances and problems. Sa'di manages to infuse his moral teachings with such lyrical charm that much of the *Bustān* reads like a moving *ghazal* in couplet form.

The culmination of Persian lyric poetry was reached about a hundred years after Sa'di with Hāfez, the most delicate and most popular of Persian poets. His *ghazal*s are typical in their content and motifs but exceptional in their combination of noble sentiments, powerful expression, elegance of diction, and felicity of imagery. His worldview encompasses many gnostic, mystical, and stoic sentiments, which were the common cultural heritage of his age. While Hāfez's satirical lines against pretense and hypocrisy lend a biting edge to his lyrics, his philosophical outlook and gnostic longings impart an exalted air of wisdom and detachment to his poems. But he is above all a poet of love who celebrates in his *ghazal*s the glory of human beauty, the passion of love, and the exhilirating qualities of wine.

Since the language of mundane love has frequently been used in lyric poetry to depict mystical longings, some critics—both native and foreign—have been led to suspect a mystical meaning in every expression of erotic love. This abuse of common sense and indulgence in the irrational has been nowhere more clearly exhibited than in the case of Hāfez. A corpus of esoteric interpretation of Hāfez has developed, complete with a fanciful glossary of mystical terms that, if followed, turns his lyrics into mystic riddles shorn of all apparent meaning and devoid of human love and passion. In reality, Hāfez satirizes the organized Sufism of his time no less than the exponents of the religious establishment.

It is true that some lines of Hāfez's poetry, as with many other *ghazal* writers, are capable of being understood on two different planes, the sensuous and the spiritual. But these instances are relatively few, and there is no reason to believe that every time the word "cup" or

27

"tresses" occurs, a mystic meaning lurks behind it. Belief in a mystical "inner meaning" of Hāfez's poetry represents the application of a *bāteni,* or esoteric principle, which distorts his meaning and flies in the face of his poetic sense. Again, Hāfez's satire of fanaticism and pretension in general, and of the pseudo-religious authorities in particular, hardly ever lends itself to mystical interpretation. This aspect of his poetry, although often mentioned, is not sufficiently stressed. Zākāni's deserved fame notwithstanding, Hāfez is the most notable satirist Persia has produced. Poignant gibes at the hypocritical shaikhs, judges, professional Sufis, and other pretenders to virtue form an integral part of his *ghazal*s and (following his model) are a common theme of Persian lyrics. The liberal Hāfez strongly felt the sting of pretense and cant; to express his outrage was as much a motive for his writing as were his aesthetic and amorous sentiments. But his subtle wit and his magnanimity keep his lyrics from being indignant or bitter. Siding with sinners and tavern-dwellers, championing the *rend*s and the *kharābātis*—the "hippies" of his time—are essentially his protests against the narrow views and bigotry of the establishment, and part of his satirical thrust (see further, below). To read mystical meanings into all this is to miss the intent and the sense of Hāfez's poetry to the detriment of his real worth.

The ascent of Persian poetry ends with Hāfez. Jāmi (d. 1492), a many-faceted poet of note, continued the tradition of the *ghazal,* as did many poets of the Safavid period (1502–1722) and the Mughal court in India. Vahshi (d. 1583), Naziri (d. 1612–13), Kalim (d. 1651–52) and Sā'eb (d. 1676–77) all wrote dainty lines and explored subtle poetic ideas, but by the time the Safavids rose to power, Persian poetry had lost much of its freshness and vigor and was becoming entangled in a web of farfetched ideas and images. The virile tones and clipped rhythms of early Persian poetry (the Khorasani style), which had given way to the passionate tenderness and fluent language of the lyric writers (the Eraqi style), now fell into languid rhythms, abstruse imagery, and often less-than-felicitous constructions (the Indian style). The outstanding example of these traits is the otherwise profound mystical poet Bidel (d. 1720), whose lyrics frequently present a real challenge for decipherment.

iv. **Didactic Poetry.** There are fewer themes less poetic or more tedious than the didactic, and yet wisdom (*andarz*) literature has long been associated with Iranian literary creations. Its roots are found in the gnomic writings of the priestly class of ancient Iran, and Middle Persian already possessed a good deal of *andarz* literature in the form of testaments, epistles, and collections of precepts. Judging from the *Shāh-nāma,* the *Khwadāy-nāmag* must have also contained a good dose of didactic writing.[27] Sasanian wisdom literature continued its existence after the advent of Islam in the form of Arabic and Persian recensions and adaptations and thus found its way into *adab* literature (see below). Fortunately, in Persian didactic writings the tedium is generally relieved by illustrative anecdotes.

Good examples of early didactic literature are Sanā'i's *Hadiqa* and Nezāmi's *Makhzan al-asrār.* 'Attār's *mathnavi*s also belong essentially to this genre, as does Rumi's major work, although their mystical intent and passionate tones give them a lyrical quality. On the other hand, the high-minded odes of the Ismaili poet and moralist Nāser-e Khosrow (d. 1061) are engaging by virtue of the poet's noble thoughts, elevated diction, and original imagery. The true gem in this field is Sa'di's *Bustān,* already mentioned.

v. **Satire.** Social satire, distinct from invective, has had limited scope in Persia, no doubt largely because of the oppressiveness of autocratic rulers and fanaticism of the religious establishment. What satire exists is often characterized by ribald or abusive language, both shunned in polite society. Three figures, however, stand out as master satirists: 'Obayd-e Zākāni (d. 1371), Hāfez, and Iraj (1874–1925).

Zākāni's satire is essentially based on humorous parody or sarcastic and derisive irony, often dressed in ribald language. His ribaldry, however, does not detract from his being one of the masters of prose style as well as one of the wittiest and most readable Persian writers. Hāfez's satire appears in succinct and poignant lines in the course of his lyrics and is directed for the most part against those who abuse religion or religious offices through their selfishness and hypocrisy. The sharpness, wit, and impact of his satire are based primarily on mocking irony, paradox, and sarcasm. He is the only major satirist whose language remains invariably pure, polished, and courteous.

Iraj, a rather casual poet and yet a satirist of high standing, belongs to the post–Constitutional period. He normally focuses his satire on situational incongruity in order to reveal the weaknesses and ills of a society stricken by ignorance, superstition, and corrupt religious and secular leadership. With an acute sense of humor his language draws successfully on colorful colloquial idioms.

Most other satire in modern times has been published in humorous

---

[27]For a discussion of the varieties of this literature and an analysis of its content, see *Cam. Hist. of Iran,* vol. 3, 398ff.

papers. Among the better known humorist-satirists of the present century are Dehkhodā (d. 1956), whose political, social, and anti-clerical satires in prose and verse won him considerable renown, and Zabih Behruz (d. 1971), whose one-act play, *Jijak 'Ali Shāh*, is a farcical satire on the Qajar court. His "Me'rāj-nāma" (The book of the ascension [of the Prophet]) and "Gand-e bādāvard" (The wind-blown stinks), parodies of classical *mathnavis*, were quite popular for many years before they were finally published in 1983 in West Germany.

vi. ***The Literary Revival and Modern Poetry.*** It was about the mid-eighteenth century that a group of poets in Isfahan, conscious of the impasse to which the belabored Safavid poetry had come, sought to restore the relative simplicity and more elegant diction of the old masters, thus initiating a revival in Persian letters. Among the early exponents of the movement were its articulate spokesmen, Lotfi 'Ali Āzar, Āsheq, and Hātef. The last is the author of the famous *Tarji' band* (Stanzaic poem); this lyrical poem of mystical purport, divided into five sections on the unity of being and the pantheistic view of the world, counts among the most noteworthy of Persian poetic compositions.

The poets of the Qajar period (1795–1925) remained faithful to the principles of the Literary Revival and maintained the linguistic clarity and eloquence associated with the old masters. Lyric poetry followed the style of Sa'di and Hāfez; panegyrics, which flourished as a result of court patronage, followed the Khorasani style (chiefly poets of the Ghaznavid and Seljuk courts). The creative energy of the poets, however, fell short of originality and was satisfied with emulating the poets of the past, grinding their worn-out clichés in well-composed and highly polished poems.

The conscious effort to return to the style of the old masters was symptomatic of a social phenomenon: a semiconscious realization of the weakness in the spirit and body politic of the nation, and a desire to counter it. The Shaikhis, and the attraction of the Babi movement for many intellectuals and patriots, may all be viewed as manifestations of a gradual social awakening, which eventually led to the reformist Constitutional Revolution. With the winning of a constitution from the Qajar king Mozaffar al-Din in 1906, the way was opened for Western-style modernization and concomitant mild changes in literary outlook and style. The pendulum of Persian history had swung once more to the west, only to reverse itself in 1979 with a vehement reaction against things alien in an attempt to remedy a social malaise, the root of which lay elsewhere.

Modern Persian poetry, which essentially continues the Qajar style, may conveniently be dated from the beginning of this century until World War II. Whereas the poets of the Qajar period produced sturdy and well-composed but unoriginal poems, the twentieth-century poets proved more receptive to fresh ideas, new forms, and original imagery.

Three poets of this period are worthy of particular note in terms of originality and attractiveness, one in the Indian subcontinent and two in Iran. Iraj (who has already been mentioned as a satirist) soon abandoned his earlier Khorasani style for a more intimate and idiomatic language, in which he wrote mostly casual and satirical poems, but also delectable lyrics. Parvin (1910–41), who remains, with Iraj, one of the two most popular poets of the period, is an eloquent writer of passionate humane feelings and ethical outlook. She is best known for her tender, fable-like *moqatta'āt*s (pieces) written in moving tones with moralizing intent. The third is Iqbāl of Lahore (1877–1938), an admirer of Rumi, who sought in a series of impassioned poems to expound his vision of Islam as a dynamic faith and a panacea for the social and political ills of the Muslim world. An intellectually endowed poet of fertile mind and reformist ambitions, his lively imagination is matched by his emotive intensity and mastery of expression. Iqbāl may well be considered the most significant poet in the classical Persian tradition since Hāfez. The present century also saw the last of the poets of note to write in the grand style of the Khorasani school, M. T. Bahār (1886–1951).

## Modernist Poetry

Modernist poetry, namely, a poetry which departs radically from the traditional school of the old masters, began to emerge only after World War II, when the deep social changes which had been developing for some time finally challenged the venerable literary tradition in a drastic fashion and eroded its foundations. It not only dispensed with the necessity of rhyme and consistent meter, but it also rejected the imagery of traditional poetry and departed noticeably from its mode of expression.

Nimā Yushij (1897–1960), the father of modernist poetry, died in relative obscurity, but after World War II a number of young poets took up his cause, fighting against the shackles of literary conventions and writing free verse, sometimes with a vengeance. The vogue gathered momentum, and by the late 1950s it had become the dominant mode of avant-garde Persian poetry. Most of the contemporary literary movements in the West, from the Symbolist to Letterist to Imagist schools, have found exponents among modernist Persian poets.

In modernist poetry, all formal canons, thematic and imagistic conventions, as well as mystical dimensions of the traditional school are by and large abandoned, and the poets (taking their cues from the West rather than from native traditions) feel free to adapt the form of their poems to the requirements of their individual tastes and artistic outlooks. Hence the great variety of styles among modernist poets.

N. Nāderpour, whose well-crafted poems are distinguished by a rich imagery no less than by the felicity of his polished language, has produced poems of considerable elegance and appeal since the mid-forties. He is also among the few modern critics who have not confused artistic integrity and achievement with commitment to definite socio-political views. A. Shāmlu (Bāmdād), who, prompted by his innovative urge, has experimented with a variety of styles, has remained a major influence among the modernist poets. An outstanding poet of this school is F. Farrokhzād, a female poet who casts her challenge against the shackles of social convention and marital morality, and the expression of her soul's search for love and fulfillment, in impassioned poems of remarkable sensuality and daring. Akhavān-e Thāleth, also a follower of the Nimā school, has produced among others, long poems of veiled protest and of epic quality. In Sepehri, a poet of serene simplicity but overweening imagery, we find an original poet singing in praise of the simple pleasures of life and basking in the contemplation of nature. Lyric poetry has found able representatives in H. Ebtehāj ("Sāya") and Simin Behbehāni. Many other poets, mostly beginning their careers in the 1950s, have become well known in the modernist school. It is a fact, however, that practically no new major poet has come to the fore since the mid-sixties.

While the core of modernist poetry remains romantic, many poets of a liberal or radical bent have been preoccupied with protest against the establishment as well as with promoting their social and political ideas. Poems of protest, however, are mostly couched in allegory, symbolic language and muffled terms, as open criticism of sensitive issues could be perilous.

Modernist poets have, no doubt, produced works of considerable freshness and beauty, more in concert with the contemporary cultural climate of Iran than traditional poetry, but the new freedom and the continuing absence of well-defined and universally accepted criteria have also led to much inept and even nonsensical writing.

## Prose Literature

Until this century, literary achievement in Persian prose was distinguished more by the style of writing than by creative aspects of the content or construction. Literary fame was garnered by imaginatively embellishing and crafting one's prose, whether informative or recreational. The stylization of prose was frequent in works on the humanities but more particularly in historiography, where the narrative lent itself easily to this form of writing; in history books the author could draw on rhetorical devices in order to heighten the praise of the patron, obfuscate his shortcomings, or gloss over his defeats. Some early histories, such as Bal'ami's *Tārikh-e Tabari* and (more notably) Bayhaqi's *Tārikh-e Mas'udi*, however, display considerable literary merit and dramatic force in many of their episodes without recourse to ornamentation.

With the passage of time, the style of writing became even more ornate, so that sometimes considerable skill is needed to extract the meaning from under a heap of rhetorical flourishes and turgid verbosity. An attractive balance between sense and artifice is struck in Sa'di's *Golestān*, noted above, only to be lost again in the contentious and florid style favored in later periods before the Revivalist Movement returned a new balance to prose.

This is not to say, however, that *belles lettres* as a genre was not cultivated. It might be better described as the literature of entertainment. Middle Persian knew tales of adventure (e.g., *Hazār Afsān*) and books of fables (e.g., *Kalila and Demna*, translated from the Indian *Panchatantra*). These varieties continued in Islamic times, with others, such as "stories of the prophets" and works of *adab*, which consisted mostly of interesting tales, witty remarks, curious observations, and attractive quotations.

It was only in modern times that prose literature began to assume a distinct status rivaling that of poetry. At the turn of the century, journalism became an instrument of social change and political reform, paving the way for the judicious use of simple, unadorned prose for fiction. The first dramas, novels, and short stories written in this prose style were all aimed at social criticism and satire and played a considerable role in raising the national consciousness and promoting social reform.

*Fiction.* After an inept and hesitant beginning with Ebrāhim Beg's *Siyāhat-nāma* (Travelog [Istanbul, 1888; first published a few years earlier in Cairo]), modern Persian prose fiction had a splendid second beginning with Jamālzāda's *Yeki bud, yeki nabud* (Berlin, 1921; English trans. *Once upon a time,* New York, 1985), a collection of six satirical stories and sketches in engaging and colorful colloquial language.

During the reign of Rezā Shah (1925–41) a number of novels were published, mostly maudlin works with pious social postures and weak techniques. Mohammad Mas'ud's first novel *Tafrihāt-e shab* (Night entertainments) made a stir by openly exposing the frustrations of the educated classes and urban civil servants with a mixture of humor and tragedy. It was followed by several others of the same kind. Hedāyat, a gifted and sensitive writer, whose frustrated latent nationalism and morbid sense of doom often led to mocking flippancy, emerged after World War II as the most outstanding fiction writer and the undisputed leader among his younger contemporaries. Although essentially a short-story writer, his short novel the *Buf-e kur* (Blind owl) has outshone by far all his other works and has exerted an enormous influence on Persian fiction. A number of his admirers, notably Al-e Ahmad, Chubak, and Behāzin, distinguished themselves in depicting the lives and circumstances of the poor, the oppressed, the ignorant, and the superstitious in a veiled or openly critical vein. In 1952 B. 'Alavi produced *Chashmhāyash* (Her eyes), a well-constructed novel of psychological insight and oblique political protest. The rather sagging and undernourished literary scene of the 1960s was enlivened for a while with M. 'A. Afghāni's *Showhar-e Āhu Khānoum* (Āhu Khānom's husband), a voluminous novel of love and betrayed loyalty, in which the circumstances of a provincial baker and his wife, mistress and children receive realistic and at the same time moving treatment. The 1970s saw the emergence of M. Dowlatābādi as a leading novelist. A writer of considerable verve and imagination, he writes mostly of the harsh life in southern and eastern deserts and oases of Persia. In his major work, *Kelidar,* a *roman fleuve* in ten volumes (1979–84), he treats of the life and times of a large array of characters, mostly poor villagers and semi-nomadic peasants and herders at the foot of the Kelidar mountains north of Nishāpur. The spectrum of experiences reflected in the pages of this marathon novel, the rich and original language, and the narrative dexterity of its author make it the most impressive Persian novel to date.

In the course of the 1970s and early 1980s, the novel, compared to the short story, has been gaining ground and increasing in number, even though well-constructed novels of merit, such as J. Mirsādeqi's *Bādhā khabar az taghyir-e fasl midādand* (The winds presaged the changing of season, Tehran, 1984) have been few.

***Drama.*** Satirical drama began brilliantly with Akhundzāda's plays;

although written in Turkish, they were conceived in the Persian cultural climate of the Caucasus and were aimed primarily at Azerbaijani readers. Some of them were translated by Ja'far Qarachadāghi who also wrote a number of plays in a similar vein. The reformist and satirical zeal exhibited in these early plays abated with the success of the Constitutional Movement in Iran and later with the restrictions imposed by autocratic rule. After World War II experiments were made with different kinds of plays, from poetical to symbolic to absurd. However, with the exception of Gholām Hosain Sā'edi ("Gowhare Morād," 1930–85), Persian drama has not been blessed with writers of the same calibre as poetry and fiction. Sā'edi, a prolific dramatist, short-story writer, and essayist of strong liberal convictions, wrote a number of socio-political and psychological dramas and has remained a strong literary influence for the past three decades.

It should be noted that Shi'ite passion plays or *ta'zia* are in verse which is generally of inferior quality and hardly rises to the level of literature.

*Prose Style.* The prose style of post World War II period has been subject to several influences and constraints. Nationalism, westernization and claims of the colloquial language have been the main forces affecting modern prose. Three different styles may be mentioned here.

The polite style of writing which finds its best representatives in books on the humanities and essays and articles in social criticism has evolved from the style of the Literary Revival. Its chief characteristic, compared to Safavid and Qajar prose, is clarity. At its best, it is also elegant. By "elegant" I mean a style of writing which is not only free from vulgarisms, verbosity, pretence, and adhers to correct grammar, but also uses apt words and phrases, is pleasing to the ear, and is informed by a quality of mind which results in firm constructions and attractive expressions. Symptomatic of the continued importance attached in Persia to this style are anthologies of essays, articles and excerpts chosen by the virtue of their stylistic qualities[28]. The practitioners of the polite/formal style generally have a good foundation in Persian classics, often revealed in their borrowings from and allusions to the old masters' writings.

This style has been generally resistant to the influence of the West and continues the classical linguistic heritage. On the other hand it

---

[28]For instance, *Namunahā'i az āthār-e fasih-e fārsi-e mo'āser* (Examples of eloquent contemporary Persian prose) selected by Jalāl Matini, vol. 1, Tehran, 1958, 2nd printing 1967; vol. 2, Tehran, 1979.

has been affected by nationalistic feelings since the turn of the century, particularly after the Constitutional Revolution. An outcome of this has been a tendency to opt for words of Persian origin rather than Arabic, and to reduce or abandon some morphological Arabic features used also in Persian, such as feminine adjectives with broken plurals (e.g. *marākez-e 'elmi* for the earlier *marākez-e 'elmiyya* "scientific centers") and of Arabic plural suffixes (e.g. *mo'allefān* instead of the now less frequent *mo'allefin* "authors"). This tendency, which has gained steadily, can be seen clearly in the writings of M. A. Forughi (d.1949), A. Bahmanyar (d.1955), and S. Nafisi (d.1966). The Persian Academy (*Farhangestān*), in which some ardent nationalists wielded considerable influence was inaugurated by Rezā Shah in 1935, and coined or proposed words of only Iranian origin.

The second type is the style which has prevailed in fiction. Whereas some writers like M. Hejāzi (d.1973), 'Ali Dashti (d.1982), and T. Modarresi (in his *Yakoliyā va tanhāyi-e u* [Yakoliyā and his loneliness], Tehran, 1964) have used polished, even melifluous prose, the general tendency has been increasingly to use idiomatic and colloquial language, and this is now, by and large, the kind of prose which prevails in dialogue. In the hands of an able writer, the medium is colorful and effective. The use of slang and dialectical forms in fiction has been an offshoot of this tendency.

The third is the journalistic style which is more difficult to define in view of its variety, but which has played a major role in the development of contemporary language. Journalists have been less constrained by the canons of literary usage and more influenced by the necessity of forging new expressions and coining novel words in order to deal with the immediacy of publishing international news and concommittant situations or ideas. An invasion of expressions based on foreign idioms characterized journalistic writing of the less conservative papers and magazines in the 1970s, when the alien-sounding editorials of some "progressive" journals and newspapers reflected a galloping Westernization and an ever-diminishing familiarity with the literary heritage of the past. The revolution of 1979 with its reaction against Western cultural elements has attempted to check this tendency.

## Translating Persian Literature

Several features of traditional Persian poetry make life difficult for its translators. One is its rhythmical musicality, which cannot be rendered satisfactorily in Western languages. Another is its ornamental aspect, often dependent on the sound and shape of words, all of which is lost in translation. A third feature is the rhyming pattern of the *qasida* and *ghazal*, where the same rhyme is employed throughout the poem. Yet another is the tendency of Persian poets to play on the associative meaning of words and their overtones, impossible to reproduce in a different idiom. With good fortune one might find a translator who can absorb the original and express it in his or her own language as genuine poetry. Such is the case with Edward Fitzgerald's translation of 'Omar Khayyām, Omar Pound's translation of Zākāni's *The Gorbi and the Mouse*, and to some extent Rückert's German translations of Sa'di. Even Matthew Arnold's "Sohrab and Rustum" (although much abridged and not entirely following Ferdowsi's plot) is, in the absence of a satisfactory translation of the *Shāh-nāma*, a treasure to be valued.

Many have tried their hand at translating Hāfez, but we must perhaps despair of ever finding an adequate translation for the rich arabesque of his thought and the music of his lines. Even Sa'di's *Golestān*, despite several translations, awaits one comparable to Arthur Ryder's translation of Kalidasa's *Shakuntala*. The *Shāh-nāma* is an excellent candidate for an effective translation in verse, perhaps on the model of Dorothy L. Sayer's translation of *Le Chanson de Roland*.

Modern Persian literature, on the other hand, having eschewed the formal and stylistic features of traditional writing, lends itself easily to translation, and some good translations of both poetry and prose are available in English and some other languages.[29]

While few of the literary products of ancient Iran remain in their original form, Persian literature on the whole offers a vast corpus of poetry and prose written in Persia, Afghanistan, India, Central Asia, Turkey, and elsewhere. Persian poetry exhibits a distinct character, reflecting a distinguished literary culture; its form, its conventions, and above all its imagery impart to it a flavor all its own. Once we have acquainted ourselves with its modes of expression, a new vista of literary delight opens before us. We can enjoy the noble sentiments, passionate feelings, and profound thoughts that Persian poets and writers have been able to express so well.

[29]See chaps. 24 and 25.

# II. PRE-ISLAMIC LITERATURES

# 2. Literary Aspects of the Avesta

Ever since the publication of Anquetil du Perron's translation of the Avesta into French in 1771, the study of Avestan literature as literature has generally taken a back seat to the study of the Avesta as a religious document.[1] Even the most rigorous philologists and linguists have often been unable to resist the temptation to discuss the religious problems posed by the Avestan texts. This is as it should be, for no serious study of Zoroastrianism in its various phases is possible without a solid knowledge of Avestan, not to mention Sanskrit, Middle Persian, and preferably the other Middle Iranian languages. The extant translations of the Avesta into European languages can be at best misleading, at worst inaccurate. And so many textual problems remain that even the most careful and up-to-date translation can mask practically insoluble philological problems.

In this brief survey of Avestan literature I will try to confine myself to the Avesta as literature, although from time to time forays into religious concepts will be necessary. I have set two goals: the first, a discussion of the Avestan language and a general overview of the contents of the Avesta; the second, a closer examination of the poetic art as it is viewed and practiced in the Avesta itself.

Avestan is one of the two Old Iranian languages in which we have substantial written records. The other is Old Persian, the language of the Achaemenian inscriptions, the forerunner of Middle Persian and, ultimately, of the Persian spoken in Iran today. Iranists tend to divide the Iranian languages into eastern and western groups, though these designations do not necessarily correspond to geographical realities. Old Persian, for example, is a western Iranian language as one might expect, but Ossetic, a language spoken in the Caucasus, is categorized as an eastern Iranian language, while Baluchi, spoken in what was historically eastern Iran, is a western Iranian language. Avestan, because it shares characterstics of both language groups, is often called a central Iranian language. The entire Iranian language family belongs to the Aryan branch of Indo-European; the other large Aryan language group is Indic, represented in its oldest stages by Vedic and classical Sanskrit.

The Avesta is a compilation of sacred Zoroastrian writings, the date of composition of which is still hotly debated among Iranists, although

---

[1]For a good study of the initial responses to the Avesta in the West, see J. Duchesne-Guillemin, *The Western Response to Zoroaster* (Oxford, 1958).

a conservative guess would have the bulk of the Avesta composed between the sixth and fourth centuries B.C. The actual collection and canonization of the Avesta took place much later, during the Sasanian era.

Two fairly distinct dialects of Avestan exist, traditionally called Gathic Avestan and Younger Avestan. The difference between the two seems to be both dialectal and diachronic.[2] The oldest section of the Avesta includes the Gathas, hymns most likely composed by the prophet Zarathushtra himself. A great debate over the dates of Zarathushtra has continued over the years. Until recently there seemed to be a developing consensus that he lived during the sixth century B.C., but Mary Boyce now argues for a much earlier date, perhaps before 1000 B.C.[3]

Zarathushtra remains a mysterious figure despite all the attempts to find clues about his life in the Avesta, later Zoroastrian sources, and classical accounts. His own compositions, the Gathas, do little to dispel the mystery. They contain only the most general autobiographical information—indeed, they center largely upon the prophet's search for a patron, a king or tribal lord who would accept his teachings and provide material support for the propagation of his revealed religion. Such a patron was found in the person of Kavi Vishtaspa, a local leader in eastern Iran. The new religion eventually spread into western Iran, though how and when it came to be the official religion of the Achaemenian Empire is still a matter of much conjecture.

If the Gathas tell us little about Zarathushtra's life, they do at least provide the basic framework of his teachings. Even so, scholars differ widely on such fundamental questions as whether Zarathushtra was a monotheist or a dualist. Was he a reformer of the old religion, or did he make a radical break with the past? Did he reject such central practices of the old religion as the sacrifice of cattle or the consumption of *haoma,* the drink which bestows immortality? If so, how is it that his followers so blithely ignored the prophet's teachings and soon after his death reintroduced these practices into the Zoroastrian religion?

That controversies over such basic questions persist may be attributed to two features of the Gathas. The first is the nature of the Gathic texts themselves. The Gathas are religious poems, not theological treatises. At times the prophet seems to be preaching to his followers,

[2]See A. Meillet, *Trois conferences sur les gatha de l'Avesta* (Paris, 1925).
[3]M. Boyce, *A History of Zoroastrianism* (Leiden, 1975), vol. 1, 189–91.

elsewhere he prays fervently to his god, Ahura Mazda, the Wise Lord. Sometimes he even seems to be reporting dialogues between Ahura Mazda and various Bounteous Immortals, the seven manifestations of Ahura Mazda's personality and activity. The tone is often one of easy familiarity: Zarathushtra can talk to Ahura Mazda as a friend would talk to a friend.

Yes, Wise One, [grant] to me Thy proper support, which an able man, possessing such, should give to his friend and which has been obtained through Thy rule that is in accord with truth. (Yasna 43.14)

This I ask Thee. Tell me truly, Lord. Someone like Thee, Wise One, should declare to me, his friend, how reverence for your kind is to be from the reverent person, and how friendly associations with truth are to be established by us, in order that it shall come to us together with good thinking. (Yasna 44.1)

I know that [reason] because of which I am powerless, Wise One: by my condition of having few cattle, as well as [that] I am a person with few men. I lament to Thee. Take notice of it, Lord, offering the support which a friend should grant to a friend. Let me see the power of good thinking allied with truth! (Yasna 46.2)[4]

Though such verses reveal with some clarity the relationship which Zarathushtra enjoyed with his god, they provide little insight into his religious system. They are in fact expressions of devotion rather than systematic theological expositions.

The second reason for the controversy over Zarathushtra's religious beliefs is the linguistic difficulty of the Gathas. The late W. B. Henning summarized the problems in the Gathas, and the consequent temptations they pose for zealous interpreters:

Inevitably, there is a large number of words in the Avesta whose meanings are unknown, and a further large number whose meanings are imperfectly known; and such unknown or imperfectly known words are particularly numerous in the Gathas. Then there are words whose meaning is not in doubt; but even they, as

---

[4]For the reader's convenience I have used the most recent translation of the Gathas into English, by S. Insler, *The Gathas of Zarathushtra*, Acta Iranica, Textes et Mémoires 1 (Tehran–Liège, 1975), 65, 67, 81.

all words, have a certain range of meanings and from that range one can select an eccentric meaning. Now, if one attributes an entirely arbitrary set of meanings to the unknown words, in such a way that this set of meanings is consistent within itself and conforms to a preconceived notion of the contents of the Gathas, and if one proceeds to select suitable extreme meanings for the known words, one can translate the Gathas in any way one likes; one can turn them into a philosophical treatise or a political note-book, a lawgiver's code or a soothsayer's utterance.[5]

To problems in vocabulary we might also add the grammatical problems with which the Gathas bristle, as anyone who has studied the texts will attest.

Despite the obstacles posed by the Gathas, however, certain features of Zarathushtra's thought are clear. Perhaps the most significant and certainly the most distinctive is his ethical dualism. There are, of course, various kinds of dualisms: light–darkness, spirit–flesh, ideal–real, good–evil. Zarathushtra's dualism is based upon the opposition of the truth and the lie. Truth implies not only veracity in speech, but also the proper order of things; the lie is not only falsehood, but also chaos and disorder. Zarathushtra expresses this dualism in the opposition of the two forces in the spiritual world: Ahura Mazda and his Bounteous Immortals are pitted against the evil demons, the *daevas*, led by the arch-fiend Angra Mainyu. The world and the souls of human beings are the battlefield upon which the two antagonistic cosmic powers seek to work their wills. Individuals must each make their own choices, and thus strengthen or foil the progress of truth.

The dualism which runs throughout the Zarathushtrian religion is expressed not only in the words of the Gathas but also in the way the words are arranged in the verses. Since Avestan is an inflected language, like Latin, Greek and Sanskrit, and unlike English and modern Persian, a certain flexibility in word order provides a wide range of possibilities for the poet. In his poems Zarathushtra takes advantage of the flexible word order to create delicate contrasts and counterpoises when discussing the relative merits and drawbacks of the truth and the lie. Sometimes the contrasts are contained very compactly in the hemistichs of one line; sometimes they are balanced between lines or stanzas. Though translations into a word-order language like English cannot do justice to this verbal juggling, the following translation of stanzas from Yasna 30 might be instructive:

[5]W. B. Henning, *Zoroaster—Politician or Witch-doctor?* (Oxford, 1951), 14.

In the beginning were the two spirits, the twins
    who in a dream became known as
Evil or good in their thoughts, words and deeds.
Those who are wise discern rightly, not those
    who are ignorant.

And in the beginning when they came together
    they created life and non-life,
So that at the end there would be for followers
    of the lie the worst existence,
And for the truth-followers the very best mind.

Of these two spirits, the evil one chose to do
    the worst deeds;
The most bounteous spirit chose truth: he clothed
    himself in the stony vault of heaven.
Those who would please the Wise Lord do so by choice,
    through the performance of true deeds.

Of the two, the demons did not discern rightly, for
    confusion came upon them while they were
    consulting together.
Thus, they chose the most evil thoughts,
And they hurried to join forces with chaos, with
    which they now plague the existence of mortals. (3–6)

In the first of these verses the contrast is contained within the verse; indeed, it runs through each line. In the second verse the same technique is employed with the additional contrast of "in the beginning" and "in the end." The effect is heightened by the fact that the contrasting adverbs "in the beginning" and "in the end" appear in the same position in the second and third lines, respectively. As a result, what the poet says is reinforced by the way he says it. The two spirits are mutually antagonistic, and they will be so forever.

The third verse is largely concerned with the correct choice of the beneficent spirit, and the fourth with the incorrect choice of the *daevas*. Thus the contrast is continued, this time in the separate verses. Through the structure of the poem the dualism which is such an important feature of the prophet's thought is emphasized. The verses of the Gathas, then, are not oriental pearls strung at random, however difficult the job of the pearlborer.

One other feature of the Gathic poetry that should be mentioned

45

is the repetition and combination of certain key vocabulary items. Repetition, of course, is an important and effective oral poetic technique, and the Gathas are oral compositions of sacred content. The repetition of key words or clusters of words recalls to the listeners other sacred verses containing these words or word groups. Repetitions thus expand the listeners' experience and enable them to place the particular verse in a wider context of associations.

It is a pity that the Gathas are so difficult, for the effort required to decipher them often obscures the fact that they are poems, not merely philological puzzles. Zarathushtra was a consummate poet, and this skill must certainly have played a large part in his ability to attract followers to his new religion. As a poet-priest, Zarathushtra stands within a well-established Aryan tradition, a point which I will take up below.

Second only to the Gathas are the Yashts, hymns to various divinities who play important roles in later Zoroastrianism. The most impressive are the hymns to Anāhitā, Mithra, the *fravashi*s, Verethraghna, Vāyu, Ashi, and the *khwarenah*. Anāhitā is the moist, strong, spotless goddess of the waters. Mithra, like his Indic counterpart Mitra, is the guardian of the contract, the god who precedes the sun in its daily journey through the heavens, and who with his ten thousand eyes is ever watchful lest individuals or nations break their solemn agreements. The *fravashi*s, often called the souls of the dead, are really heavenly alter egos of all righteous people who have lived, are living, or will live. Verethraghna is the god of victory who bears some resemblance to the Indic Indra, a dragon-slayer who is himself called Vrtrahan. Ashi, the daughter of Ahura Mazda, is the goddess of fortune. The *khwarenah* is the fortune of every person, the proper function of the individual in society. As applied to kingship, it is the divine aura which accompanies every legitimate bearer of the crown.

None of these divinities or concepts is specifically mentioned as being worthy of worship in Zarathushtra's Gathas; this fact has led some scholars to believe that the Yashts were composed at a time when radical changes had been introduced into Zarathushtra's religion. Though the language of the Yashts is "Younger Avestan," and though the Yashts are obviously of later composition than the Gathas, the religious situation which they portray bears marked similarities to the period of polytheism which preceded Zarathushtra's reform. It is thus argued that the Yashts represent the reimposition of older beliefs upon Zarathushtra's system, which then produces a new syncretic "catholic Zoroastrianism" encompassing both the new and the old religions.[6]

Further, those Yashts which are devoted to such firmly Zarathushtrian entities as Ahura Mazda and the Amesha Spentas are derivative of, and generally inferior to, the great Yashts cited above. Thus, a theory has been advanced that there are different stages of composition in the Yashts: the primitive pre-Zarathushtrian proto-Yashts, which are "Zoroastrianized" here and there, and the Zoroastrian Yashts of later composition.[7]

The Yashts as they are preserved for us in the Avesta were probably composed at approximately the same time, perhaps the mid-fifth century B.C. The priests who composed them, however, most certainly had in mind particular epithets or even entire verses that had been traditionally associated with the deities to whom the Yashts were addressed. The most interesting Yashts, those that contain the most specific and distinctive information about the deities, were probably inspired by older Yashts preserved within priestly circles. Others, the so-called Zoroastrian Yashts, which are for the most part colorless and stereotyped, may be assumed to have had no such ancient prototypes. As for the reintroduction of pre-Zarathushtrian deities into Zoroastrianism, it might be argued that Zarathushtra did not explicitly condemn these deities; he simply chose not to mention them in his Gathas. If we consider the Gathas as hymns devoted to a particular god, Ahura Mazda, then the absence of other deities should not be too surprising.

The Yashts are also an important source of information about the development of the epic in ancient Iran. Particularly interesting in this respect is the Ābān Yasht, the hymn to Anāhitā, goddess of the waters. Anāhitā is depicted as receiving the prayers of many of the heroes and villains who are prominent in the legendary history of Iran; among them are King Haoshyangha (Persian Hoshang), the founder of the Pishdadian dynasty; and Yima Khshaeta (Persian Jamshid), who ruled over a kingdom in which there was no death or old age, no sickness, no withering of plants, no hot wind or cold, and in which everyone, father and son alike, was fifteen years old.

Indeed, the Ābān Yasht reads like a Who's Who of Iranian legendary history: Azhi Dahāka, Zahhāk; Thraetaona, Faredun, the slayer of Zahhāk; the great dragon-slayer Keresāspa, the Avestan counterpart to Rostam; the Turanian villain Frangrasyan, Afrāsiyāb; Kavi

---

[6]I. Gershevitch, *The Avestan Hymn to Mithra* (Cambridge, 1967), 8–13.
[7]A. Christensen, *Les Kayanides* (Copenhagen, 1931).

Usa, Kay Kāvus; Kavi Haosravah, Kay Khosrow; the warrior Tusa. Each of these characters approaches the goddess with a request for a boon; the heroes, of course, are granted success, while the villains fail in their appeals. Unfortunately for us, their stories are not told in any detail. For specific episodes we must turn to the Pahlavi works, or to the *Shāh-nāma,* the Persian epic.

The Yashts, like the Gathas, are poems,[8] but of a somewhat different nature. While the Gathas are complex and introspective, the Yashts at their best are colorful and descriptive. For this article, which seeks to highlight Avestan literature, I have chosen as representative of the most interesting of the Yasht literature several verses from Yasht 10, the Mithra Yasht, as translated by Ilya Gershevitch:

> Grassland magnate Mithra we worship . . . whom warriors worship at the manes of their horses, requesting strength for their teams, health for themselves, much watchfulness against antagonists, ability to strike back at enemies, ability to rout lawless, hostile opponents. (10–11)

> Grassland magnate Mithra we worship . . . who is the first supernatural god to approach across the Hara, in front of the immortal swift-horsed sun; who is the first to seize the beautiful gold-painted mountain tops; from there the most mighty surveys the whole land inhabited by the Iranians, (12–13)

> where gallant rulers organize many attacks, where high sheltering mountains with ample pasture provide grass[9] for cattle; where deep lakes stand with surging waves; where navigable rivers rush wide with a swell towards Parutian Ishkata, Haraivan Margu, Sogdian Gava, and Chorasmia. (14)

> Grassland magnate Mithra we worship . . . who goes along the whole width of the earth after the setting of the glow of the sun, sweeping across the edges of this wide round earth whose limits

---

[8]It may seem strange to read a discussion of poetry without any mention of metrics. The question of meter in Younger Avestan is still a matter of hot and inconclusive debate. For the main lines of debate the reader is advised to refer to K. F. Geldner, *Über die Metrik des jungeren Avesta* (Tübingen, 1877); and W. B. Henning, "The Disintegration of the Avestic Studies," *Transactions of the Philological Society* (London, 1942), 40–56. A full bibliography on the subject may be found in G. Gropp, *Wiederholungsformen im Jung-Avesta* (Hamburg, 1966), 188–90.

[9]In the word "grass" I have followed H. W. Bailey's translation (*Zoroastrian Problems,* [Oxford, 1943], 18, n. 3) for ease of understanding. Gershevitch translates "solicitors"; see his *Hymn to Mithra,* 81, 174.

are far apart; everything he surveys between heaven and earth, (95)

holding his mace in his hand; with its hundred bosses and hundred blades [it is] a feller of men as it swings forward; strongest of weapons, it is cast in strong, yellow, gilded, iron.[10] (96)

The Yashts are also somewhat instructive in their descriptions of the "good life" in ancient Iran, as this excerpt from Yasht 17, the Art Yasht, shows:[11]

O Fortune, the beautiful, O Fortune, the brilliant,
rich, shining in splendours,
O Fortune giving good things
to those men whom thou attendest.
Well-scented is his house
in whose house the good Fortune
the giver of prosperity sets her feet,
friendly, seeking a long association.

Those men are lords with possessions
with abundant stores, provisioned
wherein is spread a couch
and there are other desirable treasures
whom thou attendest, the good Fortune.
Truly fortunate is whom thou attendest
and I also whom thou dost escort,
most mighty and powerful.

Their houses well-established
continue rich in cattle
abundantly stocked to last forever,
whom thou attendest, the good Fortune.

Their couches continue
well-spread, well-perfumed,
well-fashioned, fitted with cushions,
with feet gold adorned,
whom thou attendest, the good Fortune.

[10]Gershevitch, *Avestan Hymn*, 79–80, 121.
[11]H. W. Bailey, *Zoroastrian Problems in the Ninth-Century Books* (Oxford, 1943; new ed. 1971), 4–8.

49

Their wives surely
sit expectantly on diwans
which are beautiful, fitted with cushions,
polished, anklet-adorned,
richly adorned with ear-rings
four cornered and with gold-inlaid necklace,
"When will the house's master come to us?
When shall we rejoice joyously in his beloved person?"
Whom thou attendest, the good Fortune.

Their daughters are seated
anklet on foot, tight-waisted,
fair-bodied, long-fingered,
in form with the beauty of such
as are a delight to the beholders,
whom thou attendest, the good Fortune.

Their horses gallop,
swift, quickly snorting,[12]
they draw a swift car,
they drag at the tanned leather,
they convey the bold man, the celebrator,
swift-horsed, strong-charioted,
sharp-speared, long-shafted,
swift-arrowed, shooting afar,
hunter in pursuit of the foe,
slayer in front of the enemy,
whom thou attendest, the good Fortune.

Their camels move speedily
sharp-humped, eager,
rearing off the earth, fighting, passionate,
whom thou attendest, the good Fortune. (6–13)

Another section of the Younger Avesta is the Yasna, or worship, composed of various prayers, hymns, and other devotional material compiled and arranged for liturgical purposes. It is recited in full during the *haoma* sacrifice, the central Zoroastrian rite, with each of the components of the Yasna liturgy relating somehow to the various

[12]M. J. Dresden's translation "quickly snorting" is probably better than Bailey's "racing lightly." See "Indo-Iranian Notes," *W. B. Henning Memorial Volume* (London, 1970), 134–35.

stages of the ceremony itself. The most interesting sections of the Yasna are the Gathas, the Hom Yasht, which is a hymn to the sacred plant, the confession of faith, the four sacred prayers of Zoroastrianism, and the Yasna of the Seven Chapters, composed in the archaic Gathic dialect. Another liturgical work, the Visprad, is largely derivative of other sections of the Avesta.

The final section of the Avesta to be discussed in this brief survey is the Videvdād, or as it is often called, the Vendidād. Videvdād means "Law Against the Demons," and the title accurately indicates the contents of the book: it is for the most part a collection of rules and regulations regarding ritual purity.

The compilers of the Videvdād were most likely the Magians, a tribe of priests whose presence according to Herodotus was required at all religious functions. The Magians were notorious for three practices which struck contemporary observers as a bit bizarre: they believed that the killing of certain kinds of harmful animals was a meritorious deed; they believed that the burial or cremation of corpses was a sin, and thus insisted upon the exposure of corpses so that birds and dogs could cleanse the bones of the rotten flesh; and they advocated consanguineous marriages. These practices are all encouraged in the Videvdād.

It is perhaps appropriate that we began our discussion of the contents of the Avesta with the Gathas and end it with the Videvdād, for the Videvdād represents the ultimate application of the ethical dualism so important in the Gathas. Practically everything a human being does is now regulated by a strict code, the goal of which is the maintenance of the purity of Ahura Mazda's creation and the consequent eradication of all evil forces from the world. Many of the regulations seem foolish or impractical, but they are entirely consistent with the Mazdean dualistic outlook.

Despite the legalistic tone of the Videvdād in general, in a few passages the authors manage to transcend the dreary repetition of rules, regulations, and punishments imposed for infractions. The first chapter, for example, contains a listing of the countries of the world, or, more accurately, the territories of Iran. Even here, however, the thoroughgoing Magian dualism is apparent: for each of these territories, which are, of course, the creations of Ahura Mazda, the evil spirit Angra Mainyu has fashioned a particular "counter-creation," a heresy or plague.

Also of interest is chapter 2, the fullest Avestan account of the exploits of Yima Khshaeta, the great king who ruled over Iran during

51

its legendary golden age. This account contains the story of Yima's preparation for the first onslaught of winter, his construction of a *var*, a subterranean palace which acts as a kind of Noah's ark for the preservation of the best plants, animals, and people.

The Videvdād's closest approach to lyricism is chapter 3, a hymn to the earth:

> Who satisfies the earth with the greatest satisfaction? It is that person, O Zarathushtra, who sows the most of corn, pastures, and fruit-bearing trees. It is he who irrigates the dry land, and drains off the marsh. (23)

> For indeed that plot of ground is not satisfied which lies long uncultivated, which should be cultivated by a plowman, which desires that which is good from the woman of the house. It is like a beautiful woman who long goes childless; she lacks what is good from the male. (24)

> He who works the earth, O Zarathushtra, with left arm, with right arm and left, left brings forth her increase like a loving husband who, lying on the couch which is spread out for him, brings forth a son, an increase, for his beloved wife. (25)

> He who does not work the earth, O Zarathushtra, to him the earth says, "O man who does not work me, you shall stand, leaning on the door of another, among those who beg for food. You will be given the food which drips from the mouths of those who have a wealth of goods." (28)

> . . . What is the Mazda-worshipping religion? It is when one vigorously plows corn, O Zarathushtra, (30)

> For he who sows corn sows righteousness. For when corn is produced, the demons begin to sweat; when meal is produced, they weaken; when flour is produced, they howl; when dough is produced they break wind. The demons' mouths are burned by it; they are put to flight when corn is plentiful. (31)

Having given this necessarily superficial overview of the contents of the Avesta, I turn now to a brief discussion of the role of the poet as it is viewed within the Avesta. Unfortunately there is no Avestan Nezāmi 'Aruzi Samarqandi to discuss the education of the poet or the standards to which he should aspire. No treatise describes the tools an Avestan poet should use. We can only form some general impressions from the scattered references in the Avesta to the virtues of the eloquent man.

In Yasna 62.4, a hymn to Ātar, the god of fire, we find the following appeal:

> May you give to me, O Fire, Son of Ahura Mazda, well-being, protection, and life both swiftly and plenteously. May you give me wisdom, abundance, a quick tongue, intelligence in making choices, and ample, extensive, and imperishable mental power. May you give me progeny which is valorous, with upright stature, sleepless, watchful even when reclining on the couch, fully developed, noble, watching over the borders, eloquent, and liberal.

This passage is significant for several reasons. First of all, it is addressed to the fire, in the Aryan tradition the source of poetic inspiration. The illumination provided by fire enables the poet to discover truth and to express this truth in effective words. In the Rig Veda the fire god Agni is called Vacaspati, the lord of the spoken word. The fire is also the earthly manifestation of Cosmic Truth, Avestan *Asha*. Thus it not only illuminates, but also distinguishes that which is true from that which is false. For this reason the fire ordeal, used to determine the truth of conflicting claims, was a well-established Aryan tradition. Zarathushtra himself is said to have endured such an ordeal to prove his credentials as a prophet, and in Zoroastrianism the truth ordeal must be undergone by every righteous soul before it can be admitted to Paradise.

Another important point which the hymn to the fire brings to our attention is the association of eloquence with martial abilities. The epithets applied to the desired progeny are those normally given to effective warriors. The upright posture and the ever-watchful demeanor enable the warrior to do battle with the forces of death, which would lull him into defeat. The collocation of eloquence and martial abilities is found throughout the Avesta. In Yasht 10.25 we read,

> We worship Mithra, the profound, powerful lord, benefit-bestowing, eloquent, approving of prayers, exalted, much talented, the embodied word, the charioteer possessed of strong arms.

Now Mithra is primarily a great warrior, but his warlike abilities are complemented by his eloquence.

Indeed, eloquence is considered to be an indispensable quality for the warrior, for words which are true and correctly uttered possess an inherent power tapped by the eloquent man:

> The eloquent word of the popular leader gave his audience the impression of absolute validity; it was authoritative because one felt that it revealed the law of life. It was as irresistible and valid as the law of life itself. It was no mere beautiful sound which existed only for a moment. Once pronounced it maintained itself: it created a new situation, it turned itself into reality. Eloquence, therefore, was nothing short of creative force, a vital energy. Its essence was the mystery of creation and life.[13]

Thus, the poet is a warrior in the cosmic struggle, and his words are potent weapons. Indeed, the *manthra* of Yasht 14.45 which worships strength and victory is described in just such terms in the following verse: "These are the words which are very potent, firm, eloquent, victorious, and healing." The power of words in the struggle between the forces of the truth and the lie is revealed in their ability to defeat sickness and death, sickness being a manifestation of the aggression of evil into Ahura Mazda's world. The authors of the Videvdād knew of three kinds of healing—healing with the knife, the plant, and the *manthra*—and of these three, healing with the *manthra* is considered most effective. In a sense, the poet-physician who recites the effective *manthra* is a warrior in the battle between good and evil. Though he did not compose the words, his correct recitation of them makes him an eloquent man.

With this primacy of the role of the eloquent man in mind we may return to our discussion of Zarathushtra, and perhaps conjecture a bit about how he saw himself and how his followers in succeeding centuries were to see him. In Yasna 29, the Gatha of "the plaint of the cow," the soul of the cow addresses Ahura Mazda, "For whom did you fashion me? Who created me? Fury, violence, oppression and force overcome me. I have no shepherd other than you. Procure good pastures for me." The cow here represents all cattle, and the situation is one which must have been all too common in eastern Iran during Zarathushtra's time—the disruption of orderly pastoral life by the forces of Aeshma, the violence of nomadic plunderers. Ultimately a protector for the cow is found, as we read in verse 8 of the same Gatha:

---

[13]W. B. Kristensen, as cited in F. B. J. Kuiper, "The Ancient Aryan Verbal Contest," *Indo-Iranian Journal* 4/4 (1960), 254.

This man has been found by me; he alone listens to our teachings. It is Zarathushtra, the Spitamid; he will cause our thoughts and the thoughts of Truth to be heard. For sweetness of speech has been granted to him.

The cow responds, "Am I to be satisfied with the impotent words of a weak man? I, who desire a strong lord? When will there ever be one who will give me physical aid?"

The question, however, is merely rhetorical. For clearly Zarathushtra's words are not powerless after all. His sweetness of speech becomes the most potent weapon in the battle against the nefarious Angra Mainyu. The poet is no mere bystander in the cosmic struggle; through his unique perceptions and through the forceful beauty of his words he is an active participant in the expulsion of evil from Ahura Mazda's good world. The Videvdād portrays Zarathushtra not in his creative role as poet and prophet, but rather in his role as primal priest. Once again we are dealing with a cosmic event, Zarathushtra's birth. To the Magi, Zarathushtra was the first priest, the first one who could instruct the faithful in the proper means to achieve purification. As such he was a serious threat to the evil demons, as we read in the Videvdād:

From the northern quarter, from the northern quarters rushed forth the death-dealing Angra Mainyu, the pre-eminent *daeva*. Thus spoke the evil, death-dealing Angra Mainyu, "O Lie, rush upon, kill the holy Zarathushtra." The Lie rushed forth, the Buti *daeva*, the abandonment of Forgetfulness, the evil one.

Zarathushtra recited the Ahuna Vairya prayer.... The Lie, stunned, rushed off....

The Lie answered, "O evil Angra Mainyu, I do not envision death for him, the Spitamid Zarathushtra. The righteous Zarathushtra has a full destiny." Zarathushtra envisioned in his mind, "The evil *daevas*, the followers of the Lie, plot my death."

Zarathushtra rose and proceeded, unbroken by the difficulty of the hostile riddles posed by Evil Intention. He was bearing stones in his hand, stones the size of a house, which he had obtained from the Creator, Ahura Mazda.

Then Zarathushtra threatened Angra Mainyu, "O evil Angra Mainyu, I will smite the creation of the *daevas*, I will smite the

demon of death created by the *daevas*, I will smite the witch
Khnanthaiti until the Savior, victorious, is born from the Kansaya
Sea, from the eastern quarter, from the eastern quarters."

Then the ill-intentioned Angra Mainyu answered, "Do not destroy my creation, O righteous Zarathushtra. You are the son of
Pourushaspa. I was invoked by your mother. Renounce the
Mazda-worshipping religion to obtain the favor which Vadha-
ghana, the ruler, found.

The Spitamid Zarathushtra answered, "I will not renounce the
Mazda-worshipping religion. My bones, soul, and vital spirit will
not be separated."

To him said the ill-intentioned Angra Mainyu, "By whose words
will you overcome . . . my creation . . . ?

Zarathushtra answered, ". . . with the word proclaimed by Mazda
. . . with these words will I conquer. . . ."

Zarathushtra recited the Ahuna Vairya prayer. (19.1–10)

The hostile riddles are in fact the feeble attempts of Angra Mainyu
to overcome Zarathushtra in the truth-test, the verbal contest. But
Zarathushtra has his own potent weapons, stones the size of a house,
which we learn elsewhere are really the words of the sacred Ahuna
Vairya prayer, words created in boundless time. These words, when
correctly uttered, are victorious in every contest; they clinch every
debate. They will be similarly effective in the truth ordeal to be endured by every soul.

Through a comparison of these two texts, the Gathic plaint of the
cow and the Vidēvdād account of Zarathushtra's birth, we can see
what changes have taken place in the religion and in its views toward
the beautiful spoken word. For Zarathushtra, poetry was a creative
weapon to be employed on the side of good; for the Magi, eloquence
consisted of the ability to repeat without error the words of sacred
texts which had been repeated over the generations. In short, the
decline of Avestan as a literary medium is mirrored in the religion by
an increasing reliance upon the priests as wielders of the sacred verbal
weapon.

# 3. Manichaean Literature

In Athens, on the hill of Mars, Paul quoted one of the ancient Greek poets, Aratos of Soloi in Cilicia: "For we are also his [Zeus's] offspring" (Acts 17). In so doing he sought to attain a common ground with those to whom he was preaching: "Forasmuch then as we are the offspring of God. . . ." A good Manichaean might have uttered the same words with a pure conscience. For like the general gnostic movement of which it is considered a part, Manichaeism sought to convey to humanity a universal wisdom, *gnosis*, perceived to be the only road to the salvation of the soul, the divine spark in human beings, from the corruption and evil of this world. Only through *gnosis* could this light be restored to its original home, Paradise.

In one of the gnostic texts from Nag Hammadi in Egypt, the *Apochryphon Johannis,* the author, having mentioned the word "prison," cannot help interjecting, "the prison that is the body [Greek *sōma*]."[1] This was to the Manichaean the great tragedy of this life: the soul or Light was an exile (Middle Persian *uzdeh*), "away from its true home," imprisoned in the body, and living in a hostile, evil foreign land—this world. The believer, then, had to concentrate all efforts on the return to the "Higher Self," God, Paradise.

The fundamental etiology of this tragic situation and its happy outcome is conveniently summarized in the *Khwāstvānīft,* a lengthy confessional text for the laity, "Hearers," preserved *in extenso* only in Uighur Turkish:

> We know the light principle, the Realm of God, [and] the dark principle, the Realm of Hell. And we know what existed previously, when there was no earth and heaven. We know why God and the Devil fought, how Light and Darkness were commingled, [and] who created earth and heaven. Finally we know why earth and heaven will cease to exist, how Light and Darkness will be separated, and what then will come to be. (8A)[2]

Manichaeism, then, was above all a "soul service" (Iranian *ruwānagān,* "that which concerns the soul"; also used to denote the alms given by the Hearers to the Elect). Its one and only goal was the release of

---

[1]Sören Giversen, *Apocryphon Johannis,* Acta Theologica Danica 5 (1963), 107.

[2]Jes P. Asmussen, *Xᵘāstvānīft: Studies in Manichaeism,* Acta Theologica Danica 7 (1965), 196. On Iranian confession texts, see 235ff.

the soul (Light, God) from its material prison, to bring about its salvation, which is ultimately the salvation of God himself. The sum total of divine life under the tyranny of Darkness is the Living Soul (Augustine's *viva anima*), a designation borrowed from I Corinthians 15:45: "The first man Adam was made a living soul [*psychē zōsa*]."[3] The human being, therefore, is a collaborator with God in the great struggle toward salvation and thus has a cosmic responsibility.

## The Prophet

The founder of this great gnostic system was Mani. In his survey of the Manichaean religion in *De haeresibus ad Quodvultdeum*, 46, Augustine introduces Mani with the laconic and scarcely informative sentence, "The Manichaeans originate from a certain Persian, who was called Manes." He goes on to say elsewhere that the followers of this Manes, in order to dissociate him from insanity (*mania*) called him Manichaeus (really from Syriac Mānī Khayyā, the "Living Mani"), or Mannichaeus, with the geminate "n," which was interpreted *manna fundens*, "bestowing manna" (*Contra Faustum* 19.22). The question of Mani himself, his ancestry and origins, was of little or no interest. The exposition and refutation of his doctrines along with a general indication of his nationality were considered adequate by the Christian heresiographers. Thus, as is the case with Jesus and Zarathushtra, the copious information about Mani's teachings contrasts sharply with the meager data about the prophet himself.

Only the year of Mani's birth can be fixed with full certainty: 14 April 216 A.D. His birthplace is given as Babylonia (no doubt near Seleucia-Ctesiphon):

> I am a grateful pupil hailing from the land of Babel. I hail from the land of Babel, and I have been placed in the gate of truth. I am a singer, a pupil who was led out of the land of Babel. I was led out of the land of Babel in order to cry out a cry in the world. You, [oh] Gods, I implore, all you Gods, forgive me [my] sins through mercy. [M 4, 2 V, Parthian][4]

---

[3]On the Living Soul, see Asmussen, *Manichaean Literature* (Delmar, N.Y., 1975), 47ff.
[4]Ibid., 8–9. Abbreviations: Cat. = Mary Boyce, *A Catalogue of the Iranian Manuscripts in Manichaean Script in the German Turfan Collection*, Deutsche Akademie der Wissenschaften zu Berlin, Institut für Orientforschung, Veröffentlichung 45 (Berlin, 1960); HR II = F. W. K. Müller, *Handschriften-Reste in Estrangelo-Schrift aus Turfan, Chinesisch-Turkistan*, II, Aus dem Anhang zu den APAW aus dem Jahre 1904; MM I–III = F. C. Andreas and W. Henning, *Mitteliranische Manichaica aus Chinesisch-Turkestan*, I–III, SPAW 1932, 1933, 1934.

But on the details of his life—on his father's and his mother's families; his first public appearance; his relationship to the three Sasanian kings, Shāpur I and his sons Hormizd I and Bahrām I, during whose reigns Mani's missionary activity reached full fruition; his travels and his last years; his imprisonment; and his death sometime between 274 and 277—accounts vary widely, making it virtually impossible to ascertain precise historical facts.[5] Some light has been shed on Mani's religious background by the so-called *Cologne Mani Codex,* a Greek biography of Mani translated from Syriac. This text shows that Mani was brought up among the Judeo-Christian baptist followers of Elkhasaios,[6] a name that also appears in a Parthian text as Alkhasā.[7] Manichaean literature dwells most often, however, on the drama of the prophet's redemptive death:

The ever Powerful One stood in prayer, he implored the Father with praise: "I have cleaned the earth and spread the seed, and the fruit full of life I have brought before you. I have built a palace and a quiet monastery for your *Nous.* And the Holy Spirit I have sown in a green flower-garden and brought a delightful garland to you. Brilliant trees I have made fruitful, and I showed the road [leading] to the sons on high. I have entirely accomplished your pious order for the sake of which I was sent to this world. Take me [then] to the peace of salvation, where I shall not any longer see the figure of the enemies, nor hear their tyrannic voice. This time [viz. in distinction to the previous rebirths] give me the great garland of victory." [M 5, Parthian]

Just like a sovereign who takes off armour and garment and puts on another royal garment, thus the Apostle of Light took off the warlike dress of the body and sat down in a ship of Light and received the divine garment, the diadem of Light, and the beautiful garland. And in great joy he flew together with the Light Gods that are going to the right and to the left [of him], with harp [-sound] and song of joy, in divine miraculous power, like a

---

[5] For a brief but lucid sketch of Mani's life and teachings, see Mary Boyce, *A Reader in Manichaean Middle Persian and Parthian,* Acta Iranica 9 (Leiden/Tehran-Liège, 1975), 25f. Also see Asmussen, *X^uastvanift,* 9f., with references.

[6] See Asmussen, "Om den nyfunde græske Mani-Kodex fra Köln," *Humanitet og eksistens—en artikelsamling tilegnet Børge Diderichsen* (Copenhagen, 1976), 88–101, with a full bibliography.

[7] See Werner Sundermann, "Iranische Lebensbeschreibungen Manis," *Acta Orientalia* 36 (1974): 129f. and 148f.

swift lightning and a shooting star, to the Column of Glory, the path of the Light, and the Moon-Chariot, the meeting-place of the Gods. And he stayed [there] with God Ohrmizd the Father. [T II D 79 = M 5569, Parthian][8]

The uncertainties about Mani's biography are perhaps responsible for the fact that in later Islamic popular tradition Mani was remembered not so much as the founder of a religion, but rather as a great artist. The tradition of Mani the painter is historically well-founded, partly in the existence of Mani's *Ardahang*, a picture book (see below), and also in the Manichaeans' well-attested interest in the production of paper, in writing, and in illustration. According to this tradition, the result of the brief renaissance of Manichaeism in Central Asia during the first centuries after Mohammad, Mani is a man from China. In its Persian form the same tradition suffers exaggeration and is completely secularized. Mani becomes a painter of great renown, possessing extraordinary powers, the "master" (*sarāmad*) or "leader" (*sālār*) of the "Chinese school of painters" (*negārkhāna-ye Chini*).[9]

## The Literature

But it is a religion that Mani founded—a universal religion in the most profound sense—a religion that united and perfected the teaching of all the prophets of the past: Adam, Seth, Noah, and especially the Buddha, Zarathushtra, and Jesus. Mani, as heir to the great religious traditions, which in his thinking had failed to produce a religion for all humanity, thus became the "seal of the prophets." In a famous textual fragment, Mani compares his religion to previous ones:

The religion that I [i.e., Mani] have chosen is in ten things above and better than the other, previous religions. Firstly: the primeval religions were in one country and one language. But my religion is of that kind that it will be manifest in every country and in all languages, and it will be taught in far away countries.
Secondly: the former religions [existed] as long as they had the pure leaders, but when the leaders had been led upwards [i.e, had died], then their religions fell into disorder and became neg-

[8]Asmussen, *Manichaean Literature*, 55–56.
[9]See Asmussen, *X*ʷ*astvānīft*, 10–11. The tradition of Mani the painter still lives in Sir Muhammad Iqbāl's *Javid-nāma* of 1932.

ligent in commandments and works. And in . . . [But my religion, because of] the living [books(?)], of the Teachers, the Bishops, the Elect, and the Hearers, and of wisdom and works will stay on until the End.

Thirdly: those previous souls that in their own religion have not accomplished the works, will come to my religion [i.e., through metempsychosis], which certainly will be the door of redemption for them.

Fourthly: this revelation of mine of the two principles and my living books, my wisdom and knowledge are above and better than those of the previous religions.

Fifthly: all writings, all wisdom and all parables of the previous religions when they to this [religion of mine came . . .] [T II D 126 = M 5794, Middle Persian][10]

Perhaps this preoccupation with universality, with the common message, explains the Manichaeans' fascination with art and literature. Their beautiful paintings, intricate calligraphy, and ingeniously composed hymns that betray a deep sense of musicality, all seem to belie the Manichaean belief that life on earth is a prison, that the pleasures of this world are entrapments which keep the soul from its ultimate destination, Paradise. But Manichaean art is first and foremost purely religious, and this holds true even of literature that appears on the surface to be secular. Manichaean art is not *ars gratia artis*; it is *ars gratia Dei*:

The shining sun
and the glittering full moon
shine and glitter from the trunk
of this tree. Brilliant birds
sport there happily. Sporting
[there] are doves [and] peacocks of all
colors. . . . They sing and call of
the maidens [or, The (voices?) of the maidens sing and call].[11]

A presentiment of the pleasures and delights of Paradise. A religious poem. This is perhaps the old Iranian poetical style and imagery put into a religious context. It is possible to compare this passage with

[10]Asmussen, *Manichaean Literature*, 12.
[11]See ibid., 38.

another Iranian text, this from the Khotanese Buddhist *Book of Zambasta*:

Spring has come. In the earth it is warm. The flowers are variegated. All the trees have become overgrown. The creepers have blossomed. They sway about greatly in the breeze. The breeze from the trees smells sweetly. The lotus-pools, the springs, the ponds, the mountains are overgrown. The little birds sing many a lovely song. . . .[12]

Or with one of the Coptic psalms:

Lo, all trees and plants have become new again.
Lo, roses have spread their beauty abroad,
for the bond has been severed that does harm to their leaves.
Do thou sever the chains and bonds of our sins.
The whole air is luminous, the sphere of heaven is resplendent today,
the earth too puts forth blossom, the waves of the sea are still,
for the gloomy winter has passed that is full of trouble.
Let us escape from the iniquity of evil.[13]

According to the second-century rhetorician Theon, a fable was a "fictitious story picturing a truth." To the Manichaean, all literature exposed the truth. What remains of this literature is undoubtedly only a dim reflection of what once existed, but it is sufficient to give an accurate impression of its scope, genres, and quality. Its languages are many, a fact showing that Mani's wish for his religion to "be manifest in every country and in all languages" was largely realized. The Manichaean texts which have come to light are in Iranian (Middle Persian, Parthian, Sogdian, New Persian, and, in one fragment, Bactrian),[14] Uighur Turkish,[15] Coptic, Chinese, Greek, Latin,[16] Syriac,[17] and To-

[12]H. W. Bailey, "The Persian Language," *The Legacy of Persia*, ed. A. J. Arberry (Oxford, 1953), 189, and R. E. Emmerick, *The Book of Zambasta: A Khotanese Poem on Buddhism* (London, 1968), 286–87.

[13]Geo Widengren, *Mani and Manichaeism* (London, 1965), 90, and C. R. C. Allberry, *A Manichaean Psalm Book*, pt. 2 (Stuttgart, 1938), 8.

[14]For references to text editions, see Boyce, *Catalogue* (reference in n. 4).

[15]Republished and collected in *Sprachwissenschaftliche Ergebnisse der deutsches Turfan-Forschung*, I–II: Gesammelte Berliner Akademieschriften 1908–38 (Leipzig, 1972). See also Peter Zieme, *Manichäisch-türkische Texte*, Berliner Turfantexte (Berlin, 1975).

[16]Bibliography in Alfred Adam, *Texte zum Manichäismus* (Berlin, 1954).

[17]F. C. Burkitt, *The Religion of the Manichees* (Cambridge, 1925), 112ff.

charian B.[18] They cover the period from the third to the tenth century
A.D., and represent a comprehensive literature of varying quality,
ranging from meager products to pearls of artistry.

## Mani's Own Writings

The most important part of Manichaean literature is, of course, the
canonical books—Mani's seven scriptures in Aramaic. The canon, according to both Coptic and Chinese sources,[19] consisted of:

1. *The Living* (or *Great*) *Gospel* (Middle Persian Ewangelyon; Chinese
*Ying-lun*). This was divided into twenty-two chapters of which the
opening lines are still known:[20] "I, Mani, the Apostle of Jesus the
Friend, according to the will of the Father, the true God," and "he
[Mani] teaches the word of the Living Evangel of Eye and Ear, and
preaches the fruit of righteousness."

2. *The Treasure of Life* (Middle Persian title probably *Niyān-e Zenda-
gān*, "Treasure of the Living"). According to M915, a Sogdian fragment, this work dealt with the five gifts: charity, faith, perfection,
patience, and wisdom.[21]

3. *Treatise, Pragmateia.* No fragments of this text, nor an Iranian
title survive. To judge by the Chinese translator's gloss, it gave Mani's
view of the origin of the world.

4. *The Book of Secrets* (Middle Persian *Rāzān*). No fragments remain,
but the titles of its eighteen chapters were recorded by Ebn al-Nadim
in the *Fehrest*. They include: The Seven Spirits, The Testimony of
Adam about Jesus, The Falling from the Faith, The Prophets, and
The Resurrection.[22]

5. *The Book of the Giants* (Middle Iranian *Kawān*). This work contains
Mani's version of the story of the fallen angels and their sons, the
giants, alluded to in Genesis 6:2,4. For the elaboration of the story,
Mani relied on the tradition reflected in I Enoch or the Ethiopic
Enoch. This connection was first suggested by Isaac de Beausobre in

[18]Annemarie von Gabain and Werner Winter, *Türkische Turfantexte IX, Ein Hymnus an
den Vater Mani auf "Tocharisch" B mit alttürkischer Übersetzung*, ADAW (Berlin, 1956), no. 2
(Berlin, 1958).

[19]On the canon, see G. Haloun and W. B. Henning, "The Compendium of the Doctrines and Styles of the Teachings of Mani, the Buddha of Light," *Asia Major* 3 (1952),
204ff.

[20]M17 and M172, I; Mary Boyce, *Reader,* 32, with a reference to the Greek version
in the Cologne Mani Kodex.

[21]Haloun and Henning, *op cit.,* 206.

[22]Bayard Dodge, *The Fihrist of al-Nadim* (New York, 1970), 797–98. Also Gustav Flügel,
*Mani, seine Lehre und seine Schriften* (Leipzig, 1862), 72f. (Arabic text) and 102–103.

his *Histoire critique de Manichée et du Manichéïsme* (Amsterdam, 1734, 1739) and corroborated by W. B. Henning.[23] It is definitively proved by an Enoch quotation in the Mani Codex[24] and by the contents of Aramaic Enoch fragments from Qumran Cave 4.[25] It is only natural that Mani, having been reared in a Judeo-Christian milieu, used such literature. Aside from the Enoch literature, *Hermas' Pastor* is known in a Middle Persian version (M97),[26] and material abounds from the Gospels, often following Tatian's *Diatessaron*, and from the Pauline Epistles.[27]

6. *The Epistles* (Middle Iranian *Dibān*) are cited occasionally in Middle Persian and Sogdian texts, but no Iranian version has been preserved *in extenso*. The Coptic examples, however, indicate that these letters dealt with personal affairs as well as with doctrinal matters and organizational problems. Paul, so highly esteemed by Mani, was the model, as the following introductory lines from one of the Coptic translations shows:[28] "Manichaeos, Apostle of Jesus Christ, and Kustaios, the . . . and all other brothers who are with me, to Sisinnios!" A detailed survey of the epistles, among many others the epistles to Armenia and Sīsīn–Patī mentioned in Sogdian fragment M915, is given in the *Fehrest*.

7. *Psalms and Prayers*. Although none of the prayers has been identified, there are many fragments of Mani's two psalms in Middle Persian, Parthian, and Sogdian. These are called in Parthian *wuzurgān afriwān* (The praise of the great ones) and *Qshūdagān afriwān* (The praise of sanctification). They were addressed to the Father of Greatness, Jesus the Splendor, and very likely to other gods of the Third Creation. Mani's psalmody is "markedly formal in construction, each of the sections into which it is divided being characterized by a set phrase, recurring frequently within it."[29]

[23]*BSOAS* 9 (1943), 56ff. Also see idem, "Ein manichäisches Henochbuch," *SPAW* (1934), 27ff., and "Neue Materialen zur Geschichte des Manichäismus," *ZMDG* 90 (1936), 3–4.

[24]Marc Philolenko, "Une citation manicheene du Livre d'Hénoch," *Revue d'histoire et de philosophie religieuses* 52 (1972): 337ff.

[25]J. T. Milik, "Turfan et Qumran," *Festgabe für Karl Georg Kuhn* (Göttingen, 1971), 117ff.

[26]F. W. K. Müller, "Eine Hermas-Stelle in manichäischer Version," *SPAW* 51 (1905), 1077–83.

[27]See Werner Sundermann, "Christliche Evangelientexte in der Überlieferung der iranisch-manichäischen Literatur," *Mitteilungen des Instituts für Orientforschung* 14 (Berlin, 1968), 386ff., and Asmussen, "Iranische neutestamentliche Zitate und Texte und ihre textkritische Bedeutung," *Altorientalische Forschungen* 2 (Berlin, 1975), 85ff.

[28]Widengren, op cit., 85ff.

[29]Boyce, *Reader*, 91ff., 122f., 169f., and idem, "The Manichaean Literature in Middle Iranian," *Handbuch der Orientalistik* I, IV, 2 (Leiden/Köln, 1968), 67ff.

Four works which were not part of the canon *per se* were nevertheless regarded with reverence. One was Mani's only non-Aramaic work, the Middle Persian *Shāhbuhragān*, dedicated to the Sasanian monarch Shāpur I. Mani's *Ardahang*, a picture book portraying the most important aspects of the doctrine of the two great principles, Light and Darkness, is often mentioned in Persian literature.[30] Accompanying the *Ardahang* was a book of commentary, the Parthian *Ardahang wifrās* (Explanation of the *Ardahang*), of which some fragments remain. Finally, the *Kephalaia* (Discourses) were the sayings and teachings of Mani collected after his death by his followers. These represented a kind of Manichaean *hadith*. Again, only fragments in Iranian remain.

It is almost impossible to assign extant texts to specific works, but it is possible to get an overall picture of the topics dealt with in Mani's opus. The table of contents of Mary Boyce's *Reader* provides a convenient listing of subjects. These have to do largely with apologetic, autobiographical, cosmological, eschatological, and ethical concerns.

## Other Manichaean Literature

The noncanonical works of the Manichaeans are impressive both in their scope and in their artistic merit. The bulk of this literature is in verse, as might be expected from the Manichaean belief that the words of Mani alone were final and authoritative. A wide range of literary genres is represented: historical literature of the missionary movement,[31] biographical and hagiographical literature,[32] magical texts,[33] didactic treatises, liturgical and confessional literature, homilies, calendar tables, glossaries (Western Iranian–Sogdian), dogmatics, parables, allegories, letters, and, most notably, hymns. These unrhymed hymns followed the ancient Iranian poetical tradition of meter based upon stress rather than quantity.[34]

There is one significant, though quite understandable, omission from the Manichaean corpus: wisdom literature, so common in Middle Eastern writings, such as that of ancient Egypt, the Old Testament, and the Akkadian and later Sasanian literatures. This conspicuous

---

[30]Note, for example, Gorgani's *Vis o Ramin,* ed. M. Minovi (Tehran, 1935), 42, l. 6 and 385, where reference is made to *Arzang.*

[31]Sundermann, "Zur früher missionarischen Wirksamkeit Manis," *Acta Orient. Hung.* 24 (1971): 79ff. and 271ff.

[32]Idem, "Iranische Lebensbeschreibungen Manis," *AO* 36 (1974): 125ff.

[33]W. B. Henning, *BSOAS* 12 (1947): 39ff.

[34]Idem, "The Disintegration of the Avestic Studies," *TPS* (1942): 40ff. and "A Pahlavi Poem," *BSOAS* 13 (1950): 641ff.

absence is due to the fact that wisdom literature is largely concerned with the practical wisdom of this world: "If you are reasonable, establish a household";[35] "By knowledge shall the chambers be filled . . . make it fit for thyself in the field";[36] "Marry and establish ties of kinship in this world."[37] To the Manichaean, wisdom was not of or for this world; rather, it was devoted entirely to Paradise.

The most remarkable feature of Manichaean literature in all its genres is its rich, almost "realistic" imagery. This is clearly a Christian heritage, even in many details. For example, exactly as in the New Testament (Matt. 13:18ff., Mark 4:13ff., Luke 8:11ff.) the Parable of the Sower is told as a parable but interpreted as an allegory.[38] Manichaean imagery expressed the exact nuances of the believers' religious feelings, whether in a didactic context or in the liturgy. The teacher Mar Ammo narrates the following in a prose fragment:

> Then the spirit Bag Ard taught me "The Assembling of the Five Gates" by means of parables:

> "The gate of the eyes that is deceived when seeing what is vain, [is] like unto the man who sees a mirage in the desert: a town, a tree, water [and] many other things that demon makes him imagine and kills him. Further [it is] like unto a castle on a rock [?] to which the enemies found no access. Then the enemies arranged a feast, much singing and music. Those in the castle became greedy of seeing, [and] the enemies assaulted them from behind and took the castle. The gate of the ears [is] like unto that man who went along a secure [?] road with many treasures. Then two robbers stood near his ear, deceived him through beautiful words, took him to a place far away and killed him [and] stole his treasures. Further [it is] like unto a beautiful girl who was kept locked up in a castle, and a deceitful man who sang a sweet melody at the base of the castle wall, until that girl died of grief. The gate of the smelling nose [is] like unto the elephant when it from a mountain above the garden of the king became greedy of the smell of the flowers, fell down from the mountains in the night

[35]C. E. Sander-Hansen, *Aegyptiske Leveregler* (Copenhagen, 1952), 28 (from the wisdom book of Ptahhotep).

[36]Prov. 24:4, 27.

[37]*zan kardan ud peywand-i getig rayenidan*; see Asmussen, *Xᵘastvanift*, 31.

[38]Sundermann, "Mittelpersische und parthische kosmogonische und Parabeltexte der Manichäer," *Schriften zur Geschichte und Kultur des Alten Orient* 8, Berliner Turfantexte 4 (Berlin, 1973), 95.

and died. The gate of the [mouth is] like . . ." [M 2, Middle Persian][39]

The hymn literature likewise is richly expressive:

Who will release me from all the pits and prisons,
in which are gathered [?] lusts that are not pleasing?

Who will take me over the flood of the tossing sea—
the zone of conflict in which there is no rest?

Who will save me from the jaws of all the beasts
who destroy and terrify [?] one another without pity?
Who will lead me beyond the walls and take me over the moats,
which [are] full of fear and trembling from ravaging demons?
Who will lead me beyond rebirths, and free me from [them] all—
and from all the waves, in which there is no rest?

I weep for [my] soul, saying: May I be saved from this,
and from the terror of the beasts who devour one another![40]

There is an abundance of metaphors, but the equivalents are not at all fixed: "The Bride is the Church, the Bridegroom is the Friend of Light—the Bride is the Soul, the Bridegroom is Jesus."[41] But a certain constancy can be discerned: the Light Bridegroom (*dāmād roshn*) is Jesus,[42] who also seems to have been the most common bearer of the metaphor "Physician" (*beshaz*), a Christian tradition, but one which also fits well with Buddhist terminology for the Buddha and several of the bodhisattvas.[43] Mani also appropriated it for himself: "I am a physician from the land of Babylon." No fixed tradition maintains that Mani was a physician, but he was a physician of souls, the "Healing King," as a Chinese text has it.[44] Other Manichaean metaphors include the pearl and the treasure (*gnosis*); the merchant (Mani, the Buddha); the helmsman, the ship (Jesus, Mani, Primal Man, the Church); the sea, the harbor (the Light Realm); the shepherd and the

---

[39]Asmussen, *Manichaean Literature*, 22–23.
[40]Ibid., 83.
[41]*A Manichaean Psalm-Book* (Stuttgart, 1938), vol. 2, 154.
[42]F. Andreas and W. Henning, "Mitteliranische Manichäica aus Chinesisch-Turkestan II," *SPAW* 7 (1933): 326.
[43]Asmussen, *X^ᵘastvanift*, 321f.
[44]Asmussen, *Manichaean Literature*, 9.

sheep (the Father of Greatness, Jesus, Mani, the Apostles); musical instruments (Apostles of Light).[45]

An important category of Manichaean literature used suitable texts of foreign origin for didactic purposes. These were transmitted in local languages eastward to Central Asia and westward into the Middle East and Europe. Thus, the Manichaeans became literary intermediaries, and their contribution to European intellectual life cannot be overestimated. Everything, so to speak, could be used, even seemingly "secular" texts; the Manichaeans were masters of the art of adaptation, especially with fables and parables (Middle Iranian *āzend*).[46] The Aesop tradition, for example, is well represented in the Manichaean Uighur literature and also in one Sogdian text. This latter is the famous fable of the jealous fox (*alōpēx*) and the foolish monkey (*pithēkos*), a story first recorded by the Greek poet Archilochos in the seventh century B.C. and more recently used by La Fontaine. The Greek version is as follows:

Having danced and won favor before an assembly of animals, a monkey was elected king by them. When the fox, being jealous of him, saw a piece of meat in a snare, he took him there and said that he had found a treasure; and, instead of using it himself, he had kept it for him as a perquisite of his royal office; and he invited him to take it. The monkey went at it carelessly and was caught in the snare. When he accused the fox of laying a trap for him, the fox replied: "O monkey, fancy a fool like you being king of animals!" In this way those attempting things without due consideration not only suffer for it, but also get laughed at![47]

The so-called epimythion, the moral taken from it, is wanting in its Manichaean form but no doubt the Manichaeans found it useful advice to be careful in one's actions, especially as far as the Divine Light is concerned:

"Who will now be the right king for us? There is none better than you! All animals have approved Your Excellency as absolute king and are at the point of declaring you king. For Your Excel-

---

[45]See Victoria Arnold-Döben, *Die Bildersprache des Manichäismus* (Cologne, 1978) for a fuller treatment.

[46]For this and what follows, see Asmussen, "Der Manichäismus als Vermittler literarischen Gutes," *Temenos* 2 (Helsinki, 1966): 8ff.

[47]Asmussen, *Manichaean Literature*, 40.

lency's body is half like a man's, and half like an animal's. Let us now go quickly, and you shall seat yourself on the throne and be king over the animals!"

The foolish monkey got up and went along with the fox. When they approached the [trap?], the [fox] turned back and spoke thus to the [monkey]: "Good . . . has come before us and you have been placed before a good thing. Filled . . . you would not . . . the frame [?, the piece of meat?], but it is all presented and ready prepared for Your Excellency so that you shall eat well like a king. So if you will now take the trouble, take this frame [?] into your hands!"

The foolish monkey heard these words, at once he became very glad . . . [T I, Sogdian][48]

Another source used freely by the Manichaeans, and for which they were prime intermediaries, was the *Panchatantra*, the Sanskrit "Five Books." One example of the Manichaean use of this source is the tale of the pearl-borer, given, as expected, a Manichaean allegorical explanation:

. . . there was a quarrel, it could not be settled. So on the next day they went before a judge for a trial. The owner [of the pearls] spoke thus: "My Lord, I hired this man for one day, at a hundred gold dinars, that he should bore my pearls. He has not bored any pearls, but now demands his wages from me." The workman, in rebuttal, addressed the judge thus: "My lord, when this gentleman saw me at the side of the bazaar, he asked me: 'Hey, what work can you do?' I replied: 'Sir, whatever work you may order me [to do], I can do it all.' When he had taken me to his house, he ordered me to play on the lute. Until nightfall I played on the lute at the owner's bidding." The judge pronounced this verdict: "You hired this man to do work [for you], so why did you not order him to bore the pearls? Why did you bid him play on the lute instead? The man's wages will have to be paid in full. If again there should be any pearls to be bored, give him another hundred gold dinars, and he shall then bore your pearls on another day."

Thus under constraint, the owner of the pearls paid the hundred gold dinars; his pearls remained unbored, left for another day; and he himself was filled with shame and contrition.

[48]Ibid., 40–41.

The wise give this allegorical explanation: that man who understood all arts and crafts, represents [the body] ... The pearl-
borer is the body. The hundred [gold] dinars represents a life of
a hundred years. The owner of the pearls is the soul, and the
boring [?] of the pearls represents piety. [T I TM 418 (Sogdian
script) and M 135 (Manichaean script), Sogdian][49]

The Buddha stories also found their way into Manichaean literature. Indeed, one of the "bestsellers" of Christian European literature,
*Barlaam and Joasaph* (i.e., Brahman and Bodhisattva or Buddha), attributed to St. John Damascene of the eighth century,[50] passed
through Manichaean redactions, as is evidenced by two texts in
Uighur, one in Parthian, and one in Persian.[51] The Buddhist material
was, no doubt, shaped into a coherent whole by the Manichaeans
themselves. This series of stories centered on one major theme: The
Būdisāf's encounter with the suffering and perishability of this world
and his realization that "through wisdom, speech becomes luminous."
The Manichaean compilers must have had a number of sources at
their disposal but relied heavily on Aśvaghoṣa's *Buddhacarita* (first–
second century A.D.). The following brief Parthian text exemplifies the
Manichaean adaptation of Buddhist thought:

There was a big pond, and in it there were three fishes. The first
fish was One-Thought, the second fish was Hundred-Thoughts,
and the third fish was Thousand-Thoughts. At some time a fish-
erman came and cast his net. He caught those two fishes of many
thoughts, but he did not catch the fish One-Thought. [M 127,
Sogdian][52]

Perhaps the most startling example of the Manichaean genius in
taking advantage of non-Manichaean texts and literary forms is the
use of the Arabo-Persian *qasida* form to express Manichaean sentiments.

[With the help of] the Dhulfaqār [i.e., the sword of 'Ali] of reason
['aql] do open your speech [in plaint]!

[49]Ibid., 42.
[50]David M. Lang, *The Wisdom of Balahvar* (London, 1957), 24ff., and idem, *The Ba-
lavariani* (London, 1966), 11f.
[51]Boyce, *Catalogue*, 11.
[52]Asmussen, *Manichaean Literature*, 43.

I cry for help against this age, the age of quarrels and strife.
[They put] me, Noah-like, into an ark by force—
They throw me, Joseph-like, into the pit with violence![53]

This poem is indisputably in Islamic garb and yet deals with a characteristic theme of Manichaean theology: the suffering of the living soul in this evil and alien world.

It might be appropriate to conclude with the question of whether Manichaeaism could have prepared the way for the spread of Oriental motifs and stories in Europe. In this connection we might consider the possibility of a Manichaean source for Parsifal and thus also for the entire "Grail problem."[54] Thus, Manichaean literature may be important not only for Iranian literature, but also for the history of world literature.

[53]W. B. Henning, "Persian Poetical Manuscripts from the Time of Rudaki," *A Locust's Leg: Studies in Honour of S. H. Taqizadeh,* ed. W. B. Henning and Ehsan Yarshater (London, 1962), 89ff.

[54]See W. Hinz, "Persisches im 'Perzival,'" *AMI* 2 (1969): 177ff.

# III. CLASSICAL PERIOD

# 4. Court Poetry at the Beginning of the Classical Period

The evolution of an extensive New Persian literature in Khorasan and Transoxiana during the course of the tenth and early eleventh centuries constitutes an event of exceptional significance in the history of Iranian culture. This period saw the creation of a poetic dialect that continued as the vehicle for poetic expression well into the twentieth century. The chief genres of prose and poetry were fixed, and the national epic was given its definitive poetic recension. This period was, in short, the golden age of great beginnings. When the various developments that were then set in train had finally run their course, many Iranian poets of the nineteenth century turned back to this early period for fresh inspiration.

The importance of this development was not limited to Iran. The Central Asian Turkish dynasties—most notably the Seljuks—absorbed this Persian literary heritage and carried it to western Iran, Anatolia, and northern India in the course of their conquests. They made these areas, in S. M. Stern's phrase, "colonial territories" for Persian culture[1] and so established for the first time since the advent of Islam an extensive Islamic cultural area in which Arabic was not the unique vehicle of expression.

The royal courts of Khorasan and Transoxiana played a central role in this remarkable efflorescence of Persian poetry. From the late ninth century, when poetry was first written in New Persian, until the rise of Sufi literature in the twelfth century, virtually every major poet was either a fixture at the court of one of the ruling princes or had acquired initial training in his craft at such a court. The identification of Rudaki with the Samanids, Farrokhi and Manuchehri with the Ghaznavids, and Anvari and Mo'ezzi with the Great Seljuks—to give only a few examples from many possible ones—is so complete that mention of one automatically brings the thought of the other. The names of the Ismaili propagandist Nāser-e Khosrow or the mystic Sanā'i carry no such automatic associations since both chose to abandon the courts that had employed them as young men. Yet they learned their craft at the court, and their poetry reflects that origin. In Ferdowsi, the poet of the national epic, the *Shāh-nāma*, we en-

---

[1]S. M. Stern, "Ya'qub the Coppersmith and Persian National Sentiment," in *Iran and Islam*, ed. C. W. Bosworth (Edinburgh, 1971), 539.

counter a figure who seems to stand somewhat apart from the court. Although the facts of his biography are far from certain, he does not appear to have sought court patronage until after he was a mature man and had already undertaken his poetic rendering of the *Shāh-nāma*. Nor have any works survived to suggest that he ever composed panegyrics as a regular fixture of this or that court. Yet Ferdowsi too was dependent on the court, in that Samanid patronage of poetry and, in particular, their sponsorship of both a prose translation of the *Shāh-nāma* into New Persian and Daqiqi's unfinished poetical rendering of it prepared the ground for him. Court patrons also held out promises of a rich reward, which made the undertaking of such a monumental task both possible and attractive.

In short, one cannot understand the poetry of this period without placing it in the context of the aristocratic and courtly tradition. For subsequent periods, too, the courtly milieu retains its importance. Even after the court had ceased to be the sole sponsor of poetry, with the appearance of such poets as 'Attār and Rumi, it remained a principal one. From that time to the beginning of the modern period, no court of any size failed to attract and maintain talented and ambitious poets.

In what follows, I intend to explore some of the more important features of this tradition: the poetic milieu of the court, the formal features of the poetry composed there, and the themes and images special to the time. The focus of my remarks will be the period of Ghaznavid supremacy in the late tenth and early eleventh centuries, although I shall make some reference to earlier and later poets as well. Despite the severe limitations of our sources, this period is the first one about which we have moderately detailed knowledge. It is also one that exerted an extraordinary influence on subsequent generations of poets and patrons.

## The Beginnings

The origins of New Persian poetry are cloaked in obscurity. For many years it was assumed that the conquest of Iran by the Arabs and Islam in the mid-seventh century, and the consequent establishment of Arabic as the official language of government and religion, had cast a two-hundred-year pall of silence over the flourishing literary world of Sasanian Iran. Of course, Iranians writing in Arabic were known to have made major contributions to every field of Islamic culture, including poetry and *belles lettres,* throughout these two centuries, and to have translated extensively from Middle Persian literature into Arabic. But Persian poetry was believed to have virtually disappeared until it was revived in the late ninth century with a substantially new character, cast in the mold of Arabic prosody and Islamic sensibility. The near total absence of any extant texts in Persian from this period and the scattered and fragmentary nature of secondary accounts made this a reasonable assumption. In recent years, a more careful winnowing of what little has survived and a new interpretation of it have suggested that the situation was not so bleak as it first appeared. While the main current of literary composition was certainly in Arabic, there are also scattered indications that lyric poetry continued to be composed in a number of Iranian languages and dialects.[2]

Therefore, the earliest court poets in Persian were able to draw upon a still vital poetic tradition and did not have to revive one that was long moribund. The earliest extant examples of poetry in New Persian display an ease and fluency that hardly suggests a poetry in the process of creation or revival. Moreover, while the prosody of New Persian poetry came to be described in terms taken from Arabic—*mesrā'* (hemistich), *bayt* (distich), *qāfiya* (rhyme)—the metrical patterns are arguably more Middle Persian than Arabic in origin. The Sasanian names of some lyric forms (*tarāna, chāma, sorud*) were also employed, suggesting that they had never fallen out of use. There are still many unanswered questions about the development of the New Persian poetic language, but it clearly entails more than merely direct translation and adaptation of Arabic, as was long thought.[3]

Moreover, although Arabic was the principal, and often the exclusive, language of literary and learned composition throughout the Islamic world in the first centuries after the great conquests, one should not assume that all subjects treated in it were of Arab origin. Arabic quickly became the vehicle for an international literature, and a great deal of Sasanian Middle Persian narrative literature—including a portion of the national epic—was translated into Arabic. Arabic literature at its zenith, just before the appearance of New Persian

---

[2]See p. 10ff. on the transition of Middle Persian poetry to the New Persian. (Ed.)

[3]A number of studies on this question have appeared recently. In what follows I have drawn principally on those of G. Lazard, "The Rise of the New Persian Language," in *Cam. Hist. of Iran* (Cambridge, 1975), vol. 4, 595–632, and bibliography, 692–96; and L. P. Elwell-Sutton, *The Persian Metres* (Cambridge, 1976).

poetry, was deeply imbued with Iranian themes, images, and modes of expression. Arabic poetry was often as much Iranian as "Arab."[4]

We are still far from a thorough understanding of the complex series of events that took place in Iran during these centuries; one attempts generalizations about literary developments at one's peril. It is clear that the Islamic conquest and the wholehearted adoption of Islam and the Arabic language by Iranian writers profoundly altered the course of Iranian literature. Yet it is equally clear that the Sasanian tradition remained of great importance. New Persian literature is, in this first period of its greatness, both a self-conscious continuation of that tradition and a vital part of the Islamic literary milieu.

## Poets and Their Milieu

The principal poetic languages of the princely courts in Khorasan and Transoxiana were, as indicated above, Persian and Arabic—although Turkish and other Iranian languages had their poetry, too. The poets themselves may be divided roughly into two groups. The first is comprised of the professional court poets, those who had to undergo rigorous training in the techniques of their craft and then to demonstrate mastery of them before they could recite at court. Like the many distinguished scholars who adorned the Ghaznavid court, these poets lived by the patronage of the sultan. All the major poets of the period, such as Rudaki, Daqiqi, 'Onsori, Farrokhi, and Manuchehri, belonged to this group.

The other group is comprised of the amateurs, those who, whatever their degree of proficiency—and it was often considerable—composed poetry as an adjunct to their principal occupation at court. The majority were scribes, who shared with the poets of the first group a professional interest in both literature and the skillful use of language. Their number might also include virtually every member of the court, most notably the ruler and his viziers, since minimal competence in poetry was expected of anyone who boasted a proper education. The earliest extant anthologies of Persian poetry are, in fact, organized according to the rank of the poets, with monarchs given pride of place,

---

[4]The most recent and detailed discussion of the Iranian contribution to Arabic literature is to be found in V. Danner's "Arabic Literature in Iran," in *Cam. Hist. of Iran* (Cambridge, 1975), vol. 4, 566–94.

and the professional poets relegated to a position after that of chief ministers, religious scholars, and learned jurists.[5]

There has been an understandable tendency to blur the boundaries between these two groups. Monarchs are never court poets, nor court poets monarchs, of course, but the division between scribe and court poet is a less obvious one that has encouraged scholars to look for the origins of the latter in the ranks of the former. One authority has said, with regard to 'Onsori, chief poet of the Ghaznavid court, that like most other poets he began his career in the chancery.[6] Yet little suggests that this was true besides the similarity of their professional interests and the confusion that results from the use of one term, *shā'er*, to describe all who versify. There are, in addition, some clear indications that the two professions were regarded as quite distinct from each other. A contemporary work on the four categories of subordinates most necessary to a monarch, the *Four Discourses* of Nezāmi 'Aruzi, treats the poet's office as quite separate from that of the scribe, the astrologer, and the physician. Another contemporary work, the *Qābus-nāma*, devotes separate chapters to the professions of scribe and poet in its description of the various professions practiced in and around the court. Neither work suggests that these offices were interchangeable or that court poets were commonly recruited from the chancery.[7] Sāheb b. 'Abbād, who flourished in the latter part of the tenth century and who was an influential vizier of the Buyid dynasty as well as a noted man of letters, countered the idea that scribes made good poets in a reported comment on the poetry of Abu 'Abdallah Hosayn b. 'Ali Boghavi, "I am as astonished that a scribe should be a poet as that his poetry should circulate widely."[8]

The poetry of such amateurs did, in fact, circulate rather widely in its own time. The quotation just cited comes from an anthology gleaned from the notebooks of scribal poets who enjoyed considerable popularity, principally, one suspects, among those very bureaucrats

---

[5]The very earliest such anthology is the *Lobāb al-albāb* (A choice selection from the best minds) of Mohammad 'Owfi, ed. E. G. Browne and M. Qazvini, 2 vols. (London–Leiden, 1903–1906). In it, separate chapters are devoted to "Sultans, Kings, and Amirs," "Viziers and Chief Ministers," and "Religious Leaders, Doctors of Theology, Ministers, and Scholars" before the compiler turns to the professional poets, whose works he arranges by dynasty.

[6]E. E. Bertels, *Istoriia persidsko-tadzhikskoi literatury* (Moscow, 1960), 307.

[7]Nezāmi 'Aruzi, *Chahār maqāla*, ed. M. Qazvini, rev. M. Mo'in (Tehran, 1952). Trans. E. G. Browne as *The Four Discourses* (rev. 2nd edition, London, 1921). Kay Kā'us b. Eskandar, *Qābus-nāma*, ed. Gh. Yusefi (Tehran, 1966), trans. R. Levy as *A Mirror for Princes* (London, 1951).

[8]Tha'ālebi, *Tatemmat al-yatima*, ed. 'A. Eqbal (Tehran, 1956), pt. 2, 57.

and learned gentlemen who would modestly assert that "poetry was the least of their acquisitions." Certainly, their works did not survive in any quantity outside of this anthology. Their *divāns* were not copied from generation to generation, as were those of the court poets, and their works never provided the models for succeeding generations. Yet their contribution to the poetry of their time was not a function of the degree to which their work outlived them. As Walt Whitman aptly put it, "To have great poets, there must be great audiences, too." The amateur poets may not have produced much enduring poetry themselves, but they constituted an intelligent and appreciative audience for those who did. Their interest and their critical judgment helped to assure a very high standard for Persian letters, even as their devotion to poetry assured that no promising poets would go undiscovered for want of an opportunity to show their talent.

As I have already indicated, the literary milieu of Khorasan and Transoxiana at this time was a bilingual one, at least. Although Persian had quickly come to challenge and then surpass Arabic as a poetic language in the region, it did not replace it wholly. Arabic maintained its pre-eminence as the language of science, religion, and the chancery, and it continued to be a vehicle for poetry because scribes and scholars needed to refine their Arabic style. While many scribes and scholars composed poetry either bilingually or exclusively in Arabic, virtually no professional court poet appears to have done so. Even Manuchehri, who boasts repeatedly of the number of Arabic poets whose collected works he has memorized, and who consciously imitates the form of the Arabic *qasida,* seems never to have composed a poem in Arabic, at least not for the public record.

How the amateur poet obtained his position at court need not concern us, since he did not do so on the basis of his poetic abilities. But the question of how an aspiring court poet, particularly a young and relatively unknown one, came into the employ of a royal patron is of central importance. The process was probably fairly simple. When a young poet had gained some local reputation, he composed a panegyric in the name of the nearest likely patron and sent it to him. At the court, the merits of the poem were then judged by those best able to do so, and, depending on their opinion and the state of the patron's treasury, the poet was invited to appear at court, merely sent a gift, or left to nurse his talents in obscurity.

An anecdote in the *Four Discourses* of Nezāmi 'Aruzi relating how Farrokhi of Seistan gained a place at the court of the amir of Chaghāniyān suggests what the usual procedure may have been.[9] Farrokhi later became one of the chief adornments of the Ghaznavid court and one of the finest poets of his day, but as the anecdote begins, he had risen to no higher rank than that of stipendiary of the local amir of his own remote district of Seistan. Feeling that his talents were worth more than the amir was able to pay him, he composed a lengthy poem on the virtues of the amir of Chaghāniyān and set out to present it in person. It was early spring when he reached the capital city, and he found that the amir and all his court had gone to a valley near the city to supervise the branding of the year's harvest of colts. One official had returned to the city for supplies, and since he was knowledgeable in literary matters he had Farrokhi recite the poem for him to determine whether or not the poet should be introduced to the amir himself. The poem is too long to quote in full here, but the opening lines are of particular interest:

> I left Seistan with a caravan of silk merchants,
>> Bringing a robe woven from my soul and spun from my heart.
> Bringing a robe whose silk is composed of words;
>> Bringing a robe whose brocade my tongue has designed.
> Each thread of its warp was drawn from within me;
>> Each thread of its woof was extracted from my soul.
> Every art has gone into its making;
>> And in it there is a trace of every style. . . .

The image of the poet as a kind of silk merchant bringing rare and precious stuffs to court has a vividly emblematic quality worth reflecting on for a moment. It captures the poet's projections of himself as a skilled and painstaking craftsman, and one who is unself-conscious about both his intention to sell his wares at the best market for them and his willingness to suit them to the taste of his customer or patron:

> This robe was spun of language, wit and intellect,
>> And its designer labored long,
> So that at the head of its design, might be written
>> The praise of Abu'l-Mozaffar, amir of Chaghāniyān.

The official was impressed with the poem, but, so the story goes,

---

[9]This anecdote begins on p. 27 of the translation by Browne cited in n. 5.

he thought Farrokhi looked too uncouth to be its author. He therefore set him the further test of composing a poem on the subject of the amir's branding ground. Farrokhi labored the whole night at this task, and by morning he had composed a poem that was judged to be even finer than the first. The amir of Chaghāniyān later confirmed this opinion, and Farrokhi's career was successfully launched. The anecdote is limited to one specific case and the author has altered it in the retelling, no doubt, yet it does give reliable testimony that there was a hierarchy in patronage and that each poet who sought admission to the court was obliged to submit a masterwork to be evaluated by the poets and connoisseurs already resident there.

Manuchehri, another poet of the Ghaznavid court, may well be referring to this process when he says in a poem directed to one of his rivals:

> There are other master poets than you here,
>> With flowing words and fiery talent.
> They, who tested me unstintingly,
>> Saw my strength; they saw my mastery.[10]

An even more illuminating and detailed illustration of this is found in another of Manuchehri's poems, almost surely the very masterwork he submitted to the "master poets" to obtain admission to the Ghaznavid court.[11] It announces itself as such by the fact that it is a panegyric to 'Onsori, who was chief poet at the court at the time when Manuchehri sought admission to it. Poets neither patronized other poets nor praised their rivals, so that Manuchehri would have had little reason to compose this poem except as a proof of his skill. Moreover, the final image of the poem, in which the neophyte Manuchehri prostrates himself before the master 'Onsori, leaves little doubt as to the purpose for which it was written:

> O, Manuchehri, I fear that you, in your ignorance
>> Are sewing yourself a shroud with your own hand.
> He who beneath a crown of gems, and dressed in a brocade of verse,

---

[10]Manuchehri, *Divān*, ed. M. Dabir-Siyāqi (Tehran, 1968), 101. This is apparently the practice that Abu Mathal of Bukhara was referring to in this verse: "When the *Khᵛāja* [official] becomes familiar with my work [*kārnāma*] / He will inform the prince of its quality." (Dehkhodā, *Loghat-nāma*, under Abu Mathal Bokhāri).

[11]The selections given here in translation are all taken from chap. 2 of J. W. Clinton, *The Divān of Manuchihri Damghani: A Critical Study* (Minneapolis, 1972).

Is like a portrait of Āzar or an idol of the Brahmins—
Will you offer him your undernourished poems?
   Will you pledge your offering to censure?
Will you attempt to improve the painting on the peacock's tail,
   Or plant a pomegranate in the Garden of Eden?
Do not, in ignorance, rush before him of whom the world's
   Masters are in awe. Be not so hasty!
Your master's court is like a great bonfire,
   And you are like a camel who seeks to halt out of its own place.
An ignorant camel may fall by the wayside,
   If it is unmindful of the camel-killing lion.

What knowledge and skills was the neophyte court poet expected to have mastered? Since Manuchehri's poem provides a virtual catalogue of these, it will repay closer examination. The poem—an unusually long one of some seventy-five double lines—has a complex and varied structure. It begins with a lengthy meditation on a candle flame:

O, you who are placed upon the crown of your soul,
   My body lives by its soul, your soul lives by its body. . . .

In this, the poet demonstrates his ability to control a variety of rhetorical figures, his verbal felicity, and, in particular, his capacity for invention. He sustains our interest in his musings on the candle flame by his revelation of some new possibility of description in each succeeding line:

When you are dying, hot coals revive you.
   When you grow ill, lancing your throat heals you. . . .
You blossom before spring, and wilt before fall.
   You weep without eyes, and laugh without a mouth.

This section concludes with an extended series of similes in which the candle flame is likened to the poet in the persona of the distraught lover, thus demonstrating Manuchehri's command of that all-important range of images:

We both are weeping, pale, and by affliction melted.
   Both enflamed, both alone and sorely tried.

That which I've placed within my heart, I see upon your brow.
　　That which you've set upon your brow, has made my heart its
　　home.

Having captured our attention with this meditative introduction, the
poet now directs our eyes to the person for whom he has composed
the poem:

But you shine on and by your light I read lovingly
　　From dark to dawn the works of Abu'l-Qāsem Hasan.
The master of the masters of the age, 'Onsori.

And for the next few lines he devotes himself to straightforward
panegyric:

His poetry is like his character, both orderly and original.
　　His character is like his poetry, both beautiful and elegant.
The wealth of paradise is the reward worthy of but one of his words.
　　The treasure of Khosrow the price of a line from his pane-
　　gyrics.
As you read his poetry, you nibble sugar.
　　As you recite his lines, you inhale the fragrance of jasmine.

At this remove, particularly when robbed of the felicities of its native
language, such fulsomeness appears excessive and silly. But it was very
much to the taste of Manuchehri's contemporaries, and the ability to
compose artful praise was indispensable to the court poet. Here, Manuchehri with extraordinary subtlety demonstrates his skill as a panegyrist by turning its magnifying light on the very person who would
judge it.

This section leads quickly to the next, where Manuchehri expands
on the image of 'Onsori as the "Master of the Masters of the Age" by
naming the great masters of Arabic and Persian poetry in turn and
comparing their works invidiously with 'Onsori's. The compliment,
again, has a double intention, since it demonstrates his familiarity with
the works of these poets and at the same time he humbles them before
'Onsori. There may be a third intention as well, since by the very
allusiveness with which he names these poets ("Those two from Gor-
gān, and two from Ray, and two from Valvālji") he appears to be
testing the ability of his audience, and judge, to follow him.

Following this catalogue, Manuchehri continues his panegyric with even more astonishingly fulsome praise:

> He is the prophet sent to these poets of the ages.
> His poetry, their holy book, its substance their traditions.
> His poetry resembles paradise, for in it
> Is found all that God promised us.

Manuchehri prided himself on his knowledge of Arabic to a degree beyond that of any of his contemporaries, as is apparent in the length and variety of his list of Arab "masters." In the next section he draws attention to his intimate knowledge of pre-Islamic Arabic poetry— then, as now, a touchstone of Arabic poetic art—by an extended imitation of the vividly described journey through the desert that was one of its familiar features. Here, he also shows his skill in his description of the natural scenes he encounters and his familiarity with the constellations of the night sky. Astronomy was just one of the many fields with which the poet had to be familiar:

> Such a horse can carry me out of a valley like this one
> Or out of a fearful, stinging plain,
> So hot that its springs weep like sun-blinded eyes,
> So parched its river beds are like the gullet of Ahriman
> The desert's surface looks like an armorer's shop
> From the twisting tracks of lizards and serpents.

The journey concludes with his arrival in the presence of the object of his panegyric, to whom, as we have already seen, he pays the final compliment of suggesting that this carefully wrought tribute is hardly worthy of that great poet's notice. The desert journey—although intentionally hyperbolic from start to finish—is especially appropriate here, since it suggests the poet's willingness to undergo whatever tests are necessary to gain admission to the court.

As must be apparent from the selections quoted here, Manuchehri's masterpiece is a rich and complex work, in which the poet displays both his grasp of a large and varied body of knowledge and a thorough mastery of the art and craft of poetry. Yet even this is not an exhaustive catalogue of all the poet had to know or be able to do. Knowledge of music was recommended if not absolutely essential, since the relation of music to poetry was assumed to be an intimate one.[12] The poet had to be able to extemporize verses on whatever subject might be set—as Farrokhi did to prove that he was the poet he claimed to be. Most important, he was required to suit his style to occasions that ranged from the lighthearted to the solemn and ceremonial.

## The Forms of Poetry

Before describing in greater detail the themes and occasions of poetry, it will be useful to have a brief look at what, technically, constituted its various forms.[13] The basic structural unit of the poem was the *bayt*, or double line, which has no precise equivalent in English prosody but is nearest to the heroic couplet. Like the heroic couplet, the *bayt* is composed of two metrically equal halves. It is syntactically independent as well, with enjambment occurring only rarely. Each half-*bayt*, or *mesrā'*, is also often an independent clause. However, unlike the heroic couplet, the *bayt* was not limited to a single meter, but formed the basic unit for all the meters found in Persian poetry.[14] It provides the locus and boundaries for the many rhetorical figures characteristic of the poetry of the period.

The basis of Persian meter is syllable quantity, although stress also played an important but poorly understood role. An arrangement of three or four syllables is a foot, and a particular sequence of three to five feet constitutes a named meter. Each meter defines a half-*bayt* or *mesrā'*, such as the *motaqāreb* meter ( ͜ ͜ / ͜ ͜ / ͜ ͜ / ͜ ) and the *hazaj* meter ( ͜ ͜ ͜ / ͜ ͜ ͜ / ͜ ͜ ͜ / ͜ ). Liaison and conventions that allow several kinds of syllables to be read as long or short depending on the requirements of the meter make these meters quite flexible, and the practice of counting an overlong syllable as the metrical equivalent of two syllables means that a variation of two or three syllables within any meter is quite common.

Rhyme is principally end rhyme, and may be either by half-*bayt*, couplet-fashion, or monorhyme by *bayt*. There are also several forms,

[12]E. Yarshater, "Affinities between Persian Poetry and Music," in *Studies in Art and Literature of the Near East,* ed. P. J. Chelkowski (New York, 1974), 59–78.

[13]There are a number of works to which one may turn for a more detailed discussion of Persian prosody. The best in English is still to be found in the introduction to vol. 2 of E. G. Browne, *Lit. Hist.* Some important new information is contained in the work by Elwell-Sutton cited above, n. 3.

[14]On the forms of Persian poetry, also see the chapter on lyric poetry and the introduction to this volume. (Ed.)

more or less rare, in which rhyme is used to divide a long poem into regular stanzas (*band*).

The couplet, or *mathnavi,* is special to narrative poetry whether heroic, romantic, didactic, or instructional. The national epic, the *Shāh-nāma,* was composed in couplets. The following lines from the *Shāh-nāma,* where an approximation of the original is attempted, may impart an impression of the *mathnavi* form. Sohrāb speaks:

To Rostam will I give crown, throne, and mace,
And enthrone him in Shah Kavus' place.

When my battles are finished in Iran,
I'll here confront the Shah of Turkestan.

Afrāsiāb will leave his throne and run,
When I raise my spear before the sun.

While reign a father and son of such renown,
Who else in all the world should wear a crown?

When sun and moon fill up the sky with light,
Why should the night stars boast their crowns are bright?[15]

The *mathnavi,* in short, was employed by Persian poets to deal with the same wide range of subjects, and was manipulated with the same masterful dexterity, as was the heroic couplet by English poets of the Restoration and eighteenth century.[16]

Although narrative poetry shared important conventions of theme and sensibility with lyric poetry, it was quite different stylistically. The number of meters used for narrative was far less than for lyric. Among these a single meter—*motaqāreb*—was distinctly preferred; it was used for both the *Shāh-nāma* and Abu Shakur's didactic poem *Āfarin-nāma,* among many others. Also, the vocabulary of the *mathnavi* (the subjects of which came from a repertory established before the Islamic conquest) was restricted almost exclusively to words of Iranian origin, while lyric poetry borrowed freely from Arabic. Narrative poetry of this period had, therefore, a consciously archaic and purely Iranian quality, while lyric poetry blended Iranian with Arabic and Islamic elements. Distinct as these styles are, major poets from Rudaki to 'Onsori composed both lyric and narrative works with equal facility.

---

[15]Translation by the author.
[16]See the chapter on epic poetry in this volume for more detailed information on the *mathnavi* form. (Ed.)

The lyric forms are principally the *robā'i*, the *ghazal*, and the *qasida*. Of these, the *robā'i*—also known as the *dobayti* and *tarāna*—is surely so familiar to Western ears that it requires no further illustration. The *ghazal* is by no means well known, but it has lately gained a certain currency among contemporary American poets through the burgeoning interest in *ghazals* in Urdu—the offspring of Persian. The *qasida* is used mainly in panegyrics and generally employs a formal and lofty style; although it is far and away the most popular genre among the court poets of this period it is hardly known outside Iran beyond the circle of specialists.

The *ghazal* and *qasida* begin as virtual twins since both are written in the same rhyme scheme—monorhyme by *bayt* with the opening half-*bayt* rhyming as well. The *qasida*, however, is substantially longer than the *ghazal*; it is composed of thematically different sections, whereas a *ghazal* is devoted to a single theme, most often romantic. *Ghazals* usually run from three to five *bayts* in this period, and rarely exceed a dozen *bayts* even in later periods.[17] It is an uncommon *qasida* that contains less than twenty *bayts* and the average *qasida* in the Ghaznavid period was more than twice that length. The work by Manuchehri discussed above represents the multipartite thematic structure of the *qasida* in a clear but exceptional manner. It contains more sections than was usual and has borrowed several of them from pre-Islamic Arabic poetry.

The more usual pattern for the Ghaznavid *qasida*, in particular the panegyrics that were the court poet's chief stock in trade, was both more simple and more predictable. The first section, or *nasib*, is traditionally described as designed to attract the attention of the prince or patron, and so contains pleasing images of wine-drinking, vivid depictions of the garden in spring, or romantic scenes. Up to this point the *nasib* resembles nothing so much as a *ghazal*. However, at the place in a *ghazal* where the poet would bring the development of his theme to a close, in the *qasida* he introduces a line of transition to the second portion, which is the *madh*, or the panegyric proper. Thus Farrokhi concludes his description of the brocade of verse he has woven by saying that he intends to weave into it the name of the amir of Chaghāniyān, while Manuchehri has his star-crossed lover say he has whiled away his sleepless night poring over the *divān* of 'Onsori.

The panegyric takes up the major part of the poem, and in it the poet presents a series of brief idealized images of his patrons: 'Onsori

[17]On the *ghazal* form, see the chapter on lyric poetry in this volume. (Ed.)

as the master of masters and the prophet of his age; the sultan as a heroic warrior and paragon of justice; a vizier as a brilliant stylist and servant of unswerving loyalty. The images in this section are as much dictated by convention as those in the *nasib,* and here also the poet's task is principally to give a fresh luster to what was already long familiar. The panegyric concludes with a prayer, *do'ā,* as the final section of the poem. The *do'ā* is rarely more than a few *bayts* long, and as the function of the first two sections may be said to delight and exalt respectively, the *do'ā* serves as a charm against the inevitable process of decay and decline, and as a protection against human enemies as well:

For so long as Persian years are reckoned by the sun,
  As Arab years are by the moon,
May the lord [Sultan Mahmud] be perpetually fortunate,
  His ill-wishers in perpetual want and peril.[18]

O Lord! Give the king a thousand years of life!
  In health and happiness, in felicity and prosperity.
Preserve him and his house in thine own protection,
  From the passage of time.
From his face and those of all his nobles,
  Hold back all that is abhorrent, O Magnificence![19]

Brief as it is, the *do'ā* makes the ritual quality of these panegyrics inescapably clear and suggests that it was not simply a love of good poetry that made the panegyrist a fixture at every court.

The relative length of the various sections of the *qasida* was no more fixed than its overall length. Nor, for that matter, was it absolutely essential to have all three sections in every *qasida.* Its formal specifications were remarkably simple—monorhyme and about two dozen *bayts*—and within that not very restrictive frame, the poet was free to develop his poems as fancy suited and talents allowed.

## Poetry and the Court

The fifteenth-century anthologist Dowlatshāh, who viewed the Ghaznavid court through the distorting glass of several centuries, wrote

[18]'Onsori, *Divān,* ed. M. Dabir-Siyāqi (Tehran, 1963), 141.
[19]Manuchehri, *Divān,* 33; translation in Clinton, *Divan of Manuchihri,* 141.

89

that "Mahmud had some four hundred eminent poets in constant attendance upon him."[20] The figure is an obvious exaggeration: "The traditional Oriental figure for a large number, forty multiplied by ten," as a modern scholar has said. Yet scholarly caution may offer too strong a corrective here. Mahmud's court was large and splendid, as those of his Samanid predecessors had been. While it was not large enough to sustain anything like four hundred professional court poets, if we include, as Dowlatshāh—himself an amateur—may well have done, skilled amateurs from the ranks of princes, generals, court officials, scholars, and theologians, the figure becomes less improbable.

With such an abundance of poetic talent available, the occasions which became subjects for poetry were both many and varied. At one extreme we find the trivial and ephemeral, such as a polite plea for a gift:[21]

After having made some subtle gestures
    He approached and offered us some narcissi.
He indicated to us by all that,
    That he had obliged us for some white [silver] and yellow [gold].

or a brief rainfall that made the road muddy under the feet of Amir Nasr's horse:[22]

I bear witness that even the clouds
    And rain serve Amir Nasr.
They softened the earth of the path
    Lest it wound his mount's hooves.
May he retain three things without
    Cease—glory, sovereignty, and youth.

or a royal gift:[23]

The monarch has given me such a horse as this, but no saddle.
    A horse without a saddle is like a flagon with no handle.

[20]Dowlatshāh, *Tadhkerat al-sho'arā'*, ed. E. G. Browne (London, 1901). The passage here referred to is translated in Browne, *Lit. Hist.*, vol. 2, 120.
[21]Abu Tayyeb Tāheri (in Arabic) in Tha'ālebi, *Yatimat al-dahr*, vol. 4, translated by M. C. Barbier de Meynard as "Tableau littéraire du Khorassan et de la Transoxiane," *JA*, 5th ser., 1 (1853): 187.
[22]Abu Hosayn Morādi (in Arabic) in Tha'ālebi, *Yatimat al-dahr*, 189.
[23]Manuchehri, *Divān*, 137; and Clinton, *Divan of Manuchihri*, 82.

At the other extreme lie moments of such fearful importance as the death of a monarch:[24]

Ghaznayn is not now the city I saw last year.
What has befallen it to so reverse its state?
I see houses filled with weeping and lamentation,
    Weeping and lamentation that rend the soul.
I see streets in tumult from end to end,
    A tumult raised by horsemen dashing wildly.
I see the streets of the market filled with men,
    But the doors of merchants' shops closed and locked.

of the accession of his heir:

"A padshāh of pure descent has passed away,
    A padshāh of happy birth sits on the throne.
All the world mourns the one who has gone,
    All rejoice for him who sits now in state.
If fate has taken our lamp from us,
    It has set a candle before us in its place."
O, Lord of the Khosrows of the earth
    To the world you are both Jamshid and Qobād![25]

Predictable and recurring events filled the vast middle ground between these two extremes. The annual feasts, in particular those of the new year, Nowruz, which fell on the first day of spring, and the harvest festival of Mehragān, were favorite subjects, as were the drinking bouts and erotic interludes that were so much a feature of court life.[26] The departure of the ruler and his court on a hunt or a campaign—or their triumphant return from either—the birth of a prince, or, as we have already seen, the annual visit to the branding ground, all might provide the occasion for a poem.

[24]Farrokhi, *Divān*, 90.
[25]Ibid., 41. The first three *bayt*s cited here are, in fact, an incorporated quotation (*tazmin*) from a *qasida* composed a century earlier by the Samanid poet Rabanjani. Farrokhi is here celebrating the accession to the throne of Sultan Mahmud's elder son Mohammad. When the party of his younger son, Mas'ud (then campaigning in western Iran) gained control in Ghazna and invited him to hurry back to take the throne, the poet again rose to the occasion: "Hasten quickly, tell us when you will return / O, Prince of Princes, and Padshāh of the Just! / Khosrow of the world, King Mas'ud b. Mahmud, / He who is without peer among shahs and kings." (*Divān*, 300).
[26]E. Yarshater, "The Theme of Wine-Drinking and the Concept of the Beloved in Early Persian Poetry," *SI* 13 (1960): 43–53.

When one surveys the wonderful abundance of Iranian poetry in this golden age, two general characteristics stand out. The first is the degree to which all of this poetry reflects exclusively the world of the court. The second, closely allied to the first, is its unfailingly public and ceremonial quality. One is struck by the virtual absence of the private, personal voice. These two qualities hold true not only for the panegyrics of the court poets, but also for a very different work composed by a poet who stands somewhat beyond the court circle, namely Ferdowsi's poetic rendering of the national epic, the *Shāh-nāma* (Book of kings).[27] The *Shāh-nāma* is the most important literary creation of this period, and the one which most steadfastly defies any attempt at brief characterization. Within the capacious scope of its fifty thousand *bayt*s it traces the story of the Iranian nation, dynasty by dynasty, from the creation of the first king to the defeat of the last Sasanian monarch by the Arab armies in the mid-seventh century. As it moves forward in time, it shifts first from myth and legend to historical romance, and then to history. It constitutes an encyclopedic compendium of pre-Islamic culture, as well as a grammar and lexicon of the Persian literary language, virtually untouched by Arabic, that has continued as the vital core of New Persian. It is a sourcebook for metaphor, a reference text for models of narrative style, a glossary of human motivation. It crystallizes what was essentially Iranian within the fully developed Islamic culture in which Iran was both partner and contributor.

A number of themes recur throughout the *Shāh-nāma*. Among the most important are the ancient and enduring enmity of Turan for Iran, the dilemma posed for loyal Iranians when an unwise shah inherits the throne, the immortality of noble deeds, and, encompassing all the other themes, the inexorability of fate. These themes are woven into a number of tales of varied length that combine occasional romantic interludes with high adventure, palace intrigue, and heroic encounters. The principal figures are the kings, princes, and noble warriors of the royal court. The dominant figure among these is Rostam of Zābol, a paladin who serves many kings of Iran over some eight hundred years, and who singlehandedly saves Iran from disaster many times during that period.

Yet others exert an even more decisive influence on the course of

[27]The most recent English translation of the *Shāh-nāma* is R. Levy, *The Epic of the Kings* (London, 1967). It is, however, a selective translation, and many passages are presented in summary only. The only complete English translation is that of A. G. and E. Warner, *The Book of Kings* (London, 1920–25).

the *Shāh-nāma* although they are not so long-lived as Rostam: Kay Khosrow, the good and brave king who at last defeats Afrāsiyāb, the evil king of Turan; Siyāvosh, the noble prince who faces a moral dilemma of Hamletian dimensions, and whose decision precipitates generations of conflict; and Esfandiyār, the prince who helps convert Iran to Zoroastrianism, but whose ambition for the throne leads to defeat and death at the hands of Rostam.

In all these rich and varied tales, the *Shāh-nāma* provides the perfect embodiment of the courtly and public quality of early Persian poetry. Like Malory's *Morte d'Arthur,* its focus is that of the court and its concerns, to the exclusion of the world outside. War and feasting, hunting and feats of strength and skill, courtly romance, the struggles for succession and supremacy, these are the engines that set its narratives in motion. Moreover, these same subjects are the sources of imagery and incident as well; the everyday concerns of farmers or herdsmen or traders, the details of domestic life or the accidents of individual perception receive no attention. At dawn, the sun is an invincible warrior advancing over the mountains to put the armies of night to flight with his shining blade. The coming of spring is seen in the palace garden, where the blossoming plants are described as gems or rich brocade. Armies on the move seem to pass through a landscape devoid of life until they encounter the goal of their march—another army, a fortress, a fortified city. Religion appears as a powerful moving force in particular narratives—as when Esfandiyār enforces adherence to the teachings of the prophet Zoroaster on all Iranians, or when Islam inspires the Arabs to the conquest of Sasanian Iran. Moreover, the divinity's support of Iranian monarchy is a constant feature of the whole work. Yet both the nature of belief and the details of worship are only briefly adumbrated.[28]

The *Shāh-nāma* is also pre-eminently a public work of art, neither composed from the stuff of the poet's life nor meant to be read by individuals in private. Ferdowsi has taken traditional material—stories of great antiquity that were composed to be performed publicly—and given it a superb poetic form. It is a monumental extended eulogy to the kings and heroes of the Iranian nation down to the advent of Islam and was meant to become the common possession of all Iranians and Iranophiles.

It would be misleading to suggest that all the *qasida*s and *ghazal*s

---

[28]On the *Shāh-nāma,* see further the chapter on epic poetry and the introduction to this volume. (Ed.)

composed in this era were no more than chips off the monolith of the *Shāh-nāma*. I have already indicated that much of the poetry of the day was concerned with the trivial and the topical, and that much of it was either composed in Arabic or based on Arabic models. Yet in vital respects the poetic world of Ferdowsi and of the court panegyrists contemporary with him was one and the same. Like him, they drew upon the royal court for both subject and metaphor. Nature is for them the gorgeous and luxurious world of the palace garden, and they depict it as a concoction of rare stuffs and precious gems, red-olent of costly perfumes. The actors on their stage are all sultans and viziers and generals, or the handsome servants who attend them. The human population that resides beyond the royal precincts is virtually excluded from consideration. The love the court poets celebrate, un-like that found in the *Shāh-nāma*, is often homosexual, and more often between courtier and servant than between prince and princess. Yet, as in Ferdowsi, it is still courtly love that concerns them, not domestic.

The public celebration of royal character and noble action is the central inspiration of the major poets of the period. The *Shāh-nāma* provides an essential clue to the source of that inspiration, as well as to an understanding of why Iranian monarchs of the time were willing to spend such fortunes on their panegyrists. Shortly after Ferdowsi completed his work, Farrokhi began a lengthy *qasida* on Mahmud's conquest of Somnath in northern India by saying:

> The story of Alexander's grown old and become just another fable;
> Tell us something new, for what's new has a special sweetness.[29]

The new story he offers us is the narration of the real campaign of Mahmud, which he has cast in the heroic mold of the *Shāh-nāma*. His motive is transparently to do for Mahmud what Ferdowsi had done for Alexander—a great ruler of Iran who, like Mahmud, was of half-Iranian parentage (in Iranian legend), and who also campaigned in India. In the accession *qasida* quoted above, Farrokhi also likens Mah-mud's son and successor to the legendary Iranian kings, Jamshid and Qobād.

Although the connection between contemporary and legendary—that is, pre–Islamic—rulers and heroes is not always made so explicitly, the obvious goal of court panegyrics is to create enduring images of

---

[29]Farrokhi, *Divān*, 66. Farrokhi's poetry contains a number of comparisons between Rostam and Mahmud, all to the latter's advantage. See M. Minovi, *Ferdowsi va she'r-e u* (Ferdowsi and his poetry) (Tehran, 1967), 132–34.

the monarchs of the time that will take their places beside those of antiquity. Later generations marveled at the extraordinary generosity of the Samanid and Ghaznavid rulers toward their poets laureate. Mahmud, in particular, gave gifts of almost unbelievable richness. A century after Mahmud's death, Khāqāni wrote enviously of his largesse to 'Onsori:

> 'Onsori received a hundred purses of silver and a slave to carry each
> For composing ten *bayts* during one campaign to India.
> 'Onsori, I've heard, struck the stands of his cooking pots
> Of silver, and set his table with gold.[30]

When a sultan believes that the hope of immortal renown lies in poetry, and the *Shāh-nāma* was persuasive evidence that it did, there is less reason to wonder at his rewarding his poets with gifts worth a king's ransom.

---

[30]Khāqāni Shirvāni, *Divān*, ed. A. 'Abd al-Rasuli (Tehran, 1939), 680, and Clinton, *Divan of Manuchihri*, 46. One might mention here the 10,000 dinars that Rudaki is reported to have received for a panegyric he composed in honor of Amir Abu Ja'far in *Tārikh-e Sistān*, ed. M. Bahār (Tehran, 1935), 316–24.

# 5. Epic Poetry

Persian epic poetry is both extensive and little known. The following discussion will attempt to introduce this poetry by touching on several areas of literary and cultural interest. Beginning with a definition of epic poetry, it will move on to examine some of the background of the Persian national epic and then will focus on Ferdowsi's *Shāh-nāma* itself. The nature of the heroes and the language of the epic will be discussed, and the shift from epic to romance that took place in medieval Persian literature after the *Shāh-nāma* will be examined. Finally a word will be said about the place of *Shāh-nāma* in the Persian literary tradition.

Epic poetry in its oldest form is oral poetry, and from this unwritten form the literary epic evolved. In the present context an epic poem is understood to be an extended narrative, focusing on the deeds of high-ranking persons, with the interest generally revolving around the adventures of a few kings and great heroes. Thus it is a poetry of action, reflecting a court-centered society. Nevertheless, epic poetry always has a close connection with a particular people for whom it has a profound meaning. Likely to embody the history, the ideals, and the values of a people, it is often a cohesive force in ethnic or national consciousness. It can formulate a people's cultural and spiritual heritage and objectify it in a manner which appeals to the heart as much as to the mind. Persian epic poetry fits all of these requirements perfectly, although what survives of it today is not oral but literary. Doubtlessly a long tradition of oral poetry lies behind this, but it is a tradition lost to us today.

As Persian epic poetry is explored in terms of the above characteristics, the discussion will then focus on Ferdowsi's *Shāh-nāma,* its antecedents, and its descendants. The *Shāh-nāma* is closer than any other work in Persian literature to our definition of epic poetry and is thus the most useful pivot for a general discussion. Other works will be mentioned against the background of the *Shāh-nāma*.

To understand better this poetry and the way it fits into the framework of Persian literature, some general background information is necessary. Paradoxically, we have far more material available from the Iranian epic tradition than we have epic poetry embodying this material. Furthermore, the greater part of what remains to us of the epic tradition was written down in Islamic times by Muslim writers for Muslim audiences. This religio-cultural setting obviously influenced what was set down and how it was presented. Regardless of when they were written down, however, these stories, legends, motifs, beliefs, and attitudes have their roots deep in the past, and this past shows itself in ways both obvious and subtle. Some of these ways will be discussed later, but first, the main sources of Persian epic poetry must be considered.

The deepest roots lie in ancient Indo-European and Indo-Iranian traditions, and the traditions of the Iranians as they developed into a nation. The sources of this national tradition are often difficult to identify, but we can be reasonably certain that traces of myths and practices stemming from the common period of the Indo-Europeans can be seen in the Avesta and in the epic poetry that survives. It is probably from those times that the accounts of Jamshid, Faredun, Hōshang, Kay Khosrow, and others who play important roles in the *Shāh-nāma* have their origin.

As the Iranians moved onto the plateau that is now their homeland, they brought with them old myths and legends. In the process of territorial expansion and settlement, battles fought with the indigenous peoples also left their mark in the Iranians' memory, and accounts of these were preserved in oral tradition. Assuming that there was oral epic poetry even in this early period, it is likely that these stories existed simultaneously in several different versions. In a tradition of oral epic poetry, the concept of a "correct" version of a story, a canonized variant to be preferred over all others does not, cannot, exist. In orally transmitted epics, the story is recreated with each telling; only with the invention of writing did the concept of a fixed text develop.

In addition to ancient memories and traditions, another major source of Persian epic poetry is prehistoric religious tradition, from Zoroastrianism and other pre-Islamic religions. It is not certain how long the Iranians had been settled on the plateau when Zarathushtra appeared as a prophet in the sixth century B.C., or earlier. This would give at least fifteen hundred years for episodes from that period to work their way into the national legend and the material that Ferdowsi used as his source.

As the Iranians wandered onto the plateau, some of them began to shift from nomadism to agriculture. This development implied a more settled life, the growth of villages, and a change in their view of the world. It must have been during these transitional times that one of the great motifs of Persian epic poetry began to emerge: the theme of Iran versus Turan. In the *Shāh-nāma* we see a late and confused form of this theme, cast in terms of Iranians versus Turks, with the Oxus River forming the boundary between the two hostile peoples. The wars between these peoples occupy such a large part of the *Shāh-nāma* that they must reflect older and deeper oppositions, possibly beginning with the age-old animosity between nomads and settled people. Zoroastrianism contributed religious and ethical dimensions to this conflict, and it is no surprise that such opposition, growing out of conflicting social and religious systems, was also seen as a struggle between the forces of good and evil. In the entire national legend the Iranians have no more bitter enemies than the Turanians.

Along with national and religious traditions, a third major element entering into Persian epic poetry can be called the popular tradition. This consists of legends, stories, traditions, and fantasies about persons and places, real or imagined, that form a part of a nation's culture but are not necessarily part of the mainstream of the national tradition and its heroes. Many stories from popular tradition are grafted onto great figures in the national tradition. The sources of the popular tradition are found all over the world and are productive even today.

With some idea of the principal elements that go into Persian epic poetry, we may now turn to the major example of that poetry. The *Shāh-nāma* is an epic poem of some fifty thousand lines, written over a period of about thirty years and completed around A.D. 1000 by Abu'l-Qāsem Ferdowsi, a member of the landed gentry from the village of Tus, a few miles north of Meshed in eastern Iran. It is written in rhyming couplets in the *motaqāreb* meter: ˇ ˉ ˉ / ˇ ˉ ˉ / ˇ ˉ ˉ / ˇ ˉ (twice). Ferdowsi displays great pride in his work and takes pains to tell us that he has written this poem as a monument that will endure the ravages of time. It should be stressed that the *Shāh-nāma* is a carefully created literary epic and not a product of the oral tradition, although there is certainly much from that tradition in it.

The epic falls into natural divisions of an introduction and fifty sections of unequal length, each devoted to the reign of a king. The fifty reigns are grouped chronologically into four major dynastic divisions—the Pishdadians, the Kayanians, the Parthians, and the Sasanians—and form a chronicle of the Iranian people from the creation of the world to the Arab conquest of Iran. Overlapping the first two dynastic divisions is a special cycle of tales integrated into the mainstream of the narrative. This is the so-called Seistan cycle, part of a much larger cycle of stories originating in eastern Iran and devoted to the exploits of the great hero Rostam and his descendants. Thus it can be said that Ferdowsi cast a considerable portion, but not all, of the national legend into the form of an epic poem. The parts that he left out will be discussed later.

The *Shāh-nāma* is a poem of action. The characteristic pursuits of the Iranian nobles are hunting, feasting, and war—three closely related activities. In hunting for sport, the aggressive drives of the warrior are directed toward animals, thus satisfying the desire for action and conflict while reducing the risks involved. Feasting, with its erotic overtones, represents the other side of the coin, where the urge to violence is sublimated. Since the heroes of the *Shāh-nāma* are free of the administrative duties of kingship, they have little else to do but hunt, drink, and fight, and thus pass their time alternating between excesses of violent action and, as it were, violent indolence. They never flag in their pursuit of personal honor and glory. The kings, on the other hand, fulfill a different role and hence tend to behave with a greater degree of decorum and gravity.

We recall that it is the rule for epic poetry to focus on the deeds of a great hero. The conventions of the epic, however, allow for little psychological development in the characters, with the result that the heroes of the *Shāh-nāma* are born, not made. Cast in the heroic mold from birth, the hero's life is merely the working-out of its predestined nature. The great hero of the *Shāh-nāma* is Rostam, and his career is no exception to this rule. Descended from a long line of Seistani rulers tracing their lineage back to the mythical hero Keresāspa, Rostam, like many heroes in world literature, was born by cesarian section and showed astounding prowess practically from his first day. He matured much more quickly than other boys of his age, and while still a youth, he killed an elephant singlehandedly. Entering into a lifetime of heroic behavior, he fearlessly met all challengers, natural and supernatural. He was independent in the rule of his own territory but subservient to the ruling monarch of Iran. After a long and splendid career of service to several kings, he met an ignominious and unheroic death.

According to Northrup Frye's definition, the epic hero's power of action is superior in degree to other men's but not superior to the natural environment. In this respect too Rostam is a typical hero, endowed with superhuman strength and endurance but still subject to fatigue, the pain of wounds, and the normal human emotions of anger and love. He is not immune to the rigors of old age, and he cannot fly through the air, control the elements, or make himself invisible. Because of these limitations, we can easily identify with Rostam as a human being. If he is more powerful than we, he still cannot challenge nature or the gods, nor can we. If Rostam's pride sometimes interferes with his good sense, who of us can claim never to have had this happen? As an epic hero, Rostam is solid and dependable, with a clear idea of his own importance in the general scheme of things.

Rostam and his royal masters are not the only characters in the epic, at least in the legendary parts. While the majority of the actors are human and most of the action motivated by human concerns, supernatural agents are present as well. *Div*s (demons) are a common breed of the latter. Rostam is captured and carried off by a *div* named Akvān in a very peculiar episode, and in a famous series of adventures the great hero rids the province of Mazanderan of these creatures.

One of the most spectacular of the supernatural creatures is the Simorgh, a mythical bird who nourishes Rostam's father and protects Rostam himself. This bird, with its healing powers and its protective attitude toward great heroes, may embody a very old Iranian or Indo-Iranian belief. In his well-known battle with Esfandiyār, Rostam faces an enemy who seems to be his match. In desperation Rostam summons the Simorgh, who provides him with the magical means of killing his enemy. Such aid is not given without recompense, however, and the direct result of Rostam's victory is his own death at the hands of his brother later on.

The most pervasive of the supernatural forces is God, and He too intervenes on behalf of the hero. When Rostam is fighting Sohrāb in their tragic conflict, Rostam is hard-pressed by his adversary. Although earlier he had prayed that God take some of his excessive power from him, now he prays for added strength. The ironic result is that Rostam is victorious, only to learn, as his heroic opponent lay dying, that he has killed his own son.

One might object here that Rostam is something less than a real hero because, when he is hard-pressed, he can call upon supernatural help. There are two dimensions to this problem, one literary and the other moral. First, Rostam is an epic hero, and the job of epic heroes is to win. He does not indulge in scruples, mainly because they are irrelevant here. This is not to say that he is amoral, but only that he is required by epic convention to win, and win by whatever means necessary. Second is the moral dimension. We have seen that in both instances when Rostam is forced to call upon nonhuman help, the aid comes, but a price is exacted in return. In the one case Rostam kills his own son, and in the other he subsequently loses his own life, just as the Simorgh predicted he would if he accepted the means to kill Esfandiyār. The epic hero will win by any means, but he must also win at any cost, and in Rostam's case the cost of winning is the greatest price a person can pay.

The world of the *Shāh-nāma* is centered in Iran and extends outward in all directions. As the action flows in and out like the tide, it surges over much of the then-known world. The geographical scope of the epic is vast. Hunting expeditions and wars carry the heroes far beyond the boundaries of Iran to encounter Arabs, Byzantines, Central Asians, Chinese, Indians, and other non-Iranian peoples. Long journeys and marches are frequent; prolonged absence from home is the rule for heroes. With all of this variety, however, local color plays almost no role at all. Other than the numerous depictions of sunrise and sunset, nature is hardly described. Whether the action is in Arabia or China, the only variable is the enemy, and the terrain and climate might not exist for all we know.

It must not be thought that the whole *Shāh-nāma* is concerned with the exploits of Rostam, for historical material is present in generous measure as well. As mentioned earlier, the epic is divided into four major dynastic sections, and by the end of the second dynasty Rostam is dead and the Seistan cycle has come to an end. The last two sections, on the Parthians and Sasanians, bring the narrative out of the mythical and legendary eras and into historical periods.

The section on the Parthians is very short, while that on the Sasanians is relatively long, taking up roughly one-half of the epic. Here we are given a great deal of historical information on the Sasanians and their principal enemy, the Byzantines, plus, among other things, the amorous adventures of Bahrām Gor, the romance of Khosrow and Shirin, the story of Bahrām Chobin, and a number of throne speeches of ethical content. From this it is evident that the *Shāh-nāma* combines different kinds of material: mythical, legendary, epic, historical, ethical, and romantic.

It is worth noting that in Iran, today's audience is interested only in the earlier part of the *Shāh-nāma* and not in the Parthians and Sasanians. They rightly sense that with the death of Rostam, the truly epic part of the *Shāh-nāma* ends, and what remains is essentially a historical account with no hero to give it focus. To satisfy their audiences and prolong their sessions, the storytellers now interpolate various other tales from the Seistan cycle into their narratives of the *Shāh-nāma*. It is thus mainly the Seistan cycle that provides the true epic heroes, while the latter part of the narrative purports to give us history.

To the extent that the *Shāh-nāma* presents a linear sequence of events, many of which are linked by the process of cause and effect, and also conveys much information, it does constitute a work of history as well as an epic poem. In fact, *Shāh-nāma* means "Book of Kings," and this may be regarded as a generic as well as a specific title. Before Ferdowsi's time there was a long tradition of writing *Shāh-nāma*s, stretching back to the late Sasanian period when an official chronicle called "Book of Kings" was compiled. The intention of this latter work clearly seems to have been historical.[1]

Along with the historical material in the *Shāh-nāma*, however, there is much that falls outside of historical time. Some events described are not susceptible to any sort of verification, and with others the narrative time cannot be historical. What does it mean to us, for example, that Rostam lived several hundred years? What is the real significance of his battle with Esfandiyār? These events have a different kind of meaning for us from those connected with Khosrow II and the Byzantines. We cannot accept as true Ferdowsi's explanation of how material culture developed in the world. Nor could those who explained material culture by the myth in the *Shāh-nāma* understand the history of the world as a process. Thus the *Shāh-nāma* contains not only different kinds of material, but different modes of thought as well, and the tension that exists among these modes of thought is only resolved by the synthetic vision that the poet has imposed on his material.

Turning now to a different sort of question, that of the language of the epic, we see that the *Shāh-nāma*, like much epic poetry, is written in relatively plain language. In this case, the Persian is considered simple for two reasons: it contains a very low percentage of Arabic loanwords, and it is relatively free of rhetorical devices and complicated figurative language. These two qualities are linked: for technical reasons, it is quite difficult to write highly figured poetry in Persian while severely restricting the Arabic which can be drawn upon. The question is, why should the language of the *Shāh-nāma* be this way? The traditional answer gives Ferdowsi great credit as a nationalist but little credit as a poet. Since great nationalists do not necessarily make great poets, a different answer will be suggested below.

Ferdowsi's images are succinct and appropriate. He rarely piles image upon image, and he seldom employs extended metaphors requiring several lines. An example will help make this clear. At one point, Ferdowsi has an enemy general say to his men before battle:[2]

[1]See also p. 10 (Ed.).
[2]*Shāh-nāma*, ed. E. Bertels (Moscow, 1960–), vol. 4, 229, l. 316.

> We will make the air like a spring cloud;
>   We will rain arrows upon them.

The Persian is richer than the English, but the point comes through in translation. He uses the image of a spring cloud to express a threat to the Persians. In the first half-line we are presented with the unqualified image of a spring cloud, which might carry with it associations of abundant rain, revivification, and movement. But these are immediately eliminated by the second half-line, which focuses the image on the rain alone. We now understand that the rain will consist of arrows and that it will bring death rather than new life. It is appropriate that this image is used by an enemy, for how could an Iranian, whose new year commences with the vernal equinox, ever ironically link spring with death? Beginning with a common military cliché, *tir bārān* (raining arrows), Ferdowsi lifts it out of an anonymous and moribund state to endow it with a new freshness and create an image that goes directly to the point.

In contrast to this economy of imagery, the writers of later epics and romances tend to be more prodigal. Images in a long series or large conglomerations are characteristic of these works, as is a more general use of imagery altogether; thus, they depend on figurative writing rather than on precise description. Here then lies one of the basic differences between the epic and other kinds of narrative poetry.

This distinction leads us back to our question of why there are so few similes and metaphors in Ferdowsi's epic language compared with other Persian poetry of his time. The answer lies in the tension which exists between the need to use rhetorical devices and figurative language to render vivid the action of the heroes, and the seductive dangers inherent in the use of such language—seductive because in poetry of heroic action, the listener's attention must remain fixed on that action. The meaning of the event lies in its action. If the action is described in figurative and suggestive language, flights of associations are started up in the listener's mind, associations which add new dimensions and nuances. These in turn divert the mind to contemplation and interpretation and away from the speed, the sequences, the actions and reactions that are the stuff of this poetry. In this respect, Persian epic poetry is not autonomous. It demands the imaginative participation of the listener, as any Tehran storyteller will affirm. It will not, however, bear the kind of imaginative extension which comes with the reading of lyric poetry. The lines of epic poetry should ring like a sword on a shield, or a hammer on an anvil, not like a carillon in a bell tower.

In this sparing and very precise use of imagery I believe we can understand some of Ferdowsi's success. He knew well how to control his language in order to achieve a desired effect. He used epic language with his raw material and produced epic poetry, while others, with no less appropriate material at their disposal, were not able to restrict themselves to the linguistic leanness of the master. Precisely this ability contributes in large measure to his poetic stature.

The language and form of the *Shāh-nāma* had a profound effect on how the remaining material from the national legend—those stories not included in the *Shāh-nāma*—were preserved for posterity. The Persian national legend was enormously broad in scope and in Ferdowsi's time undoubtedly contained much material now lost to us. Hints of such material may be gained from Sogdian, Armenian, Middle Persian, and Arabic sources. All was not lost, however, for we have the numerous post-*Shāh-nāma* epics and traditional romances to supplement these hints. In outward form the later epics closely resemble the *Shāh-nāma* and are written in the same meter and rhyming couplets; traditional romances are in prose for the most part, although in some of them the verse original shows through the thin spots.

As mentioned above, imposed upon the main narrative of the *Shāh-nāma* is a cycle of stories about a family of heroes residing in Seistan who were descended from Keresāspa. Ferdowsi treats the life and adventures of Sām, his son Zāl, and Zāl's son Rostam, all members of this Seistan family. After Rostam's death there is little news of the rest of the family in the *Shāh-nāma*, yet many stories must have been current in medieval Persia, because for four or five hundred years after Ferdowsi's death, tales of the other members of the Seistan family were put into verse on the model of the *Shāh-nāma*, and thus saved from oblivion.

The earliest of the post-*Shāh-nāma* epics, completed about a half-century later, is Asadi Tusi's *Garshāsp-nāma*, which describes the deeds of Garshāsp, a descendant of the legendary King Jamshid. Likewise we have in verse the adventures of Sām, of Rostam's son Farāmarz, of his grandson Borzu, and of various other relations such as Jahāngir, Bahman, Āzarbarzin, Kush, and of one woman, Bānu Goshasp. She is a daughter of Rostam who marries the mighty Giv, son of Godarz. Both of them are prominent figures in the *Shāh-nāma*. They fall into such violent domestic strife that Rostam has to intervene and bring about peace. Their son is Bizhan, whose love for the Turanian Manizha gets him into deep trouble, and he must be rescued by Rostam.

The most extensive of the later epics is the *Borzu-nāma,* of which some manuscripts are equal in size to the *Shāh-nāma.* Borzu is the son of Sohrāb, but he is not mentioned in the latest edition of the *Shāh-nāma.* The Seistan family comes to an end with Borzu's son Shahryār, whose life is described in the *Shahryār-nāma.* Nor does this exhaust the post-*Shāh-nāma* epics, as there are several others concerned with lesser figures.

While all of these works share the epic characteristic of being focused on the deeds of one hero, they differ from the *Shāh-nāma* in their conception of the hero and the nature of his actions. This divergence from the essence of epic poetry (which also includes language, as indicated above) increased over time. The seeds of change can be seen even in the *Garshāsp-nāma,* the closest chronologically to the *Shāh-nāma.* By the time of the *Sām-nāma* of Khwāju Kermāni, written in the fifteenth century, the shift from epic to romance was complete.

The reasons for this change are not known at present; the best one can do is describe the nature of the change and hope this will provide a clue to its causes. What happened, in brief, was that one set of heroic models was substituted for another. Characters who appear in the *Shāh-nāma* as typical but minor epic figures, Sām or Farāmarz for example, are changed when they appear as the central characters of a later epic. In the case of the prose romances, we find the substitution of characters such as Dārāb, Firuz Shāh, and Khorshid Shāh for the Kayanian kings of Ferdowsi's epic.

Our admiration for the older epic heroes is based on their superhuman strength and courage and the patriotic service to which these are put. In this case the poet, the reciter, and the audience are drawn together by a collective memory of the national past. One function of this past is to set norms for the future, thus binding together the whole span of Iranian civilization in a unity of values.

As the epic hero changed to a romantic hero, the relations binding together the poet, the reciter, and the audience also changed. In Frye's terms, the powers of action of the romantic hero are superior in degree both to ours and to the natural environment. Thus, our admiration for the romantic hero is based on our desire to escape from everyday life into a fabulous world of adventure and idealized love, a world where everything turns out well, a world where the passions of mortals are magnified but where, in the process, the characters have lost their human vulnerability. The result is a hero once removed from those we can identify with as we do with an epic hero. The romantic vision of the past sets no norms for the future, and the audience is merely entertained by the stories, having little sense of participation in shared values which have formed his civilization across the centuries.[3]

Keeping in mind this very general picture of the shift from epic to romance, we may suggest some possible reasons for such a change. One could argue, for example, that after Ferdowsi's death there was a general decline in the epic spirit, which might be linked in some fashion to social and intellectual changes in the Iranian cultural area. This point of view, however, would be very difficult to defend. Alternatively, one could suggest that the writers of romances and their audiences had always been present, and that Ferdowsi was an exception. This proposition would be much easier to defend, and would better account for the evidence. No doubt there are other ways to explain the rapid disappearance of epic poetry after Ferdowsi, but any explanation must take into account the long pre-*Shāh-nāma* tradition of oral romance in Persia, a tradition which continued in full force until the twentieth century.

Finally, something should be said about the place of epic poetry within Islamic Persian literature. From one perspective, the *Shāh-nāma* stands out as a towering monument in the literary tradition. As we examine it more closely, we see that, like many monuments, over the years it has developed an extremely complex relationship with its surroundings. For one thing, the *Shāh-nāma* stands at the end of the oral epic tradition in Persian literature. Oral transmission of epic poetry went on after A.D. 1000 to be sure, but its status would never be the same, since a literary tradition now ran parallel to it. Furthermore, the existence of the *Shāh-nāma* galvanized others to write down those parts of the national legend that Ferdowsi had left out. As we have seen, these later epics looked something like the *Shāh-nāma*, but were quite different in language and spirit. In fact they form a major link between the epic and the romance traditions of medieval Persia.

The *Shāh-nāmā*, while incorporating elements of earlier romances such as *Khosrow and Shirin,* had a strong influence on subsequent romance writing. In the verse romances such as *Vis and Rāmin* and those of Nezāmi, the weight of the *Shāh-nāma* is felt everywhere: in the

---

[3]See chap. 8 on romances (Ed.).

language, in the presentation of battle scenes and descriptions of warriors and heroes, in the description of sunrise and sunset, and in the very structure of the works themselves, where such standard epic elements as single combats and long overseas journeys appear frequently. Much the same can be said of the epic's influence on the traditional prose romances where, in addition to the above, direct quotations from Ferdowsi are frequent.

Beyond the direct influence of the *Shāh-nāma* on the writing of later epics and romances, a large category of pseudo-epics was directly inspired by it. These historical or religious pieces are modeled on the form of the *Shāh-nāma* but are unlike it in the use of language and in epic spirit. The historical pseudo-epics are very numerous. For example, Hamdallāh Mostowfi brought the *Shāh-nāma* up to his own period of the fourteenth century with his *Zafar-nāma*. Many of the pseudo-epics were written about the lives of the Moghul emperors, and the practice was continued into the nineteenth century with the *George-nāma,* produced in India in honor of a visit by the British monarch.

Religious pseudo-epics are also numerous. They are for the most part concerned with the battles and successes of Mohammad and 'Ali. Here the epic form has been used to mold historical and religious material, from a very particular Iranian point of view. The result is a linking of 'Ali, Mohammad, and other religious figures prominent in the Shi'ite tradition, to the older Iranian epic heroes. This brings the religious events in question under a strong Iranian light, and presents them squarely within the tradition of epic-romantic narrative poetry.

While the *Shāh-nāma* had a powerful literary effect in subsequent centuries, it also had and continues to have a powerful psychological effect on the Iranian people through its patriotic and nationalistic sentiments. Since these are extraliterary matters, they will not be discussed here beyond observing that Ferdowsi was able to formulate the national ideals and values of the Iranians in a manner which had no parallel in their literature. His achievement was such, however, that the *Shāh-nāma* can be enjoyed as epic poetry for its own sake by those unaffected by its patriotic and nationalistic appeals. Its literary and symbolic values combine to make it a true monument, with a life of its own and a message for us all.

## Bibliography

Frye, N. *Anatomy of Criticism* (Princeton, 1971).

Jauss, H. "Levels of Identification of Hero and Audience," *New Literary History* 5 (1974): 283–317.

Merkelbach, R. "Inhalt und Form in symbolischen Erzählungen der Antike," *Eranos Jahrbuch* 35 (1966): 145–75.

Safā, Z. *Hamāsa Sarā'i dar Irān* (Tehran, 1954).

# 6. Ferdowsi and the Art of Tragic Epic

Perhaps no single man of letters, with the possible exception of Homer, has had such a profound and decisive effect on the language and life of his people as Ferdowsi has had on Persian and the survival of an Iranian cultural identity. From the plains of Iraq to the shores of the Atlantic in North Africa the tongues of the people and their diverse cultural selves were submerged to a dominant Arab identity. Some three centuries after the Arab-Muslim conquest of Iran this Arabization was still expanding.

While it is true that the encouragement of Persian letters by some local Iranian rulers such as the Samanids and the Saffarids had begun to attract Persian poets to their courts, there were also Iranian princely houses such as the Tahirids who disdained the vernacular of their native land and were zealous patrons of Arabic and Arab poets. Probably the sum total of Persian courtly verse written in the half century before Ferdowsi—notwithstanding the wealth and stature of Rudāki's works—did not amount to a fraction of Ferdowsi's *Shāh-nāma*. Nor was it the sheer volume of the *Shāh-nāma* which tipped the scale in favor of the survival and flowering of Persian as a literary language.

The choice of subject matter and the conscious use of language appropriate to it, enabled Ferdowsi to create a monument of such decisive historical impact. He set out to render into Persian verse hardly admixed with Arabic words, a late Sasanian recension of an Iranian universal history; that is to say, a comprehensive and self-revealing Iranian view of the world and of that nation's place and role in it. With this heroic stroke he succeeded in snatching from extinction a veritable lexicon of the Persian language, and endowing that language with a self-assured and enduring literary expression. With the same stroke he rescued from oblivion a mythicized and profoundly structured world outlook that embodies the process of interactions of cosmic forces, moral values and human relations with all their complexities, paradoxes, and dynamic tensions.

While it is true that much of the thematic, episodic, and character treatment of the *Shāh-nāma* may yield a wealth of meaning when subjected to various analytical grids, the comprehensive framework of the opus is primarily a reflection of the cosmological structure in its sources. In that structure the concept of Time is focal. The drama of creation, the cosmic struggles of good and evil, the unrelenting force of nature, the deeds of men—all take place not only in time but under

Time. This is a notion of time not simply as a convention of measuring the rhythm of life and nature, but extending from that external convention to a self-existing, transcending, controlling and compelling force whose operation is both tyrannical and full of paradox—and therefore, insofar as man is concerned, ultimately tragic.

The tyranny of Time and the paradox of human existence are the parameters that form the grid of *Shāh-nāma*'s structure and the matrices that shape its literary form. At the most outer level the *Shāh-nāma* can be perceived as an historical annal of royal reigns, and Ferdowsi himself may have conceived of his work as no more than a glorious history of his people. The apparent organization of the poem, as distinct from its inner structure, is simply an abbreviated account of man on earth from creation until the appearance of Kayumars, followed in ever greater detail by the narration of events of each succeeding reign. The very convention of marking time, the recording of a calendar, is established and renewed with each enthronement.

On this surface level the variety of episodes, the imbedded tales, the modulation of heroic and romantic narratives, the unravelling of sub-episodes, and the pursuit of feats of individual heroes may be seen simply as a chronological sequence of events belonging to a given period, i.e. the reign of a given monarch. On this surface level, likewise, the dimension of time appears to be linear, proceeding from a primordial state of near bliss—the enthronement of Kayumars (so quintessentially captured in that incomparable painting attributed to Soltān Mohammad in the so-called Houghton *Shāh-nāma* manuscript[1]), to a final tragedy of defeat and treachery—the fall of the Sasanian empire and the murder of Yazdgerd III.

On a deeper level, however, Time as source of all things, the giver and taker of life, and equated with fate, is the relentless mover of Ferdowsi's tragic epic. The influence of the late Sasanian Zurvanite beliefs upon Ferdowsi's sources has been noted by Zaehner,[2] and it is crucial in the definition and comprehension of this pervasive role of Time in the *Shāh-nāma*. At this inner level the direction of Time is cyclical and not linear. It is a cycle viewed from the center and not from the periphery, a cycle revolving vertically and not horizontally. Our spatial experience of it is in ascent and descent rather than round and round. And it is at this inner level of the operation of Time that

[1] *The Houghton Shahnamah* (Cambridge, Mass., 1981), vol. 1, color plate no. 8 facing p. 58.

[2] R. C. Zaehner, *The Dawn and Twilight of Zoroastrianism* (London, 1961), 240–41.

we are faced with the element of paradox. Time, as fate, brings ups and downs, which is to say that it generates both good and evil.

Again, on the surface level, the *Shāh-nāma* is the arena of combat between good and evil—man and demons, Iran and Turan. But on the inner level we are led to an increasing awareness of permeation of good with evil, to a realization of pollution and corruption and, inescapably, death as the final gift of Time. Within this encompassing frame, governed by Time and riddled with paradox, is woven an inner structure of enormous dramatic power and beauty. In a series of three-generation cycles the gradual internalization of evil is woven around the central epical theme of a tragic death and the need to avenge it.

In the first cycle encompassing Kayumars, Siyāmak, and Hushang, the evil is represented by Ahriman and his demons directly—an entirely external embodiment not even belonging to the human species. Kayumars's Elysian happiness is dashed by the death of his rash but insufficiently armed son, Siyāmak, at the hands of the Black Demon. It is left to his grandson Hushang to war against the Demon and avenge the blood of his father. The utter polarity of the struggle between absolute good and unalloyed evil is even graphically depicted in the color contrast of the naked fair-bodied Siyāmak and the pitch black Demon. There is no room for contemplation of shades of grey.

In the second cycle, spanning the generations of Faredun, Iraj, and Manuchehr, where we witness the horrendous crime of fratricide and the origin of the bad blood that runs through much of the epic, already much has happened that has left the door open for the penetration of evil into human nature. Jamshid, the bringer of world order and the giver of civilization, the conqueror of earth and sky, has fallen victim to his own hubris and exposed the world to Zahhāk's thousand-year reign of terror. Faredun himself is still in full possession of his purity and goodness, protected through the intervention of Sorush, nursed by the wondrous cow Pormāya, covered by *farrah* (divine glory), and beloved by his people. But his three sons are born of Jamshid's sisters, once polluted by Zahhāk and taught the evil arts, although ritually cleansed and made chaste by Faredun before bearing him his sons. The demons, who were corporeal and distinguished by their warts and hideous appearance before, are now abstracted into Greed and Envy (*āz* and *rashk*) and enter into the nature of Faredun's two older sons. The pitiful innocence of Iraj, the younger brother, his childlike goodness, is no match for the evil of his brothers who murder him. Faredun has to wait an extra generation for Manuchehr, born

111

of Iraj's daughter, to grow to manhood and avenge his murdered grandfather and bring solace to his great grandfather by killing his own great uncle. We see that murder and revenge, shedding of blood that demands shedding of more blood, have become a family affair. What could be a more graphic demonstration of the process of internalization of evil? Reflecting the realities of his own time Ferdowsi identifies the Turanians with Turks, but in fact it is the feud of cousins, Iranians all and the descendants of Faredun, that constitutes the heart of the epic.

In the third cycle involving Kay Kāvus, Siyāvosh, and Kay Khosrow, the rot is deeper and more complex. Kay Kāvus, the first link of the chain, is the weakest. Notwithstanding the culpability of his wife Sudāba and the dastardly treachery of Garsivaz, a brother of the Turanian arch king Afrāsiyāb, Kay Kāvus cannot be exonerated in the death of his son from an earlier wife and his crown prince. It is his capricious and suspicious nature and his weak-willed mollification of Sudāba that drives Siyāvosh into exile and to his death. Siyāvosh, the victim and middle link, is still a guileless and pure youth, but the moral boundaries of Iran and Turan, of good and evil, are hopelessly blurred. Kay Khosrow, the avenger, son of Siyāvosh, is born of his union with Farangis, the daughter of the arch-enemy Afrāsiyāb. In righting the scales of good and evil it is his own grandfather that he must kill.

In the next cycle of Goshtāsp, Esfandiyār, and Bahman the moral choices are irreconcilably at a standoff. The enormity of the paradox is overwhelming. Firstly, none of the three links is blameless. Even the middle link—heretofore innocent and therefore pathetic—now in the person of Esfandiyār, is unable to evoke our total sympathy. On the level of articulation he is pious, dutiful and self-righteous, but in his soul he is burning with resentment of his father and ambition for the throne; he is made unattractive by an overbearing royal hauteur. Goshtāsp, the father, is more than indirectly implicated in the death of his son. Knowingly and intentionally, he sends Esfandiyār on a mission that can only end in his death. And the revenge of Bahman is empty of all righteous satisfaction. It is a mere display of destructive fury against the innocent kith and kin of the slayer of his father, who is none other than Rostam, the principal hero of the *Shāh-nāma*, already dead by the treachery of his own brother. And what are we to make of the role of Rostam in this tragedy as the doer of the evil deed? For more than three hundred years he has lived in the *Shāh-nāma* as the mighty sword of the righteous in the cosmic battle against evil, only to come upon this horrible fork in the road, both avenues of which lead to perdition.

If we accept this conceptualization of the structure of the *Shāh-nāma* then we are faced with a tragic epic which is suffused with more doom and gloom than other poems of its genre. For while it is true that in many epics such as the *Gilgamesh*, the *Iliad*, the *Song of Roland*, *El Cid*, to name only a few, we are witness to the heroic death of the protagonist, in each case the death is a key to the resolution of the conflict and a promise of return, restoration, or redemption. That, as we have noted, was the scheme in the early episodes of the *Shāh-nāma*, but it became increasingly difficult to maintain it. In the end, the restoration, which is crucial to catharsis in the classic formulation of tragedy, is missing.

The tragic impact of the *Shāh-nāma*, however, is not simply the sum of its tragic episodes. It pervades the encompassing conception of the work, and the sources of it are to be found not only in the late Sasanian Zurvanite ideas, but in the conscious and unconscious paradoxes that form the personality and the emotional and intellectual outlook of Ferdowsi. If the late Sasanian Zurvanite conception of Time as Fate and Death is clearly reflected in the interrogation of Zāl by the *mobad*s or the Zoroastrian priests, as Zaehner has pointed out,[3] nowhere is the resonance between those ideas and the personality and outlook of Ferdowsi better revealed than in the letter of the Sasanian general Rostam Farrokhzād to his brother on the eve of the battle of Qādesiyya and the rout of the Iranian army before the invading Arabs.[4] We may read it as the cry of anguish of the poet himself.

The episodic outer dimension of the *Shāh-nāma* has often masked the vast underlying structure from the careless reader, however. Essentially reduced, that structure is built upon a moral view of man in the world and the gradual process of internalization of evil. On the surface it may seem that Ferdowsi's main object is to preserve the "history" of his fatherland, but the sum of the *Shāh-nāma*'s artistic worth outweighs the inherent shortcomings of the poet's conscious scheme. Broadly conceived, it belongs to the epic genre. But it is not a formal epic like the *Aeneid* or the *Lusiad*. Rather, it has the spontaneity of the *Iliad*, and its episodic character reveals its kinship with the *chansons de geste*. More than any of its kindred poems, however, the *Shāh-nāma* is beset with paradoxes and conflicts—paradoxes that

---

[3]Ibid.
[4]The *Shah-namah*, Moscow edition, Vol. 9, 313ff.

are the substance of its art and the source of its tragic nobility. If there is a unifying theme in the *Shāh-nāma* it is no simple "wrath of Achilles," but the malevolence of the universe. Yet Ferdowsi is no passive fatalist. He has an abiding faith in a just Creator; he believes in the will of man, the need for his efforts, and the worth of his good deeds.

The pervading paradox of human existence is refracted and made particular in the episodes and in the lives of mortals who, prism-like, reflect the light and shadow of character, the changes of moods and motives, and the many psychic levels of personality. In the strength, variety, and sometimes profundity of its characterization—often achieved with much economy of means—the *Shāh-nāma* is remarkable in the annals of classical literature. Very few of its many protagonists are archetypes. Alas, all too many of its noblest heroes are prey to the basest of human motives. And even the vilest among them have moments of humanity. Although outwardly many a character defies all natural bounds, none is exempt from the inner reality of human nature. The goodness of the best is possible and the evil of the most wretched is not incredible.

Nowhere is this depth of characterization more evident than in the person of Rostam, the foremost of Iranian heroes. He is essentially a man of the world. Chivalrous, intensely loyal, pious, fearless, steel-willed and obdurate, he is nevertheless subject to occasional moods of disenchantment and indifference accompanied by gargantuan gluttony. He has a mystic reverence for the crown of Iran that inspires him to all his heroic feats. But he is quick to take offence and, at the slightest bruise to his ego or threat to his independent domain, wealth or power, he reacts with the full fury and resentment of a loyal dynast. For all his "active" temperament he can be very wordy and didactic. When occasion demands it, he is wise, temperate and resourceful. Of the more than three hundred years of his life, so lovingly recounted by Ferdowsi, only one night is spent in the amorous company of a woman. It serves the purpose of siring the ill-fated Sohrāb. For the rest, he is infinitely more devoted to his horse. Sometimes he is unable to rein his pride, which results in two monstrous deeds and shapes the final tragedy of his life.

It is partly this depth of characterization that enhances and ennobles the tragic episodes of the *Shāh-nāma*. Jamshid the priest-king—world-orderer, giver of knowledge and skills—is the victim of his own hubris. The tragedy of Sohrāb is not merely in the horror of filicide but in the fear and vanity of Rostam and the repulsed tender premonitions of Sohrāb. The tragedies of Iraj and Siyāvosh evoke the cosmic anguish and the inconsolable pity of the guileless and the pure, ravaged by the wicked. Forud and Bahrām are the promise of sweet and valorous youth cut down by the senselessness of war. Esfandiyār is rent by the conflict of his formal loyalties and his piety and good sense. But it is his vanity and ambition that send him to his doom. Nor is this moving sense of the tragic reserved for the Iranians alone. Pirān, the hoary Turanian noble, shows compassion to captive Iranians and risks his own life to protect them, only, in the end, to lose it for remaining loyal to his sovereign. Even the villainous Afrāsiyāb— a prisoner of his evil nature—is pitiable and tragic in the helpless moments of self-awareness.

Ferdowsi has no set formulae for tragedy, yet in the early and mythical part of the *Shāh-nāma* an inexorable divine justice seems to balance most of the scales. Iraj and Siyāvosh are restored and triumphant in Manuchehr and Kay Khosrow, Rostam is reconciled to his fate as the price for the slaying of Sohrāb and Esfandiyār, and Afrāsiyāb cannot escape his share. The tragic impact of the *Shāh-nāma*, however, is not simply the sum of its tragic episodes. It pervades the encompassing conception of the work, and the sources of it are to be found in the conscious and unconscious paradoxes that form the personality and the emotional and intellectual outlook of Ferdowsi.

The overriding tragic fact of the poet's life is that the glory of which he sings is no more. But this is not to say that the *Shāh-nāma* is a defiant nostalgic lament. The intellectual horizon of Ferdowsi is that of a rational and devout Muslim. Mohammad and Zoroaster are venerated as if they were of the same root, but Ferdowsi's pride in Iran is his constant muse. His concept of history is thoroughly Islamic, but there is no Augustinian righteous indignation in him. The cumulative emotional tensions of his "history" are unresolved. Even in his stark treatment of the final reigns of the Sasanian empire, when the succession of evil, tyranny, rapacity, treachery and chaos is unrelieved by any sign of grace, he cannot quite bring himself to a condemnation of the Iranian empire. The only possible catharsis is in the contemplation of the ideal of justice, essential in Islam—yet already far detached from the realities of his time. Nor is the holocaust so distant as the fall of the Sasanians. Ferdowsi was undoubtedly inspired by the recent Iranism of the Samanid epoch and may even have conceived of his masterwork as an offering to that illustrious house, only to witness its demise at the hands of the Turkic Ghaznavids. The bitterness of the mythical Iranian-Turanian epic struggle that permeates the *Shāh-nāma* and gives it its dramatic tension is largely the pressing phenomenon of the poet's own time. Thus he experienced a re-en-actment of the final tragedy of his poem. The necessity of dedicating the *Shāh-nāma* to the very Turkic destroyer of the Iranian Samanids must have been bitter and demeaning. Much of the traditional de-nunciatory epilogue addressed to Mahmud of Ghazna may be accre-tions of later times, but the tone is true.

The tensions and contradictions in the experience of the poet that are reflected in the tragic paradoxes of the *Shāh-nāma* and are a source of validity, profundity, and universality of its art, are not all conscious or external. The interactions of his innate character, his inculcated traits, his social position, his changing environment, and the nature of his creative genius, all fail to achieve a synthesis. Instead, they fashion a personality marred by unresolved intellectual conflicts and spiritual anguish.

He belongs to the class of *dehqān*s, or landed gentry, and has an inherited expectation of privilege which is embittered by gradual im-poverishment. He is not yet free of the impulses of generosity and noble detachment that sometimes flourish in the serene middle pla-teaus of wealth and power; but he is already afflicted with the material obsessions, if not the greed and avarice, that characterize periods of rise and fall. Thus he seeks, and needs, the patronage and the emol-uments of the Ghaznavid court, yet he is too proud, too detached and too dedicated to his "uncommercial" art to secure that patronage in the accepted mode of the day. He is contemptuous of the servility and the parasitic existence of the court poets, of the artificiality of their panegyric verse, of the ignobleness of their self-seeking and mutual enmity. Yet he is not without the artist's vanity, envy and acrimony, and occasionally he succumbs to the temptation of proving himself in their terms.

Ferdowsi's genuine compassion for the poor and the wronged, his remarkable and persistent sense of social justice, his courageous and vocal condemnation of irresponsible rulers, his altruism and ideal-ism—in short, his profound humanity—account for some of the most moving and ennobling passages in the *Shāh-nāma* and endow it with a consistent integrity. At the same time he had the conservative impulses of the *dehqān*. His yearning for legitimacy, his outrage at the disregard of position, his abhorrence of anarchy, his fear of heresy, and his dread of unruly mobs provide the narrative with moments of eerie drama and apocalyptic visions and nightmares.

However much may be said of the formal and philosophical dif-fuseness of the *Shāh-nāma*, it is transcendentally successful as a true epic. In that sense only a comparison with the *Iliad* can be meaningful and instructive. In their origin, nature and functions, as well as in form and content, there are arresting similarities between the two poems. This is not to say that the likenesses outnumber the differences. The *Shāh-nāma* is, of course, the product of a much later and more self-conscious age, and it draws from a vast fund of literary conventions and clichés of Near Eastern cultures. But the *Shāh-nāma* and the *Iliad* partake of the fundamental mysteries of epic as art. They both represent the instantly and eternally triumphant attempts of conscious art to immortalize the glory and the identity of a people. It does not matter that neither Homer nor Ferdowsi were the very first to attempt such a task in their cultures. It is the supreme elixir of their art which accomplished the miracle. They ennobled the oral epic without losing its spontaneity. Furthermore, they did so at a time when the cement of past associations was crumbling and the common identity of their peoples was in danger of effacement. Thus by their creations Homer and Ferdowsi succeeded at once in immortalizing the past and bequeathing the future to the language and life of their nation.

The Western reader of the *Shāh-nāma* will learn much—and may gain in enjoyment—by some comparison of its similarities and differences with the *Iliad*. Although Ferdowsi works with a number of written and even 'literate' sources, at least in the first half of the *Shāh-nāma*, as in the *Iliad*, the roots of oral tradition are close to the surface. Both poems employ a simple meter, and their rhyme schemes are suited to the long narrative and aid in memorizing. The heroes in both epics are affixed with appropriate epithets and are easily recognizable even without mention of their names. Both poems make use of a certain amount of repetition to assist recapitulation. Episodes of battle and heroism are modulated by sequences of chase, ostentatious banquets and idyllic revels, and ceremonious councils and parleys. Semi-independent sub-episodes are interspersed to vary the mood and relieve the tedium of the narrative. Of these, several romances in the *Shāh-nāma*, particularly those of Zāl and Rudāba and of Bizhan and Manizha, in their exquisite lyricism, poignant intimacy and self-contained perfection, have no peers in the *Iliad*. Both poets lavish masterful attention upon the details of the martial life—the description of armor and weapons, the personal and near magical love of the heroes for their mounts and their armor, etc.—that breed and sustain a sense of epic involvement. Both poems abound in warm human touches that evoke pathos and enhance the evolving drama.

117

Transcending these more or less formal similarities are the fundamental parallels of human behavior under similar relationships and social conditions, and the recognizable range of human types in the *Iliad* and the *Shāh-nāma*. The affinities of the indispensable hero Rostam with Achilles; of the capricious, covetous, apprehensive, and envious monarch Kay Kāvus with Agamemnon; of the stolid and martial Giv with Ajax; of the wily and wise Pirān with Odysseus; of the dutiful and sacrificial Gudarz with Hector; of the impetuous and handsome Bizhan with Paris; of the youthful, loyal, and pathetic Bahrām with Patroklos; of the impulsive, sensuous, and beautiful Rudāba with Helen; of the adoring, meek, and resigned Farangis with Hecuba—these are only a few of the evocative suggestions of artistic kinship between the two epics. In the fragile social order depicted in the *Iliad* and in the first half of the *Shāh-nāma* tension and strife are never far from the surface. But Ferdowsi has endowed his cosmos with a higher morality and thus the lapses of his heroes are more grave and awful.

In addition to mortal humans, both epics are peopled by several supernatural orders of goodly spirits, demons, and magical creatures who intervene in the affairs of men and profoundly affect their fate. But the God of the *Shāh-nāma* is the unknowable God of Zoroastrians, Jews, Christians, and Muslims. Unlike the deities of the *Iliad* He is not implicated in the struggle of the mortals, though he is constantly evoked and beseeched. Only twice does an angel intervene to alter the course of battle. At other times there is only indirect confirmation of the righteous chastisement of the wayward. On the other hand prophetic dreams count for more in the *Shāh-nāma*. Fate is the unconquerable tyrant of both poems, but in the *Shāh-nāma* it is sometimes unravelled by the stars, robbing the drama of its mystery.

The *Shāh-nāma* is inordinately longer than the *Iliad*. Essentially it is made in two segments: the mythical and legendary first half, and the "historical" second half. The psychological and artistic seam cannot be concealed. The fundamental affinities with the *Iliad* are primarily true of the first half. But even there the unity of theme, the limitation of action and time, the rapid devolution of the plot, the resolution of the conflict, and the uncanny proportions of the *Iliad* are missing. Ferdowsi's "historical" mission undoubtedly scatters the artistic impact of the *Shāh-nāma* and diffuses the focus of its aesthetic concept. But the wrath of Achilles, after all, is not the sole catalyst of Homer's art. The validity and viability of the *Iliad* rests in its general relevance to the human situation. In this sense the artistic flaw of the *Shāh-nāma* is more than made up by, and perhaps makes for, its greater universality.

Thus in the *Shāh-nāma* we come across characters who have no counterparts in the *Iliad*, and one must cull the whole of Greek mythology, mystery and drama for parallels. Jamshid, the primal priest-king, the divinely inspired creator of civilization, the bringer of world order, whose hubris causes his fall and plunges mankind into evil and darkness; Zahhāk, the grotesque tyrant, the personification of irrational and demonic forces, who grips the world in a thousand-year reign of terror; Kāva, the rebellious *vox populi* triumphant in a just cause; Faredun, the ideal and wise king, compassionate pastor of his people; Siyāvosh, the tragic guileless youth, maligned, helpless, and martyred; Kay Khosrow, the messiah-king, avenger, and restorer. Every one of them is a focal realization of a master figure in the history of man's existence and aspirations.

It is this universality together with its faithful and unresolved reflection of the human paradox that is the essence of the *Shāh-nāma*'s art and the cause of its timelessness; for it permits every generation to seek its own resolution.

## Bibliography

*Editions*
Ferdowsi. *The Shahnama,* edited by E. Bertels et al. 9 volumes. Moscow, 1966–71.
Idem. *The Shahnama,* [edited by Said Nafisi et al.] 10 volumes. Tehran, 1934–36.

*Criticism*
Nöldeke, Th. *Das iranische Nationalepos* (Berlin and Leipzig, 1920); English translation "The Iranian National Epic" by L. Bogdanov in *Journal of K. R. Cama Oriental Institute,* 6 (1925): 1–161.
Yarshater, E. *Cambridge History of Iran,* vol. 3, part 1 (Cambridge, 1983; rep. 1986), 343–480.
Minovi, M. *Ferdowsi va She'r-e u* (Tehran, 1986).
Meskub, Sh. *Moqaddama'i bar Rostam va Esfandiyār* (Tehran, 1964).
Idem. *Sug-e Syihāvosh* (Tehran, 1971).
Eslāmi Nadushan, M. 'A. *Zendagi va marg-e pahlavānān dar Shāhnāma* (Tehran, 1969).
Davidson, O. "The Crown-bestower in the Iranian Book of Kings," *Acta Iranica* X (1985): 61–148.

See also Epic Poetry, bibliography.

# 7. Lyric Poetry

The earliest Persian lyrical poetry, which dates from the closing decades of the ninth and the beginnings of the tenth centuries, is characterized by a set of rules and conventions which remain typical of all
Persian odes written by later generations of poets. Not only had the
prosody established itself so solidly that it remained unshaken for
more than one thousand years, but the mode of expression had already taken a shape which proved durable. Two poetic traditions contributed to the birth and rapid growth of this poetry: first, the Iranian
tradition of the Sasanian period and its little-known continuation during the early centuries of Islam, and, second, the Arabic tradition
which became dominant in the wake of Iran's political and religious
defeat.

## The Origins of Persian Lyric Poetry

We may begin with a brief analysis of the following poem by Shahid
of Balkh (d. 936), which contains a number of the significant features:

> I swear by your life, earnestly I swear,
> That I shall not turn from you nor listen to any advice.
>
> They advise me, but I accept no advice,
> For once one has sworn, advice is of no avail.
>
> I have heard that he can go to paradise
> Who fulfills the wishes of a desirous person.
>
> A thousand partridges have not the heart of one falcon,
> A thousand slaves have not the heart of one master.
>
> Should the king of the Chinese ever see your face,
> He would bow before you and strew dinars.
>
> Should the king of the Indians ever see your hair,
> He would prostrate himself and uproot his idol temples.
>
> I am caught in a catapult of torments, like Abraham
> They want to throw me into the fire of woes.
>
> May you be healthy, O rose of spring and paradise,
> That they may recite prayers toward the Mecca of your face.[1]

[1]I am grateful to Dr. Margaret Madelung for her suggestions, especially concerning
the translations of the poems.

Even though the *ghazal*, destined to become the vehicle *par excellence* of the Persian lyric, did not reach its technical perfection until almost two centuries later, the only formal requirement missing in this poem is the pen name (*takhallos*) in the last line. The number of lines, the rhyme pattern, the forceful thrust of an idea in the first line and its elaboration and reinforcement throughout, all follow the requirements for a sound and effective *ghazal*. The two major themes—the vow to remain ever-faithful to the beloved and the praise of her unmatched beauty—are expressed in terms which reveal nothing of the actual qualities of the beloved. The lover's suffering and his refusal to yield to the advice of others who tell him to forget her, the idealization of her beauty by having the king of China bow before her, and the deep blackness of her hair, which captivates even the king of India and forces him to destroy his own temples and worship her instead, are all among the stock of stereotypical images used and reused by later generations of poets.

Not all the earliest Persian lyrics display the formal qualities of Shahid's poem. Although very little of this poetry survives, and it is difficult to pass judgment, it appears that some poets are still unsettled and in search of a definitive mode of expression. Shahid and Rudaki (d. 940) were hailed by the succeeding generation of poets as great *ghazal* writers, but the term "ghazal" in all likelihood did not stand for the fully developed form which, in the hands of the classical masters, was destined to make the genius of Persian lyrical verse manifest. It appears that it had a range of application wider than that of the classical period. From the testimony and theoretical descriptions of authors such as Shams-e Qays-e Rāzi, we may safely gather that initially the *ghazal* was a poem to be sung and accompanied by an instrument. In this sense, it was equivalent to the *qawl* (song) and was used as late as the thirteenth and fourteenth centuries.[2]

What then, was the form that served lyrical themes? Probably all existing forms were utilized, including the *qet'a* (short poem) and even the *robā'i* or the *dobayti* (quatrain). The introductory section of the panegyrics, known as the *nasib*, however, must be regarded as the principal vehicle of lyric poetry before the *ghazal* form was fully developed and firmly established in the early twelfth century.

The court of the Samanid dynasty (A.D. 864–1005), with its emphasis on Persian culture and its generous patronage of Persian poets,

[2] J. Homā'i's footnote, *Divān-e 'Othmān-e Mokhtāri* (Tehran, 1962), 569ff; Z. Mo'taman, *Tahavvol-e she'r-e fārsi* (Tehran, 1960), 199ff.

was the ideal soil to nourish the seeds of nascent Persian poetry. The general atmosphere, however, was not purely Iranian. The Persian poet, despite any inspiration he might have received from the continuing old traditions among the lower levels of his native society, was separated from his pre-Islamic ancestors by at least two centuries of silence. The dominating factors of Islam and the Arabic language had changed religious norms and world view as well as literary taste and orientation. Baghdad was the metropolis of the new culture, and many Persian scholars and administrators had long since devoted their learning and talents to the prosperity of the new civilization. Iranian poets flocked to Baghdad, composed poems in Arabic, and were engaged in cultural interchange. Even the poets enjoying the support of their Iranian patrons back in Khorasan could not escape the influence of Islam and Arabic literary traditions. No wonder, therefore, that not only Arabic words, but even Arabic imagery and figures of speech penetrated Persian poetry.

Most important among the literary borrowings was the *qasida* form, but the Persian poet derived his subjects from a world different from that of the Arab poet. Instead of the typical prelude describing the deserted camp site of the beloved and her tribe, the Persian poet had a repertoire of topics inspired by his own geographical and cultural background, and by the social life of the royal court. There were, admittedly, those who occasionally imitated the Arabic models and wept over the imaginary ruins of the dwelling place of an imaginary beloved. But on the whole, such cases remained the exception. The Iranian calendar provided royal courts with numerous occasions to celebrate great feasts. Especially important were Nowruz, New Year, the most joyous festival of the spring, and Mehrgān, observed at the beginning of autumn. Descriptions of the natural world during the springtime were the most common poetic topics. Other favored subjects were love in all its aspects, bygone youth, and the making and drinking of wine. The early Persian poets were lovers of nature and derived much of their imagery from it. They were not very concerned with the abstract realms of thought. Their diction retains a freshness and charm that is not diminished by the heavy pace of the meter and the typically slow movement of the rhythmic patterns.

## Early Forms

The tenth-century writer Rudaki is far more than a mere lyricist and court poet. In his surviving poems—which include bits of epic verse

and elegies, with didactic, contemplative, and also Bacchic themes—
there is often a melancholy complaint about the transitory character
of life, a sense of resignation to the helplessness and mortality of
human beings. In Rudaki's poems we also find the germ of Khayyāmian thought which later permeates the entire corpus of Persian poetry.

The following piece, quoted by Bayhaqi, is an example of Rudaki's
"existentialist" sorrow:

> In this transitory abode the guest
> Should not set his heart forever.
>
> You will have to sleep underneath the earth,
> Even though you now sleep on brocade.
>
> What succor from being with others
> When you needs must enter the grave alone?
>
> Under the ground your companions ants and insects;
> Open your eyes and behold, it is visible now.
>
> The one who dressed the tresses of your hair,
> Though that one received wages of gold and silver,
>
> Seeing you with cheeks turned pale,
> Himself turns cool. He is not blind.[3]

Shahid makes the same painful observation in the following epigram:

> If grief gave off smoke the same as fire
> The world would be darkened for evermore;
>
> If you went about this world from end to end
> You wouldn't find one wise man who was happy.[4]

The remedy suggested by Rudaki is the same as Khayyām's:

> Live happy, happy with the black eyed,
> For the world is naught but a tale, a wind.
>
> One should rejoice in what is coming,
> And not remember what is already past.

[3]*Tārikh-e Bayhaqi*, ed. Q. Ghani and 'A. Fayyāz (Tehran, 1945–46), 188.
[4]'Owfi, *Lubábu 'l Albáb*, vol. 2, ed. E. G. Browne and M. Qazwini (Leiden, 1906), 4;
tr. A. J. Arberry, *Literature*, 37.

I and the one with curly locks and smelling musk!
I and that moon-face of the Huri race!

Fortunate is he who gives to others and himself enjoys;
Wretched he who does not give nor does himself enjoy.

Wind and cloud is this world, alas!
Bring wine, let be what may!

The images used by Shahid in the following two *bayt*s are common to
many later lyricists:

The cloud doth weep as weeps the lover, while
Like the beloved doth the garden smile;

Afar the thunder, like myself, doth groan,
When with the dawn I rain my piteous moan.[5]

An outstanding lyricist of the second half of the tenth century is
Monjik of Termez. In a poem[6] that technically would have been a
perfect *ghazal* if it had contained the pen name, Monjik describes his
beloved as being "more beautiful than Armenian silk" and "purer
than drops of winter rain"; he describes her hair filling streets with
the scent of musk, her face, the entire region with light. With her he
feels as if he were in a temple of beauty; she should not look at the
moon lest it darken out of envy, nor walk by the garden lest the cypress
droop from shame in comparison with her graceful stature. Most of
the images used in this poem were in the process of becoming fixed
conventions.

A major poet of the late tenth century, well known as the forerunner
of Ferdowsi, is Daqiqi (d. 978). In the extant lyrical fragments he
emerges as a stronger poet than in his epic verse, with a greater wealth
of imagination and more direct, nature-related similes. Still he also
uses clichéd images, perhaps more than his predecessors. In a famous
lyric[7] he compares the black night to the hair of the beloved, the bright
day to her pure cheeks, the well-polished agate to her lips, the blossoming rose again to her cheeks, gazelle eyes and open narcissus to
her eyes, bow and arrow to eyebrows. Her body, he says in closing,
cannot be compared to a cypress, for it is the cypress that resembles

[5]'Owfi, vol. 2, 4; tr. E. G. Browne, *Lit. Hist.*, vol. 1, 454.
[6]Z. Safā, *Ganj-e sokhan* vol. 1, (Tehran, 1960), 42–43.
[7]G. Lazard, *Les Premiers poètes persans* (Tehran–Paris, 1964), vol. 1, 147.

her stature. In all of these similes Daqiqi achieves a more powerful effect by reversing the position of the images in the similes: it is not the hair, for example, that resembles the night, but rather the night that in its intense darkness looks like her hair.

In another love poem of only five distichs, Daqiqi employs the more refined technique of using metaphors; by dropping all the words denoting comparison from his similes, he connects the images more closely with each other:

O would that in the world 'twere endless day,
That from those lips I ne'er need 'bide away!

But for those scorpion curls my love doth wear
No smart like scorpion-sting my heart need bear.

But for the stars which 'neath those lips do play,
I need not count night's stars till dawn of day.

Were she not formed of all that is most fair
Some thought beyond her love my soul might share.

If I must pass my life without my friend
O God, I would my life were at an end.[8]

From among the many poets who lived during the second half of the tenth century, Rābe'a of Qozdār and Kesā'i of Marv deserve to be mentioned, the former as the first known woman poet of Iran, with a few very tender poems attributed to her, and the latter for the vivid descriptions he has left in a few epigrams.

This short lyric of Rābe'a is unforced in tone and conveys plaintive feelings:

The love of him threw me in chains again,
Struggle against them proved of no avail.

Love is a sea of invisible shores,
How can one swim in it, O clever one?

If you want to pursue love to the end,
Be content to endure much unpleasantness.

---

[8]E. G. Browne, *Lit. Hist.*, vol. 1, 461–62. The word *kowkab* (star), used twice in the third line, stands for the shining teeth of the beloved (not necessarily detectable by readers unfamiliar with this style) and for tears of the lover, misunderstood by Browne.

Ugliness you must see and imagine it is beauty,
Poison you must take and think it is sugar.

Beset with impatience I did not know
That the more one seeks to pull away, the tighter becomes the rope.[9]

The following fragment again may derive from some bitter experience:

I pray to God that you may fall in love
With one stone-hearted, unfriendly like yourself.

That you may learn the pain of passion, the brand of love and
    sorrow,
That your heart may writhe at separation and know my worth.[10]

Kesā'i shows, in addition to a reflective mood, a sensibility for refreshing natural poems and close observation of minute details:

See the rain drop on the iris,
It looks like the tear in the eye of a weeping lover.

Its leaves are the feathers of a white falcon, you would say,
The beak of the falcon having picked an unpierced pearl.

* * *

Her hand emerged from behind the veil, white like ivory,
You might say Venus and the moon are wielding swords from
    behind the clouds,

The hand's back was soft like an ermine's belly
The fingertips dyed black like the ermine's tail.

* * *

Roses are a gift of price
Sent to us from Paradise;

More divine our nature grows
In the Eden of the rose.

[9]Safā, *Ganj-e sokhan*, vol. 1, 54.
[10]'Owfi, vol. 2, 62.

Roses why for silver sell?
O rose merchant, fairly tell

What you buy instead of those
That is costlier than the rose.[11]

## The Ghaznavid Lyric

The poets of this early formative period laid down the basis of both form and conventional imagery in Persian lyric poetry. Undoubted mastery, however, was achieved by three poets who flourished during the first three decades of the eleventh century at the court of the Ghaznavid rulers Mahmud and Mas'ud. They developed a characteristic style, a fixed set of metaphors, and dozens of abundantly-used figures of speech. Above all, they created a rigid pattern of impersonal, almost abstract descriptions of the beloved, which determined the course of the later lyric. 'Onsori established himself as the undisputed master craftsman, using external embellishments and exactly measured symmetry of words to the extent that he often stifled inner vitality and poetic impulse. Farrokhi, on the other hand, is the poet of exuberant love and pleasure. His tongue is sweet, his diction unforced, and his themes manifold. His poems display the pulsing of a heart overflowing with joy. Manuchehri may be said to have combined the learning of 'Onsori with the genuine excitement and inner participation of Farrokhi. He gives colorful pictures of blooming gardens, filled in spring with the cheerful singing of birds and desolate in autumn with the sweeping wind.

'Onsori (d. 1039) was the poet laureate at Mahmud's court. His several romances are lost, and his *qasida*s consist of eulogies showered on his patrons. Even the prologues to his *qasida*s betray no attempt to escape, even for a moment, from the bonds of his task. Descriptions of spring, autumn, and the loved one's features, which are almost exclusively the themes of these short preludes, lack any signs of real feeling. Throughout his poetry every distich is carefully designed, almost every word is meticulously selected, chiseled, and set in place. He himself admits his inability to write *ghazal*s as good as those of Rudaki, and yet his impact on Persian poetry has been strong because of his unique artistic mastery and competence. The following lines from his "Question and Answer" *qasida*, translated by E. G. Browne, may give some impression of 'Onsori's art, although his verbal acro-

[11]Ibid., pp. 35–36; tr. R. A. Nicholson (in Arberry, *Literature*, 37–38).

batics are lost in the process; it should be read together with the translator's footnotes:

> To each inquiry which my wit could frame
> Last night, from those fresh lips an answer came.
>
> Said I, "One may not see thee save at night."
> "When else," said she, "would'st see the moon's clear light?"
>
> Said I, "The sun doth fear thy radiant face."
> Said she, "When thou art here, sleep comes apace!"
>
> Said I, "With hues of night stain not the day!"
> Said she, "Strain not with blood thy cheeks, I pray!"
>
> Said I, "This hair of thine right fragrant is!"
> Said she, "Why not? 'tis purest ambergris!"
>
> Said I, "Who caused thy cheeks like fire to shine?"
> Said she, "That one who grilled that heart of thine."
>
> Said I, "My eyes I cannot turn from thee!"
> "Who from the *mihrāb* turns in prayer?" quoth she.
>
> Said I, "Thy love torments me! Grant me grace!"
> Said she, "In torment is the lover's place!"
>
> Said I, "Where lies my way to rest and peace?"
> "Serve our young prince," said she, "withouten cease!"[12]

The lyrical verse of Farrokhi (d. 1037) is unprecedented in vitality and freshness. His *taghazzol*s are captivating songs of worldly love without any attempt at allegorizing or spiritualizing. Other themes—descriptions of nature, youth, and wine—are also used repeatedly. The few anecdotes about his life reveal an adventurous and rustic, yet very romantic nature. The word *del* (heart), many times personified and made to engage in debate with the poet, is, along with *'eshq* (love) and *bahār* (spring) among the most favored words of his *Divān*. The following literal translations illustrate some of these features:

> O my heart, glad tidings be yours;
> I will give you to my friend!

[12]*Divān*, ed. Y. Qarib (Tehran, 1962), qasida no. 3, 7ff; Browne, *Lit. Hist.*, vol. 2, 121–22.

May you be happy with him, and may in this world
He be happy with whom you are happy.

Beware not to say "No, do not send me,
No one has ever sent his heart to a friend."

The friend keeps demanding you from me,
Go to the friend, let be what may be!

Kiss his hands and feet and then dwell
Underneath those locks like unto a box tree,

So that you may escape the oppression of his eyes,
And get your full satisfaction from his lips.[13]

Farrokhi frequently applies a narrative style to his prologues by telling about imaginary or real events designed to evoke a greater interest in his readers.[14] In a dozen of his *qasidas*, he assumes a rather humorous, even blasphemous attitude toward the month of fasting, Ramadan, rejoicing at its passing like a host relieved when a tedious guest leaves at last.[15]

Manuchehri of Dāmghān (d. 1040) is the last and, in certain respects, the most colorful and ingenious of this period's famous trio. His power of creativity and artistic temper are manifest not so much in his selection of themes, which he shares for the most part with others, but in his bold method of treating them. Nature, as he portrays it in all seasons, is animated with crowds of birds and decorated with an unusual multitude of flowers and plants, all actively engaged in a magic play orchestrated by the poet's lively fantasy. Nor is nature restricted, as was customary, to lovely gardens at dawn; Manuchehri describes wild deserts and mountains on stormy nights with lightning and thunder and devastating floods, as well as clear skies studded with a myriad of twinkling stars. His imaginativeness in creating fresh and original similes is unparalleled in Persian poetry. The narrative approach is a typical trait of his poetry; he often utilizes the seasonal changes, describing the "armies" of spring and winter confronting each other. The ripening of grapes is also narrated—the "vine daughters" are bedded innocently and then impregnated by the uninvited but irresistible rays of the sun.

---

[13]*Divān*, ed. A. 'Abd al-Rasuli (Tehran, 1932), no. 24, 42. Throughout these lyrics the pronoun referring to the beloved can be understood as he or she.
[14]See *Divān*, nos. 50, 58, 89, 134.
[15]See *Divān*, nos. 8, 47, 71, 73, 74, 77, 85, 99, 124, 204, 207.

The introduction of a new stanzaic form, the *mosammat* (*aaaaab, cccccb,* etc.), is among Manuchehri's innovations. However, that core of true lyricism, love, is not Manuchehri's concern. Whenever love is hinted at or described, it is the formal sort of love that could develop between poets and their slaves, characterized by a harsh tone and demanding attitude. His vocabulary, which is often filled with Arabic and archaic Persian words, does not suit the serenity of intimate love and tender feelings. Despite the traits they share, Farrokhi and Manuchehri represent two different temperaments and proclivities, one hardly able to remain cool and calm and the other barely betraying any passion of love.

Following are some lines from Manuchehri's "Candle" *qasida*:

Thou whose soul upon thy forehead glitters like an aureole,
By our soul our flesh subsists, while by thy flesh subsists thy soul.

Why, if not a star, dost waken only when all others sleep?
Why, if not a lover, ever o'er thyself forlorn dost weep?

Even midst thy smiles thou weepest, and moreover strange to tell,
Thou art of thyself the lover, and the well-beloved as well!

Me most nearly thou resemblest; closely I resemble thee;
Kindly friends of all the world, but foes unto ourselves are we.

Both of us consume and spend ourselves to make our comrades
      glad,
And by us our friends are rendered happy while ourselves are sad.

Both are weeping, both are wasting, both are pale and weary-eyed,
Both are burned in isolation, both are spurned and sorely tried.

I behold upon thy head what in my heart doth hidden rest;
Thou upon thy head dost carry what I hide within my breast.

All my other friends I've tested, great and little, low and high;
Found not one with kindly feeling, found not two with loyalty.

Thou, O candle, art my friend; to thee my secrets I consign;
Thou art my familiar comrade, I am thine and thou art mine.[16]

Among the later Ghaznavid poets, Mas'ud-e Sa'd-e Salmān (d. 1121) stands out. He was attached to the court in Lahore but, suspected of

---

[16]*Divān*, qasida no. 33, 70ff.; tr. E. G. Browne, *Lit. Hist.*, vol. 2, 154–55.

participation in conspiracies, he twice fell from grace and spent nineteen of his best years, probably between forty and sixty, in prison. He is best known for his prison poems, which are thematically unique in Persian literature. In them we feel the frustration of his endless loneliness, the pain of separation from his family, the physical hardship of the prison cell, and his longing for freedom. The following lines are typical:

Heaven has so destined
That all troubles be mine.

I had not suspected that like the birds
My abode would be high up in the sky.

That stars would my companion be,
The northern breeze my messenger.

I find no one to soothe my grief,
I see no one to companion with.

All night long in fear of the flooding tears
My eyes are bereft of sleep.

Whenever I speak here on this mountain top,
The answer I receive is only an echo.[17]

Before discussing subsequent poets we should consider some developments of the Persian lyric in greater detail. One is that the similes describing different features of the beloved were used so repeatedly that they very soon became clichés; losing their true impact, they gradually replaced the very subjects of comparison that they served. A ready stock of stereotypical expressions—ruby for the lips of the beloved, moon for the face, narcissus for the eyes—came to supplant the poet's personal search for innovative images. Sharaf al-Din Rāmi, a poet who lived during the fourteenth century, even compiled a manual of such similes used in erotic poetry, as a help for both poets and students.[18]

The second development is that Persian lyricists became concerned primarily with ideal types of the garden, the battlefield, the hunt, the valor of the king, the hatefulness of the enemy. One cannot know, for example, what Maymandi's palace in Ghazna, which is glorified by

[17]*Divān-e Mas'ud-e Sa'd-e Salmān*, ed. R. Yasemi (Tehran, 1939), 93.
[18]For details see Browne, *Lit. Hist.*, vol. 2, 83ff.

'Onsori,[19] looked like in reality. The figure of the beloved—whether real or imagined—is always as upright and tall as a cypress, and moves as gracefully as that tree moves in a gentle breeze. There is no way of knowing whether the figure thus described was really tall or short, corpulent or slim, nimble or clumsy. As a result of this strict convention, not only were the real qualities of the subjects disguised, but the very existence of a living person for whom the poems were presumably composed came into question. The lack of grammatical distinction between the genders in Persian further obscured the true purport of lyric compositions. The society was not too intolerant of homosexuality, which, owing to historical conditions, flourished.[20]

Court life, with young Turkish soldier-slaves available to be used and abused by wealthy masters, furnished poetic language with an additional vocabulary borrowed from the martial arts. Words such as arrow, bow, dart, sword, lasso, and shield began to be used to describe the eye, eyelashes, eyebrows, curls of hair, and so on. The beloved was called cruel, violent, tyrannical, hostile, bloodthirsty, and even a killer; the lover, in contrast, was presented as feeble, ill, poor, wronged, despairing, wounded, bleeding, weeping, sleepless, and killed or murdered. In time, these words were detached from their historical contexts and turned into stereotypical metaphors to illustrate one-sided love relationships. It required only one more step for the Sufis to use this vocabulary to describe the God-human relationship.

## The Influence of Sufism

The lyric poetry of the Ghaznavid and Seljuk periods (eleventh and twelfth centuries) can be better understood in the light of its literary and social contexts.[21] In the early twelfth century, during the Seljuk period, the influence of Sufism sparked a major development in Persian lyrics. The earlier use of amorous quatrains by the famous Sufi master Abu Sa'id of Mehna (d. 1049) had already pointed the way for future development. He was followed by poets like Bābā Tāher of Hamadān (d. mid-eleventh century) who poured out his mystical sentiments of love and longing in simple but moving quatrains. But it is

---

[19]*Divān*, pp. 91–99, especially verses 1012–25 and 1128–31.

[20]For these and many related details see J. Rypka, *History of Iranian Literature* (Dordrecht, 1968), 85–89; see also E. Yarshater, *She'r-e fārsi dar 'ahd-e Shāhrokh* (Tehran, 1955), 62ff.

[21]See 23–28 and pp. 219ff. in this volume (*Ed.*).

with Sanā'i of Ghazna that mystical thought found a secure place in Persian poetry.

Sanā'i (d. 1131 or 1140) was a writer of panegyrics until he experienced a spiritual transformation that dramatically changed the course of his life and added a new dimension to Persian poetry. After his revelation he devoted his talent to the composition of several didactic and mystical poems. His call is to repent, to abandon all worldly attachments, and to turn to a life of strictly religious observance and abstemious behavior.[22]

The most significant literary impact of Sufism was a new concept of poetic vocabulary that gave some words double or even triple meanings. In addition to their lexical meanings, these words now symbolized mystical and religious ideas as well. Words for the beloved—for example *dust, delbar, yār, jānān, ma'shuq, mahbub*—could also refer to the divine Beloved, the Prophet, or the Sufi mentor, depending on the context. "Wine" could mean the substance of mystic love or divine teachings; "intoxication," mystical fervor; "vintner," the spiritual master, and "tavern," his monastery or convent. Beauty might apply to divine beauty, and even physical attraction could be seen as a token of heavenly beauty. Broader notions from the religious sphere and Sufi circles also enriched the poetic symbolism of lyric poetry. Thus Adam and Eve, the serpent, the apple, and paradise; Abraham, his two sons, and the story of the sacrifice; Joseph, his father and brothers, and the well; Moses and Pharaoh; King Solomon and his seal, and his ability to converse with birds and animals; the life of Jesus and the Trinity—these along with countless items from Islamic history and mythology flooded Persian poetry and created layer upon layer of new metaphorical idioms. The resulting multiplicity of meanings gave lyric poetry a weightier substance than before, but at the same time deprived it of its earlier clarity.

Returning to Sanā'i, we may point out that his *Divān* includes many poems which are open to both religious and profane interpretations. Nonetheless, Sanā'i's mystical lyrics are not wrapped in a veil of ambiguous symbols. His diction is explicitly religious and often sounds like a sermon calling upon Muslims to awaken, abandon their gaudy possessions, and cleanse their hearts of worldly desires. He strikes us as an excited preacher with an urgent message in a critical situation.

---

[22]See Rypka's general discussion on this subject, 226ff. and particularly on Sanā'i, 236ff., with references on p. 243, n. 47.

He wants to launch his personal revolution in the hearts and minds of everyone. His zeal and enthusiasm are contagious.[23]

Sanā'i's significance for Persian lyric poetry is considerable not only because he widened the range of its themes, but also because he made the *ghazal* the most cherished and most adequate vehicle of lyrical expression. Whether the classical *ghazal* form existed independently of the *qasida* before Sanā'i, or was actually the same as the *taghazzol* and only later separated itself from the rest of the *qasida,* is a matter of debate.[24] The fact is that through the influence of Sanā'i, the classical *ghazal* reached a stage of technical perfection and was used, not sporadically as before, but rather on an equal footing with the *qasida.*[25] An examination of the *divāns* after Sanā'i demonstrates numerically that the balance gradually shifted in favor of the *ghazal.*

The number of *bayt*s in Sanā'i's *Divān* generally varies from five to twelve, with several slightly shorter or longer. The pen name, also introduced by Sanā'i, is used in about half of his 408 *ghazals*, often before the last line and occasionally even in the first one. Rhyme and rhythm play a conspicuous part in Sanā'i's verse; one typical feature is his use of internal rhymes within the individual verses of many poems.

Unlike court panegyrists, Sanā'i allows himself a free choice of vocabulary: open to words that are learned or common, melodious or harsh, he is mostly pious but occasionally also vulgar and even obscene. The following is a sample of his lyrics:

> Darling, my heart I gave to thee— Good-night! I go.
> Though know'st my heartfelt sympathy— Good-night! I go.
>
> Should I behold thee ne'er again— 'Tis right, 'tis right;
> I clasp this hour of parting tight— Good-night! I go.
>
> With raven tress and visage clear,— Enchantress dear.
> Hast made my daylight dark and drear:— Good-night! I go.

[23]Browne's opinion about Sanā'i's *Divān* (*Lit. Hist.,* vol. 2, 322) that, "There are probably few unexplored mines in Persian poetry which would yield to the diligent seeker a richer store of gems" is in my view a correct appraisal.

[24]Cf. S. A. Bausani in *EI*², vol. 2, under "Ghazal," 1033ff.; and Rypka, *History,* 141–42.

[25]Farrokhi's single *ghazal* (*Divān,* 436), even if genuine, is only an isolated case and cannot prove the existence of the genre in his time. The resemblance of a few lyrical pieces to *ghazal* in the romance of *Varqa and Golshāh* by 'Ayyuqi (see Rypka, *Iran. Lit.,* 177) does not yield great support to the theory of the early *ghazal* either.

| O Light of Faith thy face thy hair— | Like doubt's despair |
| Both this and that yield torment rare— | Good-night! I go. |
| Therefore 'twixt fire and water me— | Thou thus does see, |
| Lips parched and dry, tear-raining eye:— | Good-night! I go.[26] |

Political upheavals and the rise of the Seljuk dynasty in the eleventh century had both negative and positive consequences for Persian literature. The new masters did not have the same interest in the cultivation of Persian poetry, nor did they understand it to the same degree as their predecessors. However, considering the extent of their empire, the Seljuks did serve the cause of Iranian culture by carrying Persian poetry into many new territories and creating new centers for its cultivation.

At the same time, recurrent onslaughts of Central Asian nomadic tribes followed the crumbling of Ghaznavid power, and the endless miseries and destruction they caused seem to have helped the spread of Sufism. Sufi organizations were havens of consolation, and the helpless population sought solace in the spiritual teachings of the Sufis, who had an other-worldly message for the masses. Sufi thinking and passion, however, needed a more attractive vehicle of presentation than prose discourses, which usually took a learned approach. Poetry was the ideal instrument, and the *ghazal,* the ideal form. Short enough for easy memorization, it provided Sufi gatherings with suitable texts for singing. In these gatherings and elsewhere, when overcome by a state of ecstasy, the Sufi leaders would often extemporize verses in *ghazal* form. Thus the *ghazal,* unlike the *qasida,* gave Persian literature a popular form and a source of enjoyment available to both the common and literary populations.

A cursory glance at the *divān*s of poets after Sanā'i reveals how the *ghazal* soon began to outshine the *qasida.* The two greatest composers of *qasida*s, Anvari (d. 1189) and Khāqāni (d. 1199), each left a greater number of *ghazal*s than *qasida*s. Even the noted romantic poet Nezāmi (d. 1209) wrote about 180 *ghazal*s and only seventeen *qasida*s. It should be noted that Anvari and Khāqāni were able lyric poets, but neither was a Sufi; both treat love in a clear and natural way, although their poems are not altogether free from Sufi imagery.

Before reaching the golden age of the Persian lyric, we meet with yet another fascinating figure, 'Attār (d. ca. 1220), who was both a devoted mystic and a prolific poet. As such, he is the link connecting

[26]*Divān,* Tehran, 1962, no. 216, 925; trans. Browne, *Lit. Hist.,* vol. 2, 322.

his predecessor Sanā'i with his great successor Rumi. The search for divine truth is the leitmotif of his entire corpus, and the realization that it lies beyond reach is the source of his anguish. His *ghazal*s, however, are not stylistically exciting; they are somewhat verbose and occasionally clumsy. Nonetheless, as a Sufi and as the author of several mystical *mathnavi*s, he had sufficient impact on Rumi to elicit the following tribute:

> 'Attār was the spirit,
> Sanā'i his eyes twain,
> And in time thereafter
> Came we in their train.[27]

With Rumi (d. 1273), the art of the mystical *ghazal* reached its height, but since he is the subject of a separate chapter there is no need to discuss his work here.

## Aspects of the Ghazal

In earlier *ghazal*s a unifying thread ran through all the lines with differing degrees of clarity and relevance. It gradually grew thinner and less visible to uninitiated eyes, and sometimes was lost entirely under a thick layer of combined metaphors, learned allusions, and, in Sufi *ghazal*s, excessively esoteric statements. By the thirteenth century it was practically established tradition for each distich in a *ghazal* to be a syntactically and thematically closed unit, independent of the lines before and after it. Yet this did not imply a lack of cohesion among the several distichs of a *ghazal*, or a haphazard arrangement, for there exists in the *ghazal* a vertical harmony and interdependence of ideas, though not the logical development of a philosophical argument.[28]

The reader of a *ghazal* may wonder for whom the glowing verses were written, since the poems contain no names, no hint of personal experiences or factual events, not even the normally clear indications of the sex of the beloved. The objects of adoration are paragons of beauty, but never friendly and agreeable. The poet constantly moans and complains about separation and sleepless nights; he is weeping all the time, begging for just a glance of the beloved's eyes from afar,

---

[27]Arberry, *Literature*, 92; for a fundamental study of his works and thoughts see H. Ritter, *Das Meer der Seele* (Leiden, 1955).

[28]For contrasting views on the thematic unity of the *ghazal*, see Rypka, *History*, 102 and R. Rehder, "The Unity of Ghazals of Hāfiz," *Der Islam* 51 (1974), 69–89.

walking through his or her street sweeping its dust with his eyelashes, but only meeting with cruelty and indifference.

The Persian *ghazals*, in sharp contrast to Persian romances, which abound in detailed description of erotic love, never reflect the joys of union and fulfillment. Homosexuality was probably well known in Iran, even before the coming of Islam. In a report we read that the Arab poet Tulayha, once attending the court of a Sasanian king, was amazed that the king admired a poem describing a fair boy holding a rose in his hand. Conversely, the king saw no charm in poems describing the deserted camp of a beloved woman and her tribe.[29] The tacit acceptance of amorous feelings toward male companions, combined with the inferior social status and seclusion of women in Islamic Iran, discouraged men from expressing positive feelings for women, naming their names, publicly associating with them, or treating them as equals. Under such circumstances, how could a poet talk about his love for a woman, let alone allude to her identity? This would be considered indecent and against the code of honor, and could have severe consequences for both the man and woman. On the other hand, it is evident that love between men and women is the basis of Persian lyrics, and thus these supreme lyrics retain their universal appeal.

With Sufi ideology and vocabulary penetrating lyric poetry, its ambiguity increased. Any lyrical statement became susceptible to mystical interpretation, and eroticism became confused with pure mysticism. The notion of *shāhid* (witness)—for example, a handsome boy symbolically considered to be a "witness" to Divine beauty—contributed to the confusion. Certain radical trends among the Sufis brought them the reputation of being drunkards and irreligious libertines. Repudiation of worldly attachments and absolute reliance on God's sustaining providence, which served the impoverished population as a consolation in misery, also became excuses for idleness. Lyric poetry reflected all of these conflicting ideas. Native commentators and, later, Western Orientalists saw all Persian poetry in the light of Sufism and read a symbolic meaning into every word. Consequently all Persian poets, even 'Omar Khayyām, were believed to have been Sufis.

## The High Point of Lyric Poetry

The tremendous devastation brought to eastern Iran by the Mongol invasion shifted the centers of Persian poetry to other parts of the

---

[29]'Abd al-Qāder b. 'Omar al-Baghdādī, *Khezānat al-adab* (Cairo, 1960), vol. 4, 157.

country. In particular, Shiraz in the south achieved prominence, chiefly as the result of the accomplishment of two celebrated sons, Sa'di and Hāfez.

The genius of Sa'di (d. 1292) finally made the *ghazal* triumphant over the *qasida,* a position that the *ghazal* retained until recent times. His diction is flawless. It is fluent, lucid, and melodious. His language is free of obsolete and pompous phrases, and of pretentious Arabisms. Vulgarity, occasionally used in his prose, is totally absent from his lyrics. He uses rhetorical devices, but not so that he diverts the reader's attention. Artistry serves the purpose of increasing aesthetic pleasure, not of demonstrating his craftsmanship. He weaves the figures of speech in his verse so unobtrusively and harmoniously that one unfamiliar with them would not even notice their presence. Learned and simple people alike enjoy his verse.

His message is an unending praise of beauty and love. Love and beauty are the key words of Sa'di's *ghazal,* whether beauty of body or soul, nature, or spirit. His lyrical thought is serene and buoyant, even though he is quite familiar with nights of separation and loneliness:

> Precious are these heart-burning sighs, for lo,
> This way or that, they help the days to go.
> All night I wait for one whose dawn-like face
> Lendeth fresh radiance to the morning's grace.
> My Friend's sweet face if I again might see
> I'd thank my lucky star eternally.
> Shall I then fear man's blame? The brave man's heart
> Serves as his shield to counter slander's dart.
> Who wins success hath many a failure tholed
> The New Year's Day is reached through Winter's cold.
> For Laylá many a prudent lover yearns,
> But Majnún wins her, who his harvest burns.
> I am thy slave: pursue some wilder game:
> No tether's needed for the bird that's tame.
> A strength is his who casts both worlds aside
> Which is to worldly anchorites denied.
> To-morrow is not: yesterday is spent:
> To-day, O Sa'di, take thy heart's content![30]

Love and longing in his *ghazals* are generally real and profane, but

---

[30]From the *Kolliyyāt,* as quoted by Browne, vol. 2, 534.

Sa'di was a pious, moderate Muslim well-versed in Sufi thought. Mystical yearnings are certainly frequent in his *ghazals*; but in the unified world of his inner feelings, worldly and mystical longings are so masterfully fused that only by patient attempts at analysis can one detect the various strands of the poet's thought. Technical Sufi terminology, however, is not to be found in Sa'di's lyrics. The contrast between day and night, dawn and evening, is a motif Sa'di often uses to depict the conflicting forces of good and evil, hope and despair, nearness to and remoteness from God. Elements of nature, especially the gentle breeze and the softly murmuring brook, are capable of evoking nostalgic sentiments in him.[31]

Sa'di uses traditional images (rose, bud, cypress, arrow, candle) in his descriptions, but the beloved is not so much physically described as remembered by the emotions and desires which the sight of her raises in the poet's mind. The following *ghazal* is one of Sa'di's more sensuous ones:

### The Crow of the Cock

Wherefore the cock has crowed? 'tis night,
And lovers lost in passion's bliss
Leave not until the dawn's full light
Their warm embrace and tender kiss.

My sweetheart's breasts lie sheltered in
Her silken tresses' shining curls,
Like an ivory ball nestled in
A polo stick's ebony curve.

This night is precious, keep awake!
For that living tumult lies asleep.
Beware! Those who let life pass and take
Not advantage regret and weep.

The call to prayer has not yet come
From the mosque on this Friday morn,
Nor the beating of the drum
From the Atābak's palace door.

So stray thou not from passion's bed
By heeding the cock's raucous fuss,

---

[31]On Sa'di's lyrics see Rypka, *Iran. Lit.*, 252, and A. Bausani, *Storia della letteratura persiana* (Milan, 1960), 416ff.

Her lips like cock's eye are red
And to leave them were ridiculous.[32]

Generations of poets have come under the spell of Sa'di and have expressed their indebtedness to him. Hāfez called him the "master of poetry," and the Indo-Persian poet Amir Khosrow of Delhi (d. 1325) considered himself Sa'di's successor and followed the model of the master in his lyrics.

Scores of studies on Hāfez (d. 1390) exist in many languages.[33] The interest in him is universal and diverse. Hāfez had an enormous impact on Goethe in his old age, the direct result of which was the "West-östlicher Divan," considered by many Germanists to be next in importance to *Faust*.[34] Goethe's interest in Hāfez, shared and expressed in beautiful poems by Platen and Rückert, inspired German scholars to undertake important studies on this subject.[35]

Ambiguity is one of the outstanding characteristics of the Hāfezian *ghazal* and one of the main differences between his and Sa'di's style. It may have been a deliberate technique used for a variety of reasons: to shield him against those who disliked his liberal mind and perhaps his lifestyle; or to enable him to vent his Khayyāmian skepticism. Whether motivated intellectually or by natural disposition, the ambiguity of Hāfez lends a degree of sophistication to his style that is unparalleled in Persian poetry. On account of this ambiguity, Hāfez also remains somewhat aloof and unreachable, with an aura of mystery about him; he is a fascinating challenge, as well as a source of immense aesthetic pleasure.

The Shiraz of Hāfez's time was a metropolis of religious learning and Sufi instruction. Philosophy and the sciences were vigorously cultivated. There were other important poets living in Shiraz, such as the lyricist Khwāju (d. 1352), who had a great impact on Hāfez, and the

[32]*Kolliyyāt*, ed. M. Mosaffā (Tehran, 1961), 481; trans. Barry Lerner, of the University of Chicago.

[33]For a comprehensive bibliography see M. Hillmann, *Unity in the Ghazals of Hafez* (Chicago, 1976). See also Arberry, *Literature*, 329–63; Rypka, *Iran. Lit.*, 261–63; in Persian, 'A. Dashti, *Naqshi az Hāfez*, 2nd ed. (Tehran, 1965); S. Meskub, *Dar ku-ye dost* (Tehran, 1978); 'A.-H. Zarrīnkūb, *Az kucha-ye rendān*, 2nd ed. (Tehran, 1975) and *Bā kārvān-e holla* (Tehran, 1964).

[34]"Er ist naechst dem 'Faust' das bedeutendste und zugleich persönlichste Werk des Dichters." (Ernst Beutler, introduction to *Westöstlicher Divan*, 1945, ix).

[35]See, e.g., H. H. Schaeder, "Die islamische Lehre vom vollkommenen Menschen, ihre Herkunft und ihre dichterische Gestaltung," *ZDMG* 79 (1925), 192–268; see also idem, *Goethes Erlebnis des Ostens* (Leipzig, 1938). For the interest of the English-speaking world in Hāfez, see particularly Arberry, *Literature*, 332ff.

celebrated satirist 'Obayd-e Zākāni (d. 1371); they were probably personally acquainted with Hāfez. The political situation was somewhat unsettled, however, and at times erupted in violence. And yet Shiraz, for all its political upheavals, was a city of pleasure, love, and wine; the influence of the cultural milieu and the social and political atmosphere is reflected in Hāfez's *ghazal*s.

A comparison between Hāfez and Sa'di may throw some light on their respective qualities. Sa'di's facility and ease of expression do not match the sophistication of Hāfez. Sa'di was far more prolific, his total output being several times greater than that of Hāfez. On the other hand, Hāfez seems to have worked on his poems with greater care; he may even have returned to them again and again to change some words, add or omit a line. This may explain the many variants in manuscripts copied within a few years of one another, often close to the poet's own lifetime.

The two poets also differ in their philosophy and outlook. Sa'di is a man of common sense, worldly wise, compassionate, with a taste for the pleasures of life. His *ghazal*s are generally straightforward love poems which offer no problems, no riddles, and do not put one's intellect to the test. Hāfez, by contrast, is complicated, ambivalent, demanding, and rarely within our complete grasp. Sa'di's sense of humor is more on the surface; that of Hāfez is penetrating and sarcastic. Neither man was bound to any specific Sufi order.

It is difficult to see in Hāfez a holy man, completely detached from worldly interests. The plain texts of many of his *ghazal*s are about secular love, and any attempt to interpret them differently misses the point. How else can the following *ghazal* be understood?

### Love's Language

Breeze of the morning, at the hour thou knowest,
The way thou knowest, and to her thou knowest,
  Of lovely secrets trusty messenger,
I beg thee carry this dispatch for me;
  Command I may not: this is but a prayer
Making appeal unto thy courtesy.

Speak thus, when thou upon my errand goest:
"My soul slips from my hand, so weak am I;
Unless thou heal it by the way thou knowest,
  Balm of a certain ruby, I must die."

Say further, sweetheart wind, when thus thou blowest:
  "What but thy little girdle of woven gold
  Should the firm center of my hopes enfold?
  Thy legendary waist doth it not hold,
And mystic treasures which thou only knowest?"

Say too: "Thy captive begs that thou bestowest
  The boon of thy swift falchion in his heart;
  As men for water, thirsts he to depart
By the most speedy way of death thou knowest.

"I beg thee that to no one else thou showest
  These words I send—in such a hidden way
  That none but thou may cipher what I say;
Read them in some safe place as best thou knowest."

When in her heart these words of mine thou sowest
For Hāfez, speak in any tongue thou knowest;
Turkish and Arabic in love are one—
Love speaks all languages beneath the sun.[36]

The late Persian scholar Qāsem Ghani, who studied the life and times of Hāfez, made a particular point of seeking the reflection of the political events and personalities of Hāfez's lifetime in his poetry.[37] Like rubbing a decal until the picture appears, he tested many of Hāfez's poems against the confused political events of the time until gradually, at the bottom of many of the *ghazals*, the historical faces of the ruling elite appeared as objects of praise. Taking as clues the names of several personalities explicitly mentioned in some *ghazals*, Ghani concluded that the objects of love and admiration were not only the beloved and God, but also powerful princes and dignitaries in praise of whom Hāfez used the *ghazal* instead of the *qasida*. In this connection, the terms *maʿbud*, the object of worship, *maʿshuq*, the object of love, and *mamduh*, the object of praise, suggested by Bausani, provide useful distinctions. However, one should be cautious with the conclusions from such findings. The number of such laudatory *ghazals* is less than one hundred, and the number of lines containing praise, if explicit at all, is very small, in many cases only a single line.

Some scholars, mostly modern, read in the lines of Hāfez fewer

[36]Translated by R. L. Gallienne, in *Persian Poems*, ed. A. J. Arberry (London, 1954), 75–76; see also Hillmann, *Unity*, 50ff.
[37]*Tārikh-e ʿasr-e Hāfez* (Tehran, 1942).

divine allegories than sensuous allusions. In his essay on the *Sāqi-nāma* (Wild deer *mathnavi*), Eric Schroeder, otherwise extremely sensitive to the quality of Hāfez's poetry, makes sex and sensuality a major undercurrent.[38] Nor is Schroeder alone in imposing his personal outlook on poetry that has in fact evolved from specific cultural and social values.[39]

No doubt most of the verses of Hāfez have to be understood on different levels of significance. Human love as a personal experience in the life of Hāfez need not be debated. Nor are his spiritual tendencies to be doubted. The following *ghazal*, translated by Gertrude Bell, is typical of those Hāfez poems which could be understood on both secular and spiritual planes:

### Tidings of Union

Where are the tidings of union? that I may arise—
Forth from the dust I will rise up to welcome thee!
My soul, like a homing bird, yearning for paradise,
Shall arise and soar, from the snares of the world set free.
When the voice of thy love shall call me to be thy slave,
I shall rise to a greater far than the mastery
Of life and the living, time and the mortal span:
Pour down, O Lord! from the clouds of thy guiding grace
The rain of a mercy that quickeneth on my grave,
Before, like dust that the wind bears from place to place,
I arise and flee beyond the knowledge of man.
When to my grave thou turnest thy blessed feet,
Wine and the lute thou shalt bring in thine hand to me,
Thy voice shall ring through the folds of my winding-sheet,
And I will arise and dance to thy minstrelsy.
Though I be old, clasp me one night to thy breast,
And I, when the dawn shall come to awaken me,
With the flush of youth on my cheek from thy bosom will rise.
Rise up! let mine eyes delight in thy stately grace!

---

[38]E. Schroeder, "The Wild Deer Mathnavi," *Journal of Aesthetics and Art Criticism* 11 (1952): 118–34.

[39]See, e.g., G. L. Windfuhr, "Die Struktur eines Robai," *ZDMG* (1968): 75–78 and M. Hillmann's refutation in *ZDMG* (1969): 98–101. I tend to agree with Schaeder, "So pedantische und abgeschmackt auch die Interpretation der Orientalischen Kommentatoren ist, die jeden einzelnen Ausdruck bei *Hāfiz* wie nach einer Tabelle mechanisch in die mystische Terminologie übersetzt—sie ist immerhin sinnvoller als die abendländische Versuche, Hāfiz zum 'Anakreontiker' zu machen" ("Die islamische Lehre," 249).

Thou art the goal to which all men's endeavor has pressed,
And thou the idol of Hāfez' worship; thy face
From the world and life shall bid him come forth and arise![40]

## Later Developments

With Hāfez, Persian lyrical poetry reaches its zenith, and after five full centuries of poetic advances, a decline following his death was perhaps inevitable. Yet the decline was not steep. The fifteenth century witnessed the rise of yet another remarkable poet who left his mark on the history of Persian literature. Jāmi (d. 1492), a Sufi scholar and prolific author, was also a poet of love and mysticism. After Jāmi, a new orientation of Persian poets created the so-called "Indian" school of Persian poetry which lasted almost 250 years. The poems written in this period are literary puzzles demanding mental dexterity to "unwrap" them and discover the concept within. This school terminated in the middle of the eighteenth century through the deliberate efforts of a group of poets living in Isfahan who renounced the Indian style and returned to the style of the old masters. While Iranians usually consider the Indian School decadent, Western students have shown a special liking for this poetry.[41] Important among the representatives of this school, which used the *ghazal* as its main medium, are Tāleb (d. 1626), Kalim (d. 1651–52), Sā'eb (d. 1676–77), and Bidel (d. 1720).

The panegyrists of the Revival period, which lasted through the nineteenth century, wrote *qasida*s on the model of the Samanid and Ghaznavid masters. Several excellent talents, notably Sabā (d. 1822), Nashāt (d. 1828), and Qā'āni (d. 1853), brought a new vitality to court poetry. The best lyricist, however, was probably Forughi (d. 1857), whose *ghazal*s imitate the style of Sa'di and Hāfez. Numerous poets living in our century still adhere to the old style, but even in the garb of traditional forms the lyrical experience has found new directions. Indeed, within only a few decades, a new kind of lyric poetry has been born. The muse of Persian poetry is still alive.

### Selected Bibliography

Arberry, A. J. "Orient Pearls at Random Strung," *BSOAS* 11 (1943): 688–712.

[40]Hāfez, *Divān*, 336; *Persian Poems*, 71.
[41]See E. Yarshater, *She'r*; A. Bausani, "The Development of Form in Persian Lyrics," *East and West* 9/3 (1958), 145–53.

Āryanpur, Yahyā. *Az Sabā tā Nimā*, 2 vols. Tehran, 1971.

Bausani, Alessandro. "Altāf Husain Hālī's Ideas on Ghazal," *Charisteria Orientalia* (Prague, 1956): 38–55.

———. "Contributo a una definizione dello 'stilo indiano' della poesia persiana," *AIUON* 7 (1958): 167–78.

Boyce, Mary. "A Novel Interpretation of Hāfiz," *BSOAS* 15/2 (1953): 279–88.

Broms, H. "Two Studies in the Relations of Hāfiz and the West," *Studia Orientalis* 39 (1968): 1–114.

Bürgel, J. Ch. *Drei Hafis-Studien*. Bern-Frankfort, 1975.

———. "Le Poète et la poesie dans l'oeuvre de Hāfez," *Poesia di Hāfez*, Accademia Nazionale dei Lincei, 73–98. Roma, 1978.

———. "Der Schöne Türke, immernoch missverstanden," *Orientalische Literaturzeitung* 75/2 (1980): 105–11.

Clinton, J. W. *The Divan of Manūchihrī Dāmghanī: A Critical Study*. Chicago, 1972.

Dashtī, 'Alī. *Dar qalamrow-e Sa'dī*, 3rd ed. Tehran, 1965.

De Fouchecour, C. H. *La description de la nature dans la poesie lyrique persane du XIe siècle*. Paris, 1969 (reviewed by Bürgel, *Oriens* 25–26: 364ff.).

Ethé, Hermann. *Neupersische Literatur, Grun. iran. Philol.* vol. 2, 212–368. Strassburg, 1896–1904.

Forūzānfar, Badī 'al-Zamān. *Sokhan va sokhanvarān*, 2nd ed. Tehran, 1971.

Hillmann, M. C. "Turk of Shiraz Once Again," *Iranian Studies* 8 (1975): 164–82.

———. "Hāfez and Poetic Unity Through Verse Rhythms," *JNES* 31 (1972): 1–10.

Lazard, G. *Les Premiers Poètes Persans*, vol. 2, textes persanes. Tehran–Paris, 1964.

Lescot, Roger. "Essai d'une chronologie de l'oeuvre de Hāfiz," *Bulletin d'etudes orientales* 10 (1943–1944): 57–100.

Memon, Muhammad Umar, ed. *Studies in the Urdu Gazal and Prose Fiction*. South Asian Studies. Madison: University of Wisconsin, 1979.

Reinert, Benedikt. *Hāqānī als Dichter. Poetische Logik und Phantasie*. Berlin, 1972.

Ritter, Hellmut. *Über die Bildersprache Nizāmīs*. Berlin–Leipzig, 1927.

Safā, Zabīhallāh. *Tārikh-e adabiyyāt dar Irān*. 5 vols. Tehran, 1953–83.

Schaeder, H. H. "Die islamische Lehre vom vollkommenen Menschen, ihre Herkunft und ihre dichterische Gestaltung," *ZDMG* 79 (1925): 192–268.

Schimmel, Annemarie. *Mystical Dimensions of Islam.* Chapel Hill, N.C., 1975 (especially chap. 7, 287ff.).

———. "The Emergence of the German Ghazal," *Studies in the Urdu Ghazal* (s. Memon), 168–74.

Shafiʻi Kadkani, Mohammad Rizā. *Sovar-i khayāl dar sheʻr-e fārsi.* Tehran, 1971.

Wickens, G. M. "An Analysis of Primary and Secondary Significations in the Third Ghazal of Hafiz," *BSOAS* 14 (1952): 627–38.

Yarshater, Ehsan. "The Theme of Wine-Drinking and the Concept of the Beloved in Early Persian Poetry," *Studia Islamica* 13 (1960): 43–53.

———. "Some Common Characteristics of Persian Poetry and Art," *Studia Islamica* 16 (1962): 61–71.

Yussefi, Gholām Hosayn. *Farrokhi Sistāni: Sharh-e ahvāl o ruzgār o sheʻr-e u.* Mashhad, 1962.

# 8. 'Omar Khayyām

If there is one Persian poet whose name is almost universally known in the West, it is 'Omar Khayyām. For many, indeed, he is the only Persian poet they have ever heard of. Yet the irony here is that, in the great world of Persian literature, Khayyām is a relatively minor figure; if he wrote poetry at all, it was only as the diversion of an amateur, and in any case the popular image of him in the West as a self-indulgent pleasure-lover is probably wholly false.

The main reason for this misconception is that the "Omar Khayyam" whose fame has spread throughout the Western world is not a Persian poet at all, but a mid-nineteenth-century English clergyman whose real name was Edward FitzGerald. It is FitzGerald's poem, entitled the *Rubáiyát of Omar Khayyám,* that has achieved an established and deserved place in English literature and has been translated into most European and many other languages. The poem sets out to describe a day in the life of the largely imaginary figure of 'Omar Khayyām, in tones and colors designed to appeal to a mid-Victorian audience inclined to rebel against the restricting puritanism of the Victorian ethic—though it was not until after FitzGerald's death a quarter of a century later that his poem began to catch the public imagination, whose loyalty it has not lost up to the present day:

Here with a Loaf of Bread beneath the Bough,
A Flask of Wine, a Book of Verse—and Thou
   Beside me singing in the Wilderness—
And Wilderness is Paradise enow.

* * *

"How sweet is mortal Sovranty!"—think some:
Others—"How blest the Paradise to come!"
   Ah, take the Cash in hand and waive the Rest;
Oh, the brave Music of a *distant* Drum!

* * *

And much as Wine has play'd the Infidel,
And robb'd me of my Robe of Honour—well,
   I often wonder what the Vintners buy
One half so precious as the Goods they sell.

* * *

147

And when Thyself with shining Foot shall pass
Among the Guests Star-scatter'd on the Grass,
  And in thy joyous Errand reach the Spot
Where I made one—turn down an empty Glass!

One could quote a great deal more from this much-loved poem in its various versions (all the above are from the first edition), but it would be irrelevant to our present theme. The *Rubáiyát of Omar Khayyám* tells us a good deal about Edward FitzGerald and about the social and spiritual environment in which he lived, but does it tell us anything of the real 'Omar Khayyām?

Of course there is no doubt that FitzGerald used a collection of Persian verses attributed to 'Omar Khayyām as the basis and inspiration of his poem, but like many of the literati of his day, he was indulging in a piece of conscious "Orientalism." Poets and writers of the eighteenth and nineteenth centuries saw no harm in using Oriental works in this way, or, as FitzGerald himself put it in a letter, "tesselating a very pretty Eclogue out of his [Khayyām's] scattered Quatrains." The arrival in the West of such works as the *Arabian Nights* had provided great stimulus for this kind of activity—the use of an alleged or genuine Oriental source as a medium through which to promulgate one's own ideas, especially those of a pessimistic, hedonistic, iconoclastic nature—ideas that might be too shocking if presented undisguised, but were acceptable and even welcomed in an alien garb. FitzGerald can never have supposed anyone would imagine he was offering a serious translation of the twelfth-century Persian poet's work. Even if he was trying to squeeze out what he believed to be the essence of Khayyām's thought, he would have been the first to acknowledge that the resulting poem contained as many of his own ideas as those of the Persian poet. At best he was presenting the latter's ideas in a guise recognizable and appealing to a nineteenth-century English readership.

Given this somewhat cavalier attitude toward an Eastern poet, the surprising thing is that Fitzgerald's poem should have conveyed as much as it did of the original ideas enshrined in the verses of 'Omar Khayyām. However, it is the latter with whom we are concerned and not FitzGerald, and in order to make the transition we must draw attention to one or two points.

(a) The original verses from which FitzGerald drew his inspiration do not constitute a single poem. They are a collection of isolated and separate quatrains, resembling in function, if not in form, the Greek epigram or the Japanese haiku.

(b) The quatrain or *robāʿi* is a very popular form in Persian; virtually every Persian poet has written some, and a few, like 'Omar Khayyām, have written nothing else. The brevity and pithiness of the form, and the fact that every *robāʿi* has the same meter and rhyme-scheme, means that one is very much like another; to attribute authorship correctly is much more difficult than in the case of longer poems. Printing did not exist in Khayyām's time; the survival of literary works depended at best on manuscripts copied by scribes of indifferent skill, and more often—especially in the case of minor verse like the *robāʿi*—on memory and oral transmission. It is hardly surprising that there should have appeared the phenomenon of the "wandering quatrains," that is, the attribution of a given verse to two or more different writers. For some reason Khayyām has been especially subject to this kind of thing. He has become an almost legendary composer of quatrains, and so we find many verses fathered on him that could not possibly have been written by him. Apart from appearing in the collected works of other poets (though this is not evidence one way or the other), they refer to people or events long after Khayyām's time; they use words and expressions not current in his time; and some even express ideas so contrary that they could not have come from the same pen.

(c) The two manuscripts that FitzGerald used, one from the fifteenth century and one comparatively modern, contain about six hundred different quatrains, about five times the number of stanzas in the final version of FitzGerald's poem. So, even allowing for the fact that few of FitzGerald's stanzas were straight translations or even paraphrases of single originals, and that many were conflations of two or more *robāʿi*s, it is evident that his poem represents at best a highly personal distillation of thoughts that he found (or believed he had found) embedded in a large collection of verses, with whose authenticity he was in no way concerned. He was a poet, not a scholar, and although nowadays we might feel inclined to condemn a poet for treating an Oriental original in this way, in the context of his time this was entirely acceptable.

We have dwelt at some length on this matter, because obviously the authenticity of the quatrains attributed to 'Omar Khayyām is of cardinal importance if we are to use them as a basis on which to assess his character, his outlook on the world, and indeed his skill as a poet. We have seen that FitzGerald, for reasons that are not necessarily discreditable, can offer us no guidance on these matters, and so we must bid him farewell, and concentrate now on the person of Khayyām himself. This is not such an easy task as it might appear, because in fact the source material is somewhat scanty. There is only one writer who claims to have known Khayyām personally, Nezāmi 'Aruzi, the author of the *Chahār maqāla* (Four treatises), written about 1150, some twenty years after Khayyām's death. But even he does not provide us with very much information; significantly, he deals with Khayyām not in his treatise on poets, but in the one on astronomers. So far as Nezāmi was concerned, Khayyām was famous as a scientist and philosopher; if he wrote poetry at all, it can only have been as a diversion in his leisure moments.

As a matter of fact, we do know something about Khayyām's career as a mathematician and astronomer, not only from sources like Nezāmi, but also from scientific and philosophical treatises whose attribution to Khayyām is on much safer grounds than that of his verses. We know that he was encouraged to write his most important work, a pioneering treatise on algebra, by his patron Abu Tāher, the chief magistrate of Samarqand. Although this work is not dated, it must have been written no later than 1072, when Khayyām was only twenty-four. It was about then that he entered the service of the Seljuk ruler Malekshāh, who employed him together with other distinguished astronomers in the construction of an observatory, probably at Isfahan, in 1074, and in the compilation of a set of astronomical tables as the basis of a revised calendar (known as the Maleki or Jalāli Era); experts regard this calendar as even more accurate than the Gregorian calendar compiled in Europe some five hundred years later. In his late forties he went on an extensive journey, visiting Mecca and Baghdad before finally returning to his birthplace in Nishapur, where he spent the rest of his life quietly teaching. He died there in 1131 at the age of eighty-three.

In spite of the great breadth of his learning, 'Omar Khayyām seems to have written very little. Indeed he had the reputation of being a stingy teacher, although his reputation as a scientist must have rested on something more than the handful of scientific and philosophical treatises that have come down to us. That brevity came to him more naturally than prolixity we may guess from a rare personal remark made in the preface to one of his short philosophical theses, written in 1080 at the request of a chief magistrate of Fars; in the course of the preface he apologizes for having written so concisely, "because of shortness of time and lack of opportunity to develop and expand."

The most personal note of all comes in his preface to the already mentioned work on algebra, the most substantial (and probably the earliest) of the handful of works that have reached us. Here he has some caustic things to say about the scientists and philosophers of the day; only a few of them, he complains, were "capable of engaging in scientific research. Our philosophers spend all their time in mixing true with false, and are interested in nothing but outward show; such little learning as they have they expend on material ends. When they see a man sincere and unremitting in his search for the truth, one who will have nothing to do with falsehood and pretence, they mock and despise him." We may assume that Khayyām was writing here from personal experience, and this kind of thing at an early stage in his career must have colored his attitude toward his colleagues.

Indeed there are occasional echoes of a certain arrogance toward his contemporaries in some of the stories told about him. On one occasion the governor of Ray is said to have asked what he thought of one of his colleagues' attacks on the teachings of Avicenna, whom 'Omar Khayyām, though he can never have met him (Avicenna died in 1037), was wont to claim as his teacher. "Abu'l-Barakāt doesn't understand what Avicenna is talking about," replied Khayyām. "He is incapable even of understanding his ideas, let alone of criticizing his accuracy and logic." The governor was displeased with this answer. "A wise man," he said, "uses reason to refute ideas with which he does not agree; only a fool uses abuse. You ought to employ the worthiest means, not the basest."

From stories like this, from the occasional personal observation, from the style if not the content of his scientific and philosophical writings, we begin already to get a picture of a serious-minded man, somewhat reserved and shy, and at times even contemptuous of his peers—a man with a highly logical mind, a comprehensive grasp of the learning of his time, and at the same time a disinclination to commit himself without overwhelming proof. So where do the quatrains come into all this?

We have already noted that the one contemporary reference to 'Omar Khayyām does not mention him as a poet. This of course does not necessarily mean that he did not write poetry; indeed, in the Persian context it would be the exceptional educated man who did not, a statement that is still true today. But it is a reasonable assumption that his versifying was a marginal activity, insufficient in bulk, if perhaps not inferior in quality. As we have already seen, an output of nothing but robā'is would not be regarded as qualifying someone as a poet by profession; they would be a subsidiary element in the writings of even a major poet. We can perhaps visualize a man of Khayyām's rather solemn and taciturn nature relaxing with a few intimate friends, perhaps over a bottle of wine (though one may guess that his indulgence in this forbidden but tolerated dissipation was not as thoroughgoing as some of his verses might suggest), and tossing out an occasional witty epigram by way of summing up the theme of the conversation. Such verses might well not have been written down at the time, but remembered by some of his companions and committed to paper later on.

The curious thing is that, even when Khayyām's poetical gifts are mentioned for the first time in near-contemporary sources, the subject is not the *robā'is*. An anthology of verse compiled some fifty years after Khayyām's death quotes some Arabic verses, not in the *robā'i* form, and these were added to in other works of the early thirteenth century to make up a total of some twenty-five couplets. These are the only Arabic verses attributed to Khayyām and may not be genuine, but they are in content not unlike some of his *robā'is*, even containing astronomical references such as one would expect from a professional astronomer. The first Persian *robā'i* attributed to Khayyām appears in a theological treatise written at the beginning of the thirteenth century, and four more appear in later thirteenth-century works. Even by the middle of the fourteenth century, two hundred years after Khayyām's death, the total is no more than thirty-six, a strange contrast to the 158 contained in the mid-fifteenth century manuscript used by Edward FitzGerald.

It is this discrepancy as much as anything else that gives one cause to doubt many of the quatrains that have been attributed to 'Omar Khayyām in one source or another (over two thousand at the fullest count). It almost seems as though in the course of time 'Omar Khayyām ceased to be thought of as a real person and became rather a kind of eponymous composer of quatrains under whose shelter could be accommodated a folkloric collection of verses constantly growing and fluctuating. It is hardly surprising that some sceptical scholars have denied that 'Omar Khayyām the scientist ever wrote any poetry at all. We hardly need to go as far as that, but it is not unreasonable to do what some Persian writers have done: reverse the normal process and determine which are the authentic *robā'is* of 'Omar Khayyām by first building up a picture of the man and then accepting as genuine only those verses that could have been composed by such a man. This circular argument may seem a little like cheating, but the results are not so confusing as one might expect. In fact, three different Iranian writers have done this—Mohammad 'Ali Forughi, statesman and man of letters, 'Ali Dashti, journalist, politician and littérateur, and Sādeq Hedāyat, at the time an almost unknown folklorist and writer of short stories, who subsequently became one of Iran's most distinguished novelists. What is interesting is that these three men, proceeding independently from very different premises and backgrounds and with more than two thousand quatrains to choose from, ended up with no more than 253 between them, of which 53 were selected by all three. We cannot go too far wrong if we accept these 53 as authentic and use them as a touchstone by which to test and authenticate the rest. At least it is possible, on the basis of this small selection, to make some generalizations about Khayyām's literary style, poetic skill, and personal view of life and the universe.

The first point to be noticed about Khayyām's *robā'i*s is their conciseness and pithiness. This of course is characteristic of the genre, but Khayyām's are particularly skillful in this respect. They observe carefully the structure of the *robā'i*—the build-up to the climax of the third line, followed by the fourth punchline that rounds off the thought and leaves nothing further to be said. The language is simple, almost earthy, and he avoids the use of the flowery imagery so beloved of later poets. Nor on the whole is he inclined to use the metaphorical symbolism that one finds among many classical poets, particularly those of a Sufi bent (one feature that makes it unlikely that Khayyām was a Sufi, a claim sometimes made). In fact his style is what one would expect of a rationalist, a sceptical scientist with no time for frills. There are often references to astronomical phenomena, metaphysical problems, and scientific matters, such as Khayyām would have been familiar with in his daily work. Certainly in a time when the bulk of accumulated knowledge was still comparatively small, any educated man would be expected to have some knowledge of these things, so that a reference to a particular planet or constellation is not in itself evidence that the poet was an astronomer, but it is at least consistent with such a calling.

It is not easy to convey these characteristics in a translation, but a few examples may not be out of place:

You are a compound of the elements four;
The seven planets rule your fevered life.
Drink wine, for I have said a thousand times
That you will not return; once gone, you're gone.

\* \* \*

They did not ask me, when they planned my life;
Why then blame me for what is good or bad?
Yesterday and today go on without us;
Tomorrow what's the charge against me, pray?

\* \* \*

In youth I studied for a little while;
Later I boasted of my mastery.
Yet this was all the lesson that I learned:
We come from dust, and with the wind are gone.

\* \* \*

Last night I wandered in the potter's store;
Two thousand pots were there, speaking and dumb.
One cried out suddenly, "Where's the potter now?
Where is the seller, where the purchaser?"

\* \* \*

Our darling friends have vanished one and all;
Before Death's feet they groveled and were still.
'Twas the same wine we drank in life together,
But they were drunk a round or two before.

The criteria we have adopted as the distinguishing marks of an
authentic Khayyamian quatrain force us to discard, or at least to view
with suspicion, some quatrains that inspired FitzGerald to write some
of his best-known verses. None of the following, for instance, seem to
have quite the necessary qualities, being either too consciously poetical, or verging on the mystical, or just too frivolous:

The sun has looped the rooftops with its rays,
Day's Sovereign Lord has given the sign to go.
Rise quickly and obey the muezzin's call
When he commands you, "Drink ye all of this!"

\* \* \*

I scoured the world in search of Jamshid's bowl,
Not resting days nor sleeping in the night.
And then a teacher told me the plain truth:
That world-revealing bowl is—I myself.

\* \* \*

A picnic with a loaf of wheaten bread,
A jar of wine, a roasted leg of lamb,
A lovely maid beside me in the garden,
This is a life no sultan can enjoy.

Bearing in mind that Khayyām's *robāʿi*s were detached, separate epigrams, composed in times of leisure on many different occasions and contexts, can we nevertheless extract from them some kind of consistent philosophy of life? In a sense, of course, this was what FitzGerald was trying to do, but his interpretation was overweighted, not only by his inadequate knowledge of Persian, but also by his own convictions, which kept forcing their way through. Other enquirers have sought to classify the quatrains under logical headings, notably Pierre Pascal, Sādeq Hedāyat, and 'Ali Dashti. The task is not an easy one, because most of them convey more than one idea at a time, but perhaps the following sequence of thought comes somewhere near 'Omar Khayyām's thinking.

As a rationalist scientist he is sceptical of the human capacity to know and understand the mysteries of the universe:

This circle within which we come and go
Has neither origin nor final end.
Will no one ever tell us truthfully
Whence we have come, and whither do we go?

\* \* \*

The boundless universe was born of night;
No man has ever pierced its secrets yet.
They all have much to say for their own good,
But none can tell us who he is, or why.

His contempt for the learning and learned of his day comes out strongly:

Those who embraced all knowledge and all lore,
Who lighted others on the path to learning,
Themselves are lost in darkest ignorance;
They told a story, and then went to sleep.

He is unwilling to tackle the problem of the existence of God. If there is a wise and powerful Creator, then why are the happenings in the world so arbitrary? Sometimes he seems to equate God with blind Fate or with limitless and inexorable Time:

What gain did Heaven get from making me?
What kudos did it earn from my demise?
Yet I have never heard from anyone
Why I was brought here, and why taken away.

* * *

Man is a bowl so finely made that Reason
Cannot but praise him with a thousand kisses;
Yet Time the potter, who has made this bowl
So well, then smashes it to bits again.

What is at least clear is that man is impotent and insignificant, unable to change or affect his own destiny:

Since there's no changing life a single jot,
There's little point in grieving over pain.
What you or I may do, or what we think,
Is something we ourselves can never shape.

* * *

A drop of water fell into the sea,
A speck of dust came floating down to earth.
What signifies your passage through this world?
A tiny gnat appears—and disappears.

Life is transitory, and all the pressing and urgent questions that preoccupy the mind are unimportant:

I see men sleeping on the blanket of earth,
I see men hidden deep beneath the ground;
But when I view the wastes of nothingness,
Only the lost I see, and those to come.

* * *

Long will the world last after we are gone,
When every sign and trace of us is lost.

We were not here before, and no one knew;
Though we have gone, the world will be the same.

\* \* \*

I saw a ruined palace towering high,
Where monarchs once in splendor ruled supreme;
Now on its walls a mournful ring-dove sat
And softly murmured cooing, "Where? Where? Where?"

The only certainty is death; and whether or not there is life after death, there is no possibility of return to this life:

Of all the travelers on this endless road
No one returns to tell us where it leads.
There's little in this world but greed and need;
Leave nothing here, for you will not return.

\* \* \*

The dawn is here; arise, my lovely one,
Pour slowly, slowly wine, and touch the lute.
For those who still are here will not stay long,
While those departed never will return.

Here he digresses to consider a mystery, the mystery of the compounding and dissolution of the elements. Whether or not the universe is created or has always existed—a problem that troubled many enquirers of the time but which Khayyām prefers not to face—Nature is always creating or destroying. Why does God destroy what he has so carefully created?

Our elements were merged at His command;
Why then did he disperse them once again?
For if the blend was good, why break it up?
If it was bad, whose was the fault but His?

It is at this point that Khayyām makes use of his famous metaphor of the potter and the pot. This combines more than one idea—the power and arbitrariness of the Creator, the creation of human beings by the compounding of the elements, and the dissolution of human elements into dust that serves in its turn to make further new compounds:

Each particle of dust upon this earth
Was once a moon-like face, the brow of Venus;
Wipe gently from your loved one's cheek the dust,
For this same dust was once a loved one's cheek.

* * *

When the spring showers bathe the tulip's cheek,
Then is the time to fill the cup and drink.
For this green grass whereon you play today
Tomorrow will be sprouting from your dust.

* * *

Sitting one evening in the potter's store,
I watched the potter as he spun his wheel;
Deftly he shaped a handle and a lid
From a pauper's hand and from a monarch's head.

* * *

This jar was once a mournful lover too,
Caught in the tangles of a loved one's hair;
This handle that you see upon its neck
Once, when a hand, caressed a loved one's throat.

But since there is no changing the course of destiny, why waste time
speculating about these matters? However much we speculate about
metaphysical and philosophical questions, we can never by our own
unaided efforts discover the answers:

These problems you will never understand,
So leave them to the subtle men of science.
Make here your paradise with ruby wine;
That other you may see one day—or not.

* * *

I am not here forever in this world;
How sinful then to forfeit wine and love!
The world may be eternal or created;
Once I am gone, it matters not a scrap.

* * *

The sphere of heaven turns not for the wise,
Whether you reckon the skies at seven or eight.
The craving body must die, so let it go
To the ant in the grave, or to the desert wolf.

We cannot even count on life after death, so there is no point in worrying about heaven or hell:

We are the pawns, and Heaven is the player;
This is the plain truth, and not a mode of speech;
We move about the chessboard of the world,
Then drop into the casket of the void.

* * *

The rose-clad meadow by the water's edge,
Two or three friends, a charming playmate too;
Bring out the cup, for we who drink at dawn
Care nothing for the mosque or Paradise.

* * * *

When once you hear the roses are in bloom,
Then is the time, my love, to pour the wine;
Houris and palaces and heaven and hell—
These are but fairy-tales, forget them all.

And so we come to the inevitable conclusion: All we know and can be sure of is the passing moment, so we should make the most of it:

Why should I worry whether I am rich,
Or whether life is good to me or not?
Fill up the cup, for I can never know
Whether this breath I take will be my last.

* * *

Since no one can be certain of tomorrow,
It's better not to fill the heart with care.
Drink wine by moonlight, darling, for the moon
Will shine long after this, and find us not.

* * *

159

My friend, let us forget tomorrow's grief,
Let us enjoy ourselves this passing moment.
Tomorrow when we leave this transient world
We shall be one with seven thousand years.

We shall never know whether this was really 'Omar Khayyām's view of life. Perhaps these cynical, pessimistic, at times almost blasphemous thoughts were put into verse merely in order to exorcize them. We know that Khayyām wrote seriously and thoughtfully about the very matters that in his verses he dismisses almost with scorn. He must have thought that his astronomical work and his metaphysical speculations were the things by which he would be remembered. It is an ironical comment worthy of Khayyām himself that these should now be virtually forgotten, while his verses, dismissed by him as trivia not even worth writing down, should have survived to seize the imagination of the world seven or eight centuries after they were composed.

# 9. The Romance

Among the most remarkable achievements of Persian literature are its epics, and perhaps no branch of the latter is more charming, more appealing to the general reader and to Western taste in particular than the romance or the romantic epic. Its tales have inspired the best artists of Iran to create many of the finest motifs in Persian miniature painting: Shirin bathing in a pond amidst a rocky landscape, with only a blue cloth around her loins, surprised by her princely lover; or the lonely and wretched Majnun in the desert, surrounded by animals that listen to his songs of hopeless but unshakeable love.[1]

Couples in Persian love romances, such as Khosrow and Shirin, Vāmeq and 'Adhrā, Laylā and Majnun, became prototypes of love that were referred to in Persian lyrics over and over again.[2] Some tales and motifs even reached Europe early on and influenced Western writers, as will be seen later. Yet, in spite of all their fascinating aspects, Persian romantic epics have not aroused in the West the interest they deserve, among scholars or general readers. I shall therefore try to give some idea of their development, their main representatives, and their specific features.

## Origin and Earliest Manifestations of Romantic Epic

"Romantic" usually refers to love tales, although, in principle, the fairy tale is included, and sometimes both are intertwined. By "epic" we refer to epic poetry only, though epic prose, such as the famous *Book of the Parrot,* originally translated from Sanskrit by Nakhshabi in the fourteenth century, could be discussed under the same heading.[3]

The outward shape of epic poetry in Persian is defined by two elements, namely, the distich (couplet), with two rhymes, and the meter, which remains the same throughout the poem.[4] In its inner structure, the epic characteristically combines narrative and descriptive

---

[1]A fine volume reproducing such miniatures is *Mirror of the Invisible World: Tales from the "Khamseh" of Nizami* with contributions from P. J. Chelkowski, P. P. Soucek, and R. Ettinghausen (New York, 1975).

[2]See for instance *Divān-e Shams-e Tabriz* of Jalāl al-Din Rumi, ed. Foruzānfarr, no. 532, 4–5.

[3]See chap. 4 for a full discussion of Persian epics. (Ed.)

[4]Thus, Gorgāni's *Vis and Rāmin* and Nezāmi's *Khosrow and Shirin* are written in the same meter, called *hazaj,* ˘ ‒ ‒ / ˘ ‒ ‒ / ˘ ‒ ‒ (each hemistich has eleven feet); Ferdowsi's *Shāh-nāma* (Book of kings) and Nezāmi's *Alexander Romance* are in the meter called *motaqāreb,* ˘ ‒ ‒ / ˘ ‒ ‒ / ˘ ‒ ‒ / ˘ ‒

elements. In the narration, the poet usually proceeds directly, using more or less simple language, whereas in the descriptive passages he displays all his rhetorical skill with metaphors and word play. Other elements are the monologue, the dialogue (often in the form of letters), songs, adages, and the reflections and admonitions of the poet. In his romances, Nezāmi sometimes intersperses very personal elements, such as addresses to his son, and epitaphs on relatives. He also introduced the long preface offering praise of God and the Prophet Mohammad, a eulogy of the prince to whom he dedicated the poem, and some remarks on the reasons why he has chosen the subject and composed the book.

The Persian romance, thus, incorporates all the other genres: lyric, panegyric, didactic, satirical and descriptive poetry. But the romantic epic genre is unique in building long coherent units of verse, in developing characters, and in giving the poet the possibility of displaying his skill, not only in composing verse but as a narrator, lyricist, and analyst of the human psyche, and, often, as a moralist who instructs not so much by words as by persuasive examples.

In a very particular way, the Persian romantic epic is related to the short forms, particularly the *ghazal*. What is only alluded to in the *ghazal* is fully developed in the epic; what is abstract there, is concrete here; the spirit of the *ghazal* has its flesh and blood in the romantic epics, which therefore serve as an indispensable supplement to the *ghazal*.

Whereas in Arabic literature the epic genre was virtually non-existent, in Persian literature it flourished from the very beginning. Nomadic life with its concomitant unrest and insecurity may have been unfavorable to the development of so time-consuming an art. As is well known, the poetic tradition of the pagan Arabs continued to prevail in Islamic times and apparently allowed no revolutionary innovations. On the other hand, Iran had its millennial epic tradition. This was a heroic tradition, it is true, but interspersed with romantic elements which seemed only to be awaiting independent elaboration.

Many episodes in the *Shāh-nāma*, the national epic, have a romantic tinge. Besides the love story of Khosrow and Shirin, which Nezāmi took over and endowed with its classical form, we find here those of Zāl and Rudāba, Rostam and Tahmina, Bizhan and Manizha, and other couples, with motifs of separation and faithfulness, temptation and chivalry, love and jealousy, and so on. But the stuff of the romantic epic also came from other sources. The *Alexander Romance* of Pseudo-Callisthenes is prominent among imported stories, which include Hebrew, Arabic, Indian and other Greek sources. Some were also taken from Iranian pre-Islamic sources. At least one Persian romantic epic, Gorgāni's *Vis and Rāmin*, existed in Middle Persian, but long before it reemerged other Persian romances had been written.

'Onsori, the great panegyrist at the court of Mahmud of Ghazna, is reliably reported to have composed a number of romantic epics.[5] Some short fragments of one of them, *Vāmeq and 'Adhrā'*, were recently discovered in the repaired binding of an otherwise unimportant manuscript.[6] We still do not know much about the content of this epic, yet Goethe knew even less when he wrote:

Was sie getan, was sie geübt
Das weiss kein Mensch!
Dass sie geliebt,
Das wissen wir.
Genug gesagt,
Wenn man nach Wamik und Asra fragt.[7]

Greek proper names in the text of this epic reveal its Greek origin, and the fragments show that it dealt with one of those sentimental love affairs with endless episodes of separation and final happy union so typical of the late Hellenistic novel.[8] Another of 'Onsori's romances, *Kheng bot o sorkh bot* (The white idol and the red idol), was an adaptation of an Indian legend connected with the two colossal Buddhist statues still visible at Bāmiyān, as we learn from a note in Biruni's *Chronology of Ancient Nations*.[9]

A love tale in Arabic is the source of the earliest extant Persian romantic epic, 'Ayyuqi's *Varqa and Golshāh*. Here the union of a pair of childhood sweethearts is prevented by fate and family. Dedicated to their love, they choose to live after the ideal of chaste, unshakable love until death.[10] The most famous love story of this kind is, of course, that of the Arab poet Qays, called Majnun, "the insane" (lit. "possessed by jinns"), and his beloved Laylā, "the night-eyed." This story, however, was developed and shaped in the form of a full-fledged Persian epic only in the twelfth century. Hebrew tradition, on the other hand, is

[5]Rypka, *History*, 175ff.
[6]See *Wāmiq-o-Adhrā of 'Unsuri*, ed. M. Shafi (Lahore, 1967).
[7]J. Goethe, "Noch ein Paar," *West-östlicher Divan*.
[8]G. E. von Grunebaum, *Der Islam in Mittelalter* (Zurich and Stuttgart, 1963), 389.
[9]See D. J. Boilot, *L'oeuvre d'al-Beruni: Essai bibliographique*, Institut Dominicain d'Études Orientales du Caïre, Mélanges 3 (Cairo, 1955), 204, n. 83.
[10]Called *'odhri* love, apparently from *'adhrā* (virgin); see Rypka, *Iran. Lit.*, 177.

the source of *Yusof and Zolaykhā,* whose story, condensed in the beautiful twelfth *sura* of the Koran, was cast into epic form by the poet Amāni in the eleventh century. (It had formerly been attributed to Ferdowsi.) Four centuries later, it was recast by the great poet Jāmi.

## Gorgāni

The first great achievement of the romantic epic in Iran is undoubtedly Gorgāni's *Vis and Rāmin,* written about 1050. The author tells us that he used an artless Middle Persian version as his model; Minorsky has shown that the material is Parthian in origin.[11] The plot, famous for its striking similarity to the Tristan saga, is limited to a small number of persons connected to the courts of Marv in Khorasan and Māh in western Iran (Media). In Marv, King Mobad resides with his younger brother, Rāmin, and his stepbrother and vizier, Zard. In Māh, there reigns a king named Kāran, who is eventually killed in a battle against Mobad, leaving his wife, Shahru, his son, Viru, and his daughter, Vis. But this is not the beginning. At the outset, the two courts are united in a splendid feast given by Kāran. Mobad, attracted by Shahru's beauty, has the effrontery to ask her to become his wife. She reminds him of her married state but promises to give him her daughter should she have one. This unleashes the whole drama, as the author remarks: "See into what tribulation they fell by giving away an unborn child as a bride."[12]

Vis, born soon after, is brought up by her shrewd but faithful nurse and, in accordance with an old Iranian custom, is married to her brother Viru. On the wedding day, the gaiety of the assembly is suddenly interrupted by the ominous appearance of Zard, who demands the delivery of Vis in the name of Mobad, reminding Shahru of the promise she had once made to him. Shahru is embarrassed, but Vis, showing her temperament for the first time, meets Zard with a rebuff and censures the tactlessness of Mobad's demand. But Mobad insists, and a war is waged in which Kāran loses his life.

Soon after, Mobad succeeds in persuading Shahru, by threats and gifts, to deliver Vis to him. On the way to Marv, however, the curtain of Vis's litter is raised by a sudden breeze; Rāmin, King Mobad's younger brother, who is in charge of taking Vis to the royal court,

[11]See V. Minorsky, *Iranica* (Tehran, 1964), 151ff. This and other theories on the origin of *Vis and Rāmin* are summarized by Rypka, *Iran. Lit.,* 178.

[12]English trans. G. Morrison, UNESCO Collection of Representative Works, Persian Heritage Series (New York and London, 1972), 25.

beholds her face and immediately falls in love with her. The rest of the story is a long and dramatic play of intrigues and illusive appeasements. After Rāmin wins the love of Vis with the help of her nurse, and after Vis has told Mobad more than once that she will never love him because her heart is lost to Ramin, the young couple hoodwink old Mobad and escape most of his preventive devices and punitive measures, always with the nurse playing a decisive part. Eventually, when Mobad is killed by a wild boar, Rāmin and Vis, who had run away with his treasures a little earlier, capture his castle. After this violent victory, the happy couple reign over the country with justice for the rest of their lives.

This romance is remarkable in more than one respect. Not only is it full of dramatic adventures, but it also shows Gorgāni's mastery of character delineation. His *dramatis personae* reveal their respective natures through their actions and, particularly, through their monologues and dialogues. The author himself hardly ever judges them, leaving it to the readers to form their own opinions. Clearly, however, Vis and Rāmin represent true lovers. Love overwhelms them suddenly and irresistibly, and they are ready to bear all kinds of afflictions for its sake, even though their relation is obviously unlawful. Mobad, on the other hand, is shown as a cold moralist, always presuming upon his seemingly legal claim, based on Shahru's concession. His name, which means "priest," may therefore not have been chosen at random. But in his behavior toward Vis he reveals over and over again, by heartless remarks, remonstrances, and brutal punishments followed by conciliatory gestures, fresh demands, and new self-deceptions, that he is completely incapable of loving her. Mobad's coldness even extends to the physical aspect of love: on the entreaties of Vis, the nurse puts a spell on Mobad's virility; intended to last for a month, the spell becomes irrevocable when the charm is swept away in a flood.

One of Gorgāni's fine hints at the differences between Mobad and Rāmin is his description of the wanderings of the two in search of Vis. For Rāmin, the desert is changed into a rose garden, but for Mobad, nature remains dull and repugnant until he despairs of finding Vis and returns home totally wretched. These two expressions of love are placed beside two others: Vis's matrimonial relations with her brother Viru, which is legal and not unhappy, and the brief affair between Rāmin and princess Gol (a parallel to that of Tristan and Isolde of the White Hands). Both these relations, however, pale before the total, existential love of Vis and Rāmin.

## Nezāmi

For all its literary importance, Gorgāni's epic was to be surpassed by the works of the twelfth-century poet Nezāmi, by far the greatest figure in the field of the Persian romance. Unlike Gorgāni, who does not reveal any details of his life except that he experienced an unhappy love affair, Nezāmi speaks of himself and his family several times in his romances. We know that he spent his whole life in Ganja (now Kirovabad), that he married three times (successively); that his first wife, Āfāq, bore him his son, Mohammad; and some other details. The most remarkable fact about these biographical fragments is Nezāmi's love for Āfāq, a Kipchak slave girl who was sent to him by the prince of Darband as a gift for his first romance, *Makhzan al-asrār* (Treasury of secrets). Instead of taking her as his concubine, which Islamic law would have permitted him to do, Nezāmi made her his legal spouse.

This kind and pious deed (recommended by Islamic tradition)[13] is in harmony with his humanism, which is manifest throughout his writings either in direct statements or in the actions of his characters. Thus, he says about himself:

Throughout my life I have never used violence
So much as would have hurt an ant's wing.[14]

The advice to do no harm to anyone is supplemented by the injunction to "serve humanity actively":

Carry the burden of everyone if you can:
What is better than to relieve those who carry burdens?[15]

In fact, Nezāmi's humanism is crowned by his vision of woman. He depicts woman as an equal partner of man—full of warmth and love, yet at the same time proud, strong-willed, and brave. In clear distinction to so many other Oriental tales, wickedness is shown here not as an inborn quality of female nature, but as a consequence of the corrupting atmosphere of the harem.[16] As a result, Nezāmi indicates:

[13]Chapter 13 of the Book on Marriage in the standard collection of the Prophet's reported sayings compiled by al-Bukhāri in the third/ninth century.
[14]*Laylā o Majnun*, ed. V. Dastgerdi (Tehran, 1955), 44, line 13.
[15]Ibid., 56, line 6.
[16]*Khosrow o Shirin*, ed. V. Dastgerdi, 92, line 6.

To marry one wife is enough for a man;
The husband of many is the husband of none![17]

Nezāmi's humanism is based on religious belief, but he is opposed
to fanaticism and obscurantism. In the admonitions directed to his
son Mohammad, he urges him more than once to recognize himself
in order to unite mind and spirit[18] and acquire true knowledge:

Mind and spirit are heavenly gifts,
Mind and spirit are eternal life.

Finally, Nezāmi's humanism incorporates pride and independence.
Throughout his writings, he warns against serving unjust princes:

It is better to give bread from your own table to others
Than to eat sweetmeats from the table of the vile![19]

It is part of Nezāmi's genius that he made the romance a vehicle
for expressing his ethical beliefs. In his famous *Khamsa* (Quintet), the
first epic, *Makhzan al-asrār* (Treasury of secrets), is a didactic piece
outlining twenty moral principles, each illustrated by a tale. Then
follow his three great romantic epics, *Khosrow and Shirin*, *Laylā and
Majnun*, and *Haft paykar* (The seven beauties); the last epic, *Eskandar-
nāma* (The book of Alexander), combines didactic, heroic, and romantic elements.

Of the three romances none has been more popular then *Khosrow
and Shirin* (summarized and discussed in the next chapter). Khosrow
is Khosrow Parviz, the last great Sasanian king (r. A.D. 590–628);
Shirin, his beloved, is an Armenian princess.

Shirin's true historical character remains in doubt. In the *Shāh-nāma*
she poisons her rival Maryam, yet Nezāmi expressly rejects the slightest possibility of such an act as incompatible with Shirin's nature.[20]
On the basis of Nezāmi's own statements, in which he compares the
premature death of Shirin to that of his wife Āfāq and, shortly before
his own death, speaks of Āfāq with the warmest feelings, Y. E. Bertels
concludes that Nezāmi created his Shirin, one of the greatest figures

---

[17]*Eqbāl-nāma*, ed. V. Dastgerdi, 59, line 3.
[18]Literally "reason and soul."
[19]*Haft paykar*, ed. V. Dastgerdi, 53, line 8.
[20]Ibid., 56, line 4.

in world literature, in memory of his wife.[21] In any case, Nezāmi's Shirin, although a literary fiction, personifies a higher truth than any historiographical exactness could possibly yield. That Nezāmi wanted to create a symbol of love may be gleaned from one of the introductory chapters of the romance, in which he speaks of love as the great cosmic force that keeps creation alive and the universe in motion.[22] Yet, even if we did not have these lines, every page of this romance breathes love, with its afflictions and its blisses.

A love affair is also the subject of Nezāmi's third epic, *Laylā and Majnun.* Like Varqa and Golshāh, the two fall in love while still schoolchildren. But Laylā's parents have other plans for her. They forbid her to meet Majnun and find justification for their attitude as he begins to show signs of madness. In fact, Majnun seems to be more in love with the idea of Laylā than with the person, and so becomes the Orpheus of the Arabian desert, surrounded by animals who listen to his songs of love and despair.

Nezāmi's fourth tale, *The Seven Beauties,* is certainly the most romantic of his epics. It incorporates seven independent love stories, each of which is a jewel of romantic narration. Again the hero is a Sasanian king, Bahrām Gor (r. A.D. 421–39). His nickname, Gor (Onager), is said to point to his passion for hunting this animal, but Nezāmi gives it a gloomy overtone by playing with the two meanings of gor as "onager" and "grave."[23] The tales are told by the seven beauties that Bahrām married; these are princesses from the seven climes of ancient geography, and each tale is full of references to the respective planet and things belonging to its clime. Meanwhile, however, the king's subjects are suffering from a despotic vizier who conspires with the enemy and oppresses the people, and the complaints of seven of his victims form a sobering contrast to the enchanting tales of love.

The first of the tales is set in a magic garden in the sky where a fairy of unimaginable beauty lives with her maidens. A privileged visitor to the garden immediately falls in love with the seductive lady. Allowing him to caress her all day long but sending him away in the evening, she tells him that he may appease his desire with one of the maidens but must not demand that she give herself to him completely before forty days have elapsed. The lover, however, is not capable of so much self-restraint, whereupon he loses the fairy's favor and, to

[21]Y. E. Bertels, *Izbranniye trudi: Nizami i Fuzuli* (Moscow, 1962), 225.
[22]Ibid., 117–18, 484, 485.
[23]*Haft paykar,* 68–69.

his chagrin, suddenly finds himself down on earth again. But now he knows the secret of the city of the black-clothed, one of whose inhabitants told him how to reach that fatal paradise, without, however, revealing its proviso.

Patience as a prerequisite for fulfillment is also the subject of the last story, but this time the moral is taught with humor. By his impatience, the young hero places himself in a number of ridiculous situations until he learns his lesson and is rewarded with a happy union.

Nezāmi, a master poet in every respect, was quite aware of his own excellence. In his first romance, *The Treasury of Secrets,* he speaks of his superiority over other poets and, referring to his immediate predecessor Sanā'i (who wrote only didactic epics), he states:

> Though in his mint there is speech like gold,
> My mint for gold is better than his.[24]

His skill is all-embracing. His rich vocabulary and refined use of metaphor are displayed in the descriptions of nature, beautiful bodies and clothes, buildings, and so on, and the physical setting is made to correspond with the mood of the action. The love scenes between Shirin and Khosrow, for example, take place in a lovely springtime landscape, and the reproachful dialogues in winter (a device already used by Gorgāni). Equally adept is Nezāmi's use of metaphor and animation of nature for subtle allusion. Thus, in the description of a night when Khosrow's love for Shirin becomes so ardent that her virginity seems to be in danger, Nezāmi compares the moonlit sky to a litter without its black curtain, so that no veil is left except chastity.[25] Nezāmi is also a master of dialogue, character delineation, and narrative structure. But everywhere his art is imbued with a spirit that does not allow superficial, easygoing entertainment. Nezāmi's poetry is no slight fare; it is often hard to read, but always inspired and therefore rewarding.

Whether or not Nezāmi's poetry allows an allegorical interpretation, his tales and characters stand first of all for themselves; they are representations of real life, not of mystical experience or of the soul's adventures in interior worlds. At the same time, the sensitive reader soon perceives that Nezāmi was well aware of the symbolic value of

---

[24]*Makhzan al-asrār,* ed. V. Dastgerdi, 36, line 7.

[25]*Khosrow o Shirin,* 131, line 6. Some of the rhetorical devices of Nezāmi are described by H. Ritter, *Über die Bildersprache Nizamis,* Studien zur Kultur und Kultur des islamischen Orients 5 (Berlin and Leipzig, 1927).

the situations he depicts. The encounter between Khosrow and Shirin at the fountain may serve as an example. Is not Shirin's bathing in the fountain while on her way to Khosrow a symbol of her immersion in love, the fountain of life, and is not the encounter itself—with the two lovers failing to recognize one another even as each one seeks the other—a symbol of the interior state of their love? They long for each other, but are still unaware of the true nature of the partner and therefore not ready for total union.

Nezāmi's tales point to other layers of meaning: external situations often correspond to interior development, if not in a strictly mystical sense, yet even a mystical meaning can easily be detected in some of his love tales. A short passage in *Khosrow and Shirin* is indicative of Nezāmi's awareness of the symbolic meaning of fairy tales:

> You certainly know the hidden meaning of the fairy tale
> about a woman who performed sorcery on a road.
>
> She threw a comb and a mirror on the road and put a
> spell on them.
>
> The sky caused a mountain to rise from that one and a
> forest from this one.
>
> [The meaning is:] A woman who throws away mirror and
> comb becomes mighty as mountain and forest.[26]

Shorter but of particular relevance for the symbolism of Nezāmi's poetry in general is the following verse, in which the poet makes one of his many puns on the name of Shirin, or "sweet":

> The enthralling Shirin, a cup of bitter wine in her hand—
> By this sweetness and this bitterness all humanity is intoxi-
> cated.[27]

## Amir Khosrow Dehlavi

About a century after Nezāmi, the first great imitator of his *Quintet* appeared. He was Amir Khosrow of Delhi, a Perso-Indian poet of almost incredible productivity, who is reported to have created his

---

[26]Ibid., 76.
[27]*Khosrow o Shirin*, 64, line 6.

*Quintet* in less than three years. Understandably, his poems lack the maturity and spiritual depth of Nezāmi's.

Like Nezāmi, Amir Khosrow begins with a number of introductory chapters devoted to praise of God, of Mohammad, of a patron prince, dirges for a son or a daughter, and reasons for writing the book. Amir Khosrow is no slavish imitator, however. His independence is particularly evident in his *Hasht behesht* (The eight paradises), his counterpart to Nezāmi's *Seven Beauties*. Where Nezāmi relates the life of King Bahrām with its amusements and its duties and, as mentioned above, counterbalances the love tales with seven reports of the victims of his despotic vizier, Amir Khosrow reduces the material to little more than a bundle of eight stories knit together by a scanty framework. Only one of Nezāmi's seven love tales is taken over by Amir Khosrow, although with notable modifications, and the motif of the misogynist who becomes a believer in marriage is borrowed for a totally different tale. Other stories reveal a strong Indian influence: one deals with the ability of the spirit to slip into a dead human or animal body and shows close parallels to a story in *The Book of the Parrot*.[28] Most of the stories reveal an interest in magic or in semi-technical matters, such as a magical statue which laughs at absurd or insincere human behavior,[29] an eye powder (*sorma*) which makes one invisible, music which makes one fall asleep, laugh, or weep, and so on. But a purely scientific operation also occurs: the weight of a colossal gold sculpture, too heavy to be put on a balance, is measured by putting it in a boat, determining the displacement of water, and then filling the boat with some material of the same water displacement that can be weighed easily.[30]

Amir Khosrow does not possess the overflowing poetic imagination of Nezāmi, nor his faculty of subtle character delineation. A garden or a night sky is described with two or three metaphors instead of twenty. His characters are flat, but they are rich in strange and unexplainable or morally questionable actions. Their inner struggles or developments are not envisaged by the poet, let alone commented upon with Nezāmi's deep and engaged understanding which recalls the anxiety of loving parents for the welfare of their children. But Amir Khosrow is a good narrator; his style is straightforward, always gripping, and easily readable.

[28]*Book of the Parrot*, Turkish version, twenty-eighth night: Tale of the king of China; Persian version no. 75, forty-sixth night: Tale of the king of Oyayyen.

[29]In the story of the seventh princess in the white cupola, which, like the second tale of Nezāmi, features a king who is cured of misogyny.

[30]In the tale of the second princess in the yellow cupola.

## Transformation of a Theme

One of the many brief romantic pieces in the *Shāh-nāma* is the story of Bahrām Gor and a favorite slave girl called Āzāda (Noble), a harpist. This model was taken over and altered by Nezāmi and by Amir Khosrow. Thus we have three versions of the same tale, each one typical of its author.

1. In the *Shāh-nāma* the plot is short and simple, consisting of a rapid, fatal development with almost no romantic or sentimental accessories. Bahrām and his slave girl go hunting on camelback. Two gazelles, a male and a female, appear, and he asks her which of the two she wants him to shoot. Āzāda sets the king a difficult task: he should change the female into a male by shooting two arrows into her head and tap together the hoof, the ear, and the head of the deer with a single arrow shot. Bahrām not only performs this feat but also shoots off the two horns of the male, thereby making it a female. Instead of admiring him, however, Āzāda suddenly feels compassion for the poor gazelles, whereupon the proud king, used to the hyperbolic praise of his courtiers, without a word flings her to the ground, has his camel trample her to death, and rides away. "Thereafter he never took a slave girl with him to hunt."[31]

2. In *The Seven Beauties*, Nezāmi not only changes the name of Āzāda to Fetna (Rebellion, Temptation), but omits the somewhat unpleasant change-of-sex incident. He also replaces the brutal ending with a charming continuation of the story. After Bahrām's performance, the victim of which is not a gazelle but an onager (in keeping with Bahrām's nickname), Fetna says:

> The prince has perfected this skill!
> A perfected skill—how can it be difficult?

> Whatever a man has learned,
> However difficult it be, he can do it!

Nezāmi then describes the rage of the prince and adds a warning for rulers:

> If kings are vengeful,
> they shed blood whenever they wish.

[31]*Shāh-nāma*, ed. Y. E. Bertels (Moscow), vol. 7 , 273–77.

But Bahrām refrains from killing Fetna himself:

To kill women is not a feat for lion-like men;
women are no peers of men in aggression.

Yet a moment later he says to one of his officers:

Go and dispatch this affair.
She is the rebellion [*fetna*] in our auspicious court;
To kill a rebel [*fetna*] is lawful in accordance with reason.

Fetna, however, is not killed. Instead, the officer shelters her in one of his manors, and Fetna begins to prepare for a happy change in her lot. She takes a newborn calf, puts it on her shoulders, and climbs up the sixty steps of a staircase—or, as in some miniatures, rungs of a ladder—leading to a roof terrace. This she repeats daily until the calf has become a bull. Nezāmi here interjects one of his many astrological allusions: the moon (a constant metaphor for the girl) has its exaltation (the point of highest astrological efficiency) in the sign of Taurus. Finally, the king of kings is invited to a party, the preparations for which are depicted so as to whet one's appetite, and the girl, after careful makeup and dressing, again described with the most evocative metaphors, displays to Bahrām her incredible performance. Bahrām, however, remains cool:

This is not your [inborn] power!
No, you have achieved it by learning. . . .

Now, the moment for the girl's decisive riposte has come:

The shah owes a great debt!
The bull is all learning, the onager—without learning?

Her plot works. Bahrām, who had long repented his rashness, is delighted to have her return to him again. He begs her forgiveness, and she reveals to him why she withheld her praise: out of fear of the evil eye![32]

[32]*Haft paykar,* 107–20; ibid., ed. H. Ritter and J. Rypka (Istanbul, 1934), chaps. 25 and 26. A German verse translation of the story with an introduction of mine appeared in the Viennese periodical *Bustān* 8/2 (1967): 26–35.

This happy ending convinces and conveys satisfaction to the reader because it is not trivial. Nezāmi has replaced royal brutality and irrevocable fate by successful human endeavor to overcome evil: a clever, loving girl devotes herself to a year-long task in order to regain the love of a man who had intended to kill her; an officer disobeys the brutal order of his lord and gives aid to the helpless victim guilelessly; and a king acknowledges his fault and asks the pardon of a female slave. Seldom is the humanism of Nezāmi more palpable than in the alterations he made in this story.

3. In his *Eight Paradises,* Amir Khosrow, who names the maiden Delārām (Heart's repose), has replaced the second half of the story with a totally new invention. Bahrām leaves Delārām at the place of the master shot—again the sex-changing one of Ferdowsi—whence, after days of wandering, she reaches a lonely village and finds a farmer who adopts her as his child. He is a skilled musician, who teaches her the twelve modes (*parda,* in Arabic *maqām*), and in particular the four of them, which make the hearer laugh, weep, fall asleep, or become alert. Amir Khosrow's own musical skill is quite evident here. (He was the inventor of more than one instrument and one of the inaugurators of the Indo-Muslim musical style.) When Delārām plays the barbiton, the gazelles, attracted by her melodies, fall asleep and wake up as if restored from death to life. Her fame comes to the ears of Bahrām, who goes to hear her playing. Her comment on his demonstration of the hunting art had been that it was close to sorcery but that one could imagine a person doing it better or doing something else better than he. His comment now is:

> The like of this exists,
>> everyone has a share of some magical power.
> There is no artist in any country
>> who does not find his superior somewhere.[33]

"All right," Delārām retorts, "with only one exception: a king who changes a female into a male is unsurpassable!" At that point he recognizes her, begs her pardon, and loves her more than ever.

Amir Khosrow's version of the story does not have the same charm and flavor or the inner consequences and moral intensity of Nezāmi's, yet it is perhaps the most successful among the *Eight Paradises.* It is even superior to Nezāmi's version in one respect, namely, in avoiding

[33]*Hasht behesht,* ed. Ja'far Eftekhār (Moscow, 1972), 47–71.

the somewhat incongruous vision of a girl with the muscles of a heavy-weight champion and in endowing the girl with an art which is spiritually superior to that of the king: captivating animals by the tones of a lute alone is certainly subtler than changing the sex of animals by such coarse means as an arrow shot. Finally, the last ironic words of Delārām seem to convey a double meaning. Did not the king also change her sex by denying her the tenderness a woman deserves?

## Jāmi and Others

Amir Khosrow and his older contemporary Khwāju were born in the thirteenth century. Khwāju, although overshadowed in romances by Nezāmi and Amir Khosrow, and in lyrics by his younger contemporary Hāfez, is nevertheless important as a precursor of Hāfez and an inspirer of miniatures, including those of the fourteenth-century master Jonayd, which belong to the most refined and fascinating examples of Persian paintings.[34] Khwāju's two romantic epics, *Homāy and Homāyun* and *Gol and Nowruz*, are not derivative in subject.

In the fourteenth century the all-eclipsing figure is the great Hāfez, the undisputed master of the *ghazal*, but the fifteenth century brought forth a number of important writers in the field of romance. The greatest of these writers is Jāmi, who also excelled in every other branch of Persian literature. He wrote seven epic poems called *Haft owrang* (The seven thrones, or Ursa Major). Their very number reveals the author's purpose of surpassing Nezāmi's five. Among these seven poems, three are didactic and three romantic; the seventh, dedicated to the story of Alexander the Great, is a *mixtum compositum* like Nezāmi's *Alexander Romance*.

The three romantic epics are *Laylā and Majnun*, *Yusof and Zolaykhā*, and *Salāmān and Absāl*. Of these, this last is by far the shortest, but nonetheless is typical of the poet's aims. The subject matter, said to be of Greek origin, had already been used by Avicenna as an allegory, although in a completely different way.

In Jāmi's version, a Greek king wants a son, but since he does not desire to take a wife (owing to the influence of a misogynist sage who is his counselor), he gives the sage some of his semen, and "by a scientific procedure, the thought of which embarrassed the scholars," the philosopher puts it in a place where nine months later a flawless

[34]On Jonayd see B. Gray, *Persian Painting* (Geneva, 1961), illustrations 46, 47 and commentary on 51.

175

child comes forth. Salāmān, the child, is brought up by a young and beautiful nurse called Absāl. But no sooner does he reach the age of adolescence than she falls in love with him and succeeds in seducing him. Outraged, the father tries in vain to bring his son to reason by stern admonitions. In their despair, the young couple decide to die. They go into the desert, kindle a fire, and, hand in hand, leap into the flames. But the king, who has secretly witnessed the scene, saves his son and lets Absāl burn, whereupon the prince is awakened to his royal duties and marries a woman called Zohra (Venus).

In the last chapter but one, Jāmi states that the point of the story is not its form (*surat*), but its sense (*ma'ni*), since

> There is in the shape of each story
> a portion of sense for the keen-eyed.[35]

In the last chapter, Jāmi gives the interpretation of the allegory: the king is active reason, Salāmān is the human soul, Absāl is concupiscence, and so on. It is scarcely surprising that Jāmi's *Yusuf and Zolaykhā*, too, lends itself easily to such allegorical elucidation. Like Amir Khosrow, Sa'di, and many other Persian lyric poets, Jāmi was an admirer of mystical thought—he was in fact a leading Sufi of his time—and all his romances, unlike Amir Khosrow's *Eight Paradises,* are imbued with mystical ideas.

If Jāmi's romantic epics are allegorical romances, another poet of the same century, Fattāhi (d. 1448), wrote a romantic allegory, *Dastur-e 'oshshāq* (Instructions for lovers), as well as a short prose version under the title *Hosn o Del* (Beauty and Heart). Both works are fashioned around allegorical figures, including Love, the king of the Orient, with his daughter Beauty, and Reason, the king of the Occident, with his son Heart. The plot is a rather dramatic tale of love between Beauty and Heart, with other figures, such as Guardian, Rival, and so on, taken from the stock characters of the *ghazal,* and cities called Honor, Monster, and the like. This romance was later imitated and gave rise to a new literary type.[36]

Two other *mathnavi*s of the same period, the *Hāl-nāma* (Book of ecstasy), of 'Ārefi (d. 1449) and *Shāh and gadā* (King and beggar), of Helāli (d. 1529), give an epic elaboration to the long-established bi-

[35]Jāmi, *Haft owrang,* ed. M. Modarres Gilāni (Tehran, 1959), 362.
[36]See A. Bausani, *Le letterature del Pakistan e dell'Afghanistan* (Florence and Milan, 1968), 92ff.

polar metaphor of the love between God and the soul. Thus, the mystical spirit, long since dominant in the Persian *ghazal,* conquered the romantic epic also.

## The Impact of Persian Romances on Neighboring Cultures

In the preface of his *Laylā and Majnun,* Jāmi mentions only two pre-vious versions of this story, those of Nezāmi and Amir Khosrow, but there were lesser imitations as well—written in the framework of a quintet or composed as independent romances—and still others ap-peared after his time. One of the best versions of the story was created by the poet Maktabi of Shiraz in 1489–90, a few years before Jāmi's death.

Nezāmi's influence, however, did not remain limited to Persian poets. According to Annemarie Schimmel, there are "almost innu-merable imitations of Nezāmi's *Khamsa*" by Indian poets writing in Persian. By the fifteenth and sixteenth centuries, Nezāmi's fame and fascination had long since passed the language barrier as well. The first Turkish version of *Khosrow and Shirin,* written in an eastern Turk-ish dialect by a certain Qotb, appeared in 1341.[37] This was followed by many other renderings in Turkish, including that of 'Ali Shir Navā'i, the great Timurid poet and vizier of Herat, whose romance is enriched with the fantastic adventures of Farhād, presented as a sym-bol of the loving soul of the eternal beauty embodied in Shirin.[38]

After the foundation of the Moghul Empire in India in 1525, Per-sian influence also manifested itself in Indo-Islamic literature that developed in languages like Urdu, Sindhi, and Bengali. The great number of Indian emulations of Nezāmi's *Quintet* already mentioned tended, however, to be written in Persian, since most of the Indo-Muslim poets were at least bilingual. In the seventeenth century, the poet Vajhi created a successful Urdu version of a Persian romance, a rhymed prose adaptation of Fattāhi's *Beauty and Heart.*[39]

The influence of the Persian romantic epic also penetrated other forms of literary entertainment, such as folktales and shadow plays. In a Turkish shadow play of *Khosrow and Shirin,* Farhād slays the old woman who brings him the false news of Shirin's death, and the story

---

[37]A. Bombaci, *Histoire de la littérature turque* (Paris, 1968), 96.
[38]Ibid., 123–27.
[39]See n. 36.

then comes to a happy ending.[40] In recent times, the old tale has inspired an opera and a musical comedy, as well as theater plays and movies. Nor is this longevity restricted to the subject of Khosrow and Shirin; twenty years ago, I saw an extremely dramatic Indian movie about Laylā and Majnun, and in 1971 I enjoyed a charming ballet at the Tālār-e Rudaki, Tehran, inspired by Nezāmi's *Seven Beauties* set to classical Persian music.

Some beams of this radiant sun even found their way to so distant a region as the "dark West." In the eighteenth century the tale of Turandot was dramatized by the Italian playwright Carlo Gozzi. This version was then translated by the German classical poet Friedrich von Schiller, and in the nineteenth century the story was made into a grand opera by Puccini. Even so, it is unlikely that any of these three men of the West knew of the Persian model for their material, the fourth love tale in Nezāmi's *Seven Beauties*. In recent years, scholars have attempted to trace a connection between the European Tristan sagas and the *Vis and Rāmin* romance. The parallels are quite remarkable, but the nucleus of the two tales—a love triangle among an old husband, his young wife, and her charming, brave lover, with the young couple assisted by a cunning, somewhat uncanny, and very devoted nurse—is so common in love-tale tradition, and in the human experience behind it, that an independent genesis for the two sagas does not seem impossible. In fact, no traces of transmission from Persia to Europe have come to light as yet.[41]

But this question has no bearing on the importance of the Persian romantic epic as a great achievement of world literature and a source of everlasting delight for impassioned readers. Too little known to the Western literary public, this is a treasury still to be tapped, rich in the lore, facts, and fancies of a past culture, all bathed in the irridescent colors of love, that mysterious light whose homeland was so often felt to be the Orient.[42]

---

[40]H. W. Duda, *Ferhād und Shirin: Die literarische Geschichte eines persischen Sagenstoffes* (Prague, 1933). See also F. Abdullah's article "Ferhād ile Şirin" in *Islam Ansiklopedisi*, which contains interesting material on the Turkish versions of the romance.

[41]Pierre Galland, *Genèse du roman occidental: Essais sur Tristan et Iseut et son modèle persan* (Paris, 1974), is inspired by too much enthusiasm. The author erects one hypothesis upon another but is unable to show any solid evidence for a possible transmission to medieval Europe; see my review in *Fabula* 17 (1976): 100–103.

[42]In Fattāhi's above-mentioned tale, "Heart and Beauty," King Reason dwells in the Occident, King Love in the Orient. Correspondingly, Mohammad Iqbāl, an outstanding Muslim poet and thinker of the subcontinent, contrasted the Orient as the homeland of love and the Occident as the kingdom of reason.

# 10. Nezāmi: Master Dramatist

When Goethe in his "Notes and Studies Contributing to a Better Understanding of the *West-Easterly Divan*" averred that there is no dramatic form in Persian literature,[1] he was certainly referring to drama written for theatrical performances. Goethe was right, in a way, although he did not know that at the time he was writing his *Divan*, the only indigenous Iranian dramatic form had started to flourish in the framework of the ritual theater under the popular title of *ta'ziya*.

However, in the long history of Persian literature, quite a number of dramas were written, disguised in other literary forms: these were not meant to be performed before an audience but to be read in private or recited. The term "closet drama" is quite applicable to this genre of literature. These "closet dramas" are usually longer than actual dramas written for the stage. In them, the author sometimes speaks in his own voice as a narrator and sometimes through his imaginary heroes and their actions.

One of the founding pillars of the "closet drama" in Persian literature is the twelfth-century poet Nezāmi (d. 1209). As I had occasion to state elsewhere,

> The plot [in Nezāmi's closet dramas] is carefully constructed to enhance the story's psychological complexity; the characters work and grow under the stress of action to discover things about themselves and others and to make swift decisions. The tension of their interaction is sometimes almost insupportable, but the passion and fluency of the dialogue matches the flow of dramatic events. The animals, plants, and stars, the sunrise, sunsets, and the gloom of night are so vividly described that they, too, become a dramatic force in the story. Even music is used, not only for its own beauty but to heighten the drama. It is perhaps fortunate that Nezāmi was not a playwright, for he was not forced to limit his action in space and could make all the world, known and unknown, his stage. Unconfined by time, he could present the entire lifespan of his protagonists, following them even beyond the grave into paradise.[2]

One of the essentials of any dramatic form is its structural and

---

[1]J. W. Goethe, *West-östlicher Divan: Noten und Abhandlungen*, 189.
[2]P. J. Chelkowski, Introduction to *Mirror of the Invisible World* (New York, 1975).

179

artistic unity. In the three works we shall discuss here, the long poems *Khosrow and Shirin, Laylā and Majnun,* and *Haft paykar* (The seven beauties), Nezāmi achieves this unity brilliantly. He records human life in its entirety, from birth to death. In the cases of Khosrow, Majnun, and Bahrām, the offspring have been long-awaited; their births are followed by rejoicing. Each growing hero is described as possessing outstanding qualities, but for all three, the hero's life takes a course different from that expected and desired by those around him. After a period in which he lives out his own desires and frustrations, however, the hero emerges as victor over himself; were his parents still living, they would be delighted with this transformation, but as it is, the reader may now participate in this satisfaction.

In the continental climate of the Iranian plateau, winter nights are long and cold, forming a perfect background for the entertainment of royal and princely courts by reading or reciting long stories. In these circumstances, our poet could allow himself complex and profound observations on the part of his heroes. In dramas written for actual production, the time span must be compacted and reduced to a minimum. This need does not apply to the "closet drama": the writer poeticizes, generalizes, even philosophizes. Nezāmi, as is evident from his writing, was conversant with astronomy, jurisprudence, philosophy, mathematics, the art of government, music, and other arts, and he wanted to share this knowledge with his readers.

Nezāmi does not conceal his own beliefs, emotions or thoughts, for his writing is spontaneous. He always describes what is transpiring both inwardly and outwardly with regard to the characters he has created, how they relate to each other and to the situations in which they find themselves. Although the main characters are royal and prominent tribal personages, the artisans and artists (painters, sculptors, architects and musicians) are all portrayed in great detail and play important roles in helping their masters to resolve their mental and outward struggles. Here Nezāmi makes excellent use of a dramatic mechanism in the employment of confidants. An additional dimension to the dramatic buildup of the stories comes from the delineation of simple people. With their comparable attention to genre detail, the painted illustrations of these tales of Nezāmi and his followers differ from the typical iconographic formulas of the heroic epics, and in their fashion support our argument regarding Nezāmi's romances as "closet dramas."

The dramatic functions of Nezāmi's stories are mainly responsible for the impact and influence that these tales have had upon poets in the last 750 years, as well as upon miniature painters, calligraphers, musicians, and lately upon the theater, film, and ballet. This influence has not been restricted to Iran proper but can also be observed all over Western and Central Asia, in the Caucasus, and in the Indo-Pakistan subcontinent. The themes of Shirin and Farhād, Laylā and Majnun, and Bahrām and his princesses are found in Turkish and Persian shadow plays, nineteenth-century Urdu drama, Tajik musical drama, Italian commedia dell'arte, modern Turkish and Azerbaijani dramatic plays, Persian film scripts, and contemporary Persian sculptures.[3]

In comparison with the great romantic poets of the West such as Shelley, Keats, Byron and Wordsworth, some six hundred years later,[4] Nezāmi excels in the use of the dramatic form, notably the use of the characters' speech and the construction of the plot. Achieving what Elizabeth Drew describes as "the true dramatic essence," something deeper than the surface effects of pattern language, he gives his stories what Drew would also call "some mysterious injection of energy into the dialogue, which creates value in words quite beyond their apparent significance."[5]

Nezāmi, in his poetic inspiration, frequently wanders in the borderland between the conscious and unconscious. He is closer to the modern Western drama than to the classical Greek, since he is more

[3]In the Turkish Karagöz and the Persian Pahlavān Kachal, the treatment of the romance of Shirin and Farhād occurs in the framework of the folk repertoire. The same is true in the case of the Urdu dramas known as *Sangit* and *Nautanki*—especially the dance parts, which come straight from folklore. In the Soviet Republics of Central Asia, Nezāmi's stories (or their characters) are very popular in the world of drama and theater. For example, the Tajik poets Tursunzāda and Dehāti wrote a musical drama in 1936 based on Nezāmi's *Khosrow and Shirin* and bearing the same title. In Azerbaijan, Samed Vergun (d. 1956) also wrote a play based on that story, and a "Khosrow and Shirin" composed by the modern Turkish poet Nazim Hikmet (d. 1963) was translated into Russian under the title "A Legend of Love." Farhād became a symbolic figure in a play written by the Polish playwright Makaczyk and staged in Cracow in the 1950s. The story entered the world of cinema in 1920 when Zabih Behruz in Iran published a script for a film called *The King of Iran and the Armenian Princess*. In the 1930s a noted Iranian poet and journalist, 'Abd al-Hosein Sepanta, directed a film of *Khosrow and Shirin* followed by one called *Laylā and Majnun*. As for the visual arts, Bahrām and his female musician companion were favorite subjects among artists long before they entered Nezāmi's story. They appear on gold and silver platters and later on pottery and tiles; scenes from *Laylā and Majnun* were even woven into carpets. In modern art, Farhād and Shirin are often depicted in painting and sculpture, especially by the well-known Iranian sculptor Parviz Tanāvoli.

[4]Examples of "closet dramas" written by Western romantic poets are Shelley's *The Cenci* and *Prometheus Unbound*, Keats's *Otto the Great*, Byron's *Manfred*, and Wordsworth's *The Borderers.*

[5]E. Drew, *Discovering Drama* (New York, 1937), 112.

181

concerned with sin, punishment, and reconciliation than simply with the facts of the instability of human fortunes. Though he does not write for the theater, he carries the art of narration, as Thornton Wilder would say, "to a higher power than the novel or epic poem"; he is a dramatist who "must be by instinct a storyteller."[6]

Possessing the force of immediacy, Nezāmi's language creates the setting in which the action takes place. A detailed summary of one of our stories, *Khosrow and Shirin*, will illustrate this point.

*Scene 1.* King Hormoz the Great is desperately awaiting and praying for a son. His prayers are finally answered and a very promising heir is born, whom he names Khosrow. Trained in the arts of chivalry and all the learning fit for a future monarch, he becomes the delight of the entire court. Bozorg 'Omid, counselor to the king and tutor to the prince, teaches him that "the right of the ruled must always rule."

As a young man, he violates this principle with a noisy feast in a peasant's hut after a hunt. He, his friends, and his musicians keep the villagers awake with the uproar they create; one of his servants, in a drunken state, steals grapes from the peasant's orchard and in the process frightens Khosrow's horse, which stampedes and tramples the peasant's crops.

Following the peasant's complaint, the king deprives Khosrow of his princely throne and offers it to the peasant by way of compensation. After a dramatic court scene in which Khosrow prostrates himself, the king forgives him and restores his privileges. That night, Khosrow's grandfather, Anushirvan, appears to him in a dream and promises him the swiftest horse, the throne of thrones, the best of musicians, and the most beautiful of women as his bride.

*Scene 2.* The painter Shāpur, his trusted companion, tells Khosrow of the extraordinarily lovely princess Shirin, whom he had seen in Armenia. Recognizing her as the girl promised by the apparition of Anushirvan, Khosrow orders Shāpur to bring her to him. Shāpur leaves for Armenia and ascertains the place where Shirin rides to dine *al fresco* with her maidens. In the vivid setting of that pretty valley he paints a living portrait of Khosrow and hangs it on a tree. Upon seeing it, Shirin is overcome with love for the prince. Shāpur then persuades her to mount Shabdiz, the swiftest of horses, belonging to her aunt the queen of Armenia, and to escape to Persia to join Khosrow, who has sent her a ring for recognition. She stops en route to bathe in a pond, where she is surprised by a rider; although she does not know

[6]T. Wilder, "Some Thoughts on Playwriting," in A. Centeno, ed., *The Intent of the Artist* (New York, 1970), 86.

it, this is Khosrow, clothed in a black disguise rather than his customary red (as Shāpur told her he would be) because he is escaping from his enemies.

*Scene 3.* Khosrow's enemies have falsely denounced him to the king, who wants to imprison him. Therefore Khosrow flees toward Armenia with his retinue and, preceding them, sees an exquisite girl in a pool. When it dawns on him that the naked beauty might be Shirin, it is too late, for Shirin, taken by surprise, has already mounted Shabdiz and galloped away. He rides on to the court of the queen of Armenia where he is elaborately feasted and honored. Although Shirin is not there, his friend Shāpur reveals Shirin's whereabouts to him. Khosrow then sends him back to Persia on the second fastest horse, Golgun, to bring Shirin to Armenia.

*Scene 4.* Languishing in Khosrow's palace, Shirin wishes to have a residence built to remind her of the landscape of Armenia, but hostile forces erect it in a hot and unhealthy place. Shāpur rescues her from this "prison," and they ride back to Armenia together, with Shirin on Golgun while Shabdiz remains in Khosrow's stable.

*Scene 5.* Meanwhile, as King Hormoz is dying, Khosrow returns to the Persian capital to assume his legitimate throne. Unfortunately, the two parties do not meet en route. Shortly thereafter, General Bahrām Chubin turns the people against Khosrow through false reports, so Khosrow once more sets out for Armenia, now on Shabdiz. He stops to hunt. Shirin has also gone hunting that morning; they meet and are promptly enraptured with one another.

They go to the palace, where the queen, seeing Shirin's enamored state, warns her against giving in to her desires: "Keep your jewel, and he will be addicted to you as to opium." Throughout the subsequent festivities, Shirin complies with this advice. She astonishes Khosrow by her prowess in riding and hunting and charms him during elaborate festivities, but she refuses his continual impassioned advances. One day she tells him that he must regain his kingdom and assume his royal responsibilities: "If you would enjoy my bloom, salvage your good name, and let your state flower."

*Scene 6.* Consequently, Khosrow goes to Byzantium where the emperor offers him fifty thousand men on the condition that he marries his daughter Maryam and forswear other wives. Having no alternative, he reluctantly accepts her as his queen. Chubin is then defeated, and Khosrow is reinstated on the Persian throne.

*Scene 7.* During this time and following the death of her aunt, Shirin becomes queen of Armenia and a wise ruler. Responding to Khosrow's marriage with extreme mourning and desolation, she appoints a regent and returns to her dismal residence in Persia. After her haughty refusal of a clandestine night meeting, Shāpur becomes the intermediary between her and Khosrow.

*Scene 8.* Shirin longs for the milk of flocks grazing in distant pastures, so Shāpur summons the renowned engineer and sculptor Farhād, who is famous for his great skill, strength, and ingenuity. He falls in love with Shirin at first sight and digs a canal to her palace that ends in a pool of milk. She requites him with two pearls from her ears, but since Shirin cannot return his love, he goes inconsolably to the desert. Khosrow, hearing of Farhād's devotion to Shirin, becomes embarrassed and jealous and tries to bribe him with gold to forget her. Failing in this, he promises Shirin to Farhād, provided that the engineer can perform the seemingly impossible feat of cutting a road through the mountain at Bistun. Farhād immediately embarks upon this Herculean task, which makes him famous throughout the land. Shirin visits him on the mountain and brings him a bottle of milk from her pool. He is speechless and continues to work. When her horse stumbles as she begins the descent, Farhād carries both horse and rider down the mountain to her residence, to everyone's astonishment. He works ferociously to complete his task.

Afraid that Farhād will actually succeed, Khosrow sends a messenger to tell him that Shirin has died of a fever. Farhād flings his axe so that it splits, quivering in the rock, and then hurls himself to death from the mountain. Khosrow repents his act and writes a letter to Shirin, but she is mourning Farhād's constancy and love. She has a dome built over his grave.

*Scene 9.* Shortly afterward Queen Maryam dies, and after the official mourning period Shirin writes to Khosrow and urges him to remarry, to which Khosrow responds with the wish to marry her. Meanwhile, however, he has heard of a beauty named Shekar in Isfahan and rides to meet her. At a banquet, he drinks too much, and Shekar sends one of her maidens to his bed in her stead. The girl reports about his bad breath, and Shekar tells him to eat special food and come back in a year's time. He complies, returns in a year, and brings Shekar to the capital as his bride. Shirin, in despair, no longer allows Khosrow's name to be mentioned.

*Scene 10.* Tiring of Shekar, Khosrow prepares a royal hunt for foreign potentates. A retinue of elephants, foreign guards, musicians, and banners precedes them. One cold night, finding himself in the vicinity of Shirin's palace, Khosrow sends a messenger ahead to herald his arrival. Shirin orders all doors to be locked but has his path strewn with gold coins upon fine carpets. She mounts to a roof terrace; when she sees Khosrow approaching on Shabdiz and carrying her favorite narcissus, she faints.

Khosrow is welcomed with great festivity: gold has been showered down; silks have been spread; tents have been raised and covered with jeweled canopies. In the largest tent of all stands a golden, six-legged throne especially for Khosrow. But he is locked out of the castle and stands in the courtyard, pleading for entry. Shirin, in her finest robes, speaks to him only from the roof; reproaching him for his behavior with bitter recriminations, she sends him back to Shekar. Khosrow, desolated, returns through rain and sleet to his hunting party.

*Scene 11.* Shirin is remorseful and follows Shabdiz's tracks to Khosrow's camp where, at her request, Shāpur conceals her in an adjacent tent. Khosrow's minstrel Bārbad sings of Khosrow's love in front of the tent while she prompts a second musician, Nekisa, to sing in front of hers. The song indicates that she wants to be his slave. When Khosrow, in his own voice, asks her forgiveness, she cries out, thereby disclosing her presence. He runs to her and promises marriage, as she requires him to do. Shirin returns to her palace in a golden litter, and Khosrow goes to the capital to prepare the wedding. He then sends for her with a caravan of camels and horses laden with gifts.

*Scene 12.* Shirin retires early from the wedding feast. Khosrow stays, revels with his companions, and has too much to drink. Shirin, angry at the renewal of waiting, sends a hideous hag to the royal bed in her stead. Khosrow, despite his intoxication, realizes the deception and rejects her in a fury. Shirin then goes to him herself. Thereafter, they live happily for many years. Shirin has a most beneficial influence upon his governance of the kingdom.

*Scene 13.* Shiruya, Khosrow's son by Maryam, becomes openly envious of his father. Although Khosrow has been warned that Shiruya is a threat to him, he is restrained by Bozorg Omid from killing him. One day, Shiruya has Khosrow seized and thrust into a dark prison cell, where Shirin joins him and consoles him. She watches over him at night until, on one occasion, she is overcome by sleep. Then, an assassin sneaks in and stabs Khosrow in the liver. Although thirsty and bleeding to death, he restrains himself from waking the sleeping Shirin.

*Scene 14.* Shiruya has always desired Shirin and now asks her to marry him. She consents on the condition that she may first distribute Khosrow's possessions. Kings and emperors attend Khosrow's elaborate funeral. Surprisingly, Shirin is not dressed in mourning, but in red and yellow.

*Scene 15.* When the procession reaches the royal vault, she asks permission to follow the bier inside in order to say farewell to Khosrow alone. When the doors are shut, she throws herself across his body and fatally stabs herself in the liver with a dagger, letting her blood flow over him. She is buried by his side.[7]

As stated in the introduction to *The Mirror of the Invisible World,* "The story has a constant forward drive with exposition, challenge, mystery, crises, resolution, and finally catastrophe. . . . Nezāmi makes a powerful commentary on human behavior, on its follies, its glories, its struggles, and its unbridled passions and tragedies."[8]

The love story around which the plot is constructed is beset by a multitude of complications. Khosrow and Shirin at first pass each other without recognition, and then Khosrow's forced political marriage to Maryam keeps the lovers apart. The irony here is that it was Shirin who prompted Khosrow's request for troops from the Byzantine emperor. The Farhād episode brings the story almost to a premature conclusion, but his tragic death, for which Khosrow bears responsibility, keeps the story alive. Farhād's love and devotion to Shirin are so powerfully written that many of Nezāmi's emulators made it the core of their stories, without, however, breaking the love triangle.

After Maryam dies, the theme of frustration is further drawn out by Khosrow's infatuation with Shekar. She sends a proxy to the bed of the intoxicated king, just as Shirin later sends him an old hag in her stead. In both instances, Nezāmi shares with the readers events which are as yet unknown to the protagonists. This feeling of omniscience enhances the readers' interest in the story.

The success of comic or tragic episodes in the romance depends upon believable mistakes or misunderstandings by the main characters—mistakes which the readers themselves might make. In this fashion, the sense of common humanity prevents the audience's amusement from being heartless and detached.

Costume changes are a vivid theatrical mechanism which Nezāmi uses constantly. Shirin does not recognize Khosrow when he wears

---

[7]There are about sixty-five hundred couplets to the story, written in a light and flowing *hajaz* meter. The exact date of completion for Nezāmi's *Khosrow and Shirin* is uncertain; 581/1184 seems most probable.

[8]Chelkowski, *Mirror,* 47.

black instead of his customary red, and at Khosrow's funeral Shirin wears gay, colorful clothes to mask her intended suicide.

The attempted deception in Khosrow's bed, with the subsequent masterly erotic scene of Khosrow's and Shirin's love-making, is a sort of relaxing device that prepares the readers for the tragic finale, even though many happy years elapse before the *Liebestod* takes place.

Shirin, presumably a poetic tribute to Nezāmi's first wife Āfāq, is the epitome of desirable womanhood. She is beautiful, intelligent, fearless, and loyal. Khosrow, by contrast, is ruled by his imperative passions and seems to lack her strong sense of justice, as seen in his trickery with Farhād. In the move of a master dramatist, Nezāmi utilizes the death scene to absolve Khosrow of his earlier behavior toward Shirin.

The contrast between Khosrow's weakness and Shirin's strength introduces a new dramatic dimension into the literature of the Near East in that it elevates the position of the woman relative to the stature of the man. The substance of the drama, as an image of human life with all its goals, means, gains, fulfillments, losses, decline, and death, is nonetheless under the tight control of the plot. Thus we can observe the gradual unfolding and meaning of the initial situation. In terms of psychological analysis, we observe Nezāmi, as a romantic, at his best. He displays infinite mastery in presenting the different aspects of a character, building up the impression of complexity and wholeness while leaving the analysis of the character to the imagination of the reader.

The story is kept in a state of unstable equilibrium until the action, eventually, is completed. Suspense not only arises from a particular event but is built up from the outset and maintained by continuous anticipation until the very end: it lies in the dramatic irony and tense situations of which the reader is always aware, although the state of affairs could be transformed into something entirely different at any moment. New and surprising elements introduced into an established situation also exacerbate the dramatic tension. Quick switches play an important part, the biggest shocks occurring at the end of the story; just when Khosrow and Shirin are living in a land which is flourishing because of their united efforts, Khosrow is unexpectedly imprisoned and assassinated. The reader is then taken aback by Shirin's festive robes at the funeral, only to find this a deception preliminary to her suicide.

Some have tried to compare this story to that of Romeo and Juliet. Kathleen Burrill makes the point most aptly: "The story of Farhād and Shirin is one of devoted love, but like other famous lovers—Romeo and Juliet, Laylā and Majnun, tragedy is also an essence of their experience."[9]

It is rather difficult to discuss *Laylā and Majnun,* the third poem of Nezāmi's *Khamsa* (Quintet), along the lines previously employed in the analysis of *Khosrow and Shirin. Laylā and Majnun* is a psychological drama and thus falls into a special category. One can say, however, that this tragic masterpiece of love, madness, and poetry shows Nezāmi's mastery of making a full-scale, well-organized dramatic story arise from a simple tale set in the desert. For the last 750 years, Nezāmi's treatment of this legend has been unsurpassed in the Islamic world. "Nezāmi's originality lies in psychological portrayal of the richness and complexity of the human soul when confronted with intense and abiding love."[10] However, in *Laylā and Majnun,* the common denominator of the double death is presented in reverse form; here Majnun dies on Laylā's grave.

*Seven Beauties,* the next tale of Nezāmi's *Quintet,* deals with the intricate romances of the flamboyant king Bahrām Gor. The colorful life of Bahrām serves as a framework for seven exquisite stories in which the frailties and strengths of human nature are illustrated in elaborate stage sets. The daily change of costumes and pavilion colors has, no doubt, cosmological and mystical connotations, but it is nevertheless extremely dramatic and theatrical. In the brilliant dramatic contrasts, "the stars govern and so does individual will and ingenuity. The purity of desert life redeems the dissolution of the extravagant court; justice reigns and then is abandoned through negligence; but courage overcomes treachery, and jest, arrogance."[11]

One of these seven stories entered the Italian commedia dell'arte in the middle of the eighteenth century. Carlo Gozzi, trying to save the commedia from oblivion, attempted to mix the Oriental fables with the stock characters of the commedia. The cross-breeding of Italian masks and Near Eastern fairy tales was a great success. Gozzi wrote the principal parts in full and versified a considerable part of the dialogue. The most important of Gozzi's commedia fables, which greatly helped to arrest its decline, was *Turandot*; the name is derived from "Turan-dokht" and is based upon the "Story of the Red Pavilion"

---

[9]K. R. F. Burrill, "The Farhād and Shīrīn Story and Its Further Development from Persian into Turkish Literature," in *Studies in Art and Literature of the Near East in Honor of Richard Ettinghausen,* ed. Peter Chelkowski (Utah and New York, 1974), 54.

[10]Chelkowski, *Mirror,* 67.

[11]Ibid., 115.

in the *Seven Beauties*. "The Red Pavilion," as transformed into *Turandot*, had a very interesting career. It influenced Schiller and Goethe, who brought it to the National Theater at Weimar, and Schlager and Hoffmann admired the story as a perennial war of the sexes. Finally, *Turandot* became a libretto for operas composed by Busoni and Puccini.

Departing from the "closet drama" modality of *Khosrow and Shirin*, *Laylā and Majnun*, and the *Seven Beauties*, Nezāmi wrote a heroic epic about Alexander the Great in the last poem of his Quintet, entitled the *Eskandar-nāma*. It is an imaginative and refined story, written in the traditionally prescribed frame of the heroic behavior of the protagonist. This rigid frame is softened somewhat, however, by psychological analysis, romantic conduct, and the inner struggles of the heroes with which Nezāmi had been dealing in the romances. Many of the themes of this poem, the longest of the *Quintet*, could not only fit into the framework of the "closet drama," but could even be considered suitable for staging. However, unlike the other poems we have discussed, this epic fails to achieve structural unity. In addition to the massive deviations from the mainstream, the *Eskandar-nāma* is also very uneven poetically.

In this discussion we have been concerned mainly with Nezāmi as a dramatist. Western scholars tend to attribute the development of plot and characterization in modern Iranian fiction to the impact of novels in Western languages.[12] This may be true of the overall picture, but surely taking into consideration Ferdowsi, Nezāmi, and their emulators, as well as the tradition of popular theater, these developments could be considered to have native roots.

[12]See, for example, D. N. Wilber, "Iran: Bibliographical Spectrum," in *Iran, Review of National Literature* 2/1 (Spring 1971): 164.

# 11. Jalāl al-Din Rumi: Passions of the Mystic Mind

Come!
But don't join us without music.
We have a celebration here.
Rise and beat the drums.

We are Mansur who said "I am God!"

We are in ecstasy—
Drunk, but not from wine made of grapes.

Whatever your thoughts are about us,
We are far, far from them.

This is the night of the *samā'*
When we whirl to ecstasy.
There is light now,
There is light, there is light.

This is true love,
Which means farewell to the mind.
There is farewell today, farewell.

Tonight each flaming heart is a friend of music.
Longing for your lips,
My heart pours out of my mouth.

Hush!
You are made of feeling and thought and passion;
The rest is nothing but flesh and bone.
We are the soul of the world,
Not heavy or sagging like the body.
We are the spirit's treasure,
Not bound to this earth, to time or space.

How can they talk to us of prayer rugs and piety?
We are the hunter and the hunted,
Autumn and spring,
Night and day,
Visible and hidden.

Love is our mother.
We were born of Love.[1]

These are Jalāl al-Din's words of invitation to the celebration of love and life. Rumi lived in the thirteenth century, and died in December 1273. His mystic philosophy, his humanistic love, his art and faith have remained a potent moral and intellectual force in many Islamic communities for more than seven centuries.

Hegel praised him as one of the greatest poets and most important thinkers in world history. The eminent British Orientalist Reynold A. Nicholson paid tribute to him as "the greatest mystical poet of any age." His poetry was a source of inspiration for Goethe's *West-östlicher Divan*. One of the immortals of Persian classical poetry, Jāmi, said of him "He is not a Prophet, but he has written a Holy Book," referring to his *Mathnavi,* which has also been called "The Koran of Mysticism" and "The Inner Truth of the Koran." The prominent twentieth-century poet Sir Mohammad Iqbāl of Pakistan, who proclaimed "Mawlana[2] turned the soil into nectar . . . I became drunk on his wine; now I live with his blessed breath," once advised his son: "Choose Mawlana as your guide so that God will grant you love and ardor." Gandhi used to quote his couplet: "To unite—that is why we came; / To divide—that is not our aim." In 1958, Pope John XXIII wrote a special message: "In the name of the Catholic world, I bow with respect before the memory of Mawlana."

Jalāl al-Din was born in Balkh (in present-day Afghanistan) in 1207, the son of a renowned scholar. His father was forced to flee from Balkh, because of either an impending Mongol onslaught or an intellectual-political disagreement with the sultan and his entourage. After about ten years of wandering through Persia, Iraq, Arabia, and Syria, the family settled in Konya, the capital of the Turkish Seljuk Empire. The empire was in its golden age, and the city was ensconced in high culture, well-known as a haven for scholars and poets fleeing oppression. In Konya, Jalāl al-Din achieved distinction as a theologian and Sufi (mystic). He lived there from the age of twenty-two until his death almost a half-century later.

In 1244, an encounter changed Rumi's spiritual life. In Konya he

---

[1]Unless otherwise credited, the translations quoted in this article are by Talat Sait Halman.

[2]"Mawlana," literally "our Lord, our Master," is a title of respect applied to, among others, judges and sovereigns. It is especially (and often) used in reference to Rumi, as founder of the Mawlavi order of mystics.

met a wild mystic who seemed to have come out of nowhere—Shams al-Din of Tabriz. This meeting has been referred to as *marj al-bahrayn*, "the convergence of the two seas." It is said that Rumi saw the inner secrets of love and life through the influence of Shams and came to the realization that love transcends the mind. He had at his command a vast encyclopedic knowledge; he had read in depth in Persian, Arabic, Turkish, Greek, and Hebrew. But now passion reigned supreme over his mind. Rumi's affection, perhaps love, for Shams resulted in a period of virtually constant ecstasy and excitement, of poetic creativity, of immersion in music and the *samā'*, mystical music and dance. Their friendship has been likened by the French author Maurice Barrès to the friendship of Socrates and Plato, or of Goethe and Schiller.

Shams, a compelling figure of mysterious power, put Rumi through many rigorous, and occasionally cruel, tests from which Rumi emerged obedient, selfless, deepened, and enlightened. Shams seemed to answer Jalāl al-Din's prayers for *pathei mathos*:

> I yearn for a lover who wreaks havoc by rampages,
> Whose heart burns, who drinks and spills blood, defies the stars, wages
> War against Heaven, whose fire—even when it takes a plunge
> Into the bottom of the vast sea—still flames and rages.

The symbolic acts of Shams could be quite bewildering. According to legend, proclaiming that "the science of love cannot be mastered in a religious school," Shams decided to forbid Rumi to read books, including his own father's writings. One day, sitting by the pond, Shams dropped Rumi's books one by one into the water while Rumi looked on without complaint, perhaps acquiescing in the belief that the true mystic must divest himself of all conventional learning. It is said that it was Shams who prevailed on Rumi to start and stress the *samā'* as an artistic means of experiencing ecstasy and achieving mystical communion with God, the Beloved.

After fifteen months of friendship during which Rumi was in bondage to his moral and mystic guide, Shams (whose name means "sun"—the sun that enlightened Rumi) mysteriously disappeared. Rumi was in despair, and he wrote: "Without his face, Paradise for me is hateful Hell." He composed heart-rending poems full of images of burning from separation, of unbearable longing, of spiritual exile: "Come, come, in your absence I have lost my mind and my faith."

This sequence of events was, in fact, a perfect mystic phenomenon. For Rumi, Shams constituted the embodiment of God as well as the symbol of humanity. In effect, he found God and became part of godhead. The disappearance of Shams had its correlative in God's abandonment of humanity. In Shams's absence, Rumi was to undertake an arduous mystical search. He went to Tabriz and Damascus, but failed to find the Sun of Tabriz. When he finally received word that Shams had been seen in Damascus, he sent letters in verse: "O the light of my heart, come back! O my lover and loved one, our life is in your hands. Come, I pray." Shams did not reply—like God who does not answer the prayers of the mystic. Finally Rumi's son, Soltān Valad, and other disciples went to Damascus and brought Shams back to Konya. Rumi's beloved Shams, whom he called "the flying sun," was back: symbolically Rumi had found God again, this time to merge his soul utterly and inseparably:

> The voice of love is descending from left and right:
> We are bound for paradise. Join us. Watch this sight.
>
> We were in heaven—the seraphim know us well,
> And now we must return to eternity to dwell.
>
> Between all this dust and pure life lies an abyss—
> We fell. Let's hasten back to the homeland we miss.

He wrote a poetic celebration of reunion:

> Blessed moment. Here we sit in this palace of love, you and I.
> We have two shapes, two bodies, but a single soul, you and I.
>
> The colors of the gardens and the songs of the birds
> Among the flower-beds will make us immortal, you and I.
>
> The stars of heaven will come out to gaze at us—
> We shall show the stars the moon herself, you and I.
>
> United in ecstasy, we shall no longer be you or I.
> Rescued from foolish babble, we shall rejoice, you and I.
>
> All the bright-plumed birds of paradise will plunge into grief
> When they hear us laughing merrily, you and I.

A few months after the reunion Shams was gone again. It was rumored that a band of assassins, jealous of his closeness to Rumi, murdered him for "political" reasons.[3] Rumi refused to believe that Shams had died. "How," he asked, "could the sun die?"

> He lives the eternal life, yet "He is dead!" says someone.
> He is the sun of hope. Who can claim death for such a sun?
> It is an enemy of the sun who climbs on the roof,
> Covers both his eyes and shouts: "Look, the sun is dead and gone!"

It is said that the whirling dance, to the accompaniment of the reed flute, is an expression of the lament for the absence of Shams—the death of the human God. It was after this momentous event that Rumi went in search of his true God, the god in the outermost reaches of his own soul.

The passions of the mystic mind that Rumi called "my spiritual kingdom," intensified by his pains and ecstasies, gave rise to his collection of odes and quatrains embodied in *Divān-e Shams-e Tabriz* and the complete lyrics embodied in *Divān-e kabir* in Persian. In many poems, the poet identifies himself with Shams, using Sun as his penname. Most of those fervid lyrical verses, composed in strict classical forms and meters, were extemporized by Rumi while in a state of trance, his soul enraptured, bursting into effusive euphony. It was reported by his contemporaries that "there was a pillar in his house, and when he drowned in the ocean of love, he used to take hold of that pillar and set himself revolving around it. Meanwhile, he versified and dictated, and others wrote down the verses." The great *Mathnavi*, consisting of some twenty-seven thousand couplets, was also dictated in more or less the same fashion to Rumi's friend and disciple Hosām al-Din. Sometimes they would spend entire nights with Rumi dictating and Hosām al-Din writing at a furious pace, chanting it all as he transcribed. Virtually all of Rumi's poetry was reportedly composed this way, or while doing the *samā'*, as an amanuensis called *kāteb al-asrār* (scribe of secrets) took it down.

It is small wonder that Rumi was given the supreme title, "Mawlana." His reputation rests not only on the spiritual heights he attained in his poetry, but also on having brought the dimension of aesthetics to mysticism in a systematic and comprehensive way. Poetry, music, dance, and the visual arts were integrally combined in the practices of the Mawlavi order. Not only the synesthesia of the verbal, musical, and visual mediums, but more comprehensively, the unified use of

---

[3]His coffin is in the city of Konya not far from the Mawlana Mausoleum-Museum.

intellectual, spiritual, and artistic elements constituted the hallmark of Rumi's faith.

Rumi may well be the only major philosopher in history to express and formulate an entire system of thought in verse that has intrinsic merit. This assessment is not merely a converse of Coleridge's statement in *Biographia Literaria*: "No man was ever yet a great poet without at the same time being a profound philosopher." Taken together, the *Mathnavi* and the *Divān-e kabir* represent perhaps the world's most resourceful synthesis of poetry and philosophy, embracing the lyric, narrative, epic, didactic, epigrammatic, satiric, and elegiac forms. Two other comparable achievements come to mind: *De Rerum Natura* by Lucretius and the *Divina Commedia* by Dante. Rumi's poetry is superior to *De Rerum Natura,* and his philosophy is, in many respects, more effectively articulated in substance and structure than the *Divina Commedia.* In a way, the *Mathnavi* is a forerunner of Dante's work. Dante's own description of the *Divina Commedia* is essentially applicable to the *Mathnavi*: "The poem belongs to a moral or ethical branch of philosophy, its quality is not speculative but practical, and its ultimate end is to lead into the state of felicity those now enduring the miserable life of man." Significantly, the norms of humanism that characterize the work of both poets appeared first in the Muslim mystic: at Rumi's death, Dante was only eight years old. Petrarch came a full century later, and Erasmus lived two and a half centuries later. Rumi's *Divān-e Shams* could be considered the first major "sonnet sequence" in world literature, antedating both Petrarch and Shakespeare.[4]

[4]Ironically very few surveys of humanism, of world literature, or of histories of civilization so much as cite Rumi's name. His poetry is included in very few anthologies of world poetry. Most encyclopedias give him only cursory comments or a few paragraphs at best.

The fault lies partly with Middle Eastern scholars themselves. They have long been suffering from an acute feeling of inferiority about their own culture, religious or national. They have over-admired and over-acquired the cultural norms and values of the West to the denigration of their own indigenous heritage. Those who are tradition-bound often remain reactionary. Yet, few have effectively interpreted the philosophy, the arts, and the poetry of the Middle East for the benefit of the world. Anthologies of world literature and histories of the world will, consequently, underplay or sometimes bypass the Muslim world. Rumi is a victim of the same phenomenon.

Part of the reason, however, is that Rumi's poetry has not been fortunate enough to have translators of the caliber of Edward FitzGerald, whose translation of 'Omar Khayyām is perhaps the best-known example of Persian poetry in the West. His English translators are "nineteenth-century gentlemen" chronologically or aesthetically: well-meaning, diligent, often meticulous poetasters who could find rhymes, squeeze lines into meters, and squeeze all life out of poetry. In their hands, adept at archaisms and exoticisms, a great disservice has been perpetrated against Rumi's poetry. Even his best translator, Reynold A. Nicholson, could write such monstrosities as "If so be that thou throwest a glance upon [aught in] the two worlds, do not so," which was bad style even

Rumi's poetry is a vast geography of many climates and seasonal changes. It embodies the aesthetics of ethics and metaphysics. His *Mathnavi* makes a monumental synthesis of mystic ideas ranging from Neoplatonism to Chinese thought, embracing Indian, Persian, and Greek mythology, stories from the holy books, Arab and Persian legends and folk stories; it provides a schema or even a system of philosophy, insights into psychology and the laws of physics and logic, *lumina ingeni*. Regrettably, many scholars have denuded or numbed Rumi's poetry while trying to explain his philosophy. Yet, unlike most of the works of ancient philosophy, including those of the Muslim mystics, Rumi's works are stimulating reading. As Hegel writes at the end of his *Encyclopedia,* in exploring God as absolute mind, "if we want to see the consciousness of the One . . . in its finest purity and sublimity," we cannot do better than to read Rumi's verses. There is always an excitement, a revelation, passions raging or exquisitely controlled, a symmetry of ecstasy, an order of divine madness. Rumi achieved, as Homer had done, the ultimate, the near-perfect work of his own genre. Certainly, no mystic poet has surpassed him in the seven centuries since his death.

The academy of Rumi, whose mysticism was syncretic (combining many Islamic, Arabic, Persian, Turkish, Indian as well as Neoplatonic influences), was not unlike Aristotle's lyceum. It was a sanctuary for humanism where a whole spectrum of ideas was discussed freely, with tolerance, without malice. In it, souls capable of creative surges experienced ecstasy. There, art was Godliness, poetry the word of love and faith, dance the circle of joy. Rumi was obviously right when he said about himself:

The whole wide world has yet to see
The wine that moves me to ecstasy.

He took pride in the new dimensions of mysticism he introduced:

The vendors of old goods are gone. We are
The new vendors, this is our bazaar.

in the nineteenth century. As recently as 1956, Sir Colin Garbett published such gems as "Yestreen unto a star I cried / To thee my words I trust," and "Forth shalt thou tread / And thy two feet shalt shed." A highly respected scholar of Arabic and Persian literatures, A. J. Arberry, has also tried his hand at translation. Among his versions of Rumi's quatrains, published in 1949, there are such grotesque inversions as "His music when he played / Me clapping hands He made."

He viewed conventional religious tenets and institutions as restrictions on intellectual independence and the freedom of conscience. For him, orthodoxy was inimical to true faith. He denounced it in vehement terms in a *robāʿi*:

Unless the seminaries and the minarets perish,
The wandering dervish can reach no state he can cherish.
Unless faith becomes disbelief and disbelief is faith,
No vassal of God will be a true Muslim and flourish.

He stressed the supremacy of love over formal religion:

Only fools praise and glorify the mosque
While they oppress hearts full of love and faith.

\* \* \*

Beyond belief and faithlessness there lies the space
In whose heartland this love of ours has found its place:
It holds no room for religion and sacrilege—
That's the ground where the man of wisdom rubs his face.

In Rumi's eyes, the conventions of religion inflicted pain on the people:

The holy month: The people are bewildered and in pain.
Why beat the drums? You can see it with your own eyes, it's plain.
The drums make all that clamor—like the outcry of evil.
The Lord is deaf, that's why the drums blast again and again.

No poetry is more imbued with sorrow and spiritual exile than is mystic poetry. The agony of the mystic is separation from God. But in Rumi's vision there is no place for the abysmal fallacy which, in the dogma, segregates God and human beings. His monistic Sufism holds that humanity is not only God's creation, but also God's reflection. This image, the human manifestation of God, has temporarily fallen apart from Him. Mystics always suffer from separation from the loved one, from God who is the ultimate Beloved. Theirs is a sublime love which remains unrequited until they suffer so intensely in their spiritual exile that they finally reach a blissful state of the submergence of self, the death of ego.

The mystic search for God has three stages: purification, enlightenment, and union. The Sufis must abandon all physical appetites, guide themselves to the elevation that love makes possible, and finally merge their souls into God's reality. Rumi distilled this progress into just a few words:

> Since we have passed
> The night of the flesh at last,
> We are ourselves the Guide
> And life's immortal tide.
>                    (tr. A. J. Arberry)

This spiritual triumph gives the mystic soul God-like powers:

> Such is my life, though I came into the world yesterday,
> Today I have built anew this whole crumbling world.

After the long, arduous search for God ends, the mystic has the strength to destroy temporal political power:

> I drip out of a spout drop by drop—
> But like the deluge I crush myriad palaces.

The Sufi spirit triumphs in giving joy, in creativity:

> We have a soul that creates so many joys,
> If the world crumbles we would build a new one.

According to Sufism, true love renders life supreme, victorious over crass existence, transcending the confines of material life. Rumi's vision affirms that *amor vincit omnia,* "love conquers all." One of his *robā'is* declares:

> As salt resolved in the ocean
> I was swallowed in God's sea,
> Past faith, past unbelieving,
> Past doubt, past certainty.
>
> Suddenly in my bosom
> A star shone clear and bright;

All the suns of heaven
Vanished in that star's light.
          (tr. A. J. Arberry)

Mystic pain nurtures and validates faith and optimism:

Even if the world is covered with thorns all over
The lover's heart is still a rose-garden.

Love leads the Sufi to the spring of godly life. Rumi beckoned that
spring, that terrestrial and celestial paradise, in beautiful words:

Dark is the flesh, as raven's wing,
And cold the world as wintry day:
Darkness and cold! But come, spring,
And drive these sadnesses away.
          (tr. A. J. Arberry)

Rumi hopes and prays that everyone will share in the joy of love:

Let each soul find a ladder up to the skies of joy,
Let no one's back be arched like the sky because of sorrow.

One of his most subtle *robā'is* evokes the mystery of spiritual elevation beyond the proverbial spring. But only a unique soul is capable
of it—a single branch among all the trees:

This season is not the spring, it is some other season,
The languid trances in the eyes have a different reason,
And there is another cause for the way each single branch
Dallies by itself while all the trees sway in unison.

And there is nothing like the exuberance of the mystic:

Perfect, perfect, perfect
This love is three times perfect;
Empty, empty, empty
This flesh and its lusts.
          (tr. A. J. Arberry)

The following poem certainly ranks as one of the best love poems in any language:

This is Love: to fly heavenward,
To rend, every instant, a hundred veils.
The first moment, to renounce life;
The last step, to fare without feet.
To regard this world as invisible,
Not to see what appears to one's self.
"O heart," I said, "may it bless thee
To have entered the circle of lovers,
To look beyond the range of the eye,
To penetrate the windings of the bosom!"
                      (tr. R. A. Nicholson)

In Rumi's vision, the depth of the heart is God. Reason is pitiful compared with love: "The madman of love is above all reason," and "The thrones of the sultans, pitted against love, are pieces of wood." In purifying themselves, the mystics divest themselves of earthly appetites: "The road is far from lust to love."

One of his quatrains expresses the outburst of love out of tranquillity:

Every night flowers blossom in the sky,
The universe is at peace, so am I.
Then hundreds of sighs break out in my heart
Where in cold darkness flames rise with each sigh.

Love is the antithesis or even the negation of despair and death:

Old winter's reign of death is undone,
Regret is dead; love lives again.

Love's quintessential glory found eloquent expression in lines such as, "Love is the sultan of sultans: Both worlds bow at his feet," "In the sect of love, there is neither faith nor sacrilege," "Love has no body, no mind, no heart, no soul," "Love lies out of the reach of dogma," "The light that reason sheds is a false dawn. The dawn's real beauty can be seen not by the eye, but by the heart."

Love, according to Rumi, gives the mystic access to all time and space: "I am a drop that is both a drop and the vast sea." He proudly asserts about love:

Its glory in my soul
Is as a sea profound
And in that sea is all
The world of Being drowned.
(tr. A. J. Arberry)

In a superb quatrain, he sees love as all-embracing, and his friend—a reference to both a beloved human and God—as absolute bliss:

So long as I am alive, love enlivens each day.
I am not a hunter, but this is my cherished prey.
This is my moment, my epoch, my stand through time,
My heart's calm, my peace, my friend who ends all dismay.

Rumi conceived of love as the be-all and the end-all, complete in itself, absolute in value:

Love needs only love to declare itself
As the sun needs just the sun to bare itself.

For him, love is the paramount component of mystic theology:

The religion of love is apart from all religions;
The lovers of God have no religion but God alone.

Rumi was a man of passionate mind, as he expressed it in two eloquent lines:

What miraculous worlds roll within the vast,
The all-embracing ocean of the Mind!
(tr. R. A. Nicholson)

He combined in himself the three souls—sensual, rational, and transcendental, which can also be called animal, cerebral, and inspirational. His mystic life was based on total individualism, the integral or comprehensive personality, the "self" inclusive of God:

Wisdom is light for each step;
Feeling is a sun throughout the road;
Conscience is a voice wide as the horizons.

Rumi's subjectivity, which embodies the pride of "I am not the bone,
but the marrow," finds its cogent echoes in Ludwig Feuerbach's statement: "God is the highest subjectivity of man abstracted from himself.
The essential predicates of divinity, such as personality and love, are
simply the human qualities men evaluate most highly." Yet Rumi believes that love unifies all beings: "There are hundreds of thousands
of bodies, but only one soul."

Love, according to Rumi, is the ultimate transcendence of human
consciousness—analytical and rational, intuitive and holistic, but
above all devotional and passionate. In a remarkable poem, he bursts
out with the power of love:

If you were patience, I would tear off the veil,
If you were sleep, I would wake the dead,
If you were a mountain, I would consume it with flames,
If you were an ocean, I would drink you down.

In mystic morality, both sin and virtue are transcended. In fact, they
are rendered practically meaningless by love's supreme power:

I saw all those people who were the slaves of the world,
I felt true love—and the whole world became my slave.

Such a sense of triumph, arising from the mystic struggle for perfection, celebrates the human being as an image of God:

Marvellous is the human being,
Strangely wrought in every part,
Made of dust by the creator,
Masterpiece of perfect art.
(tr. A. J. Arberry)

For Rumi, life and the universe were in a state of constant flux, a
continuing metamorphosis, a dynamic renewal. He promised the
faithful that he would recreate them:

Come, come, you will never find a friend like me.
Where's a beloved like me in all the world?
Come, don't waste your life running back and forth.
You are like a dry valley, I am the rain.
You are a city laid waste, I am the architect.
Come!

In his invitation to the mystics, he pledged fulfillment and bliss:

Live in love's ecstasy, for love is all that exists.

The absence of loved ones, the separation from God who is the
ultimate and the perfect Beloved, gave the mystics their tragic existence. The *nāy*, the traditional reed flute, with its sad, soul-piercing
strains, expresses the mystic's yearning to return to beloved God. The
opening couplets of the *Mathnavi* capture the reed's moaning:

Listen to the reed, how it tells its tales;
Bemoaning its bitter exile, it wails:

Ever since I was torn from the reed beds,
My cries tear men's and women's hearts to shreds.

Let this separation slit my sad breast
So I can reveal my longing and quest.

Everyone is my friend for his own part,
Yet none can know the secrets of my heart.

The flames of love make the reed's voice divine;
It is love's passion that rages in the wine.

The reed cries with the lovers who fell apart,
It rends the chest and tears open the heart.

Nothing kills or cures the soul like the reed;
Nothing can crave or console like the reed.

The search for ecstasy, for love, for God is the soul's noble thrust
and eventual triumph. Rumi described the soaring spirit of the dervish
as the falcon flying toward God: its most eloquent expressions are
poetry, music, and the *samā'*, which embodies the unquenchable quest
for beauty and perfection. It has no arrival, but the noblest aspiration:

Songs are only a branch of the soul that yearns for union
The branch and the root are never one and the same.

Music and dance in mystic rites were among Rumi's impressive innovations. When asked why he used music and dance even on such solemn occasions as a funeral, he replied: "When the human spirit, after years of imprisonment in the cage and dungeon of the body, is at last set free and wings its flight to the source from where it came, isn't this occasion for rejoicing and thanks and dancing?" He expressed this rejoicing in many poems:

> While the spirit's sun
> Shines gleaming bright,
> Like a note, the mystic
> Dances with delight.
> (tr. A. J. Arberry)

His son Soltān Valad wrote of Rumi's passionate fondness for *samā'*:

> Music and dance were his abiding interest;
> Day or night, he would celebrate and never rest.
> He turned from traditional faith to poesy;
> An ascetic at first, he found love's ecstasy.

Rumi's poetry revels in psychological and philosophical affirmation. He does not seek or crave inner peace. He stresses the primacy of vibrant passion and transcendent ecstasy. Repose or tranquillity are not objectives for him, but rather a subdued, subtle color in the spiritual spectrum. His is the supreme combination of Dionysian rapture and Apollonian dignity:

> My dusty body
> Is heaven's light;
> Angels are jealous
> To watch my flight.
>
> Cherubim envy
> My purity
> Before my valor
> All demons flee.
> (tr. A. J. Arberry)

When he invited the mystics to his congregation place in Konya ("This place is the Ka'ba for lovers / Whoever comes half, leaves full"), he offered them divine music:

They say the reed and the lute that charm our ears
Derive their melody from rolling spheres;
But faith that transcends imagination's bounds
Can see what sweetens all the jangled sounds.

We, who are parts of Adam, heard with him
The song of angels and seraphim.
Our memory, though dull and sad, retains
Some echo still of those unearthly strains.

O, music is the food of souls who love,
Music uplifts our spirit to realms above.
The ashes glow, the latent fires increase:
We listen and are fed with joy and peace.
(tr. R. A. Nicholson)

The *samā'*, often called *āyin-e sharif* (the blessed ceremony), is an aesthetic sight and experience as well as the mind's passionate thrust. The musicians and singers create an aura of spirituality, of divine poetry, but not before the *jānhā* (the "souls," meaning the true mystics) have discussed philosophical concepts, mystical and artistic values, telling Mawlavi stories and interlarding their talks with gracious humor. When the dervishes start to whirl rhythmically, their figures, robed in the spare and impeccable *tanura*s (skirts), are dynamic and dignified, like living statues. Each motion, each gesture has a divine significance. The sudden turns are an attempt to see God in all directions. Thumping the ground symbolizes trampling crass selfhood, crushing egotism. Jumping signifies the desire to soar toward the supreme world. Genuflection is the ultimate expression of abandoning one's soul to God. Opening the arms to the sides is the aspiration to spiritual excellence, the soul's balance, union with God, and eternal bliss. The right arm points heavenward, to God; the left arm down to the earth. This way, the whirling dervish expresses his faith in the world as well as his dream of the beloved Providence. The symbolism has been articulated as follows: "We receive from God, we give out to the people. We never keep any possessions. We soar to the sky, we pour on the ground. Our souls are on the way to God's mercy."

Although a dithyrambic ritual, the *samā'* has no indignity, no obscenity. No Sufi touches another. Sensuality is a private privilege. The "dance" itself is communal, not solitary. In seeking ecstasy, each Sufi is an integral person, purifying the soul, summoning all the passions, having communion with God, without any intermediaries—each person is a world unto himself or herself. As Rumi states it: "Listening to beautiful sounds, one finds peace of heart and achieves union with God." In all the outward serenity and inner exuberance during the *samā'*, the mystics strive to arrive at a state of ecstasy which gives them a glimpse of God:

> What nurtures our soul is the whirling dance
> Where the loved one emerges in our trance.

Rumi referred to this spiritual elevation and passionate excitement as a creative surge, as divine inspiration: "The madman of love is above all reason." Antedating Emily Dickinson's "Much madness is divinest sense" by more than six centuries, he wrote: "The mind's supreme strength is the secret of madness." Yet, he also stressed the sublimity of the passion of *samā'*: "*Samā'* is where the souls of lovers come to rest / To him who has another heart in his heart it is known best."

The man of the spirit is also the man of reality. Enamored as he was of flights of mystic fantasy, Rumi remained involved in the welfare of the people of his city, in social justice, in affairs of the state. That is why he was Mawlana (guide, lord, master) not only for his disciples but also for the laity. He denigrated temporal power:

> Be the slave of someone whose heart glitters
> Instead of wearing the crown of the sultans.

In a memorable couplet, he posited the worthlessness of public office:

> Lordship is hardly worth the pain of being deposed;
> You might enjoy it for a day, but you'll shudder for a century.

He maintained that his spiritual power is superior to royalty:

> I am not one of those kings who must step down
> From the throne to take the ride in a coffin.

Rumi, according to legend, sometimes defied and took to task an unjust sultan or vizier. Once, when the sultan sought his guidance, he answered scathingly: "What could I possibly tell you? They expected you to be the shepherd. Yet you are the wolf. They wanted you to be the guard. You turned out to be the thief."

The opening lines of his *Fihi mā fihi,* a work in prose, proclaim the scholar's independence from political power. Elaborating on a *hadith* (tradition) of the Prophet, Rumi asserts: "The deplorable scholar is the one who receives assistance, support and strength from the lords. He is the worst who does his scholarship with the anticipation of hand-outs, of respect, of position and with the fear of the lords." Because he would never compromise his intellectual sovereignty, Rumi reportedly lived and died a man without acquisitions or assets. He expressed his pride over this, according to the *Manāqeb al-'ārefin* (Virtues of the saints) by the fourteenth-century biographer Aflāki, to none other than the mighty Grand Vizier Parvāna. At an official dinner that Rumi attended, a bowl of rice and a purse containing gold coins were placed before him on Parvāna's orders. The Sufi leader contemptuously rejected the grant and recited the following couplet to the grand vizier and his retinue:

Thank God, I have no desire for delicacies or sweets;
I find no value in a purse of gold or a golden bowl.

He spurned all material pleasures and gains. For the mystic who triumphed by divesting himself of worldly possessions, poverty was a matter of pride:

Poverty is heart's ease
All else is the soul's disease.

Poverty is the sole
Treasure, and spirit's goal.
(tr. A. J. Arberry)

For Rumi, the "good man is he who serves the people." He detests the praise and the panegyrics offered to unjust rulers: "If you so much as try to extol an evil man, God's lofty spheres convulse." In a remarkable *ghazal,* he vents his fury on kings who oppress the poor people:

I am such a dark night that I am angry at the moon;
I am such a stark naked pauper that I am angry at the sultan.

They try to deceive me with gold or high station or troops;
I want no gold, no matter what, I am angry at power and position.

He advised the rulers to avoid being "a burden on the people" and "to march free like a horse instead of being a carcass that the people must carry on their backs."

Rumi gave women an exalted place: "Woman is not a creature, but creator." In the Mawlavi movement, women almost always found acceptance and fulfillment as full-fledged participants. Particularly at the time of Awliyā' Chelebi, who was Soltan Valad's son and Rumi's grandson, they took part in the ceremonies and the *samā'*.

Rumi's writings are full of criticism leveled at arrogant lords, rulers who take bribes, officials who scorn the people, merchants who cheat their customers; they also contain painful depictions of cities destroyed and villages ruined, severed heads, children stoning madmen, hunger and famine. He often advocated the principles of social justice, made references to communality of property, and stood against dogmatic formalism. For him, a theft committed by a person oppressed by poverty was a lesser crime than one committed by oppressors who keep the people in abject poverty. Once a burglar stole a valuable rug from Rumi's school. The burglar was later caught and brought before Rumi, who said: "He must have stolen because of need," and bought the rug from the burglar.

In Mawlavi ethics, intellectual achievement and enlightenment play a focal role. Love and intellect, for Rumi, are complements of each other, and their absence is often closely linked to injustice and evil: "When weapons and ignorance come together, pharaohs arise to devastate the world with their cruelty."

Rumi spoke out against conformism, loveless doctrine, the preachers and defenders of the narrowest strictures, and fanatics hell-bent to reduce religion to austere, joyless, stultifying vacuities. When criticized for his use of song in the Mawlavi ceremony, he retorted: "The song in the *samā'* is like faith in prayers." Sayyed Sharaf al-Din, a dogmatist, once took Rumi to task for having said, "From the *viola d'amore* we hear the tunes of the gate of Paradise," and added that he also hears tunes but they have no such effect on him. Rumi reportedly gave the following satirical reply: "Of course. We hear from the *viola d'amore* the tunes of the opening of the gate of Paradise. He hears the sounds of the closing." The mystic leader also stressed the vital importance of feeling in science and scholarship: "Only if they enlighten the heart and transform a man into a person of feelings can science and scholarship yield benefits. If they affect only our physical being without exalting the spirit, they are just a burden."

It is said that Rumi, who was not known to have had much interest in poetry earlier, took up verse as his major intellectual vehicle after meeting Shams-e Tabrizi, and alternately, that he did so to please his circle of colleagues and disciples. According to a third theory, he found poetry essential to disseminate his ideas to the larger community, which had a penchant for verse. Regardless of the basic motivation, the fact remains that Rumi started composing poetry at the age of thirty-seven and that in the period of about thirty years until his death, he produced a corpus of verse which is extraordinary in both quantity and quality. In his prose work *Fihi mā fihi* he referred to poetry as a means rather than an end, since his purpose was to instruct and inspire. Inasmuch as it was often ecstasy that prevailed in his poems, the prosody and the rhymes seemed to be of secondary importance. Sometimes he openly complained about the stringencies of classical meters and the straitjacket of stanzaic forms. Formal devices, in his view, were restrictive—even the words themselves fell short of transcendent significance:

Eternal King, from whose couplets and odes I am set free,
Pentameters and tetrameters had nearly murdered me.
The flood took away all those deceiving rhymes in one thrust,
Leaving them to lesser poets whose heads have a thick crust.

He praised the supremacy of feeling, passion and love over form:

I sit around racking my brains to find this or that rhyme.
My loved one tells me: "You should think of my face all the time."
We are together now, relax; these rhymes have no value.
I find the rhyme and reason of the happy state in you.

In one poem, he traces his progress from consuming love to the renunciation of dogma and rational life to the poetic arts:

When the flames of love for which I had yearned
Struck my breast and all love in my heart burned,
The mind, the school, the books became things I spurned—
And then, to verses and rhymes I turned.

Regardless of such protestations, poetry served for him as the embodiment of philosophical experience, the supreme fiction, the transcendent reality. Like mystic love, it was conceived of by Rumi as its own perfection—the perfection of the ideal. His best verses conform to the famous dictum of Archibald MacLeish: "a poem should not mean / but be." Rumi's poetry has not only profound meanings but also a concrete and impressive structural existence beyond mere form.

Heightened by effusive lyricism, combining high classical style with the vernacular, his language is rich in abstractions as well as objective and concrete statements, interlarded with folk sayings and proverbs. The fervor with which he unfurls his mystic passions safeguards his poems from the dry didacticism that characterizes so much other mystical writing.

His poetic art is truly Platonic, but it goes far beyond the Platonic norms and concepts: with its *furor poeticus,* it is the poetry of inspiration *par excellence.* It is poetry as hermetic symbolism at its best, with a marvelous coherence of myths, images, metaphors, and the interaction of the occult, the obscure, the concrete, and the worldly. It is poetry as instruction of supreme values—good, beautiful, true—that are all aspects and attributes of love and of God. It is also *mimesis,* the highest form of imitation, whereby the poet seeks to simulate, and to emulate, the divine archetype. Rumi's poetry embraces all of these categories and creates a norm which evokes Shelley's words: "Poetry is the center and circumference of all knowledge."

Ultimately poetry and love became identical and mutually inclusive in Rumi's mysticism. In his verse we find his encompassing visions of life and death, and his ethical concepts. Peace, in his view, was a focal virtue to be nurtured and defended for the individual and the community. In his lifetime he witnessed the ravages of the Mongol invasion and the Crusades. One of his most eloquent couplets proclaims:

Whatever you think of war, I am far, far from it;
Whatever you think of love, I am that, only that, all that.

It is love and the true lover that live the everlasting life. That is why Rumi invited lovers to join the magnificent exodus:

O lovers, lovers!
This is the time of exodus from the world.
In my heart's ear rumble
The huge drums of the great migration.

The mystic, according to him, "dies and returns to life every instant." That is why he asserts: "You have a deathless soul. Why on earth are you afraid of death? / You possess the light of God. How can you fit into a grave?" The real death, the abject death is "when the heart falls asleep." For the heart that remains awake in love, death is nothing more than blissful silence, the eloquent quiet. The Mawlavis refer to the "dead" dervishes merely as *khāmushān* (the quiet ones). Rumi's words on the eve of his death are an affirmation of continuing life: "Light is about to reunite with Light. I stripped myself of selfhood, and He stripped himself of his image. I am now teetering at the edge of the Land of Reunion." His poems often evoke the immortality achieved by love:

> If I should die
> I bid you carry me
> To where my love might lie
> There let me be.
>
> And if she would give
> My cold lips just one kiss,
> Believe me, I would live
> Again by this.
> (tr. A. J. Arberry)

The night of Rumi's death, commemorated on 17 December each year at Konya, is called *Sheb-e 'Arus* (Wedding night):

> Death is reunion with God:
> The night of my death
> Will be a bridal night,
> The nuptial with supreme love.

In Rumi's vision, death was the ultimate triumph:

> When my coffin starts its journey to the grave
> Don't think I am unhappy to leave this world.
> When you lower me into the pit, don't weep
> Because that is a curtain behind which lies
> Peaceful Paradise.

Rumi's funeral occasioned the saddest *samā'* Konya had seen; the city had lost its great spiritual guide, and Anatolia one of its dazzling cultural figures. It was at the same time the most joyous, because the greatest mystic of them all had at last reached his beloved God. Not only were Muslims crying at the funeral, but Christians, Jews, Greeks, and Armenians as well—people of different creeds, languages, ethnic origins. They had come to revere him as their own, because he had revered them and their prophets as his own. He symbolized, as he continues to do, the unity of humankind. "There are," he said, "hundreds of thousands of bodies—but only one Soul." Rumi himself did not initiate the Mawlavi order. It was founded in his name after his death by his son Soltān Valad and some of his disciples. Bemoaning rifts and enmities, Rumi called for peace, for a united world transcending schisms, for love of humanity and love of God.

Rumi had a humanist, universalist, humanitarian vision: "I am," he declared, "a temple for all people."

Like a compass I stand firm with one leg on my faith
And roam with the other leg all over the seventy-two nations.

Seventy-two nations hear of their secrets from us;
We are the reed whose song unites all nations and faiths.

Regrettably, no scholar has made a study of Rumi's humanism. His mausoleum, which has come to be known as "the stronghold of the lovers," even today inspires tens of thousands of visitors of many faiths. They find in the "Green Dome" a vast heritage of spiritual splendor, an overwhelming aesthetic delight, and an engrossing, humanistic ethic. One of his famous *robā'is* invites all human beings, regardless of creed, ethnic background, social status, or nationality, to his shrine:

Come, come again, whoever, whatever you may be, come:
Heathen, fire-worshiper, sinful of idolatry, come.
Come even if you broke your penitence a hundred times,
Ours is not the portal of despair or misery, come.

Proclaiming that "my faith and my nation are God," Rumi made a plea for universalism in a world torn asunder by conflicting ideologies, sectarian divisions, religious strife, jingoistic nationalism. One of his universalist statements is remarkable for its age: "Hindus, Kipchaks, Anatolians, Ethiopians—they all lie peacefully in their graves, separately, yet the same color." "The Sultan of Lovers" also wrote one of the most eloquent lines of ecumenism:

In all mosques, temples, churches I find one shrine alone.

Rumi has been claimed by several countries and cultures—Iran, Turkey, Afghanistan, the Arabs, and the Muslim communities of the Soviet Union—on grounds of genealogy, birthplace, language, cultural orientation, adopted country, burial place, or territory of impact. The strongest claims are advanced by Iran and Turkey, with considerable justification. Yet a close scrutiny of biographical and other historical documents support few of these claims in any convincing way. The internal references found in his work show that Rumi wanted no "national" identification of "citizenship" in terms of our modern concepts and definitions. He sought, rather, to belong to humanity and to transcend religious schisms and national allegiances. His mystic spirit can and must be claimed not by one country, one culture, one religion, but by all people.

# 12. The Genius of Shiraz: Sa'di and Hāfez

## Sa'di, the Master of Love Poetry

"We have almost enough of Hāfez's songs—Sa'di has been more useful for us," wrote the German poet and educator Johann Gottfried Herder toward the end of the eighteenth century. As this brief remark shows, the names of the two great poets of Shiraz were well known in Germany by the end of the eighteenth century, and in fact, they were to remain favorites of the German reading public in the century to come—and much more so than 'Omar Khayyām, whose real kingdom is the English-speaking world.

Sa'di's *Golestān*, a collection of entertaining anecdotes and aphorisms in rhymed prose sprinkled with verse, was among the first works ever translated from an Oriental language into German. There was an abridged French version available in the early seventeenth century (André du Ryer, 1634), which in turn was rendered into German and influenced some entertaining literature; then, in 1651, the German scholar Georg Gentius offered a Latin version. But the truly successful adaptation of this delightful book was produced by Adam Olearius, a member of the German embassy that came from Schleswig-Holstein to Iran (1633–39) in the hope of fostering trade relations, but sadly failed. However, the treasure that the members of the ill-fated expedition brought home was more important than trade goods: it was a number of Persian manuscripts, and Olearius, a noted poet himself, was able to render the *Golestān* into a fluent, enjoyable German style with "the help of an Old Persian by the name of Hakwirdi."

This translation, decorated with many engravings, was published in 1654, and together with the adaptations that followed, it largely shaped the European image of Persian literature during the seventeenth and eighteenth centuries. As can be understood from Herder's admiring words, it was highly appreciated by the intellectuals: Sa'di, "the pleasant teacher of morals," as he says, "seems to have plucked the flower of moralizing poetry in his language . . . as his poetry was and still is regarded as a rose of the Persian tongue." His simple but elegant style, his practical wisdom, his charming anecdotes made him a poet who appealed greatly to the Europeans, especially during the Age of Reason, and he has rightly been considered the Persian poet whose work is easiest for Westerners to understand. "His genius is less alien to the West than that of others, his imagination less overbearing," as Joseph von Hammer-Purgstall wrote in 1818, and this indefatigable Austrian orientalist chose two of Sa'di's verses to be engraved on his tombstone (1856).

In spite of all the admiration expressed for the author, little was, and still is, known about Sa'di's life, for we no longer assume that his biography can be reconstructed from his works. Most scholars supposed that Mosleh al-Din 'Abdallāh was born in the late twelfth century in Shiraz, but Jan Rypka and Arthur J. Arberry have pleaded for a birth date around 1210. That sounds more plausible for the date of his death, 1292. Although saintly and pious people in the Middle East have often lived to a ripe old age of more than a hundred years, a birth date that makes him about eighty years old at the time of his death seems to be more acceptable.

Sa'di's lifetime falls in a period of major political and social changes in Iran and the whole Middle East. The Abbasid caliphate in Baghdad was weak, and the countries around it had become more or less independent, though they were still nominally under the caliph's rule. Shiraz, where the poet was born, was ruled during the earlier part of Sa'di's life by Abu Bakr b. Sa'd the Salghurid (r. 1226–60), who was wise enough not to resist the Mongol attack and thus avoided the complete destruction of the city. It was during the last years of Abu Bakr's reign that Sa'di returned to his native town from long journeys. He had performed the pilgrimage and may have traveled to other parts of the world as well, although one has to take with a grain of salt the stories in which he boasts of his adventures in faraway places: he speaks of his visit to Kāshghar and claims to have killed one of the guards in the Hindu temple of Somnath in Kathiawar. One of his nicest so-called autobiographical stories is found in the *Golestān* (II, 31): he was imprisoned by the Crusaders and had to dig trenches in Tripoli until a Muslim merchant bought and freed him; but then his previous form of slavery was replaced by a worse one, since he had to marry his benefactor's daughter. . . .

One usually assumes that Sa'di traveled for some thirty years. During this period he had truly become a *jahāndida*, someone who had seen and experienced the world. It was these experiences and his gift of acute observation, combined with a delightful, lively style, that made him such a wonderful storyteller. He showed this talent after his return to Shiraz about 1256. In the following year he dedicated his *Bustān,* a book on moral virtues in the form of moralizing anecdotes in verse, to Abu Bakr b. Sa'd, and in the next year completed the *Golestān.* That was in the year 1258, when the Mongols brought death

and destruction to the Middle East, ruining Baghdad, the capital of
the Islamic world, and killing the last Abbasid caliph. But the *Golestān*
does not reflect the terrors of the time; it is perfectly measured and
exudes wise serenity, as if the Mongols were not destroying large parts
of Iran and the Muslim East. It was perhaps this serenity of Sa'di
which, in a certain way, inspired the German poet Goethe to migrate
spiritually to the "peaceful East" some 650 years later, at a time when
Europe was shattered by the Napoleonic wars and, afterward, the war
of freedom in Germany. At that point, Persian poetry became
Goethe's consolation, and Sa'di's verse was among the sources that
inspired him, just as it may have consoled some of the poet's contemporaries hundreds of years earlier.

Abu Bakr b. Sa'd died in 1260. His son Sa'd, who had stayed in
Baghdad, succeeded him but died a few days later on his way home.
Sa'di's elegy for him is one of his finest *qasidas*, expressing his deeply
felt grief in exquisite wording, with the recurrent line:

> I do not know what news the letter brings—
> But I found blood on its title page . . .

He was right to deplore the end of the Sa'dite dynasty (in whose honor
he had probably assumed his nom de plume, Sa'di), for a time of
confusion and trouble followed, and finally Shiraz became a Mongol
province in 1286. Sa'di continued writing poetry till at least 1281—
the time of the last datable poem. Although he tended to the way of
the Sufis, he was on good terms with the most influential official of
his time, the *sāheb-e divān* Shams al-Din Jovayni, to whom he dedicated
his *Sāheb-nāma,* which contains both encomia and practical advice for
the politician. When he died in 1292, he was buried in the convent
where he spent his later years. His tomb fell to ruins, and the German
traveler Engelbert Kaempfer noted with regret its desolated state when
he visited Shiraz in 1683. The art-loving Karim Khan Zand had the
mausoleum repaired in the mid-eighteenth century, but this new
structure also slowly crumbled; finally a radiant turquoise-colored
building was erected to mark the last resting place of the great son of
Shiraz.

In East and West, Sa'di is known best for his *Golestān,* a book that
was used traditionally as an introduction to Persian language and
literature. It is, as the poet himself claims in his introduction, a garden
whose leaves are not carried away by the autumnal storms and whose
eternal spring cannot be destroyed by the turning of time. Indeed,

his *Golestān* has survived all the gardens of Shiraz and still seems to resemble a charming terrace of flowers. It is divided, like a true Persian garden, into eight parts (eight being the perfect number of paradisiacal bliss, corresponding to the eight gates of Paradise). Each chapter describes human situations and depicts in anecdotes, intermingled with verse, the behavior of kings or beggars, of lovers or sages, during days of youth and old age. The stories do not offer inflexible ethical rules but, rather, guidelines that teach the readers to behave in such a way as is advisable and practical in a given situation, so that they may apply the relevant rules to their own situations. The book looks easy at first sight, but on closer inspection one discovers the refined rhetorical art: the interior rhythm of the sentences and the fine balance between prose and poetry, the elegant puns that are barely audible to the untutored ear. All these are qualities that have made the *Golestān* a favorite of Persian readers. "Aphorisms and jokes, legends and anecdotes, now serious and sensible, now frivolous and witty, but always entertaining and pleasing"—that is how Hans Heinrich Schaeder characterizes this work, which, as he rightly states, is a true mirror of Persian character.

Numerous commentaries have been written on the *Golestān* as well as the *Bustān,* not only in Iran but even more in Turkey (Sham'i, Sudi, Soruri in the sixteenth century) and in India. Turkish translations of both works appeared as early as the late fourteenth century, and in later times there were versions of the *Golestān* in the various Indian languages such as Urdu and Sindhi, as well as in Pashto. Copies of both works were often penned by the masters of calligraphy and sometimes decorated with miniatures of great beauty. In Europe Sir William Jones, the pioneer of Oriental studies in Britain, recommended the *Golestān,* in his *Grammar of the Persian Language* (1787), as an ideal book for everyone interested in Persian. It is therefore not astonishing that the *Golestān* in particular was imitated by major Persian writers, the most outstanding example being Jāmi's *Bahārestān,* which nonetheless lacks the artistic simplicity and sweetness of the original work. Likewise the clear and simple language of the *Bustān* in the plain meter of *motaqāreb* was easy to remember, and through it many of Sa'di's stories became as familiar as household goods in the Persianate areas.

Western readers usually enjoy the *Golestān* in the numerous translations now available, but they are rarely aware of and able to appreciate another aspect of Sa'di's art, namely the lyrics and panegyrics for which the poet is famed in the world of Persian influence. Some of his *qasidas*—such as the threnody on Sa'd b. Abu Bakr—are masterpieces of powerful imagination and technical perfection; but even more delightful and far more important are his *ghazals*. It is in this field, that is, the writing of sonnet-like love poems, that the historian of literature sees Sa'di's very special role in the development of Persian poetry. Until his time, most poets had expressed erotic or romantic feelings mainly in the introductory parts of their *qasidas*, and had only infrequently sung of their love in independent *ghazals*. No doubt, Sanā'i and 'Attār had used the *ghazal* as a medium to express love: in Sanā'i's case, both worldly and heavenly; with 'Attār, predominantly mystical love. There are other poets as well, such as Anvari, Khāqāni, and Nezāmi, who utilized this short poetical form with its seven to twelve distichs for similar purposes. Nonetheless, it is Sa'di's success in expressing love, joy, and suffering in delightful, soft, undulating phrases that marks the emergence of the *ghazal* as a major form of Persian poetry. Many of his *ghazals* are distinguished by a unity of the underlying theme, which is no longer the case with later poets, such as Hāfez, or with the poets of the Indian style after about 1580.

The classical *ghazal,* of which the supreme examples are those of Rumi, Sa'di, and Hāfez, can best be compared to something like chamber music—it is a form of poetry in which the sound of the words, the elegance and transparency of the phrases lead the reader into an enchanted world where the figures move in perfect harmony. Sa'di was, no doubt, the first to create *ghazals* in this limpid, elegant style and thus set the example for generations to come. To be sure, his contemporary Rumi has also sung hundreds of *ghazals* that express his passion, but his style is so unique, born out of his very personal experience, that it cannot serve as a model, while Sa'di was able to create forms that remained exemplars of lyric poetry. One realizes his very special charm, especially when returning to his verse from the complicated *ghazals* in the Indian style that sometimes resemble enigmas: reading a few *ghazals* by Sa'di, then, conveys a feeling of delight and happiness, like looking at a well-groomed garden on a spring day, or listening to a string quartet by Haydn.

In his poetry Sa'di employs all the vocabulary and imagery that became standard *topoi* in the following centuries: allusions to Koranic expressions and persons, stories taken from the Iranian tradition as collected in Ferdowsi's *Shāh-nāma*. Images from nature, from birds and beasts, flowers and stones, water and sun, moon and clouds are likewise part and parcel of his poetical cosmos. All the typical ingredients of Persian lyrics are skillfully blended in his verse without becoming too involved and without the aim of dazzling the reader, as is the case with many of the later poets. That Sa'di also had a less serious side and was not averse to ribald writing becomes clear from the small collection of his *hazaliyyāt* (*facetiae*). These are not exactly what an eighteenth-century Western reader expected from the author of the *Golestān,* who seemed such a paragon of decent behavior, and quite a few scholars have dismissed the *hazaliyyāt* as wrongly attributed to the poet. However, this type of poetry was quite normal in medieval Iran (as elsewhere), and even Rumi, taking up some of Sanā'i's anecdotes and inventing new ones, now and then offered his readers somewhat off-color stories.

Nonetheless, Sa'di displays in all his works a wisdom and an understanding of the human mind. Many of his lines and aphorisms have therefore become proverbial and are frequently quoted in speech and writing. Typically, even Ralph Waldo Emerson was enchanted by Gladwin's translation of the *Golestān* (1806), and recommended Sa'di to his American readers, comparing his practical wisdom to that of Benjamin Franklin. Sa'di's display of "practical morals" certainly makes his work easier to translate than that of other poets, be they Rumi with his ecstatic verse or Hāfez and his gem-like lyrics. Sa'di's pleasant common sense was gladly accepted everywhere. But at the time that his fame grew in Europe, not many of his admirers asked what lay behind his verse. Did he sing in his *ghazals* of worldly love, or was it divine love, as the Sufis usually do under the veil of mundane imagery? Or was it, as has been claimed lately, political poetry in the guise of love songs? Perhaps all three interpretations are true to a certain degree, as in the case of Hāfez, his great compatriot, for it is the peculiarity of Persian poetry that it oscillates between heavenly and worldly delights and that many images can be understood at different levels. But Sa'di remains the master of love poetry and the greatest stylist that Persia has produced.

## Hāfez, the Supreme Lyricist

While Sa'di's *qasida* and *ghazal* are neatly separated and the content of his lyrics seems to be rather clear, the ambiguity becomes much stronger in the verse of Hāfez, whose fame as the paramount Persian lyrical poet has never been questioned. He too hailed from Shiraz, and it will not be out of place to remember that the city had been the center of a strong Sufi tradition. Sa'di lived, it is told, close to the sanctuary of Ibn Khafif, the famous ascetic who died in 982 and was the last to visit Hallāj in his prison in Baghdad before the martyr mystic was cruelly executed in 922. The Hallajian tradition apparently continued under the surface in Shiraz as it did in northeastern Iran. Was it not Hallāj's brief story in the *Kitāb al-tawāsin* that told about the moth longing to cast itself into the flame in order to reach complete *fanā'*, annihilation, in the fire of love, in the consuming presence of the Beloved? From Hallāj's work this story came to Iran, and most conspicuously to Shiraz, where it surfaced again in the poetry of the Shirazian writers, notably Sa'di. It became one of the favorite metaphors for the following generations of Persian poets until it was transformed, on the basis of Sa'di's verse, into one of the greatest German poems, Goethe's *Selige Sehnsucht*.

There was still another Hallajian master in Shiraz. That was Rozbehān Baqli (d. 1209), whose chain of initiation goes back to Ibn Khafif. Baqli interpreted the "paradoxes" of the early Sufis, but he also described in incredibly beautiful and highly elusive words the mysteries of chaste love. Thus Shiraz was fertile soil for mystical thought. The great masterworks of mystical epics, to be sure, were composed in the east of Iran by Sanā'i (*Hadiqat al-haqiqa*) and 'Attār of Nishāpur, whose great *mathnavi*s still enchant and puzzle the reader. In Anatolia, the mystic Jalāl al-Din Rumi from Balkh in Afghanistan, who was Sa'di's contemporary, continued this trend. On the other hand, writers from Shiraz excelled in lyrical poetry as limpid as the water of the Allahu Akbar pass that Hāfez praised in one of his *ghazal*s.

Times changed in the decades that separated Sa'di and Hāfez. Mohammad Shams al-Din, who is known under his pen name Hāfez (Koran-memorizer) because he was well versed in theological studies and knew the Koran by heart, was born about 1320. It seems that he was attached to a Sufi order, although his poetry contains many elegant attacks against the Sufis and ascetics who feign piety. The poet was apparently married, since one of his poems can be interpreted as an elegy on the death of his wife, and another one complains about the death of his son.

Little is known about Hāfez's relations with the rulers of his times. Among them, Abu Eshāq Inju (r. 1343–53) and Shah Shojā' the Mozaffarid (r. 1358–85) were interested in literary pursuits. Between these two cultured rulers, however, lies the time of the fanatic Mobārez al-Din (1353–58), a bigoted ascetic, who enjoyed executing people under the pretext of religion. He is alluded to by Hāfez as *mohtaseb*, the much-hated censor who indulged in controlling not only the business in the bazaars but, even more, the morals of the people. Understandably, Hāfez celebrated Shah Shojā''s ascension to the throne, for he, among other things, abolished the prohibitions introduced by his father. Nevertheless, for a short while the relations between the king and the poet seem to have been somewhat strained. Shah Shojā''s death was followed by a time of confusion, caused by the invasion of Timur in the eastern lands of the Muslim world. He also came to Shiraz, and a famous anecdote, spun out of one of Hāfez's *ghazals*, tells of the meeting between the proud and cruel but artistically-minded Timur and the aging poet. Shortly afterward, at the very end of 1389, Hāfez passed away in his home town.

Even though he was sometimes declared a heretic, Hāfez was soon acknowledged as the leading master of lyrical poetry. In addition, his verse was given a mystical interpretation, and his small *divān* became not only a source of joy for lovers of poetry but even more a treasury of mystical thought and an unfailing resource for prognostication. To our day, his mausoleum is frequented by visitors, many of whom like to open there the *divān* of the poet to find out what the future may hold in store for them.

Hāfez's *ghazals*, in contrast to those of Sa'di, lack an apparent coherence. The distichs often seem to be bound to each other merely by the meter and the rhyme-word, and much ink has been lavished to argue that they are constructed according to a musical principle (counterpoint), or should rather be compared to a carpet design that extends to all sides around a central motif. The latter was Goethe's impression, which he expressed in one of the finest poems in the *West-östlicher Divan*: for him, Hāfez's song is "turning like the starry spheres," with beginning, center, and end mysteriously united by the same movement.

Likewise, the real meaning of Hāfez's verse has been a matter of dispute. Some commentators have understood him to be a perfect Anacreontic, praising wine and love without inhibition, and cursing the narrow-minded ascetics and theologians. The Turkish commentator Sudi belongs to this group, which strongly influenced the early European critics, especially those who became acquainted with Hāfez through the Turkish tradition. Here, Joseph von Hammer-Purgstall is the leading figure; he translated the entire *divān* of Hāfez, which appeared in two volumes in 1812–13 and inspired Goethe to compose his *West-östlicher Divan* of 1819. Following Hammer-Purgstall's rather mundane interpretation of Hāfez, a considerable number of mediocre German poets of the nineteenth century adopted his name as a trademark for their drinking poems and love songs, and especially for their attacks against the clergy. Others—mainly in Iran and India—have rather seen in Hāfez "the Tongue of the Unseen," the interpreter of invisible mysteries. Many stories, especially from the Indian subcontinent, tell that this or that person owned only two or three books to which he would revert time and again: the Koran, the *divān* of Hāfez, and Rumi's *Mathnavi*.

Goethe understood Hāfez perfectly well. A great poet and thinker himself, he knew that the word *qua* word has a mystical quality and that a verse can convey something far beyond its external meaning, can point to a transcendental truth without being in need of an allegorical interpretation that puts, as it were, heavy chains of metaphysics around the wings of a butterfly. The true poetical word reveals and hides at the same time; it enables the reader to sense things that transcend the simple statements found in a verse. That holds true for most poetic masterpieces.

Lately, one has investigated some of Hāfez's verse not so much for expressions of love, let alone mystical love, as for his skillful way of couching praise of a prince in the vocabulary of erotic poetry. In this technique Hāfez was certainly outstanding. Indeed, the special charm of his verse consists in the fact that he uses the traditional vocabulary to such perfection that every interpretation seems to make complete sense. The beautiful but cruel beloved from whom he expects a sign of love—just a little note to catch his heart's bird by snare-like letters— may be a real young boy, fourteen years old and moon-faced, similar to the moon in the fourteenth night, or still a child who can "murder" his lover without being held responsible. It can also be the Divine beloved from whom one implores a sign of grace, a word of consolation, but who remains inaccessible, hiding Himself behind the numberless manifestations of His beauty and majesty, and can be reached only if the lover annihilates himself completely in Him. Again, the cruel beloved can be the prince or king whose whims nobody knows and on whose kindness the poet is dependent. (Poetry was, after all, mainly written for a reward, and the medieval poet usually had to rely upon his patron's generosity for his more or less modest sustenance.) The human beloved can be praised for his beauty because in him the eternal beauty of the Divine beloved is reflected (he is indeed the *shāhed*, the visible witness to this invisible beauty); the prince, in turn, has to be flattered by the same expressions as the heavenly and the earthly beloved. In fact, the unbearded *shāhed* and the prince are loci of manifestation for the contrasting qualities of the Divine beloved,

His *jamāl* and His *jalāl*, His eternal beauty and kindness, and His terrifying majesty that reveals itself in His cruelty toward those who love Him most and are willing to suffer on the path toward Him. If this interpretation of a Persian *ghazal*, and especially of a *ghazal* by Hāfez, seems far-fetched, one should read the description that the Indian historian Barani, an exact contemporary of Hāfez, gives of the role of the king as the representative of God's *jamāl* and *jalāl*.

It may be difficult for a modern reader to appreciate this multi-faceted quality of Hāfez's poetry. However, one has always to keep in mind that the Persian spirit was at that point deeply permeated by Sufi thought and thus by the belief that the divine presence is felt in the different manifestations of life. The rose that blooms in the garden points to the eternal rose (and Rozbehān Baqli, Hāfez's compatriot, was once blessed by a vision of the Divine Glory in the form of clouds of roses that overwhelmed him). The nightingale is in the same position as the human heart that longs and cries for the view of the rose-like cheek of the beloved, for the bird is an age-old symbol of the human soul, as it was used in 'Attār's famous *Manteq al-tayr*, where the thirty birds are the embodiments of human souls in their search for the presence of the divine Simorgh. Already Sa'di had taught his listeners, on the basis of Koranic verses, that every leaf on the tree is a sign of God's power and praises His greatness; and following him, Hāfez transforms the gardens of Shiraz, the promenade of Mosallā, into reflections of Paradise on earth. Thus, readers can interpret his verse according to their own levels of knowledge, or of wisdom. But that is not all. Many poets after Hāfez have used the same vocabulary, the same imagery that he did, and certainly enjoyed the variety of meaning that a single elegant verse could convey. They tried to polish the political diction even more, refining it and delighting in rare rhymes and difficult meters. But Hāfez, who does not look for such artistry, remains the greatest artist when it comes to the application of rhetorical devices, which he uses with surprising effortlessness. No other poet can vie with him in the intelligent use of those figures that transform prose into poetry—be it *hosn-e ta'lil* (fantastic etiology), or *morā'āt al-nazir* (the harmonious choice of related images), elegant metaphors, or daring hyperboles. No word stands alone but is always connected to the others by a network of relations that becomes visible only through a careful analysis of each verse.

Let us take for example one of Hāfez's most famous verses, the often mistreated *tork-e shirāzi*, the "Turk of Shiraz" who appears in European translations in insipid disguises. The translators did not

realize that the beauty of this verse—like most others by Hāfez—
depends on the equilibrium of the images; not on the fact that the
poet calls on a charming "barmaid" to be kind to him and that he
would pawn two imperial cities for the little mole on his/her face:

> If this Turk of Shiraz would take my heart in his hand,
> I would give for his Hindu mole Samarkand and Bukhara.

The verse is a masterpiece of rhetoric: there is first the contrast between the Turk, always the beautiful but cruel, white beloved, and the
Hindu, who appears in Persian poetry from the eleventh century as
the embodiment of blackness and lowliness and is usually the slave of
the Turkish ruler. One has to keep these conventions in mind to fully
understand the irony in the verse: the poet will offer the two mightiest
cities of the great Turkish kingdom, Samarkand and Bukhara, for the
slave-like black mole on his Turkish beloved's cheek. Beside the major
contrast of white and black, ruler and slave, three names of places
(Shiraz and the two Turkish cities) as well as three parts of the body
(heart, hand, and mole) are elegantly woven together. What makes
this verse so masterful, then, is not so much the content as the perfection of the rhetoric.

This brings us to another aspect of Hāfez: he is the undisputed
master of musical and poetical rhetorical perfection. It is often said
that one cannot change a word, a syllable in his poetry—not only does
every allusion and metaphor have its exact place, but also every sound,
which accounts for the mellifluous rhythm of his verses. Each verse
reveals to the patient reader a jewelry work of words, most fastidiously
wrought, behind which the meaning—mundane or religious—lies hidden. Thus his verse has the perfection of a diamond that reflects in
each of its facets the light in a different color. The comparison with
the diamond is apt for another reason as well. Hāfez is not a romantic
poet; rather, it is the clear-cut, polished quality of his verse that is so
fascinating, and at the same time so difficult to assess for a Western
reader who is used, at least from the eighteenth century, to *Erlebnis-
lyrik*—that is, the poetry that translates a real experience of the writer
into verse—and who no longer understands the "learned," intellectual
character of most of Persian poetry in which many sentiments are
filtered, as it were, through the mind until one perfect line contains
their quintessence. This density of expression and meaning is of necessity lost in translation. For no translation can ever hope to reflect
the perfection of Hāfez's verbal plays and at the same time the var-

iegated meanings and the sweet lilt of his verse. That was probably the reason why Herder, quoted in the beginning, did not like Hāfez, whose verse he came to know through the Latin translations by Sir William Jones—adaptations which, understandably, lacked the graceful elegance of the original. It took a poet like Goethe to discover behind the rather unpolished translations by Hammer-Purgstall the greatness of Hāfez, who appeared to him as his "twin," nay rather, to whom even the comparison with himself seemed too daring. It was thanks to his German echo of Hāfez's *divān* that the name of the poet of Shiraz became almost a household word in Germany; and his remarks about the characteristics of Persian poetry, which excels by its "wit" (in the classical sense of the word), are still valid. At about the same time, the young German orientalist Friedrich Rückert published a collection called *Östliche Rosen* (Eastern roses), which contains some verses that incorporate the spirit of Hāfez much better than all later versions (including Rückert's own masterful verse translation of some eighty *ghazals*). It was Rückert who, in a wordplay worthy of Hāfez, translated the character of his poetry into German:

Hafis, wo er scheinet Übersinnliches
nur zu reden, redet über Sinnliches;
oder redet er, wo über Sinnliches
er zu reden scheint, nur Übersinnliches?
Sein Geheimnis ist unübersinnlich,
Denn sein Sinnliches ist übersinnlich.

Hāfez's poetry, he says, looks sensual and is supra-sensual; when he seems to talk about things spiritual, his spirituality is sensual as his sensuality is spiritual, and it is impossible to disentangle the two levels of meaning, which belong to each other. Rückert has certainly caught the true secret of Hāfez's verse, that secret making him the most beloved lyricist in the history of Persian literature. And whatever our own interpretation of his verse, there is no doubt that his lyrics are unique, indeed. Does it really matter, then, if we do not know whether the beloved around whose beauty his poetic cosmos revolves was a prince, a young boy, or the Divine Beloved?

# 13. Persian Satire, Parody and Burlesque: A General Notion of Genre

This chapter is concerned with the various forms of the literature of reduction as they exist in Persian.[1] We shall concentrate on some of the works of representative authors with the hope that the methods and ideas of Persian satire will become clearer for students of literature.

It is an oversimplification to classify the entire body of Persian satirical writing before the late nineteenth century, with the exception of the works of 'Obayd-e Zākāni, as "poetic invective."[2] For our purposes, however, the fundamental change in the nature of Persian satire that comes with the writings of 'Obayd is worth noting.

The tradition of *hejā'* (lampoon, invective) and *hazl* (ribaldry) in classical Arabic poetry had been well established[3] by the time the great Persian poets of the Samanid (tenth century), Ghaznavid (eleventh and twelfth centuries) and Seljuk (eleventh and twelfth centuries) periods tried their hands at it. In fact, much of this type of poetry in Persian can be traced back to Arabic models. *Hejā'* as practiced by one of its most imaginative pre-'Obayd proponents, Suzani of Samarqand (d. 1174), consists of *ad hominem* attacks on the poet's, or his patron's, rivals and enemies. In this respect this early form of satire was considered the exact opposite of *madh*, or panegyric; the mechanical reversal of the language of one would automatically yield the other.[4]

In his *hejā'* Suzani essentially uses taboo words as weapons in order to lower the social or ritual status[5] of his victim. Typical of this verbal aggression are implied or open references to a man's wife or daughter, accusations of illegitimacy, disparaging references to the victim's ancestry (especially allusions to intimacy with animals), casting doubt upon the victim's sexual preferences, innuendo based on cuckoldry, and attacks of a coprophobic nature on ritual purity. His *hazl* consists

---

[1]For the basic definitions of these types of literature see the exhaustive *Parodie, Travestie und Pastiche* by W. Karrer (Munich, 1977).

[2]H. Kamshad, *Mod. Prose*, 38.

[3]Abu 'Ali b. Rashiq al-Qayrawāni (d. 1064), *Al-'Omda* (Beirut, 1972), 172.

[4]Kay Kāvus, *Qābus-nāma*, ed. Gh.-H. Yusefi (Tehran, 1967), 191. See also M. Kiyanush, *Qodama' o naqd-e adabi* (Tehran, 1975), 104–105.

[5]"Ritual status" refers to physical and spiritual purity within the Islamic context. It has been observed that much of Islamic satire deals with physical uncleanliness because it is a reaction to the strict codes of purification in Islamic culture. See A. Boudiba, *La Sexualité en Islam* (Paris, 1975), 202.

of oblique references to various parts of the body and bodily functions as well as *tafākhor* (boasting) about the size of his sexual organs, ("I'm Suzani, soft [wax]-hearted and granite-phallused").[6]

What distinguishes Suzani's *hejā'* and *hazl* is the fact that many of his poems are burlesques of perfectly serious odes written by his most famous victim, the Ghaznavid poet Sanā'i (d. 1150). Suzani's concept of satire is not only *ad hominem*, but also literary in nature. In his *hazl*, this literary tendency extends primarily to the mechanical aspects of poetry, such as prosody and rhyme. The burlesque of Sanā'i's poems is achieved through the rhythmic associations of the elevated literary language of the original with the ribaldry of Suzani's mock-lyric inventions. Sanā'i begins one of his odes: "O nightingale! The thought of you gives such pleasure";[7] by contrast, Suzani, addressing the agent of his passion rather than the bird of love, says "O fleshy, crimson, veiny, and hard beyond measure!"[8]

## 'Obayd-e Zākāni

When we come to the writings of 'Obayd-e Zākāni, we are confronted with a definite break in the traditions outlined above. Of course one cannot deny that various forms of crude verbal aggression are present in 'Obayd's works, and it could be argued that 'Obayd continues on the path of Suzani and the great thirteenth-century writer of *hazl*, Saʿdi.[9] But some of 'Obayd's works suggest a kind of literary detour, and here he seems to have made the transition from self-serving lampoon and ribaldry to genuine literary and social satire.[10]

Although 'Obayd himself terms the work "*hazl*,"[11] his *Akhlāq al-ashrāf* (The ethics of the nobles, 1340) goes far beyond traditional *hazl* and *hejā'*. Not only do 'Obayd's methods differ from those of Suzani, in

---

[6]Suzani Samarquandi, *Divān*, ed. Shāh-Hosayni (Tehran, 1957), 390.

[7]Sanā'i, *Divān*, ed. Rezavi (Tehran, n.d.), 917.

[8]Suzani Samarqandi, *Divān*, 397.

[9]Saʿdi also wrote a *Facetiae* of some fifteen manuscript pages.

[10]To Gilbert Highet this difference appears to be a difference of intent; see *The Anatomy of Satire* (Princeton, 1962), 26. Lampoon is a kind of parasite that cannot stand on its own, feeding upon the writer's ill-will toward the adversary. Genuine satire, on the other hand, is independent of its target and arises out of a desire to reform a perceived injustice or evil.

[11]'Obayd-e Zākāni, Introduction to *Treatise on the Ethics of the Nobles*. All quotations from this work as well as others by 'Obayd are taken from a complete translation of a composite text, which is being prepared for the author's doctoral dissertation. For a description and translation of some of 'Obayd's works, see Browne, *Lit. Hist.*, vol. 3, 230–57.

that he writes *hazl* in the form of a serious treatise on ethics,[12] but the range of his targets is qualitatively different from that of his predecessors. He is not concerned with an individual literary rival or his works, but with a class of people, the ruling elite of post-Mongol Iran. According to 'Obayd, this class of *ashāb* or *ashrāf*, because of a mellowing (*taltif*) of their temperaments, have invented a "preferred" or "contemporary" ethical point of view (*madhhab-e mokhtār*) to replace the traditional or "outmoded" one (*madhhab-e mansukh*).

The treatise, whose very title is a fine bit of irony,[13] is divided into seven sections, each containing the two antithetical ethical points of view on various principles of traditional ethics. This sevenfold division can be seen as a direct reference to the eightfold division of a more famous *pand* (didactic) work, the *Golestān* (Rose garden) of Sa'di. Certainly 'Obayd has Sa'di in mind when he expresses his purpose in writing the *Ethics*:

> It is the hope of this author that in writing this
> short treatise:
> One day some sympathetic soul will, somewhere,
> grace this wretched one's deeds with a simple prayer.[14]

The eightfold division of Sa'di's work alludes to the belief that heaven has eight gates.[15] Sa'di tells us he is going to recreate a "celestial rose garden" with the beauty of his earthly writing. 'Obayd's choice of seven chapters, although not explicit in the *Ethics,* rests upon the Koranic notion that hell has seven gates.[16] In his introduction, then, 'Obayd indicates that his vision is directed not toward the sacred but to the profane depths of his society, to an ethical hell which has already been achieved on earth.

To justify their point of view, the creators of this hell, the contemporary elite, use the traditional tools of moralists, namely, Koranic citation, the sayings of the Prophets, various platitudes, and *sententiae,*

---

[12]It can be shown that 'Obayd, despite his claims of inability to understand such learned treatises, was quite familiar with the *Akhlāq-e Nasiri* (Nasirian ethics) written by Nasir al-Din Tusi (d. 1274).

[13]In *Akhlāq al-ashrāf* one finds echoes of the title of a treatise by Nasir al-Din Tusi, namely the *Awsāf al-ashrāf* (Characteristics of the nobles).

[14]'Obayd, *Akhlāq al-Ashrāf* (Ethics), introduction. Compare the introduction to the *Golestān*: "But were a sympathetic soul to someday offer a prayer over dervishes' deeds." Sa'di, *Golestān*, ed. M. Khaza'eli (2nd printing, Tehran, 1969), 172.

[15]Cf. the saying of the Prophet: "As for heaven, it has eight gates," ibid., 172.

[16]See the Koran (15:44), "It [hell] hath seven gates."

anecdotes, and poetry. The traditional concept of chastity, for example, is held to be outmoded because

> Anyone who makes chastity a life principle will get nothing out of it in the end; as it has been revealed in holy Scripture: "Verily life in this world is but idle play and diversion and cheap glitter and vain boasting among you, and vying to see who can accumulate the most wealth and offspring." (Koran 57:19) From here they [the elite] argue that idle play and diversion cannot be accomplished without a little indecency and resorting to expedients forbidden by law. . . . Therefore, they who practice chastity, who are decent, will be excluded from activities basic to life and cannot be numbered among the living.[17]

'Obayd's ironic attack on the new morality of post-Mongol Iran also extends to the politics of terror practiced by Ilkhanid underlings who were, at the time, busy grabbing the territorial leftovers of their masters. In his chapter "On Justice," 'Obayd cautions against excessive fairness on the part of kings and princes:

> That misguided ruler who [God forbid!] practices Justice, who refrains from striking people and killing them, who does not attack their goods and livelihoods, and who doesn't get roaring drunk and subject his subordinates to his unrestrained debauched behavior and abuse, surely will not be feared by the people.

Since fear is the basis of all social and bureaucratic hierarchies, its absence, he argues, will lead to a complete breakdown of world order.

'Obayd satirizes some of the excesses of the learned style of his time by using its rhetorical gestures to praise sodomy, which seems to have been a widely accepted practice among the elite:

> Although some members of the lower orders scoff at sodomy, calling it perverted generosity and rumpwise virility, their opinion has no credibility, for they speak in ignorance of the saying, "Giving freely of oneself is the highest form of generosity." Whosoever allows opportunity to wither and die because of some stroke of

---

[17]'Obayd, *Ethics*, chap. 3, "On Chastity."

bad luck, has allowed the keys of success to slip through his hands and shall remain for an eternity in degradation and misfortune:

> To bite the hand in frustration—that's his lot,
> Who did not strike while the iron was hot![18]

In another work, *Rish-nāma* (The book of the beard), the comic aspects of male homosexuality appear in 'Obayd's retelling of the story of Adam's fall from clean-shaven grace:

> For as long as Adam remained in heaven as a beardless youth, the angels bowed down to him. As soon as he grew a beard, however, the angels, who had never seen one before, began to make fun of him with barbed comments [*rish-khand*]. The poor fellow was so affected that he jumped out of heaven and sought refuge in the deserts of earth and was forever burdened by misfortune.[19]

It is in 'Obayd's works that this admixture of the grossly comical and the canonical or apocryphal is fully developed for the first time in Persian satire. Indeed, his satirical works contain much that might be termed the "profanation of the sacred."[20] This type of satire, as we shall see, reappears in a much more virulent form in the works of the twentieth-century author Zabih Behruz, although 'Obayd's wry composites of the sacred and the profane never reach the level of direct attacks on Islam itself, as they do with Behruz.

'Obayd's unlimited sense of the absurd also allowed him to see the possibilities for social satire in a kind of philological tract, *Ta'rifāt* ([The list of learned] definitions). These lists were very popular among students and teachers at the various centers of learning in Iran, for they facilitated the acquisition of the jargon and technical vocabulary of philosophical, scholastic, and scientific discussions. Since the language of science at the time was Arabic, this type of literature usually consisted of a column of Arabic words "to be defined," and their Persian definitions. 'Obayd's parody is achieved first through the "Arabization" of colloquial Persian words (by adding the Arabic definite article

---

[18]Ibid.
[19]'Obayd, *Rish-nāma*, "Hekāyat 2."
[20]See M. C. Hyers, "The Comic Profanation of the Sacred," in *Holy Laughter* (New York, 1969), 9–27.

"al"), thereby admitting them to their unaccustomed place in the "to be defined" column, and also through ironic definition and litotes:

Al-Pleasant-natured: The irreligious person
Al-Beard: Hand-hold for the contemplative[21]

'Obayd also defines traditional vocabulary culled from the Koran and works of science, philosophy, theosophy, and so on. In his *Definitions,* 'Obayd divides traditional jargon into ten categories, each dealing with a class or group of people in society. He takes aim at the Turkic horde by applying apocalyptic vocabulary to them:[22]

Gog and Magog: A Turkic tribe turning its attention to a province
The Hour-long Earthquake: The period of their advent
Famine: The results of their coming.

In spite of 'Obayd's influence on later authors of Persian satire and his popularity, his reputation has suffered because he indulged in *hazl*. As a result of the firmly established view in literary and clerical circles that literature should be essentially didactic, with the aim of maintaining Islamic ideals of morality and ethics, the works of 'Obayd-e Zākāni were, and continue to be, condemned as self-serving vulgarity. 'Obayd did not in fact reject the concept that literature must be fundamentally didactic and morally prescriptive; he merely believed that it could be entertaining. In one of his most imaginative works, *Sad Pand* (The treatise of one hundred counsels, 1350), 'Obayd mocks the type of aphoristic and gnomic wisdom literature which was so popular with classical Persian authors and, in doing so, creates a work designed to instruct as well as amuse.

In a brief introduction he specifically mentions two morally prescriptive treatises of pre-Islamic origin that have "influenced" his own writing, *The Advice of Plato to His Student Aristotle* and *The Book of Advice of Anoshirvān*.[23] In a very general way, both of these treatises offer advice or define traditional values concerning the classical ethical system. For example, in *The Advice of Plato,* "wisdom" consists of main-

[21]'Obayd, *Definitions.*
[22]'Obayd, *Ten Chapters.*
[23]*Vasiyat-nāma-ye aflātun* in *Akhlāq-e Nasiri* (Tehran, 1961), 317–20; *Pand-nama-ye Anushirvan,* which forms the eighth chapter (pp. 51–55) of the *Qābus-nāma* (see n. 4).

taining an emotional and physical distance from the vicissitudes of life:

> Do not consider anyone a wise man who is made happy by the pleasures of the world or who is rendered impatient and despondent by its hardships.[24]

Both advise that honesty and candor are to be preferred to flattery and humor: "Speak the truth even if it be bitter";[25] "Refrain from joking with people."[26] In these two treatises, as in all aphoristic literature, life is seen in its entirety; its details are pushed into the background, and its universality is stressed: "Think about what you were originally, and what will become of you after death".[27] "If you don't want to live without friends and helpers, don't hold grudges."[28]

'Obayd's one hundred counsels formally resemble the sayings and aphorisms of the two works mentioned above. They are couched in simple Persian, making them easy to memorize and use at the appropriate moment. Like the sage advice of Anoshirvān they are numbered consecutively and, more often than not, warn against rather than advocate certain types of behavior. The *Treatise of One Hundred Counsels* adheres very closely to the formal conventions of the works that it parodies, but it differs from them in its content. Whereas the advice of Plato and Anoshirvān stress universal truths and stoic indifference, the *Treatise of One Hundred Counsels* emphasizes the details of everyday living and urges one not to be aloof from life, but to participate fully in its pleasures: "Don't put off today's pleasure till tomorrow."[29] No aspect of life is too insignificant or too mundane to be excluded from 'Obayd's ironic advice:

> Don't choose to live on a street on which there is a minaret so that you will be safe from harsh-voiced muezzins.

> When it comes to honesty and loyalty, try not to be excessive so that you will not become afflicted with piles or other diseases.

and

[24]*Akhlāq-e Nāsiri*, 318.
[25]*Qābus-nāma*, 52, n. 10.
[26]*Akhlāq-e Nāsiri*, 320.
[27]Ibid., 318.
[28]*Qābus-nāma*, 54, n. 33.
[29]*Hundred Counsels* (from an unpublished composite manuscript prepared for the author's Ph.D. thesis).

Masturbation is preferable to swollen testicles.[30]

Some of 'Obayd's counsels ironically confirm or contradict advice given in the two "serious" treatises. *The Advice of Plato* encourages one to "be awake at all times, for many are the paths on which evil travels,"[31] while 'Obayd suggests:

> Whenever you find a man sleeping prone—as long as he doesn't wake up—take advantage of the opportunity fate has bestowed on you.[32]

In 'Obayd's wry promotion of the principles of unprincipled behavior one can also detect elements of social satire. To those striving to become *ghāzis*, or great warriors in the cause of fighting the infidels, he has this to say:

> Beat defenseless old women with a suitably large club, so that you too can achieve the rank of a *ghāzi*.[33]

For ambitious adolescents who are interested in becoming successful in life, he has the following advice:

> Under no circumstances deny your friends or your enemies, your relatives or strangers, access to your rump, so that, when you grow old, you too will be able to become a theologian, a preacher, a world hero, or a royal chamberlain.[34]

To those interested in maintaining both their good reputations and the fabric of polite society, 'Obayd offers practical counsel:

> Take care to mount your neighbor's daughter from behind and not to go near the seal of her virginity, so that you will have fulfilled your duty to propriety, clemency, piety, and neighborliness, and so that the girl will not be vulnerable to slanderous accusations on her wedding night and can hold her head up high in public.[35]

[30]Ibid., nos. 22, 89, 33.
[31]*Akhlāq-e Nāsiri*, 317.
[32]*Hundred Counsels*, n. 41.
[33]Ibid., n. 37.
[34]Ibid., n. 46.
[35]Ibid., n. 51.

In his penultimate counsel 'Obayd alludes to the underlying seriousness of his treatise. He seems to address those who condemn his writing and to anticipate the reaction against his candor:

> Never underestimate satire and never look at the satirist with contempt.[36]

## Hāfez

In marked contrast to 'Obayd is his contemporary Hāfez (d. 1390) who, though not known as a satirist, was concerned with the hypocrisy of his times. In some of his odes one can see the development of a kind of defensive wit in reaction to the extravagances of religious zealots and hypocritical divines. These divines, or shaikhs, with their "lawful cheer" were for Hāfez, an admitted sinner, the most unprincipled members of society, whose outward shows of piety were motivated by the promise of a sensual afterlife:

> The zealot seeks a heavenly dwelling-place
> Houris to welcome him to Paradise.[37]

Concerned about his reputation rather than his spiritual well-being, the zealot cultivates the symbols of piety: Hāfez, however, worships in an outwardly impious manner, welcoming a bad reputation:

> Zealot avaunt! invite me not to wend to Heaven my way:
>     A man of Heaven not made was I by God upon His Day.
> Not one grain of the sheaves of life is stored by those who've trod
>     This pathway of mortality, and sown no seed for God.
> For thee the beads, the place of prayer, strict rule, and virtue's road;
>     For me the wine-house, and the bell, the church, the monk's
>         abode.[38]

In his poetry Hāfez prefers the seemingly sinful state of a confirmed drunkard to avoid what is, for him, the far more serious sins of hypocrisy and bloody oppression:

---

[36]Ibid., n. 99.
[37]*Selected Poems of Hāfez*, trans. G. L. Bell (London, 1897), 106.
[38]*Hāfez of Shiraz: Selections from His Poems*, trans. by Herman Bicknell (London, 1875), 77.

Better the drunkard void of fraud and wiles
    Than virtue's braggart who by fraud beguiles.
I am no hypocrite, no toper sly:
    Attest it He who secrets doth espy
Let us obey God's laws, and injure none,
    Nor teach as good what we are taught to shun.
If once, or oft, we drain the wine-cup's flood,
    The vine's blood flows there, it is not thy blood.
There is no fault which causes none a tear:
    Let it a fault be, who is faultless here?[39]

He also condemns those who use the sensational descriptions of heaven in the Koran to entice the gullible into hypocritical belief:

Be gay, drink wine, and revel;
But not, like others, care,
O Hāfez, from the Koran
To weave a wily snare.[40]

Although the majority of Hāfez's satirical allusions, like those of 'Obayd, are directed against a class of hypocritical divines, Sufis, preachers, and so on, some of his bitterest attacks on the two-faced nature of his society are reserved for the founder of the Mozaffarid dynasty, Amir Mobārez al-Din Mozaffar (1314–58). Amir Mobārez al-Din captured Shiraz from Hāfez's famous patron Shaikh Abu Eshāq in 1354. A historian of the Mozaffarids, writing some sixty years later, describes the aftermath of the amir's advent this way:

He [Amir Mobārez al-Din] established the foundations of justice and the general welfare of the peasants and devoted his energies to the training and education of divines and men of learning. He encouraged the people to listen to the sayings of the Prophet, the explication of the Koran, and the principles of Islamic jurisprudence. In his application of the Koranic injunction, "order what is lawful and prohibit the proscribed," he went a bit too far, with the result that no one had the nerve to even mention vice, immorality, or actions prohibited by law. Shah Shojā' [his son] composed a quatrain about this state of affairs:

[39]Ibid., 95.
[40]Ibid., 19.

235

In the age's revelry, drunkenness is now a crime;
The zither's unlawful, the hand no longer strikes the chime;
Profligates have all given up their wine-worship;
Except "the commissar," who, wineless, is high all the time.[41]

This poem indicates that the word *mohtaseb* (public morals officer or, as we have translated here, "commissar") was ironically applied to the amir, who, in fact, personally carried out the duties of a public censor. Hāfez alludes ironically to the *mohtaseb's* prohibitive activities when describing his own open, "profligate" form of worship:

Why speak of the shame that may fall to my lot? It blazons with glory my name:
Why ask after glory appointed in me to bring but the burden of shame?
A wine-drinker am I, to giddiness prone, whose glances and manners are free;
And where among those who inhabit this town is one who resembles not me?
Withhold from the *mohtaseb's* knowledge, I pray, the story of error like mine;
He also with ardor that equals my own unceasingly searches for wine.[42]

In another ode the poet describes the disastrous consequences of the abrupt change of government in Shiraz. Gone is the wine-loving, profligate poet-king, Shah Shaikh Abu Eshāq, to whom Hāfez was truly attached,[43] and here to take his place and plague Hāfez's free spirit is the overzealous, superficial commissar:

Though wine incites to jocund mirth, and winds through flowers are sighing,
While drinking, let the harp be mute; the *mohtaseb* is prying.
If e'er thy genial lot bestow a mate and flagon cheery,
With prudence to the goblet turn; the days of life are dreary.

[41]M. Kotobi, *Tārikh-e Āl-e Mozaffar* (Tehran, 1956), 41–42. See also Browne, *Lit. Hist.*, vol. 3, 164; in the first line of Shah Shojā''s poem Browne reads *bast-ast* (closed) for *past-ast* (is low, demeaned). The second reading seems preferable. In the second line he reads *na qanun* (not the harp) for *be-qānun* (lawful); again the second reading seems preferable.
[42]Bicknell, *Hāfez of Shiraz*, 53–54.
[43]A.-H. Zarrinkub, *Az kucha-ye rendan* (Tehran, 1970), 41.

\* \* \*

Come, wash we from our cowls with tears the wine-flecks yet remaining:
It is the time of piety, a season for abstaining.[44]

As 'Abd al-Hosayn Zarrinkub points out, the reign of the 'commissar' descended upon Shiraz like a nightmare.[45] Amir Mobārez al-Din, like many who "see the light" late in life,[46] was extremely scrupulous in rooting out all overt forms of sacrilege and impiety, in the belief that public reform yielded private morality. This public zeal encouraged his followers not only to emulate him, but also to surpass him in the field of heretic-hunting. Hāfez mocked these counterfeit attitudes "not only by making wine the main topic of his odes, but also by attacking the 'commissar' on an ideological plane and in some of his odes entering the precincts of philosophy with discussions of the notion of causation."[47]

The poet alludes to matters of doctrine traditionally considered to be outside of the realm of philosophical discussion. In one verse he mentions the so-called "Plastic Pen" (*qalam-e son'*), which is a reference to a Koranic phrase[48] used in poetry as a symbol of divine infallibility:

"The Plastic Pen," my *pir* declared, "no fault decreed":
Admire that sight of his, too pure a fault to heed.[49]

Hāfez's *pir*, or Sufi master, teaches that a world created by Allah can have no faults. Hāfez admires his ability to overlook the world's imperfections, which, to the poet, are all too obvious. Many have tried to prove that Hāfez was quite within the bounds of piety or merely being irreverent in this verse and not by any means making fun of principles of Islamic creed relating to the Creation. Be this as it may, it is interesting to note that this verse was recently recoined to provide ironic comment on a case of mass self-deception. In 1948, the sup-

---

[44]Ibid., 73. See also 'A. Eqbāl, *Tārikh-e Moghul* (Tehran, 1968), 425.

[45]Zarrinkub, *Kucha*, 57.

[46]According to a chronicle sympathetic to the Mozaffarids, *Mavāheb-e elahi dar tārikh-e Āl-e Mozaffar*, ed. S. Nafisi (Tehran, 1948), 208–29, Amir Mobārez decided to give up his sinful ways and allow the "lamp of repentence to blaze away in the pure solitude of his enlightened consciousness" in 1352, six years before he died.

[47]Zarrinkub, *Kucha*, 71–72.

[48]Koran 27:88, "the doing (*son'*) of Allah who perfecteth all things."

[49]Bicknell, *Hāfez of Shiraz*, 150.

pressed satirical newspaper *Bābā Shāmāl* raised the question of whether or not the *Majles-e Shurā,* or Parliament, really existed:

Our *pir* maintains that we have a genuine Parliament
Admire that sight of his, too pure a fault to heed![50]

## Modern Satire

A jump from the fourteenth century to modern times will perhaps seem somewhat precipitous, and one may ask what happened in the intervening six centuries. For our purposes, the answer is, "Very little." It is not until the last half of the Qajar period (1848–1924), with the rise of clandestine and expatriate presses, that legitimate Persian satire reappears. Much of the satire contained in pamphlets and newspapers is directed against the corrupt practices of the Qajar rulers. Again it is public displays of morality and faith and private immorality that compel Persian authors to create new forms of satirical responses while at the same time borrowing from the rich *hazl* tradition.

Examples of the satirical newspapers and ephemera of the Constitutional period form the content of Edward G. Browne's *Press and Poetry of Modern Persia.* The nature of political and social satire in Iran at the turn of the century is faithfully recorded in Browne's remarkable compilation, which is based in part on the work of Mirza Mohammad 'Ali Khan Tarbiyat. According to Browne's note to Tarbiyat's introduction, the first satirical Persian newspaper was *Ehtiyāj* (Need), published in Tabriz in 1898–99 and suppressed after seven editions.[51] Browne translates a poem from the satirical weekly *Sur-e Esrāfil* (Clarion call of Esrāfil) published from May 1907 to June 1908. In the poem, the poet (thought to be 'Ali Akbar Dehkhodā, d. 1956) addresses one "Kablāy" or "Karbalā'i" (one who has visited the tombs of Shi'ite martyrs at Karbalā' in Iraq). The third stanza makes good satiric sense, if we accept the suggestion that Kablāy is the hypocritical ex-shah, Mohammad 'Ali:

Times a hundred I've told you your project will fail, O Kablāy!
While half of the nation [is] wrapped in a veil, O Kablāy!
Can Islam in you and your circle prevail?

[50]*Bābā Shamal* n. 125 (Shahrivar Mah, 1326/1948), 2 (microfilm).
[51]E. G. Browne, *The Press and Poetry of Modern Persia* (Cambridge, 1914), 15, n. 1.

With fresh words of folly your friends you'll regale.
You limb of the Devil and Son of a Gun, O Kablāy![52]

A reactionary *mojtahed*, Shaykh Fazlallāh, is the butt of a poem appearing in another important satirical paper, *Nasim-e shemāl*. Browne's translation admirably conveys the colloquial force of the poem's attack on the willingness of certain clerical elements to sell out their country:

Hājji, the market's brisk, the bidding high;
Here comes the auctioneer! Who'll buy? Who'll buy?
 I'm here the Persian land to sell or pawn,
 The pride and honour of each Musulmān
 Both Qum and Rasht, both Qazvin and Kāshān,
 Yazd, Khvānsār, every city of Iran;
All's up for auction at a figure fair;
Come, gentlemen, where is a bidder, where?

Of liberals I am the stalwart foe:
I'd like to kill them all, as well you know!
I represent Shaykh Fazlallah and Co.
Brokers, who hawk Religion to and fro,
 Here is the carcass, Gentlemen, draw near!
 Who'll buy? Who'll buy? Here comes the auctioneer.[53]

Some of the finest prose satire of the modern period is found in the essays entitled *Charand parand* (Balderdash), by 'Ali Akhbar Dehkhodā (1879–1956), who in his early career contributed to the *Sur-e Esrāfil*. Dehkhodā's "simplified" prose style is characterized by the use of colloquialisms and a mock serious-newspaper format. This simplicity is deceptive, however, for his writings abound in the rhetorical devices of irony. Choosing not to attack his favorite targets (corrupt politicians and clergy) directly, he uses apophasis and puts his criticisms in the mouth of a friend:

You'll probably want to write that our elite's political parties are established on the basis of their pro-Russian or pro-English sympathies. You'll probably want to write that our clergy have given up auctioning off their endowed properties and have begun to sell out their country instead.[54]

[52]Ibid., 181.
[53]Ibid., 215. Set as in Browne's translation.
[54]A. Dehkhodā, *Charand parand* (Tehran, 1952), 12–13.

In an announcement of "a new invention," Dehkhodā reveals his unique ability to combine seemingly unconnected issues of the day into a penetrating satirical whole:

An Austrian doctor by the name of Aufschneider, having heard stories about the bread in Tehran, has invented a steel casing for the teeth, which is designed to guard against the loss of enamel and to prevent decay. Once this device is put into place, the mouth achieves the status of a grist mill driven by a four-horsepower engine, able to pulverize stone and brick (both baked and un-baked).
Address inquiries to:
Lazarette Gasse, Heilanstalt, Nr. 21.[55]

Satire of the excessive zeal of public officials in enforcing the moral code reappears in the modern period in the form of popular songs and poems, many of which are the manifestations of an "under-ground" literary response to the formal modes of late Qajar literature. One of the poets of this period, Ashraf al-Din Hosayni (d. 1933), borrows a line from 'Obayd and encourages all to "take up buffoon-ery," for the hypocrisy of the times "is making buffoons of us all."[56] Mohammad 'Ali Jamālzāda quotes one of these anti-establishment poems in his *Dār al-majānin* (Lunatic asylum):

O wine drinkers! Your lives have been shot to hell,
For the police are instructed your breath to smell!
Take my advice and "supposit" your spirits.
So that they'll smell your . . . in order to tell![57]

Influenced by translations and their readings in European litera-ture, some Persian authors in the first half of this century turned to the short story to present comical aspects of the culture of Persian-speaking people. Perhaps one of the most successful of these authors is Jamālzāda. In "Fārsi shakar ast" (Persian is sugar, 1921), he pro-duces what can be described as a comedy of manners, in which certain social types are compared and contrasted primarily through the lan-guage they speak. Resembling social satires that rely on some com-

---

[55]Ibid., 10.
[56]*Nasim-e shemāl* (Tehran), 34.
[57]M. 'A. Jamālzāda, *Dār al-majānin* (Tehran, 1942), 17.

munal activity such as a pilgrimage or a voyage to achieve the ironic juxtaposition of disparate levels of understanding, "Persian is Sugar" describes the enforced familiarity brought about by the incarceration of four unlikely cellmates. In the beginning of the story the narrator, who is returning to Iran after five years of "aimless wandering," is detained by border officials because of his suspicious (i.e., "foreign") appearance. He is put into a room where he soon finds he is not alone. His cellmates include a superficially Westernized Iranian who is busy reading the compulsory *roman*, a turbaned divine who is squatting in a corner reciting prayers, and a local youth who has been imprisoned to serve as an example to the rebellious populace. The youth, who sees no point in talking to his two "foreign" cellmates, addresses the learned divine: "O Shaikh, for love o' God, tell me what I've done to deserve this." The shaikh replies: "O ye, who believe! Give not thy sinful and frail soul to anger and rage for: 'Those who control their wrath and are forgiving. . . .'"[58] The divine goes on with his sermon oblivious of the fact that the youth cannot understand a word of it. Out of desperation, he turns to the Western-oriented gentleman with the compulsory *roman* in order to "pour out his soul": "Excuse me, sir! I'm really lost. You know us poor folk can't get things so quickly. The shaikh, it's clear he's out of it—he doesn't get a word I say. He's an Arab. For God's sake—I beseach you—tell me why they've thrown me in this cell!"[59] The gentleman with his newly acquired egalitarian gestures draws close to the youth and says:

O comrade and fellow countryman! Why have they put us here? I also have been delving into this question for hours. I can *absolument* find nothing to explain it. Nothing *positif*, nothing *negatif*. *Absolument!* Isn't it really *comique* that I, a licentiate from the best *famille*, have been taken for a . . a *criminel?* . . . But from one thousand years of *despotisme* and illegarity and *"arbitraire"* which are the fructations of it, one can have no other expectancy.[60]

Like the shaikh before him, the gentleman goes on and on with his cant without noticing that the confused local is so frightened that he begins to scream and howl uncontrollably. Finally the narrator takes pity on him and soothes him with a "genuine" Persian palliative: "My

---

[58]Jamālzāda, *Yaki bud yaki nabud*, 27.
[59]Ibid., 31.
[60]Ibid., 31–32. The translator has attempted to capture here the flavor of the original passage; hence the garbled and unintelligible words.

poor boy! I'm no foreigner—and God damn anybody who's given himself airs! I'm a Persian and a fellow Muslim. How can you let yourself get so shaken? What's really happened after all?"[61]

No survey of Persian satire could be instructive without a discussion of the works of Zabih Behruz (d. 1971).[62] In his *Mirror of Inner Truths and Key to Intellects,* he writes in the tradition of literary satire developed by 'Obayd. The work not only parodies serious treatises with ornate titles written by Persian literati, but also attacks the belief held by many of these literati in the omniscience and infallibility of Western Orientalists. Like 'Obayd, Behruz directs his vision downward to the more mundane—his book, he claims, is a realistic reflection of what he sees:

Because I saw a world covered all 'round
With a corruption and ignorance profound,
I did compose a book filled with stench and rot;
(As for roses and sweet wine I, ah, cared not!)
To the discerning, after all, verbal jewels
Are the same on gold crown or in cesspools![63]

Using the inflated prose style of what many call "sick Persian," he introduces us to the late Professor Benjamin Scholkonheim (lit. "Herr Loosen-his-pants-heim"), the greatest Orientalist of his time. Dr. Scholkonheim, although a renowned expert on Persian literature and a Hāfez specialist of note, first gained fame in the world of Orientalism as an archaeologist, "For, as the late Professor was wont to say, he would regularly conduct conversations with himself in seventy specialized 'Orientalist' tongues and could jot down as well, with remarkable ease and fluency, the most complicated of hieroglyphics and cuneiform inscriptions."[64] Behruz, whose artificial verbosity so successfully mimics the mannerisms of learned style that, at times, one forgets he is being ironic, continues:

[61]Ibid., 35.

[62]The majority of Behruz's satirical works exist in manuscript form. All translations have been done by this author. *Jijak 'Ali Shāh,* a satirical play in three acts, ridiculing the practices of the court of Qajar Iran, appeared in published form (Tehran, n.d.). After this article was written, an edition of Behruz's satirical poems and parodies under the title of *Me'rāj-nāma* and including "Gand-e Bādāvard" and "Mer'āt al-Sarāyer" was published in Germany (Enteshārāt-e Mard-e Emrūz, 1984).

[63]Z. Behruz, *Mer'āt al-Sarā'er wa Meftāh al-Zamā'er* (Mirror), 1 (published in *Majalla-ye Ārmān* 1:8–10 [1310/1931], repr. *Rāhnemā–ye Ketāb* 14:9–12 [Jan.–March, 1972]: 721–33).

[64]Ibid.

That which makes the late Professor's total sincerity and inexhaustible perseverance crystal-clear to the scholars and learned of all communities and nations is the patience and devotion he demonstrated over a period of several years of continuous research and excavation around the tomb of Esther in Hamadan. These efforts eventually led to the discovery of the twelfth chapter of the book of Genesis composed in Abraham's (upon whom be peace) own hand as well as the war memorial, which was raised by Mordecai on a site adjacent to the temple to celebrate a victory over his enemies and which was inscribed with those awesome words: "Arrasa tanjahu", or "salvation lies in wife-mongering."[65]

Aside from his literary satire, Behruz has also produced some imaginative satire on the eschatology, popular beliefs, and theology of Islam. His *Me'rāj-nāma* (Book of the Ascension)[66] is a parody of a kind of devotional poetry written on the Prophet Mohammad's night journey to heaven. The poem, which consists of some five hundred couplets, follows the structural pattern of this type of poetry very closely. The first section is devoted to praise of God and his marvelous attributes, but instead of the usual praise, Behruz confounds our expectations by contrasting seemingly contradictory Koranic descriptions of Allah. He is both "Unique, Eternal, and Forgiving" and "Avenging, Hard-headed and Canny."[67] Behruz sets the tone of the entire poem in this introductory section when he elaborates ironically on the nature of Allah:

> At times such bounty does He bestow,
> That one can't count it nor check its flow!
> At times to babe parched in desert dry
> A hint of water He will deny . . .
> Justice is paired with wrath and deceit,
> Mercy tempered with revenge so sweet,
> Seen with these many traits as montage,
> He's nothing but a holy hodgepodge![68]

[65]Ibid.
[66]Behruz, *Me'rāj-nāma* (unpublished manuscript). All quotations from this work are taken from an unpublished translation by this author.
[67]Ibid., ll. 1, 2.
[68]Ibid., ll. 9, 10, 12, 13.

After the traditional encomium to Allah, it was customary in this type of poetry to praise his Creation:

> With neither blueprint nor protractor
>> Created this world, our Benefactor.
> Though it's a marvel as *Gestalt*,
>> With its "Good and Evil" one finds fault.[69]

Following the pattern, Behruz turns next to the words of God. In his mock praise of the Koran he alludes to the verses which proclaim its inimitability:

> The book of heaven is called "Forqān,"
>> Authored by the God of jinn and man
> Despite myriad things on his mind,
>> Just think! He's penned a book of this kind!
> Even if, I swear, men, jinn, and Shaytān [Satan]
>> Gathered and with spirit, joy and élan, . . . [and]
> Kept on pondering its perfection,
>> Free of pain, grief, and indigestion,
> Of this precious book's verses *not one*
>> Would come, no matter what wool they spun![70]

Behruz calls the next section of his poem, in which he satirizes popular beliefs in the salutary and miraculous properties of relics, "On the Miracles of the Prophet." To illustrate the miraculous powers of the Prophet's saliva, he either creates or borrows from apocryphal literature a prodigy of battlefield medicine. One of the Prophet's soldiers was badly wounded in a critical battle with the enemies of Islam, when:

> Of holy saliva, just a drop,
>> Fell on that wound, the bloodflow to stop.
> From that drop of digestive juice
>> Sprang forth such skin, ready for use,
> That were you to use a microscope,
>> Would you find a trace or scar? Nope!
> Would that L. Pasteur had been alive

[69]Ibid., ll. 33, 34.
[70]Ibid., ll. 43–45, 47, 48.

And from the Prophet's sputum contrive,
Cures for ev'ry conceivable pain
To spite the skeptics with their disdain![71]

In a story about an Arab youth who goes to heaven to search out his ill-fated mate, the poet turns to the eschatology of Islam. For Behruz the terrifying descriptions of the tortures of hell and the seductive details of the pleasures of paradise found in the Koran are extensions of the contradictory conception of God revealed in the beginning of the poem. To mock the notion of a heaven where sensual pleasures continue *ad infinitum,* he uses the reductionist method of 'Obayd and mixes the scatalogical with the eschatological. Rezvān, the groundskeeper of heaven, gives the youth, whom he feels is an ill-mannered "Arabling," the address of his bride's celestial mansion and says:

Go now and do what you want to do
    You have her address, but God help you,
If you so much as befoul the road,
    Anywhere in this sweet smelling abode!
For here, since the beginning of time,
    Relieving oneself has been a crime,
In ev'ry direction all that one sees
    Is free from the slightest bit of feces.[72]

It is perhaps misleading to call Behruz's satires and parodies, which depend on a knowledge of classical Persian literature, the Koran, the sayings of the prophets and Orientalist lore, "modern." One can say that in many ways he was a conservative in his approach to satire and that his works represent a return to what today in Iranian student circles is politely called "obscure." Behruz's satiric vision, however, is all-embracing; he mocked fundamental constituents of the Persian cultural complex, and for this reason his writings will never lose their relevance to those who are familiar with that complex. Writers like Dehkhodā and Jamālzāda, on the other hand, whose works are more topical, become less comprehensible as the events they describe grow vague in the popular consciousness. They have created a kind of immediacy in Persian satire. It is this immediacy, which we might call

[71]Ibid., ll. 65–68.
[72]Ibid., ll. 479–82.

245

"modernism," that has led to the popularity of satirical columns in newspapers, satirical television and radio programs, and satirical novels.

Since much of the televized, broadcast, and printed culture in Iran is urban in orientation, most of the topics chosen for such satires are the typical problems of urban life: traffic, pollution, taxis, rent increases. Some authors, however, have managed to deal with the problems of rural Iran or have been able to expand their vision to encompass the problems of rapid modernization. One of these authors is Ebrahim Golestān who, in addition to being a fine filmmaker, is the author of a novel-*cum*-screenplay called *Asrār-e ganj-e darra-ye jenni* (The secrets of the treasure of the enchanted valley, 1973).

Golestān's novel is the story of a poor farmer who, while ploughing his rocky fields located near an isolated village, uncovers a vast, underground treasure trove. He mutilates the treasure, which includes the golden remains of some ancient civilization, in order to bring bits and pieces of it to Tehran. With the help of a jeweler the farmer converts the treasure into cash. The jeweler and his wife introduce the farmer to the wonders of conspicuous consumption and not only urge him to buy all the latest furniture and appliances for his unelectrified farmhouse, but also arouse his lust for their servant girl. He sheds his peasant clothes and emerges as "modern man," *homo consumerus*, ready to trade his subterranean wealth for anything "Western" or "automatic." Golestān describes his metamorphosis in these terms:

> The [village] man was no longer wearing his secondhand suit. On the advice of the jeweler's wife he had his clothes cut by a tailor in the latest style. The inner man also seemed to have changed. He had taken so many of his treasures to the bazaar that apparently he had freed himself from traditional, everyday financial restrictions. Crossing these material boundaries created a newfound existence for him. Although on the surface spending money was an amusement, it was actually a kind of self-amplification, self-increment; buying was power, substance and identity, a way of imposing himself on the real world.[73]

Golestān's "camera" prose seems to be particularly well-suited for caricature, and, like Jamālzāda, he is merciless in his attacks on any

---

[73]E. Golestān, *Asrār-e ganj-e darra-ye jenni* (translated by this author), 77.

kind of facade brought about by grotesque forms of misapplied Westernism:

> The young relative of the jeweler's wife was not bothered by work. He thought of nothing else but becoming an "expert in the arts." It didn't matter in which "art," it was only enough that he have an artist's reputation. Of course a cinematic career seemed to take precedence over all others, and for this he picked up some of the jargon of the trade. His visions of his own future were equipped with a director's sun hat; a viewfinder hanging around his neck; a pair of black glasses for ordinary occasions; blacker glasses for filming. . . . What was bothering the youth now, however, was the question of whether or not he should grow a beard; and if he did, whether it would be a goatee or a full beard. He patiently waited for success to find him, but at the same time he hoped that they would start coming to interview him soon so that he could answer in the fashion of the times: "You see . . . sex, today . . . new developments in the interesting utilization of creativity . . . the pulsating magnificence of bitter, biting satire . . . rebellion . . . Jean Luc Godard . . . the message of mass communications. . . ." And again, "You see," and again, "satire . . . tradition . . . the young generation. . . ." In fact he didn't know anything about any of these, except "sex," and even that only to a certain extent, namely by himself.[74]

It is difficult to conclude an essay whose function is to provide an introduction to Persian satire. What perhaps becomes clear, after the briefest of surveys, is that despite strong cultural and institutional opposition to such literature, satire has been and continues to be a very popular mode of expression in Persian, and that it deserves the kind of attention that esoteric, epic and didactic Persian literature has received in the past. It is hoped that this essay has given some insight into the scope and nature of Persian satirical writings, and not merely served to define the personal tastes of the author.

The tradition of satirical-humorous papers like *Molla Nasr al-Din* and *Nasim-e shemāl* has continued with inevitable gaps and interruptions into the present. Under Rezā Shah political satire, which had been rampant before his accession, subsided and gave way to innoc-

[74]Ibid., 77–78.

uous social and domestic satire, *facetiae,* and verbal humor. *Towfiq,* a humorous paper published early in Rezā Shah's reign (1921–27), well represented this phase. With the lifting of censorship and the confused and fluid situation that followed the abdication of Rezā Shah, a suitable environment was again at hand for political satire. *Bābā Shāmāl,* a creation of the remarkably witty engineer Rezā Ganje'i, took advantage of the situation, and during 1944–45 and 1948–49 it offered one of the best examples of Persian satire and humor. Its stand was liberal and patriotic, and its humor was literate and urbane.

In post-Mossādeq periods this tradition was continued, although with less rigor, by a revived *Towfiq,* reissued in 1962. Its publication, however, was suspended because of its lampoons and cartoons against the government. The tradition has been kept alive since the 1979 revolution, generally by expatriate papers, mostly ephemeral, but without leaving a vacuum thus far.

# 14. The Indian or Safavid Style: Progress or Decline?*

The last phase of traditional Persian poetry before its return to the styles of the old masters occurred in the Safavid period. The quality of this poetry has been a matter of controversy. In the estimation of Jan Rypka, "The literature of the Safavid period is usually regarded as a literature of decline."[1] In 1911, in a letter to E. G. Browne, Mirza Mohammad Qazvini, the noted Persian scholar, pronounced an even harsher judgment: "Under this dynasty," he wrote, "learning, culture, poetry, and mysticism completely deserted Persia. . . ."[2]

The first question we must face is whether this was, in fact, the case. Did Persian poetry and prose under the Safavids sink into the literary doldrums, as so many critics have judged, or, rather, was this an age of positive literary merit? And if our response should be negative, how are we to account for the decline of literature in the face of the political strength, economic prosperity, and the flourishing of other arts in Safavid Persia?

The answer to these questions involves several basic considerations, which have to do not only with the quality and relative merit of Safavid literature, but also with the evolution of Persian literature as a whole.

It would be useful to define at the outset what we mean by Safavid literature. Roughly, this literature comprises imaginative prose and poetry written in Persian during the sixteenth and seventeenth centuries. The time span coincides more or less with the reign of the Safavid dynasty in Persia (1501–1722) and that of the Great Moghuls in India up to the death of Awrangzib (1658-1707). One may extend the period for about half a century, during which time Persian literature in both countries continued its previous course. In Persia this would bring us to the establishment of the Zand dynasty (1750); in India, to the end of the effective rule by the Great Moghuls (1761); and in the Ottoman Empire, to about the death of Mahmud I (1754).

From the geographical point of view, this literature was produced in a vast stretch of land extending from Turkey to Central Asia and the Indian subcontinent. In Muslim India the language of poetry was

*Based on a lecture given at the Isfahan Symposium, Harvard University, January, 1974, and subsequently published in *Iranian Studies* 7/1–2 (Winter–Spring 1974).

[1]J. Rypka, *History of Iranian Literatures*, (Dordrecht, Holland, 1956), 292.
[2]E. G. Browne, *A Literary History of Persia* (Cambridge, 1928), vol. 4, 26. Unless otherwise noted, this is the volume referred to hereafter.

chiefly, and in the north almost exclusively, Persian.[3] In the Turkic-speaking countries, both Turkic (namely, Turkish, Turki, and Chagatay) and Persian poetry were written, but, except for folk poetry, they were both modeled on poetry emanating from Persia. In the words of E. J. W. Gibb, "The first Ottoman poets—and their successors through many generations—strove with all their strength to write what is little else than Persian poetry in Turkish words. . . . Of national feeling in poetry they dreamed not; poetry was to them one and indivisible."[4] This is true, in fact, of the whole literature of the non-Arab Muslim peoples that Gibb calls West Asian. "The question as to what language a writer in this West-Asian literature should use," he points out, "whether this should be Persian, Ottoman, Turki, Urdu, or Pushtu, was generally, but not always, determined by the locality in which he happened to find himself."[5] To the Ottoman people, poetry was, he continues, "a single entity, no more affected by question of race or language than was theology or science. Therefore they might, and they did write these verses sometimes in Turkish, sometimes in Persian, accident generally deciding which, but in either case the spirit and the matter were the same, nothing differing except the words."[6]

The amount of Persian literature produced during these two and a half centuries is immense. No comparable amount of literature is available from other periods of the same duration. The greater share of this writing is poetry, which gravitates heavily toward lyric poetry, with the *ghazal* as its outstanding form. Imaginative prose literature is inconspicuous, almost insignificant, compared to the poetry of the period, and it has been deliberately ignored in the following discussion.

Although no reliable statistics are available, a general impression prevails that the greater part of this poetry was produced in the subcontinent,[7] hence the appellation of the "Indian school" or "Indian style" of Persian poetry.

Here we may consider the place that India occupies in the literature of this period. From the beginning the Muslim courts of India provided generous support for Persian literature. Of the earlier Persian poets, such major figures as Mas'ud-e Sa'd (d. 1121), Sanā'i (d. ca. 1150), Amir Khosrow of Delhi (d. 1325), and Hasan of Delhi

---

[3] For Arabic and Turkish literature produced in India, see A. Schimmel, *Islamic Literatures of India* (Wiesbaden, 1973), 6ff, 25–26, and chap. 13, below. In 1582 by royal decree Persian was also made the official language of the government.

[4] E. J. W. Gibb, *Ott. Poetry* (London, 1902; repr. 1965), vol. 1, 29.

[5] Ibid., vol. 2, xxxiv–v.

[6] Ibid., xxxv-vi.

[7] Schimmel, *Literatures*, 1, 8.

(d. 1327) were attached to the Muslim courts of India. The Safavid period coincided with the establishment and expansion of the Great Moghul Empire, by far the most important and the most cultivated Indian kingdom in Islamic times. Bābor (d. 1530), the founder of the dynasty, was a Timurid prince, brought up in Persian cultural traditions. His descendants expanded their realm, and their courts became brilliant centers of Persian art and culture, but above all, of Persian poetry. Most of these Timurid princes wrote poetry themselves and exercised critical judgment on the poets of their courts. The numerous biographies of poets compiled under the Great Moghuls are replete with references to the munificence shown by these kings, their viziers, and their nobles toward the poets. On occasion, their largesse extended even so far as to reward a poet with the equivalent of his weight in gold or silver. Their generosity reached not only the poets attached to their courts, but also many more, who, having heard of their patronage, sent them poems from various parts of India, Persia, and Transoxiana. Akbar (1556–1605), whose reign coincided with that of Shah 'Abbās the Great, assembled a galaxy of Persian poets in his court.[8] So did Akbar's successor, Jahāngir (1605–28), and Shāh Jahān (1628–59), who succeeded Jahāngir. In their cultivation of literary art, these monarchs were aided by a number of learned viziers, courtiers, and advisors whose intrinsic interest in poetry and whose critical judgment did much to encourage new talents.[9]

No wonder, then, that anyone in Persia who aspired to the writing of poetry conceived the desire of traveling to India and trying his fortune there. India became the Mecca of poets and artists.[10] A great

[8]See 'Abd al-Qāder Badā'uni, *Montakhab al-tavārikh* (Calcutta, 1869), vol. 3, 170ff; Shebli No'māni, *She'r al-'ajam*, Persian trans. F. Dā'i (Tehran, 1955), vol. 3, 4.

[9]In this respect the names of several individuals come immediately to mind. These include Bayrām Khānkhānān of the court of Homāyun (d. 1555); Abu'l-Fath Gilāni, a dignitary of Akbar's period; Shaikh Abu'l Fazl, a learned and liberal vizier of Akbar and a younger brother of the poet Fayzi; 'Abd al-Rahim Khānkhānān, the son of Bayrām, who succeeded to the title of his father and served Akbar and Jahāngir; and Zafar Khan Ahsan, the governor of Kashmir under Shāh Jahān. For an account of these and several other personalities, see Shebli, *She'r*, vol. 3, 3–15.

[10]The following lines by Sā'eb: "There is no head wherein the desire for thee dances not, / Even as the determination to visit India is in every heart." (trans. E. G. Browne, *Lit. Hist.*, vol. 4, 165) and by 'Abd al-Razzāq Fayyāz Lāhiji, the son-in-law of the philosopher Mollā Sadrā Shirāzi:

> Great is India, the Mecca for all in need,
> Particularly for those who seek safety.

> A journey to India is incumbent upon any man
> Who has acquired adequate knowledge and skill.

(quoted by P. Bayzā'i, introduction to the *Divān* of Kalim [Tehran, 1957], 5) express a widespread sentiment.

many Persian talents left their country for India, and the vast majority of them were well rewarded. Even the poet Hazin (d. 1766), who showed great aversion to India, eventually found refuge in the subcontinent following the Afghan invasion of Isfahan. It is in deference to the large number of poets in India writing in Persian that as noted above the third major style of Persian poetry is called Indian (the other two being Khorasani and Eraqi).

Of late, a number of Persian critics have advanced a case for calling the poetry of the period under discussion the "Safavi" or "Isfahani" school, on the grounds that it was largely fostered in Isfahan at the time of the Safavids.[11] The argument is cogent enough. With the shift of the Safavid capital to Isfahan in 1598, the city prospered and became the focus of the poets who represented the Safavid style. However, it seems to me that there is little reason to press this point too hard. To call the style "Indian" is the least compliment one could pay a country that so generously received and supported Persian artists and men of letters for several centuries.

## Controversy over Safavid Poetry

The quality of this poetry has been a subject of controversy, and the views expressed on it by critics of different periods and different orientations are sometimes diametrically opposed. Sām Mirzā (a brother of Shah Tahmāsp), who compiled a biography of his contemporary poets, the *Tohfa-ye Sāmi* (Gift of Sām), considers them superior to the poets of the past. He finds them equal to Khosrow of Delhi, Sa'di, and Anvari, and even superior to Ferdowsi and Sanā'i.[12] As to his view on the status of the poets, he declares them "chosen by God and recipients of endless [divine] light." And to drive his point home, he refers to a line by the twelfth-century poet Nezāmi, in which he counts poets second only to prophets in the human hierarchy.[13]

This is somewhat typical of the exaggerated views expressed by the contemporary authors of the *tadhkeras* (notices of the poets) concerning the poetry of their time.[14]

[11]See, e.g., A. Firuzkuhi's impassioned argument in his introduction to the *Divān* of Sā'eb, 2nd ed. (Tehran, 1957), 4–5 and R. Bayzā'i, introduction to the *Divān* of Kalim (Tehran, 1957), 13.

[12]Ed. R. Homāyun Farrokh (Tehran, n.d.), 3–4.

[13]Ibid., 3.

[14]Cf. Abu'l Fazl 'Allāmi's comment: "Poets strike out a road to the inaccessible realm of thought, and divine grace beams forth in their genius.' *Ā'in-e Akbari*, vol. 1, trans. H. Blochman (Calcutta, 1873), 548.

However, we obtain a very different view from Hazin, a brilliant, versatile, and encyclopedic writer and poet of the last phase of Safavid rule, who also compiled a *tadhkera* of his contemporary poets. He laments the decline of poetry in his time and deplores the banality of hackneyed poets, the abundance of incompetent versifiers, and the currency of plagiarism. His scathing criticism also extends to the writers of *tadhkeras*, whose faults include ignorance, distortion of facts, lack of critical aptitude, and unconscionable vulgarity. He sums up his views of the writings of his period with a hemistich: "The substance is wrong, the meaning is wrong, and the style is wrong; all is wrong."[15] His view of the status of poetry itself is no less negative:

> It is not hidden from the knowledgeable that the art of poetry, in comparison to the lofty arts and higher achievements, is marked by a lowly station. . . . The lower type of poetry is exceedingly worthless and mean and, in fact, derogatory to its composer; the middle type of poetry is only a waste of time and its existence and nonexistence are equal; to commit oneself to the perfect type of poetry, even if it should issue from a pure soul, would be useless in an uncritical age. . . . For many years now, [competent] criticism and understanding of poetry have become very difficult, in fact impossible, in the same way that writing [good] poetry has disappeared, and the pretensions of the claimants are all based on bombast.[16]

Much of Hazin's criticism, however, derives from his pessimistic nature and gloomy view of his own age. Otherwise, Hazin was himself a practitioner of the Safavid style, and not only arranged five *divāns* of his own poetry,[17] but considered his contemporary poets important enough to compile a laudatory biography of them.

The first effective criticism of Safavid poetry came from a group of Revivalist poets, who, toward the middle of the eighteenth century, turned away from the Indian style to a simpler, more lucid style and purer diction that simulated the style of the earlier Persian poets. A leading figure of the group was Lotf 'Ali Beg Āzar (1711–81), the author of the well-known *tadhkera* called *Ātashkada* (Fire-temple). The unmistakable distaste of Āzar for the style of the Safavid poets becomes clear in his comments on them, as well as in his scanty selections

---

[15]*Tadhkera-ye Hazin*, 2nd ed. (Isfahan, 1955), 5–6.
[16]Ibid., 7.
[17]M. Sereshk (M. Shāfi'i Kadkani), *Hazin-e Lāhiji* (Mashhad, 1963), 29.

of their works. His comment on Sā'eb, the outstanding poet of the Safavid period, sums up the attitude of the group:

> From the beginning of his writing poetry, the way to the firm imagery of the eloquent poets of the past had been blocked, and the undisputed rules followed by the old masters had been lost. After . . . Sā'eb, who was the instigator of this new distasteful style, the level of poetry continued daily in decline, until this time of ours, when . . . thanks be to God, their fabrications have completely fallen into disuse and the rule of the old masters revived. . . . Most of Sā'eb's poems were seen by me, and the following lines were selected only with great effort.[18]

Āzar's comment on Tāleb-e Āmoli, a major poet of the period and the poet laureate of the Moghul emperor Jahāngir, is also typical: "He is among the notables and compiled a *divān*. He has a peculiar style in poetry, which is not to the liking of eloquent poets."[19]

Āzar set the tone for other critics to assail the Indian style and to call for a return to the earlier style of poetry. His line of criticism, for instance, was continued by Maftun Donboli (d. 1827), a poet, historian, biographer, and critic of the early Qajar period. In his comment on the poet Moshtāq, a champion of the Revivalist cause, Maftun quite floridly airs the same views as those held by Āzar:

> When the meadow carpet of poetry became trampled by the insipid metaphors and vapid illustrations of Showkat,[20] Sā'eb, Vahid,[21] and their like and lost its freshness and splendor, Moshtāq came to stroll in the garden of poetry and rolled up their style like a bud and spread out a carpet of poetry woven in keep-

[18]Ed. H. Sādāt-e Nāseri, vol. 1 (Tehran, 1957), 123–25. Two manuscripts have the following instead of what has been quoted above: "He [i.e., Sā'eb] has a peculiar style in poetry, which has no resemblance to that of the eloquent poets of the past. Although he was not inclined to write panegyrics and quatrains, he has a *divān* of nearly one hundred thousand lines, which was examined by me, and after much consideration, the following lines were selected" (ibid., 127, n. 2).

[19]Ibid., vol. 2, 870–71.

[20]Showkat of Bukhara (d. 1695–96), a poet who enjoyed great reputation in Turkey and Central Asia and served as a model to many Ottoman poets; see E. J. W. Gibb, *Ott. Poetry*, vol. 4, 96–97.

[21]Mohammad Tāher Vahid Qazvini (d. 1708–09), a Safavid poet, statesman, and historiographer and a contemporary and friend of Sā'eb. See H. Ethé, "Neupersische Literatur," *Grundriss der iranischen Philologie* (Stuttgart, 1891–1904), vol. 2, 312, 342 and Ch. Rieu, *Catalogue of Persian MSS*, vol. 1 (London, 1879), 189b.

ing with his own taste. . . . The sweet-singing nightingales of his time [i.e., his contemporary poets] followed him.[22]

The most vituperative attack on the Safavid poets and their style, however, comes from the poet, anthologist, biographer, historian, and courtier Rezā Qoli Khān Hedāyat (1800–1872) in the introduction to his *Majma' al-fosahā'* (The meeting place of the eloquent), which is the best-known *tadhkera* of Persian poets. The language he employs is so harsh as to leave no doubt that aversion to the Safavid style had escalated by his time. Hedāyat maintains that:

After the Seljuk poets no progress was obtained in poetry; on the contrary, it declined daily from the highest level until it reached a middle stage with the poetry of Salmān Sāvaji and his like. A number of poets belonging to this stage attempted lyric poetry, but except for Khwāja Shams al-Din Mohammad Hāfez, whose *ghazals* have been well appreciated by the admirers of form and substance, there is hardly a *divān* inherited from them that could be enjoyed or would be worth hearing.

He goes on to say:

Gradually the poetry declined further from the middle stages and reached a low level. Under the Turkmans and the Safavids, reprehensible styles appeared . . . and since there were no binding rules for lyrics, the poets, following their sick natures and distorted tastes, began to write confused, vain, and nonsensical poems. They infused their poetry with insipid meanings instead of inspired truths, ugly contents . . . instead of fine rhetorical devices and attractive innovations. . . . But, since every defect is followed by a perfection, and each separation by a reunion . . . toward the end of the rule of the Lurs [namely, the Zand dynasty] several individuals directed their tastes toward reviving the style of the old masters and demonstrated awareness of the tastelessness of the style of the later poets and their banal ways . . . and endeavored . . . to divert people from their blameworthy style.[23]

---

[22]Quoted by M. T. Bahār from *Hadā'eq al-janān* in *Sabk shenāsi*, 2nd ed. (Tehran, 1958), vol. 3, 318.

[23]*Majma' al-fosahā'*, ed. M. Mosaffā (Tehran, 1957), vol. 1, 9–10.

This trend of thought continues into our own time, whose taste and critical standards have been largely shaped by the sensibilities of the Qajar poets. It has found its most steadfast contemporary exponent in the last poet laureate of Persia, Mohammad Taqi Bahār (1886–1951). In a series of lectures on the "Literary Revival" (*bazgāsht-e adabi*), which were later published in the journal *Armaghān*,[24] he denigrated the Indian style and considered the period of Fath 'Ali Shāh "a brilliant period of poetry, similar to that of Sultan Mahmud of Ghazna."[25] His views on the subject are expressed succinctly in a polemical poem addressed to a fellow poet, of which the pertinent stanzas, literally translated, read:

The Indian style possessed novelty,
But had very many failings,
It was infirm and spineless,
Its ideas were feeble, its imagery odd.
The poems were crowded with ideas, but unattractive;
They were wanting in eloquence.[26]

This assessment of Safavid poetry, coupled with an ever firmer appreciation of the Khorasani and Eraqi styles, gained increasing general acceptance and became the prevailing critical judgment expressed in treatises on Persian literature.[27]

This view of Safavid literature, however, has by no means been shared by everyone. Not only did the poets of the period consider their age one of great literary merit, but also the Indian and Ottoman critics, who by far outnumbered the Persian ones,[28] upheld their estimation of Safavid poets. The literary turnabout, which took place in Persia and which led to the rejection of the Indian style, did not occur outside the country. On the contrary, in India, Afghanistan, Central Asia, and Turkey, where Persian poetry received the added admiration reserved for imported goods, the Safavid trend continued without any major setback until recent times, when the impact of the West

---

[24]All these lectures are now published together in *Bahār o adab-e fārsi*, a collection of one hundred of Bahār's articles, carefully edited by M. Golbon, with an introduction by Gh.-H. Yusofi, 2 vols. (Tehran, 1972); see 43ff.

[25]Ibid., 49.

[26]*Divān*, vol. 2 (Tehran, 1957), 228. The poem is a response to Sarmad, who had expressed different views.

[27]A recent expression of this view appears in Y. Āryānpur, *Az Sabā ta Nimā* (Tehran, 1972), vol. 1, 7–13.

[28]See Browne, *Lit. Hist.*, vol. 4, 163; Gibb, *Ott. Poetry*, vol. 3, 247–48.

brought about considerable social transformation in these regions. Literary criticism in these countries, when negative, was directed not against the prevailing style, which was considered valid, but against the failings of individual poets within this style.[29]

The latest and, by far, the most outstanding of these critics is Shebli No'māni (d. 1914), whose *She'r al-'ajam* in Urdu, despite some methodological shortcomings, remains to this day one of the liveliest and most readable general estimates of Persian literature from the earliest times to the end of the seventeenth century. An indication of Shebli's opinion is provided by the fact that he devotes the entire third volume of his work to seven major poets of the Safavid period. Contrary to the views expressed by Hedāyat and Bahār, he considers these poets outstanding and their style an improvement on that of the earliest poets. He shows great appreciation for their concise expression of subtle feelings and their ingenuity in expressing and illustrating delicate lyrical thoughts. His enthusiasm for the merits of these poets is abundantly reflected in his remarks on them. For instance, he writes of 'Orfi: "Hosayn Thanā'i, Mohtasham, and Sanjar Kāshāni improved the *qasida* considerably, but 'Orfi lifted it from earth to sky."[30] He considers even Anvari no match for 'Orfi.[31]

By reading Shebli, one gets the distinct impression that the decline in Persian poetry began not in the fifteenth century or even earlier, as most modern critics would have it, but in the eighteenth century, after the demise of the great poets of the Safavid and Moghul era. To him, only the contrived poetry of Nāser 'Ali, Bidel, and their like constitutes a decline.[32]

The same exalted view of Safavid poetry prevailed in the Ottoman Empire, where Jāmi, 'Orfi, Sā'eb, and Showkat provided in turn the highest literary models.[33] An example of the reverent attitude toward the Safavid style is reflected in E. J. W. Gibb's comment on some of its representatives. Of Fozuli, a trilingual poet of the sixteenth century

[29]Among the excellent examples of such criticism are Serāj al-Din 'Ali Khān Ārezu's *Tanbih al-ghāfelin*, directed against Hazin's poetry, and the rejoinder to Ārezu by Gholām 'Ali Āzad Belagrāmi in his *Khezāna-ye 'āmera*. See Sereshk, *Hazin*, 40ff.

[30]*She'r al-'ajam*, vol. 5, 22.

[31]Ibid.

[32]Bidel's works, however, which have often been singled out as a notorious example of obtuseness and bombast in Persian lyric poetry, had a major impact in Central Asia into the 1920s. In fact, they gave rise to a mystico-poetic cult in Afghanistan and Transoxiana. This phenomenon is reflected in the expression *Bidel-khwāni* (reading of Bidel), which refers to weekly meetings at which Bidel's works were read and commented upon.

[33]Gibb, *Ott. Poetry,* vol. 1, 6; vol. 3, 247–48.

(d. 1562–63), who is hardly known in Persia, he writes: "There is no greater name in all Turkish literature than Fozuli of Baghdad," and counts him among "men who in any age and in any nation would have taken their place among the Immortals." Gibb writes further, "He composed with equal ease and elegance in Turkish, Persian, and Arabic, his Turkish poems being highly favored by the critics of Rum [i.e., Asia Minor], his Persian *divān* being the delight of the poets of every land."[34] He describes Showkat of Bukhara, a Persian poet of the seventeenth century (d. 1695–96), who represents the exaggerated style of the late Safavid school and is little known in Persia, as "deservedly famous for his marvelous ingenuity and fertility in the invention of fresh and picturesque images and similes," and further that "he continued for more than half a century to be the guiding star for the majority of Ottoman poets."[35] I have already referred to the respect shown to Bidel in Central Asia and Afghanistan well into the twentieth century.[36]

Of the Western critics, Ethé, Browne, and Rypka concur with the general estimate that from the middle of the seventeenth century, Persian poetry in both Persia and India entered a course of sharp decline, a course that had already begun in the fifteenth century.[37] Browne, however, when comparing Sā'eb with the poets of the Revival period, finds himself in agreement with Shebli rather than with Persian critics, in his admiration for this poet.[38] Further, while he regards the sixteenth and seventeenth centuries as a fairly barren period in Persia, he does not extend this view to India and speaks of "a brilliant group of poets from Persia . . . [who] adorned the court of the 'Great Moghuls' in India."[39]

Interestingly enough, of late, a certain reaction has appeared in Persia itself against the categorical rejection of the Indian style poetry. The most recent editors of Āzar's *Ātashkada* and Hedāyat's *Majma' al-fosahā'* have challenged the remarks of their respective authors about Safavid poets and have sought to correct their views.[40] The most thor-

---

[34]Ibid., vol. 3, 70, 71, 78.

[35]Ibid., vol. 1, 130; vol. 4, 95–97, 185.

[36]See above, n. 32.

[37]Ethé, "Neupersische Literatur," 309–11; Rypka, *Iran. Lit.*, 496–97; Browne, *Lit. Hist.*, vol. 4, 24ff.

[38]Browne, *Lit. Hist.*, vol. 4, 164–65, 265ff. See a similar view expressed earlier by Charles Rieu, who remarks on Sā'eb: "By common consent the creator of a new style of poetry, and the greatest of modern Persian poets," *Catalogue*, 693.

[39]Browne, *Lit. Hist.*, vol. 4, 25.

[40]See *Ātashkada* (Tehran, 1957), vol. 1, 124; *Majma' al-fosahā* (Tehran, 1957), vol. 1, 19 of the introduction.

ough defense of the Indian style, however, is penned by Amiri Firuz-kuhi, an able contemporary lyricist and a literary scholar, in the introduction to his edition of Sā'eb's *Divān*: "This glossing over of the facts, indeed this injustice and bias-peddling . . . and particularly the ignorant or hostile judgment of Āzar . . . has not only caused Sā'eb to be relegated to the rank of worthless poets, but also managed to hide half the body of the country's literature under masses . . . of ignorance and neglect."[41]

The controversial nature of Safavid poetry thus becomes evident, and the problems it poses involve the critic in more than a mere assessment of this poetry. In order to gain a clearer view of Safavid poetry and its worth, we may do well to remember that value judgments on literary products are, to a certain extent, a matter of taste, and taste varies with time. The critical writings of each age inevitably bear the imprint of its norms and follow its aesthetic criteria. Were a Sā'eb or a Kalim to review the poems of a Vesāl or Qā'āni, poets of the Revivalist school, they would probably find them wordy, tasteless, and destitute of poetic ideas. A clear instance of this divergence of tastes is provided by the comments of Nezāmi 'Aruzi (twelfth century) and Dowlatshāh (fifteenth century) on Rudaki's well-known poem, *Buy-e juy-e mowliyān āyad hami*: the former considers it "inimitable," the latter, "insipid."[42]

## The Self-Image of Safavid Literature

Each age creates its own literary canons, and no apologies are needed for our adherence to the criteria of our own time, so long as we allow for other approaches and points of view.

The literary tenets of the Safavid era differed decidedly from our own. The Safavid poets wrote with an exalted view of their poetry. Despite the homage paid to some earlier poets, they were very much enthralled with the poetry of their own time. They exhibited greater confidence in the quality of their work than, say, the poets of the Ghaznavid court, who looked up with admiration to the pioneer poets of an earlier period. Not only were the poets convinced of the superior quality of their works, but they also considered their period one of

[41]*Divān*, 2nd ed. (Tehran, 1957), 2. Amiri's eloquent defense heartened several other admirers of Safavid poetry in their efforts to revive interest in it. See e.g., Bayzā'i, introduction to Kalim's *Divān*, 12.

[42]Dowlatshāh, *Tadhkerat al-sho'arā'* (Leiden, 1901), 31–34; 'Aruzi, *Chahār maqāla*, ed. M. Qazvini (Leiden, 1910), 32.

literary prosperity and fertility. In their estimation, this age had given birth to thousands of fresh poetic ideas and its poetry had excelled that of other periods by the subtlety of its thought, the richness of its substance, and the novelty of its imagery. The major poets of the period, notably Fayzi, Kalim, and Sā'eb, considered themselves poets of a very high order,[43] and 'Orfi felt that his own works marked the apogee of Persian poetry.[44]

It is also a measure of the self-confidence of the Safavid poets that they frequently responded to and imitated one another's poems, for they considered the verses of their contemporaries important or attractive enough to adopt their meters and rhymes in poems of their own.[45]

Also, explicit praise for contemporary poets was not infrequent.[46] Within his own lifetime, Sā'eb grew into such an eminent figure that many people traveled to Isfahan to visit him. Two fellow-poets compiled anthologies of his vast output.[47] Indian rulers and notables also commissioned anthologies of the works of poets they sponsored.[48]

Again, the Safavid poet repeatedly shows consciousness of a specific aspect of his poetry that to him appeared original and inventive, an

---

[43]See Shebli, *She'r al-'Ajam,* vol. 3, 32, 60, 152; for Kalim see, for instance, *Divān,* 281 (*ghazal* no. 484); for Sā'eb, see *Divān,* 215 and also 871, where in a *qasida* in praise of Zafar Khan, he considers himself excelling the poets of all ages and challenges the boasts of his contemporaries 'Orfi, Now'i, and Sanjar.

[44]See Shebli, *She'r al-'Ajam,* vol. 3, 70–71, where a number of verses reflecting 'Orfi's exaggerated view of himself are brought together.

[45]This is a practice of long standing in Persian literature. One usually responds to a poem that one considers of special quality, and this attention is always a compliment to the original poet. The responding poet sometimes explicitly mentions the author of the original poem; this is particularly the case with Sā'eb, who generously refers to the poems that have moved him. In less confident periods, the poets respond to well-known poets of the past. In modern times Ferdowsi, Sa'di, and Hāfez have been the poets most frequently responded to. The technical terms for the practice are *tazmin* and *esteqbāl.* The first refers to the inclusion of a citation from the original poet, the second to imitating his meter and rhyme.

[46]For some examples see Shebli, *She'r al-'Ajam,* vol. 3, 82 (Fayzi's comment on 'Orfi in a private letter) and 163–67; Firuzkuhi, introduction to the *Divān* of Sā'eb, 33–34; 'Abd al-Bāqi Nahāvandi, *Ma'āther-e Rahimi,* vol. 3 (Calcutta, 1931), 115; the *Divān* of Naziri, 618, 622.

[47]See Firuzkuhi, the *Divān* of Sā'eb, 11, 27.

[48]Such an anthology was made, for instance, by Zafar Khan Ahsan (see above), a patron of Qodsi, Kalim, Sā'eb and some other poets. See Bayzā'i, introduction to the *Divān* of Kalim, 6, who quotes from Mohammad Afzal Sarkhosh's *Kalamāt al-sho'arā',* a contemporary *tadhkera.*

aspect that he believed raised his above the level of earlier poetry. Briefly, this aspect was the discovery and expression of new poetic ideas.[49]

## Nature and Norms of Safavid Poetry

Concern for novel ideas and impressive constructions dates back to the Timurid period. Some forerunners in this respect were Kamāl Khojandi, Kātebi, Besāti, Khiyāli, Amir Shāhi, and Āzari, all poets of the first half of the fifteenth century. The following lines show the consciousness of the poets themselves of their effort:

O Shāhi, describe the beloved's lips by some new image
There is no pleasure in oft-heard words.
(Amir Shāhi)

O Kamāl, even if I concur that the poems of your peers
Are all, like miracles, divinely inspired,

When they are void of distinctive images,
It is futile to imagine that they find renown.
(Kamāl Khojandi)[50]

But it is in the Safavid period that this tendency reaches its culmination, to the point that it affects the quality of poetry and helps shape a new style.

The poet can satisfy his search for an original poetic idea in a number of ways:

(1) *By hitting upon a novel simile or metaphor.* Sā'eb, for example, advises his fellow men to be "as open-faced as the secrets of the drunk." Another line by him reads:

Like a bow, whose share of the hunt is a [mere] yawn,
Whatever I have is for others.

---

[49]Pride in the innovative merit of their poetry finds adequate expression in the works of the poets. See, for some examples, Shebli, *She'r al-'Ajam*, vol. 3, 10, 80, 165; M. Mosaffā, *Divān* of Naziri, notes, pp. 618, 620; Shereshk, *Hazin*, 53ff.

[50]The critics of the period were also alive to the issue, and not always in agreement, as evident from Dowlatshāh's comment on Kamāl Khojandi: "The learned men of letters maintain that the subtleties of the Shaikh [Kamāl] have removed his poetry from sincere feelings and passion." *Tadhkera*, 328. For further details and examples, see E. Yarshater, *She'r-re fārsi dar 'ahd-e Shāhrokh* (Tehran, 1953), 144ff.

Or consider the following line by Naziri:

> Like a sputtering candle flame,
> Life hesitates to leave me, knowing that you dwell in my heart.

Or, again, the following line by Sā'eb:

> It is a mere line from the book of the wanderings of Majnun,
> The whirlwind afoot on the skirt of this desert.

(2) *By creating a new variation of an older image or theme.* There are literally thousands of variations on such familiar images introduced by earlier poets as: the particle of dust (*dharra*), which, despite its nothingness, strives to rise to the sun; the legendary bird *homā*, whose favor may raise a beggar to the throne; the tulip and its black spot, which resembles the burnt-out heart of the lover; the tavern, inhabited by carefree drinkers who have washed their hands of our bigoted world; the unattainable mirage, eluding us like success; the desert thorns, which prick and sting the lover's blistering foot; the lover's heart, chained in the curls of the beloved; wretched Reason withdrawing before imperious Love; the dew losing its life to a moment of the sun's kindness; the noble cypress, foregoing the benefit of fruits and standing free from the hazards of the seasons; lightning striking the dried grass just as the beloved's glance strikes the lover's heart. One can mention, in fact, the whole repertory of images employed in Persian lyrics of the Eraqi school. As an example of variations on the old theme of the candle burning itself down like a lover, the following line by Kalim may be cited:

> Should I keep thus sinking into myself from the weight
>     of sorrow,
> I shall end up, like a candle, having my skirt as a
>     collar.[51]

Or the following from Hazin, as a variation on the theme of love being more burning than lightning and more consuming than fire:

---

[51]Kalim, *Divān*, 90.

The lightning flees with burnt breath [in shame] from
   my land;
The flame is mere dust, arisen from my ashes.[52]

On the theme of the mystic Mansur b. Hosayn al-Hallāj, who in his
rapture claimed divinity, Sā'eb, in a disparaging comment, offers this
novel variation:

Mansur's bowl was empty, thus it reverberated;
Otherwise, in the tavern of oneness no one is even
   conscious of himself.[53]

(3) *By capturing and expressing some subtle feeling or situation.* The following line by Naziri may illustrate the point:

So as not to shame her by her unfounded indignation
I confess to uncommitted sins.[54]

The following lines on the theme of the lover's jealousy against real
or imagined claimants may also be quoted in this respect:[55]

I would not soften your heart by my laments,
Fearing that someone else's lament may sway you.
                ('Orfi)

Jealousy kills me everytime I hear a stranger sigh
Fearing he sighs for love of you.
                (Bahā'i 'Āmeli)

Though she came to visit me, I died;
Wondering from whom she had asked the way to my house.
                ('Ali Qoli Mayli)

I ask everyone I meet about her,
But to myself I whisper, O God, let him be ignorant.
                (Vahid Qazvini)

[52]Sereshk, *Hazin,* 86.
[53]Sā'eb, *Divān,* 181.
[54]Naziri, *Divān,* ed. M. Mosaffā (Tehran, 1961), 231.
[55]Most of the following lines are taken from an anthology which I made for myself
when I was a graduate student.

Behold my jealousy; even He who fulfills desires
Has not heard your name from my lips during prayer.
('Orfi)

Out of love for my beloved I am even jealous of myself;
I have passed the point of being jealous only of others.
(Naziri)

I am dying of jealousy; how many times can I witness
The wine cup touching its lip to yours and giving up its life.[56]
(Tāleb Āmoli)

(4) *By offering a clever, witty remark,*[57] as in:

What a profitable theft is stealing a kiss;
It doubles if it is reclaimed!
(Sā'eb)

When you left me last night, I did not sense it;
For you are life, and the passing of life makes no sound.
(Hazin)

The only thing which troubles me about the Day of
    Resurrection is this,
That one has to look once more on the faces of humanity.
(Sā'eb)

If one cannot walk without sight, how then
Can you pass the world by when you close your eyes to it.
(Kalim)

(5) *By employing a keen observation.* Notice, for instance, the following line by Kalim, in which he compares the white hair growing under dyed hair to teeth in a mocking laugh at old age:

[56]*Ghāleb tohi konad* has a double meaning: literally, "that it empties its vessel" and figuratively, "that its soul departs from its body." As in many verses of the period, both meanings apply, the figurative sense revealing a new level of meaning and affording the reader a pleasurable surprise.

[57]Recourse to *double entendre* (*ihām*), which is very frequent in Safavid poetry but hardly translatable, may be classified under this category. Most rhetorical devices, in fact, are manifestly "witty."

When white roots peep out from under hennaed hair,
It is a toothy grin mocking your beard.[58]

(6) *By enlivening common phenomena with an unexpected interpretation,*
as in the explanation offered by Faghāni for the presence of dew drops
on the rosebud at dawn:

Each dawn the rosebud, saturated with dew,
Cleanses its lips in order to call your name in prayer.[59]

Or this line by Sā'eb, which interprets white hair in an unusual manner:

The milk I had sucked as an infant
Turned into white hair and shot out [on my head] through
    the strains and stresses of the spheres.

Or the following line by Ghani Kashmiri, which is highly contrived:

The narcissus dared to speak of your eyes; Zephyr struck
    her in the mouth.
Now she suffers from toothache and must suck water
    through a straw.[60]

(7) *By invoking a paradox.* For instance, Naziri, in a supreme maso-
chistic gesture, claims that he gave up challenging Fortune, since he
found it infirm in its enmity:

I throw down my shield, since Fortune is feeble in its
    hostility,
I am not to challenge an unmanly enemy.[61]

In another line he seeks justice from enemies, not friends:

---

[58]Kalim, *Divān*, 1. Kalim's *qasida* in praise of the first Imam (*Divān*, 1–3) is replete
with remarks based on the keen observation of daily life.
[59]Faghāni, *Divān*, ed. S. Khwānsāri (Tehran, 1937), 3.
[60]Traditionally the eyes of the beloved are likened to the narcissus. The poet twists
this cliché by saying that the narcissus should not dare to aspire to such resemblance.
Since it has, however, it has been hit in the mouth; the idea is to offer a poetic *raison
d'être* for the flower's stalk.
[61]Naziri, *Divān*, 279.

No truth is left in friends because of envy,
If you seek justice, seek it from enemies.[62]

Hazin uses a fine paradox in his jibe at religious hypocrisy:

O Brahman, you have no weight before us,
Since our feigned faith excels your unbelief.[63]

And Shifā'i complains that his beloved is not cruel enough:

This is yet another oppression that you do not hurt your
    lovers enough
So that they become accustomed to cruelty.[64]

(8) *By reaching a new level of poetic exaggeration;* for instance, in the
following line by Sā'eb:

So many hearts have melted by beholding you,
That it is hard to cross your street without a ship.[65]

Or this line of Qodsi:

A flood descended [so mighty] that it sank the sea in its
    whirlpool;
Which lover removed his sleeve from his drenched eyelashes?

Or this line by Faghāni:

You visited the lover's dream, and he rubbed your feet
So much to his eyes, that your feet took on the tone of henna.[66]

Or this line by Naziri:

I have become so feeble from the agony of awaiting you
That my glance has no strength to reach your face.

[62]Ibid., 42.
[63]Sereshk, *Hazin*, 80.
[64]Shebli, *She'r al-'Ajam*, vol. 5, 63.
[65]Sā'eb, *Divān*, 216.
[66]In the world of Persian lyrics, the lover sheds tears of blood.

Or this line by Kalim:

My black fortune has so darkened the spheres
That bats now press the sun hard to their bosoms.

(9) *By illuminating an aphorism or a common belief by an apt illustration,*
as in the following lines:

Love befriends a grieved heart more readily:
A smoke-crowned lamp is more quickly kindled.
(Naziri)

It is foolish to lean back on the enemy's obeisance:
The flood by kissing its feet brings down the wall.
(Sā'eb)

Befriending the weak illumines the heart:
When wax allies itself with wick, it radiates in the gathering.[67]
(Sā'eb)

Leaving this troubled world is better than entering it:
The rosebud enters the garden with constrained heart and
    departs smiling.
(Sā'eb)

Many such lines sound like, or have indeed become, proverbs, containing as they do vivid sensory parallels which have both literal and figurative meanings.[68] This may be further illustrated by some lines from Sā'eb, the great master of this art:

If God should will it, the enemy will become the source
    of benefit:
The source of the paste in a glassmaker's workshop is
    stone.

Everyone who like the candle exalts his head with a
    crown of gold

---

[67]*Sham'-e mahfel* has a double meaning: literally, the candle of the gathering; figuratively, the center of attraction. Both meanings are exploited by the poet.

[68]For instance, in the proverb "An empty shotgun scares two people," both the literal and the figurative meanings apply.

Will oft-times sit [immersed] in his tears up to the
neck.[69]

When a man grows old, his greed grows young:
Slumber becomes heavy at the time of dawn.

All this talk of faith and unbelief leads to one end:
The dream is the same, only interpretations differ.

Only light-headed people grow excited by every empty word:
A slight breeze makes a bamboo grove reverberate.

An old palm tree has more roots than a young one:
Older men are more strongly attached to the world.

From the insignificance of dust on top of the wall I concluded
That a nobody does not become a somebody by sitting on high
places.

Revolution of the sphere does not distinguish good from evil:
The millstone does not separate wheat from barley.

In the field of free choice, like a child on a hobbyhorse,
We are mounted in our own eyes, but [in fact] are on foot.

One could mention a few more methods as well as a number of
rhetorical figures used by the poet with the same aim in view. And
yet the poet's endeavor to generate surprise and excite admiration
often involves a more complex technique. To impress the reader, the
poet often has recourse to a combination of the means mentioned
above.

This point may need some elaboration. In order to appreciate Persian lyric poetry we must remember that the poet's quest is not merely,
or even chiefly, to express a sentiment or a thought, but to formulate
the idea in an impressive manner. The pleasure derived from Persian
poetry involves a marked element of aesthetic surprise.[70] A poet must

[69]Trans. E. G. Browne, *Lit. Hist.*, vol. 4, 276.

[70]Cf. Avicenna on "wonder" (*ta'jib*) as an element of aesthetic appreciation: "And in
imagination there is something of [a sense] of wonder, which is absent in demonstrable
truth. . . . Imagination [which is the basis of the art of poetry] is a yielding to wonder
and the pleasures that are in the utterance itself." "Al-She'r," in *al-Shefā': al-Manteq*, ed.
A. Badawi (Cairo, 1966), 22–23. He uses the word *mo'jeb*, "causing wonder," in reference
to the pleasurable quality of poetry. Cf. also a similar approach by Nasir al-Din Tusi,
*Asās al-eqtebās*, ed. M. Rezavi (Tehran, 1947), 590.

make his readers admire and marvel at his mastery, besides being moved by it. This mastery consists of not only the ability to conceive a poetic idea, but also the ability to transmit it by a well-constructed, elegant expression. Not expression alone, but apt, admirable expression is the poet's aim. The key to the understanding of aptness in this context is "ingenuity." In order to construct an ingenious expression, the poet draws on a large set of rhetorical devices. Chief among these are *tanāsob* or *morā'āt-e nazir* (harmony of images or congruence of poetic ideas), *tazādd* (antithesis), *mobālagha* (hyperbole), *ihām* (*double entendre* or amphibology), *talmih* (allusion), *ersāl-e mathal* (illustrative reasoning or argument by illustration or analogy), *hosn'e ta'lil* (poetic explanation), *kenaya* (symbolic statement) and *jenās* (homonymy or play on the resemblance of words).

A simple image, symbol, or trope is hardly sufficient; the poet often uses these as material for more elaborate constructs. As the seventeenth century wears on, the poet uses not only rhetorical figures abundantly, but he tends to combine and cross them, twist and turn them around, substituting in the process allusion for expression, evocation for declaration, and intimation for statement. The final product is sometimes reminiscent of paintings in the style of Synthetic Cubism by Picasso, Gris or Braque, where hints of objects and figures (or parts of them) are meshed, dovetailed, and otherwise combined into an evocative picture. Bidel's constructs, in which he frequently breaks, combines, and orchestrates his crowded imagery, often have the effect of an ingenious contrapuntal composition, whose various strands have become difficult to follow.

Such complex constructions take place generally within the span of a line, even a mere hemistich. The line is the unit of lyric poetry, and compactness is essential to its effect. Dramatic climax or conclusion is alien to the artistic design of Persian lyrics. They follow an entirely different literary design, which consists of a series of clever, independent strokes, held together by the formal cohesion of the poem.

To call rhetorical devices "embellishments," as they often are, is misleading. Much of Persian poetry is essentially rhetorical, and rhetoric is a conceptual rather than a formal feature of it. The stringent requirements of rhythm and rhyme add their own challenges to the conceptual organization of poetic ideas. The effortless ease and fluency of a Ferdowsi, a Sa'di, or a Hāfez do not represent an absence of such sophistications. Their mastery, rather, disguises their inimitable craftsmanship. A poet who succeeds in the face of the tyranny of form and the exigency of rhetorical formulation excites our admiration, as does the flawless performance of an acrobat or a magician.

It is well known that Persian poets, almost without exception, indulge in braggadocio and conceit. Whereas the conceit of an Arab poet encompasses a broad spectrum of achievements, the Persian poet boasts almost exclusively of one quality: his gift and mastery as a poet. Were it not for the dexterous character of his art, such self-glorification might strike us as excessive and odd. As it is, the poet is only too well aware of the nature of his craft, and like his audience, marvels from time to time at his own achievement.

It was also this overriding concern for creating "impressive" constructs that prompted the Timurid poets to achieve feats of formal acrobatics. Kātebi (d. 1435) wrote three *mathnavis*; one features double rhyme in every line, the second combines a rhyme and an alliterative wordplay (*jenās*) in each line, and the third can be read in two different meters throughout. Ahli of Shiraz (d. 1535) responded to the challenge by composing a *mathnavi* called *Sehr-e halāl* (White magic), which combines all three of these artifices![71]

Kātebi also wrote a *qasida* in which he took it upon himself to use the Persian equivalents of "camel" (*shotor*) and "room" (*hojra*) in each hemistich, and his contemporary, Lotf Allāh Nishāburi, composed a *qasida* that, along with the normal rhyme, repeats the names of the four elements at the end of each line.[72] In the ever-difficult field of chronograms, Kamāl Kajkuli wrote an elegy, of which the Chagatai vizier Amir 'Ali Shir says, "Such deeds are in fact beyond human aspiration; it is therefore believed that he had conquered the planet Mars."[73] The remark is not surprising in view of the fact that multiple dates can be extracted from several lines of the poem. 'Ali Shir's translator into Persian wonders what he would have said if he had heard the *qasida* that Sahāb wrote after 'Ali Shir's death. From each of the first hemistichs the date of 'Ali Shir's birth can be extracted, and from each of the second, the date of his death.[74] And yet such poems look pale when compared to a variety of *Mowashshahāt*[75] and virtuoso compositions, such as those employing only dotted or undotted letters throughout.[76] It is yet another measure of the preoccupation of the

[71]For details, see Yarshater, *She'r-e fārsi dar 'ahd-e Shāhrokh*, (Tehran, 1955), 190ff.
[72]Ibid., 122.
[73]*Majāles al-nafā'es*, ed. A. Hekmat (Tehran, 1944), 14.
[74]Ibid., 207.
[75]Poems that produce additional poems, lines, names or dates, when some specified letters or words of the poem (e.g., the first letter of each line) are put together.
[76]For further details, see Yarshater, *She'r-e fārsi*, 119ff., 131.

times that the writing of verse-riddles became a frequent occupation of the poets.

In the Safavid period attempts at formal virtuosity subsided in the interest of conceptual sophistication. The poets were too busy coining and combining ingenious images to play too much with metrics or the formal aspects of the language or writing. However, it is also a fact that the lyric writers of this period were not satisfied with a mere rhyme and generally add a *radif* (a word or phrase which is repeated throughout the poem after the rhyme). In the whole body of Sā'eb's *Divān*—and it is a copious one—there are no more than a couple of *ghazal*s without a *radif*.[77]

The arduousness of the poet's task and the constraints placed upon his art should not lead us to believe, however, that his message was restricted or his tongue tied. The Persian poet simply operated within this particular framework, determined by some basic elements of his culture. What cultural or social circumstances helped shape the formal and conceptual frame of Persian poetry is outside the scope of this paper, but it may be noted that a certain correspondence between the canons of political behavior and social ethics, on the one hand, and literary norms on the other, is worth investigating.

When poetry was first written in Persian, judging by what is left of early Samanid poetry, content was stressed. The creation of poetic ideas and fresh imagery was more important than the manner of their formulation. In the course of time, however, the ingenious formulation of thought gained importance and finally became the dominant aspect of poetry. In this respect, the development of Persian literature as a whole may be studied from the vantage point of the interplay or tension between the spontaneity of expression, on the one hand, and the formal exigency and rhetorical demands of the craft, on the other.

## Aspects of Safavid Poetry

From the fourteenth century, almost during the lifetime of Hāfez, a deepening interest in the intellectual, witty formulation of thought sets in. Many lines in this poetry are remarkable, if not in purity of diction and musicality, at least in keenness of perception, wittiness of expression, and skillful orchestration of ideas within a line. Those who

[77]Examples of verbal and chronographic virtuosity, however, can be found also in the Safavid period. See Ethé, "Neupersische Literatur," 309–11 for the description of a congratulatory *qasida* by Vahmi, a poet of the court of Shāh Jahān, which puts Sā'eb's poems to shame.

have the leisure to acquaint themselves with the vast poetical output of this period will find scattered gems of considerable beauty in the works of Safavid poets. Striving for novelty and for subtle and ingenious ideas has on many occasions succeeded in producing terse, pithy, epigrammatic lines or clusters of lines that are not to be found in the poetry of other periods. Anyone who compiles an anthology of single lines of Persian poets is bound to select a large number from this period, with Sā'eb in the forefront. Browne need not have felt ashamed of his choice.[78]

In this sense, and only in this sense, Safavid poetry represents a certain advance. One cannot help being awed at the sheer conceptual dexterity that seems at times beyond human ability. The skill with which the poets of the Indian style weave various strands of thought into an evocative, multi-faceted web, subtly connecting the different levels of meaning or crossing from one to another, leaves the reader breathless. The effect might be compared to the first aerial view of a busy intersection of multiple roads in an American highway system.

It is this particular achievement that raises Safavid poetry above the level of a mere continuation of Timurid poetry. The intensity of this quality has also bestowed on Safavid poetry the title of a new style, even though its beginning lies in Timurid times.

This advance was made, however, at a price. The quality of thought and the directness of expression suffered, and the emotive aspect of poetry sank under masses of artifice. Metaphors based on highly tenuous relationships become permissible—far-fetched comparisons whose comprehension taxes the imagination of the reader. Eventually, as Alessandro Bausani points out in his ingenious discussion of the Indian style techniques,

as the comparison becomes more and more hyperbolical, even the last thin thread of formal resemblance is snapped, and we arrive at totally free images like, for example, in the following by Bidel (d. 1721) "Turbulent, the wave's pen writes the story of the sea" . . . where the choice of comparison between "wave" and "pen" is completely free and personal.[79]

---

[78]Browne, *Lit. Hist.*, vol. 4, 164.

[79]Bausani, *Le letterature del Pakistan e dell'Afghanistan*, rev. ed. (Florence and Milan, 1968), 49. See also his *Storia della letteratura Persiana* (Florence and Milan, 1968), 294ff. and "Contributo a una definizione dello 'stile indiano' della poesia persiana," *Annali*, n.s. 7 (1958), 167ff.

Pulling at diverse images with elusive links and building intricate, dazzling structures on precarious foundations, the poets become jugglers of images and tropes rather than interpreters of feelings. With this deepening pursuit of mental acrobatics and the unrelenting attempt to impress and amaze, they get further and further away from real life experience, and their poems become more and more abstract.

In this sense, Safavid poetry represents a decline. Eventually it becomes caught in a web of complex rhetorical devices from which it cannot be extricated. It ends in contrived artificiality and in puzzle-like constructions, a maze of metaphors and forced imagery that cloy. The sheer intellectual exercise required to catch all the meanings and multiple relationships is exhausting. We search for some simple expression of heartfelt emotion, but it is only rarely that we find it. The poets, although ostensibly communicating their inner feelings to us, are in fact engaged in a "game." The game eventually becomes so complex and demands so much mental effort that it kills the pleasure of playing.

The flight from simplicity and the reluctance to engage in direct expression are also reflected in a number of syntactical features of the verse. These include reversing the logical order of a sentence, an argument or an exposition, so that the poet would not be in danger of being understood too easily and the readers would not be robbed of their pleasure in unraveling a complex structure and gaining an aesthetic release when the meaning finally dawned on them. Such a reversal may be effected, for example, by placing a conditional clause after the main clause, or by transposing the expected order of a simile, or by making a verbal complement follow the verb, against the normal grammatical order. All three of these are exemplified in a *ghazal* of Hazin, partially translated here:[80]

Spring clouds rolled in the sweat of shame
In the face of the affluence of my tear-raining eyelashes.

Even as the dust which springs from the startled flight of a gazelle,
Peace flees startled from my restless heart.

The heart of envy makes the tulip's heart bleed,
If your brand should blossom on my side.[81]

[80]Language peculiarities cannot be brought out easily in a translation. Only an approximation of the syntactical haziness may be expected here.

[81]In the original, the subject of the verb in the first hemistich is the brand; the poet is twisting around a simile likening the tulip's black spot and the beloved's brand.

Like wild rue, would crackle in the fire of your love,
My spark even in the days when it dwelled in flint.[82]

## Linguistic Shortcomings

Coupled with this contrived mode of expression are certain linguistic shortcomings, which are particularly annoying to the educated modern reader. First, the syntax is occasionally impaired. Second, the words are very often inadequate, that is to say, although the meaning comes through, it is not well expressed in all aspects. Finally, the poems of the period strike our ears musically as somewhat drawn out and languid. We miss those well-placed shifts of tone and those artistically appealing arrangements of long and short syllables that make the music of the classical poetry so attractive.

In pre-Timurid times not only is there a correct correspondence between word and meaning, but the choice of words is generally governed by an aesthetic sensibility that rejects some words and favors others. Modern taste, insofar as the music of line and the choice of words are concerned, is educated by the style of the classical poets, and therefore the language of the Safavid period strikes us as somewhat wanting.

Here we may also consider the question of the infiltration of the popular language into poetry, which some critics have associated with the erosion of the classical style, although this question is essentially distinct from the language deficiency referred to above. It has been suggested that in the Safavid period, because of excessive preoccupation with religious training and a disruption of the normal curriculum, those who wrote poetry were not so familiar with the works of classical writers as their predecessors.[83] Therefore the language of the streets crept into poetry and robbed it of its more elegant and musical diction. There is some truth in this. The language of poetry in both India and Iran does reveal many aspects of the spoken language, as against the polished language of writing. Bausani, who has presented us with one of the more comprehensive discussions of the Indian style,

---

[82]In the original, the spark, which is the subject of both verbs, comes at the end of the line. The idea is to give a poetic explanation of the spark's scintillation. Likening the spark to the crackling of wild rue on fire implies that the spark was jumping for joy with the knowledge that the lover would borrow the fire from the stone as an expression of his love. The line is not only complicated, but somewhat defective in language. The poet is trying to do too much within a single line.

[83]See Browne, *Lit. Hist.* 24ff., where M. Qazvini's view to this effect is also cited; also Bahār, *Sabk shenāsi*, vol. 2, 49.

attributes this penetration of popular language into poetry to a "breakdown of formal harmony" that took effect in the Safavid period.[84] He writes:

> One of the most important catalysts in the formation of the Indian style was its liberation from the influence of a critical environment. Such a liberation was possible on two grounds: one geographical, namely the transfer [of the literary center] to India, where different social conditions and different tastes prevailed and where Persian was not the native tongue of many local poets; and the other social, namely the disinterest on the part of the Safavids in poetry, and the replacement at the court, in the sphere of spiritual influence, of the class of secretaries and literary men by that of the Shi'ite clergy, which had little or no particular taste for classical poetry.[85]

There is no doubt that poets of the Safavid period did not exhibit the same basic concern for linguistic purity and elegance as did Ghazā'eri or Anvari or Shams-e Qays or their like; therefore, the introduction of familiar expressions did not meet with much highbrow discouragement, although this is not to say that literary criticism had abated. In fact in Persia, but to an even greater degree in India and Turkey, comments on the merits and demerits of literary compositions continued to flourish, and the *tadhkera*s of the period display a keener interest in literary criticism than previously.[86] Their major preoccupation, however, was with the ingenuity of poetic thought rather than with refined diction.

Under the Safavids the emergence of the Shi'ite *olamā'* as an influential pressure group perhaps helped to maintain and promote the relaxation of classical restrictions. It would be more difficult to assign a role in this respect to India, since in a foreign country written works are bound to command greater respect as models than the spoken language, as witnessed also by the course of poetry in the Ottoman Empire. The Persian poets of India did no more than follow the trends set in Persia. Major poets like Fayzi, 'Orfi, Naziri, Zohuri, Tāleb, Asir, Kalim, Qodsi, and Sā'eb, who are the best representatives of the Indian style, were at the same time all products of a continuous, uninterrupted Persian tradition. Fayzi, who alone among all these poets

---

[84]Bausani, *La letteratura Persiana*, 296; *Le letterature del Pakistan e dell'Afghanistan*, 51ff.
[85]*La letteratura Persiana*, 294.
[86]See above, 259f.

was born in India, does not differ on that score from the others. In fact his language, like that of his contemporary 'Orfi, is closer to that of the earlier masters, since he was closer to them in time.

The important point to bear in mind is that the gradual encroachment of popular language and the decline of classical linguistic and rhetorical standards date back to social upheavals caused by Mongol and Tatar invasions.[87] Even though the movement reaches its culmination toward the end of the Safavid period this is not a demarcation line. To realize the gradual development of this tendency, it is sufficient to remember that: (1) the *ghazal,* which became especially popular from the thirteenth century, was by its very nature more easily susceptible than the *qasida* to the use of intimate language, as were lyric *mathnavis;* (2) the spread of Sufi thought and practice and the popularity of mystic orders in the period between the Mongol invasion and Safavid supremacy further helped to diffuse these two genres among the ordinary people and make them far less elitist than before; (3) the weakening of literary discipline among the secretarial class had its faint beginnings in the thirteenth century, when the Mongol holocaust caused considerable disruption of normal life, and the subsequent Tatar and Turkman invasions and frequent wars among rival princes and pretenders hardly helped to restore the situation. No wonder, then, that the erosion of classical "eloquence" has frequent examples in the fifteenth century.[88]

However, from a literary point of view the admission of popular idiom is neither detrimental nor meritorious. Rumi is not a lesser poet because of his frequent use of everyday language, and Iraj visibly gains by it. It is the linguistic "infirmity" met in both poetry and prose during this period that deserves notice and must be considered one of the features of Safavid literature.

The question of language, however, cannot be separated from other issues affecting the poetry of the period. After all, language is only a mirror of thought, and in a way the two are the same: weakness in language reflects weakness in thought. Logical thinking cannot be separated from good syntax.

Attributing progress to Safavid poetry in one respect and decline

---

[87]Cf. Bertels's view, which also places the erosion of classical style earlier than the Safavid period and associates it with the poetical activity of the urban population as against the feudal aristocracy. See "K voprosu ob 'indiiskom stile' v persidskoi poezii," in *Charisteria Orientalia* (collection of papers dedicated to J. Rypka), ed. F. Tauber, V. Kubíčková, and I. Hrbek (Prague, 1956), 59, and below, 282.

[88]See above, 261.

in another may appear to be an equivocal appraisal. This has not been my intention; rather, I have tried to demonstrate that questions about artistic developments, or any human affairs for that matter, can hardly be answered satisfactorily by a simple yes or no. A purist may see in the rococo style a downward trend compared to the classical style of the Renaissance, and yet one cannot deny that the rococo, within its own frame of reference, has satisfied some sophisticated tastes and has contributed to the enrichment of the arts. Or again, one might prefer the clarity and firmness of the *naskh* or *tholth* style of Arab-Persian calligraphy, but who can deny the fascination of the dancing turns and twists of the *shekasta*?

Still, the steadfast inquirer may legitimately ask for an overall evaluation of Safavid literature. The answer to that question is provided by the simple fact that the Safavid era marks the last phase of the full cycle of the Persian classical tradition. A remarkable literature makes its last efforts during this period and then fades out in exhaustion. The Revivalist poetry of the next two centuries represents the last rally before the final rout.

With the last of the poets writing in the Indian style (and not with Jāmi, as is often assumed) the genuine classical period comes to an end.[89] Naturally the assumption of such a cycle cannot be divorced from a consideration of the creative energies of the people who produced the literature. The exhaustion that characterizes the tail-end of Safavid literature is, in fact, evident not only in the arts, which declined sharply after Shah 'Abbās, but also in the whole sphere of social and cultural life.

## Parallelism between Poetry and the Other Arts

Here we may briefly consider the question of parallelism between poetry and the other arts. First we may wonder whether the Safavid period (which in its first half was conspicuous for Persian painting, architecture, and textiles) represents the peak of these arts as is sometimes assumed. Would it not be more plausible to think of the early Safavid period as marking not so much the zenith of these arts as the

---

[89]The mistaken view that Jāmi (d. 1492) either marks the end of the classical period or is the last great poet of the classical tradition is based partly on the one-sided view of the Revivalist critics who chose to ignore the Safavid period, and partly on the lack of appreciation for the fact that Persian poetry continues its course without interruption, but with expected modification, to the end of the Safavid period, and outside of Iran for still longer.

artistic prosperity that followed the high tide of the Timurid era? Nor did the decline of these arts wait for the downfall of the Safavids. It is already evident after the reign of Shah 'Abbās. Richard Ettinghausen has drawn attention to the decline of heroic painting and the currency of a more delicate, more decorative, but less robust and less expressive art under the Safavids.[90] One wonders whether even the best monuments of the Safavid era could be considered an improvement on the mausoleum of Mohammad Oljāytu (d. 1316), one of the last Ilkhans, in Soltāniyya, or the Blue Mosque of Tabriz (fifteenth century), which was built under the Qara Qoyunlu Turkmans.

However, even if we place the apogee of Persian painting and architecture in the fifteenth century, prior to the rise of the Safavids, we do not find parallel chronological developments between literature and the other arts, since the fifteenth century was already a period of literary decline. Our problem could perhaps be resolved by a different approach, recognizing that different arts, even though they follow the same evolutionary courses, do not share the same starting point or the same tempo. The mature age of one art may coincide with the youth or infancy of another. Therefore, even though we find the same pattern in the progression of the arts, their phases do not coincide. By "starting point," in this context, I mean the time when an art takes off and begins a rising movement toward a peak. Different arts may be stimulated by different agents and at different times. For instance, the impetus that Persian painting received from Chinese painting in the thirteenth century is not paralleled in literature. Nor does the stimulus of Arabic poetry in the rebirth of Persian literature in the ninth century find a parallel in painting or architecture.

The important point, however, is that the Safavid period as a whole betokens a general cultural exhaustion, the effect of which becomes evident in all the arts. The first half of this era (the sixteenth century) gives us the last glow, in some areas even the brightest gleam; the second half (the seventeenth century), the inevitable extinction.

## What Caused Persian Literature to Decline?

Now we may take up the question that we put to ourselves at the start and turn from "how" to "why." What caused the decline of Persian literature at this particular period?

---

[90]*Highlights of Persian Art*, ed. R. Ettinghausen and E. Yarshater (New York, 1982), 261ff.

There is no doubt that the Safavid period as a whole was one of political strength. The country had been ruled by feuding princes, had suffered under continuous warfare and was now brought under a firm and unified control. As in Sasanian times, the unification of church and state cemented the fragmented Persian society with a strong common cause. The economic situation, which had been disastrous prior to the advent of the Safavids and during the earlier period of their reign, was finally stabilized, and the nation began to prosper under Shah Tahmāsp. The era of Shah 'Abbās the Great witnessed the expansion of trade, a large and successful program for constructing roads and public buildings, and an open-minded, economic-oriented foreign policy. How are we to explain the decline of literature despite political stabilization and economic prosperity?

Several explanations have been offered to account for this phenomenon, and we may review these first. One is that the Safavid court was not as interested in poetry as were the former Persian courts. Their preoccupations with the promotion of Shi'ism prevented the Safavid kings from heeding poetry, and, the argument goes, since the advance of poetry in Persia has always been largely dependent upon court patronage, poetry suffered.

This view, which is based on a persistent fallacy common to almost all histories of Persian literature, is closely connected to the customary but superficial periodization of Persian literature according to dynastic events. As such, it hardly sheds any light on the subject. For one thing, the Safavid kings were not as insensitive to poetry as some critics have made them appear. Shah Esmā'il was himself a poet of considerable merit in Azeri Turkish. Shah Tahmāsp was a patron of the arts, and even if he preferred religious poetry to panegyrics toward the end of his reign, still he did encourage poets.[91] According to Eskandar Beg, we owe Mohtasham's moving elegy on the martyrdom of Hosayn and the events of Karbalā to Shah Tahmāsp, who reportedly frowned upon a *qasida* in his praise sent to him by Mohtasham and suggested poems in praise of the Shi'ite saints.[92] His brother, Bahrām Mirzā, who was given the governorship of Khorāsān in 1549, was a poet, musician, and calligrapher; he sponsored many artists who worked in his library.[93] Bahrām Mirza's son, Ebrāhim Mirza (d. 1577), who married

[91]See Eskandar Monshi, *Tārikh-e 'alamārā-ye 'Abbāsi* (Tehran, 1955), vol. 2, 178.
[92]Ibid. Eskandar Beg reports that some fifty to sixty religious poems were quickly offered by various poets, following Mohtasham's lead.
[93]See Qādi Ahmad, *Calligraphers and Painters,* introd. B. N. Zakhoder, trans. V. Minorsky (Washington, D.C., 1959), 3–4.

Shah Tahmāsp's daughter and held the position of master of ceremonies (*ishshak aghasi*) at the court, was also a man of learning, a calligrapher and poet, with a *divān* of five thousand verses to his name.[94] Yet another example of the attention shown to poetry by the Safavid princes is Sām Mirza, to whom I have already referred; he was a brother of Shah Tahmāsp and the author of *Tohfa-ye Sāmi*, a biography of contemporary poets. Shah 'Abbās the Great frequented the poets, listened to their poetry, and bestowed the title of poet laureate on Shefā'i (d. 1628); and the custom continued to the end of the Safavid dynasty. He is said to have paid a poet (Shāmi) the equivalent of his weight in gold as a mark of his appreciation.[95] Nasrallāh Falsafi has brought together all instances of Shah 'Abbās's attentions to the poets.[96] From these and similar examples one can see that although the Safavid kings were perhaps not inordinate patrons of poetry, they cannot be made the scapegoat for any decline in literature. Besides, the generous courts of the great Moghuls in India provided all the patronage the poets could wish for. If courtly patronage could be responsible for advance or decline of the quality of poetry, this period should have produced poetry second to none.

Should one need any further proof of the irrelevance of court patronage to the quality of poetry, one may consider that neither Nezāmi, Sa'di, nor Hāfez belonged to any courts noteworthy for their patronage. Nor, for that matter, did Khayyām or Rumi, who completely ignored court patronage. Mahmud's indifference to Persian epics did not hamper the creation of the *Shāh-nāma*. On the other hand, Jāmi, who was honored during his lifetime perhaps more than any other Persian poet—and not only in Persia, but also in the Ottoman Empire—did not produce anything but derivative poetry. Altogether the effect of court patronage has been unduly exaggerated in treatises on Persian literature. The renaissance of Persian literature in the tenth century was essentially not a product of Samanid patronage or institutions (even though it was helped by them), but rather an aspect of a larger historical phenomenon that also gave rise to local dynasties and their institutions.

In fact, during the Safavid period poetry was a very popular art. It is enough to remember that Sām Mirzā records more than seven hundred contemporary poets of the period of Shah Esmā'il and Shah Tahmāsp, and Nasrabādi, who wrote under Shah Solaymān, records

[94]Ibid., 5.
[95]Eskandar Beg, *'Alamārā*, vol. 1, 515–16; Nasrabādi, *Tadhkera*, 212.
[96]*Zendegāni-e Shāh 'Abbās-e Avval* (Tehran, 1955), vol. 2, 28ff.

some seven hundred of his contemporary poets. Abu'l-Fazl 'Allāmi, the author of *Ā'in-e Akbari*, a valuable work on Akbar's life, court, and institutions, states that "thousands of poets are continually at court" and mentions fifty-nine poets whom he had personally introduced to Akbar.[97] Badā'uni, in his *Montakhab al-tavārikh*, enumerates 38 shaikhs attached to the same court, 69 scholars, 15 physicians and philosophers, but 167 poets.[98] Even Hazin, who takes a dim view of poetry and the poets of his time and considers the great majority of them hack writers unworthy of being recorded, manages to record the biographies of one hundred poets, all Shi'ites and all residents of Persia! Therefore, we may put the dynastic explanation of Safavid poetry comfortably to rest.

Another explanation offered sometimes, though less frequently, to account for the peculiarities of the Safavid style, is a geographical one. Mirzoev, for instance,[99] as well as some Persian critics,[100] links the excessive subtlety and the far-fetched character of this poetry with features of Indian life and culture.

In the same way, but with a different end in mind, Shebli also considers the Indian environment responsible for the superior quality of Indian style poetry. To him, the Indian climate has a beneficial effect on everything imported to India. For instance, Persian and Turkish physical beauty reach their perfection in India, and the British born in India, according to him, turn out handsomer than those born in their homeland. Also, it is in India that Persian architecture, cuisine, and embroidery find their most refined examples. In the same manner, the Indian climate imparts to Persian poetry a new delicacy and tenderness, which become evident if we compare the poetry of 'Orfi, Naziri, Tāleb, and Qodsi, who wrote mainly in India, to that of Shefā'i and Mohtasham who lived and wrote in Persia.[101]

On imports other than poetry, I am unable to pass judgment. But insofar as poetry is concerned, the effect of Indian climate does not appear to have set any trends. The great majority of the Indian poets received their training in Persia and wrote poetry before they sought patronage on Indian soil. Sā'eb, who represents this poetry more than

[97]Browne, *Lit. Hist.*, vol. 1, 548–611. He adds, "There are, however, many others who were not presented, but who sent from distant places to his Majesty encomiums composed by them" (p. 611).

[98]Browne, *Lit. Hist.*, 249.

[99]See J. Bečka in Rypka, *Iran. Lit.*, 496, 537, n. 51; and Bausani, *Le letterature*, 45–46.

[100]For instance, Y. Aryānpur, *Az Sabā*, vol. 1, 8. See also Bahār, *Sabk shenāsi*, vol. 3, 46.

[101]Shebli, *She'r al-'ajam*, vol. 5, 163–64.

any other figure, did not live in India more than six years. The fact, however, which works most effectively against this explanation (as well as the previous one) is that this style of poetry had its beginning neither in the Safavid period nor in India. It began in Persia and was already noticeable during the Timurid period. In 1953 I published a book on Persian poetry of the Shāh Rokh period, that is, the first half of the fifteenth century, and subtitled it "The Beginning of Decline in Persian Literature." The chapter that deals with the characteristics of this poetry[102] could with little modification be applied equally to Safavid poetry. As Bertels points out:

> It is characteristic that the movement [i.e., the Indian style] does not adhere to any particular geographic region and that the poets following this style were to be found in Herat as well as in Tabriz and Shiraz. Some of them making their way to India and becoming acquainted with the poetry flourishing there on occasion came to intensify still further the typical traits of the style, but we can still state that the style could hardly have developed in India as such.[103]

A third explanation is basically a religious one. It holds the religious policy of the Safavids and the attendant weakening of Sufism responsible for the decline of literature. This view is put forth in its clearest form by Mohammad Qazvini in a letter to E. G. Browne. He wrote of the Safavid kings:

> In regard to the Sufis particularly they employed every kind of severity and vexation. . . . Now the close connection between poetry and *Belles Lettres,* on the one hand, and Sufism and Mysticism on the other, at any rate in Persia, is obvious, so that the extinction of one necessarily involves the extinction and destruction of the other. Hence it was that under this dynasty learning, culture, poetry and mysticism completely deserted Persia. . . . In place of great poets and philosophers there arose theologians, great indeed, but harsh, dry, fanatical and formal.[104]

---

[102]Yarshater, *She'r-e fārsi,* 104–39. H. Khāleqi Rād, "Payehā-ye sabk-e hendi dar ghazaliyyāt-e Jāmi," *Rahnema-ye ketāb* 16 (1973): 21–33, tries to show that characteristics of the Indian style are already discernible in Jāmi's lyrics. Cf. Rypka, *Iran. Lit.,* 295.

[103]Bertels, "Indiiskom stile," 58–59.

[104]Browne, *Lit. Hist.,* 26–28.

Minorsky, too, brings mysticism into his explanation of the dearth of great poets in this period, although in a different vein. In fact, his theory has more of a politico-economic basis. He favors a search for the social, political, and economic background of mysticism in a given period,[105] but in general regards the spread of mystical tendencies in Persia as a reverberation of the frustrations and distresses imposed by the vicissitudes of Persian history. Unlike Browne, he finds the decline of mysticism and literature under the Safavids natural and a possible result of people's occupation with new opportunities. He writes rather cautiously:

> The explanation of this fact would perhaps be that the mysticism which penetrated Persian poetry, or gave it a special coloring, was linked to times of distresses and frustration. At a time when the people were fighting for their national existence and when possibilities were opening up for useful enterprise and the improvement of general conditions, the mystical routine no longer corresponded to the conditions of the time.[106]

Rypka, referring to Minorsky's view (and somewhat amplifying it) states:

> Mysticism—after all an intrinsic feature of Persian literature—is usually a reverberation of wretched and necessitous circumstances, whereas under the Safavids the Iranians were first of all engaged in upholding their own position, then in expanding their property and in pursuing other aims of a practical nature. The religious orders died out under the pressure of Safavid policy, and with them the Sufi conceptions and speculations, which were contested and suspected by the *mojtaheds* with the most intense hatred.[107]

Such theories are hardly tenable. They may explain the increase in volume of religious poetry, but not the character of the period's lit-

---

[105]V. Minorsky, "Persia: Religion and History," in *Iranica* (Tehran, 1964), 247–48 (originally published under the title, "Iran: Opposition, Martyrdom and Revolt," in *Unity and Variety in Muslim Civilization*, ed. E. G. von Grunebaum [Chicago, 1955], 183–201).

[106]Ibid., 253.

[107]Rypka, *Iran. Lit.*, 294. Rypka has perhaps read a little more into Minorsky's view than his succinct passage indicates—possibly on account of his own sympathies.

erature. Mystic orders suffered in Safavid Persia, but not for long. Shi'ite orders soon began to blossom, as shown by their comfortable existence in the Qajar period. In any event, official religious sanction has never been a necessary condition for the expansion of mysticism. Sufism contains a streak of social protest and has often prospered under adverse conditions. Besides, mystical themes do continue in the *divān*s of Safavid poets, notably that of Sā'eb, at times in extreme or at least pronounced forms.[108] Even if we accept the severity of atmosphere in Persia for the Sufis, no such restrictions prevailed in the Ottoman Empire, Central Asia, Afghanistan, or India. And as we have seen, the poetry of the period is indivisible.

As to absorption in economic or political activities, this did not prevent a plethora of poets in Persia or India from pouring forth numerous volumes of verse. It is hard to see why it should have adversely affected its quality.

Yet another theory seeks to explain the literary climate of the Safavid period by the economic depression that affected Persia, when the sea passage to India was discovered by the Portuguese and the Italian trading colonies on the Black Sea disappeared.[109] According to Jiří Bečka the political and economic decline at the beginning of the sixteenth century resulted in "increased formalism, a highly contrived form of poetry and prose, marked by still stronger Arab influence."[110]

This view, which somewhat contradicts Minorsky's opinion, hardly takes into consideration the situation in countries other than Persia. Nor does it account for the popularity of poetry in this period. Further, the correlation between economic depression and increased formalism and artificiality is not entirely clear. One might expect perhaps more expressive poetry, revealing some of the accompanying hardships felt by the society.

Two other theories may be mentioned here. One is somewhat marginal and emphasizes the general view that strong, central governments in Persia have always worked against literary prosperity.[111] Supposedly based on the evidence of Persian history, it is in fact mainly deduced from the Safavid circumstance. Islamic Persia, however, has been politically fragmented most of the time, and therefore

---

[108]See, for instance, Sā'eb, *Divān,* 181; Faghāni, 145; Naziri, 2; for Hazin, see Sereshk, *Hazin,* 23.

[109]Rypka, *Iran. Lit.,* 293–94.

[110]Ibid., 496.

[111]Ibid., 293.

there is little evidence to the contrary on which to build a plausible theory.

The other view, advanced by Bertels, does not attempt to explain any "decline" of Persian letters under the Safavids, but tends to explain the character of Safavid poetry, which he does regard with some sympathy, by the social conditions of the period. He writes:

> Whereas at one time poetry was a sort of prerogative of the feudal aristocracy, in the sixteenth century it became (in the *ghazal*) increasingly associated with the urban population and with the merchants and artisans, and hence a number of new traits asserted themselves, notable among them the "lowering of imagery," the use of similes and metaphors uncommon in court circles, the introduction into the *ghazals* of motifs that did not entirely correspond to the refined tastes of the feudal strata.[112]

Similarly, assuming a reflection of social order in poetry, Rypka draws parallels between the treatment of the lover by the beloved, as pictured in the lyrics, and the treatment of subjects by their God-kings.[113]

Of course, no one can deny the impact of social conditions on literary products. But the social theory offered by Bertels and others is far too sketchy to provide a viable explanation of the development of Persian literature. To associate the convoluted Indian style with common people rather than with the sophistication of the court does not appear particularly credible. Indeed, one might expect the contrary. Farrokhi and Sa'di were not exactly aristocrats, and the Samanid princes were hardly more feudal than the Safavid kings, who were almost worshiped by their subjects. One may explain the passage of the popular language into poetry by the popular character of its practitioners, but to ascribe the whole character of Safavid poetry to some ill-defined social conditions taxes the imagination. Further, if it is meant that some new social condition in the Safavid period made for its special literary character, it must be borne in mind that Persian social conditions underwent little significant change from the ninth to the twentieth century. As long as Islam remained the effective framework of the social system, the society stayed fairly static. Neither the frequent Turkish and Tatar invasions, nor the advent of the militant Safavids, nor the rise of Nāder Shāh in the eighteenth century (which

[112]Bertels, "Indiiskom stile," 58–59.
[113]Rypka, *Iran. Lit.*, 295.

was often dubbed by contemporary writers as the Revolution of Persia)[114] brought about major transformations in the social structure of the country. Violent changes in dynastic rule, even when backed up by radical religious slogans, should not be mistaken for fundamental changes in social conditions. There have been ripples, but no great waves. This circumstance in itself might explain the continuation of the basic molds and concepts of Persian poetry from the time of its inception until well into the twentieth century.

## The Old Age of Classical Persian Poetry

This survey apparently leaves us with no explanation for the decline of the classical tradition at the end of the Safavid period. It seems to me, however, that in all the accounts presented so far, a simple explanation has been left out. We have been offered every possible reason for the weakening state of an octogenarian without mentioning his age. Persian poetry does no more than follow a general pattern of development common to all arts. It begins with the simplicity and directness that characterize the earlier stages of an art and leads to the complexity and exaggerated formalism that plague all arts toward their end, when creative energy is expended.

At the dawn of an art form, as in the springtime of a nascent culture, the pulsations of an active and searching spirit give birth to new forms and new ideas. If it is allowed to follow its own course and is not stifled or diverted by other currents, in time it gains the elegance and the maturity characteristic of middle age. Elegance leads to refinement, and this already contains the seeds of decay. Gradually sophistication and formalism replace the expression of heartfelt sentiments. Art becomes over-intellectualized; clever, but no longer inspired. In the end it is halted in "perpetual turning up of new facets of a now crystallized and undevelopable thought-stock. . . . It begets no more, but only reinterprets, and herein lies the negativeness common to all periods of this character."[115]

This pattern is not limited to the arts alone. It is also discernible in the development of Sufism from the simple and emotive asceticism of early mystics to the formalism of an Ibn al-'Arabi to the conventional,

---

[114]E.g., *Histoire de Thamas Kouli-kan nouveau roi de Perse ou Histoire de la dernière révolution de Perse arrivée en 1732* (Paris, 1742). Jonas Hanaway adds to his account of the British trade (London, 1754) the title, *The Revolutions of Persia during the Present Century.*

[115]O. Spengler, *The Decline of the West*, trans. C. Atkinson, abridged by A. Helps (New York, 1965), 244, 181.

superstitious, and lifeless practices of some late dervishes. The course of Islamic sciences provides yet another example.

One may well question whether this is an adequate explanation. The answer is that this is a morphological explanation, rather than a causal one. No art form, and indeed no culture, has continued in strength forever. Sooner or later an inward erosion sets in, and the art or style loses its creative capacity and its inner vitality. The explanation offered above only recognizes the Safavid period as the final phase of a sustained effort at literary creativity that constitutes the classical period. This last phase of literary activity coincides with the Safavid politico-economic *tour de force*. Isfahan, which Herbert described as "Yea, the greatest and best built City throughout the Orient,"[116] is symbolic of the comprehensive effort that occasions the ascendency of the Safavids. The fuel that fed the fire, however, was far from robust and was also in short supply, and soon no more than flickers remained of the old flame.

What dictates the particular time span of an art form, or the duration of creative energies among a people, is hard to determine, but this is no reason to be satisfied with superficial analyses or inadequate theories.

After Shah 'Abbās the Great, Persian poetry shows signs of debility. By the end of the Safavid rule it has actualized all its inward possibilities. It exhausts itself in a maze of contrived ideas and artifices and dies of senility. The Isfahan that Morier visited in 1811 symbolizes the state of inner frailty and evident exhaustion that Persia was destined to experience in the wake of the Safavid exuberance:

> The great city of Ispahan, which Chardin described as being twenty-four miles in circumference, were it to be weeded . . . of its ruins, would now dwindle to about a quarter of that circumference. One might suppose that God's curse had extended over parts of the city, as it did over Babylon. Houses, bazaars, mosques, palaces, whole streets are to be seen in total abandonment; and I have rode [sic] for miles among the ruins, without meeting with any living creature, except perhaps a jackal peeping over a wall or a fox running to his hole.[117]

---

[116]Herbert, *Travels into Africa and Asia* (London, 1638), 153.

[117]James Morier, *A Second Journey Through Persia . . . Between 1810 and 1826* (London, 1818), 134. And this despite the "great pride in the improvement of the city and its environ" that was taken by Amin al-Dowla, the governor of the city (ibid., 132).

Has there been a rebirth? There has surely been a new start. Whether this start heralds the rise of a new tradition headed for a peak is for time to tell.

# IV. CONTEMPORARY LITERATURE OF IRAN

# 15. Persian Prose Fiction (1921–77):
# An Iranian Mirror and Conscience

In what may be the first "age of prose" in the thousand-year course of imaginative literature in the neo-Persian language on the Iranian plateau, modern fiction is a dynamic and variegated contemporary literary medium and thus constitutes one of the "Highlights of Persian Literature."

In recent years, the growing significance of Persian fiction has not gone unnoticed, critical writing in Iran and abroad illuminating aspects of its development and major achievements.[1] But, to date, a survey of the course of this body of literature with due emphasis on works written in the 1970s has not been attempted.

In this essay, which is basically chronological in its organization, section 1 cursorily treats the apparently sudden emergence of modern Persian fiction in the first two decades of the twentieth century and considers native antecedents and foreign influences. Section 2 touches upon the course of historical, journalistic, and sentimental fiction during the reign of Rezā Shah Pahlavi (1921–41) and the concomitant appearance of Sādeq Hedāyat, Iran's most important twentieth-century author. Section 3 describes the proliferation of the short story as a form for literary and social expression during World War II and its aftermath up to the reestablishment of Mohammad Rezā Pahlavi's monarchical control in August 1953. Section 4 surveys the major figures and fictional forms during the subsequent period of Pahlavi rule (1953–77), and section 5 attempts a partial assessment of the significance of this body of fiction. The essay has an implicit, twofold thesis: first, that what began as a self-consciously adaptive and derivative form of expression has become a truly Persian and Iranian literary form; and second, that Persian fiction from 1953 to 1977 was a pri-

---

[1] A bibliography of critical writing on and published translations from modern Persian literature appears in "Major Voices in Contemporary Persian Literature," ed. M. C. Hillmann, *Literature East and West* 20 (1980): 328–51. Hereafter the volume is referred to as "Major Voices." Also, "Literature and Society in Iran," ed. M. C. Hillmann, *Iranian Studies* 15 (1982), includes important fiction in translation not available in "Major Voices" or elsewhere, and critical essays on various writers and works. This volume is hereafter referred to as "Literature and Society in Iran." Kamshad, *Modern Persian Prose Literature* (Cambridge, 1966) provides a critique of Persian fiction up to the early 1960s with special emphasis and a long essay on Hedāyat; E. Yarshater's essay, "The Modern Literary Idiom" in *Iran Faces the Seventies*, ed. E. Yarshater (New York, 1971), reviews Persian fiction up to the late 1960s.

mary arena or medium for the display of the Persian literary genius and for the representation of the Iranian intellectual self-image, individual and collective aspirations, and social criticism.

## The Emergence of Modern Persian Fiction (1900–1920)

The beginning of the modern era in Persian prose fiction was signaled by the publication in Berlin in 1921 of a collection of six anecdotal tales called *Yeki bud yeki nabud* (Once upon a time). Their author, Mohammad 'Ali Jamālzāda (b. 1892), had been educated in Europe and was a nationalistic expatriate.

"Fārsi shekar ast" (Persian is [as sweet as] sugar) is the first and most famous of the stories in *Once Upon a Time*.[2] A brief satirical anecdote, it depicts the lack of communication among a group of Iranians being detained by Customs at Enzeli during a period of political turmoil in Rasht and the capital to the south. In the detention room, the narrator observes an Iranian student just back from Europe speaking an affected, nearly incomprehensible Frenchified Persian. The student and an equally affected molla, whose Persian is mostly Arabic, confuse a villager from Enzeli who seeks information and solace from the others. The molla's retreat into the past, the student's refuge in foreignness, and the villager's confusion with the identity of the present are stereotypical characterizations still pertinent more than a half-century after Jamālzāda recorded them.

Behind "Persian Is Sugar" and the other stories in *Once Upon a Time* lay a specific intent made explicit by Jamālzāda in the preface to the volume. There he observed that Iran, a nation with a proud literary history, had fallen behind other literature-producing societies because of the traditional sentiments that the norms of the ancients must be blindly followed and that literature is produced for the elite.[3] This conservatism with respect to literary innovations led Iranian writers to recoil at the thought of two tenets that Jamālzāda believed lay at the core of successful contemporary European literatures: the use of language as spoken by the people and the paramount importance of

[2]The stories of *Once Upon a Time* are summarized and discussed in Y. Mashiah, "Once Upon a Time—A Study of *Yaki bud yaki nabud*," *Acta Orientalia* 33 (1971): 109–43. "Persian Is Sugar" appears in translation in "Major Voices," 13–20.

[3]M.'A. Jamālzāda, "Dibacha" (Preface), *Yaki bud yaki nabud*, 7th ed. (Tehran, 1966), 1ff. This preface has been discussed and translated in H. Dargahi, "The Shaping of Modern Persian Short Story: Jamālzāda's 'Preface' to *Yiki Bud, Yiki Nabud*," *The Literary Review* 18/1 (Fall, 1974): 18–37.

fiction as a literary medium.[4] These convictions, Jamālzāda tells the reader, persuaded him to publish the six stories in the hope that they might stimulate other writers to begin using the colloquial language as a medium and to use fiction as a form in their literary endeavors. A sort of manifesto for modern Persian fiction, Jamālzāda's preface and the stories that followed it heralded a new era in imaginative Persian literature.

To be sure, the way was in part prepared for Jamālzāda and those who followed by developments in the opening decades of the century. First, *Siyāhat-nāma-ye Ebrāhim Beg* (The Travels of Ebrāhim Beg), had been published about 1902. A first-person, satirical narrative of a foreign-born Iranian returning to his backward, corrupt homeland, that volume had established lengthy novel-type fiction as a Persian literary vehicle.[5] Its impact on the Iranian intelligentsia on the eve of the Iranian Constitutional Revolution further illustrated the potential significance of prose fiction in influencing social action. The same held true for a second kind of influential prose fiction: the literary translation of James Morier's *The Adventures of Hajji Baba of Ispahan* (London, 1824). With its satiric criticism of Persian mores and morals, these translations were not without effect upon the Iranian reading public, about to challenge the authority of the Qajar monarchy. Third, in 1909, *Shams o Toghrā* (Shams and Toghrā) appeared, a first example of what became a popular form of historical narrative, in which the Iranian people as a nation were coaxed to united action through the portrayal of glories in the Iranian national past. Fourth, there was the emergence of modern, *engagé*, journalistic writing, particularly through 'Ali Akbar Dehkhodā (1879–1956), whose articles and narrative sketches in the *Sur-e Esrāfil* newspaper (1907) exhibited "a keen appreciation of social conditions and revealed a critical sense of humor."[6] Although not fiction, through its succinctness and simplicity this journalistic writing helped shape Persian prose as a comprehensive medium for the public at large.

---

[4]Ibid., 25–29.

[5]According to Hafez Farman-Farmayan, "the first instance of a Persian novel based on Western models was by the ubiquitous dilettante Nāser al-Din Shah; it was called *Hekāyat-e pir o javān* and was written in 1876. The manuscript lies in the National Library (MS no. 492) and establishes its author as the father of the modern Persian novel." See H. Farman-Farmayan, "The Forces of Modernization in Nineteenth-Century Iran: A Historical Survey," in *Beginnings of Modernization in the Middle East: The Nineteenth Century*, ed. W. R. Polk and R. L. Chambers (Chicago, 1968), 143.

[6]M. Rahman, "Social Satire in Modern Persian Literature," *Bulletin of the Institute of Islamic Studies* 2 and 3 (1958 and 1959): 69.

Of course, other antecedents and circumstances in the millenium of imaginative Persian literature were conducive to the development of modern prose fiction, for narrative has figured prominently in Persian since the emergence of the neo-Persian language as a literary vehicle in the middle of the ninth century.[7] Still, in large measure, the course that Persian fiction was to pursue, and which Jamālzāda charted in part in *Once Upon a Time*, drew its inspiration from abroad, from the kinds of prose fiction described by Jamālzāda in his preface. Precisely because the new fiction was both an adaptation and innovation inspired from abroad and an oblique development out of the Persian literary past in a wholly new guise, it did not conflict with a threatened tradition to the same extent as did modern Persian verse, which also made a debut in 1921 with the publication of parts of *Afsāna* (Myth) by Nimā Yushij (1895–1960). This does not mean that the course of modern Persian fiction was smooth, because Iranian readers, except for those familiar with European literature, were unprepared for the modes, content, and forms of this new fiction. As one scholar describes it:

> For centuries and centuries Persian literature remained, so to say, impersonal. The artist was always supposed to follow the lines which had been laid down before him, and to produce a work in the admitted and respected social cadre. He could seldom be seen in his work; he was to follow the precepts of accepted morality, the exigencies of his readers who were exclusively members of the ruling class and of the intellectual elite.

And ". . . the artist has always preferred imagination to observation."[8]

The new fiction put a premium on realistic portrayal and the personal vision of the individual artist. Naturally, it was difficult for some readers to cope with this development. It forced them out of complacency and demanded individual responses for which acquaintance with the conventions of the traditional literature offered no bases or vocabulary.

---

[7]Kamshad, *Prose Lit.*, 3–53, offers a convenient survey of "The Historical Background" to modern Persian prose, "The Qajars and Reform (1796–1925)," and other developments up to the publication of Jamālzāda's *Once Upon a Time*. A specific Persian narrative tradition inviting study *vis-à-vis* the development of modern Persian fiction is introduced by W. L. Hanaway, Jr. in "Formal Elements in the Persian Popular Romances," *Review of National Literatures* 2/1 (Spring 1971): 139–60.

[8]S. Nafisi, "A General Survey of the Existing Situation in Persian Literature," *Bulletin of the Institute of Islamic Studies* 1 (1957): 15–16.

Jamālzāda, for example, published no fiction for twenty years after *Once Upon a Time* for three reasons: (1) the realistic portrayal of Iranian society was offensive to the government, (2) religious and other conservative elements in Iranian society found Jamālzāda's social criticism "blasphemy offensive to national pride," and (3) the author himself did not feel the great commitment to literary engagement that has characterized most post-World War II fiction writers—as Jamālzāda put it later, he did not want to give up the pleasures of youth for the trials of writing, but decided to leave that occupation for middle age.[9]

## The Era of Rezā Shah (1921–41)

In the two decades of Rezā Shah Pahlavi's rule (1921–41), attempts at historical novels, journalistic social protest fiction, and sentimental social commentary in fiction proved of contemporary appeal and significance. But for various reasons, such as their very adaptive and imitative qualities as experiments in still-foreign forms, none of these attempts has proved enduring from a critical point of view. First were the historical tales, such as *Dāmgostarān yā enteqām khāhān-e Mazdak* (The plotters or avengers of Mazdak, 1921), *Dāstān-e bāstān* (The story of yore, 1921), and *Dāstān-e Māni-ye naqqāsh* (The story of Manes the painter, 1927), a genre well suited to official propagation of nationalism and the new emphasis on pre-Islamic traditions. Second, journalistic social protest fiction was represented by works such as *Tehran-e makhuf* (Horrible Tehran, 1922), *Ruzgār-e siyāh* (Black days, 1931), and three books by Mohammad Mas'ud (d. 1947), *Tafrihāt-e shab* (Night entertainments, 1932), *Dar talāsh-e ma'āsh* (In search of a livelihood, 1932), and *Ashraf-e makhluqāt* (The noblest of creatures, 1934), which were severe indictments of urban aimlessness and decadence. Third, in a series of three books by Mohammad Hejāzi (1899–1977), *Homā* (1927), *Patrichehr* (1929), and *Zibā* (1931), women—an important and fashionable subject during the period of secularization leading to Rezā Shah's 1936 banning of traditional Moslem veiling of women in public—were portrayed from a sentimental, sometimes sensational upper-class vantage point.

But in 1930, after four years' residence in France, a young intellectual aristocrat by the name of Sādeq Hedāyat (1903–51) returned to

---

[9]Kamshad, *Prose Lit.*, 94–95; M. 'A. Jamālzāda, "Sharh-e hāl" (Autobiography), *Nashriyya-ye dāneshkāda-ye adabiyyāt-e Tabriz* 6/3 (1954).

Iran and published a collection of eight stories entitled *Zenda be-gur* (Buried alive). A second collection of eleven stories entitled *Se qatra khun* (Three drops of blood) appeared in 1932. A year later came a satire called *'Alaviyya Khānom* (Madame 'Alaviyya), a collection of *qaziyya*s (narratives) called *Vagh vagh sāhāb* (Mr. Bow Wow) written in collaboration with Mas'ud Farzād, and a third collection of seven short stories called *Sāya rowshan* (Chiaroscuro). Then in 1937, during a trip to India, Hedāyat produced a limited private edition of a short novel called *Buf-e kur* (*The Blind Owl*).

Thus, in seven short years, the major figure in modern Persian fiction came center-stage and produced some forty short stories and two longer pieces of fiction, together with numerous works of nonfiction. Hedāyat's short stories exhibit no technical advances in terms of form or stylistic sophistication; it is, rather, Hedāyat's personal vision of the misery of modern humanity that gives his work its vitality. In his stories, the Iranian landscape is peopled with characters who embody this vision of helplessness and hopelessness. Their fates verify the author's pessimism. None of Hedāyat's works so dramatically portrays fatalistic alienation, frustration, and misery as his most famous and most discussed work, the controversial short novel *The Blind Owl*, whose title character and protagonist has been interpreted by some as a fictionalized version of Hedāyat himself. In *The Blind Owl*, fear of and craving for death, longing for and revulsion from sexual expression, the apparent merging of past and present and of the conscious and subconscious, and the rich textures of Iranian lore and imagery all combine to create an engrossing atmosphere of mystery and urgency that critics have only recently begun to illumine.[10]

## The New Age of Prose (1941–53)

In September 1941, the Allied Occupation Forces precipitated the abdication and exile of Rezā Shah, and World War II set into motion forces that have since figured in nearly every aspect of Iranian life, including imaginative literature.

Almost on the morrow of Rezā Shah's abdication and exile, *The Blind*

---

[10]Available in D. P. Costello's translation as *The Blind Owl* (London, 1957; New York, 1957, 1969). The novel is given its first, multi-faceted critical airing in English in *Hedayat's 'The Blind Owl' Forty Years After*, ed. M. C. Hillmann (Austin, Tex., 1978). This volume also includes a list of other Hedayāt fiction in translation, to which two more recent translations need to be added: *Sādeq Hedayat: An Anthology*, ed. by E. Yarshater (Boulder, Colo., 1979); and *Haji Aqa*, trans. by G. M. Wickens (Austin, Tex., 1980).

*Owl* appeared in its first public Iranian edition, immediately becoming Iran's most controversial and influential piece of fiction. At the same time, after four years incarceration following his conviction for activity contrary to an Iranian anti-Communist law passed in 1931, Bozorg 'Alavi (b. 1904) was freed and published a collection of stories called *Varaq-pārahā-ye zendān* (Scraps of paper from prison). His first collection of six stories called *Chamedān* (Suitcase) had appeared in early 1935.[11] A year later appeared *Panjāh o se nafar* (Fifty-three people), a collection of narratives detailing the experiences of the people convicted along with 'Alavi. In 1942, Hedāyat published *Sag-e velgard* (The stray dog), his fourth and last collection of short stories.

Although, at the other end of the spectrum from 'Alavi, who had committed himself to communist ideology, even Hedāyat was caught up in the fervor of open social criticism that characterized the war years. His last major work, *Hājji Āqā* (1945), was a biting, satirical portrait of a traditional character stereotype.[12]

In 1944, Mahmud E'temādzāda (b. 1915), subsequently better known by his pen name Behāzin, published a collection of stories entitled *Parākanda* (Scattered pieces). He was a professional translator who had gone to France on a government scholarship at the age of seventeen to study naval engineering and later served in the Iranian Ministry of Education. A year later, Sādeq Chubak (b. 1916), a translator and officer with the Iranian Army General Staff who was about to join the British Embassy Information Department in a similar capacity, published *Khayma-shab-bāzi* (The puppet show), a collection of eleven stories. In 1946, Jalāl Āl-e Ahmad (1923–69), a Persian teacher who had completed course requirements for a Ph.D. in Persian literature at the University of Tehran, produced his first collection of twelve stories, *Did o bāzdid* (The exchange of visits).

As new writers of promise, Behāzin, Chubak, and Āl-e Ahmad joined Hedāyat, 'Alavi and Jamālzāda—who had ended his twenty-year literary silence with *Dār al-majānin* (The lunatic asylum) and the collection *'Amu Hosayn 'Ali* in 1942—as the major figures of a new age of prose. Modern Persian fiction had thus come of age with the variegated voices of Jamālzāda's anecdotes of manners, Hedāyāt's surrealistic *The Blind Owl* and stories in a Jungian psychological mode, 'Alavi's sociological portraits, Behāzin's socialist realism, Chubak's nat-

---

[11]These stories are summarized and discussed by G. M. Wickens, "Bozorg Alavi's Portmanteau," *University of Toronto Quarterly* 28 (January 1959): 116–33.

[12]A later narrative, *Tup-e morvāri* (The pearl cannon, 1947), was not published in its entirety till 1978, only to be banned in early 1979.

uralism, and Āl-e Ahmad's realism. Even the Iranian academic world formally proclaimed the dawn of this new era at the First Congress of Iranian Writers, held at the University of Tehran in 1946.

The fictional mainstream from 1946 to 1953 provided a forum for the ideological views of politically active writers in various socialist groups and parties. In 1947 Āl-e Ahmad published a second collection of stories called *Az ranji ke mibarim* (Our suffering). A year later he published *Setār,* and in 1952 his *Zan-e ziyādi* (The unwanted woman) appeared, reprinted in an expanded edition in 1964.

Behāzin's second collection of stories, *Besu-ye mardom* (Toward the people), was published in 1948, followed by his first and only novel, *Dokhtar-e ra'iyyat* (The serf's daughter, 1951), a tale of class struggle set in his native Gilan during the 1910s and 1920s. In this story the title character survives the oppression of the landlords and can even maintain hope for the future as she breaks away from the peasantry to enter the working class.

'Alavi published another collection of stories, called *Nāmahā va dāstānhā-ye digar* (Letters and other stories) in 1952 and later that year published his only novel, *Chashmhāyash* (Her eyes). Depicting life during the Rezā Shah period, *Her Eyes* centers on the career of a famous painter called Mākān (a fictional character based in part upon Kamāl al-Molk, d. 1938), who was exiled from Tehran to a small town for his anti-government activities. The novel also revolves around the life of the woman whose portrait by Mākān attracted attention (thus the title) and whose sacrificial marriage to a general saves Mākān from permanent incarceration.

The most important literary event of the period, however, was not the publication of a work or works; rather, it was Hedāyat's suicide in Paris in April 1951, which symbolized both the ultimate despair of the Hedayatesque vision and the violence of the age. Reformer and social thinker Ahmad Kasravi (1890–1946) and social critic and journalistic novelist Mohammad Mas'ud (d. 1947) had both been assassinated earlier.

## Later Developments in Persian Fiction (1953–77)

In late August 1953, Mohammad Rezā Shah Pahlavi returned to Iran after forced departure a week earlier as a result of pressure exerted by Prime Minister Mohammad Mosāddeq (d. 1967) and his nationalist government. From his return onward, Mohammad Rezā Pahlavi commenced a consolidation of power, development of ties with the United

States, centralization and expansion of the bureaucracy, accelerated industrialization, mass secular education, and the fostering of nationalism under the aegis of the Pahlavi name. This broad movement was of paramount importance in every sphere, including imaginative literature, for the next quarter century.

For each of the five remaining major fiction-writers from the earlier 1921–41 and 1941–53 periods—Jamālzāda, 'Alavi, Behāzin, Chubak, and Āl-e Ahmad—the new era meant distinctive reactions and new roles. For two of them, Jamālzāda and 'Alavi, the new era meant an end to their significance as major writers of fiction.

Having resumed literary activity during the war and untouched by subsequent political circumstances in Iran, Jamālzāda was prolific in fiction- and essay-writing into the 1970s. But none of his later publications captured the imagination of the so-called *rowshanfekr* (intelligentsia) readership or provoked the respect and emulation that *Once Upon a Time* had. Jamālzāda was the precursor of the maturity of Persian fiction, but, as a result of his long separation from Iran and residence in Switzerland as well as, perhaps, his own predilections, he was thought to have failed to match steps with changing taste and developing sophistication. His anecdotal stories were perceived as lacking contemporary settings and social criticism and were presumably dated for readers with sociological views of fiction and an interest in more rigorous organization and penetrating characterization.

'Alavi was in East Berlin as a visiting professor at Humboldt University when Mosāddeq fell. Facing imprisonment in Iran because of his Tudeh (Communist) Party activities, he remained in East Germany as a professor of Iranian languages and literatures; in later years he turned his major attention from fiction toward scholarship and translation from German into Persian. In Iran, although his earlier works remained popular among the non-establishment intelligentsia during the pre-Khomayni years, their themes and their author, now reportedly at work on a long autobiographical novel, were often viewed as belonging to another age and critically weak.

Hedāyat, despite his suicide in 1951, survived as an influential and relevant voice in the post-Mosāddeq era and the dominant voice in Persian fiction into the 1970s. However, some critics have felt that, important as Hedāyat's works were when they first appeared, only *The Blind Owl* and a handful of short stories are likely to pass the test of time.[13]

[13]E. Yarshater, "The Modern Literary Idiom," 284–85; R. Barāheni, *Qessa nevisi* (Storywriting), 2nd ed. (Tehran, 1969), 440.

Like Jamālzāda, Hedāyat and 'Alavi, Behāzin received his higher education in Europe. (It may be indicative of the growing indigenousness of Persian fiction that, although knowledge of a Western European language remains an important tool for nearly all Iranian writers of fiction, none of the major post-Mosāddeq writers of fiction has been educated abroad.) For Behāzin, education in France was important for two specific reasons: first, his acquaintance with French language and literature had effects on his own writing style; second, his knowledge of French enabled him to "resist the quarrelsomeness of office and politics and, as an escape from humiliation, to turn to translation by which the family's livelihood has been secured for years."[14] Thus, although Behāzin desisted from presenting explicitly leftist views in his writing after 1953, he was able to avoid direct involvement with the system and retain a positive reputation among non-establishment readers (enhanced by brief periods of incarceration) in the 1970s. In any case, besides numerous translations, Behāzin continued creative writing after 1953. A collection of essays and reminiscences called *Naqsh-e parand* (Design in silk) was published in 1955. Then came scattered stories in *Payām-e novin* and elsewhere, which were gathered in his most important collection, *Mohra-ye mār* (The snake's magic bead), published in 1966. Another collection of tales entitled *Shahr-e khodā* (City of God) was published in 1970, followed by a collection of earlier fiction called *Dāstānhā-ye montakhab* (Collected stories, 1972) and reprintings of *The Serf's Daughter* (1974) and *The Snake's Magic Bead* (1975).

In 1949, Sādeq Chubak became the librarian at the National Iranian Oil Company, a position he held till retirement in 1974. With a firm reputation as a short-story writer and with no inclination for any sort of political or even public literary activity, Chubak bided his time after the publication of his second collection of stories, *Antari keh lutiyash morda bud* (The chimpanzee whose master had died, 1949). He did not publish another major piece of fiction till 1963 when his novel *Tangsir* appeared. Based on incidents to which Chubak and his father were witness in Bushire in 1922 and previously presented in a short story by Rasul Parvizi (1957), *Tangsir* is the story of a Tangestani who, frustrated in his attempts to seek redress against four Bushire notables who have cheated him, takes justice into his own hands, slays the four, and then seeks to flee Iran by boat with his wife and child. A departure

---

[14]Behāzin, "Dar chand kalama" (In a few words), *Dāstānhā-ye montakhab-e Behāzin* (Selected stories of Behāzin) (Tehran, 1973), iii.

from Chubak's earlier naturalistic stories, *Tangsir* was followed by two further collections of naturalistic stories entitled *Ruz-e avval-e qabr* (The first day in the grave, 1965) and *Cherāgh-e ākhar* (The last alms, 1966). Then, in 1966 Chubak's lengthiest piece of fiction, *Sang-e sabur* (The patient stone), appeared. A grim, naturalistic tableau in multiple stream-of-consciousness technique and one of the most moving pieces of fiction in the Persian language, *The Patient Stone* relates a series of murders of prostitutes by a psychopathic religious fanatic waging a one-man crusade against venereal disease. The story focuses on one of his victims and her son and neighbors in the slum dwelling where they live. One of the neighbors is a destitute teacher and aspiring writer who epitomizes the plight of modern humanity, cut off from his roots and, as it were, thrown into space.

Having remained in Iran through the 1960s, unlike 'Alavi and Ja-mālzāda, and having outlived Hedāyat, Chubak pursued his own course of development.[15] Undeterred by—but very conscious of—political circumstances, he successfully bridged the generation gap in Persian fiction.[16]

The youngest of the major writers of fiction from the war years, a political activist with the Tudeh Party and then with the Third Force Party, Āl-e Ahmad ended direct participation in politics in 1953 and concentrated his efforts on essay and fiction writing. He emerged in the 1960s as the leading spokesperson for the non-establishment intelligentsia, a role no single writer has been able to fill since his death in 1969 at age forty-six. In early 1955, he published *Sargozasht-e kan-duhā* (The story of the beehives), an allegory in a "once upon a time" folktale format of foreign exploitation of Iranian oil. His best-known piece of fiction, *Modir-e madrasa* (The school principal, 1958),[17] is an indictment of the Iranian elementary education system told in a first-person narrative exhibiting the taut, succinct, angry prose that became Āl-e Ahmad's trademark. In 1961, *Nun w'al-qalam* (The letter "N" and the pen) was published, another "once upon a time" tale

[15]Chubak was Iran's most important writer of fiction in the 1960s. But he has published nothing since.

[16]This view of Chubak's significance is rejected by some (unconvincing) critics, among them: 'A. Dastghayb, *Naqd-e āthār-e Sādeq Chubak* (A critical study of the works of Sādeq Chubak, Tehran, 1974); N. Ebrāhimi, "Nazari shetabzada dar bara-ye nevisandegan-e mo'aser-e Iran (A hurried look at contemporary writers of Iran), *Ferdowsi* no. 1048 (27 Day 1972): 28; M. Kiyanush, *Barrasi-ye she'r o nathr-e fārsi-ye mo'āser* (An examination of contemporary Persian poetry and prose, Tehran, 1968), 186–97; P. Naqibi, "Yak ketāb-e bi-payan (A book without a message [*The Patient Stone*]), *Ferdowsi* no. 812 (12 Ordibehesht 1967): 14–16.

[17]Trans. J. K. Newton (Chicago, 1974).

presenting Āl-e Ahmad's view of the defeat of Iranian leftist movements after World War II.[18] Then, in 1962 came the most important of his numerous nonfiction writings, *Gharbzadegi* (Plagued by the West),[19] a description of Iran's growing subservience to and imitation of the West. Āl-e Ahmad's longest published work, *Nefrin-e zamin* (The cursing of the earth), appeared in 1968. A continuation of sorts of *The School Principal, The Cursing of the Earth* uses a fictionalized narrative to criticize aspects of land reform, mechanization of agriculture, education, and military conscription, all of which contribute to the loss of roots on the part of the people in the community as the old order is replaced by the new.[20] Of a contemplated volume of short stories entitled *Nasl-e jadid* (The new generation), only five appeared under the title *Panj dāstān* (Five stories) not long after Āl-e Ahmad's death. Finally, in late 1981 *Sangi bar guri* (A stone on a grave) was published; this short autobiographical narrative tells the story of the childlessness of Āl-e Ahmad's marriage to Simin Dāneshvar (b. 1921), a well-known fiction writer in her own right.

By the mid-1950s it was apparent that Persian prose fiction was moving beyond the imitation and adaptation of Western models. Readers were beginning to expect it to provide a clear reflection of the language and lives of the Iranian people. Three writers, Hedāyat, Chubak, and Āl-e Ahmad, played the leading roles in making fiction the primary form of imaginative literary expression and the most "social" artistic medium in Iran.[21] By the mid-1970s, the importance of these three writers had not diminished, but they had been joined by a host of others, notable among them Ebrāhim Golestān, Ahmad Mahmud, Bahrām Sādeqi, Jamāl Mirsādeqi, Gholām Hosayn Sā'edi, Samad Behrangi, Nāder Ebrāhimi, Mahmud Dowlatābādi, and Hushang Golshiri.

Ebrāhim Golestān (b. 1922), has been a translator, cinematographer, publisher, and (from 1958 to 1967) paramour and literary guide to Iran's premier poetess Forugh Farrokhzād (1935–67). He has made his distinctive fictional voice known with the publication of fewer than thirty stories in four collections: *Āzar māh-e ākhar-e pā'iz* (Āzar, the last month of autumn, 1948), *Shekār-e sāya* (Shadow-hunting, 1955), *Juy o*

---

[18]*The Letter "N" and the Pen* summarized and discussed in M. C. Hillmann, "Al-e Ahmad's Fictional Legacy," *Iranian Studies* 9 (1976): 252–60.

[19]Trans. P. Sprachman, Modern Persian Literature Series, no. 5 (Delmar, N.Y., 1982).

[20]A plot summary of *The Cursing of the Earth* by M. R. Ghanoonparvar appears in "Major Voices," 240–44.

[21]Barāheni, *Qessa nevisi*, 77–78, 450–52.

*divār o teshna* (Stream and wall and thirst, 1967–68) and *Madd o mah* (Tide and moon, 1969). His single piece of longer fiction is *Asrār-e ganj-e darra-ye jenni* (The secrets of the treasure of the haunted valley, 1974), an allegorical depiction of the baseness of Iranian society from ruler to ruled.[22]

Golestān demonstrates a conscious sense of form in short fiction often lacking in earlier fiction excepting Chubak's; he also has a conscious sense of prose style. Having translated some Twain and Hemingway into Persian, he helped pave the way for other writers to experiment beyond the earlier innovative simplicity, directness, and colloquialism in Jamālzāda and Hedāyat and even beyond the reportorial realism of Āl-e Ahmad and the dense naturalism of Chubak. His experimental use of rhythmic cadence to establish and complement narrative pace is achieved mainly through the phrasing of traditional quantitative prosodic feet, the repetition of words, particularly verbs, and the balance of parallel structure. A particularly effective story by Golestān is "Safar-e 'Esmat" ('Esmat's trip, 1965), in which a prostitute repenting her past at a religious shrine is invited by a molla she meets there to become one of the "sisters" of the shrine who minister to the male pilgrims. The story is a *tour de force* of situational irony enhanced by Golestān's distinctive style.[23]

Bahrām Sādeqi (d. 1984), a physician by training, is also primarily a short-story writer. He began publishing short stories in the mid-1950s in *Sokhan* magazine and elsewhere but did not publish a collection until 1970, when twenty-six of his stories, including his longer story "Malakut" (Heavenly kingdom, 1961), appeared under the title *Sangar o qomqomahā-ye khāli* (The trench and empty flasks). Some critics consider Sādeq the most effective Iranian short-story writer of the 1960s and 1970s.[24] Not atypical of his style and thematic concerns is the story "Ba kāmal-e ta'ssof" (With deepest regrets, 1958). A lonely, frustrated, white-collar worker, whose obsession with death has led to the habit of reading all obituary notices in the newspaper, one day reads what he thinks his own obituary—a confusion caused by a typographical error in the surname. He attends what he thinks is his own wake and there makes a speech condemning the hypocrisy of those present.[25]

[22]Paul Sprachman's article on the novel appears in "Literature and Society in Iran."
[23]Available in Carter Bryant's translation in "Major Voices," 191–95.
[24]See N. Ebrāhimi, "Nazari shetābzada dar bāra-ye nevisandegān-e mo'āser-e Irān," *Ferdowsi* no. 1049 (4 Bahman 1972): 34.
[25]Available in M. E. Mottahadeh's translation in *The Literary Review* 18/1 (Fall 1974): 129–43.

Jamāl Mirsādeqi (b. 1932–33), another productive fiction writer during the 1960s, has been called "one of the best-known short-story writers of contemporary Iran whose works consistently dealt with socially significant themes." His stories focus on "generational conflict, traditional versus modern values, and liberty of conscience versus prejudice."[26]

Of the writers of fiction who began their careers in the late 1950s and early 1960s, the most prominent is Gholām Hosayn Sā'edi (1935–85), psychiatrist, amateur ethnographer, editor, and Iran's leading dramatist (under the pen name Gowhar Morād). He was extremely productive till the mid-1970s, when censorship of his works became strict and he was incarcerated for a period of months, gaining release in June, 1975. Sā'edi authored some thirty books during the later Pahlavi years, among them a novel called *Tup* (The cannon, 1967) and six collections of short stories: *Shabneshini-ye bā shokuh* (The splendid soiree, 1960), *'Azādārān-e Bayal* (The mourners of Bayal, 1964), *Dandil* (1966), *Vāhemahā-ye bināfm o neshān* (Vague fears, 1967), *Tars o larz* (Fear and trembling, 1968), and *Gur o gahvāra* (The grave and the cradle, 1972). An interest in the common person, rural and urban, and in the psychological probing of characters is combined with a rich, realistic texture, often with a dramatic point of view, in many of Sā'edi's stories.

The most famous among them is the fifth tale in *The Mourners of Bayal*, which Sā'edi made into a screenplay calld *Gāv* (The cow) in 1969; produced by Dāryush Mehrju'i, the movie ranks among Iran's best. *The Cow* is the story of a villager whose ownership of a cow gives him both status and income in his village, but the cow dies, and its owner, unable to cope with the loss, begins to behave like the cow, ultimately forcing his friends to lead him, cow-like, to the city in hopes that something can be done. Like his cow, the villager dies.[27]

Samad Behrangi (1939–68), who spent his brief adult years as a Persian teacher in villages and towns of Azerbaijan, began writing fiction, collecting folk tales, and translating Turkish stories into Persian in the late 1950s. His publication in 1964 of a story called "Talkhun" established him as a modernist writer of promise. A year later

---

[26]M. Estelami, "[Book Review] *Shabcheragh* (The luminous stone). By Jamal Mirsādeqi." *Iranian Studies* 9 (1976): 299. Mirsādeqi's "Barfhā, saghā, kalāghhā (The snow, the dogs, the crows)" appears in *Modern Persian Short Stories*, trans. M. S. Southgate (Washington, D.C., 1980), 62–74.

[27]M. Ghadessy's translation of the story, The Cow: Screenplay appears in "Sociology of the Iranian Writer," *Iranian Studies* 18 (1985). Several Sā'edi stories are anthologized in translation in *Dandil* (New York, 1981).

came the first volume of *Afsānahā-ye Āzarbāyjān* (Tales of Azerbaijan), Persian translations of Turkish folktales in collaboration with Behruz Dehqāni; the second volume appeared in 1968. In 1966 his first children's story "Olduz o kalāghhā" (Olduz and the crows) was published, followed by a number of other stories, including "Māhi-ye siyāh-e kuchulu (The little black fish, 1968), his most popular story.[28] Posthumously, his children's stories were collected in *Qessahā-ye Behrang* (The stories of Behrang, 1969). His other fiction was collected in *Talkhun o dāstānhā-ye digar* (Talkhun and other stories, 1970). Overtly didactic, with a focus on societal ills perceived for children, Behrangi's stories are not likely to endure as fiction but owing to his sudden death by drowning in September 1968, and the importance given in Iran to social content in literary criticism among non-establishment readers, Behrangi has become a cult figure. To be sure, his children's stories provided impetus for the broadening of that form, and for fables as well, during the late 1960s and early 1970s.

If total social commitment and the subordination of questions of art and craft to it constitute the basis of Behrangi's appeal to *rowshanfekr* readers, the lack of these elements in the most prolific serious short-story writer of the 1960s and early 1970s, Nāder Ebrāhimi (b. 1935), means that the respect of such readership was only grudgingly given. As one critic puts it:

> Ebrāhimi's books from beginning to end are a stage for his experiments in various contexts of fiction-writing: (1) half-philosophical stories in classical belletristic prose with conclusions that the reader can predict beforehand; (2) sad animal fables with simple prose that are more suitable for children; (3) surrealistic stories with a tense style in which words or situations are sometimes played with stubbornly; (4) adventure stories concerning renegades—khans and Turkmans—whose form is often reminiscent of some American writers and which have skillful descriptions; and (5) realistic stories that also show another face of the writer—a partisan writer with class consciousness.[29]

---

[28]"The Little Black Fish" has been translated several times, most recently by Eric Hooglund and Mary Hoogland in an anthology of five Behrangi stories entitled *The Little Black Fish and Other Modern Persian Stories* (Washington, D.C., 1976).

[29]*Bāzāfarini-e vāqe'iyyāt: 11 dāstān az 11 nevisanda-ye mo'āser* (The recreation of reality: 11 stories from 11 contemporary writers), comp. M. 'A. Sepānlu (Tehran, 1970–71), 126.

Numerous collections of Ebrāhimi's stories have been published: *Kāshāna'i barāye shab* (A house for the night) and *Ārash dar qalamrow-e tardid* (Arash in the realm of doubt, 1963), *Masābā o ro'yā-ye Gājerāt* (Masaba and the Gujarati dream, 1964), *Makānhā-ye 'omumi* (Public places, 1966), *Afsāna-ye bārān* (A tale of rain, 1968), *Hazārpā-ye siyāh o qessahā-ye sahrā* (The black centipede and desert tales, 1969), *Tazādhā-ye daruni* (Internal contradictions, 1971), and *Dah dāstān-e kutāh* (Ten short stories, 1972). Volumes of single stories include *Bār-e digar shahri keh dust midāshtam* (Once again the city I loved, 1967) and *Ensān, jenāyat o ehtemāl* (Humankind, crime, and probability, 1972). A selection of his earlier stories appeared under the title *Dar sarzamin-e kuchek-e man* (In my small land) in 1968. Ebrāhimi was still contributing experimental stories to *Ferdowsi* magazine during its last days (i.e., 1974). His very productivity and variety of fictional forms make it difficult to characterize his work through a single example, but "Bād, bād-e Mehregān" (The wind of Mehregan, 1967) shows his skill in one sort of story. Set at the University of Tehran in the early 1960s and later, it is a story of student dedication to causes; he depicts their energetic devotion to political dissent in one period, and the same energy expended on emotional discussion of poetic theory in another.[30]

But the 1960s and early 1970s, served as much more than the backdrop for important fictional works by major voices such as Chubak, Āl-e Ahmad, Golestān, Sā'edi, and Ebrāhimi. It marked, first, the broadening of the production of Persian fiction beyond the coterie of major figures all mutually acquainted and centered in Tehran. The proliferation of literary magazines from the mid-1950s onward had much to do with the increased output of stories and the rise of new authors. *Payām-e novin, Ketāb-e hafta, Andisha o honar, Ārash, Ferdowsi, Jong-e Esfahān,* and *Alefbā* all were prominent in this regard, although defunct by the middle of the 1970s. *Sokhan,* where short fiction had been published since the magazine's founding in 1943, ceased publication early in post-Pahlavi 1979.

These and other magazines provided a handy vehicle for the exposure of new work to readers and critics. Among the short-story writers they published are those cited above and the following: Mahshid Amirshāhi, Shamim Bahār, Amin Faqiri, 'Esmā'il Fasih, Mahmud Kiyānush, Bābā Moqaddam, 'Abbās Pahlavān, Rasul Parvizi, Shāpur Qarib, Manuchehr Safā (Gh. Dāvud), Khosrow Shāhāni, Nā-

---

[30]"The Wind of Mehregan" appears in a translation by M. R. Ghanoonparvar and D. L. Wilcox in "Major Voices," 218–39.

ser Taqav'i, and Feraydun Tonakāboni (F. T. Amuzegār). The works of these and other short-story writers run the gamut from traditional anecdotal tales to "amorphous, surrealistic, and 'absurd' fiction," with their authors classifiable, in one critic's terms, as realists (following Hedāyat's lead), traditionalists (*à la* Jamālzāda), and experimentalists (i.e., modernists who take their cues from contemporary literary developments abroad).[31]

Secondly, the 1960s marked the coming of age of the Persian novel. Āl-e Ahmad's *The Letter "N" and the Pen* (1961), Chubak's *Tangsir* (1963) and *The Patient Stone* (1966), Sā'edi's *The Cannon* (1967), Dāneshvar's *Mourning* (1969), and Golestān's *The Secrets of the Treasure of the Haunted Valley* (1974) have been cited above in other contexts. Three other major novels are: 'Ali Mohammad Afghāni's *Showhar-e Āhu Khānom* (Āhu Khānom's Husband, 1961), Hushang Golshiri's *Shāzda Ehtejāb* (Prince Ehtejab, 1969), and Rezā Barāheni's *Ruzgār-e duzakhi-ye Āqā-ye Ayāz* (The infernal times of Āqā-ye Ayāz, 1972).

In 1961, 'Ali Mohammad Afghāni (b. 1925), a former military officer, was granted a pardon after a 1954 death sentence had been commuted to life imprisonment for treason; when he published *Āhu Khānom's Husband* the following year, both the literary establishment and non-establishment intelligentsia acclaimed it as a milestone in Persian fiction. This monumental novel of more than eight hundred pages covers a period of eight years, from 1934 into World War II, in the lives of a prosperous Kermanshah baker, his wife, and the woman he falls in love with. Ultimately, it will be judged less as a critical success than as an important step in the development of Persian fiction, for it offers testimony that the Persian language has the resources, and the Iranian environment the content, to flesh out a lengthy saga.[32]

Hushang Golshiri (b. 1938), high school teacher, editor of *Jong-e Esfahān*, and author of short story collections *Methl-e hamisha* (Like always, 1973) and *Namāzkhāna-ye kuchek-e man* (My small chapel,. 1975), ended the decade of the 1960s on a most promising note with the

[31]Mas'ud Zavārzadeh, "The Persian Short Story since the Second World War: An Overview," *Muslim World* 58 (1968): 314.
[32]For an evaluation of the novel see E. Yarshater, "The Modern Literary Idiom," 308–10. This novel was followed in 1966 by another lengthy one, *Shādkāmān-e darra-ye Qarasu* (The happy ones of the Qara Su Valley), a love story combined with social criticism and exhibiting the same stylistic and structural strengths and weaknesses seen in *Āhu Khānom's Husband*. A plot summary of *Āhu Khānom's Husband* and bio-bibliographical notes on Afghāni appear in "Major Voices," 162–66. Afghāni's last Pahlavi-era novel is *Shalgham miva-ye beheshte* (Turnips are fruits of heaven, 1976).

publication of *Shāzda Ehtejāb*. In this stream-of-consciousness tale, the title character, a descendant of princely feudal lords, is left with hereditary tuberculosis and the photographs of relatives on the walls of his room, neither of which he can cope with or control. The novel, one of the most successful in the use of some Western techniques of writing, effectively depicts the tyranny of certain Qajar princes.[33]

Rezā Barāheni (b. 1936), English professor, literary critic, minor poet, and, for a time, controversial expatriate, was as ambitious in his first lengthy piece of fiction, *The Infernal Times of Āqā-ye Ayāz*, as were Afghāni and Golshiri. A pseudo-historical narrative printed in Tehran by Amir Kabir but never distributed, thus little read in Iran, *Ayāz* forms the first part in a projected trilogy. In it the author brings together the Arabic-speaking gnostic martyr Mansur Hallāj (857–922), the Ghaznavid monarch Mahmud (970–1030), Mahmud's slave and presumed catamite Ayāz, and Samad Behrangi in a telescoped historical and allegorical setting. Ayāz recounts his shocking story of gore and sex, thematically portraying the history of the Iranian nation as a people literally and figuratively sodomized.[34]

One of the most popular serious novels of post–World War II Iran seems to be Simin Dāneshvar's *Suvashun* (Mourning, 1969), which is set in Shiraz during that war. The novel describes various reactions to the Allied occupation of Fars province: many Shirazis are willing to sell themselves, so to speak, to the British. Also depicted are conflicts between landlord and peasant, and the different environments of city, village, and tribal life. Specifically, *Mourning* is the story of an educated landowning family in which the husband/father Yusof, unwilling to submit to pressure from the occupying forces and their Iranian supporters, and also untraditional in his just treatment of peasants, is assassinated on a trip to his village. Particularly significant in *Mourning* is its point of view. This story of a male-dominated society is told by a woman, Yusof's wife Zari, who at one point muses:

If only the world were in the hands of women, women who had given birth or, in other words, have created and know the worth of what they create and who also appreciate forbearance, patience, monotony, and being unable to do anything. Perhaps be-

---

[33]M. R. Buffington's translation of *Shāzda Ehtejāb* appears in "Major Voices," 250–303.

[34]Carter Bryant's translation of the opening section of *The Infernal Times of Āqā-ye Ayyāz* appears in *New Writing from the Middle East*, ed. L. Hamalian and J. D. Yohannan (New York, 1978), 292–326.

cause men have never literally been creators, they are always ready to throw themselves into water and fire in order to create something. If the world were in the hands of women, where would war be?[35]

A third phenomenon of fiction writing during the 1960s was the growing self-consciousness of writers as professionals sharing common responsibilities and aims. The formation of the Association of Iranian Writers in 1968, and group efforts to deal with problems of censorship were two aspects of this united self-consciousness. A third aspect, that of a common sense of social purpose, is discussed below in the context of the sociology of the Iranian writer of fiction. An equally important aspect of the new self-consciousness had to do with literary criticism. The 1960s saw the development in Iran of literary critical debate and writing that went far beyond existing biographical, historical, and impressionistic approaches to criticism. It essayed both to formulate modernist literary theories and to assess traditional and modernist literary works through sociological and formalistic analysis.

Earlier criticism, such as P. N. Khānlari's "Nathr-e fārsi dar dowra-ye akhir" (Persian prose in recent times, 1946)[36] and Āl-e Ahmad's "Hedāyat-e Buf-e kur" (The Hedāyat of *The Blind Owl*, 1951),[37] cannot be ignored in spite of the more rigorous and analytical criticism from the early 1960s onward. Nor has the new criticism been met with total approval. Much of it is often viewed as self-serving, because many of the major critics are poets and writers of fiction themselves and therefore competing for reader approval in both roles. Further, the level of social commitment expected in fiction in the 1960s and 1970s sometimes clouds other literary critical criteria and leads to evaluation of works, on the one hand, and enunciation of critical theory, on the other hand, that often seem one-sided or derivative. Barāheni's 1968 *Storywriting* was a milestone in Persian fiction criticism both in its detailed discussions of traditional elements of narration, such as char-

[35]Simin Dāneshvar, *Suvashun*, 9th ed. (Tehran, 1978), 195. According to *Ferdowsi* no. 1082 (3 Mehr 1972): 22, the novel's reception among readers was unprecedented in the history of Persian fiction. Khwārazmi Publishers announced a ninth printing of 33,000 copies in October–November 1979 and asserted that more than 120,000 copies of the book had been sold to date.

[36]*Nakhostin kongera-ye nevisandegān-e Iran* (The First Congress of Writers of Iran, Tehran, 1947), 128–75.

[37]In *Haft maqāla az adabiyyat-e mo'aser* (Seven essays on contemporary literature, Tehran, n.d.), translated by A. A. Eftekhary in *Hedayat's 'The Blind Owl' Forty Years After*, 27–42.

acter, plot, setting and theme, and in its analysis of the works of a single author, Sādeq Chubak.

In any case, the new self-consciousness of writers and readers concerning critical questions at least gave the literary scene a new vocabulary and brought Persian fiction closer to the mainstream of contemporary world literature.

## Critical Retrospect

The major landmarks of modern Persian fiction are conspicuous enough: Jamālzāda's *Once Upon a Time* stories (1921), Hedāyat's short stories of the 1930s and *The Blind Owl* (1937, 1941), the emergence of Chubak and Āl-e Ahmad as short-story writers during and after World War II; then 'Alavi with *Her Eyes,* Behāzin with *The Serf's Daughter,* and Āl-e Ahmad with *The School Principal* in the 1950s; the maturation of the short story form in the 1950s and 1960s in the works of Chubak, Golestān, Sā'edi, Ebrāhimi, and others; the surprise appearance of Afghāni's monumental *Āhu Khānom's Husband* and Chubak's two novels *Tangsir* and *The Patient Stone* in the 1960s; the promising note of Golshiri's *Prince Ehtejāb* and Dāneshvar's *Mourning* at the close of the decade; the appearance of several promising short-story writers in the early 1970s, and the publication of novels such as Golestān's *The Secrets of the Treasure of the Haunted Valley* and Goli Taraqqi's *Khāb-e zamestāni* (Winter sleep, 1973). At the very least, some thirty collections of short stories and fifteen or so pieces of longer fiction warrant scrutiny in any comprehensive survey of the more than half-century of developments in modern Persian fiction. An in-depth study of the course of twentieth-century Persian fiction would involve more than a hundred works, exclusive of short fiction not yet anthologized.

Modern Persian fiction from its very beginnings has been *engagé,* social commitment in fiction becoming a conscious *ta'ahhod-e adabi* (literary commitment) for writers during the 1960s. This fact, as well as the realization that imaginative literature generally offers a self-image of the society that produces it, make the sociological consideration of modern Persian fiction a relevant concern in any assessment of its achievement.[38]

The consideration of literature in sociological terms is a traditional focus of attention in literary study, but the question is a complex one:

[38]See M. C. Hillmann, "The Modernist Trend in Persian Literature and Its Social Impact," in *Iranian Studies,* 15 (1982): 7–29.

First, there is the sociology of the writer and the profession and institutions of literature, the whole question of the economic basis of literary production, the social provenance and status of the writer, his ideology, which may find expression in extra-literary pronouncements and activities. Then there is the problem of the social content, the implications and social purpose of the works of literature themselves. Lastly, there are the problems of the audience and the actual social significance of literature. The question how far literature is actually determined by or dependent on its social setting, on social change and development, is one which, in one way or another, will enter into all three divisions of our problem: the sociology of the writer, the social content of the works themselves, and the influence of literature on society.[39]

An inkling of the social content of Persian fiction has already been intimated above in references to individual short stories and novels. Altogether there are a dozen or so major themes in Persian fiction. These include, for example, the alienation of the individual and the abjectness of the modern human condition in an Iranian setting; criticisms of aspects of the institution and popular practices of Islam;[40] the oppression of rural and urban lower classes and of women; contemporary mores and sexual and psychological maladjustment; negative portrayal of the political system and representation of the allegedly corrupting effects of power at all levels; the decadence of the aristocracy; the cynicism of the non-establishment intelligentsia; depiction of the people, particularly the middle class, as individualistic, acquisitive, and self-interested; the representation of the manifold aspects of and tensions deriving from the confrontation of Iran with the West; and the tyranny of father and other authority figures in various private and public spheres that have been discussed under such headings as "ruler-subject relations," "masculine history," and "son killing."[41] Aspects of social history, local color, depiction of customs and dialects of distinct groups of Iranian people, and the like are another source of important social content in Persian fiction.

[39]R. Wellek and A. Warren, *Theory of Literature* (New York, 1956), 95–96.

[40]M. C. Hillmann, "Revolution, Islam, and Contemporary Persian Literature," in *Iran: Essays on a Revolution in the Making*, ed. A. Jabbari and R. Olson (Lexington, Ky., 1981), discusses Iranian writers' attitudes toward Islam in detail.

[41]See M. C. Hillmann, "Language and Social Distinctions in Iran," in *Continuity and Change in Iran*, ed. N. Keddie and M. Bonine (Binghamton, N.Y., 1981), 327–40; R. Barāheni, "Masculine History," in *The Crowned Cannibals* (New York, 1977), 19–84; and M. Southgate, introduction to *Modern Persian Short Stories*, ix–xii.

As for the influence of Persian fiction upon Iranian society at large, despite its popularity among some university students and non-establishment literati in Iran, it remains, in a word, negligible. To be sure, in the vacuum of Iranian studies, writers such as Jamālzāda and Hedāyat are understandably assumed both to have "international reputations" and to be known in Iran "to the members of all classes."[42] Even Hedāyat, very clearly an unknown writer in France at the time of his death in 1951 and appreciated during his life by a very small group of Iranian writers and intellectuals, has no significant reputation outside of Iran. His popularity in Iran certainly has not extended "to the members of all classes" because, very simply, Iranian readers of fiction are a miniscule minority in a society where the majority is illiterate. These observations lead to a regrettable fact that cannot be overemphasized: native Iranian interpretive fiction is not "popular" in Iran or abroad. In Iran this fiction, with notable exceptions, did not even compete favorably with Western fiction in translation or with Iranian escape fiction during the Pahlavi Era.

The question of the writer and his or her role in society in the study of modern Persian literature is a particularly complicated one because the context in which the Iranian writer has operated during the first three-quarters of the twentieth century has been so changeable. Basically, twentieth-century Persian fiction would seem amenable to a sixfold periodization, with the writer's role(s) distinctive and different in each period: (1) the Constitutional period and its aftermath (1900–1921); (2) the Rezā Shah period (1921–41) with its superficial Westernization, secularization, stifling of expression, and grim censorship; (3) the period from late 1941 to August 1953, in which freedom of expression and some development of middle-class involvement in social questions occurred; (4) late 1953 to 1970 during which Mohammad Rezā Shah consolidated his position and power, and established a new context of censorship and information control; (5) the period 1971–77, in which the government tightened control and began actively to incarcerate "dissident" writers, to merge distinctions between those writers and a rising number of actual revolutionaries and guerillas, and to reinstitute what non-establishment intellectuals consider the tone of the Rezā Shah period; and (6) 1978 and after.

[42] J. A. Bill, *The Politics of Iran* (Columbus, Ohio, 1972), 75–76. Iranian writers do not share Bill's view; cf. Jalāl Āl-e Ahmad, "Chand nokta darbāra-ye moshakhkhasāt-e kolliye adabiyyāt-e mo'āser-e Iran" (1961), translated as "Characteristics of Contemporary Literature in Iran" by P. Dutz in *Iranian Society: An Anthology of Writings* by Jalāl Āl-e Ahmad, comp. and ed. M. C. Hillmann (Lexington, Ky., 1982), 89–98.

In recognizing the great difference in the political and social climate between the 1941–53 and 1953–70 periods, it has been natural for Iranologists to suppose a change in the kinds of writing and stances of writers during the latter period *vis-à-vis* the earlier one. An asserted "esoteric" and "symbolic" style was the major recourse for those writers who did not forsake their craft, put it in the service of the system, or turn to uncommitted writing.[43]

As for those who opted out, 'Alavi was the only major literary figure who actually left Iran. Another sort of "opting out" is supposedly represented by Behāzin, who is said to have "switched to translation."[44] But with three collections of short stories and one of essays published between 1955 and 1972, active involvement in the Association of Iranian Writers, and brief periods of incarceration in the 1970s, Behāzin was most productive as an *engagé* writer during the post-Mosāddeq, pre-Khomayni era. The very productivity of the writers is significant. First, political constraints, to a point, were a stimulus to *engagé* writing, commitment, and social criticism in imaginative literature, rather than a deterrent. Second, social criticism in imaginative literature in the highly controlled Pahlavi political environment was used by the system both as a sign of some progressiveness and as a means of reducing the pressure of discontent. Imaginative literature had a limited impact, and its social import, however thinly veiled, was nonetheless indirect and made ambiguous by the very artifice of art. Third, imaginative Persian literature became the substitute for overt activity when the latter was judged dangerous and/or ineffectual.

Equally important is an appreciation of the manifold functions of the writers in contemporary Persian literature. First, because no writer of serious imaginative literature in Iran has yet been able to support him- or herself through original fiction, drama, or verse, the bulk of contemporary Iranian writers either have done their writing as a sideline to their basic work, often government employment, or have found a means of livelihood in some other area of writing, such as translation, journalism, or editorial work. Second, the translator of works of imaginative literature in Iran, owing to the importance and popularity of Western literature in translation, is as much an artist and stylist as an author of fiction or poetry. Third, the translator, in choosing works to translate, may demonstrate as much social concern and challenge the status quo as directly as in his or her own writing, while achieving

[43]Bill, *Politics of Iran*, 75–76.
[44]Ibid., 75.

a distance of a single remove from any direct displeasure from the system.

A more important issue concerns the view that the most influential *engagé* writers "changed their method and style" with the reestablishment of monarchical control in August 1953. Indicative of the complexity of the question and of governmental response to modernist Persian literature are the careers of Āl-e Ahmad and Chubak. Āl-e Ahmad's most productive years as a mature writer began with the publication of *The School Principal* in 1958, which is, if anything, direct, explicit social criticism, although mild in comparison with his essay "Plagued by the West" (1962) or with *The Cursing of the Earth* (1968), a multi-faceted direct social criticism of the "White Revolution" era. Nor did Chubak change his attitude or language from his earliest stories through *The Patient Stone* (1966). No one who has read *Tangsir* or *The Patient Stone* can fail to comprehend the relevance of the novels, even if a historical setting is used in both. The historical setting is also used by Modarresi in *Sharifjān Sharifjān* (1965), Āl-e Ahmad in *The Letter "N" and the Pen* (1961), Sā'edi in *The Cannon* (1967), and Dāneshvar in *Mourning* (1969). Perhaps a historical setting has proved a useful device in post-Mosāddeq fiction, but it surely does not constitute esoteric writing or a change in method of style, especially when one realizes that earlier works such as *The Serf's Daughter* (1951) and *Her Eyes* (1952) are similarly "historical."

There is no denying that a new context of official control over the press, and over publication of literary works, developed in the 1970s. This new censorship was not a sudden thing, and perhaps began with the death of Āl-e Ahmad in September 1969, when writers, editors, and friends discovered that the government was not prepared to allow the commemorative ceremonies and publications planned in his honor. It increased in intensity after the Siyāhkal incident in the spring of 1971, during which a number of radical guerillas were trapped and slain by the security forces. Its results can be seen in the subsequent disappearance of non-establishment literary magazines and the incarceration of such established fiction writers as Behāzin, Sā'edi, Golshiri, Tonakāboni, and Dowlatābādi, as well as others, poets and essayists. Although the unraveling of the circumstances of the arrest and incarceration of Iranian literary figures from 1971 onward is basically not a literary question, even in the context of a consideration of the sociology of the Iranian fiction writer, the fact that a number of modernist Iranian writers had similar experiences in this regard may point up significant common stances and circumstances among these writers during the Pahlavi years.

First is the fact that in the 1971–77 period, for reasons other than advocacy of the overthrow of the government, or violation of the law, Iranian writers were subject to surveillance, questioning, and incarceration. Such government action seemed to have as its purpose not the permanent silencing of a writer, but a lesson to the writer in question (and his or her fellow writers) to follow carefully the guidelines or boundaries beyond which even veiled social criticism could not go. Further, such government action reminded the literary audience that writers of imaginative literature had no independent social base. Government control of the printed media, and the supervision and censorship of written material before publication, were the means by which most writers were constantly reminded of the limits; short-term incarceration without formal charges and subsequent limitation of employment and travel opportunities were not uncommon punishments for infringement. These measures clearly demonstrated the regime's sensitivity to the potential effects of imaginative modernist *engagé* literature.

Social commitment in imaginative literature highlights a certain ideological common ground shared by many modernist Iranian writers and their readers, together with common non-creative literary activities that these writers seem drawn to. First, although these writers were products of the government educational system and generally in government employ, they were explicitly non-establishment and implicitly anti-establishment in their loyalties during the Pahlavi era. Thus, they gravitated toward journals without obvious government connections, and most of the major figures in modernist literature have, like Āl-e Ahmad and Sā'edi, assumed editorial responsibilities with such magazines. Second, although modernist writers generally attach importance to a good command of at least one major Western European language, are generally active as translators of Western works, and seem to bring a Western orientation to their analysis, exposition, and literary forms, they are explicitly anti-*gharbzāda* (*gharbzāda* meaning "afflicted by and infatuated with the West") and culturally nationalistic. They may at the same time be thoroughly critical of those native traditions, such as aspects of the institution of Islam, cultural orientations toward hierarchy, and royalist traditions, that they view as responsible for many contemporary social and political ills. Often they translate writers whose works seem to them to

315

stand in a similar relation to the status quo in France or the United States. Third, although works of imaginative literature in Iran rarely provide their authors with significant income and although the reading public is extremely small and does not even include a significant segment of the educated populace, modernist writers conceive of themselves as professional writers and as a basic intelligentsia. This attitude seems, in part, to account for the involvement of many writers in speaking out and writing on subjects beyond their primary literary form, and their audience seems to expect a prominent lyric poet, for example, to appear in print with his or her views on art in general, Israel and the Arabs, contemporary morality, the plight of the poor and the illiterate, and the effects of Westernization.

Another important aspect of Pahlavi-era Persian literature is what appears to be the non-revolutionary orientation of most Iranian modernist writers. This assertion runs counter to a radical view which classifies that literature as either "revolutionary" or "submissive," and Hedāyat, Āl-e Ahmad, and Sā'edi, among others, as "revolutionary artists."[45] This radical analysis seems not to consider that modern Persian fiction may be more complex and amenable to a fourfold, rather than a twofold, classification, namely, revolutionary, reformist, uncommitted, and submissive/panegyric. Modernist *engagé* writers (even those with formal ties with the Pahlavi establishment) were generally reformist. When it is argued, for example, that a story such as Behrangi's "The Little Black Fish" thematically presents "the need for armed struggle in order to create lasting benefits for all the people,"[46] the dispassionate reader recognizes the hyperbole inherent in that radical position.

Private and public statements by major Iranian writers of fiction and their very participation in the Pahlavi system, as well as their flexibility in responding to constraints through innuendo, symbolism, and allegory when direct social criticism may mean censorship or worse, indicate that they were not revolutionaries during the 1953–

---

[45]T. Ricks, "Samad Behrangi and Contemporary Iran: The Artist in Revolutionary Struggle," in *The Little Black Fish and Other Modern Persian Stories*, 95–124; an expanded version of this essay, with the title "Contemporary Iranian Political Economy and History: An Overview," appears in *The Review of Iranian Political Economy and History* 1/1 (December 1976): 24–54.

[46]Ibid., 117. G. J. J. de Vries provides an insightful critique of Ricks' views in "Book Reviews," *Edebiyat* 2 (1977): 121–28, reprinted in "Major Voices," 323–27.

77 period.[47] That they remained writers in Iran during the 1971–77 period also may imply that professionally the situation was not literally intolerable. Of course, how modernist, *engagé* writers will respond in the future to increased pressures and constraints and to the new sociopolitical context that the political turmoil since 1978 and the establishment of the Islamic Republic in early 1979 have created, is unpredictable. Nevertheless, the existence of constraints during the 1971–77 period and official Pahlavi sensitivity to the social content of recent Persian fiction are further evidence that this body of literature is a committed and relevant literary medium. In fact, this literature has constituted the clearest mirror of the Iranian intellectuals' self-image and conscience, and, according to one critic writing in 1970, "may now be considered the richest source of reference for the social scientist."[48]

## Postscript

The fall of the Pahlavi monarchy and the establishment of the Islamic Republic of Iran did not bring an abrupt end to the Pahlavi-era modes of fiction which are the subject of this essay. Even while new sorts of fictional subjects and stances, including that of the Iranian short story writer and novelist and their characters in exile, mark the 1980s, Afghāni, Barāheni, Dowlatābādi, Fasih, Golshiri, Mahmud, and Mirsādeqi, among others, have published fiction in the 1980s continuing earlier directions. They have brought the Iranian novel to preeminence over the short story, while the readership of fiction in Iran greatly expanded by the mid-1980s.

---

[47]The possibly exceptional case of the controversial Iranian critic, poet, and novelist Rezā Barāheni, whose self-exile from Iran ended in early 1979, is reviewed in "Major Voices," 304–13. In the slightly more open atmosphere of the fall of 1977, the Association of Iranian Writers sponsored the evenings of lectures and poetry readings at the Goethe Institute in Tehran. A number of presentations were daring, but the basic thrust was reformist, not revolutionary. See *Dah shab: Shabhā-ye shā'erān o nevisandegān dar anjoman-e farhangi-ye Iran o Ālmān* (Ten nights: evenings of poets and writers . . . , comp. Nāser Mo'azzen, Tehran, 1978).

[48]Cf. Yarshater, "The Modern Literary Idiom," 310, 317.

# 16. Sādeq Hedāyat

## A. An Appraisal*

Sādeq Hedāyat was born in Tehran in 1903 and committed suicide in Paris in 1951. Within the span of some twenty-five years of literary activity he published a substantial number of short stories, two short novels, a novelette, two historical dramas, a puppet play, a travelogue, and a collection of satirical parodies and sketches. His writings also include literary criticisms, studies in Persian folklore, and translations from Middle Persian and French.[1]

Hailed by his admirers as the most significant writer that Persia has produced in modern times, and attacked by his detractors as a decadent writer of little talent and less art, Hedāyat was long a controversial figure who aroused strong emotions in both camps. The conservative critics, brought up in the school of the old masters of Persian literature and accustomed to their elitist and elegant style, saw in Hedāyat's writings a corrosion of long cherished aesthetic values and a travesty of good taste. Hedāyat's ungainly prose, his profanity, and his use of themes and techniques alien to Persian tradition grated on their literary sensibilities. But there was also a more profound, if less visible, reason for the antagonisms that he aroused. Hedāyat's breaking of many literary taboos posed a symbolic threat to the fabric of the established order. After World War II the increasing admiration of the younger generations and the intellectuals for Hedāyat's writings served only to heighten the animosity of the literary establishment toward him.

These critics in fact missed the point in judging Hedāyat by literary standards and social values that had passed their prime and were about to crumble. Hedāyat's significance lies not so much in his intrinsic merits as a writer as in his capturing the mood of a society in transition and giving vent to the underlying sentiments of a new generation—a generation that felt helpless in the face of external pressures and internal policies. The frustration of the hopes and yearnings evoked during the Constitutional Movement (ca. 1900–1921) for the renovation of a glorious past found expression in Hedāyat's sense of

*Published first in E. Yarshater ed., *Sadeq Hedayat: An Anthology.* (Modern Persian Literature Series, no. 2), Westview, Boulder, Colo., 1979.

[1]For a complete bibliography of Hedāyat see H. Kamshad, *Modern Persian Prose Literature* (Cambridge, 1966), 202–8, and M. Golbon, *Ketab-shenāsi-ye Sādeq Hedāyat* (A bibliography of S. H., Tehran, 1976). See also p. 296 n. 10 and p. 514 in this volume.

gloom and disheartened fatalism. He set the trend for a whole generation of upcoming writers who saw in his nostalgic melancholy and pessimism an expression of their own thwarted hopes and aspirations.

However, it would be an oversimplification to seek an explanation of Hedāyat's cynicism and morbidity in his environment or the circumstances of his personal life alone. It was largely his particular disposition that tinted the world in dark colors. The thought of suicide had been with him from an early age. He had attempted to drown himself as a youth. One of his earliest short stories, "Buried Alive" (1930), which depicts a sick man's weariness of life, withdrawal from the world, and flirtation with death, well reflects Hedāyat's personal morbid tendencies.

A key element of Hedāyat's tormented feelings is his strong, if distorted, sense of nationalism, which at times borders on chauvinism. His attraction to the study of Middle Persian Zoroastrian literature was no doubt motivated by a belief in ancient Persian virtues and a desire to catch glimpses of a past unsullied by the corruption of alien influences. His pride in a glorious ancient Iran can be seen in *Parvin, dokhtar-e Sāsān* (Parvin, daughter of Sāsān), a drama of mawkish sentimentality, which had as its theme the defeat of the Persians at the hands of the invading Arab armies in the seventh century, and the atrocities suffered by noble, cultivated Persians. This emotionally tinged preoccupation with Persia's failed glory runs through many of Hedāyat's works.

Characteristically, however, Hedāyat passes lightly over Iran's historical achievements and past splendors to concentrate on the anger and dejection born of defeat; it is on the blows and injuries received from the Arabs, the Mongols and other invaders of Persia, rather than on Persian conquests and cultural contributions, that he lingers. It is revealing that one of the works Hedāyat translated from Middle Persian is *Zand-e Vahman Yasht,* an apocalyptic treatise about the end of the world, that describes the setbacks, defeats, and indignities which the followers of the Good Religion are destined to suffer before the coming of the Savior, who in the course of a final battle punishes the wicked, smites the forces of evil, and restores the world to its original purity.

Hedāyat's sentimentality and his tendency to despair often surface in a cynical or flippant attitude. The inherited order of things, the official and the established, which for him symbolized the triumph of evil, became the targets of his sneers or his mocking satire. Nowhere is this better seen than in his denigration of some of the more de-

319

graded aspects of religious practice. In *'Alaviyya Khānom* (1933),[2] one of his most successful works, Hedāyat gradually unveils the pervasive moral hypocrisy and sexual promiscuity among a seemingly pious group of pilgrims to the holy city of Mashhad. The torrential terms of abuse and the cascades of obscenity pouring out of the mouths of some of the characters in this novelette indicate aggressive feelings that the shy and mild-mannered Hedāyat could only express in his writings. Such feelings, however, appear more frequently in the form of self-mortification and self-pity, or as ridicule. In *Vagh vagh sāhāb* (Mr. Bow Wow), a series of parodies, mocking narratives, and facetious sketches (with Mas'ud Farzād, 1933), for instance, he ridicules the contemporary literary and social scene by perverting its norms and caricaturing its practices.

One of his later works, *Hāji Āqā* (1945),[3] a loosely knit, almost plotless story, centers on a character who symbolizes the unprincipled exploiters who increase their wealth and secure their pleasures at the expense of the poor and the ignorant. The work was written at a time when the leftist groups were at the height of their activities in Iran. They saw in Hedāyat's concern for the abused and the downtrodden a vindication of their own stand and were ever anxious to draw him closer to themselves and involve him in their activities. Structurally, *Hāji Āqā* is not one of Hedāyat's most successful works; indeed, in some respects it resembles a political tract. However, it does cast light on the inner thoughts of Hedāyat. Hāji Āqā as a type represents the moral bankruptcy and social decline of the establishment, and elicits Hedāyat's mocking jibes and persistent rancor. The work not only contains some of the best of Hedāyat's humor, but also shows glimpses of hope, instances of defiant courage, and even an implicit repudiation of Hedāyat's own often expressed fatalism. In a bit of cynical advice proffered by Hāji Āqā to his son we read: "People must obey and believe in fate so that we can make sure of enslaving them."

Hedāyat, however, never became a political activist. His suicide six years after the publication of *Hāji Āqā* only showed that his recurrent depression had set in again. Neither his growing fame nor all the praise and adulation he had begun to receive at home and abroad could sustain his failing faith in life.

One source of Hedāyat's appeal derives from his marked humanity,

[2]Translated by G. Kapuscinski and M. Hambly as "The Pilgrim" in *Sadeq Hedayat: An Anthology*, ed. E. Yarshater (Delmar, N.Y., 1982), 1–40.
[3]Trans. G. M. Wickens as *Hāji Āqā, the Portrait of an Iranian Confidence Man* (Austin, Tex., 1979).

or rather, his profound sympathy with the poor and the deprived. The privileged, the greedy, and the corrupt are targets of his loathing and resentment, but the weak and the suffering draw his loving care and compassion. Observant and sensitive, Hedāyat penetrated their lives and captured their idiom. If his technique is Western, his chief characters belong to the heart of Persian society. His detailed descriptions of their circumstances, pain, and anguish seldom fail to draw us into their worlds—so much so that even some of his more fantastic stories appear plausible.

Although Hedāyat was born to a high-ranking family which had produced leading civil servants and political figures from the early nineteenth century onward, his affinity with the underdog is reflected even in his earliest works. In the short story "Davud the Hunchback" (1930),[4] he depicted the sufferings of a poor, lonely, deformed hunchback who is mocked and ridiculed by everyone. Even when the hunchback tries to find comfort in the companionship of a stray dog which he finds crumpled in a corner, consolation is denied him; the dog is dead.

Hedāyat's interest in folklore no doubt fed his interest in the habits, beliefs and superstitions of the poorer strata of the society. His deep and lasting sympathy with animals, best seen in the somewhat maudlin story *Sag-e velgard* (The stray dog, 1942)[5] showed itself in one of his earliest pieces of nonfiction, "Men and Animals" (1924), a clumsy and inept treatise which attacks the eating of meat for the cruelty involved in the slaughtering of animals. Three years later he published in Berlin an enlarged and more convincing version called *Favā'ed-e giyāh-khwāri* (The merits of vegetarianism). Hedāyat's compassion for suffering animals is an extension of his empathy with the downtrodden and the distressed. In all of them he saw a reflection of his own suffering and endowed his characters with his own torment.

Hedāyat is an uneven writer. His adolescent sentimentality, his occasionally flimsy plots and his drawn-out, gloomy monologues sometimes sound sophomoric. At his best, he is an effective and penetrating writer and a skilled artist. His prose lacks the elegance and musicality of the best Persian literary style; but his plain language, taken from everyday speech, is well-suited to his characters and his realistic descriptions. Even in his fantastic stories, Hedāyat wrote graphically. Despite his often awkward prose, he knows how to tell a story. His

[4]Trans. H. S. G. Darke in E. Yarshater, ed., *Anthology*, 173–78.
[5]Trans. B. Spooner, ibid., 119–26.

dialogues are well constructed and convincing and his mastery of the colorful idiom of ordinary people is particularly remarkable. In stories like "The Pilgrimage" and "Dāsh Ākol" part of the reader's enjoyment comes from Hedāyat's skill in the gleeful use of idiomatic colloquialisms. To a Western reader this aspect of Hedāyat's art may appear of minor consequence, but to Persian readers it presented an innovative use of the language in writing. Mohammad 'Ali Jamālzāda had used it earlier in his pioneering *Yeki bud yeki nabud* (Once upon a time), and some of Hedāyat's followers, notably Sādeq Chubak and Jamāl Mirsādeqi, have perfected the technique since. However, by combining his mastery of succulent idioms and slang with engaging plots, Hedāyat broke the barriers of literary conventions more effectively than others.

In technique, Hedāyat was influenced by Western writers. Persian literary tradition, which excels above all in the lyric, the epic, and the didactic genres, does not offer appropriate prototypes for modern fiction or drama. Hedāyat was sent to Belgium as a young man to study dentistry, but soon gave up his interest in formal studies, and turned into an avid reader. He was attracted early to de Maupassant and Chekhov, but it was Kafka whom he admired most. Part of Hedāyat's novelty was his attempt to adapt post-romantic Western styles to Persian fiction writing.

However, Hedāyat was far from a derivative writer. Despite his continued fascination with some of his Western contemporaries, he emerges as an authentic voice of independent spirit, firmly grounded in Persian culture and sentiment. His best work, and the most widely read novel in Persian, *Buf-e kur* (The blind owl, 1937),[6] is a work of considerable artistic merit. In the dreamlike atmosphere of the book, distinction between the real and the imagined is often blurred in the floating and intermingling threads of events. The reader must surrender to the author's carefully conceived but elusive plan, his enthralling meanderings between a world of haunting fantasy and the stark realism of the protagonist's life.

Hedāyat's importance in Persian literature derives primarily from his pioneering work and the enormous influence he has exercised on Persian writers since World War II. Despite his oddities and notwithstanding the harsh criticism leveled against his work as being perverted and alien to Persian tradition, Hedāyat owes much of his popularity to the fact that he is essentially a writer of moods and sentiments that are deeply rooted in Persian life and tradition.

[6]Trans. D. P. Costello (London, 1957; New York, 1957).

First, the melancholy tenor of his writings is common not only to Persian lyric poetry and Persian music—the two most intimate voices of the Persian soul—but also to the Persian religious outlook in Islamic times, with its emphasis on the passions and martyrdom of the saints. An account of the genesis of this mood is beyond the scope of this chapter, but, if no other reason, the vicissitudes of Persian historical experience appear to fully justify it. Although Hedāyat's grim despondency exaggerates the mood, nevertheless it is an expression of a genuine and widely shared Persian feeling.

Second, Hedāyat's fatalism, perhaps best expressed in his short story "Bonbast" (Dead end),[7] coincides with a cherished mode of thinking in Islamic Persia. Islam preached a belief in the absolute will of God and in predestination as a manifestation of God's will, and Persian literature is replete with the notion of the futility of human struggle against destiny. Hedāyat's personal predicament favored this belief. It is succinctly reflected in a recurrent phrase in "Dead End": "it had to happen." In those fleeting moments of hope, when Hedāyat denounced a belief in fate, as in *Hāji Āqā*, he was indeed writing against the grain.

Third, Hedāyat's ardent, if often distorted, romantic pride in the Persian past ties him intimately to his native culture. Since the turn of the century the Persian national consciousness had increasingly stressed, on the one hand, the decline of the present, and on the other, the splendid accomplishments, real or fancied, of ancient and medieval times. Both Hedāyat's romantic view of the past and his cynical notion of the present find a ready response among his countrymen, who display the same ambivalent feelings toward their society. Love turned into resentment and disgust colors the attitude of many Persian intellectuals and is echoed only too often in the works of modern Persian writers.

Finally, Hedāyat's sarcastic humor and mocking parodies express the impotent rage and thwarted expectations that underlie much of the satirical and abusive literature of Persia through the centuries. Thus, in the last analysis Hedāyat is a thoroughly Persian writer who voices native attitudes in a new guise. While breaking with the tradition in genre, technique, and style, he reflects the basic sentiments of that tradition.

---

[7]Trans. by P. Mead in E. Yarshater, ed., *Anthology,* 103–18.

## B. Sādeq Hedāyat's Composite Landscapes: Western Exposure

In a culture that is acutely sensitive to the discrepancies between inner and outer, between the corrupting influences of the outside world, the world of getting and spending, and the purity of an innocent inner being, the life of Sādeq Hedāyat represents an exemplary fealty to that inner self. In fact, it may be difficult for Western readers to understand the kind of loyalty and respect (and controversy) Hedāyat inspired, particularly in the fifties and sixties when his reputation took on mythic qualities. He was the aristocrat who refused to benefit from family connections and remained in low-level positions of the government bureaucracy to the end of his life; he was a writer whose harsh naturalism showed no sign of seeking popularity, a thinker who refused to compromise on extreme positions (his intense Schopenhauerian pessimism, his specific repugnance for Islam), which few readers can have agreed with. It was a life marked (in his vegetarianism, his life-long bachelorhood) by exclusion from the sign-system that normally defines community. A eulogistic notice printed on the back cover of Parastu paperback editions of Hedāyat's works in Iran eloquently sums up the Iranian fascination with Hedāyat as both artist and persona:

> Sādeq Hedāyat's life and the works that he wrote were of a piece—unpretentious and straightforward. He lived like a shadow among us, and like a shadow, he disappeared . . . but a shadow that, once cast, we can never forget. It is always there for us to rest in its shade. His life was a tragedy, but a tragedy that his very being made inevitable. He was acquainted with all our hopes and fears, and unclasped a secret book that may turn out to be an instrument of prophecy, a prophecy in which a nation can see the way it has been living.

The passage does not tell us that Hedāyat committed suicide in 1951. We are expected to know that already, and the lyric refusal to draw connections of cause and effect creates a rhetoric of intimacy and helps evoke the mythic atmosphere. Behind it we feel that the abrasive naturalism of his short stories is linked with the lack of pretense he showed in his career, and the image of the shadow is itself a favored one in Hedāyat's writing. Here it seems to be a relative of the shadow in Hedāyat's greatest work, *Buf-e kur* (The blind owl), where it is imagined as taking on substantial form. In this context it becomes a figure for the paradoxical mark left by the writer, whose retirement from the world of affairs is in fact a delayed mode of communication with it.

The hint of social context that creeps in at the concluding phrase of this eulogy makes Hedāyat, momentarily, not simply a melancholy individual whose sufferings contain a mysterious significance, but a sacrificial figure, whose pain is somehow an expression of—or intensification of—the pain of his society. It is hard to avoid sensing in much of the praise for Hedāyat during the fifties and sixties an unexplained intensity—perhaps, in part, the expression of a localized pessimism aimed at the social order in the shah's Iran.

The corpus of texts we have from Hedāyat would be remarkable no matter who had written them, but the historical importance of the texts and the reputation of their author are even more interesting in light of his family background. Hassan Kamshad's *Modern Persian Prose Literature* reminds us that the Hedāyats, a landowning family from the northern province of Mazanderan, typified the class that came into prominence in Qajar times when a centralized government bureaucracy was being developed.[8] Sādeq Hedāyat's great-grandfather, Rezā Qoli Khan (1800–1872) was himself a famous literary figure, court adviser, compiler of a famous anthology (*Majma' al-fosahā'*, or Concourse of the eloquent), and poet. The altered rules of art and society, as well as a relative decline in family fortunes, are evident in the career of Rezā Qoli Khan's great-grandson, who was also clearly recognized as the center of a literary community, but one that had drifted from the courtly world, and in which the virtues of a writer were measured by his willingness to utter unpleasant truths. His membership in the community of respected writers was secured by his refusal to participate in the systems of patronage made available by the powerful.

What happened in between was a complex process of entry into the modern world and the mixed effects of Western influences. During the second half of the nineteenth century such institutions as the *Dār al-Fonun*, a college on the Western model, became central to the process of introducing new knowledge and making translations of Western scientific works possible. Sādeq Hedāyat's uncle was the director of the Dār al-Fonun, as his great-grandfather had been, and Hedāyat attended it in his turn. It is difficult to say what he thought of it: the mad narrator of "Three Drops of Blood" was a student there, and another of its graduates is the melancholy scholar Mirza Hosayn 'Ali in "The Man Who Killed His 'Self'" from the same collection.

[8]Kamshad, *Modern Persian Prose*, 137–201.

Attitudes toward Western influences became increasingly ambivalent in the early twentieth century, when Western technology (the press) and political concepts (nationhood, parliamentary distribution of power) were used against Western transgression (such as the tobacco monopoly) in the Constitutional Revolution. Hedāyat was born in 1903; the Constitutional Revolution was constant news from 1905 to 1911, and the accession of Rezā Shah took place in 1921: the writer's formative years covered a period of political awakening that ended in ever-dwindling expectations. Jalāl Āl-e Ahmad observes in a famous essay on Hedāyat that his generation was one that knew only growing corruption and lost hopes, "wretchedness and misery"[9] (*foqr* and *maskanat,* the terms the narrator of *The Blind Owl* uses to describe the landscape of desolation that surrounds him). The Western orientation of Hedāyat's reading in this period is clear enough from his juvenalia, articles written in Persian that constantly cite the European classics he studies in the Dār al-Fonun and the French École St. Louis.

In one sense, then, the years he spent in Europe (1926 to 1930) were superfluous. He knew French; he had read the French curriculum. The ostensible purpose of his trip was to study dentistry in Belgium, but he seems to have abandoned that project early on. Possibly the value of those years lay less with his studies than with the fact that this was a time when he was responsible only to himself. There are paintings dating from this period, and the content of the seemingly autobiographical stories set in Europe suggest a life of idleness. But to judge from the bulk of very polished writing he published immediately after his return to Iran, he must have worked nearly full-time in a lonely apprenticeship with the tradition of the European short story.

His return from Europe in 1930 initiated an extraordinary outburst of creativity. Most important are the three collections of short stories published in as many years—*Zenda be-gur* (Buried alive, 1930), *Se qatra khun* (Three drops of blood, 1932), and *Sāya-rowshan* (Chiaroscuro, 1933). To the modern reader they are uncomfortably intense and often marked with gratuitous violence, but each collection is full of memorable characters and has a sharp visual focus and distinct narrative shape, all of which has made them models for the Persian short story. These are his most substantial writings from this period, but they are less than half the total output. There are uncollected short stories, two heroic plays set in the last days of the Sasanian empire, a

---

[9]Translated in *Hedayat's "The Blind Owl" Forty Years After,* 27–42.

blasphemous satirical play for puppets *Afsāna-ye āfarinesh* (The story of creation), which was published only much later in France, a short travel book *Esfahān nesf-e jahān* (Isfahan, half the world), and a series of ephemeral satires written in collaboration with Mas'ud Farzād. The satires are throwaway pieces in a mocking, wheedling voice, which offer us a glimpse of a more spontaneous Hedāyat utterly unlike the controlled, measured person of his serious writing. There is in addition a compendium of folk beliefs and folk customs, *Nayrangestān* (an untranslatable word that means something like "superstition," or perhaps "the house of deception"). Hedāyat was in fact a major figure in the revival of interest in folklore, which has been an integral part of Iranian cultural self-awareness.

Folklore is at the center of a complex of interests that recur in varying permutations throughout Hedāyat's work. It is first a language that evades the ceremonial prevarications of official literature, thus providing a counterweight to the aesthetics of court poetry. Indirectly, folklore dovetails with Hedāyat's religious skepticism, and in particular his distrust of the authority of Islam. His interpretation of 'Omar Khayyām in his edition of the quatrains, for instance, which was published during this period, is an attempt to see in Khayyām a skeptic much like himself. Folklore represents a tenuous link with an earlier Iran, a purer world before the coming of the foreign invasion of Arabic culture. This celebration of an uncorrupted Iran at the back of history may seem far removed from the processes of Westernization, but there is a peculiar cultural dialectic at work here, one nearly universal in the Third World, in which articles researching an indigenous folk culture are often ballasted by citations of European folklorists and philologists. The collection of folklore is itself an imported project, an outgrowth of European Romanticism, which is linked intimately with the notion (also Romantic) of the nation-state.

The same cultural dialectic applies to his innovations as a writer of short stories. Hedāyat did indeed, as is often said, simplify Persian prose, creating almost single-handedly a written dialect responsive to the rhythms and diction of spoken Persian. This previously absent middle style was a creation possible only by analogy with relatively recent developments in European narrative voice. We would be mistaken to see in this a compromise of his abilities as a writer, since creativity is always a process of grafting previously existing elements onto new contexts. The innovations of these stories are harder for us to perceive today because they have become so familiar to both Iranian and Western readers. Thus it is necessary for us to imagine them

327

against a different background. There had been an extensive tradition of historical romance with epic Iranian settings and, beginning with Mohammad 'Ali Jamālzāda's *Yeki bud yeki nabud* (Once upon a time, 1921), a local color tradition.[10] What is new in Hedāyat's short stories of the thirties is a more precise definition of narratorial authority. This technique establishes the speaker's point of view objectively, explicitly, and allows a style that mediates between the pose of neutral observation and the kind of narrated, third-person monologue exemplified by Joyce's *Dubliners*; with Hedāyat's style we are always able to reconstruct where, so to speak, the narratorial camera is located.

The characteristic Hedāyat short story of this period opens with an Iranian scene, portrayed in considerable detail through the eyes of a particular observer. We follow the central character through a more or less routine series of events whose importance escalates, usually to a catastrophic end, often of seemingly unmotivated violence. That violence, the most troublesome aspect of his stories for contemporary readers to come to terms with, is often attributed to Hedāyat's personal pessimism, but it might have as much to do with the narrative demand for closure in a style that otherwise tends to produce sardonic anticlimaxes. A good example from Hedāyat's first collection is the opening of "Dāvud-e guzhposht" (Dāvud the Hunchback), a story whose visible Western elements are relatively specific since it is probably modeled after Thomas Mann's "Little Herr Friedemann."

"No, no. I can never go on with this. I must renounce it entirely. Others can get happiness out of it, but not me. . . . For me it can only bring misery and suffering. Never, never. . . ."

Dāvud was muttering to himself under his breath; he was tapping the ground with the yellow stick he had in his hand, and he was walking with difficulty, as if it was not easy for him to keep his center of gravity. His chest stuck out like a drum; on top of it a large face was sunk between narrow shoulders. Seen from close up, he looked harsh, dried up, repellent, with his thin compressed lips, scanty arched eyebrows, dropping eyelashes, prominent yellow and bony cheeks. If you looked at him from a distance you would see the coat on his back sticking up like a muslin head shawl; long misshapen hands, a wide hat pulled down over his forehead. Above all, the serious air he assumed as he

[10]See H. Daragahi, "The Shaping of the Modern Persian Short Story: Jamālzāda's 'Preface' to *Yeki Bud, Yeki Nabud*," *The Literary Review* 18/1 (Fall 1974): 18–37.

prodded the ground violently with his stick made him look even more ridiculous [*u-ra mozhek karda bud*].[11]

The narrative opens with a close-up that allows us to hear the central figure before we know who he is.

The theme of the opening quotation turns out to be sexual guilt, a subject that never ceases to be fundamental in Hedāyat's writing. As a more or less universal experience, this theme projects something we identify with spontaneously on an otherwise distanced figure. Notice how easy it would be for the grotesque figure of Dāvud to become another exotic figure on the landscape, and how even the objective details, which are described in the language of an unsympathetic observer (e.g., *u-ra mozhek karda bud*), never break the thread of identification with the protagonist. In the passage that follows, the camera pulls back further:

He had started out from the corner of Khiyabān-e Pahlavi and was walking along an avenue outside the town in the direction of the Dowlat Gate. It was near sunset; the air was warm. Ahead of him, to the left, earthen walls and the fading light of these last evening moments. To his right some half-finished brick houses showed up at intervals at the edge of a ditch. . . .

The eye for detail goes beyond what the character notices, and this anchoring in detail helps avoid sentimentality as we move inward in the next paragraph: "Dāvud was thinking how from his earliest childhood up to now he had always been an object either of ridicule or pity. . . ."

"Dāvud the Hunchback" is not one of those stories in which the concluding moments are violent. Dāvud walks to the edge of town— a location that repeats geographically his own outsider's status in the community—where he passes a dying dog (dogs, valued in pre-Islamic times and despised as unclean thereafter, are central in Hedāyat's bestiary); a glance from the dog strikes him as "the first candid look [*negāh-e sāda va rāst*]" he has had in his life. He then converses inconsequentially with a woman to whom he has once proposed marriage, and in the mood of depression which follows he bends down to hug the dog and finds that it has died. Here the violence is attenuated;

[11] Translated by H. D. G. Law in *Life and Letters* 63/148 (1949): 255–59, with minor changes in transcription.

elsewhere it is concentrated and focal. Abji Khānom in the story of that name (in the collection of "Buried Alive") drowns herself during her beautiful sister's wedding feast; Dash Akol (hero of the story by that name in *Three Drops of Blood*) is killed in a brawl. In "Changāl" (The claw), a parodic naturalization of Grimm's fairy tale, "The Juniper," (in Persian "Bolbol-e sar gashte"),[12] the narrative concludes with Ahmad taking on the character of his wicked father, killing his sister Robāba and, for unexplained reasons, dying himself. The recurrence of this reversal of the romance pattern, in which a man and woman die together, is so insistent in Hedāyat's short stories that it may occur independently of visible cause and effect. There are a few stories whose endings are Chekhovian and underplayed ("Hājji Morād," for example, or "Madeleine"), but the stories that have been taken as representative basically follow a pattern in which unexpected violence intrudes on a scene of daily life as if to show us its sinister underside, or even to reproach us for not having seen it sooner.

If I emphasize the patterned quality of these remarkable stories, it is not to call into question their impressive variety or the texture and linguistic clarity of their style. It is a patterning that continues, coherent and recognizable but strangely altered, and is reassembled at a whole new level of complexity and compression in Hedāyat's greatest work, *The Blind Owl* (1937). The beauty of reading *The Blind Owl* in conjunction with the short stories is that it allows us to see familiar themes unfold: to look back through *The Blind Owl* at the short stories is to see the shape of *The Blind Owl*, coherently prefigured, even seemingly inevitable. Looking the other direction, the leap is a mystery.

*The Blind Owl* was privately printed in India, in a *samizdat* mimeographed form, during the trip that occupied the center point of Hedāyat's career. He went to Bombay in 1936 to study Pahlavi, the pre-Islamic language of Iran, with the Parsee scholar Behramgore Anklesaria. It has been suggested that *The Blind Owl* was a long-term project perhaps finished before the trip, and that a major purpose for his leaving Iran was to publish it in India. The explicit sexual scene it concludes with and passages that flirt with blasphemy made it impossible to publish in Iran under Rezā Shah; it appeared in Iran (serialized in a Tehran newspaper) only in 1941, after the shah's abdication.

It is shocking in form as well as content. *The Blind Owl* is not in any traditional sense a novel, unless we take the term loosely to include

---

[12]Sobhi (F. Mohtadi), *Afsānahā-ye kohan*, 6th ed. (Tehran, 1963), vol. 1, 36–45.

any narrative over a certain length. Nor is it a single narrative, but two separate accounts of distantly similar events, both of which circle around the death of a woman. In the first the speaker, who seems to have evolved from the tortured voices of the narrators in the title stories of "Buried Alive" and "Three Drops of Blood," portrays himself as a painter in a dismal, picturesque landscape on the edge of a town later identified as Ray, a suburb of Tehran. The narrative is not so much a plot as a seemingly random sequence of events that takes on meaning only in retrospect. A woman whose sketch he has painted from imagination materializes in reality and then disappears, initiating a vain search for her. She then appears at his doorway, enters his house, lies on his bed, and for unexplained reasons, dies. He succeeds in painting a portrait of her face in death and while burying the body finds an antique vase in the gravesite. The vase turns out to have on it a portrait identical to the one he has just painted. The language of sensual love has thus been transformed into a language of art. With this, the first part ends; the reader intuits its rightness as parable without necessarily taking the time to work out its possible allegorical ramifications.

In the second part a voice, evidently that of the same speaker, begins to describe a different world in which, rather than being an artist, he is simply a convalescent confined to a room from which he looks out at a city scene. Again, the story is one of frustrated love, but here it is the speaker's mixed passion and resentment toward his young wife. Although less happens in it, part 2 is considerably longer than part 1. The mode is realism, and in long stretches the narrator addresses himself to religious hypocrisy and develops a philosophy of pessimism much like what Hedāyat has developed elsewhere in his writings. This is one of the major sources for the commonplace belief that Hedāyat's life and writings were "of a piece."

The events of part 2 are minimal, but arranged in such a way that the thread of narrative anticipation is never broken. The speaker surmises that a grotesque old man (described in the same terms as a figure who appears regularly in part 1) is having an affair with his wife. In the climactic scene, the speaker makes love with her in disguise, and in an act of violence, which he portrays (unconvincingly) as an accident, kills her. Here the language of sensuality merges with the language of violence. In a further merger, in a scene following the climax, the speaker looks into a mirror and sees not his own face, but the face of the grotesque old man.

It is as if the two parts of *The Blind Owl* function to link the three elements of love, violence, and art, the nodal points in which the mundanity and propriety of daily life are broken. The metaphorical net that links those three elements provides the coherence that was missing in the gratuitously violent endings of the short stories, as if *The Blind Owl* were an emendation or framework designed to probe the unspoken coherence of the previous works. Similarly, the objectivity and exactitude of the narrative point of view, which characterizes the short stories, becomes strangely exaggerated and mystifying in *The Blind Owl* until it begins to color our understanding of the narrator. Pictorial vividness gradually merges with obsessive over-definition, so that the same distinctive short-story technique, here intensified, allows us to see that the narrator is insane.

The question of Western influence on *The Blind Owl*, more visible here than in his short stories, was at one time considered a sensitive one, as if it compromised Hedāyat's creativity to acknowledge that he had the good sense to recognize useful styles and adapt them to his purposes. Āl-e Ahmad, and after him Menoutchehr Mohandessi, noticed that passages from Rilke's *Notebooks of Malte Laurids Brigge* were paraphrased without acknowledgment in the text of *The Blind Owl*, whether as silent homage or as a mysterious act of forgetfulness, we do not know.[13] Other figures are important to Hedāyat's writing in a more pervasive way: Freud and Edgar Allan Poe, the one as a mode of vision and the other as a source of motifs and themes. The Freudian mechanisms of condensation, displacement, and reversal are unmistakably present in Hedāyat's conscious construction of his speaker's distorted portrayal of his experience. What Poe provided was a lexicon of romance tropes in brief form, which allowed Hedāyat to see where the turgid structures constantly reappearing in his short stories came from.

But more important than specific influences are the affinities we can discern between *The Blind Owl* and Western modernists he did not read, writings that create a new narrative self-consciousness the same way he did, out of the cast-off parts of an exhausted naturalism. *The Blind Owl* is more an experimental construct than we have indicated: it is not enough to say that part 1 is a fantasy version of what part 2 narrates in a relatively realistic mode. There are evident lapses into hallucination in the second part too, as well as refusals of symmetry that make it impossible simply to mesh the two. This form produces

---

[13]See Āl-e Ahmad's "Hedāyat-e Buf-e kur," 83, English translation, 31; M. Mohandessi, "Hedāyat and Rilke," *Comparative Literature* 23/3 (Summer 1971): 209–16. Mohandessi's study is reprinted in shortened form in *Hedāyat's "Blind Owl" Forty Years After,* 118–24.

a supplement to the inexplicable parts, those corners inaccessible to the light of exegesis. The result of such asymmetries is to put the readers face-to-face with writing itself, forcing them to confront the individual phrase, transition of mood, or voice independent of its context, in the manner of the French *nouveau roman*. Kafka's critiques of language and the limits of referentiality became popular in Europe in the thirties, but Hedāyat discovered them only later; it was a discovery that must have validated his own experiments, and his long essay on Kafka, "Payām-e Kafkā" (The message of Kafka, written in 1948 in conjunction with a series of translations of Kafka into Persian) stands as a marker at the end of his career, as the essay on Khayyām stands, symmetrically, at the beginning.

After Hedāyat's return from India there is a change in style suggesting that he has played out a particular series of themes. Meanwhile, the years that followed Rezā Shah's departure were years of buoyancy and enthusiasm in the intellectual community. A literature of direct statement and political engagement became briefly possible, and Hedāyat was very much a part of that movement. He produced another collection of short stories, *Sag-e velgard* (The stray dog, 1942), in the vein of his three earlier collections, but with an attempt to develop a style of longer engaged narration. "Fardā" (Tomorrow, 1946) is a somber exercise in stream of consciousness, not as a formal experiment but as a committed device that allows us to hear (in a pair of monologues) the thoughts of two workers in a printing house as they drift off to sleep at night, thinking about unionization and the daily affairs that divert them from it.

More substantial still is *Hāji Āqā* (1945), Hedāyat's portrait of a sinister capitalist, a wily, ignorant Tehran bazaari, reactionary and hypocritical, whom we observe in his courtyard making shady business deals with visitors and brow-beating members of his family. For the Soviet Orientalist D. S. Komissarov, *Hāji Āqā* is Hedāyat's masterpiece,[14] but Western readers are likely to have reservations. Hāji Āqā is a caricature too single-minded to be credible, too evil to be comic. Gianroberto Scarcia has suggested that Hāji Āqā's counterparts in reality are more evil still because they possess a charm that conceals that sinister guile. The result, despite Hedāyat's continuing inventiveness in character and setting, is a flattening of the very social issues we want to understand. A climactic scene, for instance, in which Hājji Āqā and a representative of the local clergy discuss the necessity of

---

[14]D. S. Komissarov, *Sâdek Khedâyat: Zhizn' i tvorchestvo* (Moscow, 1967), 58.

keeping the people ignorant and superstitious, reduces social injustice to a simple willed conspiracy and leaves no room for the possibility that history might be more complex.

*Tup-e morvāri* (The pearl cannon, 1947) is perhaps a more successful satire. It is complex, funny, and so scurrilous that it could not be published until 1979; *Hāji Āqā* and *Tup-e morvāri* were taken off the shelves somewhat later that year. The book is an imaginary history of the pearl cannon, a Tehran landmark that Shah 'Abbās took from the Portuguese on the island of Hormoz in 1622. The tale is recounted in a variation of the buffoonish voice Hedāyat had been developing for many years in the ephemeral satires of *Vagh vagh sāhāb* and which continued in scattered pieces throughout the forties. It is full of marvelous comic anachronisms (when Columbus hears the cannon go off in 1492 on San Salvador, his first thought is to search out the communists who must have set it off); at times it approaches the inventiveness and narrative fluidity of *The Blind Owl*.

We have been speaking of Hedāyat both as a central figure in Iranian literature and as an eccentric whose discoveries and innovations are in themselves shocking and uncanny, alien even to Iranian readers. Perhaps the fact that the same figure can be at once eccentric and central should remind us that the spatial metaphors with which we attempt to describe cultural phenomena are limited; whenever we look closely at his work we are likely to find unpredictable cultural precedents. Hedāyat's repugnance for the Arab heritage of Persian culture did not prevent him from writing in a language balanced and counterweighted with Arabic loan words, and real parallels can be drawn between the morbidity of his personal thematics and the martyrology of Shi'ism. The omnipresence of his Western reading as a shaping force is beyond dispute. I wonder in fact if we have not taken from Hedāyat's career the wrong lesson. At a time when Iranian culture is widely dispersed throughout the globe, and extraterritoriality is the fate of still another generation of Iranian intellectuals, it may be less useful for us to point out his vision of a pure Iran, free of various anti-Iranian contaminants, than to examine the openness and receptivity that made his writing possible. Instead of uncompromising purity, we might focus on his radical eclecticism and his willingness to improvise.

## Bibliography

For translations of Hedāyat's works, see p. 514.
There are three major treatments of Hedāyat's biography: V. Monteil,

*Sādeq Hedāyat* (Tehran, 1952), the concluding chapter of H. Kamshad, *Modern Persian Prose,* and D. S. Komissarov's very thorough study, *Sādek Khedāyat: Zhizn' i tvorchestvo* (Moscow, 1967). All three of these books, as well as Hedāyat's *"The Blind Owl" Forty Years After,* include full bibliographies of Hedāyat's works. There is, in addition, an exemplary bibliography of works by and about Hedāyat, which brings together for the first time the extraordinary multiplicity of analyses, testimonials, and attacks available in Persian: *Ketābshenāsi-ye Sādeq-e Hedāyat,* ed. M. Golbon (Tehran, 1976).

# 17. Contemporary Poetry in Iran

When the precursor of modern Persian poetry Nimā Yushij (1895–1959) challenged the methods and practices of the old school poets, the traditionalists tried, in various ways, to curb any possible spread of his influence. And for a time they seemed to succeed. Modern poetry was simply ignored or presented as some kind of outrageous mannerism to be made fun of. Today, less than two decades after Nimā's death, the picture seems to have been reversed. It is the traditional poets who have receded to the background, their voices heard mostly in exclusive poetry sessions, local P.E.N. club meetings, or in the pages of partisan journals such as the newly launched and avowedly "anti-modern" *Gowhar*.[1]

Even though the modern movement had its most influential leader in Nimā Yushij,[2] the new Persian poetry did not reach its full fruition until the early 1960s, when several new literary journals appeared, notably the quarterly review *Ārash*.[3] From the early issues it was clear that *Ārash* aimed at publishing the best in contemporary poetry and prose—original or experimental but not sloppy, literary but not stilted, international in outlook but not xenophilic. Whether by design or naturally, the journal also became an outlet for the friends and followers of Nimā Yushij to champion the cause of the master. Not only were a good many of Nimā's unpublished or inaccessible works made available for the journal's growing readership, but *Ārash* was also the first to publish some of the best tributes made to the once-neglected father of modern poetry, including Āl-e Ahmad's engaging portrayal, "The Old Man Was Our Eye."

In a way, paying tribute to Nimā has been the major common denominator of contemporary Persian poetry over the past two decades. Otherwise, the best of the new poets, even those who have been most vociferous in championing the Nimā school, exhibit a wide range of poetic tendencies, while others have more or less broken away from Nimā's legacy. The diversity has indeed been quite salutary for contemporary Persian poetry and a significant factor in its growth and maturity. After all, Nimā's range—with all his knowledge of prosody, philology and music, and his admirable dedication to poetry—was that

---

[1] This chapter was written in 1975 (Ed.).

[2] Needless to say, the new movement in poetry was not launched suddenly or single-handedly. Earlier, such poets as Iraj, Dehkhodā, Bahār, 'Eshqi, and a few others had started to deviate from the conventions of the traditional verse.

[3] Now called *Daftarhā-ye zamāna* and published irregularly under the same editorship.

of one person and rather limited. His was not a poetry of illumination or "cosmic consciousness" like the work of some of the best Persian classical masters, such as Rumi or Hāfez, but primarily a poetry of mood and musicality, of original lines and fresh images.

In the following pages I will talk about the works of those poets who represent the diversity just mentioned: (1) the Nimā school; (2) the new "romantics"; (3) the beginnings of a breakthrough; (4) the significant coalescence represented by the poetry of Sohrāb Sepehri; and (5) Forugh Farrokhzād and prospects for the future.[4]

## The Nimā School

Among the new Persian poets, Ahmad Shāmlu (pseudonym A. Bāmndād, b. 1926) has admitted unequivocal indebtedness to Nimā Yushij: "It was Nimā who led me this way. I mean, it was Nimā who showed me what poetry really is." The influence of Nimā on Shāmlu's poetry has been such that one can even trace in it some of the recurrent concerns and attitudes found in Nimā's work. For example, the theme of hopeful anticipation in the face of a lifeless stillness that runs through Shāmlu's poetry is reminiscent of a good number of Nimā's later poems. In one of his earlier works Shāmlu pictures a battered sailing ship lying inactive on the Caspian coast. The convalescent speaker has wishful visions of

> The fishermen
> making their way to the battered ship
> The hammer feeling the nail
> The saw singing with the wood,

and finally seeing "the sunk-in-the-sand on the sea."

The same theme is central to the skillfully written popular poem "Pariya" (The fairies), in which the adroit juxtaposition of the folkloric and colloquial with the literary, the varying cadences, irregular and yet coordinated, and the rare tonal interplay of elegaic despair and festive hopefulness combine to create a virtuoso piece of beauty and poignancy; it is an example of how Nimā's innovations have helped in extending the possibilities of Persian poetry.

[4]For a bio-bibliography of the major new poets, see E. Yarshater's entries in *Cassell's Encyclopedia of World Literature* (rev. ed., 1973) under the individual poets. See also his article "The Modern Literary Idiom," in *Iran Faces the Seventies* (New York: Praeger, 1971).

In Shāmlu's most recent poems, collected in *Marthiyahā-ye khāk* and *Ebrāhim dar Ātash*, there is less of hopeful waiting and anticipation and more of an increasing preoccupation with the passage of time, with the futility of waiting, of "turning around tomorrow and tomorrow."

The following poem, called "Marthiya" (Threnody), is not only an evocation of this theme but also an example of Shāmlu's recent attempts to strip the poem to its stark purity:

On the leaden background of the dawn
the rider
      is standing still
the wind dishevels
          the long mane of his horse.
God, O God
the riders should not stand still
at a time when warning is given.

                         \* \* \*

By the burnt-down shed
the girl
      is standing still
her thin skirt
        moving in the wind.

God, O God
the girls should not stand still
when the men
tired and despairing
        are growing old.

While writing, by and large, in the manner of Nimā and Shāmlu, the poetry of Mahmud Āzād (b. 1932) has a distinguishing lyrical tone, reminiscent, above all, of Hāfez. The title piece of *Ā'inahā tohist* (The mirrors are empty), has as an epigram the Hāfezian lines, "Nobody is in the mood for drunkenness / Where have all the dreg-drainers gone?" and contains terrifying imagery of moribund stillness:

They have looted the dolls.
There are no faces in town.
The shops are open, open and empty and dark
The harrassed businessmen complain about the wind,
                    the rain, the idlers.

The harrassed businessmen say:
—What a rain, first time ever!
It was a big rain, you know. . . .

And the buyers, unbelieving, survey the whole town:

behind the shopwindows
they have cans and paper flowers.
From the waters of the store tiles
they have wiped away the pictures of trouts.

In town they have buried the vines.
In town the minstrels have thrown away
their empty casks, on the pavement

In town they have closed the eyes.

What keeps this and other similar poems from being a mere expression of despair or political protest is Āzād's lyrical tone and delicate musicality. As such, he is closer to Nimā than Shāmlu or Turkey's celebrated poet Nazim Hikmet. Āzād seems to have read a good deal of classical Persian lyric poetry and has retained its tone and mood, while throwing away its recurrent symbolism and imagery. For motifs such as "the moth and the candle" he has substituted a repertoire of equally recurring but nonsymbolic words and images (more in the manner of classical Japanese poets than the 1920s Imagists) such as the garden, the rain, the blossom, the wind, the river, the sun. The result has been such typical Āzād poems as the following four-liner entitled "Yād" (Remembrance):

The birds are gone to see the winds
The blossoms to see the white waters
Only a bare land is left and the gardens of mind
And a memory of your love, O kinder than the sun.

The imagery of Āzād's more recent works—"Bahār zā'i-ye āhu" (Spring calving of the deer), "Fasl-e khoftan" (The season of sleeping)—is more subdued. In such poems as "Be man sokut biyāmuz" (Teach me silence), he seems to have found a new direction with influences, above all, from the later poetry of Farrokhzād.

Some of the poems of M. 'Omid (Mahdi Akhavān-Thāleth, b. 1928) would not have been distinguishable from the poetry of Shāmlu,

Āzād, and others of the Nimā school were it not for a certain characteristic wit and irony. So much at home is 'Omid with this device
that at times his poetry becomes merely charming or clever, reminiscent of some of the lesser poets of the classical and post-Safavid periods. At other times, however, as in the title poem of his first
important collection, *Zamestān* (Winter), 'Omid uses wit in its best
modern sense. Sometimes he combines the form of the classical love
poetry with Nimāesque cadences and his own original imagery and
mode of diction. Such poems he calls *ghazals*, numbered to distinguish
one from the other, of which the following, "Ghazal 8," is quite representative:

> Tell me, lady, why did I dream of you last night?
> Where were we
>             where were we going so late at night
> but not alone.
> It seemed there was a child walking,
>                         hand in your hand
> who sometimes eyed us: as if plaintive
> that you nestled against me, half-drunk;
> sometimes like two feathers, you and I
>     seated on the soft wind in flight,
> sometimes like two autumn leaves
> that started life in spring and went together
>                     to the end.
> And even now, far from others, upon a quiet lake
> We give ourselves to a shallow wave, barely a ripple
>                         in the soft wind,
> flowing toward the far-off seclusion of
>                     the lake
> with no care for beginning or end.
>
>                     * * *
>
> And so, in that dream of a night, or a
>                         while,
> free, bereft of any fear
> we went on and on
> and a while we were silent, except a word
>                     or smile or glance.
> What a dream it was!
> Tell me, where were you going so late at night?

And where before had we met?
And when did our paths come together, tell!
And how did we first break the ice, how did we
                    warm and grow fond of each other?
What a dream it was!
Why did I dream of you, lady, tell me!

And we kept on going . . .
till we came to an orchard-lane, narrow and winding
                    and dark.
Suddenly around a bend you stopped.
I stood close by.
You faced a stone house
that stood as a mountain citadel
and yet, soft and humble from its walls
blue lilacs and violet sweetbriars
leaned down to the middle of the lane
so low some branches lay their
                    faces on the ground
and, at that moment, the door of the house
—the color of oak and its knocker
                    of ebony—
seemed to be waiting for raps brimming
                    pleasure
its heart trembling, like mine, for
                    joy or naught.
Your knock upon the door
echoed in the hall behind,
in seclusion of blue lilacs
you answered my whistle, bent over
                    and laughed,
and your teeth were the white of fish-scales.
For a moment you stared silently in my eyes
and I saw in your eyes both devils and angels.
You leaned over
a moment full of intrigue
and cleverly blended blossom-kisses with
                    scolding eyes
and I, fearing that the door might open, watched,
                    with chagrin, the little child
—his plaintive look seemed to taunt us—

then a sound from the hall . . . as if someone were
                            slowly opening the door.
But you held to your scowls and blossom-kisses.
Hurriedly but full of joy I kissed your lips
and kissed again . . . and again . . . and again,
and then, without farewell, turned the corner
                            of the lane, drunk.
What a delicious dream it was!
Now, waking, I am in rapture, head to toe.
But lady, delicate dream lady
tell me, why did you come to my dream at night—
in the day you are the moon and gone.

## The New Romantics

This poem, one of 'Omid's best *ghazal*s, exemplifies an interesting development in modern Persian poetry. The dictionary meaning of *ghazal* is love, lovemaking, or courting, indicating the original purpose and content of this poetic form. The apotheosis of the *ghazal*, of course, was achieved with such masters as 'Erāqi, Rumi, Sa'di and Hāfez, who also found in its passionate language a fitting vehicle for the expression of mystical yearnings and ecstasies. With the decline of Sufism, the *ghazal* became tame and mundane, but it never lost its strong appeal. About the time Nimā was writing his experimental poems, M. H. Shahriyār was publishing *ghazal*s of great poignancy and originality that elicited the admiration of Nimā himself, even though technically speaking the poets were poles apart. It did not take long before the blend and modification one might expect took place. Such poets as Tavallali, Shaybāni, Golchin, early Farrokhzād, Nāderpur, Sāya, Moshiri, and others wrote poems—sometimes in the manner of the traditional *ghazal*, but more often in the more flexible *dobayti* (quatrain) form—which reestablished the original, nonmystical concern of lyrical poetry as a vehicle for the poet's personal emotions.

The limitations of this kind of poetry are obvious; in fact some of the poets in this group, in spite of initial contributions to modern poetic idiom, have remained quite reactionary. A notable exception has been Nāder Nāderpur (b. 1929), perhaps the only poet whose work has been welcomed both in the experimental *Ārash* and the relatively conservative journal of "contemporary art and literature," *Sokhan*. Nāderpur is a highly gifted poet and for years has maintained a large readership. But the problem with the kind of popular modern poetry that Nāderpur's works represent is that it does not seem to have anything pressing to say. It sometimes arouses one's admiration for its inventive imagery, lulls the heart, pleases the senses, or elicits some stock emotional responses. Otherwise, its pains and passions are skin-deep, as are its joys and pleasures.

Besides Nāderpur, a good number of other gifted poets belong to what may be called the new romantic school of Persian poetry. To the names mentioned above can be added Rahmāni, Ro'yā'i, Kho'i, Ātashi, Sereshk, and others. Some of these poets have distinguished themselves with a degree of originality, but the distinctions have mainly been in secondary factors. For instance, Sāya was long noted for his concise, indigenous images—in the manner of early 'Omid—such as the following:

My bed
is a lone empty shell
while you, the pearl,
hang around
others' necks.

Nosrat Rahmāni, a self-styled *poète maudit*, intersperses his poems with a catalogue of ordinary, deliberately "non-poetic" objects of the house, the street, the brothel, and the opium den. Finally, there is Yadallāh Ro'yā'i, whose lines, notably in his *Daryā'i* poems, can carry the reader away on a tidal wave of auditory images; he is a poet, above all, of magnetic musicality and elegant cadences.

## The Beginnings of a Breakthrough

Sharply different from the new romantics is a group of poets for whom lyricism, musicality and imagistic evocativeness is of secondary importance and whose poems are usually based on the juxtaposition of realistically perceived pictures and images, often in colloquial idiom and open form in the manner of the mid-century American objectivist poets:

Heads or tails?
        Heads
Heads or tails?
        Tails
The coin spiraled up through the smoke

turned on the orbit of moments
ran down the tower-hill of Time
rolled on the counter:
Di.....nnn...ggg—ding.
If heads, we'll get a message
If tails, Lord O Lord—
   Again the tedious caresses of desire.

The drunkards in the bar can't wait
The din of heads or tails fills the air.

A coin broke the silence of the jukebox:
Now one can dance a frantic twist.

Tired of the schedule of the desk, pen, job
Tired of the pallor of it all
One can drink another beer.

Heads or tails?
   Heads
The coin spiraled up through the smoke
turned on the orbit of moments.

Suddenly the rat of a doubt raises a head
scurries around the corners of my mind, repeating:
May the tower of Time devour your coin, man!
Both sides of the coin are tails.

The poem, entitled "Shir yā khatt" (Heads or tails), is by Farrokh
Tamimi. Poems of similar style can be found in the works of Esmā'il
Shāhrudi (Āyanda), T. Saffārzāda, Y. Amini (Maftun), Manuchehr
Neyestāni and Mohammad 'Ali Sepānlu, who have also, in some de-
gree, broken away from the trend represented by Nimā and Shāmlu.

The most controversial poet of the post-Nimā era, and the chief
practitioner of the so-called New Wave (*Mowj-e now*) poetry is Ahmad
Rezā Ahmadi (b. 1940), author of collections characteristically titled
*Ruznāma-ye shishe'i* (The glass newspaper), *Vaqt-e khub-e masā'eb* (The
good time of troubles), and "Man faqat sefidi-ye abr rā geristam" (I
wept only the whiteness of the cloud). Ahmadi's refusal to let form be
an impediment to the act of writing poetry has been so complete that
even his more sympathetic fellow poets have been led to comment on
his excesses. "Dear Ahmad Rezā," the late Forugh Farrokhzād once
wrote him in a personal letter, "This total disregard of form that you

have chosen to adopt isn't freedom. It is just a kind of convenience, not unlike the professional nose-thumber who turns his back to all ethical matters. Destruction *per se* is never admirable unless it leads to creation."

What often holds Ahmadi's seemingly formless poetry together and makes it different from the bland "prose poems" of others is a disarmingly innocent confusion of metaphoric language:

I had a huge stepmother
as big as God
my stepmother never beat me
my stepmother never pinched me
my stepmother loved me
and I loved my stepmother
my dad was afraid of my stepmother
at night in the plantation of the sky
my stepmother and I smoked the hookah
my stepmother would get high on hookah puffs
in my father's house hookah was forbidden
God danced with my stepmother
God was friends with us
God was our playmate, he never cheated
at nights he told us stories
his stories would put me to sleep
my stepmother would laugh
God wouldn't get mad
His stories were as nice as winter-night roasted nuts
I liked God's stories more than those in the Koran
          or the Torah or the Gospels
God was alone
except for my stepmother and myself He had no friends.

While reflecting the poetic manner of Ahmadi and other New Wave poets, the poem just cited is not a typical one in that it stands on a fairly straightforward narrative line and character portraiture, and is therefore quite easy to comprehend. The following piece, called "The Seventh Nude" (what "nude" and why "the seventh"?) is more representative:

The day you came
I had written down every address

in bad handwriting.
And you lost all the houses.
You didn't tell me.
The neighbors did.
You came late
the window smelled of the damp
you didn't tell me
that it was raining outside.
I closed the window.
The neighbors didn't see you
grow old.
The neighbors were saying that.
If you now were
you'd remember the chairs.
We didn't grow old
but we didn't climb the stairs
                    anymore.
The bread was delivered
                    to the house.

An Ahmadi poem that seems at the same time to be a suggestive manifesto opens with the line, "I have always wanted to live with three words." They are "tree, bird, sky." Aware of his linguistic paucity, the speaker asks his mother to buy him some more words in the market. "Live with those words," she answers, "talk to each other / tell stories / having a few words is not a shame." At the end she recapitulates, "Words won't solve your problem, Ahmad Rezā." This strategy—to evoke poetic feeling with the utmost economy and simplicity of language—can at times result in lines of uncanny irony as in the following excerpts from a poem called "Rāhhā-ye āsheqāna" (Love paths):

The Paths of Love
—weary and old—
were returning with the autumn
of life's early mornings
the innocence of our childhood
embroidered
on their gowns.

In the long run Ahmadi is not, with all his modernity, much different from the neoromantic lyricists in that he tries, like them, to capture a personal feeling and evoke it in the reader. But he does so in the manner of late symbolists and surrealists, from Wallace Stevens ("rosy chocolate and gilded umbrella") to the so-called "New York School" poets (John Ashberry, Frank O'Hara, and the group associated with *The Paris Review*). As such, it is a credit to Ahmadi's poetic gifts that his lines seldom give the impression of sheer mannerism or self-conscious cleverness. As I suggested earlier, this is due to Ahmadi's continuously fresh lyricism, a quality that ultimately links him, despite many indications to the contrary, to the indigenous traditions of Persian poetry, from Āzād and Nimā all the way back to the early *ghazals*.

Traditionally, reactions against realism have flourished more in France and other Romance-language countries than elsewhere, and some of the poets discussed so far have exhibited these trends in different degrees. Nimā himself was quite at home with the French language and had no doubt been influenced by French poets, as were a good number of younger poets, among them Nāderpur, Honarmandi, and Ro'yā'i. Shāmlu has been a leading Persian translator of Garcia Lorca's poems and has reflected the Spanish poet's influence in his own works. One result of this phenomenon has been that modern Persian poets have rarely learned from, or been influenced by, intimate or intensely confessional works such as Whitman's "Song of Myself," Lowell's "Life Studies," Ginsberg's "Howl" and "Kaddish," or Eliot's early poems, to mention only a few diverse styles.

Two notable exceptions are Forugh Farrokhzād and Sohrāb Sepehri, very different from each other in their poetic development and yet similar in their concern with what might be called a poetry of illumination, as well as a concern with moral purpose (as distinct from strictly aesthetic or political ones) in the domain of art.

## The Poetry of Sohrāb Sepehri

The work of Sohrāb Sepehri (1928–81)[5] reveals an interesting contrast to many of the poets discussed or mentioned thus far, not so much in the form or imagery of individual lines as in the overall manner of poetic execution and, along with it, in personal concerns and loyalties. First and foremost, Sepehri was an artist—both painter and poet—who had a sharp and sensitive eye for the things of the phenomenal

[5]The article was written before Sepehri's death. The date of his death has been added by the Editor.

347

world, nature in particular. Furthermore, he was committed at once to artistic ingenuity and moral/philosophical concerns.

The latter aspect is different from the kind of avant-garde art (literature or plastic arts) in which the artist hopes his deliberately vague, half-finished or "open-ended" form will provoke the viewer's or reader's subliminal mind to supply depth and enrichment. Ahmadi's work, as was seen, is often poetry of this kind. Sepehri, on the other hand, had a definite philosophy or message (if one is permitted to use these words), and he painted a picture or supplied a poetic image accordingly. The result may be corner-painting, in the manner of classical Japanese and Chinese artists, in which the vastness or mystery of space or the void is heightened by brief suggestive brushwork. Or, as was seen in Sepehri's later art, a totally opposite technique: for example, tree trunks—and nothing but tree trunks—forcing themselves into the viewer's attention.

With the gifts of an inventive painter, and a genuinely religious temperament, Sepehri—an eminently modern poet who kept himself free from the entanglements of the "literary scene"—distinguished himself from many of his contemporaries. Little concerned with literary or ideological fashions or the predilections of the young, poetry-reading intelligentsia, he was able to eschew the overly prized ingredients of relevance or "social consciousness," elegance of diction, and innuendos of wit, irony, and ambiguity. Instead, by following his own poetic and spiritual direction, he wrote poems of lucid vision and execution from beginning to end. A poem like the characteristic "Sadā-ye pāy-e āb" (The sound of water's footsteps) (in *Hasht Ketāb*, Tehran, 1978) is of such unabashed ecstasy and abandon, his praise of nature, light (*nur*), truth (*haqiqat*), and love (*'eshq*) so direct, that the first literary parallel one thinks of, in spite of the poem's unmistakably modern form, is the poetry of the thirteenth-century mystic, Jalāl al-Din Rumi:

> I am from Kashan . . .
> I am a Moslem
> my Mecca is a red rose
> my prayer spread the stream, my holy clay the light
> my prayer rug the field
> I do ablutions to the rhythm of
>     the rain upon the windowpane
> In my prayer runs the moon, runs the light
> the particles of my prayer have turned translucent

I answer to the prayer call of the wind's muezzin
upon the minaret of the cypress tree
I say my prayer in the mosque of grass
and follow the sitting and rising of the wave.

My Ka'ba is by the water
beneath the acacia trees, and moves
like a breeze from orchard to orchard
from city to city
the Sacred Stone of my Ka'ba
is the garden's light.

I am from Kashan
my profession is painting
now and then I make a cage with colors
and sell it to you
so that its prison song of mountain poppies
will keep company with your loneliness
what a hope! I know
my canvas is inanimate
the pond of my art has no goldfish

I am from Kashan
my lineage may go back to a patch of grass in India
to a vessel made of Moroccan clay
to a whore who lived in Bukhara.
My father died after two arrivals of swallows
after two snowfalls, after sleeping twice
on the patio
when father died the sky was blue
my mother jumped up from sleep, my sister became
beautiful
when my father died cops were poets
the shopkeeper asked me: how many
melons do you want?
I asked him: how much is joy?
My father was a painter
he also made mandolins, played the mandolin
and was a calligrapher.

Our garden was on the other side of knowledge, in
the shade
a place where the feeling interlaced with grass

the convergence point of glance, the cage, and the
                                        looking-glass
our garden was, perhaps, an arc from the green
                                        circle of happiness
the hard fruits I chewed, in dream, were God's.
Those days the water I drank had no philosophy
the berries I picked had no knowledge
as soon as a pomegranate cracked
it became the stand of desire's fountain
when a bird sang, the joy of my listening trembled
whenever loneliness pressed its face against the
                                        windowpane
light came and put its arm around my shoulder
love came and told jokes—
what was life but a raining of new years
a pine full of starlings
light and joy standing in line
taking free rides to the pond full of music.

Then slowly the child tiptoed on the street of
                                        dragonflies and faded out of sight
I packed my belongings and left the city of carefree
my heart heavy with the nostalgia of dragonflies
I went to the world's party
to grief
to the garden of gnosis
to the patio of knowledge
I walked by the staircase of religion
and went as far as the street of doubt
as far as the cool air of desirelessness
as far as the rainy night of love
as far as the woman
as far as pleasure's lamp
I heard the wingbeats of loneliness
and I saw many things
I saw a child who smelled the moonlight
I saw a cage without a door
where light fluttered its wings
a ladder upon which love climbed
to heaven's rooftop
a woman who rubbed the sunbeam in a mortar

at noon they had bread on their table, fresh
      basil leaves, a tray of dew, a bright bowl
              of ease

I saw many things upon the earth:
I saw a beggar who went from door to door
singing the larks' song
I saw a poet who addressed the lily
      of the valley as "lady" . . .
I saw a train carrying light
I saw a train carrying politics (and going so empty)
I saw a train carrying morning-glory seeds and
              canary songs
and a plane, through its window
a thousand feet high, I could see the earth:
I could see the hoopoe's crest
the butterfly's beauty-spots
the passage of a fly across the alley of loneliness
the luminous wish of a sparrow descending from a pine
the coming-of-age of the sun
and the bright embrace of the doll with the dawn.

Stairs that led to lust
stairs that led to the cellar of alcohol,
to the ordained putrification of the rose
to the perception of the arithmetics of life
stairs that led to the rooftop of illumination
stairs that led to the platform of the apocalypse.

Further below I saw my mother
washing the teacups in the memory of the river.
The city
was covered with cement geometry
the rooftops of hundreds of buses had no pigeons
a flowershop owner auctioned his flowers.
Between two flowerstems of despair a poet
hung a rope
a boy threw stones at the school door
a child spit out apricot stones at father's
              faded prayer rug
and a goat drank water from the Caspian of the
              world map.

351

The wheel of a cart longing for the halt of the
        horse the horse for the driver's sleep
        the driver for death.

        I could see love, I could see the wave
        the snow, the friendship
        the word
        the water, reflections upon the water
        the cool canopy of the cells in the blaze
                      of blood
        the damp direction of life
        the east of man's inner sorrow
        the season of strolling in the woman's alley
        the smell of solitude in the season's lane.
In summer's hand a fan.

The journey of the seedling to the flower
the journey of the ivy to the other house
the journey of the moon to the pine . . .

And I saw the people
I saw the cities
the fields, the mountains
water and soil
light and dark
and plants in light, and plants in dark
animals in light, and animals in dark
man in light, and man in dark.

I am from Kashan
but my city is not Kashan
my city is lost
I have built a house on the other side of night
with love and earth.
In this house I am close to the wet loneliness of
                                grass
I hear the sound of gardens breathing
the sound of the darkness raining from a leaf
the light clearing its throat behind the tree
the sneeze of water from every crack of the rock
the whisper of the swallow from spring's rooftop
the sound, so pure, of the window of silence
the sound, so light, of love shedding skin . . .

the density of longing gathered in the wing
the bursting of the soul's resistence.
I hear the footsteps of desire
and the ordained sound from the passageways of blood
the throbbing of the wild pigeon's early dawn
the heartbeats of Friday night
the flow of the carnation on the mind
the sound of the rain on love's wet eyelids
the song of pomegranate orchards
the smash of the glass of happiness at night
the ripping of beauty's paper
the comings and goings of the wind in
    the wandering exile's bowl.

I am near the beginning of earth
I take the pulse of flowers
I am acquainted with water's wet fate,
    trees' green course
my soul flows to the direction that is new
my soul is so young
it coughs with joy
my soul is a loafer
it counts raindrops, the brick-tiles
sometimes, like a stream pebble, my soul is washed
    clean and shines
I haven't seen two pine trees hate each other
I haven't seen a poplar sell its shadow
the elm tree gives its branch to the crow
    at no charge
wherever there is a leaf I rejoice
the field poppy has bathed me in the verve of life.

I don't know
why they say: a horse is a noble beast
a dove is pretty
and nobody keeps a hawk
why is a clover in bloom lesser than a red tulip . . .

Maybe our mission is not to fathom the "secret"
    of the rose
our mission is to swim in the essence of the rose
to wash our hands, before dinner, in the ecstasy

of a leaf
to be born at dawn with the sun
to give wings to rapture, to let the passions take
flight
to recognize the sky between the two syllables of
"being"
to unburden the sparrow from the load of knowledge
to take back the name from the cloud,
the pine, the gnat, the summer
to climb to the altitude of love upon the wet feet
of the rain
to open the door to man, to light, the plant, the
moth
Maybe our mission is
to pause between the morning glory and century
and run to the call of truth.

Not only in this poem[6] but also in a good number of others, notably those contained in *Hajm-e sabz* (The green mass, 1965), Sepehri reveals a cosmic or religious consciousness ("religious" in its original, authentic sense; elsewhere I have called it neo-Sufic[7] to distinguish it from ritualized or organized Sufism), and the concern of a truly religious mind with love, compassion, and kindness to sentient beings. In the hands of a lesser poet such themes, particularly in the context of twentieth-century poetic tastes and sensibilities, could be embarrassingly sentimental or irritatingly preachy. It is a tribute to Sepehri's gifts that he was always capable of saving his lines from such pitfalls.

An objection made against Sepehri is that he was not a "people's poet" (in the sense that, say, the Turkish Nazim Hikmet was), that he lacks social consciousness. If the latter phrase is intended to mean political involvement, the objection is valid. In contemporary Iran, it should be pointed out, dissenting political expression is extremely difficult, if not impossible. But literary artists can, as some have tried to do, get the political message across through the use of fable, allegory and folklore (e.g., Āl-e Ahmad, Behrangi, and Sā'edi in prose, Shāmlu in poetry). But Sepehri bypassed such available channels. Social or political themes *per se* never constitute the subject of his poetry. When such concerns are expressed, they blend so ineluctably with the rest

---

[6]A longer version of this poem can be found in *Mundus Artium* 1 and 2 (1972).

[7]"The Neo-Sufic Poetry of Sohrāb Sepehri," *Books Abroad* (Winter 1973). Some of the following paragraphs are based on that article.

of the fabric of the poem as to be unnoticeable. For instance, when we find the poet distressed, say, by the "era of the Ascension of Steel," the "cement geometry of the city" (whose train is "carrying politics, running so empty"), he wonders in the same breath why "nobody takes a crow of the field seriously." And:

Why don't people know
that the nasturtium blossom is not a coincidence
that in the eyes of today's hummingbird flow
                    yesterday's rivers?

## Forugh Farrokhzād

Forugh Farrokhzād (1935–67) is perhaps the only important figure among the new poets whose work, *in toto*, reflects the whole spectrum of change and development in contemporary Persian poetry and is therefore worth a more detailed treatment. Her first published volumes were *Asir* (The captive), *Divār* (The wall), and *'Osyān* (The revolt), whose themes are well indicated by the titles—the captivity of the sensitive individual, the poet herself, within the walls of tradition and intolerance, which create the feeling of the necessity of revolt. The language of these volumes is extremely personal and more realistic than romantic/symbolist. The tone often fluctuates between the outcries of a creative artist on the one hand, and the desires and frustrations of a young woman, on the other.

With her fourth collection of poems, *Tavallodi digar* (A second birth), Farrokhzād entered a distinctly new phase and proved to have matured into a poet of rare originality and vision.[8] In this volume, and in the poems that appeared in the pages of *Ārash* (1964–67), one finds that this poetic sensibility has grown in all directions, stretching with it the poetic form. Whether in the caustic satire of "Ay marz-e porgohar" (O, bejeweled homeland!) or the moving observations of "Delam barāye bāghcha misuzad" (I feel sad for the garden) and "Paranda faqat yak paranda bud" (The bird was merely a bird), one encounters a highly sensitive and aware poet, whose language is at once unadorned and intense:

---

[8]*Tavallodi digar* and a selection of other poems by Farrokhzād have been translated by J. Kessler and A. Banani as *Bride of Acacias*, Modern Persian Literature Series no. 3 (Delmar, N.Y., 1982). The work has been rendered into English also by Hasan Javadi and Susan Sallée in *Another Birth* (Emoryville, Cal., 1981). Ed.

The bird said, "What a smell, what a sun, ah
spring has arrived
and I'll go find my mate."

The bird flew away, like a message, from the
veranda
the bird was small
the bird wasn't thinking
the bird didn't read newspapers
the bird wasn't in debt
the bird didn't know many people

The bird flew in the air
passed over the stoplights
reached carefree heights
and madly experienced
the blue moments

The bird, ah the bird, was merely a bird.

Many of the poems published in *A Second Birth* belong to a period of
earnest self-examination. In them, Farrokhzād emerges as a poet of
fusions rather than effusions, of processes rather than mere things,
whose earlier emotional eruptions with their inevitable repetitiveness
have given way to a marked density of poetic substance:

Today is the first day of autumn
I know the secret of seasons
I understand the language of moments
the Savior is asleep in the grave
and the earth, the accepting earth,
is a beckon for repose.
(From "At the Threshold of A Cold Season")

I go to the veranda and with my fingers
feel the taut skin of the night

The lights of contact are out
The lights of contact are out

Nobody will introduce me
to the sun
nobody will take me to the party of sparrows

Remember to fly
the bird will die.

(From "I Feel Sad")

As can be seen, the newly acquired complexity is balanced with a certain plainness of language. Far from being a deliberate device, Farrokhzād's simplicity is the inevitable expression of a mind that has consciously thrown away the garb of social fronts and falsities. No wonder, then, that sometimes the poet finds the language of a child or a sheer *naïf* the most convenient vehicle of expression:

I have dreamed
that someone is coming
I have dreamed of a crimson star
and every sign—my fluttering eyelids
my pairing shoes—
all the signs are telling of something
and I'll be struck blind
if I am lying
I have dreamed of that crimson star
even in my waking
someone is coming
someone is coming

Someone different
Someone better
someone who isn't like anyone, isn't like Father
like Jonah
like John
like Mother,
but is just like the one that should be
and he is even taller than the trees at the Masons'
and his face
is even brighter than the coming Imam's
and he is not afraid of Sayyed Javad's brother
who's gone
and become a cop
and he is not even afraid of Sayyed Javad himself
who owns all the rooms in our house.

And his name is
(just as Mother calls in the beginning and the end
                              of her prayer)
the Judge-of-all-Judges
the Way-of-all-Ways
and can read all the hard words in the third grade
                                            book
with eyes closed
and can subtract a thousand
from twenty million
without a mistake
and can buy at Sayyed Javad's grocery store
whatever he wants, on credit
and can make the word ALLAH
which used to shine
green as the dawn
to be lit again across the skies of the Meftahiyan
                              Mosque[9]
                (From "Someone Who Isn't Like Anyone")

This is very different from the poetry of those who decorate their lines, even if with a good deal of skill and delicacy, by means of elegant or ingenious imagery (Nāderpur, Kasrā'i, Ātashi, Sepanlu, Barāheni, Ro'yā'i and others) or those who use the folkloric and ethnological images with a certain self-consciousness.

"To be a poet is to be human," Farrokhzād said in an interview not long before her death.[10] ". . . I know some people whose daily activities have nothing to do with their poetry. Only when they are writing poetry do they become poets. The rest of the time they are greedy, cruel, sloppy, jealous, and petty. I for one don't believe in what they say. And when they clench their fists and make noise—in their poems and so-called essays—I get revolted and lose all faith in their work." This statement is significant in two ways. First, it gives an astute picture of what was happening in the mid-sixties at the very culmination of the development of the new poetry, which was at once a sign of the vitality of the new renaissance and a prelude to its undoing: poets-

---

[9]For a more complete version of this poem, see Farzan, "Forough Farrokhzād, Modern Persian Poet," *Books Abroad* (Autumn 1968); for a word-for-word translation of the same poem, see "Someone Like No One Else," trans. T. M. Ricks, *The Literary Review*, special Iran number (Fall 1974).

[10]With the editors of *Ārash*, summer of 1965.

*cum*-critics jumping at each other's throats (mainly in the pages of the now defunct weekly *Ferdowsi*), making resounding claims about a certain poet's incompetence or "illiteracy" or, sometimes in a short span of time and voiced by the same critic, about the same illiterate poet's genius and, by contrast, another's mediocrity.

Second, Farrokhzād's statement sheds some light on her own poetry and position at the time. Here was a poet who, very much like the great Persian poets of the past, had arrived at a stage where she realized that the poetry she wanted to write was not (to paraphrase Farrokhzād herself) a separate thing, an urn to be wrought or a work to be done, but ineluctably diffused within the poet. The result was such poems as "Āyahā-ye zamini" (The earth texts), an apocalyptic poem full of terrifying images of darkness and suffocating airlessness, and, toward the end, the faint glimpse of hope and regeneration:

Then
the sun grew cold
and the blessing ceased upon the lands

Across the plains the grass turned to dust
and the fish dried up in the sea
and thenceforth the earth
did not accept its dead.

At every tarnished window
the night tossed back and forth
like a restless phantom
and the roads lost their direction
in the dark.

Nobody thought of love anymore
nobody thought of triumph
and nobody
ever thought of anything anymore.

Emptiness descended upon the lonely earth
blood smelled of hashish and opium
women gave birth
to babies without heads
and the cribs took their shame
to cemeteries.

What dark and bitter times
the power of bread had won,

making the hungry and haggard prophets
flee the divine promised lands;
the lost lambs of Jesus
heard no shepherd's call
across the silent dismay of plains.

Motions and colors and pictures
were reflected upside down
in the eyes of mirrors
and over the heads of wicked clowns
and the sordid faces of prostitutes
there glowed neon halos
in the shape of flaming parasols.

The marshes of alcohol,
steaming rancid vapor
sucked in the numb multitude of intellectuals
and the vicious mice
chewed away the gilded books
stacked in old closets.

People,
the ravaged crowd of people
gaunt and dazed and dejected,
wandered from one exile to another
carrying their inauspicious dead,
the aching desire for murder
bloated in their hands.

At times, a tiny spark let loose great havoc
within the lifeless crowd
they charged upon one another
men reached for their knives
and slashed each other's throats
and upon a bed of blood
slept with child-girls.

Always in the ceremony of hanging
when the executioner
gouged the shying eyes of a victim
they sat and watched silently
their old sagging limbs
quivered tautly with delight.

Perhaps even now behind the ravaged eyes
in the abysmal freeze
something indistinct, half-alive, had survived
and with its last exhausted moves
wanted to believe
in the pure song of waters
perhaps—and yet what an unending emptiness
the sun had died
and nobody knew the name
of the sad pigeon of faith
that had flown away.

Ah, the prisoner's voice!
Will the plaint of your despair
ever burrow
from any side of this cursed night
a new way toward light?

Ah, the prisoner's voice—
O the last voice of voices.

Several things are worth pointing out about "The Earth Texts."
First, even though its theme of despair/hope might remind the reader
of similar concerns discussed earlier in this article, the resemblance
is very superficial. Unlike comparable poems of, say, Nimā or Shāmlu,
the condition of despair depicted here has little to do with a specific
social or political situation, but with the condition of the world at large
and of humanity's, including the poet's, spiritual condition. Second,
the Koranic/biblical language of the poem indicates that at about this
time, Farrokhzād is using different modes of form and diction for
different purposes. Third, the complete absence of the first-person
pronoun "I" is extremely rare in Farrokhzād's poetry, whether early
or late. The implications of these characteristics will be noted later on.
Finally, if one were to trace any modern influence in form, language,
content, and meaning in this poem (and several other later poems),
one would most likely come up not with the name of any European
poet, but with that of the Anglo-American T. S. Eliot. The implications of these characteristics to the development of contemporary Persian poetry will be pointed out later, after citing a still different
Farrokhzād poem, written in the traditional *mathnavi* form, and with
an exquisitely ambiguous erotic/mystical language, entitled "Āsheqāna" (Love song):

O
From whose vision
The night has gathered color
From whose fragrance my heart has become heavy, heady

Your being spread upon my eyes
purging me of my sorrows
washing me clean
        like the body of the earth with raindrops.

The beating of my burning body
Afire in my lashes' shadows
More bountiful than the sea of wheatfields
More fertile than the golden boughs of trees

Opener of the door to the sun
Amidst the sudden blackout of doubt
No more fear for me, Lord
No pain but the pain of bliss.

The tight cubicle of my heart
        and such light.
From under a tombstone
        such sound rejoicing of life.

Your two eyes, my meadows
The fire of your eyes, branded on my eyes
Had I you in me before
Had I you in me before.

It is a dark pain
        the sorrow of wanting
The indignity of stooping
Laying one's head on any heartless chest
Taking the pulse of the heart with hate
Seeking caresses, receiving snake bites
Finding poison in fake smiles
Paying the thieves
        getting lost in thieves' highways and bazaars.

* * *

Ah, with you my light commingled
By you from the graveyard resurrected
You have arrived from the skies of farthest stars

with wings splashing gold dust.
From you my loneliness quelled
My body scented with smells of embrace.
You the water of the river of my bosom
The flood of the dry bed of my veins.
In the cold darkness of this world
I'll take steps with your steps.

O you who are hiding beneath my skin
Seething in the blood of my skin
My hair ablaze with your tenderness
My cheeks burning with the prism of your lovingness
Stranger to my masks and clothes
Familiar with my body's garden paths.

A rising without setting
The sun of the southern lands

Ah, fresher than the early dawns
More revirescent than Aprils
This is not love anymore
          this is dazzlement
A burning chandelier in the silence of the dark.
With love I have turned
          to a total abandon from head to toe.
This is not I, this is not I anymore
Alas the wasted life I lived with the *I*

Ah, your lips the essence of longing of my lips
My mouth made in the image of your kiss
My body shuddering with the pleasures of bliss
The lines of your body the stuff of my dress
How I wish that I would burst
and break the dam between desire and fulfillment.
I would rise on my feet
as a heavy cloud—and weep.
The tight cubicle of my heart
          and such heady smoke of holy incense.
In the requiem eve of mosque
          such melodies of the harp
Empty space and such flights
Such songs amidst a silent night.

\* \* \*

O your glance the lullaby of enchantment
The rocking cradle of distressed children
Your breath the breeze of sinking into sleep
The quietude of my fear's tremblings
Sleeping in the smile of my tomorrows
Traveling in my world's unseen depths.

You blended me with the beatitude of poetry
               you made my poems into glows and embers
You blazed my love's fever
You burned my verse in fire.

As mentioned earlier, the work of Forugh Farrokhzād demonstrates, besides the making of an unusually good poet, the range and diversity of the new Persian poetry. Starting with more or less traditional forms and rather banal but obviously genuine concern with the desires and frustrations of self-fulfillment, she surprises her readers with a poetic "second birth," in which, while still concerned with the "I," she shows a growing awareness of people and the world around her, and herself *vis-à-vis* this world. She does not become an "objective" poet, but internalizes her observations. The self remains but becomes a larger entity, with more possibilities of sorrow and joy. Damnation and salvation knock simultaneously on the door of consciousness. It is up to the poet to choose any one of these possibilities: to look the conflict earnestly in the face; to see an escape; to lay blame, as she had in the earlier works, on the family, the husband or tradition; or, as other poets were doing, to become a Marxist and blame the environment and political system. Farrokhzād, we find, chooses the first alternative. She becomes, in a way, a truth-seeking wayfarer, a *sālek* (to borrow a term from the Sufis). "I have lost my life," she says in a letter to Ebrāhim Golestān (*Ārash* II, 13) ". . . I want to start anew." Having started to see the vanity of socially sanctioned pursuits and pleasures, for some time she still clings to the vanity difficult for an attractive woman to abandon; but the poet is changing and developing, and time is running short. Thus, at twenty-seven, when she sees two lines between her brows, her reaction is: "No more illusions. Finally I have found myself."

These changes in the poet's life are reflected in her poetry. They are changes with many facets and phases, and the poet records all of them, now in the form of a satire, now a tender lyric, a compassionate portraiture, a childhood nostalgia, a spiritual longing, a feeling of ordinary loneliness, a vision of the dark night of the soul, or a passionate, quasi-erotic desire to surrender to the One. An extremely varied and flexible means of expression is needed to accommodate all this. But fortunately around this time (early to mid-1960s) the poet had at her disposal the liberating prosodic innovations of Nimā and of those who have followed him. Then there are the *mathnavi*s and *ghazal*s of such past masters as Rumi and, finally, the whole legacy of modern world poetry (the poet had knowledge of English, so she could read Anglo-American poets first-hand; above all, she read T. S. Eliot). Not only could she write poems comparable to the best of modern world poetry, but she was also able to discard any single existing model or practice, whether traditional or new.

Besides being the best representative of the new Persian poetry in all its change and development, Farrokhzād was also, during the first half of the 1960s, a pivotal force and a salutary example. I do not think it was a coincidence that, after her death and a year or two of post-mortem unity among the poets, modern Persian poetry lost its vigor and vitality. There might have been other reasons, but Farrokhzād's absence was certainly one: there was no longer a poet of passionate earnestness and sincerity in whom "poetry had been diffused"; for whom art was not something extraneous to be manipulated or worked on, to be used for self-aggrandizement or sheer self-expression. And, therefore, there was no longer a model poet to emulate, to be scolded by, or to be encouraged and inspired by.

Since the latter part of the 1960s, many of the newly launched periodicals, both in Tehran and the provinces, have ceased publication; many of the practicing poets have been ensconced in well-paying jobs in the Iranian Radio-Television and other government-run agencies. This, or tighter censorship, may have caused the disturbing paucity of literary production, particularly poetry. Even such poets as Sepehri, for whom political censorship or lack thereof seems to make little difference, have become virtually silent. Very few books of any genuineness or literary merit are being published. By contrast, there has been a proliferation of translations from the works of Western authors and an inordinately heavy emphasis on the visual, plastic and dramatic arts.

This is quite unfortunate because few nations in the contemporary world enjoy the possibilities available to the Iranian writer or poet to produce works of extraordinary richness and depth, indications of which we have seen, in these pages, in the works of Farrokhzād, Sepehri, and others. The possibilities in question are varied and can be summarized briefly. First, a *living* past literature: the written Persian language has changed very little since Ferdowsi's, Khayyām's or Rumi's time; second, a unique milieu, contemporary Iran is a meeting-place of stunning contrasts. The present-day Iranian may be seen emerging from the twilight of an active bazaar—unchanged for centuries—or may be seen dodging a donkey to maneuver his automobile, if he has one, or vice versa. Third is the availability and awareness, through the relative affluence of the country and expanding communication, of current developments in Western art and culture. Finally, on the one hand there is a historical capacity for a renewed, sagacious simplicity, the good life of contentment and peace; and on the other a sense of cultural loss, the temptation to adopt the Western consumerist mode of equating the pursuit of pleasure with the pursuit of happiness, and the resulting confusion and conflict. What a fitting metaphor this is for the inner human conflict![11]

[11]For an update of the developments in recent years see Michael Hillmann's article "The Modernist Trend in Persian Literature and its Social Impact," *Iranian Studies* 15 (1982): 7–30. (Ed.)

# 18. Forugh Farrokhzād

She was a lonely woman, an intriguingly unyielding rebel; an adventuress of both body and mind; an iconoclast who asked (and sometimes answered) the wrong questions. Relentlessly, she trespassed boundaries and explored new domains. Zestfully, she demanded of life the gratification of her desires—intellectual, emotional, and sensual—troubling herself less and less about so-called moral proprieties. In short, Forugh Farrokhzād was a woman in quest of union and communion:

> I come from the land of dolls
> From under the shade of paper trees
> in the garden of a picture book
> From the droughts of barren trials of friendship and love[1]

Forugh Farrokhzād was born in Tehran on January 5, 1935, the third of seven children. She only finished the ninth grade in formal schooling before being transferred to a girls' school to study painting and sewing. She married at sixteen, was a mother at seventeen, and divorced at nineteen. Perhaps she knew that the "sucking, frozen"[2] mouth of death awaited her, that she had to fully and quickly use the little time allotted to her. At the height of her creativity, at the age of thirty-two, Forugh died in a car accident.[3]

But Forugh had conquered time. Not long before she died, in a poem published posthumously, she no longer dreads the recycling of nature and the arrival of yet another spring. Her art is a promise of blossoming and growth, eternity itself:

---

[1]Jascha Kessler with Amin Banani, trans., *Bride of Acacias* (Selected Poems of Forugh Farrokhzād) (New York: Caravan Press, 1982), 105.

[2]What peak, and what heights?
Don't all these winding paths
converge and close
in that sucking, frozen mouth?
From the poem "Green Delusion," in Kessler and Banani, 68.

[3]For the poet's biography, see: Amir Esmā'ili and Abolqāsem Sedārat, *Jāvedāneh, Forugh Farrokhzād* (Tehran, 1972); Michael C. Hillmann, "Forugh Farrokhzad: Modern Iranian Poet," in *Middle Eastern Muslim Women Speak*, Elizabeth Fernea and Basima Bezirgan, eds. (Austin: University of Texas, 1977), 291–317; and Mehri Bharier, "Forugh Farrokhzad: Persian Poetess and Feminist," M.A. thesis (Durham University, 1978).

Perhaps those two hands were true, those two young hands
buried below the neverending snow
And next year, when Spring
sleeps with the sky beyond the window
and shoots thrust from her body
the green shoots of empty branches
will blossom, O my dearest one, my dearest only one[4]

Forugh not only grows through her art, she also portrays that growth in her writing.[5] Finding herself in an ever-changing reality, she records the development of her consciousness and identity, experienced within, but not limited by, the society in which she lived.[6] No other writer in modern Persian literature has portrayed change with such detail, candor, and passion. Forugh's entire canon of work might be considered the first *Bildungsroman* written by and about a woman in Iran. Though a genre of novel, and though its tradition is almost exclusively associated with male characters, the *Bildungsroman* best defines Forugh's ceaseless developmental journey. Her five collections of poetry, viewed as a whole, constitute nothing less than a tale of self-discovery and growth.

Forugh's life and art testify to the eventual, although agonized, triumph of a woman and an artist discovering her individuality. For this poet not only had the audacity to trespass boundaries and to follow her inner promptings, she also had the temerity to express them openly and frankly in her poetry. Her unconventional life is revealed in her poems with candor—an exuberant sincerity that was, and continues to be, considered dangerous. In other words, Forugh not only challenged many issues on a personal level but, by publicizing them, she questioned them on a cultural level as well. Needless to add, she paid dearly for her independence, her dislike of blind obedience, and her stubborn claims to passion. Accounts of her life, as well as her art, attest to anxiety, feelings of dislocation, and conflicts, mingled with loneliness, notoriety, and hardship:

It was I who laughed at futile slurs,
the one that was branded by shame

[4]Kessler and Banani, 102.

[5]For English translations of Farrokhzād's work see: Kessler and Banani; Hassan Javadi and Susan Sallee, trans., *Another Birth* (Emerville, Cal.: Albany Press, 1981); David Martin, trans., *A Rebirth* (Lexington, Ky.: Mazda Press, 1985).

[6]For Farrokhzād's major stages of development as a poet see: Farzaneh Milani, "Formation, Confrontation, and Emancipation," in *A Rebirth*, 123–33.

I shall be what I'm called to be, I said
But oh, the misery that "woman" is my name[7]

Rebellion is the very stuff of Forugh's life and the galvanizing principle behind her art. From first to last, her poems, in spite of their plurality of content and approach, have a certain rebelliousness in common. She always aims her eloquently barbed words against benumbed compliance and stultifying habits:

—A star?
—Yes, hundreds and hundreds but
all beyond the walled-in nights
. . .
—I must say something
I must say something
in the shivering moment at daybreak
when space blends with something strange
like the portents of puberty
I want
to surrender to some revolt
I want
to pour down out of that vast cloud
I want
to say no no no[8]

Refusing to imprison herself in ascribed moulds and aspirations, Forugh ceaselessly carried the burden of self-creation. Every time she found herself caught between two equally imperative but irreconcilable drives, she eventually chose exploration of new territories, whatever the cost. She would not resolve her conflicts by allowing herself to be lulled into conformity:

Perhaps addiction to existence
and habitual tranquilizers
have dragged our pure and simple desires
into the pit of degeneration
Perhaps the spirit's been exiled

[7]Kessler and Banani, 132.
[8]Ibid., 53.

into solitary on a desert island
Perhaps I merely dreamed the cricket's voice[9]

This rupture with tradition is perhaps most visible (and least tolerated) in Forugh's mutiny against conventional man-woman relationships. She is one of the few women writers in Iran to seek erotic, emotional, and intellectual possibilities outside of matrimony. Describing her emotions and the experiences of both her body and her mind—avoiding semantic obliquity, obtrusive stylistic devices, and traditional artifices of concealment—she explores patterns of heterosexual relationships in an unprecedented manner. No other Persian woman has offered more detailed and candid descriptions of such relationships nor a more individualized, less restrained portrayal of men.

The substitution of abstractions for individuals or the subordination of characters to types—a literary tradition practiced all too often—has no appeal for this poet. Even the criterion of objectivity and its techniques are repeatedly abrogated. The self-interest of the observer does not invalidate her portrayals. In fact, it adds a delicately human dimension to them.

Forugh's presentation of men is complex and variegated. As her poetic consciousness gradually changes, her selection of companions undergoes similar modifications. As a result, images of men in her early poetry are very different from those in her later ones.

In her first collections—*Asir* (The captive) 1955, *Divār* (The wall) 1956, and *'Osyān* (Rebellion) 1957—men are presented as physical creatures, led by erotic instincts and frightened of intimacy:

He was taught nothing but desire
interested in nothing but appearance
wherever he went, they whispered in his ears
woman is created for your desires[10]

In her early poetry there is a perpetual search for a man who can appreciate her as a total human being rather than as a mere body to be desired. But the men around her are so sensitized to sexuality in its most limited sense that they will not risk intimacy. Thus they are indiscriminate in their sexual enjoyment, more interested in diversity

[9]Ibid., 64.
[10]Forugh Farrokhzād, *Asir* (The captive, Teheran, 1354/1975), 58.

than in any sustained relationship. The quality of relationships is over-shadowed—even abandoned—in favor of promiscuity. Indiscriminate lovers and love affairs are confused with deeper physical and emotional demands:

He wants wine-biding kisses from me
how can I deny his waiting lips?
He thinks of pleasure alone, unaware
of my search for more eternal pleasures

I want from him sincerity of love
to sacrifice my whole existence
he wants my fiery body
to consume his anguish[11]

And again:

You show affection for no one
unless you have her in your embrace
and when you open your arms
soon, she is forgotten[12]

In many poems of the early period men are seen in exaggerated conformity to codes of masculinity. They are terrorized, yet mystified, by signs of emotion, softness, or intimacy. They try so hard to be "real" men that they become caricatures of masculinity. Full of pretenses, yet addicted to approval, intense anxiety and vulnerability lurk behind their façade of strength.

Although desired and sought after in her early poetry, men are, to use Forugh's metaphors, "unfaithful" and "egotistical" "oppressor" and "warden." Acutely aware of her need for masculine companionship and love, she comes repeatedly to the bitter realization that men cannot fulfill her needs. In the unfortunate absence of real, sustained satisfaction, her search takes an increasingly desperate form. In many poems the speaker voices her lassitude and despair over yet another failed affair. Suffering from narrow choices and inner conflicts, the poet finds herself imprisoned in mismatched alliances.

While the men in her early poems give out mixed, confusing signals, Forugh's own poetic persona is no less fraught with contradictions. In

[11]Ibid., 40.
[12]Forugh Farrokhzād, *'Osyān* (Rebellion, Teheran, 1355/1976), 104.

371

the first three collections, she exhibits an intriguing blend of certainties and doubts. On the one hand, there are the burning flames of body and mind—both thirsty. On the other hand, there are limiting (and internalized) social norms and sanctions. In these poems the persona is a woman alone, at the threshold of a fascinating, yet frightening, journey; a woman both basking in and terrified by her passions; a woman attracted to and yet repelled by love affairs and lovers. She can neither deny herself the privilege of listening to her adventuresome heart, nor free herself from what she has been taught in regard to self-respect and morality. Thus she vacillates between two sets of values and aspirations, society's and her own, unable to relinquish either, or to integrate the two.

The titles of her early books—*The Captive, The Wall,* and *Rebellion*—are indicative of their general mood. A "captive" bird endlessly flutters its wings against the bars of its cage and "walls" and, though terrified by the prospect of open space and "rebellion," awaits the moment of flight:

I wait for that one careless instant
From this dark prison to wing away
and laugh in the keeper's face
At your side my life beginning its new day

I think of this knowing I shall never
be able to escape this plight
For even if the keeper should let me go
I've lost all my strength for the flight[13]

In her early poetry Forugh is attracted to women's independence and intellectual growth, but she cannot abandon the traditional virtues expected of a woman: purity expressed by chastity, devotion expressed by commitment to domestic concerns. Confronted with issues of economic security, the future of her only child, and the exacting glances of the "other," she voices the painful tension between independence and, conversely, domestic security and traditional women's roles:[14]

---

[13]Kessler and Banani, 123.

[14]Some of these fears proved not to be unfounded. Following the publication of *The Captive,* Forugh left her husband and lost custody of her only child. This pained her to the end of her life. Furthermore, throughout her short literary career, she worked in an atmosphere of contempt and bitter criticism from many critics. Maligned during her life, she only came to fame posthumously.

Bind my feet in chains again
so that tricks and deceits won't make me fall
so that colorful temptations
won't bind me with yet another chain[15]

Implicitly, and at times explicitly, she seeks a conflict-free sanctuary, a refuge from the burden of responsibility and doubt. She is tempted by socially-validated codes of conduct and convenient, mapped-out paths. She is tired of swimming against the current, but her body, stretched to new experiences, never returns to its original dimension; her mind, exposed to new horizons, refuses confinement.

*The Captive, The Wall,* and *Rebellion* are fraught with conflicts: between sensuality and the safety of puritanical morality, between freedom and its accompanying anxieties and uncertainties. There is resentment of men's absolute right to give free rein to their sexual whims, and her demand that pleasure be women's right as well. And yet relations that do not extend beyond the immediate passionate union to a mutually-cherished, longterm relationship, are unsatisfying. In short, the boundaries between delight and disgust, between attraction and aversion are not clear.

In her early poetry Forugh is a marginal character who has adopted new values without quite rejecting the old ones. And all the men around her, too, display ambivalent attitudes to both sets of values. The introduction to *The Captive,* written by a male author, exemplifies this ambivalence. Instead of discussing Forugh's revolutionary demand for the verbal and emotional space denied women throughout the centuries in Iranian culture, or praising her attempt to appropriate new emotional and sexual terrain between the sexes, he apologetically reminds the reader: "Let he who has no sin cast the first stone at the sinner."[16] A sinner Forugh believes herself to be, and a sinner she is believed to be by her staunchest supporter at the time, let alone others.

The relationships portrayed in the early poetry lack the intimacy and spontaneity essential to real friendship. If the demands of the man are carnal, selfish, and emotionless, the ideals of the woman are based on fantasies (which are too delicate) and ambivalence (which is destructive). Small wonder if these relationships, in spite of their element of free choice, are not conducive to trust and communication.

---

[15]*Asir,* 113.
[16]Shojāʿ al-Din Shafā, "Preface" to *Asir,* 4.

Their purpose is functional. He desires her body; she desires his long-term commitment: sex in exchange for loyalty:

> You, with your sincere heart, woman
> don't seek loyalty in a man
> He does not know the meaning of love
> don't ever tell him the secrets of your heart[17]

These conflicts, confusions, and aberrations are transitory manifestations of a basic reappraisal of norms on a very intimate level. They show the agonies and ambiguities which accompany a transition from one cultural pattern to another:

> After all that madness, ah my god
> is it possible I've returned to my senses
> And it seems that "she" has died in me,
> so tired and silent am I, all hopelessness
>
> Melancholy, interrogating the mirror,
> What do you think of me now, what?
> But in the mirror I see, oh god
> nothing I was, not even the shadow of that
>
> Like the Hindu dancer, on my own grave
> with such deliberate grace I dance
> To brighten this hut the light of a hundred
> burning desires I've given with extravagance[18]

Forugh's first three collections resemble the agonies of a pregnant woman at the moment of delivery. The pain is mingled with a promise of birth and regeneration. Indeed, in *Tavallodi digar* (Born again) 1964, Forugh emerges as a different character, one privileged with emotional and intellectual complexities, actively involved in a redefinition of her life, and more at peace with herself than ever before. The vacuum created by the dissolution of inadequate social values is filled with her own new substitutes. Where earlier she defined herself by her relationship with a man, or her lack of one, she now seeks self-assertion and self-realization. Where earlier her value depended on

[17]*Asir*, 110.
[18]Kessler and Banani, 129.

her ties with others, she now projects herself in wider horizons—emotional, intellectual, and sexual. Perhaps the most fascinating aspect of *Born Again* is the birth of a female character rejoicing in her new options, a warrior who has fought for every step of her path to freedom.

Forugh's technical development is closely linked to her growth as a poet who seeks to transcend traditional limitations. Although in the 1950s, when she was writing her first poems, the modernistic poetic movement had gained prominence in Iran, Forugh continued to write traditional verse. Nimā had already published "Afsāna" (A myth) in 1922, which not only heralded a new beginning in the history of Persian poetry but also led to more daring experimentation by Nimā and his followers and, ultimately, to the birth of modernistic poetry. Nonetheless, a sense of dissatisfaction with classical poetics permeates only a few poems in Forugh's first three collections. Of the eighty-six early poems, only twelve lack consistent rhymed couplets and adherence to classical formal traditions.

If the shattering of classical restraints did not find its way into Forugh's poetry until the publication of *Born Again*, it is because the poet had been on a journey of her own, taking her own time to change. Forugh's own comments about the influence of Nimā on her poetry are self-explanatory: "I discovered Nimā quite late or rather at the right time—in other words, after many experiments, temptations, and a period of vagrancy and search."[19]

The freedom in form of almost all of the poems of *Born Again* and *Imān beyāvarim be āghāz-e fasl-e sard* (Let us believe in the oncoming of the cold season) attests to long years of formal confrontation with language, a diligent practice of the craft mingled with years of reflection and inner growth. Truly, the most significant aspect of these volumes rests in the birth of a protean self, capable of embracing life in its plurality and, inevitably, in need of new avenues of expression.

It is through the development of poetic personae that the poet freed herself from rules of classical versification. Forugh had reached a point where her poetic impulses could no longer be contained within traditional boundaries. The breadth of her content required new words, new images, and a well developed sense of irony. She allowed

---

[19]M. Āzād, "An Interview with Forugh Farrokhzād," in *Ārash*, ed. Sirus Tāhbāz (Tehran, 1345/1966), 37.

the inner landscape of each poem to reveal itself of its own accord and to determine the particular form the poem would assume.[20]

Later poems, although markedly different from the earlier poetry, represent no abrupt break. Rather, they constitute a natural culmination, the result of an evolution that progressively demolished the confinement in and obedience to traditional prosodic rules. Forugh's progression toward free-form lines and meters was an organic necessity rather than a capricious imitation of the modernistic abdication of traditional poetics: "I want to say that even after reading Nimā, I wrote many bad poems. I needed to develop within myself and this growth needed time."[21]

Forugh's rebelliousness is thus conveyed throughout her poetry. In the early writings, it takes the shape of disdain for worn-out, conventional subject matter, coupled with an attempt to express herself openly. In the later writings, the adventurer in life becomes an adventurer in language and poetic forms as well. Regularity of line length and strophic organization is abandoned in favor of a free-flowing structure. A language refreshing in its burgeoning colloquialism, a style marked by inclusion of new words, peculiarities of syntax, and exclamatory sentences and interjections further heighten the intensity already imparted to her work by candor.[22]

In later poems, there is further transformation, as her personal rage, suppressed emotions, and social frustrations become integrated with a more public perspective. Identifications between the poet and other women are replaced by a move toward larger human concerns and preoccupations. Furthermore, she can now celebrate the formation of new relationships—meaningful and regenerative, enriching rather than confining both partners:

> It's not a question of weakly splicing two names
> and pairing them in the fusty pages of some register

[20]All poems published posthumously are in free verse. Only two poems in *Born Again* are written in traditional forms. Forugh's selection of formal structure for the two poems, "Lovingly" ('Āsheqāna) and "Swamp" (Mordāb) further prove that now the form of the poems evolves out of intrinsic requirements of the poem as a whole. In an interview with the poet Āzād, she explains why she wrote the poem "Lovingly" in the *mathnavi* form: "In 'Lovingly' I wanted to express an intensity of love that no longer exists. . . . That feeling viewed within the context of today's particularities was and continues to be a forlorn feeling. Sometimes, in order to express forlorn feelings, one has to resort to times forlorn." (Ibid., 47).

[21]Ibid., 39.

[22]For a detailed study of stylistic characteristics of Farrokhzād's poetry see: Ardavān Hamid Dāvarān, "Modern English and Persian Poetry: A Comparative Study," Ph.D. diss. (University of California, Berkeley, 1973).

It's a question of my hair,
gay with the singed poppies of your kisses
and the secret loyalty of our bodies
and our nakedness glinting
like the scales of fish in water
It's a question of the silvery life of a song
sung by a little fountain at dawn[23]

In this poem, titled "Garden Conquered," morality is a personal discovery rather than blindly institutional. Intimacy is experienced rather than sought or idealized. Love is not determined by motives of security, power, or possessions. Pleasure is reciprocated in kind, and sexuality is not turned into a bargaining table. There is no exchange of sexual favors for economic support, loyalty, or matrimony. Companionship, sexual gratification, and devotion are freely sought and freely given by both partners.

The poetic persona of "Garden Conquered" is the very opposite of the passive woman which has been (and, to some extent, continues to be) the female sexual ideal. To show desire and gratification is no longer a male prerogative. Women can choose now; and men can enjoy the privilege of being truly desired. Both can revel in the non-utilitarian quality of an erotic partnership. This new relationship is between two consenting, fulfilled partners:

The crow that soared
over us
and vanished into a drifting cloud's troubled thoughts
its voice a short spear arching across the horizon
will carry news of us to the city
Everybody knows
Everybody knows
you and I saw the garden
through that dour, cold embrasure
and picked the apple
from that happy branch out of bounds
Everyone's afraid
Everyone's afraid, but you and I
who were joined to the lamp, the water, the mirror
and were not afraid[24]

[23]Kessler and Banani, 71.
[24]Ibid.

The lovers through the "dour, cold embrasure" see the apple and, to pick it up, they enter the garden. Contrary to the legend of Adam and Eve, their plucking of the forbidden fruit admits them to the garden rather than expels them. Subtly, the poet turns the familiar myth around. It is not the woman who tempts the man. Instead, they pick the apple together and deliberately. Neither is responsible for the other; there is no devil. They both enjoy (rather than regret) their "fall." With their lovelocked hands they can even "bridge the nights":

It's not a question of anxious whispers in the dark
It's a question of daylight and open windows
and fresh air
and a furnace where useless things are burned
and a world pregnant with new seedlings
and birth and perfect ripening and pride
It's a question of our lovelocked hands
that have bridged the nights
with the message of perfume and light and the moving air[25]

"Garden Conquered" is more than a love poem. It is the story of two lovers who evade social constraint not by escaping or defying it so much as by declaring it irrelevant. This poem, as well as many others in *Born Again* and *Let Us Believe in the Oncoming of the Cold Season* (published posthumously in 1974), is an eloquent affirmation of the possibility of friendship and communication between a man and a woman, a relationship based neither on a marriage license nor on physical or economic needs alone. It speaks of emotional, intellectual, and sensual compatibility, of love, and of common concerns.

Men as depicted in the last two collections are quite different from the egotistical bird-jailer who inhabits Forugh's first three collections. They, too, are freed from roles traditionally assigned to them. Freed from the tight mould of "masculinity," men can desire and be desired, no longer forced to hide their own needs and feelings.

In her later work, Forugh condemns the mental devastation and self-alienation of her earlier experiences, describing them as "a desperate exertion between two different stages of life, the last pantings before some kind of liberation."[26] Struggling for independence and a strong sense of self, in and out of relationships with men, she discovers

[25]Ibid., 72.
[26]Āzād, 39.

new possibilities and alternatives to ensure her personal growth. She resigns herself to the fact that romance alone is inadequate to fulfill all her needs. Moments of intense sensuous beatitude do not necessarily offer more than temporary physical intimacy:

Night approaching
and darkness after night
and after dark
eyes
hands
and breathing breathing breathing
and water sounding
dripping drop drop drop from the spigot
then two dots of red
two cigarettes
the clock's ticktock
and two hearts
and two solitudes[27]

Although a great deal of contemporary Persian poetry deals exclusively with love, Forugh openly and bitterly criticizes the nature of its treatment:

Modern Persian poetry rarely has known what it is to love truly. In it, love is so magnified, so plaintive, and so anguished that it does not match the nervous and hasty lines of today's life. Or else it is so primitive and so full of the pain of celibacy that it automatically reminds one of male cats in season on sunny roofs.[28]

Certainly, some of Forugh's own early poetry falls, in some ways, within the category of these love poems she criticizes. Yet, her treatment of heterosexual love, on the whole and especially in her later poems, is unique, standing apart from those described above. Repeatedly, she laments the destructive limitation imposed on men and women by traditionally-ascribed roles and relations. With subtlety, yet convincingly, she shows how the lack of real intimacy hurts both sexes. Men and women share different versions of the same problem:

[27]Kessler and Banani, 70.
[28]"A few writings and scattered words about poets and poetry," in *Ārash*, 16.

Half of her secret, from herself hidden
And ashamed of his face, simply human

Yet addicted to the scent of her mate
From street to street she runs, hunting her mate

Sometimes finding him, but doubting it's he
Her mate, someone lonelier yet than she

Both trembling and fearful of each other
Ungrateful, bittertongued to each other

Their love a madness that must be condemned
Their union a suspect dream that must end[29]

[29]Kessler and Banani, 55.

# 19. Modern Persian Drama

Modern Persian drama is a novel and vibrant genre. Born in the last century, it has developed rapidly and has finally achieved literary status in the course of the last two decades. Though modeled after Western dramatic form, its inspiration often comes from Persian folklore, which is itself rooted in ancient traditions. However, the differences in mood and content from Western drama on the one hand, and from popular Persian folk shows on the other, set the genre apart. It is neither an adaptation of Western drama nor descended from a continuing dramatic tradition, but rather an original art form.

## Historical Background

There is no conclusive evidence for a continuing theatrical tradition in Iran. Formal drama apparently did not exist in Achaemenid Persia. Although drama that developed from religious festivities and rites was familiar in ancient Greece, Egypt, Babylon and India, similar rites such as the Mithrakana[1] and the Magophonia[2] in Persia did not lead to the development of a formal dramatic genre.

Greek theater was introduced in Iran with Alexander's conquest and continued to be performed through Parthian times.[3] However, this practice, representing an alien art form, was understandably not continued in the Sasanian Empire, where a national spirit dominated. Theater was not included among the arts that enjoyed popularity at the Sasanian court, such as music, dance and minstrelsy,[4] nor is there an indication of any kind of indigenous theater which might have been inspired by Greek drama. None of the historians reporting on the period mentions theaters or dramatic performances,[5] and no plays or fragments of plays have been found to date.

[1]See M. J. Vermaseren, *Mithras, the Secret God*, trans. T. and V. Megaw (New York, 1963), 21.

[2]See W. B. Henning, "The Murder of the Magi," *JRAS* (1944), 133–44.

[3]See, for example, Plutarch, *The Age of Alexander*, trans. I. Scott-Kilvert (Harmondsworth, Eng., 1973), 324–25, 327–28, 329ff. and *The Lives of the Noble Grecians and Romans*, trans. J. Dryden (New York, 1932), 673–774.

[4]A description of these arts can be found in "Khusrow, Son of Kawad, and a Page," *Selected Texts from Pre-Islamic Iran*, trans. C. J. Brunner, special supplement to *The Asia Society Grapevine*, no. 2 (1977).

[5]See Mas'udi, *Les Prairies d'or*, ed. and trans. Barbier de Meynard and Pavet de Courteille (Paris, 1864), vol. 2, 152–53; Ibn Qutayba, *'Ujûn al Ahbâr*, ed. and trans. C. Brockelmann, in *Zeitschrift für Assyriologie und verwandte Gebiete* (Berlin, 1900), vol. 1–4; *Chronique de Abou-Djafar-Mohammed-ben-Djarîr-ben Yezîd Tabarî, d'après la version persane d'Abou 'Ali Mohammed Bel'amî*, trans. H. Zotenberg (Paris, 1958), vol. 2; and Biruni, *Āthār al-bāqīyeh*, trans. Dānā Seresht (Tehran, 1948), especially 100–206.

After the Arab invasions in the seventh century A.D. and the Islamization of Iran, drama was again conspicuously absent from the Iranian renaissance that culminated in the ninth and tenth centuries at the court of the Samanids.

Popular and oral forms of theater, however, do exist in post-Islamic Iran. In modern times these fall into two groups: the religious theater (*ta'ziya*) on the one hand, and various forms of popular amusement shows on the other. *Ta'ziya* is a ritual theater focusing on the martyrdom of the Shi'ite Imam Hoseyn at Karbalā in A.D. 680 and related events. It is the only indigenous drama in the world of Islam and presents many interesting traits in its dramaturgy. It resembles the passion plays of medieval Europe in the simplicity of its stagecraft and conventions, in the abolishing of space and time limitations, and in the total involvement of its audiences.[6] It appears that the origin of *ta'ziya* lies in pre-Islamic customs, and particularly in the mourning rites for Siyāvosh in eastern Iran.[7]

Popular amusement shows have many forms, which include *naqqāli* (storytelling), *Shāh-nāma khwāni* (reciting episodes from Ferdowsi's epic), *ru howzi* (spectacles performed on a platform covering the garden pool), *taqlid* (satirical comedies ridiculing some stock character of Persian life), and *siyāh bāzi* (clowneries performed by a black jester for his white master). These shows consist of many variations on a basic plot; their stylized acting technique resembles that of the Italian commedia dell' arte. Other amusement shows are *khiyāl bāzi* (shadow plays resembling the Turkish *karagöz*) *'arusak bāzi* (puppet shows), and *khayma shab bāzi* (marionette shows).[8]

Formal theater gradually found a place in Persian letters under the influence of the West. The introduction of the printing press in 1812 made books, newspapers, and pamphlets available to an increasing number of readers. Numerous translations of European works—among them plays by Shakespeare and Molière—were undertaken and rapidly gained popularity. Simultaneously, original plays patterned on Western models began to appear. The precursors of these

[6]For detailed descriptions of *ta'ziya* see Gobineau, "Le Théâtre en Perse," *Les Religions et les philosophies dans l'Asie centrale* (Paris, 1866), 359–79; S. Homāyuni, *Ta'ziya o ta'ziya khwāni* (Tehran, 1975), 7–107; and *Ta'ziyeh: Ritual and Drama in Iran*, ed. P. Chelkowski (New York, 1979).

[7]E. Yarshater, "Ta'ziyeh and Pre-Islamic Mourning Rites in Iran," in *Ta'ziyeh: Ritual and Drama in Iran*, 89–91.

[8]A full discussion of popular Persian theater can be found in B. Bayzā'i, *Nemāyesh dar Irān* (Tehran, 1965–66), 44–115. See also J. Cejpek, "Dramatic Folk-Literature in Iran," in Rypka, *Iran. Lit.*, 682–93.

were comedies containing witty criticisms of society and political institutions, including seven plays written in Azari Turkish by Ākhund-zāda (a reform-minded liberal residing in Tiflis), which were translated into Persian in 1874,[9] and three plays until recently attributed to Mirza Malkom Khān (a prominent Persian political figure) published in Berlin in 1921.[10]

Playwriting increased after the declaration of the Constitution in 1906, and gained further momentum under Rezā Shah.[11] The plays of this period, however, written either for the purpose of political propaganda or in response to rising nationalistic sentiment, were weak dramatically. Stages were few and very simple. In general, plays were produced by Iranians who had acquired experience of the theater abroad.

Theatrical techniques improved only after Rezā Shah's abdication in 1941, when freedom from censorship, accompanied by a great deal of intellectual activity, resulted in many excellent productions. A number of theatrical companies of leftist persuasion came into being. Some groups attempted to arrange Persian tales for the theater with varying degrees of success; in any case, they achieved considerable progress in stagecraft. Even after the government closed the leftist theaters, talent and vitality continued in the Dehqān, Ferdowsi, Bārbad, and Sa'di theaters of Tehran. Repertoires included translations from Ibsen, Chekhov, Strindberg, Shaw, and O'Neill as well as original Persian plays. Talented actors such as 'Abd al-Hosayn Nushin and Mohammad Khayrkhāh received acclaim. A school of dramatic art was established under 'Ali Nasr, and acting gradually gained recognition as a profession.

The fall of Mosāddeq in 1953 coincided with the beginning of a new era in the socioeconomic growth of Iran. Government control became tighter and theater was on the decline for several years. But the return of economic well-being was accompanied by an increased number of productions. Criticism of the regime was not tolerated, so theater groups strove for artistic merit rather than political or social comment. The Faculty of Arts of Tehran University offered courses in dramatic art for the first time; these included playwriting, directing,

---

[9]Kamshad, *Modern Prose*, 28.

[10]H. Algar, *Mirza Malkum Khān, A Biographical Study in Iranian Modernism* (Berkeley, 1973), 264–77.

[11]Playwrights of this period and titles of their major works can be found in Jannati 'Atā'i, *Bonyād-e nemāyesh dar Irān* (Tehran, 1955), 58–88, and in E. Yarshater, "Development of Persian Drama in the Context of Cultural Confrontation in Iran," in *Iran: Continuity and Variety*, ed. P. Chelkowski (New York, 1971), 30–31.

and acting. Under the Fulbright program, three American professors were invited to Tehran to lecture on American drama. This led to the production at the university of plays by Tennessee Williams, Herman Melville, Eugene O'Neill, and Arthur Miller.

## Flourishing of Drama in the 1960s

In the 1960s, Persian theater received considerable encouragement from the government. The Department of Fine Arts (later the Ministry of Arts and Culture) founded a School of Acting and a School of Dramatic Arts, and Tehran University's Department of Fine Arts added a drama section in 1965. A Theater Bureau was created within the Ministry of Arts and Culture to sponsor and supervise the production of original as well as translated plays. A state-supported national television was established, in addition to the privately owned Televizion-e Irān, and an increasing number of one-act plays were written and produced for television. The National Television operated a theater workshop (*kārgāh-e namāyesh*) that promoted the production of experimental plays, both Western and native, for television and the stage. The commercial theaters continued to be active, and two state-supported theaters were established in Tehran, providing playwrights with new outlets and opportunities. The Shiraz Arts Festival, inaugurated in 1967, generated much interest in the theater year after year. It featured *ta'ziya*s staged on a grand scale, revivals of Western avant-garde plays, and premieres of many original Persian plays. Performances at the Festival were followed by round-table discussions on theory and aesthetics in which large and enthusiastic audiences took part.

This impetus, together with the model of a new theater in the West, saw the emergence of several new and gifted playwrights, among whom Bahrām Bayzā'i, Gholām Hosayn Sā'edi (who writes under the pen name Gowhar-e Morād) and 'Abbās Na'lbandiyān are leading figures. The works of 'Ali Nasiriyān, Bahman Forsi, Arsalān Puryā, Bizhan Mofid and Esmā'il Khalaj have also been received with interest. While dramatic styles and inspiration vary from author to author, one general trend is apparent: the casting of familiar themes from Persian literature and folklore into modern dramatic form. Together, the works of the new dramatists are considered to have raised Persian theater to a literary genre.

The conditions that brought about the consolidation of the new dramatic art in the 1960s were threefold. In the first place, the long period of experimentation with Western dramatic form, going back to the turn of the century, had gained momentum over the years and accelerated considerably in the preceding decade. Secondly, the drastic change in the economic and social structure of Iran resulted on the one hand in government sanction and incentives for the theater, and on the other in the emergence of a middle class that provided adept audiences for playwrights who had learned their art in the new drama schools and workshops.

A third factor must be seen in the model provided by the avant-garde theater of the West. Born in the 1950s and characterized by freedom of form, this theater addressed itself to the emotions rather than to the intellect. In their works, such authors as Ionesco, Beckett, Dürenmatt, Genêt, and Pinter reacted against the stringent intellectualization of traditional Western theater and the plethora of rules encumbering it since the Renaissance. In an attempt to return to the essence of dramatic art, they abandoned rational dialogue as the primary mode of expression. Turning away from the exact representation of life, from carefully worked-out plot development and characterization, they gave new importance to nonverbal expression. Their works reflected the theories proposed by Antonin Artaud in his book, *Le Théâtre et son double*,[12] the experience of Brecht, and familiarity with the theater of the Far East. Artaud had called for a theater speaking a "physical language," one whose impact would be strong enough to bring about a collective purge of emotions in the audience, comparable to the rejuvenating effect of plague epidemics. Berthold Brecht used music, dance, and sets as modes of dramatic expression to accompany the dialogues; his plays proceeded through a succession of visual tableaux, and through an original technique known as the "alienation effect," aimed at destroying the illusion of reality.[13]

Some of the avant-garde plays of the West were translated into Persian shortly after their European premieres; they reached Iran at a time when the intellectual and artistic climate was feverish with activity and experimentation. This artistic form was much closer to the native Persian dramatic sense than the plays of Shakespeare, Molière, Ibsen, or Shaw could ever have been. Indeed, the "low" forms of comedy found in Persian folk theater are all based on nonverbal, nonintellectual expression: they rely on mime, clowneries, slapstick humor, and

---

[12](Paris, 1938; repr. 1964), 9–69.

[13]This technique consists of the actors periodically interrupting the action to remind the spectators that they are only actors. In this way, they prevent the identification of the events unfolding on stage with life.

highly stylized actions and situations. In this sense they are closer to what Artaud called "pure" dramatic art than Western ideological theater. It is not surprising that the new playwrights of Iran, now receiving considerable encouragement and support, were inspired to use this form as a model for expressing their own talents. In the following sections, the art of the three leading figures of this new Persian theater will be examined.[14]

## Bahrām Bayzā'i

As a writer, Bahrām Bayzā'i finds his inspiration and his models in Persian folklore and traditions. A good example of his art can be seen in his collection of three one-act plays published in 1963, entitled *'Arusakhā* (The puppets), *Ghorub dar diyāri gharib* (Evening in an alien land) and *Qessa-ye māh-e penhān* (The story of the hidden moon). Here Bayzā'i faithfully follows the form of the traditional Persian marionette show, *khayma shab bāzi*. As in the marionette play, the characters are called Hero, Girl, Demon, and Puppeteer; a fifth character, Black Man, comes from another popular folk show, the *siyāh bāzi*. As in the marionette play, Puppeteer opens each one of the plays with a soliloquy in which he presents to the audience the characters that he "has made with his own hands," and announces the basic plot; he frequently engages in dialogues with the other characters during the action. The wind, thunder, and lightning that periodically underscore the action are also borrowed from the *khayma shab bāzi*, which often ended with the sudden noise of wind and thunder and the appearance of a giant who picked up the puppets and carried them away. The fall of the curtain in the second play is accompanied by Black Man leading the audience into a rhythmical snapping of fingers, a common practice in many Persian folk shows. A transparent backdrop is used in the first play, on which the shadows of Hero and Demon are seen engaging in combat; this technique is reminiscent of the shadow theater.

The central theme of these three plays is the human condition and the individual's inability to influence his or her destiny. This idea, so pervasive in Persian literature and popular religion, often underlies the shadow plays as well. But while in the shadow plays it serves merely

[14]See E. Yarshater, "Modern Literary Idiom," in *Iran Faces the Seventies,* ed. E. Yarshater (New York, 1971), 311ff., and idem, "Persian Drama," in *The Reader's Encyclopedia of World Drama,* ed. J. Gassner and E. Quinn (New York, 1969), 647ff. for a discussion of the rise of dramatic art in modern Iran.

as a basis for many comic illustrations, Bayzā'i gives it a tragic and carefully structured dramatic treatment. Humanity's inescapable destiny is to suffer through solitude, love, and war, and each of these elements in turn receives special treatment in one of his plays.

Solitude is the main theme in *The Puppets*, where Hero expresses, like Shakespeare's King Lear or Vigny's Moïse, the isolation of the hero:

I'm tired . . .
Of wandering about in the world,
Of having no home of my own.
When did I have a moment's respite:
. . . There's a mountain over there
With a spring at its foot
And a green oasis spreading by the spring.
. . . But they are deserted:
When I reached them
No one was there![15]

Embittered at having waged many futile wars, Hero refuses to fight the Demon who is threatening the city. He is compelled to do so, however, in order not to disappoint the girl he secretly loves. He kills the Demon but is himself mortally wounded.

Solitude is also the lot of the other characters. As Hero leaves the scene to meet his death, he says to his friend Black Man:

I didn't mean to leave you behind alone,
May God have mercy on your loneliness![16]

And Black Man himself, together with Puppeteer, warns the Young Man who is eager to follow in Hero's footsteps that his sword will be heavy:

You'll have to carry it 'til the end of your life,
Under the scorching sun,
With a burning in your chest,
With heavy feet,
And the bitter solitude of the hero.[17]

[15]*Seh nemāyeshnāme-ye ʿarūsaki* (Tehran, 1963), 11.
[16]Ibid., 24.
[17]Ibid., 25–26.

*Evening in an Alien Land* focuses on the theme of love. Hero loves Girl; he will build her an abode by the Green Lake where they will live happily, but first he has to kill the Demon who inhabits the shores of the Lake. He sets out to do this, but finds out that Demon is only another suffering human and refuses to fight him. Angered at his characters' refusal to carry out the parts that he has alloted them, Puppeteer destroys Hero and Demon, and Girl dies of grief. Black Man arrives on the scene and points an accusing finger at Puppeteer, who angrily thumps his fists on the stage and demolishes everything. Then, appalled at his own actions, he falls to the ground, picks up one of his motionless puppets in his hands and sadly exclaims, "We have destroyed each other, you and I!" Thus love, in spite of the beautiful feelings that it engenders, results not in happiness but in death and destruction.

In *The Story of the Hidden Moon*, the central theme is war. Hero and Demon have been at war for years, a war so old that nobody can remember how it started. "The people have forgotten the legends," and in the city desolation and calamity prevail:

No flower has bloomed for years
The vines bear sour grapes . . .
The termites chew at the city in the dark.[18]

Deafening cries break the air, and Black Man hurries in to announce that Hero and Demon have died at each other's hand, that war has come to an end. Amid the rejoicing of the people and Black Man's grief at the loss of his friend Hero, an enigmatic traveler promises to bring Hero back to life. All that is needed is for someone to express the wish, but there is one condition: Demon will have to come back to life, too. Black Man refuses to express the wish and leaves, despite Traveler's objections that his concern is not peace, but rather his secret love for Girl. Girl arrives on the scene; she, too, hesitates to express the wish until Traveler promises that he will take life back from Hero and Demon if they prefer not to live. Girl expresses the wish and the two come back to life amid thunder and frightening cries. Black Man, angered by this, rushes in and kills Traveler, who is now unable to keep his promise to Girl when she returns to tell him that Hero and Demon do not want to live. Girl and Black Man turn to each other in

[18]Ibid., 83.

388

consternation, while the curtain falls and Puppeteer comments that "war will continue for ever and ever."

The *dramatis personae* are archetypes representing single, exaggerated aspects of human nature. Girl is beautiful, pure, and sincere; Hero is noble and brave; Black Man and Monster are the innocent, suffering victims; Puppeteer and Traveler symbolize destiny. Puppeteer turns out to be the real villain in the second play. After he has killed everyone and destroyed everything, he exclaims:

> Never, never did I believe
> That I could be the Monster myself.[19]

Destiny is not willed; it is itself in the hands of chance and uncontrolled events, as Puppeteer himself remarks:

> I am merely a spectator
> Watching the story of Life and Death
> I am the one who starts the show
> But the end is unknown.[20]

Embodying the themes in this manner, the characters are stylized, unreal. They bring an element of magic and mystery to the plays. There is no attempt on the part of Bayzā'i to recreate life; rather, the spectator is constantly reminded that the characters and the play are fictitious. Puppeteer greets the spectators, introduces the characters and the plot, and periodically interrupts the action to make comments. This Brechtian device reminds the audience that they are at a show and destroys any illusion of reality that may have been emerging. Puppeteer's comments are frequently of a foreboding nature; they announce an imminent catastrophe and reinforce the unreal atmosphere:

> What is Black Man trying to say?
> His words have left no color
> On Girl's cheeks.[21]

The language in the three plays is stylized and poetic. The dialogues

[19]Ibid., 71.
[20]Ibid., 87.
[21]Ibid., 51.

progress through rich imagery and flowing rhythm, as exemplified in the following passage:

> Hero: In the field I can see a blue morning glory
>       Blooming in the sunshine
>       The sun has imparted its light to the flower
>       And the flower has given its fragrance to the light.
>       The sun is my love,
>       And the morning glory your body.
> Girl: The morning glory is ready for you . . .
> Hero: And my hand has come to pick it.[22]

Often, the *dramatis personae* abandon the response type of dialogue; instead, they echo and continue each other's thoughts like instruments in a musical composition:

> Girl: Night has come again
> Black Man: And grown darker
> Girl: The candles are not lit
> Black Man: And the torches are out
> Girl: If you light a fire
> Black Man: Its light will die in the dark
> Girl: Why should one light a fire
> Black Man: There where the light will die
> Girl: Everyone in town is asleep
> Black Man: And all the city gates are locked
> Girl: Locked gates and sleeping people![23]

Bayzā'i uses images of nature that are traditionally found in Persian literature and miniature painting: the sky, the moon, springs and flowing streams, flowers, trees and gazelles, vineyards and wine. The frequent, at times monotonous, repetition of words and motifs impart to the dialogue a quality reminiscent of Persian music. In addition, certain vague allusions create a haunting sense of mystery that accompanies the action:

> This was a cry,
> And this cry has always existed.

[22]Ibid., 36.
[23]Ibid., 78.

Why didn't we, who were always here,
Ever hear the cry before?[24]

or:

—Do you know this man?
—No.
—I hear he arrived in the city today . . .
—But it seems to me that I've seen him somewhere, long ago.
—Where does he come from?
—No one knows.
—Where is he going?
—No one knows.[25]

Through the diction of poetry, Bayzā'i forges a dramatic style that is original and vibrant, despite some stiltedness. Lengthy dialogues at times result in static scenes that are not very effective dramatically. This is especially true of the first play, where the only real action—the fight between Hero and Monster—is superimposed on the dialogue by projecting the shadows of the protagonists on a backdrop. However, the total effect of the *Three Puppet Shows* is one of beauty and simplicity.

Bayzā'i's message is a despairing one: destiny is absurd, and the only respite from suffering is death. This pessimistic view is also expressed in his other plays. *Pahlavān Akbar mimirad* (Akbar the Champion dies), published in 1965 and staged in 1966, is a play drawing on traditional Persian life. It portrays a champion wrestler who can easily defeat a young opponent, but who prefers to keep the promise he has made to an old woman. This woman happens to be his challenger's mother but rather than break his word and cause her grief, Akbar prefers to accept defeat and leave the city. In doing so he follows the chivalrous tradition of his profession, but his cruel fate creates a tragic atmosphere in which the hero's suffering and loneliness seem futile.

In 1966 Bayzā'i published two more plays: *Donyā-ye matbu'āti-ye āqā-ye Asrāri* (Mr. Asrāri's publishing world) and *Soltān-e mār* (The snake prince). The first of these is a biting criticism of the corruption and fraud that prevails in the publishing world. Mr. Asrāri is the director

[24]Ibid., 78.
[25]Ibid., 79–80.

of a thriving magazine; he publishes the stories of one of his talented young typesetters under the name of his nephew. This ploy yields financial success for the company. Trouble broods when the typesetter, whose silence has been bought, disappears. But clever manipulation on the part of Asrāri and his nephew soon brings the typesetter back, desperate and pleading to be allowed to return to his former job. This play is patterned after traditional Western theater, with some episodes reflecting the influence of the theater of the absurd. The sets and characters are realistic, the plot is linear, and the action derives essentially from the dialogue. The pace of the play is fast, and the tone satirical.

*The Snake Prince* is somewhat less pessimistic. Cast in mythological times, it is an allegory focusing on government oppression and political corruption. The Snake Prince is an ugly and hated tyrant, but he is redeemed by a beautiful maiden who loves him and breaks the spell under which he was held. Shedding his snakeskin, he turns out not only to be a handsome young man, but also a hero who saves his people from the greed of two foreign countries that had intrigued to divide the land between themselves. Here the dramatic techniques are bold and innovative: the stage, borrowed from the *ta'ziya*, is a circular platform around which the audience is seated; music and dance periodically punctuate the action and contribute to the drama; the *dramatis personae* are an interesting mixture of humans and supernatural beings (*div*s) from ancient Iranian mythology.

These plays were followed by *Majles-e divān-e Balkh* (The court at Balkh) in 1969, a historical play showing the inhabitants of the city victimized by corrupt government officials; *Hashtomin safar-e Sendbād* (Sindbad's eighth journey) in 1971, an allegory on destiny and fate inspired by the *Arabian Nights; Gomshodegān* (The lost ones), published in 1978 but written in 1969; and *Chahār sanduq* (The four trunks), published in 1979.

Bayzā'i is also known in Iran for his films, which include *Āhu, Salandar, Talhak o digarān* (Ahu, Salandar, Talhak, and others), *Ragbār* (Downpour), *Laylā, dokhtar-e Edris* (Leila, daughter of Edris), *Ghariba o meh* (The stranger and the fog), and *Kalāgh* (The crow). He has also written two monographs on the theater: *Namāyesh dar Irān* (Theater in Iran) in 1965, and *Namāyesh dar Chin* (Theater in China) in 1970.

## Gowhar-e Morād

Gowhar-e Morād is the pen name of Gholām Hosayn Sā'edi, the most prolific and perhaps the most effective of the new playwrights of Iran.

A psychiatrist by profession, he has published fifteen full-length plays, two collections of one-act plays, and a collection of pantomimes. He is also the author of short stories, novels, and film scripts published under his real name. Because of sociopolitical implications in his work and alleged political activity, he was arrested several times and spent months in prison. Released in 1975 he traveled to the United States in 1978 for a brief visit at the invitation of a group of American writers and publishers who had petitioned and interceded on his behalf. Subsequently he spent some time in England, and then returned to Iran, where he published his most recent play shortly before the Islamic Revolution.

Direct political commentary is central to his collection of one-act plays entitled *Panj namāyesh-nāma az enqelāb-e mashrutiyyat* (Five plays concerning the Constitutional Revolution), published in 1966. Partisan plays set in the town of Tabriz during the period following the Constitutional Revolution of 1906, they depict the plight of the people victimized by the corrupt upper classes. A second collection of one-act plays, *Khāna rowshani* (Housewarming, 1967), centers on social themes and psychological exploration. In his collection of pantomimes, *Dah lāl bāzi* (Ten pantomimes, 1963) Sā'edi presents a series of macabre, surrealist fantasies, picturing individuals trapped in painfully absurd situations, impotent against merciless fate. Here, social criticism is symbolically expressed in the characters and the situations.[26]

In Sā'edi's full-length plays, criticism similarly ranges from direct attack to symbolic diction. For example, *Kalāta gol* (The flower hamlet, 1961) is a realistic description of the struggle of a landlord against a despotic government about to confiscate his property, while *Chub be-dasthā-ye Varazil* (The stick-wielders of Varazil, 1965) is an allegory focusing on villagers whose farms are threatened by wild boars from a neighboring forest. They turn for help to Matāvos, a man of foreign origin, who sends hunters to their rescue. The hunters rid the village of the wild boars but turn out to be a greater burden to the village, on whose resources they draw more heavily than the beasts. Lending a hand to the villagers again, Matāvos helps them hire a new group of hunters. Aiming their rifles at the first hunters, the new ones suddenly turn to join them, and the play ends dramatically as both groups point their rifles at the panic-stricken villagers. The symbolism is clear:

---

[26]A more detailed account of the plays in these three collections can be found in E. Naby, "Gowhar Murad: A Persian Playwright," M.A. thesis (Columbia University, 1971), 32–66.

the hunters represent government officials who take their directives from a foreign power; the villagers are the people of Iran struggling against natural hardships and government exploitation. With this work Sā'edi emerges as an *engagé* playwright, taking up the cause of the oppressed against their oppressors. Furthermore, he displays here a vigorous dramatic style, characterized by social criticism couched in the study of human nature, boldly drawn characters stemming from contemporary Persian life, tightly structured plots serving as vehicles for allegory, stylized sets and dialogues, and an unmistakably Persian landscape.

The strengthening of this style can be observed in his *Ā-ye bi kolāh ā-ye bā kolāh* (Long "A," short "A"), published in 1967 and staged the following year in Tehran, where it received wide acclaim. This satire on human nature portrays a group of people so entrapped in their social roles that they refuse to heed the warnings of the enlightened ones among them and unknowingly submit to destruction. It is a two-act comedy that ends in catastrophe. An old man sees a double-headed monster enter a vacant house on his block and wakes up his neighbors in alarm. Fear-inspired deliberations ensue on the street, punctuated by the sarcastic remarks of the Man on the Balcony, but the group is unable to decide on any action. The first act ends with the comic revelation that the robber is only an old woman carrying a huge rag puppet. The second act is a replica of the first one, with some variations: the old man sees a large number of robbers enter the house, and the deliberations stem from the neighbors' refusal to believe him. Their skepticism leads them to abuse the old man and to drive out the Man on the Balcony, after which they all go back to sleep. The curtain falls as the robbers pour out of the house one after the other to attack the neighborhood.

The form of this play, two symmetrical acts in which a simple plot is repeated with some variations, resembles that of Samuel Beckett's *Waiting for Godot.* As in Beckett's play, the focus is on the deliberations of the characters on stage, rather than on plot development. But the similarity stops here. Beckett's play is imbued with a metaphysical aura; it raises questions about humanity and its destiny on earth. The themes are expressed concretely, leaving the audience restless and disturbed. In their mechanical, clownish quality, the characters seem to exist only through their physical presence on stage. In Sā'edi's play, by contrast, the framework is realistic. We are in the realm not of metaphysics but of psychology. The twelve main characters—as opposed to four in Beckett's play—are boldly portrayed. They represent types commonly found in today's Iranian society: an old man and his semi-emancipated daughter, a doctor, a mechanic, a school janitor, a reporter, a police officer. In casting them, the author seems to have been inspired by the characters of the *ta'ziya*, in whom a single, dominant moral trait is exaggerated. Here, fear is embodied in the Old Man, self-consciousness in the Young Girl, pedantry in the Doctor, common sense in the Man on the Balcony. As in the *ta'ziya* also, the characters express themselves through pantomime, facial expression, and stylized movements as much as through dialogue. This technique is particularly striking in the scene at the end of the second act, where the characters physically restrain the Old Man, whom they believe to be mad, while the Doctor examines him and administers a shot and sleeping pills. The pantomime and the verbal invectives become truly farcical.

Stylization is also apparent in the dialogue. The language is the everyday idiom of the people, with the characters, using the speech patterns typical of their respective trades or status in society. For example, the Mechanic's Mother constantly utters pious formulas, typical of superstitious old women: God protect us. . . . God reward you. . . . May God forgive those who torment others. . . ."[27] The Man on the Balcony is consistently blunt, direct, and sarcastic:

And you believe me, every word I say. But you dilly-dally and procrastinate. And you want to know why? Because you're afraid. You're cowards, the whole bunch of you. . . .[28]

The Doctor speaks in long, flowery phrases laced with medical terms:

A heavy dinner . . . has blurred your thinking processes, in addition to which you suffer from hypertrophy of the prostate, which forces you to awaken every few hours. And all of these organic and psychological factors interacting on each other are the reason for your hallucinations and phantasmagories.[29]

Speech variations are most striking in the scene where a reporter arrives on stage and each character tries to make the best possible impression. The Mechanic states his identity with trite detail:

[27]*Āy-e bi kolāh, āy-e bā kolāh* (Tehran, 1967), 19ff.
[28]Ibid., 42.
[29]Ibid., 22.

> I, 'Abbās Fallāh, mechanic of the Pars Garage, and bearer of the birth certificate number 4536, firmly believe that the decision . . .[30]

The Man shows his mediocrity by uttering incoherent, stereotyped trivialities:

> I am in favor of radical changes in social affairs and I'm convinced that basic and essential security—the basic and essential—the basic and—[31]

while the Young Girl, when asked for her opinion, answers with a silly, immature: "Well I—I don't have any special opinion."[32]

However, the characters also possess psychological reality; they develop as the play progresses. Each one of their actions, each one of their movements on stage is determined by their psychology. This technique, often found in Western theater, is used here with considerable skill. The dramatic tension that results is interspersed with humorous episodes and witty remarks that provide comic relief. The absurdity of the situation, where the characters in their pajamas deliberate on the street in the middle of the night, engage in petty arguments, and throw nonsensical accusations at each other, is clearly inspired from the Theater of the Absurd. However Sā'edi, unlike Ionesco for example, does not abandon logic and coherence in the dialogues themselves. An interesting *jeu de scène*, directly borrowed from Ionesco's *Le Maître,* has the Man on the Balcony, his back turned to the audience, reporting to the other characters what he alone can observe to be happening backstage.

With the characterization and the themes carefully structured around the central satire of people in society, dramatic tension is admirably maintained. However, because of the absurdity of the situation and the sarcastic tone dominating the dialogues, the final catastrophe must be viewed more as pathos than as tragedy in the classical sense. The *dramatis personae* are everyday people seen in their everyday lives; they are not Aristotelian heroes. The first act ends as a farce, and farce also dominates in the second act as the Old Man is victimized by his neighbors. But because the second act opens with the burglars tiptoeing on stage and going to hide in the vacant house,

[30]Ibid., 48–49.
[31]Ibid., 48.
[32]Ibid., 48.

a sense of doom constantly underlies the farce, culminating in the invasion of the neighborhood by the burglars as the curtain falls on the sleeping houses. This play succeeds as entertainment because it has unity, a quick pace, adept characterization, and also because it treats serious themes in a light, farcical manner. It must be viewed as good comedy rather than serious tragedy, and as such, it also has literary value.

In his subsequent plays, Sā'edi relies increasingly on techniques inspired from the Theater of the Absurd and on nonrealistic expression. These include *Parvarbandān* (The fattened lot, 1969), which focuses on the generation gap in modern Iran; *Dikta o zāviya* (Dictation and angle, 1970); *Jāneshin* (The successor, 1970); *Vāy bar maghlub* (Woe to the vanquished, 1970); *Chashm dar barābar-e chashm* (An eye for an eye, 1971);[33] *Āqebat-e qalam farsā'i* (An end to endless writing) and *In dar ān dar* (This door, that door), published together in 1975; and *Māh-e 'asal* (The honeymoon, 1978), his most recent published play, portraying a newly married couple at odds with a grotesque "guest" who symbolizes the secret police, SAVAK.

Mention must also be made of Sā'edi's films, two of which have won international acclaim. *Gāv* (The cow) directed by Dāryush Mehrju'i, won prizes at the International Film Festivals of Venice and Chicago in 1971; *Dāyera-ye minā* (The enamel cycle), also directed by Mehrju'i, won a prize at the International Film Festival in Paris in 1978 and received excellent reviews when it was shown subsequently in New York.

## 'Abbās Na'lbandiyān

'Abbās Na'lbandiyān made his debut as a dramatist with a play performed at the Arts Festival of Shiraz in 1968, *Pazhuheshi zharf o sotorg va now dar sangvārahā-ye dowra-ye bist o panjom-e zaminshenāsi* (A modern, profound, and important research in the fossils of the twenty-fifth geological era). The setting is a cave filled with fog, representing the afterworld. Ghostlike characters enter one after the other through the mist, shouting "Zamenhof!" They have strange names, all of which result from different combinations of the same five Persian letters: *kh, sh, ā, g* and *y*. They come from all walks of life: politician, soldier, pauper, prostitute, cuckold, playboy, and poet. They are about to start

---

[33]For a translation of this play, see L. Stevenson, "An Eye for an Eye, A Modern Persian Play," M.A. thesis (Columbia University, 1981).

on a long journey, each one searching for someone he or she loves. Urged by the others to "tell his story" each relates, with varying degrees of coherence, his or her sad experience in life. In the first act, the cuckold is chosen by the others to be their leader. In the second act, the director of the play appears on stage, angrily admonishing the actors for their poor acting. He is accompanied by twelve assistant directors who carry torches and periodically salute him with a loud "Heil!" He leaves the stage as abruptly as he entered, after having threatened to torture the actors. Storytelling and deliberations on the journey resume. The last character to appear on the scene is the poet,[34] who recites absurd verses passionately. The others dance in a frenzy around him, urging him to tell them the secret, "the Truth," but he doesn't know the Truth. The stage fills with fog as they all gesticulate and shout, their voices drowned by the chords of Mozart's *Jupiter Symphony,* and the curtain falls.

This play has a vague metaphysical quality. The model used by Na'lbandiyān is possibly *Manteq al-tayr* (Discourse of the birds), a mystical allegory by the twelfth–thirteenth-century Persian poet, 'Attār. The subject of this work is the quest of the birds for the mythical Simorgh; the birds represent the Sufi pilgrims and the Simorgh, God or Truth. The birds decide to start on their journey and elect the hoopoe as their leader. Long deliberations ensue; the birds procrastinate, and in the end only thirty birds continue the quest. Having reached the end of their journey, the birds see only themselves: *si morgh,* or "thirty birds." In Na'lbandiyān's play, the *dramatis personae* are also looking for "the Truth" and are clearly likened to birds. They plead with the poet, "Tell us the story . . . so that our flying wings may find some respite here."[35] The poet himself talks about his mentor (whom he calls *shaikh* or *morshed,* both of which are Sufi expressions) in terms that bring to mind the life that the brethren of Sufi orders led in their monasteries (*khānaqāh*s) under the direction of their mentor:

We spent our time deliberating and scrutinizing and reflecting and meditating, and our road was a single one. . . . He spoke and we listened. . . . We proceeded from darkness to light: from the night we plunged into the heart of the day. . . . We were there

---

[34]Some aspects of the poet are reminiscent of Christ; see E. Yarshater, "Modern Literary Idiom," 315–16.

[35]'Abbās Na'lbandiyān, *Pazhuheshi . . .* (Tehran, 1968), 79.

with him. And it was he who began all the stories. We were only lovers of the Truth.[36]

And when the characters surround the poet, whirling in a mad dance, they recall the elaborate dancing ritual of the order of the whirling dervishes, founded by the mystic poet Jalāl al-Din Rumi in the thirteenth century. However, the difference with Sufi philosophy is striking. In *Manteq al-tayr*, the long road traveled by the birds leads to reunion with God; there is the affirmation, when the thirty birds find only themselves, that human beings, together with their fellow travelers, are themselves a part of "the Truth." Here, quite the contrary, the message is a desperate one: having been disappointed by politics, war, love, and life, the characters implore the poet to tell them "the Truth." But his answer is a pitiful "I don't know": their quest was senseless and their deliberations absurd.

Some of Na'lbandiyān's dramatic techniques are clearly inspired by the West: the unspecified search and sense of expectancy from Kafka; encounters in the afterworld of people who had nothing in common on earth, from Sartre's *No Exit*; the director and his assistants appearing on stage from Pirandello's *Six Characters in Search of an Author*. The poet unable to give any message resembles the orator uttering unintelligible syllables at the end of Ionesco's *The Chairs*; the title which has no relation whatsoever to the action reminds us of Ionesco's *Bald Soprano*; the posters hanging from the ceiling are reminiscent of Brecht's theater; the symmetry in the form of two almost identical acts seems to come, here again, from Beckett's *Waiting for Godot*. The influence of the Theater of the Absurd is particularly strong: the "stories" told by the *dramatis personae* do not constitute a cohesive scheme; rather, they serve as vehicles for allusions, pantomime, dance, music, and visual symbols through which the themes are expressed. As in the Theater of the Absurd, the intent is to reach the spectators through their senses and their emotions rather than through their intellect alone. In the dialogues, logical argumentation is abandoned: instead, painful cries, shreds of phrases, and numerous allusions bring to the spectators a physical, visceral sense of the absurdity of life:

You steal soul-rendering breezes, you steal soft words, you steal shoes and wheat and cotton.[37]

[36]Ibid., 80.
[37]Ibid., 26.

The poet passionately recites:

> For the sake of my warm tears
> For the sake of my yellow complexion
> For the sake of the covenant I made with you
> . . . for the sake of patience and the forehead.[38]

The cry "Zamenhof!" is itself an allusion to the futility of universal communication, since Dr. Ludwig Zamenhof was the person who developed Esperanto, a language that never succeeded in establishing itself as the international idiom.

As in Samuel Beckett's theater, the themes are concretely expressed in a number of visual items: cruelty is represented in the whip brandished by the soldier against the poet, in the torches of the twelve assistant directors. A thick rope hangs around each of the characters' necks, symbolizing the inescapability of fate. The cuckold has a horn growing from his forehead, the soldier a pistol and a sword sheath hanging from his waist. The characters, like Beckett's Vladimir, Estragon, and Pozzo, have no psychological depth, no reality, although their preoccupations and concerns come from contemporary Persian life. They are dehumanized caricatures of human beings who bring to the spectator the physical evidence of their miserable plight. The play leaves the spectator bewildered and shocked, but awakened from the stupor of everyday life. Here the stage truly "speaks its own physical language," as called for by Artaud.

Other techniques are truly original. One of these is the use of the fog that fills the stage periodically. It blots out sets, characters, and scenes, then retracts but never completely disappears. On the one hand it accentuates the pervasive sense of mystery in the play, on the other hand it has a role similar to that of both the chorus and the *deus ex machina* of Greek tragedy. When it unexpectedly fills the stage, it seems to punctuate the action and has the effect of a silent comment. When the poet is overpowered by the soldier at the end of the play, the fog, suddenly expunging the entire scene, brings a contrived resolution to the crisis. Another innovative technique is the choreography of the movements of characters on stage; they culminate in a circular dance as the play draws to a close.

Throughout the play, music sets the mood as it would in a film.

[38]Ibid., 75–76.

400

Rimsky-Korsakov's *Capriccio espagnol* adds a light touch to a happy interlude in one of the "stories"; a military march by Berlioz precedes the entrance of the despot; Mozart's *Jupiter Symphony* brings pathos to the confession of the poet. The recurring fanfare of drums, cymbals, and trumpets, the sudden bursts of thunder and lightning have a similar function: they underscore the events happening on stage.

This play is a tragedy focusing on the desperate and absurd quest for truth and meaning in life. Its strength comes from the concentration on the central theme: the rejection of all ideals, be they political, philosophical, or romantic. The techniques of theatrical expression are bold, but the many motifs borrowed from a variety of sources dilute the dramatic style. The play is far from having the beautiful simplicity of a tragedy by Beckett or an *anti-pièce* by Ionesco. Nevertheless, its impact is strong: visual effects, sounds, music, and dance interwoven with words and allusions affect the audience's senses, emotions, and intellect. Its ambitious scope is reminiscent of a grand-style *ta'ziya*. The spectators cannot remain passive; they are constantly shocked, puzzled, or engaged in deciphering the allusions and events unfolding on the stage. The play succeeds in imparting a message of despair.

Na'lbandiyān subsequently wrote four more plays: *Agar Fāust yek kam ma'refat be-kharj dāda bud* (If only Faust had shown a little wisdom), published in 1969; *Sandali kenār-e panjera begozārim o beneshinim o be shab-e derāz-e tārik-e khāmush-e sard-e biyābān negāh konim* (Let's pull a chair next to the window and sit and stare at the long, dark, black, cold night in the desert), a one-act play published in 1970; *Qessa-ye gharib-e safar-e Shād Shin-e Shād Shangul be diyār-e ādam koshān o amradān o jozāmiyān o dozdān o divānegān o ruspiyān o kāf keshān* (The strange story of Shad Shin son of Shad Shangul's journey to the land of murderers, beardless queens, lepers, thieves, madmen, prostitutes, and pimps) in 1972, followed the same year by *Nāgahān* (Suddenly). These publications were all sponsored and copyrighted by the Shiraz Arts Festival Organization. In the first three of these plays, the author uses essentially the same techniques for dramatic expression as he did in *A Modern, Profound and Important Research in the Fossils of the Twenty-fifth Geological Era*. In *Suddenly*, his style is more realistic: there is no striving for the grandiose, and the play is stripped of effects borrowed from Western dramatists. In all his works he conveys the same despairing message: the human condition is absurd, and individuals cannot escape their cruel fate.

## Assessment

After several centuries of gestation within the oral and folk forms of the art, and after a good deal of experimentation influenced by the West, Persian theater achieved maturity in the 1960s and became unquestionably a part of Persian literature. Often borrowing its form from the West, it nonetheless succeeds in remaining essentially Persian in inspiration and outlook. Pessimism pervades this theater, echoing some of the classical themes of Persian literature as well as the familiar attitude of twentieth-century Western thought. Coming at a time when material abundance was dominating Iranian life, this pessimism also seems to reflect a subconscious skepticism on the part of the dramatist. Accelerated modernization was causing tremendous upheavals in daily life; in literature and the arts, the confrontation between centuries-old traditions and Western models was acutely felt. The pessimism that Bayzā'i expresses with sadness, Gowhar-e Morād with sarcasm, and Na'lbandiyān with discordant cries mirrors the pains and tribulations of a society in flux.

While the lack of perspective may make it difficult to predict which plays will survive the test of time, or what course the genre will take, of its dramatic and artistic merits there can be little doubt. What is certain is that its life has been short. In the 1970s, dramatic creation decreased as the Pahlavi regime's grip on writers became harsher. A prolific writer like Gowhar-e Morād published only three plays after 1972; Bayzā'i published two, and Na'lbandiyān none. At present, theater is in a state of hiatus, but one can surmise that drama will resume when political stability returns to Iran.

# V. PERSIAN LITERATURE
# OUTSIDE IRAN

# 20. Persian Poetry in the Indo-Pakistani Subcontinent

Shortly before the year 1300, Amir Khosrow of India wrote that all languages were preserved in his homeland in their purest state, so that the Persian spoken in India was much purer and more refined than that in Iran, Afghanistan, or Central Asia.

Amir Khosrow (1256–1325), son of a Turkish father and a mother of Indian extraction, is certainly an excellent witness to the situation of the Persian language and literature. He is considered the outstanding medieval Indo-Persian poet and at the same time the inaugurator of Hindustani music. But he was by no means the first great poet in the subcontinent to write in Persian; rather, he perfected a tradition that had been alive for more than two centuries.

The first Muslim conquests in the subcontinent took place in 711–712, when the young Mohammad b. al-Qāsem entered Sind from Iraq and subdued the Indus valley up to Multan. For three hundred years, Sind remained the first stronghold of Islam in the subcontinent, smaller settlements of Arab merchants on the western and southern coasts of India notwithstanding. With Mahmud of Ghazna's seventeen invasions into India between 999 and 1026 the situation changed; a considerable part of the northwestern subcontinent fell under Muslim rule, and soon the city of Lahore became an important center of Persian culture.

Under Mahmud, Ghazna was the most important gathering place for poets and scholars, and Lahore, considered the door to India, came to be known as "little Ghazna." It was in Lahore that the great Sufi Hojviri settled after long wandering. This scholarly mystic was the author of the first major Persian work on Sufism, his *Kashf al-mahjub* (Unveiling of the veiled), which is a superb treatise on early mystical ideas and practices. When Hojviri—called Datā Ganj Bakhsh by the people of the Panjab—died about 1071, his tomb became a place of pilgrimage, and it is said that every Sufi who came to India from Iran and Turan first solicited Datā Sahib's permission to proceed farther into the subcontinent.

At about the same time the first major poets appeared in Muslim India. Abu'l-Faraj Runi (d. 1091) was so successful in the art of the *qasida* that even a master like Anvari appreciated his verse very much. For example, a verse such as

405

> When I want scent you are color [*rang*]; when I want
>   peace you are war [*jang*],
> When I go straight, you are lame [*lang*]—what kind
>   of character have you got?

with its nice internal rhyme and pairs of contrasts prefigures countless compositions of the same kind in Indo-Persian poetry.

Even more important was Mas'ud-e Sa'd-e Salmān (1046–ca. 1131), a wealthy landlord who suffered from the changing political situations and was incarcerated for several years in the fortress of Nāy, from whence he poured out his longing for his beloved Lahore in touching verses:

> O Lahore, woe to you!—Without me, how are you?
> Without the radiant sun—how are you? . . .
> You were a meadow, and I the lion of the meadow—
> How have you been with me! And how are you without me?
> Your lap becomes emptied of friends, one by one—
> With hidden foes in the skirt—how are you? . . .

Toward the end of his imprisonment, he sighed:

> No single hair of mine was white the day
> When Fate cast me in jail and broke my back.
> And I remained in grief and sorrow so
> That now no single hair of mine is black.

Mas'ud thus inaugurated the genre of *habsiyyāt* (prison poems) in the Indo-Persian tradition, in which category some of the finest poems written through the centuries belong—from Mas'ud's heartfelt *qasida*s to Ghāleb's touching poem written from jail in 1847. Urdu literature, too, is rich in this particular genre. However, Mas'ud is noted not only for his *habsiyyāt*; his panegyric poetry shows all the skill a good Persian poet could muster. Particularly interesting is his utilization (for the first and probably only time) of indigenous Indian forms such as *bārā-māsa*, poems on the twelve months, or those connected with the days of the month or the week. All these forms, which were used in Sanskrit and Indian popular languages to express the feelings of a loving woman during the various seasons of the year, were converted by Mas'ud into panegyrics for princes and cleverly filled with the traditional imagery of Persian. He also composed some poems of the *shahr-*

*āshub* type (praising the people of a town), and his verse was so well known that Sanā'i carefully collected his poetry.

No outstanding poet emerged between Mas'ud's death in about 1131 and the birth of Amir Khosrow 125 years later, but a good number of historians and prose writers writing in Persian were active in India during this period. With the beginning of the Mongol on-slaught on the Middle East, several leading intellectuals sought shelter in places like Multan, Ucch, and Bhakkar at Qabācha's court whence they were brought to Delhi by the victorious ruler Iltutmish. Among them was 'Owfi, the author of the *Lobāb al-albāb* (Quintessence of the hearts), a most useful biographical handbook of poets, which he ded-icated to Qabācha's vizier. His second work, the *Jawāme' al-hekāyāt* (Compendium of anecdotes), is dedicated to Iltutmish's vizier in Delhi. At the same time 'Owfi left Ucch for Delhi, so too did Menhāj al-Serāj (d. 1260), whose *Tabaqāt-e Nāseri* is the first major historical work in Persian composed in India. He thus inaugurated the art of historical writing that flourished in the late thirteenth and fourteenth centuries. This process culminated with Barani's *Tārikh-e Firozshāhi*, which ex-presses the author's strictly orthodox, elitist bias and yet is one of the most fascinating and beautifully written chronicles of Islamic India. About the same time 'Esāmi, exiled to Dowlatābād like so many other members of the Delhi society, wrote the *Fotuh al-salātin* (Conquests of the sultans), a rhymed chronicle that was imitated through the cen-turies.

In the course of the thirteenth century poetry once more flourished, largely because of the influence of the mystical orders which had spread into India in that period. For example, Fakhr al-Din 'Erāqi, a singer of enchanting love songs, lived for twenty-five years at the *dar-gāh* (court) of Bahā' al-Din Zakariyyā, the Sohravardi saint of Multan, and developed his art in this milieu even though the Sohravardiyya order was generally not inclined to mystical poetry and music. On the other hand, the Cheshtiyya, established in India by Mo'in al-Din Cheshti in Ajmer and his friend Bakhtiyār Kaki in Delhi, were in favor of music and poetry, and encouraged the Cheshti saints to produce some of the finest poems in the Indo-Persian tradition. Jamāl al-Din Hānsvi's (d. 1260) simple verses are remembered, as are his succinct Arabic adages. Amir Khosrow belongs to the Cheshti-influenced group as does his close friend Hasan Sejzi Dehlavi, who has been called "the Sa'di of India" because of the lucidity and graceful move-ment of his verse. His line, *"Mā qebla rāst kardim be samt-e kajkolāhi"* (We have turned our direction of worship toward the place of the one with his cap awry), is still proverbial. With his *Favā'ed al-fo'ād* (Things profitable to the heart), a collection of sayings by his master Nezām al-Din Owliyā', Hasan invented the genre of *malfuzāt* (collected sayings), which became predominant in the history of Sufi literature in India.

Compared to Hasan's sweet verse, Amir Khosrow's poetry seems to foreshadow the later, more complicated *sabk-e hendi,* or "Indian style." Amir Khosrow was primarily a court poet and was clever enough to write panegyrics for all seven sultans under whom he lived and who were often deadly adversaries. At the same time he was close enough to Nezām al-Din Owliyā', the leading Cheshti saint of Delhi, to imbibe his mystical spirituality, which is especially conspicuous in the introductory religious poems of such great epics as his *Majnun o Laylā.*

Amir Khosrow excelled in both lyrical and epic poetry. He tried to emulate Nezāmi's *Khamsa* (Quintet) in his own *Khamsa,* a work which has been illustrated time and again in India as well as in Iran. He also introduced a new genre into Persian, namely the epic dealing with contemporary events. Examples are *Duval Rāni Khezr Khān,* which tells the love story of Prince Khezr with a Hindu princess; his *Toghloq-nāma,* in which he describes the victories of Ghiyāth al-Din Toghloq; and the *Qerān al-Sa'dayn* (Conjunction of the two lucky stars), telling of the short-lived reconciliation between Sultan Balban's son Boghrā Khan with his own son, Mo'ezz al-Din Kay Qobād, who had inherited his grandfather's throne. From the historical and social viewpoint his *Noh sepehr* (Nine spheres) is particularly interesting because in it the poet, an ardent lover of his Indian homeland, describes the peculiarities of India in high-flown verse. Moreover, each of the nine spheres is written in a different meter although only seven classical meters were used for *mathnavi*s, as Agha Ahmad 'Ali discusses in his *Haft āsmān* (Seven heavens), a handbook of Indo-Persian *mathnavi*s written in the nineteenth century. It should be mentioned in passing that imitations of Nezāmi's *Khamsa,* as begun by Amir Khosrow, became almost a genre in their own right in India; all imitations of his *Makhzan al-asrār* (Treasury of [divine] secrets) have titles ending in *-ār,* beginning with Amir Khosrow's *Matla' al-anwār* (Rising-places of the lights).

One may regard Amir Khosrow's epics, especially the historical ones, as too studded with rhetorical devices that make it next to impossible to decipher the historical facts. He is best in his lyrics, although these too are much more complicated than the lyrical poetry written in Iran proper during the same period. Khosrow is a master of every possible rhetorical play and impresses the reader with ingenious inversions of images and the incredible ease with which he plays with words. He also plays elegantly on the *double entendre* of Persian and Hindi words (although the question of whether or not he composed Hindi verses himself is still not resolved). His skill in Arabic is visible in some of his *qasidas*. Sometimes he uses Indian themes, as in the famous first lines of his collected poems, *Abr mi bārad* (The cloud rains):

> The cloud weeps, and I become separated from my friend—
> How can I separate my heart from my heart's friend on such a day?

> The cloud is weeping, and I and the friend are standing, bidding
>     farewell—
> I weeping separately, the cloud separately, the friend
>     separately . . .

This is a lovely adaptation of Indian love songs set in the rainy season. He also alludes to Hindu customs such as suttee in images that are closer to reality than those usually used by Persian poets. Many of Amir Khosrow's poems are singable; they still form an important constituent of *qawwāli* sessions and of Hindustani music in general. Among them is the *ghazal* "Khabar-ast now rasida" with its central line:

> All the gazelles of the steppe have put their heads on their
>     hands
> in the hope that one day you will come to hunt them. . . .

There is also the elegant *na't* in praise of the prophet ascribed to him, "*Namidānam che manzel bud shabgāhi ke man budam*" (I do not know what station it was where I was present at night) with its superb ending, "Mohammad was the candle of the assembly in that nightly place where I was."

While Amir Khosrow's poetry seems closely related to the court, other poets in the mystical orders developed the typical diction of intoxicated mysticism. Among them is Amir Khosrow's contemporary, Bu 'Ali Qalandar of Panipat, whose *mathnavis* are clearly influenced by Rumi's work. In his lyrics, he sang of nothing but love:

> Were there no love and were there no grief of love—
> Who would have said or heard such lovely words?

409

Were there no love, no one would come to God,
Eternal beauty would not lift its veil . . .

In the following two centuries, during which Muslim kingdoms extended to Bengal and to the Deccan, a vast amount of literature was
produced, but little of it is of first quality. In 1330 the Cheshti Sufi
Nakhshabi retold the Sanskrit fables known as the *Tuti-nāma* (Parrot
book), which became a kind of bestseller and was not only translated
from his Persian version into various other languages but was also
illustrated with fine miniatures. The powerful mystical poems by
Mas'ud Beg, who was executed in 1381 for his too-daring statements
about mystical unity, are worthy of a deeper investigation, while the
saint of the Deccan, Gisudarāz, follows more the classical tradition
and expresses in his lyrics a warm, radiant love. His most famous
poem, "*Ānān ke be-jam'-e eshq mastand . . . ,*" is inscribed around the
dome of his mausoleum in Gulbarga:

Those who are intoxicated from the goblet of Love
Are out of their minds due to the wine of *alast* [Koran 7:171]

Sometimes they strive for piety and ritual prayer,
Sometimes they drink wine and are idol-worshipers.

Whatever they saw on the tablet of Existence,
They washed it off, except the image of the Beloved. . . .

The *qasida*s of Badr of Chāch from the Farghāna are notorious for
their linguistic difficulties but have been admired in the subcontinent
for centuries and have thus influenced Indian taste. The Muslims in
India, who for the most part used Persian as the language of literature
and administration as well as for higher conversation, were perfectly
capable of producing and appreciating complicated literary forms.
Slowly, however, they lost touch with the perfectly lucid style of Persia,
where the poets, even in moments of highest inspiration, could rely
upon a living language that was spoken all around them.

Nevertheless, the poetry of Rumi and Hāfez remained the source
of poetical inspiration all over the subcontinent. In the fifteenth century in Bengal "even the holy Brahmins recite the *Mathnavi* [of
Rumi]," and both the *Divān* of Hāfez and the *Mathnavi* frequently
served as semi-sacred books from which prognostication was taken.
Beyond this, many Indian poets wandered through Islamic lands, and
their friendship and correspondence with masters like Jāmi certainly

left an impact on Indo-Persian poetry. The powerful minister of the Bahmanid kingdom, Mahmud Gavān from Rasht, a friend of Jāmi, composed a fine handbook of epistolography, following Amir Khosrow's example. He also erected in Bidar a typically Timurid *madrasa,* thus perpetuating Iranian influence in the Deccan. Likewise the court poet of the Lodis, Jamāli Kanboh, traveled all over the Muslim world and produced, besides Hindi compositions, some fine Persian poems. His line addressed to the Prophet has gained special fame because it sums up the Muslim attitude that the Prophet is superior to all other previous messengers of God:

> Moses went out of his mind by a single revelation of
>    the Attributes—
> You see the essence of the Essence and still smile!

During the Lodi period, Persian was adopted by many Hindus who worked in the royal service. After the Moghuls entered India, and Bābor established the foundation of the empire with the battle of Panipat in 1526, Persian remained the common language of the elite. Even though Bābor wrote his autobiography in Chagatay Turkish, he, like every educated man, was able to compose verse in Persian. The maintenance of the Turkish heritage of the "House of Timur," as the Moghuls called themselves, did not impede the growth of Persian literature during the next three centuries. On the contrary, with Homāyun's return from Iran to India in 1554, Persian artists such as 'Abd al-Samad and Mir Sayyed 'Ali were brought to India to create, in cooperation with indigenous artists, the incomparable style of Moghul miniature painting. Likewise, poets began to come to the subcontinent because Shah Tahmāsp in his later years was not much interested in artists, panegyrists, and lyric poets. Therefore one observes a constant emigration of Persian poets to India in the last quarter of the sixteenth century.

Moghul India was indeed the promised land for Persian poets. Not only did Emperor Akbar and his family members attract and encourage poets and artists; the military aristocracy did the same. It was initially Khānkhānān 'Abd al-Rahim, himself a gifted poet in Turki, Persian, and Hindi, who became the Maecenas of hundreds of artists; the *Ma'āther-e Rahimi,* a remarkable chronicle in three volumes, enumerates all the poets who wrote for him.

The kingdoms of the Deccan, where culture reached an apex at the same time as in the Moghul Empire, proved a fertile ground for poets

411

even though in Golconda the interest in Arabic and Dakhni Urdu was sometimes greater than the interest in Persian. The talented Zohuri, for instance, describes the mirth and music of Ahmadnagar and Bijapur in his highly sophisticated prose and poetry. His *Seh nathr-e Zohuri* (Three essays), written as an appendix to Sultan Ebrāhim II 'Adelshāh's book on music and poetry, the *Ketāb-e nowras,* shows the perfection of his witty rhetorical skill, while his *Sāqi-nāma* (Book of the cup-bearer) reflects the joys of a seemingly undisturbed period of wealth and peace.

To describe Persian poetry at the Moghul court one might use Hermann Ethé's apt though somewhat ambiguous term "The Indian summer of Persian poetry." Indeed, the verses written by poets like 'Orfi and Bidel are as different from the classical Hafezian style as a colorful forest in autumn differs from the blooming trees of May. The colors become stronger, but behind the outward glamour the awareness of winter's approach is palpable. In this sense, the translations from Sanskrit into Persian made on Akbar's request may have contributed to an "Indianization" of Persian in the centers of the empire.

The Indian style, developed out of the 'Erāqi style and beginning with Amir Khosrow, is noted for its intrinsic difficulties. The poets are no longer content with the traditional way of combining images and topics by following the classical rules of *morā'āt-e nazir* (harmony of images) and *hosn-e ta'lil* (poetic explanation); rather, they fill the inherited rhetorical devices with fresh contents and thus attain surprising results. Images are broken into pieces and put back together like pictures of a kaleidoscope; abstract concepts are introduced, and the use of verbs in the infinitive (often even plurals of infinitives) is frequent. One finds a tendency to use proverbial sayings in the second half of a verse, but, on the other hand, the poets tend to introduce items from daily life or terms from Hindi.[1] Miniature painting and poetical description go together: about the same time that an artist painted Emperor Jahāngir sitting on an hourglass, poets too used the image of the hourglass. Even Aurangzib sighed:

> The grief of the world is overpowering, and I have only
>     a single small heart—
> How can I put the sand of the desert into an hourglass?

The same is true for spectacles: we see painters wearing eyeglasses

[1]See also chap. 14, p. 261ff. (Ed.)

when they are portrayed, and the poets find eyeglasses a wonderful symbol for the intellectual knowledge that stands between people and God, revealing some things and yet separating the people from their goal. They may joke:

> One should make for me spectacles from the wine bottle
> So that in my high age I can read the line of the cup,

or describe narcissi with dew-drops as "eyes with spectacles." They also praise the beauty of a work of art by saying that the sky has put on the sun and moon as spectacles in order to see the dainty work in inlay and ivory properly.

The royal velvet, so skillfully woven in Lahore and Gujarat, becomes a contrast-image to the *buriyā*, the reed mat of the dervishes. It was probably out of a false etymology that one of the most frequently used images in Indo-Persian poetry developed: velvet, *kamkhā*, was sometimes read as *kam-khʷāb*, "with little sleep," and since the Persian idiom describes velvet of great softness with the words *khʷābash khub ast*, "its 'sleep' is nice," the poets invented more and more eccentric combinations between the velvet and sleep—for example, the velvet, disturbed by the nightingale's complaints, gets up like thorns to stare with a thousand eyes at the poet. A typical example of the inversions and impossible contrasts of which Indian style is so fond is a Kashmiri poet's quatrain:

> The silk of our flame is woven from water,
> Our linen is woven at night from moonlight.
>
> You ask for sleep in love—O heart, go
> To the velvet factory where they weave sleep!

Likewise, Chinese celadon ware, an item of great rarity imported to the Moghul court, offered the poets farfetched comparisons with the strange hair-style of the Chinese emperor, as the celadon ware has fine cracks that resembled hairs on its surface.

The poets tried to introduce everyday objects into their poetry by strangely twisting them: "Seek a far-fetched meaning, bring a distant word," says Naziri. Thus, a poetry which may be called mannerist developed, and is reminiscent (in some ways) of the extreme *badi'* style of ninth-century Arabic poetry in which objects were described with exotic comparisons.

413

Of course, the poets of Moghul India continued to write *qasida*s, *ghazal*s, and *mathnavi*s, as they had inherited these forms from the classics, and in some of their verses they achieve great beauty. But one usually feels a lonesome, somewhat tragic mood behind the glittering surface, and it is not surprising that one of the favorite expressions during those years is *shekast,* "broken, breaking"; it occurs at the same time that the *shekasta* style of calligraphy developed in India and Iran. No doubt the Sufi tradition, particularly the Naqshbandiyya, who became influential in the latter part of the seventeenth century, played a role in the choice of such images, for according to them, the human being has to be broken in order to reach the treasure that is hidden within.

The beginning of the *sabk-e hendi* is usually connected with the names of Fayzi and 'Orfi. Fayzi, Akbar's court poet and brother of his biographer Abu'l-Fazl, was of Indian origin, and his poetry is somewhat in the tradition of Jāmi. It is very skillful, reads well, and displays the author's superb intellectual capacity. Comparisons between Fayzi and 'Orfi, who was from Shiraz, have been a favorite topic for historians of literature for centuries. 'Orfi's style is more majestic, powerful, and filled with high-sounding hyperbole. Although he has been criticized severely for his haughtiness as well as for the difficulties of his poetry, he seems much more impressive than Fayzi. Badā'uni, who hated Fayzi, happily states (though probably with some exaggeration) that 'Orfi's poems were sold in every corner of the bazaar while Fayzi had to pay all the expenses of the copyists and even then had to give the poems away! Indeed, a *qasida* like 'Orfi's *Hasb-e hāl* ("personal circumstance"), "*Az dar-e dost che guyam be che 'onvān raftam*" (How shall I describe the way I left my beloved), with its constant tension between hope and despair is one of the great poems of the Persian language:

> From my friend's door—how can I tell how I went?
> Having come there all longing, I went, all deprivation. . . .
>
> I came in the morning like a nightingale in the meadow of *Nowruz*[2]
> In the evening I went like one who mourns, from the dust of the
>     martyrs. . . .
>
> I am that Joseph who, not having gone to Egypt,
> Came out of the well, and went to prison. . . .

[2]The first day of the Spring and the Persian New Year.

Longing for pain, so typical of mystical poetry, is superbly expressed in 'Orfi's *ghazal* calling for suffering:

Come, O Pain, for I have the wish to flee from rest,
The wish to be joined with grief, to be cut off from joy!

Come, O Love, and make me debased in the world
For I have the wish to hear some good advice from those
    without pain!

Come, O Death, and befriend me! for without him, how
    long can I stand it?
I wallowed in blood—now, I have to wish to rest!

Both Fayzi and 'Orfi died relatively young, but more poets came in the following decades. Zohuri, the court poet of the Deccani princes, has already been mentioned; the Persian poet Sā'eb spent six years in India and impressed the literary scene there. Among the more famous poets one may single out Naziri, in whose work the complications of the Indian style are very conspicuous, and Tāleb-e Āmoli, some of whose lines have become proverbial, such as:

I closed my lips from speaking so that one would say
The mouth was a wound in my face, which became healed.

Or his lovely hemistich, "The rose remains fresher in your hand than on the twig."

Perhaps the most versatile poet of the later Moghul period was Kalim. He composed *mathnavi*s on various events during the reign of Shāh Jahān; for instance, he wrote a fine description of the famine in the Deccan "when both worlds were like an hourglass that became empty and full from living and dead," and about young Aurangzib's fight with a raging elephant. Kalim's descriptions are elegant and witty, and in his *ghazal*s longing and resignation are expressed in unforgettable images:

We are unaware of the beginning and the end of the world:
The first and last page of the old book has fallen away!

* * *

Not only does that young smiling rose flee in terror from me—
The thorn in this desert drags away my skirt.

415

His clinging to me is [like] the attachment of wave and shore:
Moment for moment with me, every instant fleeing from me. . . .

Among the other poets of this period, Qodsi Mashhadi may be singled out because of his famous poem in honor of the Prophet, a poem still popular in India. Its beginning, "Welcome, O Meccan, Medinan, Arabic lord," is very typical of the Indian tendency to underline the Arabian origin of the Prophet.

Besides the innumerable poets, we also find a great many prose writers during the heyday of Moghul rule. There are chroniclers of Akbar's life—Badā'uni with his critical approach, and Abu'l-Fazl, whose admiration of Akbar sometimes colors his judgment; then follow the authors of works on the time of Jahāngir (who himself left his delightful Persian memoirs, the *Tozok-e Jahāngiri*) and even more of Shāh Jahān—chronicles in which rhetoric sometimes overshadows historical data. Theologians and members of Sufi orders also continued their literary activities; as they had collected the sayings of their masters from Hasan Sejzi's time, they now composed detailed histories of the orders to introduce friends and novices into the spiritual heritage of each master. Others composed *tadhkera*s enumerating poets of earlier days, under romantic titles like *Meykhāna* (Tavern), *Butkhāna* (Temple) and *Golzār* (Flower garden). Later, the titles were often constructed so that they supplied the date of the composition of a book. Translations and commentaries of classical mystical works were written in great numbers, such as studies on Ibn al-'Arabi and commentaries on Rumi's *Mathnavi*.

Persian poetry and prose also flourished in places far away from the seat of government, as in Bengal and Sind. Sind, especially, can boast of some fine Persian poets, among them Mir Ma'sum Nāmi, known as a calligrapher who designed many of Akbar's inscriptions. He also served as Akbar's ambassador, and was both a noted physician and a fine historian of his home province of Sind, which had been annexed to the Delhi Empire in 1591.

The later years of Shāh Jahān were a watershed in Indian Islamic culture. During his reign his heir apparent Dārā Shokuh, who was executed in 1659 for alleged heresy, composed a number of books on Sufi topics in Persian and, more importantly, translated fifty Upanishads from the Sanskrit into Persian. This translation formed the basis of Anquetil Duperron's translation of the Upanishads into Latin, which, on its appearance in 1801, evoked enthusiastic admiration among European intellectuals and greatly influenced the image of India in the West.

In Dārā's entourage we find not only the Hindu Chandar Bhān Brahman, who gives interesting Persian accounts of his master's life, but also Sarmad, one of the strangest figures in Indo-Muslim literature. Born a Persian Jew, Sarmad studied with Molla Sadrā in Shiraz, embraced Islam, became a merchant and left for India. In the city of Thatta he fell in love with a Hindu boy, and probably under the shock of an overwhelming experience, began to wander around, *qalandar*-style. In Dārā's presence he shocked people by walking around stark naked and defending Eblis (Satan) as the true defender of Divine Unity, as mystics like Hallāj and Ahmad Ghazāli had done before him:

The One who gave you the royal glory [*shokuh*, allusion to Dārā's name]
Gave us all the implements of confusion.

He gave a dress to everyone whose fault he saw—
To the immaculate He gave the dress of nudity!

\* \* \*

Sarmad, do not talk about Ka'ba and monastery,
Do not walk in the street of doubt like those gone astray!

Go, learn the art of servantship from Satan:
Choose one direction of prayer, and do not prostrate yourself before anyone else!

With Aurangzib's ascension to the throne the situation changed. The emperor, whose attitude toward fine arts and worldly joys hardened in the course of time, disliked court historiography and panegyric poets; many of them went to other areas to sell their talents, or the poets twisted the complicated Indian style into even more eerie figures and cobweb-like forms to create a world of fantasy into which they could escape from the realities of life as that life became increasingly difficult. The emperor himself, fighting thirty years against the Deccan states, never returned to Delhi, and the constant wars impoverished the empire, whose borders had now been extended to the point where they could not be defended. It is not surprising that with Aurangzib's death in 1707 (he was nearly ninety years old) the Moghul Empire broke up, and the next 150 years saw the disintegration of one of the mightiest kingdoms on earth, which finally came under British control.

During this process, which began in the late years of Aurangzib, Persian-writing poets invented a world of their own; Ghanimat-e Kanjohi fled into the realm of romantic mystical tales in his *Mathnavi, Neyrang-e 'eshq* (Love's magic), with its long chains of anaphoras. Nāser 'Ali Serhendi's style is almost incomprehensible even for a born Persian, as becomes clear from the sarcastic remarks of the Iranian refugee, 'Ali Hazin, who reached India in 1738: "Of the poetry of Nāser 'Ali and the prose of Bidel nothing can be understood! If I should bring them to Iran there would be nothing better to make my friends mock!" 'Ali Hazin's pure Persian style was, in turn, not at all appreciated by the Indian poets.

The greatest master of the late *sabk-e hendi* is Mirza Bidel (d. 1721), a mystically-minded man, whose voluminous *divān* and prose writings have never been studied in full in the West because of their insurmountable difficulties. He composed a *mathnavi* in mystical style, called *Tur-e ma'refat* (Sinai of knowledge), which speaks of his experiences during his journeys and offers his thoughts on nature. His *Char 'onsor* (Four elements) in mixed poetry and prose has been called a kind of mystical autobiography, difficult to disentangle, but filled with interesting thoughts. Later generations, especially Iqbāl, have found in Bidel a forerunner of their own dynamic world view. Likewise his work, largely unknown in Iran, has become the favorite of the Persian-reading public in Afghanistan and Tajikistan.

Bidel's diction reveals its beauty only to the very persevering reader; his way of twisting images and creating novel combinations of thoughts makes many of his lyrics incomprehensible even after careful reading. Yet suddenly one comes across verses in which content and form are so perfect, and the meaning so deep, that one willingly reads on in the hope of discovering more gems. Longing, despair, and hoping against hopelessness are the essential ingredients of his verse:

Out of longing and desire for you the shifting sand dunes in
the breast of the desert are trembling like a helpless heart.

\* \* \*

Here, the morning of old age results in giving up one's hope—
Here, the woof and warp of the shroud is the white hair.

Turning the general notion of the joyful morning into something fearful and threatening is typical of Bidel, as of many poets in Moghul India. Sometimes he simply longs for rest and sighs:

Even the dead man thinks of resurrection—
How difficult it is to rest!

And yet, he does not want eternal rest:

It is said that paradise is eternal rest—
A place where the heart no longer trembles with a scar—what
    kind of place is that!

From such verses one understands why Iqbāl regards Bidel as a formative element in his life, contributing to his own theory that even eternal life is a constant development of the soul.

Bidel is the last great representative of the Indian style, even though during the eighteenth century many writers continued to use Persian for their writings. But other languages were being introduced as literary media: in the North, Urdu spread rapidly after its southern form (Dakhni) had been in use in the Golconda and Bijapur kingdoms for at least two centuries: in Delhi, it now largely replaced Persian, at least for truly expressive poetry. The influence of Persian prosody, rhetoric, and style on classical Urdu, however, is evident even to the casual reader. And as the Moghul Empire broke up after Aurangzib's death the linguistic unity that had been achieved by using Persian as the language of higher culture was shattered as well: in the provinces, mystical poetry of great beauty was composed in Sindhi and Panjabi while Pashto had developed its own poetry somewhat earlier; in Bengal, Muslim Bengali works once more became popular.

Persian, however, still held sway over the urban population. One of the best introductions to the rhetoric, prosody, and stylistic peculiarities of Persian, particularly Indian Persian, was printed in Lucknow in 1821 on the letter-press that the enterprising king of Oudh, Ghāzi al-Din Haydar, had installed. This *Haft qolzom* was briefly analyzed by the Austrian Orientalist Joseph von Hammer-Purgstall, while its seventh book was translated in congenial style by the leading German Orientalist-poet Friedrich Rückert; it is still an indispensable introduction into the trickiest aspects of Persian poetry, including the art of chronograms.

At the time that this work was published, the last great writer in Indian Persian was already a noted poet. He was Mirza Asadallāh

Ghāleb (1797–1869), now praised particularly for his small Urdu *divān*, which he, however, dismissed as "colorless" compared to his "colorful pictures" in Persian. Ghāleb claimed to write in a purely Persian style, not an Indo-Persian one, and spent much time fighting with other poets about the correct use of Persian words and phrases. For the modern reader, however, this poetry is more reminiscent of Naziri or Tāleb than of Hāfez, even though in his *qasida*s he relied heavily on the classical works of Anvari, Khāqāni, Zahir Fāryābi, and others. His great *Hymn of Divine Unity* (with *"andākhta"* at the end of each line as its *radif*) is modeled after 'Orfi's similar poem but surpasses the earlier poem by far in difficulty. In his *qasida*s Ghāleb displays all his rhetorical skill and sometimes achieves wonderful results even though his style is very heavy. The same is true of his *ghazal*s, some of which have almost become proverbs in Indo-Pakistan; thus his lines on the fate of Hallāj, the martyr of love, who has always served as the model for suffering lovers and rebels against the establishment:

> The secret that is in the breast is not a sermon—
> You can say it on the gallows, but not on the *menbar*![3]

He expands images of the *sabk-e hendi*:

> Come and behold the fervor of my longing to see you—
> Come and behold my dropping from my eyelashes like tears!

But sometimes his verse is simple and singable:

> Farewell and union have each its own delight:
> Go away a thousand times and come a hundred thousand times!

In 1835 the Macauley edict abolished Persian as the official language in those parts of India that were under the British East India Company, and introduced English instead. This was a heavy blow for Muslim culture, for Persian had been, even in its late, complicated forms, the unifying element for the Indian intelligentsia, including Hindus who were often well-versed in the poetry of Hāfez and Rumi. Now this binding element was gone, and literature in the regional languages was encouraged.

Yet the tradition remained alive among the educated classes, and

[3]Pulpit, normally wooden, used in mosques for preaching.

when Muhammad Iqbāl (1877–1938) wanted to address a larger audience both in and outside of India, he turned to Persian, composing his *Asrār-e khodī* (Secrets of the self) in 1915 in the language of Rumi, whom he considered his spiritual guide. From that time onward he used the classical Persian language for most of his literary works, including the *Jāvid-nāma* (Book of Eternity), an account of his heavenly journey in the company of Rumi. Iqbāl's style is much simpler than that of his predecessors; the prophetic message which he had to convey could not be given in complicated forms and images, but had to be straightforward, expressed in verses that were easy to remember. Therefore one only rarely meets with the clichés of the Indian style in his work. The traditional images become, for him, vessels for new content, and his novel interpretation of the tulip and the falcon, of Farhād and of Hallāj is fascinating for those who have followed the development of Persian poetry in the subcontinent. And even though Iqbāl excuses himself for the possible flaws of his verse by stating that he "is an Indian, Persian is not his mother tongue," it is a fact that he rejuvenated Persian poetry in the subcontinent and gave it a new, powerful bent that strongly contrasts with the "broken" imagery of the traditional Indian style. For he had a message, and it was this very message of resurrection and new life that formed his language and turned it, once more, into a living, organic idiom. Unfortunately there was no other poet who could continue his work in Persian, even though his thoughts have been taken over by Urdu poets. It seems that with Iqbāl the history of Persian in the subcontinent finds its end, as a candle flickers up once more to full glow shortly before it is extinguished.

# 21. Iqbāl's Persian Poetry

Persian was the language of higher education and literature in India from the Middle Ages to 1835, when its use for educational and administrative purposes was abolished by the Macauley edict. But the classical language, which had also deeply influenced the development of Urdu and provided its rhetorical and poetical forms, remained the common heritage of the educated Muslim up to the first decades of the twentieth century. Mirza Asadallāh Ghāleb (d. 1869) was much prouder of his achievements in Persian poetry than of those in Urdu, which were widely acclaimed and today constitute the center of interest for all Ghāleb-lovers in East and West.

Aware of this central role of Persian in Indo-Muslim culture, Muhammad Iqbāl (1877–1938), "the spiritual father of Pakistan," understandably turned to Persian at a critical point in his literary career, namely when he gave up the traditional, mystically-tinged world view of his earlier days to unveil "The Secrets of the Self," *Asrār-e khodi,* in 1915.

In the *Secrets,* Iqbāl states, "I am of India; Persian is not my native tongue, . . . ." but it is astonishing to see how deeply he was aware of the artistic possibilities of Persian. One knows from his correspondence with Solaymān Nadwi how carefully he would choose his words and how he always found classical authors to document his use of rare expressions and choice words. Iqbāl composed the *Asrār-e khodi* in Persian because he rightly believed that only then would the poem have an appeal beyond the borders of India and be read by Persians and Turks as well as by European Orientalists (who for the most part were not conversant in Urdu).

It may be that the decision to use the classical language was made when, as the poet tells in the *Secrets,* a vision of Rumi appeared to him, "bade him arise and sing," and began to guide him on the new path, remaining his true Khezr to the very end of his life.

Like every educated Indian Muslim Iqbāl was well acqainted with Rumi's ideas, but like millions of his compatriots he understood the *Mathnavi* in the light of Ibn 'Arabi's theories, and called "the excellent Rumi," in his doctoral thesis of 1907, "the great prophet of pantheism." His attitude changed after his return from Europe to Lahore in 1908, when the influences and impressions of his stays in Cambridge and Germany slowly transformed his thinking. It may be that Shebli No'māni's biography of Rumi, which Iqbāl must have read during

those critical years, persuaded him that there was much more dyna-
mism in Rumi's work than he had realized, and at the end of this
period Rumi indeed appears as the master who teaches his Indian
disciple the message of love and progress, and of constant growth
through love.

The very fact that all of Iqbāl's *mathnavi*s are written in the meter
of Rumi's *Mathnavi-e ma'navi* shows his indebtedness to the great medieval master; however, one should not forget that almost every post-
thirteenth century poet who had to deal with metaphysical topics chose
the simple *ramal mosaddas* meter, and that most poets skillfully inserted
verses from the *Mathnavi* into their own, as Iqbāl did time and again.

In Iqbāl's case, the use of Persian for the revolutionary poem *Asrār-
e khodi,* published during World War I, seems at first sight ironical. In
the first edition of this poem he mercilessly attacked Hāfez and his
school, about whom he had written a few years earlier in his *Stray
Reflections,* "In words like cut jewels Hāfez put the sweet unconscious
spirituality of the nightingales." (Nr. 119). He had carefully studied
the different editions of the *Divān-e Hāfez* and preferred that of Hermann Brockhaus with the Turkish commentary of Sudi. He had also
gone through a vast amount of literature about the poet, from which
he preferred the *Latā'ef-e ghaybi* of Mirza Mohammad Dārābi and
Wilburforce Clarke's English rendering. He sometimes inserted allusions to Hāfez's verses into his own poetry, and four years after the
publication of the *Secrets,* he admitted in a letter, "If literary standard
means that beauty is beauty, be its results useful or pernicious, then
Hāfez belongs to the best poets of the world." But this beautiful poetry
seemed to him extremely dangerous for the spiritual health of the
Muslim community: interpreted either at face value or under the spell
of Ibn 'Arabi's teachings, such poetry seemed to divert the Muslims
from the right path, from the way of constant struggle with the lower
self, and lure them into the delightful rose gardens of Shiraz where,
lulled into slumber by melodious, undulating verse, they would forget
their duties. "The wine of the Sufi and poet has carried you away
from yourself," says Iqbāl in the *Zabur-e 'ajam* (Persian Psalms), where
he also remarks that Hāfez's poetry "did not sharpen the sword of
the Self." During the period he worked on the *Secrets,* Iqbāl criticized
other masters of classical Persian Sufism in very strong words, but the
sharp reactions of many admirers of classical Persian poetry to his
verdict later made him delete the most critical verses from the *Secrets
of the Self.*

Iqbāl could not but be influenced by the spell of Persian. The majority of his poetical works are written in the language of Hāfez and Rumi, and the longer he wrote the more he began to insert lines of classical Persian poetry into his own verse. 'Erāqi, once despised, appears in a positive role in *The Reconstruction of Religious Thought in Islam*; Sanā'i, formerly neglected or misinterpreted by Iqbāl, inspired him to a beautiful Persian ode during his visit to Ghazna in 1932. Amir Khosrow, 'Orfi, and especially Naziri appear in his verse, while Nāser-e Khosrow and Sayyed 'Ali Hamadhāni became actors in the *Jāvid-nāma*.

Iqbāl's Persian works display an astonishing variety of themes. After the *Secrets*, which ushered in a new period of rediscovering the human Self, the next *mathnavi* in Persian was *Romuz-e bikhodi* (Mysteries of selflessness), in which the poet discusses the role of the individual in the ideal Muslim community as well as this community itself. It is probably Iqbāl's most difficult Persian work since it contains a utopian vision of the Islamic community as the living witness of God's unity, which should be, like the Prophet, "mercy for the worlds."

The third work in the uninterrupted sequence in Persian was the *Payām-e mashreq* (Message of the East), conceived as an answer to Goethe's *West-östlicher Divan*. In this work Iqbāl displays his skill not only as a preacher who utilizes the time-hallowed *mathnavi* form for his religio-political and psychological ideals, but also as a lyrical poet of high rank. The quatrains of the first part of this collection, *Lāla-ye tur*, point to his favorite symbol, the tulip of Sinai, which is a synonym for the flame; the wild tulip that struggles to manifest its life in the desert is one of the images he uses time and again for himself and his role in the community. The quatrains in this collection follow the *dobayti* style rather than the classical *robā'i* models, and he liked to preserve this slightly looser form in all his later quatrains. In the *ghazals* of *The Message of the East*, Iqbāl uses traditional images, which he then twists ingeniously so as to apply them to his central topics, the development of the self and the upward movement of the soul. At times he achieves wonderful results in this art, some of his *ghazals* conveying enraptured rhythm and powerful imagery.

He seems strongest in the topical poems of the central part of the *Message of the East*, which includes some of his most lyrical lines. Some of his lyrical poems are novel in form and content, such as the "Fragrance of the Rose." In the powerful "Conquest of Nature," the creation myth is retold and interpreted in the light of Iqbāl's philosophy of the Self, with Iblis acting as the power that helps man to self-realization, while in the quick rhythm of the "Cameldriver's Song" the

424

poet's longing to reach the sacred cities of Islam is well expressed. Iqbāl's dramatic talent shows itself in the "Dialogue between God and Man" and the conversation between "Poet and Houri," a poem inspired by Goethe. In the *Message of the East* Iqbāl reaches the first apex of his Persian poetry. He is capable of using the language for all purposes; he makes it pliable and (especially in the short political aphorisms in the latter part of the book) fills inherited forms and images with a new spirit.

A year after the appearance of *Message of the East* Iqbāl published his first collection of Urdu poems, *Bāng-e darā* (The sound of the caravan bell), which was followed by a great harvest of Persian verse. In 1927, the *Persian Psalms* appeared, offering a collection of prayer poems, some of which give witness of Iqbāl's deep religious feeling. Particularly important for his relations with classical Persian thought is the final part of the *Psalms*, the "Golshān-e rāz-e jadid" (The new rose garden of secrets), a modern answer to Shabestari's famous Sufi poem, which has been analyzed in great depth by Alessandro Bausani.

Since his early days Iqbāl had been collecting material for a work comparable to Goethe's *Faust*, Dante's *Divine Comedy*, and Milton's *Paradise Lost*. This poem appeared in 1932 as the *Jāvid-nāma*, dedicated to the poet's young son Jāvid. Once more Rumi acts as the poet's guide, comparable to Dante's Virgil, leading him through the different spheres in which Iqbāl discusses religious and political problems with the masters of bygone days, with Muslim leaders, Hindu sages, and ancient mythical figures, until he finally reaches the Divine Presence in which all words end. The *Jāvid-nāma* is interspersed with lyrical verse, taken partly from Iqbāl's earlier poems, and in one or two cases from other authors, such as Tāhera Qurrat al-'Ayn's famous song. It is no doubt Iqbāl's *magnum opus*, the one into which he distilled his most sublime thoughts, his aspirations, and his dreams. Its motto is, not surprisingly, taken from Rumi—the famous *ghazal* with the refrain *—m ārzu'st*, "I wish," which expresses Iqbāl's central concern, the longing for the true man of God whom the shaikh went out to seek with a lantern.

The *Jāvid-nāma* is generally regarded as a very difficult work and is, like all good classical Persian poems, heavily fraught with meaning. Not that Iqbāl uses the traditional punning, or enjoys playing with the different meanings of a word. Indeed, his rhetoric is comparatively simple, and he rarely indulges in the involved phrases of which the poets of the Indian style were so proud. Poetry, as one should always remember, was for him a way of promulgating his ideas, not a playful display of his rhetorical skills. As he wrote in a letter in 1935: "I have no interest in the art of poetry, but I have some special intentions and to explain them I have chosen the way of poetry because of the traditions of this country." The plain words themselves are filled with such deep meaning that superficial reading cannot reveal their significance; every phrase creates a spinoff of allusions to the history of religion, politics, Sufism, and other fields. Only by studying the ramifications of the seemingly simple words and discovering ever new cross-relations can one really enjoy the *Jāvid-nāma*. Even the average Persian reader has difficulties understanding all of Iqbāl's allusions, especially since his thought centers on problems connected with India. But every reader must confess that the *Jāvid-nāma* has its place among the great Persian epics.

One can well understand that after completing the *Jāvid-nāma* Iqbāl did not produce another major work in Persian. The two large collections of poetry which were printed in the following years, *Bāl-e Jibril* (Gabriel's wing, 1936) and *Zarb-e kalim* (The stroke of Moses, 1937), are in Urdu. In between, one finds two minor collections of Persian poems, one called *Pas che bāyad kard* (What shall now be done), and the other, *Mosāfer* (The traveler). The first deals with some of the problems that intrigued the Muslim lands in the early thirties, while the second reflects Iqbāl's impressions during a journey to Afghanistan. His posthumously published *Armaghān-e Hejāz* (A gift from Hejaz) contains mainly short poems, the majority in Persian, among which some quatrains are most memorable.

Since Iqbāl did not think of himself primarily as a poet, he avoided unnecessary embellishment of his verses. Hating the device of *l'art pour l'art* he tried to write poetry that could build up a healthy individual's mind and strengthen the community of believers. The rhetorical devices that he used for these purposes are often reminiscent of Rumi. There are numerous repetitions, as is common in poetry meant to be sung; often a strong hiatus between the two halves of a hemistich is used for a more impressive rhythm, which, combined with internal rhyme, makes the lines easy to memorize. The strong use of contrasting pairs of concepts, common in Sufi poetry, is part of Iqbāl's poetical technique. More than that, it serves to express his conviction that life is a constant tension between the poles of *jalāl* and *jamāl*, "divine power" and "divine beauty," the interplay of which guarantees the continuation of life, like inhaling and exhaling in breathing. The device of *tazādd* (contrast) was widely used in classical Sufi poetry. Beside these outward forms, which make Iqbāl's poems memorable and singable, he also displays a great talent for attracting his listener's attention with a traditional motif, like the tulip or the falcon (both his and Rumi's favorite soul bird) and then transforming the accustomed image into the expression of some unexpected meaning that serves his personal philosophy.

Some Pakistanis have praised Iqbāl as *Rumi-ye 'asr,* the Rumi of our age, and one of the best studies of his work, by A. H. 'Erfāni, bears this very title. Yet comparisons are generally lame, and Iqbāl himself knew that he could be compared neither to Rumi nor to Goethe; his background and the situation into which he was born were entirely different. He is certainly much closer to Rumi than to any other Persian-writing poet, and he understood and interpreted Rumi's wisdom better than most mystics, poets, and philosophers of the last six hundred years. The stress on the dynamic character of love is doubtlessly the most important factor both poets have in common.

For quite a long time Iqbāl's poetry was not readily accepted by the Persians who perhaps saw in him a late representative of the Indian style that 'Ali Hazin had criticized so bitterly in the eighteenth century. Indeed, the outstanding poet of his style, Mirza Bidel, was praised by Iqbāl as one of his spiritual guides. However, Persian readers eventually became aware that Iqbāl is a poet who not only had a message of revival and development but also had a command over the language of Rumi and his followers rarely found in our century anywhere in the world.

This combination of strength and elegance, of deep content and attractive form, certainly makes Iqbāl one of the leading Persian poets of the twentieth century. As he himself wrote in the year 1915:

I have no need of the ear of today—
I am the voice of the poet of tomorrow!

# 22. The Persian Literature of Afghanistan, 1911–78, in the Context of Its Political and Intellectual History[1]

In the English language, the primary connotation of literature has changed from its fourteenth-century meaning of "polite learning through reading" to its present meaning of "imaginative forms of writing."[2] But in Afghanistan, where oral literature is still the major form of cultural expression and literacy the preserve of a minority, literature while referring to production of literary works still retains its connotation of literary culture. This is no paradox, for oral and *not* written literature is still the major form of cultural expression in Afghanistan. Writing, despite the expanding rate of literacy, has remained the preserve of a minority of the population.

Written literature, with which we are exclusively concerned here, has been a domain as well as an instrument of cultural and political contention. The challenge facing Afghan writers, put simply, has been that of effecting a synthesis between the heritage of classical Persian and genres of expression first developed in the West. To unravel the complexities of the picture, it is imperative that we continuously place literary texts and their authors in their historical context.

## Established Literary Theory and Practice

Mawlavi 'Abd al-Ra'uf, a religious scholar attached to the court of King Habiballāh (1901–19) argued in 1911 that Muslim thinkers divide literature (*adabiyyāt*) into twelve branches. According to him, the Arabic word *adab* has had the duel meaning of cleverness and the delineation of the boundaries of things. The principle object of the literary sciences is the comprehension of language, especially Arabic. Three primary branches of literature, devoted to the understanding of the words and grammar of Arabic, are mere preliminary steps to

---

[1]Persian is one of the two official languages of Afghanistan. Literature produced in Pashtu, the other official language, shares the same context but otherwise differs from the literature produced in Persian. In view of the Afghan pronunciation of Persian and the manner in which Afghan Persian words are normally transcribed, *w* instead of *v* is used in the transcription of Persian words in this article. Arabic *al-*, however, is rendered as such.

[2]See Raymond Williams, *Key Words* (New York, 1976), 150–54.

428

the fourth and major task: the comprehension of the Holy Koran, considered the model and highest form of literary achievement. The writing of poetry and prose, each divided into a number of genres, constitute the remaining divisions of the literary sciences.

To Mawlavi 'Abd al-Ra'uf, literature "encompasses most of the branches of knowledge that occupy the majority of the learned members of mankind. All of theology . . . is included in it. So are all the Greek sciences, whether devoted to the person and attributes of God the Almighty, the Angels, and the world of souls, or to astronomy and the remaining mathematical sciences" (*Serāj al-Akhbār*, 6/1:17). He made it clear, however, that this all-embracing definition is not the only meaning attached to the word. "To most learned people," he stated, "the words *adab* and *adabiyyāt* imply the knowledge of courtly manners [a word derived from the same root] as well as methods of dealing with superiors and with those senior and junior to one in authority or age. It also implies compliance with the rules of the *shari'at* [Muslim sacred law]" (ibid).

Despite their small numerical size, the Afghan literati at the turn of the century considered themselves to be heirs to a well-grounded tradition of the arts of comprehension and composition. All writings having excellence of form or expression were considered to be contained within one single cultural tradition, that of Islam, and were subsumed under the label of literature. But the emphasis on the interconnection between literature and manners, both of which are called *adab*, highlighted the connotation of the word as literary and courtly culture. At the same time, however, the knowledge of words was considered a means to the ultimate comprehension of the word of God, the Holy Koran.

'Abdal'āh Qāri's (1871–1943) training provides an example of a close fit between the theory and practice of literature. Qāri belonged to a Kabuli family respected for its long history of learning. After initial instruction from his father, he studied with Hāfezj Wardak, a distinguished grammarian. He went on to study Arabic literary sciences and acquired mastery of all the relevant branches. He committed the Holy Koran to memory and acquired eminence in the *nasta'liq* style of calligraphy. At the age of twenty, he was appointed Prince Habiballāh's literary and religious adviser. His entire life, except for two brief trips in the entourage of the Prince to India, was spent in Afghanistan. Qāri composed his first poem (a *qasida*) in 1891 but his stature as a poet grew with his poem of 1894, welcoming Prince Nasrallāh from his trip to England in 1894. In 1896, after sixteen years of bloody conquests, King 'Abd al-Rahmān (1880–1901) instituted a yearly ritual celebrating the theme of national unity, and this gave Qāri the opportunity to write a poem which brought him wide acclaim. When Prince Habiballāh succeeded his father on the throne, he appointed Qāri tutor of his eldest son. Qāri's *Divān* (collection of poems) was published in 1923 in Lahore.[3]

The stages of training traversed by Mawlavi 'Abd al-Ra'uf, who belonged to an eminent Kandahari religious family, must have been very similar to those of Qāri. Yet Mawlavi 'Abd al-Ra'uf's official preoccupation was with the *shari'at* (Islamic law) rather than with literature. The emphasis on literary skills in the system of learning, while indispensable to the mastery of other sciences, should not be viewed as the only aim of the system. The career of Molla Faiz Mohammad Hazāra, whose three-volume history of Afghanistan is the single most important source for the events of the nineteenth century, illustrates another aspect of the system. The details of Faiz Mohammad's early training are not known, but we do know that he studied with Molla Mohammad Sarwar Eshaqzai, a member of Prince Nasrallāh's staff who, in 1892, secured for Faiz Mohammad an appointment on the staff of the prince. Faiz Mohammad's task, in addition to being a secretary, was to copy books. His initial yearly salary of two hundred rupees was increased by one hundred and twenty rupees after five years of service. In 1907, when he was entrusted with the writing of *Serāj al-Tawārikh* (The lantern of history) his salary was increased to one thousand rupees, a rather substantial sum at the time.[4]

The nexus between literary training and employment in the court was a direct one for Qāri, Mawlavi 'Abd al-Ra'uf, and Faiz Mohammad. Mahmud Tarzi's (1865–1933) early training throws a different type of light on the connection between power and culture. Tarzi was a member of the royal lineage. In 1869 his father enjoyed an annual stipend of fifty-five hundred rupees; he was an accomplished poet with a distinct and innovative style, a calligrapher and painter. Tarzi's education was entrusted to the special care of Molla Akram Hotak, a companion and member of his father's literary circle. In 1879, when the second Anglo-Afghan war broke out, Tarzi was studying Arabic grammar and reading commentaries on the poetry of Jalāl al-Din Rumi. To reach this stage he had to have read the *Golestān* and *Bustān*

---

[3]Guyā E'temādi, "Qāri 'Abdallāh Khān Malek al-Sho'arā'," *Āryānā* 1/6 (1943): 4–14.
[4]*Serāj al-Tawārikh* (1333 L.H./1915), vol. 3, 868.

of Sa'di, the *Khamsa* of Nezāmi, Jāmi's *Yusof and Zolaikhā,* Kāshefi's *Anwār-Sohaili,* and a series of other well-known works.[5]

Ideally, with the end of the war in 1880, Tarzi would have resumed his education. That, however, was not to be. In 1882, his father's household was forced into exile and, after staying three years in Karachi, the family settled in Damascus on a pension from the Ottoman Sultan. When Tarzi was permitted to return to Afghanistan in 1905, he had spent twenty-three years abroad. During these years, Tarzi had devoted considerable thought to the assessment of his literary education, and the changed circumstances of the country were to provide him with a format for the propagation of his ideas.

Before dealing with Tarzi's new literary ideas, it will be useful to summarize the major characteristics of the established literary theory and practice. The Islamic conceptualization of literature allowed for the dissociation of language and ethnicity. Qāri, a Tajik, Faiz Mohammad, a Hazāra, and Tarzi, a Pashtun, all learned their linguistic skills in Persian from masters who were ethnically Pashtun. The students or masters could as easily have belonged to one of the other ethno-linguistic groups in the country. In a country where at least thirty-two languages, belonging to four linguistic families, are spoken, agreement on common tenets of literature and education was important.

These shared principles of taste were engendered through the reading of particular texts, standardized methods of teaching, and well-defined institutions. We have already mentioned the names of some of the major texts and authors. The relation between the readers and the texts was not individualized but mediated through the masters, who, in turn, were links in widespread networks of scholarly and religious connections. Each master passed the brightest of his students to his own masters or to other well-known masters, and the serious students travelled widely in search of their ideal master(s).

Only a small number of students, of course, had the ability or willingness to go through all the stages of this very demanding process of learning. Most of them stopped after their first lessons of grammar with the village molla, whose own knowledge was usually limited to elementary literacy and a smattering of Arabic. But even the most ill-informed village molla knew the names of some of the best *madrasas* (Islamic schools of learning) and the names of some of the most em-

[5]See Rawān Farhādi's introduction to *Maqālāt-e Mahmud Tarzi dar Serāj al-Akhbār-e Afghāniyya* (Kabul, 1977): 9; for a list of the classic textbooks which were to be studied by aspiring students see *Nezām-nāma-ye makāteb-e khānagi* (Regulations regarding unofficial schools) (Kabul, 1302/1923), 5.

inent contemporary masters, and he could inspire his students to move in search of more qualified teachers. Moreover, passages of poetry and prose from the classic authors were frequently recited by the village mollas in their preachings. Literacy, therefore, was not a necessary requisite for partaking in the literary heritage.

Nor were the mosques and *madrasa*s the only agencies in the formation and propagation of standards of literary taste. The *majles* (gathering), whether formal literary discussion group or social party, was an even more important means of legitimation. A monarch, prince, or man of means could convene a *majles* at regular intervals for discussing the works of a specific literary figure or for general discussion of literary topics. The connection between literature and literary culture, however, was so strong that any social occasion could turn into a discussion of literature, where poetry fitting the occasion would be recited.

The poetry, on such occasions, was not always from the literary giants of the distant past. The man whose poetry has most captivated the imagination of the Afghans in the last two centuries is Mirzā 'Abd al-Qāder Bidel (1644–1720). *Majāles* (pl. of *majles*) convened by Mahmud Tarzi's father, for instance, were almost completely devoted to the recitation of Bidel's poetry. These sessions, according to Tarzi's later testimony, could last up to six hours of uninterrupted readings.[6] Tarzi's father and many other poets followed the literary canons of Bidel's poetry, and it is reasonable to assume that members of the *majles* prevailed on their host and other poets to entertain them with their own compositions. Discussion of established literature thus led not only to its appreciation but also to its reproduction.

The courts of the Afghan rulers and princes had always had a literary component to them. The changed conditions at the turn of the century, however, allowed for one of these courtly gatherings to be transformed into a committee for literary criticism. Prince Nasrallāh, the king's brother and the second most powerful man in the country, was like many Afghans a devotee of Bidel. He used to convene a regular *majles* (session) to recite his poems and to authenticate

---

[6]*Serāj al-Akhbār* 6/22 (1917): 7. Mahmud Tarzi's works include *'Elm wa eslāmiyyat* (Science and Islam) (Kabul, 1330/1912); *Āyā che bāyad kard* (What is to be done?) (Kabul, 1330/1912); *Rawza-ye hekam* (Garden of wisdom) (Kabul, 1331/1913); *Az har dahān sokhani va'z har chaman samani* (A saying from everyone and a flower from every garden) (Kabul, 1331/1913); *Parāganda* (Scattered [pieces]) (Kabul, 1332/1914); *Siāhat-nāma-ye se qet'a-ye ruy-e zamin* (Journeys in three continents) (Kabul, 1333/1915); *Mo'allem-e hekmat* (Master of wisdom) (Kabul, 1334/1916); *Watan* (Homeland) (Kabul, 1335/1916–17).

all of Bidel's poetry. The availability of the printing press, introduced in the country in the 1870s, made it possible for the deliberations of the prince's *majles* to reach a wider audience. By 1919, when Prince Nasrallāh lost his bid for the throne to his nephew, his group had published a volume of Bidel's poetry beginning with the first four letters of the alphabet.

Thus the printing press could serve as a bridge between mosques, *madrasas* and *majāles* and the reading public, and thereby reinforce the existing standards of literary theory and practice. Indeed between 1870 and 1911, the printing press in Afghanistan, which put out religious and literary products, fulfilled this function. However, returning from his long exile, Mahmud Tarzi was to use the printing press for a rather novel task.

## Mahmud Tarzi's Literary Challenge

Mawlavi 'Abd al-Ra'uf, a prominent product of the old school, published his conservative essay on literature, which expounded traditional concepts in the first issue of *Serāj al-Akhbār*—a bi-weekly publication managed by Mahmud Tarzi and the only newspaper in the country between 1911 and 1918. The nature of the readers' reception to 'Abd al-Ra'uf's piece can only be guessed, but Tarzi's reaction was decidedly negative. He immediately made it clear that, to him, the word literature conveyed a totally different meaning, referring to "the products of the artistic imagination of contemporary eastern and western writers in poetry and prose."[7] Works of literature, as illustrated by the translation of a German poem and a French novel, were to entertain the readers of the paper and broaden their horizon.

Representing a new medium of literary communication, the paper was, as far as Tarzi could determine, not to be used for reinforcing the culturally established standards of literary taste but for questioning them. Tarzi was too cautious to openly articulate his policy at the very inception of the publication; six years later, however, he was more candid. In a series of articles entitled "What is literature?" he drew a sharp contrast between the underlying approaches of "eastern" and "western" writers:

> Eastern storytellers, in order to please their audience, have relied on exaggeration, spending their energies on the creation of exceptional superstitious entitites. Not finding the events of daily

[7]*Serāj al-Akhbār* 1/2 (1911): 7.

life worthy of their attention, they have had recourse to the supernatural. They have invented strange creatures called "fairies"
and have made them fly like birds! . . . European novelists, on the
other hand, concentrate their attention on the routine events of
their environment. They use their imagination and their writing
skills for the depiction of events that are within the realm of
possibility and not those that are impossible![8]

European authors, he insisted, avoided purple prose in their narratives, modelling their writings on conversational patterns of daily life.

Literature, in Tarzi's scheme, was to be a vehicle of cultural change
rather than cultural continuity. He was not merely broadening the
meaning of literature to encompass the works of imagination of other
cultures; he was insisting that European models of literary expression
were superior to those in his own culture and better suited to modern
conditions. The audience to whom Tarzi primarily addressed himself
were the younger members of the court, the bureaucratic officials,
and the students in the newly-established modern schools, the first of
which had been established in 1907. The membership of these groups
in all probability did not exceed two thousand individuals, a small
minority. But their strategic location in relation to state power more
than compensated for their numerical weakness and made their response to Tarzi's ideas of long-term consequence. Tarzi's advocacy of
a new definition of literature, therefore, marks the beginnings of the
new Afghan official culture, in which the fact of writing in the Persian
language is less important than the fact that the writing is produced
in an Afghan context.

Despite Tarzi's call for easily comprehensible styles of writing the
connotation of literature as literary culture did not change but, instead, was reinforced. Tarzi's opposition to the established norms of
literary theory and practice meant that *Serāj al-Akhbār* could not become the connecting link among the established channels of literary
communication.

The literary theory enunciated by Mawlavi 'Abd al-Ra'uf was by no
means confined to Afghanistan. Aspiring literati in India, Iran, and
Transoxiana were nurtured on the same texts through very similar
institutions, and absorbed the shared standards of literary preference
and critique. Prior to the eighteenth century, the literati in these areas
had participated in multiple networks of connections in what was truly
a common cultural heritage.

[8]*Serāj al-Akhbār* 8/5 (1918): 4–6.

The British conquest of India—resulting in the decline of Muslim hegemony in India and the replacement of Persian as the literary language and the language of bureaucracy—periodic outbursts of civil wars and foreign invasions of Afghanistan and Iran, and the increasing subjugation of the states of Transoxiana to the Czarist empire, all put severe limits on the reproduction of these ties. Literary contacts between the literati of Iran and Afghanistan, as shown in the complete neglect of Bidel in Iran, were minimized.[9] None of the major Afghan literary figures in the first quarter of the twentieth century had spent any time in Iran.

The connections with India and Transoxiana, however, remained strong, and the style known as *Sabk-e Hendi* (the Indian style) was the dominant style of poetry writing in the country for a long time. The published editions of classic texts in Arabic and Persian were also first made available through the medium of commercial companies that specialized in the printing of these books in India. The appearance of *Serāj al-Akhbār* reinforced these connections. Underneath the official culture that was being formulated and propagated by the nationalist intellectuals, many other strands of interconnections continued. The intellectuals, however, had a near monopoly of publication inside Afghanistan, and to understand their products we need to have a clear grasp of Tarzi's role and impact.

## The Literary Content of Serāj al-Akhbār

Between 1911 and 1918, while writing most of the essays in the paper and managing every aspect of its production, Tarzi also wrote a textbook on world geography, produced four collections of literary essays and an account of his travels, wrote a number of pamphlets, and translated a five-volume history of the 1905 Russo-Japanese war and four novels of Jules Verne (1828–1905). In subsequent years no Afghan intellectual has been able to match him in using literature as a means of defining the cultural agenda of the entire country. And literature, of course, meant both poetry and prose.

The very introduction of the new medium enabled Tarzi to bring to his audience new genres of writing. From editorial and news reports to novels, every form of writing in the paper was new. An Afghan reader may not find much of literary value in Tarzi's writing style, but

[9]For a summary treatment of these themes see Rawān Farhādi's "Afghanistan: Literature," *Encyclopedia Iranica* I/6: 564–66.

would probably judge it clear and succinct. How his contemporaries, who were products of the established Islamic institutions, reacted to his prose is not known. It is quite possible they considered it rather vulgar.

Afghans were first introduced to the short story, novelette, novel, literary essay, and foreign poetry through the pages of *Serāj al-Akhbār*. However, Tarzi did not content himself with these achievements, and attempted to redefine the style and content of the dominant medium of expression, poetry.

The place occupied by love, beauty, wine, and flowers in classical Persian poetry offended his sensibilities as an advocate of modern education. Colonialism, patriotism, progress, and technology were to provide the alternative key symbols of the new poetry. His call for change is best illustrated in a poem which, ironically, argues for the relegation of poetry to the pastimes of the past:

Bygone is the time for poems and
Bygone is the time for magic and sorcery

Now is time for action, effort and will
Bygone are carelessness and laziness

This century is the century of cars, railways, and electricity
Bygone is the cadence of a camel ride.[10]

Fully aware of the stylistic austerity of his poetry compared to the elegant standards of the past, Tarzi justified his approach on the basis of its relevance to the needs of the times. However, he may have considerably underestimated the imaginative powers of his readers. The evidence for this assertion comes from the reactions of several generations of Afghans to his translation of Jules Verne's science fiction. Tarzi, who first translated these novels for the pleasure of the king, referred to them as 'technical novels' and justified their publication as guides to the knowledge of world geography. I would argue that the books appealed to Afghan readers because of their fantastic dimension, a quality much in tune with the structure of fairy tales.

Jules Verne's works were not the only door to fantasy opened by Tarzi. In his travel diary, entitled "Journeys in Three Continents," while expressing his image of the good life, he also recounted his

---

[10]For a summary of Tarzi's major works, see my weekly column "Readings on Afghanistan" in *Kabul Times*, 1975–76. His poetry is dealt with in the issue of May 3, 1976.

sexual exploits in Cairo, Damascus, and Istanbul. This is the only time until today that, to my knowledge, an Afghan author has dealt with the subject of sex autobiographically in print.[11] But Tarzi's frankness in discussing sex did not extend to his analysis of politics. Not only did he avoid direct criticism of the king and his entourage, but every action of Habiballāh was praised, although he was mostly preoccupied with his large harem and given to aping English dress. The break between the role of court poet and reformist journalist was not as radical as it may have appeared at first sight. Indeed, the largest number of poems published in *Serāj al-Akhbār* were written in praise of the king by the court poet, Shir Ahmad, a man now confined to oblivion.

Criticism of power took place only through the medium of symbols, at culturally marked occasions of the year. Despite his advocacy of directness of expression, Tarzi resorted to such stratagems. An ode to the king, composed by the court poet, filled the entire first page of the twenty-first issue of the fifth year of the paper. But pages 5–8 of the same issue were devoted to a poem celebrating the justice of 'Omar, the second caliph of Islam. This poem, describing the encounter of 'Omar with a poor widow in the dead of the night, was most probably written by Tarzi. The widow argues that 'Omar's ignorance of the plight of her children makes him unfit for leadership. 'Omar, however, is shown to be aware of the burdens of his office and cognizant of the circumstances of the widow. The story is a curt reminder to the king that his role as a Muslim ruler is not confined to celebration but that he should aspire to the standards of justice established by the Prophet of Islam and his companions. The symbolic power of the poem is not contained in its form or content alone; it is juxtaposed with two pictures of the king's 1907 trip to India, where the glaring contrast between the legacy of 'Omar and the deeds of Habiballāh are revealed to all who care to see.

Tarzi's own practice shows that established cultural symbols could be deployed for the furtherance of reformist goals. Indeed, in his political writings, Islam, portrayed as a religion and culture condoning the pursuit of scientific activity and progress, occupies an important place.[12] Islamic symbols, however, are largely absent in his poetry and literary essays. The only time he has recourse to God is in his discus-

[11] For a detailed description of the diary see ibid., April 29, May 31, and June 23, 1976.

[12] I have treated this issue in "Literature as Politics: The Case of Mahmud Tarzi," *Afghanistan* 29/3 (1976): 63–72.

sion of social compassion, when the rich are reminded that, had the Almighty wished it, the stations of the rich and the poor could easily have been reversed.[13]

## The Success and Failure of the Intellectuals, 1919–29

Nineteen hundred and nineteen was an eventful year for Tarzi. At the beginning of the year, opposition of some elements in the court had forced him to discontinue the publication of the paper. With the assassination of Habiballāh and the accession to the throne of King Amānallāh (1919–29), an adherent of his reformist ideas as well as his son-in-law, Tarzi became foreign minister. Amānallāh quickly declared Afghanistan fully sovereign and went to war with Great Britain in 1880, which dominated the foreign relations of Afghanistan. Despite the ambiguous outcome of the war, negotiations resulted in the recognition of the full independence of Afghanistan. Tarzi headed the Afghan delegation at these negotiations, and his two terms as minister of foreign affairs and as ambassador to France removed him from effective participation in the cultural scene.

How did the Afghan intellectuals respond to Tarzi's literary agenda? To answer this question I will differentiate between formats of presentation, genres of writing, and dominant symbols of expression.

*Serāj al-Akhbār* was simultaneously a newspaper, a literary magazine, a philosophical and scientific journal, and a political tract. In the newspapers which succeeded it, however, a tendency toward specialization in one of these functions is evident. *Afghān,* published under the editorship of Mohammed Ja'far in Kabul, was the first daily newspaper in the country and largely restricted itself to reporting and commenting on current events. *Haqiqat* (Truth), on the other hand, was merely the government's organ of propaganda during the rebellion of 1924 in the southern province. With the suppression of the rebellion the paper, which was edited by Borhān al-Din Koshkaki (1891–1954), ceased publication.

Most of the newspapers of this period had an average life-span of one year, but after 1919 Afghanistan was never to be a one-newspaper country. Tarzi's new format of expression was clearly destined to endure. But did the hold of the format also imply the hold of the new genres of expression?

---

[13]*Az har dahān sokhani va'z har chaman samani* (A word from every mouth and a flower from every garden) (Kabul, 1331 L.H./1913), 73–74.

Tarzi introduced the Afghans to the short story, novelette, and novel, but not a single Afghan author experimented with these genres of writing, and not a single book-length translation of a literary work of a Muslim or European writer was undertaken in this period. An examination of the material published in *Amān-e Afghān* (The Afghan peace), the successor to *Serāj al-Akhbār*, shows, in fact, a distinct tendency toward becoming an organ of government propaganda.

This intellectual failure was a result of the political success of the intellectuals. 'Abd al-Hādi Dāwi (1894–1983), Tarzi's assistant in *Serāj al-Akhbār* and the first editor of the *Amān-e Afghān*, was then appointed to a succession of diplomatic posts and became minister of commerce in 1925. Mir Gholām Mohammed Ghobār (1896–1978), who displayed remarkable creativity during his editorship of the *Setāra-ye Afghān* (The Afghan star), was also quickly recruited into the ranks of the bureaucracy. The small number of the intellectuals—indicated by the total student body of 1,590 students enrolled in 13 schools in the country in 1930—was simultaneously the cause of their strength and their weakness.

In addition to introducing his readers to new genres of prose, Tarzi had urged his compatriots to infuse their writing with new symbols. Between 1911 and 1918, the only major poet to respond positively to Tarzi's call was 'Abd al-Ghani Mostaghni (1875–1933), among whose contemporaries only 'Abdallāh Qāri is his match in literary stature. But, unlike Tarzi's own poetry, Mostaghni's poetry was not single-stranded. He did pay tribute to modern education and newspapers, but he also composed odes to Habiballāh. His *ghazals* are deeply evocative of Bidel and display all the artistic characteristics of the Indian style of poetry. Qāri, who has a poem in praise of Tarzi in his published collection of poetry, only published one *ghazal* in the *Serāj al-Akhbār*, a work of exquisite craftsmanship but replete with all the symbols Tarzi objected to.[14]

Education, patriotism, and Islam, however, were clearly the dominant symbols during Amānallāh's decade, celebrated both in verse and in prose. Examination of some brief passages from the period makes the centrality of these themes clear.

"We are today the most backward of nations," wrote Dāwi, "but if we had been equipped with the weapon of education we would have been in the forefront of the modern caravan."[15] Education clearly was

---

[14]*Serāj al-Akhbār* 7/20 (1918): 12.
[15]*Amān-e Afghān* 1/5 (1920): 3.

viewed as the panacea, but united action of the citizenry could only result from the bonds of patriotism and religion. The stress on Islam, however, was coupled with a critique of Western civilization and an assertion of Eastern unity.

"As though by force of gravity or magic," argued an author in *Amān-e Afghān*, "the imagination of the East has been overwhelmed by the West. We have been made ignorant of ourselves and our neighbors. Our fascination with the West has caused us to forget our own sensibilities. But the sound of the collapse of Europe has brought about the awakening of Asia. We have to be awake! We easterners should rise, make each other aware, and unite together. We should strengthen our mutual social bonds and follow the lead of Japan."[16] Ghobār, sensing the possibility of another World War, went even further, arguing that "despite the deaths of hundreds of thousands of people in the five years of the war the morbid imagination of Europe is still pervaded by a sense of savagery and barbarism."[17]

Acquisition of Afghan independence and the sense of disenchantment with the West had two major literary consequences. First, the establishment of diplomatic relations between Afghanistan and Iran was celebrated by poets with odes to the common cultural heritage of the two countries. Even more significantly, articles and poems from *Akhgar, Mashreq, Chehranomā*, and other Iranian publications were reprinted in the Afghan press, contributing to the Afghan awareness of literary trends in Iran. Second, and perhaps more importantly, the intellectuals, unlike Tarzi, felt more at ease with their own cultural legacy and made extensive use of Islamic symbols for the furtherance of their social and political goals. The case of Mohyi al-Din Anis, the most innovative intellectual of this decade, best illustrates this contention.

Anis, who grew up in Egypt, made his first political intervention through the literary medium. In 1924, he published in Herat "Nedā-ye Talaba-ye ma'āref yā hoquq-e mellat" (Voice of the students or rights of the nation), innovatively making use of dialogical principles to attack notions of despotism and elitism, and to make a sustained argument for democratic notions of government. The dialogues are carried on among individuals with real-life counterparts, and the cultural setting is fully integrated into the text. At critical junctures the proper Islamic justifications for a democratic form of government are

[16]*Amān-e Afghān* 2/8 (1921): 4.
[17]*Setāra-ye Afghān* 1/13 (1921): 2.

offered. The book can be read in multiple ways, and its literary format is as important as its clear and succinct arguments.

In 1927, Anis was given permission to publish the bi-weekly paper *Anis* (Companion), a publication directed at intellectuals and bureaucrats. Although pages of *Anis* were filled with discussions of the nexus of rights and obligations binding the citizens and the government in a democratic state, the editor did not shy from making his points through the poetry of the great Sufi mystics. The editorial of June 10, 1928, entitled "Betaraf-e hajj-e haqiqi" (Toward true pilgrimage), consists of a long poem by Jalāl al-Din Rumi, describing the process through which Bāyazid Bestāmi, a great Sufi master, is led to the discovery that the house of God is in the hearts of the people and not in a building made of bricks and mortar.[18]

The relevance of literature to the contemporary situation, as *Anis*'s practice shows, did not need to be at the cost of the entire heritage of the language. Change in the conditions of literary production, however, did not result from a dialogue among intellectuals but from political upheaval. In January of 1929 Amānallāh's regime succumbed to a rural rebellion, and the king, along with Tarzi, was forced into exile. The country plunged into a nine-month civil war, at the end of which General Nāder (1929–33), a distant cousin of Amānallāh, established a new dynasty.

## A Literary Renaissance: The 1930s and 1940s

The new power elite did not take a tolerant attitude toward the intellectuals. A total ban of Tarzi's name and ideas was put into effect, lasting until the 1960s. Dāwi, Ghobār, and others languished in jail or internal exile, and Anis and many others perished during their stay in prison. Yet, at the same time, the intellectuals were encouraged in their literary efforts and supported by the state. To take account of this complex picture we will, once again, take stock of the formats and institutional channels for the expression of ideas, genres of writing, and dominant symbols.

Focus on the formats and institutional channels of expression shows that the opposition of the state was to the person rather than to the. cultural agenda of the politically active intellectuals. By the end of the first decade of the new dynasty, a department of press, publishing two dailies in the capital city alone, had been established; a literary society

[18]*Anis* 2/10 (1928): 1–3.

(*anjoman-e adabi*), with its own journals, had been founded; and the number of educational institutions greatly expanded. The founding of the College of Letters within the framework of Kabul University in 1944 signaled the state's participation in the management of literary production.

By 1940, the majority of the individuals devoted to intellectual pursuits were salaried functionaries of the state. There was also a clear trend toward increasing literacy and, thereby, a potential increase in the number of readers. The number of students jumped from 1,590 in 1930 to 60,000 in 1949, reaching 497,911 in 1967 and peaking to 928,000 in 1976. The expansion was not merely quantitative. The establishment of the Literary Society in 1930 quickly led to the launching of the first literary and historical journal, an almanac, and, after an interval of some years, an encyclopedia. The production and management of these novel means of presentation and representation were carried out by a small group of Afghan intellectuals, who took over the editorship of the dailies and management of Radio Kabul (created in 1940) in the 1940s.

It was during these years that Afghan authors started experimenting with the genres of writing to which Tarzi had introduced them. Short stories, novelettes, novels, literary essays, and literary and historical criticism were all taken up in earnest. Still, poetry remained the most valued mode of expression. Writing was viewed as craftsmanship, and its aesthetic qualities were stressed. The shift in emphasis from the dominant symbols of the Amānallāh period is nowhere more evident than in the choice of theme for a poetry contest sponsored by the journal *Kabul*, the organ of the Literary Society. The subject was Spring and the first prize went to 'Abdallāh Qāri. To stress the role of the state as a patron of literature King Zāher, resurrected the title of poet laureate (*malek al-sho'arā'*), which had not been used for centuries, and bestowed it on Qāri.

The choice of Qāri as the bearer of this old title was quite fitting, for he was truly the connecting link with the classical heritage of the land. When the first modern school was established in Kabul in 1907, Qāri was appointed to teach the fundamentals of language and literature. During his nearly three decades of tenure as a teacher, Qāri published at least seven textbooks on various aspects of the Persian and Arabic languages and literatures. In a country where textbooks are the most important source of reading, Qāri's accomplishment in setting and nurturing the literary tastes of generations of students cannot be exaggerated. The literary achievements of the authors of the 1930s and 1940s, who were either his students or had studied his texts, can therefore be directly linked to his efforts.

Beyond the aesthetic themes, history and culture were undoubtedly the sources of key symbols for the Afghan intellectuals of this period. Their originality was not in the mere investigation of the past but in their success in convincing their readers that depite all the traumas of history Afghanistan possesses a continuously resilient culture, capable of responding to the challenges posed by foreigners and capable of absorbing them. 'Abd al-Ra'uf Binawā (d. 1985), Seddiq Farhang (b. 1914), Ghobār, after his release from jail, 'Abd al-Hayy Habibi (d. 1984), Ahmad 'Ali Kohzād, Khalilallāh Khalili (b. 1909), 'Abd al-Rahmān Pazhwāk (b. 1917), Sayyid Qāsem Reshtyā (b. 1913), Ebrāhim Safā (b. 1908), Osmān Sedqi (b. 1918), Muhammad Qadir Taraki (1910–82) and other members of the group were not mere historians, journalists, and literary critics. Their writings were permeated by history, and their mooring in the classical Persian heritage allowed them to creatively adapt the language to new genres of writing.

The short stories and dramas of Pazhwāk are models of literary achievement. Drawing on folklore, history, and myth, he forged a style of narrative still indebted to the classical tradition, yet distinctly his own. His widely read renderings of the stories of Rudāba and Zāl from the *Shāh-nāma* of Ferdowsi, the "Shāhzāda-ye Bost" (Prince of Bost) from the folklore of Kandahar, *Wazifa* (Duty) from eighteenth-century history, and the "Dokhtar-e kuchi" (Nomad girl) from nomadic mythology are all considered masterpieces of Persian prose in Afghanistan.[19] Pazhwāk, during his editorship of one of the two daily newspapers of the capital, showed that directness of expression in journalism could be combined with elegant writing. He also wrote some dramas but was soon absorbed in diplomatic duties from the late 1940s on.

The role of 'Abd al-Ghafur Breshnā (1907–74) and of 'Abd al-Rashid Latifi in playwriting was similar to that of Pazhwāk's in short stories. Breshnā, who was trained in painting in Germany, was the most prominent painter of this period and drew on history both in his paintings and writings. Latifi, who served as the editor of one of the dailies of Kabul, also wrote plays for theater and played a critical role in the training of actors. Breshnā and Latifi both served as directors of Radio Kabul, enlarging the reach of literature to a wider

---

[19]Most of these stories were first published in *Āryānā*, the literary organ of the *Anjonman*, which began publication in 1943. A selection bearing the title of *Afsānaha-ye Mardom* (Stories of the people) was subsequently published as a book.

audience through the broadcast of special literary programs. The use of new formats of presentation was, no doubt, a contributing factor in the literary achievements of these authors in the realm of prose. Their poetry, however, is a critical testimony to their pivotal role as connecting links with the classical heritage of the language. The aging Qāri and Sufi 'Abd al-Haqq Bitāb (1888–1971), on whom the title of poet-laureate was bestowed after Qāri's death, were the leading poets of the period. Both Bitāb, who became professor of Persian literature at the College of Letters after its establishment in 1944, and Qāri were representatives of the classical tradition and dwelled on well-established poetic themes.

The younger generation, without sacrificing the literary standards of elegance imbibed from Qāri and Bitāb, confronted the politics of cultural production. Pazhwāk's ode to patriotism,[20] to take one example, shows the subtle deployment of key symbols. Alexander the Great, facing unexpectedly strong resistance in Afghanistan, seeks the solution of the puzzle from his mother and Aristotle, who ask for a sample of the men and the soil. During their first interview in a Greek palace, the Afghan leaders display the appropriate reasonableness of the conquered. Before their next interview, however, a clod of soil from Afghanistan is hidden under the carpet and upon entering the room the demeanor of the Afghan nobles changes. With sudden fury they voice their demand for equality, forcing Aristotle and Alexander's mother to the conclusion that the resistance is embedded in the Afghan soil. Only then does Pazhwāk deliver his message: a speck of the dust of his homeland will have more effect on a patriot than a thousand barrels on a fancier of wine.

By any criteria Pazhwāk's poems are fine literary achievements, but, as poetically acknowledged by him, they are pale reflections of Khalili's eloquent verses. Khalili, writing in the lofty Khorasani style, has been the undisputed *ostād* (master) of poetry in Afghanistan during the last five decades. Two volumes of his poetry have been published in Iran, and he has been thoroughly conversant with literary trends in Iran and the Arab world. His poetry ranges widely, and he has responded to the demands made on the poet by intellectuals and by the court.

His panegyrics to King Zāher were written at the same time as his description of Afghanistan as a "country sunk in debt." "Our way is difficult, the atmosphere dark and our destination too distant," was his assessment of the reformist experiments of the 1960s. Describing

---

[20]Beginning with *Hazār khom na-konad mast may-parastān rā.*

444

proverbs as hackneyed expressions of the past, he has demanded new slogans fitting novel social relations, and he has protested the injustice of a system where petty thieves are punished while powerful robbers go unheeded. Yet, the sight of Mecca has moved him into pouring verses that any Sufi master would have been proud to claim as his own. And at other junctures, he has been so stirred by the sight of beautiful women as to bemoan the failing powers of an aging body suffering from unsatiated desires.

The strand unifying these diverse symbolic ventures is Khalili's unique ability to work words into riveting images lending themselves to multiple interpretations. His poem of 1943 entitled "Dāstān-e Ja-hānsuz wa Ghazna" (The story of Jahānsuz and Ghazni)[21] provides a particularly apt example. Alā' al-Din Jahānsuz (The world-burner) acquired his epithet because he burned Ghazni in retaliation for the slaying of his brother, after the Ghaznavid emperor Bahrām Shah had granted his brother sanctuary. Revenge, a key symbol in Afghan culture, is the central theme of the poem, 'Alā' al-Din invokes the tenets of the Islamic and national codes of honor, which bind an emperor to his princes, in justification of his move on Ghazni and Bahrām Shah, stressing the might of his army rather than the justice of his action.

Khalili juxtaposes major symbols, such as mountains and palaces, hunters and lions, with such effectiveness as to totally engage the emotions of his readers. The poem can be read over and over again for its sheer literary power. Yet, it can also be read as a metaphor for Khalili's personal life, as well as for the relations between the State and the intellectuals. Khalili, whose father was killed by King Amā-nallāh, played an active role in the rebellion of 1929 and was confined to internal exile at the beginning of the new dynasty. Therefore his warning against the misuse of power and the sin of hubris can also be construed as a protest against the treatment of the intellectuals by the regime.

The warning fell on receptive ears. By the end of the 1940s, not only did Khalili become a member of the cabinet, but even Dāwi was released from jail and appointed to a succession of important governmental posts. Were these the signs of the dawn of a new working relation between the intellectuals and the royal family?

## Conformist Literature, 1950–63

The 1950s were marked by two simultaneous transitions: younger members of the royal family assumed control of the state apparatus,

[21]*Āryānā* 1/9 (1943): 55–56.

and a younger group of intellectuals took charge of the means of cultural production. During the period that Prince Dāwud was prime minister (1953–63), a large-scale influx of foreign aid transformed the central government, which became the dominant political and economic force of the society. The bureaucracy mushroomed, and the expenditure on educational and cultural institutions was significantly increased.

The managers of these expanded institutions had either been born or come to maturity during the rule of the new dynasty. Ebrāhim 'Abbāsi (b. 1926), Sayyid Faqir 'Alawi (b. 1920), Sabāh al-Din Koshkaki (b. 1933), Shafi' Rahgozar, and Sayyid Khalil (b. 1930) served as the editors of the two major dailies of the capital during the 1950s and 1960s. They were younger men who had acquired their education in Kabul University or in journalism in the West. None had ever been imprisoned and none, to my knowledge, indulged in the writing of poetry. Nor did any of them acquire eminence for the literary quality of his prose. But, through the serialization of novelettes (to the writing of which even Rahgozar was attracted) and novels, the dailies played an important role in the popularization of these genres of writing. An examination of six of these works, published as books after their appearance in the dailies, reveals a number of constant themes. *Shām-e-tārik wa sobh-e rawshan* (The dark night and the bright dawn, 1948), *Begom* (a woman's name, n.d.), *Tolu'-e sahr* (The rise of the dawn, 1949), *Forudgāh-e eshq* (The valley of love, 1952), *Hākem* (Governor, 1956), and *Shām-e gharibān* (The dusk of the exiled, n.d.) were respectively authored by Solaimān 'Ali Jāghori, 'Aziz al-Rahmān, Gholām Hosain Fa'āl, Shafi' Rahgozar, and Halim Hātefi.

The state is depicted as the agency of progressive social change, with education providing the key to the development of patriotism. With three of the authors choosing 1928 as the time of their narration, the symbol of "dawn" is explicitly linked with the raise of the new dynasty. Criticism is directed at prevailing social rather than political relations. Unequal distribution of resources is described, but the contradictions are always happily resolved. Gender relations are, however, treated much more realistically. Women, to be sure, are idealized as patriots and seekers of education, but the oppression of women by men is usually dramatically illustrated. This emphasis on gender was not accidental. Prince Dāwud and his brother Prince Na'im, both married to the sisters of the king, appeared with their unveiled wives in public in 1959, stunning the Afghans. Indeed, earlier attempts at changing gender relations had contributed to Amānallāh's downfall.

But Dāwud's perception of the shift in the public mood was sound and, except for one violent reaction, this public gesture was welcomed.

Prior to 1959, Afghan women had already made use of the new formats of literary expression. Makhfi Badakhshi, to take one example, had published a large number of her poems in the 1930s and 1940s. But in the early 1960s women acquired their own distinctive formats, such as the magazine *Mirman* (Lady). Nafisa Mobārez (b. 1931), a member of a prominent literary family, served as the first editor of the magazine and defined its direction. Roqiyya Abu Bakr (b. 1921), a member of another prominent literary family with a visible public career of her own, was probably the leading female writer of the 1950s and 1960s. Besides authoring short stories and literary essays, Abu Bakr also translated Tolstoy's *Anna Karenina*. Her translation of Tolstoy is symptomatic of the increasing awareness and response of Afghan writers to the trends in world literature. The actual number of translations from Western languages into Persian in Afghanistan has been rather small. Iranian translations, published in cheap paper editions, however, more than compensated for the shortage of reading material. Indeed, in the 1960s and 1970s, the full range of Iranian literary publications was an integral part of the Afghan intellectual scene.

## Committed and Creative Literature, 1963–78

The final judgment on the publishability of any form of writing during the last five decades has been pronounced by individuals officially in charge of censorship. There have been only two intervals during which the stringent application of this rule has been relaxed, 1951–52 and 1963–73. In these periods a lively press, calling itself "national" as opposed to "governmental," has dominated the intellectual scene. The literary quality of the writing during the first interlude was uniformly high, but the picture during the second break was more complex.

During the first period, Ghobār, Dr. 'Abd al-Rahmān Mahmudi (b. 1909), Gol Pāchā Olfat, and Faiz Muhammad Angār were given permission to publish their own newspapers. All of these individuals were liberal democrats, holding the superiority of constitutional government to dictatorship as self-evident, and they expressed themselves clearly on that central issue. The publication of these papers is a landmark in the development of writing critical editorials, social and economic essays, and reports on contemporary events.

But they also made very effective use of poetry and satire. *Watan* (Homeland), published by Ghobār, only printed a few poems during its one year of publication. A classic poem from Jāmi, narrating the story of a monster blaming his ugliness on the mirror, was probably the most poignant symbolic justification offered by the intellectuals in defense of their critical attitude toward the regime.[22] But the paper made it plain that critical discourse was not its own justification. A poem entitled "Vatanparasti-ye kādheb" (False patriotism) warned that radical phrases could be used as a mask for corruption, and demanded behavior corresponding to the stated ideals.[23]

Satire, as the following examples show, was also wielded as an instrument of criticism. "Q: Where is the place of emergence of geniuses? A: Afghanistan, of course. Only through hard work, sustained effort, and demonstrated ability do people in other places acquire reputations for soundness, the prerequisite of high office. Without scientific investigation and research the emergence of genius in such places is therefore impossible. But in our country average people are suddenly propelled to high places. This is certain evidence of their God-granted intelligence and genius. The existence of such people until the coming of the day of judgment should be a source of pride for our country and nation!"[24]

In a column entitled "Az farhang-e vatan" (From our national culture) *Watan* provided its own definition of the following and other words: "the national assemby: a large empty chamber; new laws: lost; an open session: not known to anyone; a closed session: no one should know; the duty of assembly: postponed until tomorrow; which tomorrow: the unknown future."[25] The phrases mostly rhymed in Persian, and their composition required skill in the manipulation of the words.

But the regime responded to criticism by reverting to a more authoritarian posture. Ghobār, Mahmudi, and many others of the intellectual activists were imprisoned, and the writing of conformist literature became the norm. Yet in 1963, after Dāwud had stepped down, the king, who had finally assumed charge of ruling, was ready to engage in a bolder experiment with liberalism. Censorship was relaxed and between 1963 and 1973 close to thirty "national" papers saw the light. None of these papers achieved a continuous record of

[22]*Watan* 1/10 (1951): 3.
[23]*Watan* 1/6 (1951): 2.
[24]*Watan* 1/2 (1951): 2.
[25]*Watan* 1/11 (1951): 2.

publication, the average ranging from several weeks to five years, but at any given moment a number of papers did exist.

The great variety in the formats of presentation, genres of writing, and range of key symbols makes summary treatment impossible. The impinging of politics on literature, however, can be vividly captured through the letters of two poets protesting the publication of their poems in two of these papers. Khalili as politician was judged a reactionary by the activist intellectuals, but Khalili as poet was continuously complimented through the publication of his poems in the "national" press. Khalili normally did not object, but when *Mosāwāt* (Equality) attributed a poem called "Kazebān-e khod-gharaz" (The self-serving liars), he denied authorship of the poem in a letter to another paper. The editor of *Mosāwāt*, ackowledging that Khalili did not share the politics of the paper, refused to believe Khalili's disclaimer; to convince the readers of his access to Khalili's unpublished poems, he printed a poem from Khalili's period of internal exile in which he had painted a very critical portrait of the royal family.[26]

The publication of "Bahār-e Balkh," a poem praising the spring of Balkh, in *Kārawān* (Caravan) resulted in a different type of protest. Wāsef Bākhtari's letter read: "I wrote the poem at a time when I equated art with imitation of the predecessors, repetition of their trite phrases, and borrowing of theme and language from others."[27] Alleging that *Kārawān*'s anti-progressive character was recognized by all, he claimed that publication in such a paper could only bring shame to a true intellectual.

Form, format, and meaning of discourse had become an object of intense struggle among intellectuals whose work, despite all their insistence on the unity of theory and practice, consisted of craftsmanship of words. Departure from the millenium-old established forms of poetry, not surprisingly, became a clear trend in this context. Afghan poets, following the lead of the Iranians, broke away from rhymed structure and began writing free verse.

Bāreq Shafi' (b. 1932) and Solaimān Lā'eq (b. 1930) had embarked on the new path of writing in the late 1950s and had won their literary spurs through the award of official literary prizes. Bāreq, a man without a university education, and Lā'eq, a graduate of the College of Letters, had both served as editors of literary magazines. In the 1960s,

---

[26]The poem appeared in *Mosāwāt* 2/9 (1968): 2; the commentary was published in ibid. 2/11 (1968): 2.

[27]The poem appeared in *Kārawān* 1/17 (1969): 1; the letter of protest was published in ibid. 1/27 (1969): 2.

however, they assumed the mantle of revolutionary poets and served as managing editors of *Khalq* (Masses) and *Parcham* (Banner), the organs of the Soviet-oriented leftist movement. The publication permit of *Khalq* was withdrawn within weeks, but *Parcham* was permitted publication for two years. In prose these papers followed the model of *Tudeh*, the Iranian communist party, but largely confined their publication of poetry and literary prose to the writings of Bāreq and Lā'eq.

The poetry of these two men, despite their self-image as revolutionaries, is permeated with the key symbols of Afghan culture. We can take Bāreq's poem entitled "Efrit-e ertejā" (The sorcerer of reaction) as an example. He wrote:

Oh devil
Gone are those ill-omened moments
When your dark thoughts like black stars
With hellish eyes full of sin
Were displaying themselves in the clear sky of the imagination of the masses.[28]

Lā'eq was the publisher of *Parcham* but confined his own strictly literary work in the paper to one short piece and some poems in Pashtu and Persian. For inspiration, Lā'eq drew on epic and folk poetry and stories, history, and myth. In this as well as in effective deployment of language Lā'eq's range of writings approaches the breadth of Pazhwāk's work.

Bāreq and Lā'eq were not the only poets who looked upon writing as a revolutionary activity. In its nine issues, *Sho'la-ye jāwid* (The eternal flame), a Maoist-oriented paper, alloted considerable space to poetry. Before its publication permit was withdrawn the paper published two poems from Wāsef Bākhtari, three poems from Moztareb Bākhtari, and two poems from Dr. Rahim Mahmudi, the publisher of the paper. As the publication of the paper coincided with May 1, there is an understandable emphasis on proletarian internationalism. The attempts by these three poets to engage the same theme provides an interesting test in the effective deployment of the power of the language. Wāsef Bākhtari in his poem called "Hamāsa-ye Sho'lahā" (Epic of the flames),[29] written in free verse, makes use of the opposition

[28]*Parcham* 1/5 (1968): 4.
[29]*Sho'la-ye jāwid* 1/2 (1968): 2.

between light and dark in telling his comrades that the ultimate victory will be theirs. Moztereb Bākhtari, who, along with Wāsef Bākhtari, emerged as one of the most accomplished younger poets of the 1960s, is equally agile in the use of words. Rahim Mahmudi's effort, as a result of his weaker mastery of the language, only faintly echoes the message preached by his two fellow-travellers.

Politics, however, was not the consuming passion of all poets. Some of the intellectuals felt that the production of literature was a vocation that did not need to be politically compromised or justified. *Sapidadam* (Dawn), which advertised itself as a "neutral publication," became the outlet for the publication of Afghan and foreign literature and literary criticism. The contributions of Mahmud Fārāni, a graduate of the College of Letters, are especially impressive. A contemporary of Bāreq and Lā'eq, he, too, has been a major innovator in the use of free verse; but he is the only poet of the 1960s whose treatment of themes parallels the concerns of Khalili.

If I have conveyed the impression of continuity in the language of poetry of the 1960s, it is because I have focused on the works of the best writers of the period. In general, the literary quality of the "national" papers as well as the "governmental" papers was rather poor. But there were other innovations in the use of language that are worthy of notice. Hājji Esmā'il Siāh, through the publication of his poetry in 1931, had played a major role in the continuation of the classical tradition of satirical poetry. *Tarjomān* (Interpreter), published by Dr. Rahim Nawin, became an instrument for the propagation of politically critical satire between 1968 and 1972. The paper provides rich commentary on the current events of the period.

In July of 1973 when Prince Dāwud seized political power and declared Afghanistan a republic, the boisterous press was muzzled. Censorship was imposed once again, resulting in the dominance of a dull official press. But the debates in the College of Letters continued to be lively. *Adab* (Literature), the journal of the College, has been from its inception a major forum for the discussion of literature. Bitāb, Ahmad Jāwid, Rahim Elhām (b. 1931), Neghat Sayyedi (b. 1933), and Sayyed Bahā' al-Din Majruh not only played an important role through their teaching, but also set literary standards through the writing of poetry and prose. The 1970s saw contributions by Asadallāh Habib, a novelist, Makhdum Rahim, a poet, and Gholām Ghaws Shojā'i, a philosopher and literary critic. After graduating from the College, they respectively went for further training to the Soviet Union, Iran, and the Federal Republic of Germany, and upon returning to teaching, they brought renewed emphasis on literary criticism and literary theory.

"International conferences," so-called because of the participation of foreign scholars, provided the major public forum where relatively free exchange of ideas on Afghan history and literature took place. In addition, such conferences became the meeting place for Afghan intellectuals of different generations and an occasion for the publication of books. 'Abd al-Ra'uf Binawā (1913–85), Habibi, 'Abd al-Ghafur Rawān-Farhādi (b. 1929), Reshtyā, Sedqi, 'Abd al-Hakim Tabibi, the latter four recalled from ambassadorships, were brought together with younger and older figures from Kabul University, the media, and the bureaucracy. On these occasions Rawān-Farhādi and Bahā' al-Din Majruh, as members of the intermediate generation, played a particularly important role in mediating between those older and younger than themselves, and in renewing their emphasis on the quality of creative writing.

Rawān, despite his demanding administrative and diplomatic duties, had found time for writing sermons for the radio, commentaries on current events, and translations of literary essays and a French novel. Between 1974 and 1978 he devoted full attention to intellectual pursuits. He rendered Tagore's *Gitangeli* into Persian verse, basing his translation on the Bengali, English, French, and Urdu editions of the work. The care devoted to the task and the literary quality of the language employed should rank this work among the most creative examples of translation in the Persian language. His compilation and publication of Tarzi's essays from *Serāj al-Akhbār* was also an important step in restoring the knowledge of this central Afghan figure.

Majruh's *Azhdahā-ye khodi* (Ego-monster), first published in Persian and then in Pashtu, is in my opinion the single most important literary work of the last four decades in Afghanistan. Majruh, relying on his French training in philosophy and psychology and on his profound knowledge of Afghan folklore and Sufi literature, has crafted a simultaneously beautiful and moving narrative. Through the metaphor of the journey and other culturally established symbols, Majruh warns his readers about the dangers of despotism and the evils of prejudice. In a conference in 1977 devoted to the discussion of Sayyed Jamāl al-Din Afghāni, Majruh delivered a paper entitled "The message of the Sufi of Herat to the West" and proposed holding the first conference of Occidentalists.

At the moment when some of the Western-educated Afghans were confronting through the medium of literature the cultural implications of their dual worlds of upbringing and education, the agenda was changed by politics once again. On April 27, 1978 the Khalq party seized power in a coup, and the Afghans were embroiled in a whirlwind of events. The shape of the literature of the future is being determined in the course of the struggle over the culture of today.

### Bibliography

For a general survey of the bibliographical references of the Persian literature of Afghanistan see Donald Wilber, *Annotated Bibliography of Afghanistan*, 4th ed., revised by Jamil Hanafi, Human Relations Area File Press (Washington, D.C., 1982), chap. 8: Languages and Literature, 377–439; and Keith McLachlan and William Whittaker, *A Bibliography of Afghanistan* (Cambridge, 1983), chap. 13: Language and Literature, 550–99. See also M. S. Mawlā'i, *Bargozida-ye she'r-e mo'āser-e Afghānestān* (A selection of contemporary poetry in Afghanistan; containing brief biographies with select poetry of Āyina, Elhām, Bāreq Shafi'i, Pazhwāk, Tawfiq, Khalili, Rahgozar, Sedqi, Safā, Tāleb Qandahāri, Fārāni, Lā'eq, Māyel, Nawid, and Nahmat), intr. by P. Khānlari and M. S. Mawlā'i (Tehran, 1350/1971). *Rāhnemā-ye Ketāb* 7 (Winter 1343 Š./1964): 215–61 (articles by S. Saljuqi and I. Afshār and samples of contemporary prose and poetry by Pazhwāk, Sohayl, Māyel Heravi, Khalili, Āyina, Elhām, Bāreq Shafi'i, Bitāb, Dāwi, Khalil, Rahgozar, Saljuqi, Shāyeq, Sham'riz, Sedqi, Safā, Ziā'i, Ghobār, Fārāni, Faizi, and Qārizāda). M. Schinasi, *Afghanistan at the Beginning of the Twentieth Century: Nationalism and Journalism in Afghanistan. A Study of Seraj ul-Akhbar (1911–18)* (Naples, 1979). Ch. Pahlavān, "Negāhi ba andishahā-ye ejtemā'i o farhangi-e Mahmud Tarzi," *Āyanda* 9/8–9 (1362 Š./1983): 595–601. R. Farhādi, "Afghanistan: Literature," in *Encyclopaedia Iranica*, vol. 1 (London, 1984), 564–66. *Ed.*

# 23. Modern Tajik Literature

Modern Tajik literature has developed under diverse influences. Besides the classical and modern Persian and folkloric foundations, Russia has exerted immense influence on Tajik thought and letters: first, as a result of the tsarist conquest of Central Asia, and, then, far more directly, through the Bolshevik Revolution and the Communist social and economic system that emerged from it. The Soviet era, in particular, has been decisive. It has offered Tajik writers new subject matter and modes of expression, but it has also required them to conform to ideological standards at times so narrowly interpreted as to impede true creativity.*

## Turn of the Century

At the end of the nineteenth century and the beginning of the twentieth Tajik literature was not distinguished from Persian literature and was largely beholden to its Iranian and Central Asian heritage. Traditional forms and meters predominated, and the literary language, often abstract and filled with Arabic words and constructions, was but little affected by the vernacular. As in Persia, poetry was by far the favorite medium of expression, while prose was reserved for short tales of amusement or edification, travel accounts, and, to the extent permitted, social and political theorizing. This literary conservatism was reinforced by an oppressive political and social system maintained by the amirs of Bukhara, whose capital was one of the main centers of Tajik (and Turkic) intellectual life. The rulers of the Manghit dynasty, who had occupied the throne since the middle of the eighteenth century and who preserved their political autonomy from Russia until after the Revolution of 1917, showed little sympathy for innovation in any field of endeavor and dealt summarily with all opposition. Muslim clergymen were staunch allies of the amirs in literary and cultural matters. As the keepers of the holy tradition and as interpreters of the Shari'at, they enjoyed enormous influence in a society that was largely illiterate and where, consequently, few persons had access to the diversity of opinion offered by the written word. As learned men and as teachers in the *madrasas* (traditional religious schools) and the *maktabs* (traditional schools for children at the elementary level), the

*In this chapter some allowance has been made for the more common transcription of Tajik names (e.g., Sadriddin Aini for Sadr al-Din 'Ayni).

clergy also enjoyed an almost complete monopoly over formal education and were, hence, in a unique position to influence successive generations of intellectuals. Not surprisingly, the literature patronized by the amirs and the mollas had nothing to do with political commentary and social reform; they preferred poems in praise of the dynasty, mystical pieces, and glosses on the sacred writings.[1]

The works of Ahmad Donish (= Dānesh, 1827–97) made the first major breach in the intellectual and cultural bulwark constructed by the amirs and the mollas. Donish[2] was a singular figure in Bukhara— a free-thinker (within the limits of that time and place) with a cosmopolitan range of interests, who was better acquainted with European cultural and material accomplishments than perhaps any other Bukharan of his day. Despite his reputation as a non-conformist, the amir was forced to acknowledge Donish's special gifts and employed him in various capacities. In 1857, 1869, and 1874 he sent him on official missions to St. Petersburg, where, through the intermediary of Russian society and institutions, Donish had his closest contact with Western Europe.

As a writer Donish was best known during his lifetime for his prose works, and it is upon them—a prose of ideas rather than *belles lettres*— that his reputation rests today. His most important work was *Navāder al-vaqāye'* (Rare events), which he composed in the 1870s and 1880s.[3] In a volume of over 750 manuscript pages he dealt with the most diverse topics—philosophy and morals, the structure of the state and the qualities of the ruler, the importance of industry and the liberal professions, and the family and the raising of children. It provides remarkable insights into Central Asian intellectual and social life, but it is, on the whole, somber in mood, for Donish was overwhelmed by the ignorance and backwardness he saw on all sides. He was struck

[1]General accounts of the cultural and intellectual life of Bukhara in this period are contained in Rasul Hodizoda, *Adabiyyāt-e tājik dar nima-ye dovvomi 'asr-e XIX* (Dushanbe, 1968), vol. 1, 7–126; Iosif S. Braginskii, *Ocherki iz istorii tadzhikskoi literatury* (Stalinabad, 1956), 376–418. Of enormous value are the memoirs of Sadr al-Din (Sadriddin) Aini; see below, n. 11.

[2]Recent studies of Donish's life and works are: Zarif Rajabov, *Ma'āref-parvar Ahmad-e Donish* (Dushanbe, 1964); Rasul Khadizade, *Akhmad Donish i tadzhikskaia prosvetitel'skaia literatura* (Moscow, 1968); Rasul Hādizāda, *Ahmad-e Donish* (Dushanbe, 1976); Gianroberto Scarcia, "Note su alcuni motivi della cultura tagica e su Ahmad Daniš," *Annali* (Istituto Universitario Orientale di Napoli) 11 (1961): 84–103; G. A. Ashurov and M. D. Dinorshoev, "O prosvetitel'skoi sotsial'noi filosofii Akhmada Donisha," *Izvestiia Akademii Nauk Tadzhikskoi SSR* (Otdelenie Obshchestvennykh Nauk) 3/93 (1978): 48–59.

[3]Excerpts have been published in Russian translation in Akhmad Donish, *Puteshestvie iz Bukhary v Peterburg* (Stalinabad, 1960), 125–273.

over and over by the immense gap in technology and standards of living between Europe and Central Asia. But he remained hopeful that all the ills around him could be remedied by "enlightenment," that is, by rational thought and knowledge applied sympathetically and consistently in every branch of human endeavor. He had no illusions about the enormity of the task that faced would-be reformers, for he discerned fundamental structural differences between the Eastern and the Western mentality which would impede the adoption of European ideas and methods in Central Asia. To overcome these obstacles he looked to a strong-willed but enlightened ruler to force Central Asia into the modern world. In the hope that the amirs of Bukhara would assume the task he addressed his work to them.[4] But he became thoroughly disillusioned by their failure to rise above the backwardness around them, and in his later years he wrote a bitter condemnation of the Manghit dynasty in *Tarjama-ye hāl-e amirāni-e Bokhārā-ye sharif* (Biographies of the amirs of noble Bukhara), which, out of prudence, he circulated only among close friends.[5]

Not the least of Donish's contributions to the revival of Tajik intellectual life was his creation of a small circle of younger writers who shared his enlightened views and disseminated them among their own pupils. Perhaps the most talented of Donish's disciples was the poet Shams al-Din (Shamsiddin) Makhdum, better known as Shāhin (1859–94).[6] He was skilled in all the traditional forms and meters of poetry, which he turned into vehicles for advanced ideas. His *ghazals* are remarkable examples of subtle political commentary. He also composed a version of *Laylā and Majnun,* in which the traditional love story was interwoven with praise for learning. Another of Donish's followers was Mohammad Seddiq Hayrat (1878–1902),[7] who wrote lyrical poetry distinguished by simplicity of language and sincerity of feeling. Yet another disciple, Tāshkhwāja (Toshkhoja) Asiri (1864–1915),[8] combined an admiration for traditional poetic expression in

[4]Donish concerns himself directly with these questions in his so-called "Political Tract," which was an autonomous part of *Navāder al-vaqāye*; ibid., 33–122. The work is analyzed in Zarif Radzhabov, O *"Politicheskom traktate" Akhmada Donisha* (Dushanbe, 1976).

[5]Zarif Radzhabov, *Iz istorii obshchestvenno-politicheskoi mysli tadzhikskogo naroda vo vtoroi polovine XIX i v nachale XX vv.* (Stalinabad, 1957), 157–80; Rajabov, *Ma'āref-parvar,* 127–71. See also the introduction to the edition by I. A. Najafova (ed.), *Traktat Akhmada Donisha "Istoriia mangitskoi dinastii"* (Dushanbe, 1967).

[6]Radzhabov, *Iz istorii obshchestvenno-politicheskoi mysli,* 206–18.

[7]Relatively little has been written about Hayrat. A sympathetic appreciation of his character and work may be found in S. Aini, *Sobranie sochinenii* (Moscow, 1974), vol. 5, 168–80.

[8]Z. Radzhabov, *Poet-prosvetitel' tadzhikskogo naroda—Asiri* (Dushanbe, 1974), 27–54.

the style of Bidel with a defense of secular learning. In such works as the *mathnavi, Khetāb ba mosalmān* (Appeal to Muslims), he followed Donish's example of criticizing the mollas for their rejection of everything that was new.

In the first two decades of the twentieth century Tajik writers were attracted to the growing intellectual ferment among the Muslim peoples throughout the Russian Empire. From the Crimea and the Caucasus eastward a consciousness of religious and cultural individuality combined with an impatience with material backwardness had set in motion a strong movement for school reform and general public "enlightenment" among Tatar, Azerbaijani, Uzbek, and other Turkic intellectuals. Known as Jadidism, from the emphasis placed upon new methods of education, this movement also attracted adherents among Tajik intellectuals who moved in the same circles as Uzbeks and Tatars in Bukhara, Samarkand, and other cities.[9] The fact that the Jadids, as these reformers came to be known, were often Pan-Turks did not deter Tajiks from joining in their activities, for at this period a distinct Tajik national consciousness did not exist. Many Tajik writers were, in fact, bilingual, composing in Uzbek as well as in their own language. Any ethnic rivalry that might have existed among Central Asian intellectuals was assuaged by the supra-national character of Jadidism, which expressed itself in strong Pan-Islamic sentiments. Eager to disseminate their ideas as widely as possible, the Turkic Jadids created a vigorous newspaper press. Their initiative had important consequences for Tajik intellectual and literary life, for it led to the founding of the Tajik-language press. Although the Jadid newspapers in Central Asia appeared mainly in Uzbek, several of them such as *Samarkand* (1913, Samarkand) and *Ā'ina* (*Oina*, The Mirror [Samarkand, 1913–15]) carried articles and poetry in Tajik. *Bokhārā-ye sharif* (Noble Bukhara [Bukhara, 1912–13]) was the principal Tajik newspaper.[10]

The outstanding Tajik representative of the Jadid movement was Sadriddin Aini (1878–1954).[11] He was to achieve his greatest fame

[9]Radzhabov, *Iz istorii obshchestvenno-politicheskoi mysli*, 383–436; Braginskii, *Ocherki iz istorii tadzhikskoi literatury*, 394–409; Hélène Carrère d'Encausse, *Réforme et révolution chez les musulmans de l'empire russe. Bukhara 1867–1924* (Paris, 1966), 150–67.

[10]Alexandre Bennigsen and Chantal Lemercier-Quelquejay, *La presse et le mouvement national chez les musulmans de Russie avant 1920* (Paris and The Hague, 1964), 156–69.

[11]The literature on Aini is extensive. Among the newer general studies are: Iosif Braginskii, *Sadriddin Aini*, 2nd enlarged edition (Moscow, 1978), and Jiří Bečka, *Sadriddin Ayni, Father of Modern Tajik Culture* (Naples, 1980). The standard Tajik edition of Aini's works is *Kulliyāt*, 15 vols. (Stalinabad-Dushanbe, 1958–77). A selection has appeared in Russian: *Sobranie sochinenii*, 6 vols. (Moscow, 1971–75). The best sources on

after 1917 as the pioneer of Soviet Tajik prose, but his earlier writings had already marked a significant turn away from traditional intellectual and literary pursuits. He received his formal education at several *madrasas* in Bukhara in the 1890s. None offered him the intellectual stimulation he sought; their rigid curricula, dominated by conservative religious ideals, and their emphasis upon rote learning repelled him. He resorted, instead, to self-education. He and a few fellow students met in secret to study "secular" subjects—history and literature—and to read newspapers, an activity forbidden by the amir. His patron, Sharifjān Makhdum, introduced him to the literary salon held regularly in his home, where leading intellectuals, including Donish, gathered to discuss literature and the important issues of the day. At the same time, Aini read avidly, especially in Persian and Central Asian literatures, which were the dominant influences on his own creativity before 1917. He also became acquainted with the works of Donish. *Rare Events,* in particular, was a revelation to him. Donish's faith in progress and his reliance on reason and knowledge as the means of achieving it transformed him, by his own account, into an "enlightener," and advocate of the "new method" schools of the Jadids.

If Aini's vocation was that of teacher, his avocation was poetry.[12] In effect, he had been raised on poetry from childhood when his father read the classics and recited folktales in verse to him. His mature reading focused on Hāfez, Jāmi, Navā'i, Fozuli, and Bidel, and he honed his critical sense and his skill in versification in long discussions with his friend, the poet Hayrat. About 1895 Aini began to write poetry of his own. Reticent, he used various pseudonyms and shared his thoughts only with Hayrat. Some of his pieces were love poems written in the classical manner, while others were conventional word games and imitations of the *ghazals* of Bidel.[13] But others were melancholy; they expressed deep loneliness and a pervasive sense of the

---

Aini's life and ideas are his own writings. The first complete edition of his memoirs was *Yāddāshthā,* 4 vols. (Stalinabad, 1949–54). A good edition in one volume, introduced and edited with a glossary of words not familiar to Persian readers by Sa'idi Sirjāni was published in Tehran, 1984. There have been numerous Russian editions, usually under the title, *Bukhara.* A recent edition is in S. Aini, *Sobranie sochinenii,* vols. 4 and 5 (Moscow, 1974). Aini also wrote a short autobiography, *Mokhtasar-e tarjema-ye hāl-e khodam.* The Russian version is entitled, *O moei zhizni;* see S. Aini, *Sobranie sochinenii* (Moscow, 1971), vol. 1, 35–120. There is also an English version: *Pages from My Own Story* (Moscow, 1958).

[12]On Aini's early poetry, see Khamid Niiazov, *Put' Sadriddina Aini—poeta* (Moscow, 1965), 34–47.

[13]The influence of Bidel on Tajik writers remained strong during this period. See Hodizoda, *Adabiyyāt-e tājik dar nima-ye dovvom-e 'asr-e* xix, 126–36.

injustice of life. Occasionally, Aini turned to satire and parody, which were much in vogue among Central Asian writers of the time as instruments of social commentary. Whatever their subject, all these poems displayed a freshness of conception and a mastery of the *'aruz*. Aini's reputation as a talented poet grew, and his work began to be included in anthologies.

After 1905 Aini became increasingly absorbed in social issues, a preoccupation that began to be reflected in his poetry.[14] Until the Bolshevik Revolution the guiding principles of both his teaching and his writing were Islam (in the purified form advocated by Donish) and Jadidism. His commitment to social and religious reform was strengthened by contact with the new currents of thought that were emerging throughout the Muslim Middle East. He became a faithful reader of the Muslim press—the classic Jadid newspaper, *Tarjomān* (Terjüman), which had been published in the Crimea since 1883, the bitingly satirical *Molla Nasr al-Din* (Nasreddin) of Jalil Mohammadqolizāda (Mamedkulizade), which began publication in Tiflis in 1906, and various newspapers from Egypt and India. He took the initiative in founding a new-method school in Bukhara for Tajik children in 1908 and composed a textbook for it the following year, *Tahdhib al-sibyān* (The education of children). It contained edifying stories and poems which were fully in keeping with literary tradition and Islamic teachings, but they were also intended to instill in their young readers a special reverence for school as a "holy place" where "salvation" from such worldly evils as ignorance might be found.

During this time Aini continued to write poems in both Tajik and Uzbek on traditional themes, but increasingly their subject matter revealed his new concern with problems of education and culture. Sometimes sadness showed through as the poet meditated on human irrationality and ignorance. In "Fāje'a-ye shi'a va sonni" (The tragedy of Shi'ites and Sunnites), a poem written in 1910 shortly after a bloody clash between Sunnites and Shi'ites in Bukhara, he expressed horror at the killing of Muslim by Muslim in the name of faith.[15] In "Hasrat" (Grief, 1913), a long poem in Uzbek, he lamented the lack of modern educational opportunities for the peoples of Central Asia and warned that if reforms were delayed much longer Turkestan would be transformed into a "graveyard." These and other poems preserved traditional forms, but they showed a tendency toward a simpler, more

---

[14]Niiazov, *Put' Sadriddina Aini*, 48–62.
[15]Ibid., 56–59.

colloquial diction. Many were first published in *Bokhāra-ye sharif* and *Ā'ina*.

World War I, though physically far removed from Central Asia, nonetheless upset the normal pattern of existence of many Bukharan intellectuals. For Aini, these were years spent in search of refuge from the agents of the amir, who had never ceased to equate independent thought with sedition. In spite of the danger, Aini continued to work on behalf of Jadid cultural causes. At the beginning of 1917 he published a second edition of his school textbook. He included new material, notably a story written in the form of letters between a young man far from home and his family. It was Aini's first important work of realistic prose, the genre upon which his literary reputation would mainly rest. His characters are living beings who reveal their individuality through the distinctive way in which they express thoughts and emotions.

## The Impact of the Russian Revolution

The Russian Revolution of 1917 and the Soviet regime that followed set the development of Tajik literature on a new course.[16] The recognition of a distinct Tajik political and ethnic nation separated the Tajiks from other Central Asians, thereby providing a framework within which the "national" talent could be concentrated (the Autonomous Tajik Soviet Socialist Republic was established in 1924 and the Union Republic, comprising the eastern part of the old Amirate of Bukhara and the Pamir region, in 1929). A new Tajik literary language, based upon classical Persian, but drawing heavily upon the grammatical patterns and vocabulary of the vernacular, was gradually created. The economic and social goals of the new regime, embodied in five-year plans of rapid industrialization and the collectivization of agriculture and the eradication of "obsolete" customs and mentalities, offered writers new artistic opportunities, but imposed upon them new functions and responsibilities. Soviet Russian literature increasingly served as a model for the nascent Soviet Tajik literature in both content and form.

During the 1920s the efforts of Communist ideologists to mobilize Tajik (and other Central Asian) writers for the building of a "new life"

[16]Useful general surveys of Soviet Tajik literature are: *Ocherk istorii tadzhikskoi sovetskoi literatury* (Moscow, 1961), 28–220, and Jiří Bečka, "Tajik Literature from the 16th Century to the Present," in Jan Rypka, et al., *History of Iranian Literature* (Dordrecht, Holland, 1968), 546–605.

were frustrated in part by serious political differences between Turkic and Tajik intellectuals. Supporters of Pan-Turkic and Pan-Islamic ideas, many of them adherents of Jadidism, vigorously opposed the new political system and cultural norms and, in an effort to maintain the "unity" of "Turkic Central Asia," they denied the existence of a separate Tajik nation. Sadriddin Aini and other Tajik writers just as vigorously defended the ethnic individuality of their people. Tajik and other Central Asian writers also disagreed on problems of literary creativity. At one extreme were those who clung to tradition in form and subject matter and who rejected innovations in language. At the other extreme were the adherents of the so-called proletarian culture, who demanded that literature serve the practical needs of society and who denied the importance of form and artistic inspiration. To promote their ideas the latter organized the Association of Proletarian Writers of Tajikistan in 1930. The party leadership viewed these disputes with mounting concern. Yet, despite its attempts to bring "order" to literary life, the 1920s remained a period of wide-ranging creative debate and experimentation that Tajik writers would not experience again. With the formal establishment of the Union of Tajik Writers in 1933 the party at last acquired an instrument capable of directing all aspects of literary production. The Union brought out the first Tajik literary review, *Barāye adabiyyāt-e sosyālisti* (For a socialist literature, 1932–37), a title which clearly expressed the goals of the Union.[17] At the first congress of Soviet writers in Moscow in 1934 the poet Abu'l-Qāsem Lāhuti expressed solidarity with the aims of the "new literature" on behalf of the writers' organization of Tajikistan. Overflowing in his praise of the new social and economic order, he urged his fellow delegates to create "works worthy of socialism."[18]

The Union of Writers was responsible for promoting the ideological and esthetic principles (they were never separate) of socialist realism, which were crucial in determining an author's choice of subject and his handling of plot and character. First and foremost the writer had to remember that he could never be neutral toward his subject. Rather, he was expected to depict social life and the individual personality in accordance with certain well-defined criteria: he must remain close to the life of the working masses; he must provide a correct interpretation of current party policy; and he must follow party directives in

[17]From 1938 to 1964 the review was entitled *Sharq-e sorkh* (The red east) and since 1964 *Sadā-ye sharq* (Voice of the east).

[18]B. Nikitine, "La littérature des Musulmans en U.R.S.S.," *Revue des études islamiques* 3 (1934): 349–54.

his creative activity (*partiiaviiat,* or in Russian, *partiinost'* ).[19] Observance of these guidelines would enable the writer to fulfill his social responsibilities. He could thus demonstrate how social change took place and why it must lead inevitably to the creation of a better, communist society, and he could separate the "progressive forces" from all their opponents, heaping praise on the former and excoriating the latter. Finally, these guidelines would remind the writer that his art was not merely a reflection of reality but was a powerful instrument for changing that reality.

## The New Poetry

For Tajik poetry as for Tajik literature in general, the 1920s were a time of transition. The creative theories and artistic values of the leading poets had been formed in the pre-1917 era, and they adjusted to the new circumstances with varying degrees of success. For many, the revolution was simply a continuation of the reform movements of the Jadids and of other enlightened opponents of despotism. Unable to grasp the all-encompassing nature of the political and economic changes that were taking hold in Central Asia, they remained faithful to traditional lyricism based on classical form and meter and devoid of social aims. Typical of the unassimilated was Mohammad Zafar Khān Jowhari (Javhari, 1860–1945).[20] An admirer of Bidel, he remained a lyric poet, imbuing his work with abstract images and a flowing, ornate language suffused with Arabic words. Not surprisingly, he published little after the installation of the new literary order. Payrow (Pairav) Solaymāni (1899–1933),[21] a younger poet of promise, succeeded where Javhari had failed. From the traditional, lyrical poetry he wrote early in his career, he turned to socially relevant themes, as in "Shokufa-ye 'Erfān" (The blossom of knowledge, 1926), and to new techniques. Although he respected the canons of the '*aruz,* he experimented boldly with the free verse of Mayakovsky and introduced the dialogue of ordinary speech into his work.

Two major figures of Soviet Tajik literature warmly embraced the new social poetry. Even before the Bolsheviks had triumphed in Bukhara Sadriddin Aini had written several poems to rally support for

[19]For a recent discussion of *partiiaviiat,* see Atakahān Saifollāev, '*Aqidahā-ye adabi-e Lenin va adabiyyāt-e tājik* (Dushanbe, 1973).

[20]*Ocherk istorii tadzhikskoi sovetskoi literatury,* 44–45.

[21]Ibid., 48–53; Sohib Tabarov, "Payrow—hamzamān-e mā," *Sadā-ye sharq* 3 (1982): 101–109.

the revolution.[22] His "Sorud-e Azādi" (Hymn of freedom, 1918), which was based on "La Marseillaise," was completely new for Tajik poetry; its content and its rhythm were radical departures from tradition. Aini composed two other poems in 1918 in the same vein, one harsh and uncompromising and dedicated to his brother who had been executed by the amir's men, and the other a hymn of praise to the revolution, "Be sharaf-e enqelāb-e Oktobr" (To the glorious revolution of October). In the 1920s and later, Aini continued to write an occasional poem, usually on a utilitarian theme such as the benefits of collectivist agriculture, but his major contributions to the development of Tajik literature were henceforth to be in prose.

One of the most consistent practitioners of the "new poetry" throughout his long career was Abu'l-Qāsem Lāhuti (1887–1957), the first major Soviet Tajik poet.[23] A Persian revolutionary, born in Kermānshāh in western Iran, and a leading poet of the Constitution Period (1906–11), Lāhuti fled to the Soviet Union after the failure of an uprising led by him in Tabriz in 1922. He finally settled in Dushanbe (from 1929 to 1961, Stalinabad) in 1925. Much of his inspiration came from the radical economic and social transformation of Tajik and Soviet society. In sometimes strident verse he celebrated the successes of socialist construction, the struggles against the "nationalists" (or *basmachi,* a general term of opprobrium for the opponents of the new order), and the spread of literacy. But at the same time he composed *ghazal*s of exquisite delicacy. His singular contribution to Tajik poetry was undoubtedly the adaptation of classical genres and meters to the requirements of socialist realism. In order to deal effectively with the new subject matter of poetry Lāhuti reworked traditional epic genres such as the *dāstān* into poems with contemporary, realistic themes. A master of the *ghazal, robā'i,* and *mokhammas* and of all the meters of the *'aruz,* he led the way in elaborating new stanzaic structures and in diversifying the rhyme scheme. He used meters that were not part of the classical tradition, such as syllabic verse, and through his translation of Shakespeare's *Othello* he introduced blank verse into Tajik poetry. A good example of his technique is the *dāstān, Tāj va bayraq* (The crown and the banner, 1935). An epic poem about socialist construc-

---

[22]On Aini's poetry written during the Civil War and in subsequent decades, see Niiazov, 70–124. On the treatment of the revolution in Bukhara in Aini's works in general, see Namāz Hotamov, *En'ekās-e revoliusiya-e khalqi-e sovieti-ye Bokhārā dar asarhā-ye Sadriddin Aini* (Dushanbe, 1980).

[23]On Lāhuti, see the introduction by Zāya (Zoia) Osmanova to A. Lakhuti, *Izbrannoe* (Moscow, 1959), and *Ocherk istorii tadzhikskoi sovetskoi literatury,* 274–336. The standard edition is Abu'l Qāsem Lāhuti, *Kolliyyāt,* 6 vols. (Stalinabad-Dushanbe, 1960–63).

tion in agriculture, it describes the competition between work brigades on a kolkhoz in terms of the monumental battles depicted in the old legends, but Lāhuti conceived of it as a "parallel" (*nazira*) to the *Shāh-nāma* and used the meter of the latter.

A new generation of poets, whose intellectual and artistic values had been formed after the revolution, came to the fore in the late 1930s. They adhered faithfully to the canons of civic poetry, drawing upon the fulfillment of economic plans and foreign policy objectives for their themes and writing in a language that was close to the vernacular and accessible to a mass audience. Their poems extolled the exploits of the peasant and worker, who, as the builders of the new Communist economic and social order, were treated in heroic terms. Among other pervasive themes were the contrast between the backward and oppressive past and the bright future, the eradication of old mentalities, and the emancipation of women. No event was too small—the completion of a bridge or prize day at a village school—to be considered a fitting subject for versification. All were occasions for meditating on the dramatic changes taking place in the lives of ordinary Tajiks.

The leading poet of this generation was Mirzā Tursunzāda (1911–77).[24] His best work combined a strong attachment to traditional form and meter with socially conscious subject matter. He admired the music and color of classical Persian verse, as is evident in longer poems written in the late 1930s, and his style was greatly influenced by the concision and directness of folk poetry, of which he was a passionate collector. But the majority of his poems dealt with contemporary themes. For example, his first major work, *Khazān va bahār* (Autumn and spring, 1937), contrasted the hard life of the peasantry under the old regime with the self-fulfillment assured them by the kolkhoz. In this and numerous other works Tursunzāda took up the challenge of the party to create the new, positive hero of collectivist society and the new woman, who rejected her traditional passive role in society and became a leader in production and community life.

During World War II Tursunzāda and his fellow poets of several generations joined together in a common effort to mobilize the home front psychologically for the war of survival against Nazi Germany.

---

[24]Iurii Babaev, *Mirzo Tursun-zade. Kratkii ocherk zhizni i tvorchestva* (Stalinabad, 1961); Iu. Babaev, *Pevets solnechnykh vershin* (Dushanbe, 1978). Tursunzāda's most important works have appeared in Russian translation in *Izbrannye proizvedeniia*, 2 vols. (Moscow, 1971). The most recent selection in Tajik is Mirzā Tursunzāda, *Asar-e montakhab*, 2 vols. (Dushanbe, 1981). There is also a bilingual Russian-English selection of his poetry: Mirzo Tursun-zadeh, *My Day and Age* (Moscow, 1977).

Much of the resulting poetry excelled in militancy, but few pieces survived the war artistically. Tursunzāda himself composed tirelessly on the theme of the brotherhood of Soviet peoples as in the *mathnavi*, *Pesar-e vatan* (Son of the fatherland, 1942). Aini contributed "Mārsh-e enteqām" (The march of vengeance, 1941), which rendered the hard beat of marching columns of men by short, resounding rhythms. Typical of Lāhuti's numerous works were the militant *Dāstān-e ghalaba-ye Tanya* (The story of Tanya's victory, 1942), about a young partisan executed by the enemy, and the *ghazal* "Be modāfa'a-ye Leningrad" (To the defense of Leningrad, 1942), which conveyed the nobility of patriotism and sacrifice in more personal tones.

In a period not distinguished by literary innovation the work of Mirsa'id Mirshakār (b. 1912), who was to become a leading poet after the war, stands out.[25] Many of his shorter pieces, like "Qasam-e Teshabāi" (Teshabāi's oath, 1942), which praised the heroism of the Tajik soldier and his Russian brothers in defense of their Soviet homeland, are indistinguishable from a myriad of similar poems by others. His finest work draws upon the folklore and ordinary life of his native Pamir region. The *dāstān*, *Ādamāni az bām-e jahān* (Men from the roof of the world, 1943), is an extraordinarily moving portrait of the Tajik miner, and *Qeshlāq-e telā'i (tilloi)* (The golden village, 1940; revised version 1944) fused legend and contemporary social change. Using the classical meters Mirshakār retold the story of villagers who set out in search of the legendary "Happy Land" and who, after many hardships, returned home to discover that the happy land was in fact their native village, which in their absence had been transformed into a prosperous, free community under the new Soviet system.

In the decade after the end of the war utilitarian themes continued to predominate, but the relative relaxation of the war years gave way to close ideological scrutiny of literary production. Writers found it prudent to conform to the directives of Andrei Zhdanov, the chief cultural theoretician of the Soviet Communist Party, and his successors, who elaborated an extreme version of socialist realism. Even Lāhuti, who had done yeoman service for the regime, was taken to task when he failed to observe the new rules. The particular object of official displeasure was his long poem about Lenin's sojourn in Razliv in 1917, *Pari-ye bakht* (The fairy of happiness, 1948). Its theme was certainly acceptable, but its form and images were judged to be too "allegorical" and "archaic" because they were "beholden" to classical

---

[25]*Ocherk istorii tadzhikskoi sovetskoi literatury*, 421–58.

Persian poetics. The majority of authors, however, stayed safely within approved guidelines, celebrating the accomplishments of industry and agriculture and creating a genre that might be called "production poetry."

Mirzā Tursunzāda wrote of these things, too, but his was the more serene style of the epic. Much of his work dealt with the liberation movements of the peoples of Asia and Africa and were intended to serve the interests of Soviet foreign policy. Typical of this output were *Qessa-ye Hendustān* (The ballad of India, 1947), a salute to India's independence combined with a denunciation of "Western imperialism," and *Dokhtar-e muqaddas* (The holy girl, 1951), which was dedicated to the emancipation of Indian women.

A work of a different order written during the same period is Tursunzāda's masterpiece, *Hasan-e arābakash* (Hasan the cart-driver, 1954). It portrays the transformation of Tajikistan in the 1920s and 1930s through the experiences of Hasan and his sweetheart, Sadaf. Hasan has had to adjust his way of life to rapidly changing social and economic conditions. Reluctantly, he realizes that his horse and cart must make way for modern means of transport, and he learns to be a truck-driver. His decision symbolizes the adjustment that every Tajik had to make as he confronted an increasingly unfamiliar world. In this modest way, then, Hasan was no less a new man or positive hero than the ubiquitous kolkhoz leader and party activist. Sadaf is clearly the new woman, for her ambition is to become a teacher and spread learning among those most in need, but Tursunzāda avoids stridency in depicting her integration into the new society. In composition Tursunzāda adhered closely to the classical tradition of Tajik-Persian poetry—the *'aruz* meter and the *mathnavi* form. A critical and ideological success, *Hasan-e arābakash* was instrumental in establishing the *dāstān* as a major genre of Soviet Tajik poetry.[26]

## The New Prose

Prose during the 1920s and 1930s underwent changes similar to those of poetry. Most striking perhaps was the transition from the lyricism characteristic of classical storytelling and folktales to a realistic, at times pedestrian, treatment of plot and character. Just as poets, so were prose writers expected to promote economic and social projects.

---

[26]Tursunzāda's contribution to the development of the *dāstān* is discussed by Jiří Bečka, "The Tajik Soviet Doston and Mirzo Tursunzoda," *Archív Orientální*, 44 (1976): 213–39.

Essential to their success and to the development of a realistic prose was the creation of a suitable literary language. Writers strove to bring the language of fiction close to that of the vernacular by emphasizing simplicity and clarity of expression. The object was to make literature (that is, the ideas it purveyed) accessible to the greatest number of people.

The dominant figure of Tajik prose during this period was Sadriddin Aini. His contributions to the development of the modern Tajik literary language and prose style were decisive. The three novels he published between 1924 and 1934 document the stages of development of socialist realism and clearly establish him as the founder of Tajik realist prose.[27]

Aini's *Ādina yā sargozasht-e Tājiki kambaghal* (Ādina, or the adventures of a poor Tajik, 1924), a short novel about the mountain peasants of eastern Bukhara and the changes brought about in their traditional way of life by the revolution, illustrates the transition from older prose techniques to the new. Many features of traditional prose—the loose construction, the accumulation of casual incidents, the abundance of poetic quotations, and the idealized pair of lovers (Ādina and Golbibi)—remain. Yet, *Ādina* was unlike anything that had appeared before in Tajik prose: the main characters were poor peasants, the past was recent and unheroic, and the images and style were down-to-earth.[28]

In *Dākhunda* (Dākhunda, 1928), the first full-length Tajik novel, the positive hero made his appearance in Tajik fiction.[29] Yādgār, the main character, was a poor peasant, but unlike the more conventionally crafted Ādina, who accepted fate passively, he struggled to reshape the world in accordance with Communist values. Artistically, Yādgār is a more successful creation than Ādina. The latter was a static figure, whereas the former evolves from a submissive mountaineer concerned only with obtaining his share of life's good things into a self-conscious revolutionary intent upon improving the life of his community. But this is no five-year-plan novel written according to some ideological formula. Tradition retains its hold on Aini as he introduces numerous

[27]For general studies on Aini's prose, see: Abdukarim Rakhmatullaev, *Proza Aini* (Dushanbe, 1970); Iosif Braginskii, *Problemy tvorchestva Sadriddina Aini* (Dushanbe, 1974), 68–90; and S. Halimov, *Sadriddin Aini va ba'zi mas'alahā-ye enkeshāf-e zabān-e adabiye tājik* (Dushanbe, 1974).

[28]Aini's language and style are analyzed by Kh. Hosaynov, *Zabān va oslub-e "Ādina"-ye ostād Aini* (Dushanbe, 1973).

[29]A. Saifollāev, *Romān-e ostād Sadriddin Aini "Dākhunda"* (Dushanbe, 1966) is a comprehensive discussion of themes and characters.

digressions and meditations that betray his earlier didactic impulses, and his portrayal of life in the village is a masterpiece of affectionate details.

*Gholāmān* (The slaves, 1934) chronicles the life of Tajik peasants from the early nineteenth century to the triumph of the kolkhoz in the 1930s.[30] Perhaps Aini's finest novel and certainly the major work of Tajik fiction before World War II, it combines his deep knowledge of Tajik history and keen understanding of Tajik rural life with continued faith in the new economic order as the key to prosperity and social justice. It also brings Aini's art closer to the ideals of socialist realism. He contrasts the individualistic labor of the old society, which brought neither material rewards nor spiritual satisfaction, with the collective labor of the new, which, though often hard, ennobled man. Here, too, the "new man" of Soviet society reaches maturity in the persons of the kolkhoz member, Hasan Ergashev, the son of slaves, and Fatima, a Komsomol member and a tractor driver. Their superior moral and social qualities and optimistic view of life, which were the products of a new conception of work, stamp them as the people of the future. But they are not merely embodiments of an idea. In Aini's hands, they are creatures of flesh and blood.

Aini also drew upon the Tajik past and his own recollections for his two other major prose works. The short novel, *Marg-e sudkhor* (The usurer's death, 1937),[31] a tale of miserliness and hypocrisy set against the background of Bukharan society of the turn of the century, provides a new dimension to Aini's creativity—psychological depth. His memoirs,[32] which brought the story of his life down to the first years of the twentieth century, are in effect a rich panorama of Central Asian life in the traditional form of Tajik prose—a series of short stories and sketches, each capable of standing alone. The method is realist, but not necessarily socialist, and the new man is Aini himself, who overcomes hardships and injustice through inner strength drawn from his native heritage.

In spite of Aini's example, short fiction predominated until the end of World War II. Influenced by the didacticism and concision of the

---

[30]*Tā'rikh-e adabiyyāt-e soveti-ye tājik*, vol. 2: L. N. Demidchik, *Nasr-e sālhā-ye 30* (Dushanbe, 1978): 65–128.

[31]Ibid., 136–49. N. Ma'sumi, *Ocherkho oid ba enkeshāf-e zabān-e tājik* (Stalinabad, 1959) is a detailed analysis of Aini's contribution to the creation of the modern Tajik literary language in the novel. The influence of traditional Persian prose on Aini and his attention to historical detail are discussed in Jiří Bečka, "Tradition in *Margi sudxur*, the Novel by Sadriddin Ayni," *Archív Orientální* 35 (1967): 352–71.

[32] See n. 11.

traditional *hekāya*, the authors of short stories and sketches concentrated on the contemporary problems of Tajik society, using loosely constructed plots and stereotyped characters. In depicting workers and peasants building the new society and overcoming class enemies, authors were satisfied with externals and ignored inner feelings and motivations. The war simply exacerbated these shortcomings. Although it offered new opportunities for original work and although the regime, desperate for popular support, allowed Tajik (and other Central Asian) writers to celebrate the deeds of national heroes of the past, short fiction continued to serve limited, if crucial, ends—to arouse and sustain a common Soviet patriotism and to exhort the populace to all manner of material sacrifices.[33] The war produced no major accomplishment in Tajik prose.

The novel came into its own after the war, but, in the first decade or so of peace, writers generally conformed to the current precepts of socialist realism. Plot and character continued to be subordinated to immediate civic purposes, often with unfortunate artistic consequences. The main themes of the novel—the heroic defense of the Soviet fatherland by all its peoples, the reconstruction and strengthening of the socialist economy, and the victorious revolutionary and working-class movement—amply suggest what the function of the novelist was supposed to be. Since "good" had to triumph over "evil" and the "new" over the "old," an author's work often assumed the form of a documentary or a sociological treatise. Plots were schematic, and conflicts were resolved in a facile manner. Character development was generally rudimentary. Heroes and villains were sharply delineated. The former came from the working classes and became leaders in their particular branch of production or moved on to important managerial or party responsibilities. The positive hero, about whom many volumes had been (and would be) written,[34] now made his appearance full-blown. Of the many qualities he had to possess, one was essential—he must work within the guidelines set by the party; individual initiative that ignored direction from above, however well motivated, was frowned upon. He also had to show complete devotion to the tasks of building socialism, and he had to work with the masses and grow with them, without, however, forgetting that his primary responsibility

[33]Jalāl Sharifov, *En'ekās-e jang-e bozorg-e vatani dar nasr-e tājik* (Dushanbe, 1981), 8–41.

[34]A comprehensive discussion of the question is Zoia Osmanova, *Khudozhestvennaia kontseptsiia lichnosti v literaturakh Sovetskogo Vostoka (traditsiia i sovremennost')* (Moscow, 1972).

469

was to lead. Finally, he had to be a model of self-discipline, lest personal feelings and desires interfere with the accomplishment of his mission. He was almost always a product of Soviet institutions or party influences, and while he might occasionally be allowed to falter, he never failed to triumph in the end. Although this "new man" was by no means unattractive (one is reminded of the stock hero of many a Western movie), his adherence to a strict, almost puritanical, code of behavior made him something less than flesh and blood. The villains, too, were often no less stilted. Like the heroes, they were composite figures embodying a particular idea or representing an entire social class. They were invariably drawn from all those groups that stood for pre-Soviet values—landowners, old village leaders, nationalists, the Muslim clergy, and anyone associated with Western capitalism or espousing Western intellectual values. Rarely did any of these people exhibit saving graces.

The works of three novelists—Sātim Ulughzāda (b. 1911), Jalāl Ekrāmi (b. 1909), and Rahim Jalil (b. 1909)—are representative of the period.

Sātim Ulughzāda's first important prose work was the short novel, *Yārān-e bā kemmat* (Noble friends, 1947), which described the faithfulness of Tajik wives to their husbands at the front during the war. It is the story of Zaynab, who remarries when she learns that her husband has been killed. But when she hears that he has survived and is a cripple, she returns to him and restores his faith that he can once again contribute to society. The author's exploration of the psychological motivations of his main characters raises this novel somewhat above the ordinary. Although only partially successful, this experiment was a sign of the new directions that the Tajik novel would eventually take. But for the time being, Ulughzāda stuck to proven formulas. His *Now ābād* (The new land, 1953) is a typical "production novel." It covers all the familiar themes of life on the kolkhoz—the introduction of new farming methods, changes for the better in the status of formerly dispossessed classes, the all-pervasive contest between the old and the new, and the inspired leadership of party activists. The plot revolves around the struggle between, on the one hand, the autocratic heads of two kolkhozes, who resist their merger, despite the economic advantages, because of the loss of power this action would entail, and, on the other, the secretary of the kolkhoz party organization, the hero of the novel, who has dedicated his life to the common good. The conflict, not surprisingly, is resolved in favor of the latter, for, as the author makes clear from the beginning, he

470

was "in step with history."[35] In the autobiographical *Sobh-e javāni-ye mā* (The dawn of our youth, 1954) the leitmotiv is the transformation of whole communities and individual psyches brought about by revolutionary struggle. A panorama of Tajik rural life, Ulughzāda's favorite theme, the novel is composed of a series of short stories held together by the main character, Sobir. Through the eyes of this young peasant we witness the destruction of the old society by revolution and civil war, and the emergence of the new people who will lead the rural classes to self-fulfillment.[36]

In 1940 Jalāl Ekrāmi[37] published the first version of his novel about the beginnings of collectivization in Tajikistan, *Shādi*, named after its hero. Clearly inspired by Sholokhov's *Virgin Soil Upturned*,[38] the author traced the changes in the peasant mentality: from intense individualism and suspicion of all things new, to a sense of social solidarity and confidence in the future. A second volume (1957) showed the further development of the kolkhoz after World War II. The plot centers around the conflict between the innovators, who sought to introduce new methods of production, and their enemies, who clung stubbornly to the ways of traditional peasant agriculture. Shādi, who had distinguished himself in the war, was now the head of the kolkhoz and stood with the innovators. As a Communist who had identified himself with the peasant masses, he is a typical hero of Soviet fiction of the period. Despite carefully crafted, accurate descriptions of many aspects of rural life, the novel is in the end unsuccessful. The resolution of the central conflict is contrived—we do not know what caused the conservatives finally to see the light—and the personality of the hero remains one-dimensional—work molds his character, and production goals are his only passion. In other novels Ekrāmi was inspired by the revolutionary past. *Dokhtar-e ātash* (The daughter of fire, 1961), an examination of the life of the common people of Bukhara in the first two decades of the twentieth century, emphasizes the importance of the working-class movement as the chief catalyst in transforming Central Asian society. He is concerned specifically with the emancipation of the new Tajik woman. She has cast off the veil and partici-

[35]*Ta'rikh-e adabiyyāt-e soveti-ye tājik*, vol. 4: M. Shokurov, *Nasr-e sālhā-ye 1945–1974* (Dushanbe, 1980), 102–6, 117–22; Larisa Demidchik and Mohammadjān Shokurov, "Mehr-e zendagi va insān," *Sadā-ye sharq* 8 (1981): 129–42.

[36]Shokurov, *Nasr-e sālhā-ye 1945–1974*, 220–29; K. Iusufov, *Sotim Ulughzāda va povesti tarjumaiholii u "Subhi javonii mo"* (Dushanbe, 1968).

[37]For a general appreciation of Ekrāmi as a novelist, see Sh. Huseinzoda, *Jalāl Ekrāmi* (Stalinabad, 1959); Shokurov, *Nasr-e sālhā-ye 1945–1974*, 107–14.

[38]Georgii Lomidze, *V poiskakh novogo* (Moscow, 1963), 173–80.

pates fully in the social life and government of post-revolutionary Bukhara, thereby contributing to her own emancipation.[39] The novels of Rahim Jalil also conform to approved patterns of plot and character development.[40] *Ādamān-e jāvid* (Immortal people, 1949), one of the most popular postwar novels, described the conflict in northern Tajikistan in the mid-1920s between "progressive forces"— those who strove to establish the new Soviet economic and political order—and their opponents—the "nationalists." *Shurāb* (Shurāb, 1959), which derives its title from the mining district of northern Tajikistan, contrasts the harsh exploitation of the miners in pre-revolutionary times with the well-being and dignity assured them by the Soviet system. In both novels Jalil describes the life of the miners in almost monographic detail, but the reader can immediately distinguish heroes from villains and is never in doubt about the outcome of the conflict.

## Development of Drama

A Tajik drama in the modern sense of the term did not exist before 1929.[41] "Plays" were presented before that date, but the performers were folk poets and dance groups who followed the oral tradition and had no written texts. The beginnings of a modern drama coincided with the efforts of Soviet authorities to popularize their economic and social programs among the mass of the people. They counted upon plays—oral performances—especially to reach a population that was still largely illiterate. Accordingly, they established a Tajik national theater in Stalinabad in 1929, and in the same year the first Tajik plays, simple, didactic pieces, began to be presented. Subsequently, drama took its place beside poetry and fiction as an instrument of public policy. Plot and character did not differ from those of the *dāstān* and the novel. These similarities were all the more natural because the leading playwrights were also poets and novelists.

Between the early 1930s and the late 1950s the major plays were dramas of political struggle and economic modernization. Before World War II, for example, Mirzā Torsunzāda exposed the "nationalist" ambitions of certain groups of intellectuals in *Hokm* (The verdict, 1933); Jalāl Ekrāmi composed the first Tajik play about factory life,

---

[39]B. Khodāidādov, *Roman-e Jalāl Ekrāmi "Dokhtar-e ātash"* (Dushanbe, 1967).

[40]Shokurov, *Nasr-e sālhā-ye 1945–1974*, 264–79.

[41]N. Klado, "Dramaturgiia Sovetskogo Tadzhikistana," in *Tadzhikskaia sovetskaia dramaturgiia* (Moscow, 1957), 380–93.

*Doshman* (The enemy, 1933); and Sātim Ulughzāda examined the perennial conflict between the old and the new on the kolkhoz in *Shādmān* (Shādmān, 1939). Plots and characters in all these were simple
and direct, and the language was colloquial, and in *Shādmān* even in
dialectic. The war years brought new themes, but no significant
changes in technique. Typical of the utilitarian subject matter were
Ekrāmi's *Del-e mādar* (A mother's heart, 1942), which lauded the spirit
of sacrifice among the civilian population, and *Khāna-ye Nāder* (Nāder's house, 1943), which celebrated the victory of Stalingrad as a
united effort of all the Soviet nationalities.

In the immediate postwar period drama remained less innovative
than either poetry or fiction. Nonetheless, several works of uncommon
interest appeared, notably Mirshakār's *Shahr-e man* (My city, 1951) and
*Fāje'a-ye Osmānov* (Osmānov's tragedy, 1957). Both deal with the sensitive question of national feeling. On the surface the first play seems
to be standard fare about the planning and building of a new city, but
in the disputes between a senior architect and his younger colleague
we are treated to an engaging debate over what style is most in keeping
with the Tajik national character. The younger man, who favors the
functional lines of modern architecture, finally prevails. But in *Fāje'a-
ye Osmānov*, which examines the creative isolation of a composer who
abandoned the native musical tradition, Mirshakār asserted the pre-
rogatives of the Tajik style.

## New Trends

The death of Stalin and the processes of de-Stalinization encouraged
writers to diversify their subject matter and to experiment with form.
Yet, the party never ceased to remind them of their duty to stand in
the front ranks of those struggling to achieve the victory of Communism. In a somewhat more relaxed climate of creativity since the
late 1950s and early 1960s Tajik authors have produced a remarkable
variety of works ranging from the timeworn specimens of earlier decades to innovative probings of the individual psyche and of the seemingly ordinary events of daily life.[42]

In poetry Mirshakār's long poem, *Dasht-e laband* (The lazy steppe,
1961), dealt in thoroughly conventional ways with the opening up of
virgin lands and the struggle to establish a kolkhoz. But the work of

[42]A recent examination of the nature of civic poetry is Iusuf Akbarov, "Ruhi grazh-
danii she'r," *Sadā-ye sharq* 4 (1981): 135–45.

Ghaffār Mirzā (b. 1929), perhaps the most important of the poets who began their careers after World War II, suggested that something new was in the air. His *Sisad-o shast-o shesh pahlu* (366 Degrees, 1962) is a free-moving, unusually frank conversation of the poet with the reader about the events of the year just past. Abandoning the *'aruz*, he experiments boldly with form, allowing the hero of the poem, who is both observer and participant, to hold together its loosely connected parts.

Indicative of new trends in the novel was Ekrāmi's *Man gonahgāram* (I am guilty, 1957). It was the first Tajik novel to concern itself primarily with the more intimate problems of family life. But at the same time Ekrāmi was careful to maintain the proper ideological perspective by showing the struggle between the old mentality and the new, by emphasizing the nobility of the heroes, and by assuring the triumph of the "progressives." Less conventional was Fazl al-Din Mohammadiev's (b. 1928)[43] treatment of the generation gap, *Ādamāni kohna* (Old people, 1962). The elderly had usually been depicted condescendingly either as impediments to progress or as good-natured remnants of an obsolete past. The emphasis was invariably upon the young as the true bearers of Communism and the creators of the new world of the future. Mohammadiev broke with tradition. He did not turn his sons against their fathers. Instead, he showed how the young continued the struggles of the preceding generation and how both were united by a commitment to the same noble ideals. His short novel, *Dar ān dunyā* (In that world, 1966), also suggests how far the Tajik novel had traveled since the 1930s. It is a story of a pilgrimage to Mecca by Muslims from Soviet Central Asia as told by a doctor, an atheist, who accompanies the faithful. Through his eyes we see superstition and irrationality, corruption and commercialism at every step of this "journey to another world." Mohammadiev does not miss the opportunity to indulge in satire at the expense of the Muslim clergy and of religion in general. But gone are the days of frontal assaults on faith. The author is restrained, even delicate at times, in his handling of what is clearly a sensitive issue. Yet, these matters are merely the outer shell of the novel. They are the occasion for reflection on eternal themes: the meaning of human existence and the nature of happiness. On the surface, then, the novel is an anti-clerical tract, but its essence is a philosophical meditation.

---

[43]Mas'ud Mollājānov, "Tiramāh-e bārāvar," *Sadā-ye sharq* 1 (1982): 105–11; Shokurov, *Nasr-e sālhā-ye 1945–1974*, 169–84.

Tajik playwrights have also embraced new themes and have made their heroes, and even their villains, more human and, hence, more believable, as they probed deeply into the motivations behind individual behavior. Characteristic of their fresh approach was Sātim Ulughzāda's comedy, *Gowhar-e shabcharāgh* (The marvelous jewel, 1962), which portrays the foibles of ordinary people in a light-hearted manner far removed from the plodding censure of the Stalin era.

Since the 1930s Tajik literature, like all the national literatures of the Soviet Union, has felt the homogenizing influences of ideological control exercised by the Communist Party. Yet, Tajik poets, novelists, and playwrights have succeeded in preserving the distinctive characteristics of their own literature, which set it apart from other Soviet literatures. They have continued to draw inspiration from classical Persian literature and from a rich folklore, and they have interpreted the contemporary life of their people in accordance with national traditions and sensibilities.

# VI. TRANSLATION OF
# PERSIAN LITERATURE

# 24. Persian Literature in Translation

For all practical purposes, the European discovery of Persian literature came about in the seventeenth century, during the Age of Enlightenment. Serious study of it was launched a century later in the Age of Reason, and its chief exploitation was conducted in the nineteenth century during the Romantic Age. In the present century (which may very well come to be known as the Age of Anti-Reason), the interest in Persian literature has proliferated along both familiar and novel lines. These basic historical facts about the adaptation of Persian literature in the West must be borne in mind in any attempt to understand the Western reader's knowledge of that literature, for the knowledge has never been wholly disengaged from the European auspices under which it was perceived. The prepossessions of each age have left an indelible stamp upon the images of those Persian writers with whom the age was concerned.

Thus, because Sa'di's moral didacticism appealed to the Enlightenment and the Age of Reason, both the choice of selections from his works and the manner in which they were translated reflect the bias of those times. Similarly, Hāfez in the Age of Reason could only be perceived as a sort of pseudo-classical lyrist—the "Persian Anacreon." In the later Romantic Age, he was permitted to show his consanguinity with mystics. In the present century, his "intellectual nihilism," as A. J. Arberry calls it, lines him up with the flouters of reason. The neo-classical era not only regarded Ferdowsi as the "Persian Homer," but it specifically viewed him in the reflected light of Alexander Pope's popular version of the Greek poet. With perhaps an equal justification, a later time finds in the mythology of the *Shāh-nāma* a Frazerian and Jungian unconscious lying beneath the national epic level.

Surely it is naive to believe that mere accretion of historical and linguistic knowledge necessarily brings us closer to a "true" perception of Persian literature. Whatever we have learned in the past three hundred years about Persian literature—the Islamic phase of which came to full flowering during the half-millennium from about A.D. 1000 to 1500—has been learned in the context of our own varying cultural prejudices. The "truth" about it has always been tentative and always relative to a certain time and place.

This epistemological consideration will appear less constricting if we observe that it applies equally to the developing reputations of writers in their own countries and in their own languages. Shake-

speare, even in his English career, has been subject to the same va-
garies of interpretation as beset a writer translated from a foreign
language. It would take a bold critic to maintain that the present age
has a better understanding of the "essential" Shakespeare than any
earlier age merely because it has more information about him. If,
indeed, knowledge can deliver us from the prepossessions of other
times, it should also, presumably, be able to liberate us from the bonds
of our own arrogance. A similar modesty should prevail in our view
of the career of a translated writer. Translation, after all, merely adds
one more cultural variable to those provided by time and circumstance.

Without pushing this relativism too far, the present essay will attempt to trace the morphology, as it were, of Western, and especially
English, perceptions of Persian writers during the three centuries that
they have been known in Europe and America. Except in the case of
the most egregiously inept ones, no evaluation of the translations will
be offered.[1]

## The Neoclassical Beginnings

The Enlightenment discovered Persian and other exotic literatures
through its humanistic curiosity. Its great contribution to cultural history was its glimmer of awareness that even the non-Christian religions
were legitimate efforts to regulate ethical life, and that the art of
letters was not the exclusive prerogative of either Christian Europe or
pagan Greece and Rome. Even before André du Ryer made his French
translation of the Koran in 1647, he had rendered portions of Sa'di's
*Golestān* into the same language (1634). In England, George Sale's
influential translation of the Koran (1734) was preceded by Thomas
Hyde's study of the Zoroastrian religion and his renditions (in Latin)
of poems by Hāfez and 'Omar Khayyām. In 1644 there had also
appeared a French translation of the *Anvār-e sohayli* (The Lights of
Canopus), a Persian version of the fables of Pilpay.

It was Sa'di, however, who most captivated the imagination of the
Enlightenment. In 1651, his *Golestān* was published as the *Rosarium* in

---

[1]A good compendious bibliography of translations from Persian is D. L. Wilber's
"Iran: Bibliographical Spectrum" in the Iran number of *Review of National Literatures*
2/1 (Spring 1971): 161–81. A fairly complete bibliography of the classical literature
appears in the present writer's *Persian Poetry in England and America: A Two Hundred Year
History,* Persian Studies Series no. 4 (Delmar, N.Y., 1977). The content of much of this
essay is derived from that book.

a Latin translation by the Dutch Orientalist George Gentius, and in 1654 as *Der Persianischer Rosenthal* in a German version by Adam Olearius, who later appended *Der Baumgarten* (The *Bustān*) in a translation made from a Dutch version.[2] These works, and a book of travels by John Chardin, were the main sources for the vogue of Sa'di in the next century. Voltaire was to present his *Zadig* as a translation from Sa'di, and both Johann Herder in Germany and Joseph Addison in England were to adapt, in their own languages, fables from the *Bustān* and the *Golestān*. Benjamin Franklin, too, persuaded by the neoclassical precept that literature should both delight and instruct, was to take a *Bustān* parable on toleration (which had come via Gentius into the work of the seventeenth-century English divine Jeremy Taylor) and try to pass it off as a missing chapter of Genesis.

In the last quarter of the eighteenth century, events conspired to shift the center of Oriental studies from the continent to England. In part this was due to the philological labors of Sir William Jones, who rendered selections from various Persian authors into Greek, Latin, French, and English. His excited correspondence with the Polish ambassador Baron Reviczky, who had made Latin versions of Hāfez, was to generate the European vogue for that poet. But a more important factor sparking interest in Hāfez and other Persian poets was a fairly unexpected geopolitical development. Just when Jones was threatening to drown his Persian books deeper than plummet ever sounded because of lack of patronage, Pitt's India Act of 1784 was passed, bringing the commercial activities of the East India Company under closer supervision of the crown. The cultivation of the Persian language, which was the court language of India, and of Persian literature, which informed the entire Islamic civilization of that land, now became a patriotic necessity. A flurry of linguistic and literary activity ensued, and to Jones's *Persian Grammar* were added, as working tools, a Persian-English dictionary, various handbooks, and numerous translations from Persian authors. The purpose of these books was frankly utilitarian, but as their content was often literary, the names of Ferdowsi, Sa'di, and Hāfez soon became household words in England, occasionally preempted as *noms de plume* by poetasters unable to make it on their own.

Since it was under Indian rather than Persian auspices that the

[2]The earliest history of European translations from Persian is covered by H. A. R. Gibb, "Literature," in *The Legacy of Islam*, ed. T. Arnold (Oxford, 1931; repr. 1960); and by A. F. J. Remy in *The Influence of India and Persia on the Poetry of Germany* (New York, 1901).

481

Persian authors were being offered, Indian taste largely determined which authors were to be cultivated. Jāmi, a favorite in India, was thus rated more highly than Rumi or Nezāmi, who were relatively neglected. 'Attār's *Pand-nāma*, a compendium of ethics, was translated, but his more characteristic mystical writings would have to bide their time. Ferdowsi's eminence was never doubted, and so he had his fair share of editions and partial translations. Sa'di, because his fame extended over the entire Islamic world, was perhaps the most popular. His works, the mystical writings excepted, however, were rightly regarded as the best means of acquiring a proper understanding of Muslim manners and morals. Throughout the following century—even after 1834, when Persian was replaced by English as the official tongue of India—the *Golestān* continued to be required reading for all who went to India. New translations of it came out in every generation. Sa'di's social realism—called Machiavellian if it was disapproved—was regularly drawn upon to plumb the baffling psychology of his coreligionists in India. When Napoleonic politics brought Persia itself into the English orbit in the early nineteenth century, Sa'di also had to interpret the character of his compatriots. He retained this political usefulness well into the twentieth century: during the occupation of Iran by British and Russian troops in World War II, a parable of his was made to serve the purpose of anti-German propaganda by British intelligence.

For the cultivation of Hāfez, there was certainly reason enough in his Indian popularity and in the traditional use of his *Divān* as a book of auguries. His status as a favorite of English translators, however, may have had more to do with literary than with socioeconomic history.

## Romantic Enthusiasm

By the late eighteenth century, coinciding with the increased importance of India in Britain's commercial life, the philosophy of Romanticism began to levy its claims upon European writers and to displace the neoclassical aesthetics that had dictated taste for a century or more. The old devotion to reason and aversion to religious enthusiasm yielded to the celebration of emotion and intuition. In England, Pope's didactic and satiric modes gave way to the imaginative lyricism of Burns and Blake. The heroic couplet was supplanted by blank verse, the sonnet, and stanzaic forms. In subsequent generations, as Wordsworth, Coleridge, and Southey, then Byron, Shelley, and Keats extended the rebellion against the restraints of neoclassicism, the Persian lyric poets, especially Hāfez, found a hospitable reception. All the more so, perhaps, because most of the Romantic poets had been brought up on the works of Sir William Jones!

The neoclassical bias was well expressed by Edward Gibbon, whose epic history bemoaned the decline of the classical world. Gibbon was not deficient in scholarship on Islamic civilization, but with regard to literary matters, he had no doubt that "the classics have much to teach and . . . the Orientals have much to learn. . . ." He had in mind "the temperate dignity of style, the graceful proportions of art, the forms of visible and intellectual beauty, the just delineation of character and passion, the rhetoric of narrative and argument, the regular fabric of epic and dramatic poetry."[3] With such preconceptions it is no wonder that eighteenth-century translators typed the Persian poets as a species of Greeks or felt constrained to apologize for the "excess of ornament and inflation of style" that were regarded as characteristics of Persian poetry.

But the counterforce was stronger. Gibbon's friend Sir William Jones was all for rejuvenating the dying life of English poetry by infusing it with the very materials of Asian verse. He prophesied that "if the languages of the Eastern nations were studied in our great seminaries of learning . . . , we should be furnished with a new set of images and similitudes; and a number of excellent compositions would be brought to light, which future scholars might explain and future poets imitate."[4] And so James Ross, translator of the *Golestān*, explained that the Persian expression "moon-face" was not so silly as it seemed to English readers, because it was not intended to describe the symmetry of the beloved's features but rather her silvery whiteness and her virgin purity. Another new translator clung stubbornly to the Persian idioms, even the puns, because otherwise the poetry of the original would be, he said, "all evaporated." This Romantic flexibility was of course destined to prevail over neoclassical rigidity, and in the next generation, Alfred Tennyson, schooled by Jones, would deliberately employ Persian imagery even in poems that were not Oriental in theme.

In this developing history, an influential role was played by the Germans, just as in the previous century the French had been dominant. In fact, H. A. R. Gibb has assigned to Germany the chief re-

[3]*History of the Decline and Fall of the Roman Empire,* ed. William Smith (London, 1881), vol. 6, 403 note.
[4]Jones, *Works,* with a Life by Lord Teignmouth (London, 1807), vol. 10, 359.

sponsibility for adapting Islamic poetry to European Romanticism. Herder's Orientalism had been at first largely a humanistic response to a newly discovered chapter of history, but when Jones's translations became available to him, he made adaptations of Persian and Indian works that were to pave the way for the Romantic flowering of the *orientalische Richtung* in Goethe, Rückert, Platen, and Bodenstedt. The interest in Persian poetry evinced by so important a figure in German cultural history as the philosopher Hegel testifies to the new uses to which the foreign literary importations were being put. German philosophy, now given over to organicism, intuitionism, and even mysticism, found an ally in Persian Sufism. Meanwhile German philologists such as Tholuck, von Hammer-Purgstall, Brockhaus, and Rosenzweig-Schwannau were producing texts and translations of Persian literature for the use of not only German but also English and American writers.

The leading popularizers of Persian literature in England and America in the mid-nineteenth century often took their cue from the Germans. Edward B. Cowell, who taught FitzGerald to read Persian, owed his later interpretations to German sources; Samuel Robinson, a businessman who was an amateur of Persian, owed both texts and translations to them. The two most widely read anthologies of Asian literature—Louisa Costello's *The Rose-Garden of Persia* in England, and William R. Alger's *The Poetry of the Orient* in America—contained numerous English translations of German versions of Persian poetry. Under German influence, the mystic Rumi began to be noticed. Hāfez, formerly the "Persian Anacreon," was now the voice of weeping and loud lament. Before the Romantic Agony played itself out, he was to become the hero of the *fin de siècle* decadents. Even in Transcendentalist America, which was generally resistant to such tendencies, the wine of Hāfez was no longer simply "Moore's best Port," but stood for intellectual emancipation and expansion of the mind.

## Colonialists and Amateurs

In the West, the substance of Persian literature has been given its widest currency not by translators proper but by adapters of others' translations such as Goethe, the two Arnolds, and Emerson. Against such licence, academic scholars (including Browne, Nicholson, Arberry, Levy, and Jackson) have exerted a rectifying influence, besides providing a number of important translations of their own. It is, however, from an intermediary group, the *sahib*s of the British colonial enterprise, that the most substantial activity in translation has come.

Such a civil servant was Herman Bicknell, whose translations from Hāfez in 1875 were the most numerous to date. It was another civil servant, H. Wilberforce-Clarke, who rendered the complete *Divān* into English in 1891. Among the various translations of the *Golestān*, the most favored were the work of governmental agents, among them Francis Gladwin, James Ross, and Edward B. Eastwick. Even the version wrongly attributed to Sir Richard Burton (probably by Edward Rehatsek) came out of Burton's checkered career in the service of the empire. Alexander Rogers's translation of Ferdowsi, Jāmi, the *Anvār-e sohayli,* and other works had a similar origin, as did Sir Edwin Arnold's various translations and adaptations.

Britain's commitments in Asia not only provided a training ground for the linguistic skills required in translation, but also guaranteed a reading audience for what would otherwise have been a rather esoteric foreign literature. The fairly limited American contribution to this body of Near Eastern literature—and, conversely, the rather large American contribution to, say, Japanese studies in the twentieth century—point up this governing geopolitical influence in Western Orientalism.

If another category of cultivators of Persian literature were to be cited, it would have to be the amateurs. Although Gertrude L. Bell was later to be employed in government service, her popular renditions of Hāfez grew out of a girlhood infatuation with FitzGerald's *Rubaiyat*. The second complete version of the *Divān* of Hāfez, in 1901, was also the work of a pure amateur, John Payne. The *chef d'oeuvre* in this field was of course Edward FitzGerald's *Rubaiyat of Omar Khayyam,* undoubtedly the single most significant development in the English history of Persian literature. From its appearance in 1859, it was fraught with meaning for the future cultivation of that literature, not only by the English-speaking world but also by much of the rest of the world. For the most part it was FitzGerald's version that was translated into various languages of the world—not the Persian quatrains of Khayyām.[5] After an unnoticed debut, his rendition acquired a life of its own that was to have a strong bearing on the social and philosophical attitudes of several generations of European readers.

Perfectly naturalized in English, the *Rubaiyat* became for more than half a century the most popular poem in that language. Understandably, but erroneously, it was regarded as an English poem. It has

---

[5]See A. G. Potter, *A Bibliography of the Rubaiyat of Omar Khayyam* (London, 1929); for the subsequent history, consult "Bibliography" of *Persian Poetry in England and America.*

continued, inexplicably, to be denoted an "adaptation," a "transcription," a "modification," even a "transmogrification" of the original, but the fact is that it is a translation. It may not be literal, certainly it is not complete or always accurate; but then, on behalf of what translation can all of of these claims be made? Its relation to its sources has been well detailed, first by Edward Heron-Allen and later by A. J. Arberry, and its spiritual affinity with the Persian author warranted by A. Christensen.[6] FitzGerald occasionally joined together several quatrains to form one of his own, expanded two lines of 'Omar into four of his own, arranged the quatrains in his own order, and even allowed a strain from other Persian poets to waft in. But the music of the original is largely there, as is much of its local color and a fair portion of its message. If he stubbornly rejected a Sufi interpretation of the quatrains, he is probably on surer ground than are Robert Graves and Ali Shah who affirmed it. For most Europeans it may even be said that his *Rubaiyat* is Persian poetry.

Its effect upon the cultivation of other Persian poets cannot, however, be said to have been salutary. During the vogue of the *Rubaiyat* in the late nineteenth and early twentieth centuries, all other Persian poets except Ferdowsi were seen in its rather garish light. Hāfez was viewed as a later 'Omar, a skeptic and a hedonist; not merely his *robā'i*s, but also his *ghazal*s were rendered as quatrains (by, for example, Clarence Streit). The same was done, by Thomas Wright, to Sa'di, whose homely philosophy hardly lent itself to such accommodation. Lesser figures like Bābā Taher and Kamāl al-Din were pulled completely out of their orbits by the magnetism of 'Omar. If Rumi's quatrains resisted this tug, it was because their translator, A. J. Arberry, was deliberately seeking to combat the tyranny of 'Omar Khayyām.[7]

The fame of FitzGerald's translation did, however, direct the attention of scholars of Persian to the author, who had hitherto been regarded as mainly a scientist-mathematician. New translations of the *Rubaiyat* began to appear purporting to set aright FitzGerald's presumed distortions. As new manuscripts of 'Omar Khayyām surfaced, the image of the poet altered; but when other scholars shed doubts upon the authenticity of the new manuscripts, the image once again

---

[6]E. Heron-Allen, *Edward FitzGerald's Rubaiyat of Omar Khayyam with Their Original Persian Sources* (London, 1899); A. J. Arberry, *The Romance of the Rubaiyat* (New York, 1959); and A. Christensen, *Critical Studies in the Rubaiyat of Umar-i-Khayyām* (Copenhagen, 1927). See also chap. 7 of this book, in which L. P. Elwell-Sutton discusses 'Omar Khayyām's poetry, and FitzGerald's treatment thereof, in detail.

[7]See *Persian Poetry in England and America*, 218–27.

became shadowy. Perhaps the climax of all this activity was the 1967 Robert Grave–'Omar Ali Shah translation, which, using a Sufi lexicon to interpret the wine, the saki (*sāqi*) and other sensuous images, made 'Omar Khayyām a pious mystic. This was but the latest of a series of backlashes against the hedonistic and skeptical stress placed upon 'Omar's thought by FitzGerald and his followers. Since, however, the authenticity of the Ali Shah manuscript has also been severely challenged, matters may be said to remain *in statuo quo.*

In its heyday, the *Rubaiyat* factory ground out not only endless reissues of FitzGerald's four—or five—editions, but also numerous new translations and adaptations, some of which were so tendentious and eccentric as to deserve a lunatic-fringe tag. With some justification, a recent critic regrets the fame of the *Rubaiyat* because it has meant the neglect of more significant Persian poets.[8]

Attempts to find a FitzGerald for Rumi, Hāfez, or Ferdowsi have met with no success. Ferdowsi and Nezāmi have indeed received special attention from art critics interested in the illuminated manuscripts of their works; Rumi and 'Attār have been appropriated by advocates of the Sufi path; and Jāmi's *Yusof and Zulaykhā* in a German translation has been drawn upon by the great novelist Thomas Mann for his *Joseph in Egypt.* But no translation from the Persian, however useful or scholarly, has met with a literary success comparable to FitzGerald's *Rubaiyat* of 'Omar Khayyām. Even FitzGerald failed to do for Jāmi and 'Attār what he did for 'Omar. His *Salaman and Absal* was rendered, as he himself admitted, in too Miltonic a blank verse, and more of the original was left out than kept, as Arberry's later study shows. His *Bird-Parliament,* a version of the *Manteq al-tayr,* he himself rightly described as only "a paraphrase of a syllabus" of the original.

This, of course, does not mean that there have not been important translations of the leading Persian writers. Academic scholarship has given us a complete English translation of the *Shāh-nāma* by the brothers Warner to match Mohl's French and Pizzi's Italian versions; a complete edition and English translation of Rumi's *Mathnavi* by Nicholson; and an authentic English translation of Sa'di's *Bustān* by Wickens to replace the earlier versions by Wilberforce-Clarke and Davie. To the further extension and refurbishing of the English reputation of Rumi, Professor Arberry devoted the last years of his life. Some of the classics of Persian prose, too, have seen needed English translation: Kay Kāvus's *Mirror for Princes* (by Levy), the *Siyāsat-nāma* of Nizām al-Molk

---

[8]A. Ahmad, introduction to *Ghazals of Ghalib* (New York, 1971).

(by Darke), and *The Nasirean Ethics* of Tusi (by Wickens), to name only a few.[9]

In the above-mentioned works, however, whether prose or verse, the essential element is content. In lyric poetry, on the other hand, form is of the essence. The truly vexing question in the translation of Persian literature has been what to do with the *ghazal* form. Hence, the critical figure has always been Hāfez.

## The Lyricists

Sir William Jones early set the fashion of finding an ode-like equivalent for the *ghazal* with his famed "Persian Song of Hāfez," in which the following first two lines of the Persian text became the accompanying six of the English:

If that Shiraz Turk would take my heart in hand,
For his/her black mole I would give Samarkand and Bukhara.

Sweet maid, if thou wouldst charm my sight,
And bid these arms thy neck enfold;
That rosy cheek and lily hand
Would give thy poet more delight
Than all Bocara's vaunted gold,
Than all the gems of Samarcand.[10]

---

[9]For a fuller list of translated prose works, see the bibliography in R. Levy, *An Introduction to Persian Literature* (New York, 1969). Considerable boost has been given to the translations of Persian literature by the Persian Heritage Series which was founded in 1962 by Ehsan Yarshater and has been edited by him since. The Series aims "at making the best of Persian classics available in major western languages," for "the intelligent reader who seeks to broaden his artistic and artistic horizon through an acquaintance with major world literature." A number of Persian classics have been published in this series. They include 'Attār, *Muslim Saints and Mystics*, tr. A. J. Arberry; Nezāmi, *Chosroes et Chirine*, 2 vols., tr. Henri Massé; Rumi, *Mystical Poems*, tr. A. J. Arberry; Tusi, *The Nasirean Ethics*, tr. G. M. Wickens; Nezāmi, *Le Sette principesse*, tr. A. Bausani; Ferdowsi, *The Epics of the Kings*, (abridged tr. of the *Shāh-nāma*), tr. Reuben Levy; 'Aruzi, *Les quatre discours*, tr. I. de Gestines; Faramarz, *Samak-e 'Ayyar*, tr. F. Razavi; Gurgani, *Vis and Ramin*, tr. G. Morrison; Bighami, *Love and War*, tr. W. Hanaway, Jr.; Rumi, *Licht und Reigen*, tr. J. Ch. Burgel; 'Attār, *Ilahinama*, tr. J. A. Boyle; Samarkandi, *Le Livre des sept viziers*, tr. D. Bogdanovic; Hāfez, *Divān* (Hafizu-Shishu), (in Japanese), tr. T. Kuriyanagi; Anon, *Iskandarnamah*, tr. M. Southgate; Nezām al-Molk, *The Book of Government*, revised tr. H. Darke; Nezāmi, *Khosrau and Shirin* (in Japanese), tr. A. Okada; Naser-e Khosrow, *Book of Travels*, tr. W. Thackston; Sa'di, *Bustān*, tr. G. M. Wickens.

Another collection, Modern Persian Literature Series, also founded and edited by Ehsan Yarshatar since 1978 "is devoted to translations of works of modern Persian poets and writers."

[10]Jones, *Works*, vol. 10, 251.

That Jones was capable, if he wanted, of retaining the *ghazal* form is demonstrated by his rendition of what he called "An Ode of Jami," of which these are the first two couplets:

> How sweet the gale of morning breathes:
>    Sweet news of my delight he brings;
> News, that the rose will soon approach
>    The tuneful bird of night, he brings.
> Soon will a thousand parted souls
>    be led, his captives, through the sky,
> Since tidings, which in every heart
>    must ardent flames excite, he brings.[11]

The monorhyme ("delight," "night," "excite"), the *radif* or refrain ("he brings"), and the caesural breaks have all been preserved; even the *takhallos* or pen name of the author is given in the closing couplet. Yet it is all too apparent that the thought is being forced into a preordained form, and Jones wisely eschewed the method as a general rule. When it was tried again later, on Hāfez—by Payne's "isometric" rendition of the entire *Divān* and by Walter Leaf's selections from it—there was almost total failure on the part of the former and only occasional success on the part of the latter. By and large, translators have chosen a stanzaic equivalent or a linear biblical prose as the most feasible media for the *ghazal*s of Hāfez.

Edward B. Cowell, who was the chief interpreter of Hāfez for the mid-Victorians, began with Jones's metrical, rhymed stanzas but later passed on to an unrhymed, unmetrical linear translation, as exemplified by these excerpts from his two versions of the same *ghazal* made at different times in his career:

> Haste, Saki, O haste! with the joy-giving bowl,
> Thee the poet invokes from the depth of his soul.
> At first, love seemed easy and all appeared gay,
> But what troubles have since vexed my wearisome way.

But:

> Hither, hither, o cupbearer, hand round and give the cup;
> For love at first showed easy, but difficulties have come![12]

[11]*British Poets, Including Translations* (Chiswick, 1822), vol. 74, 100.
[12]*Asiatic Journal,* 3rd ser. III, 222 (May 1844): 354; and *Fraser's Magazine* 50 (Sept. 1854): 288ff.

The problem, however, was not simply the external form of the *ghazal*. Even when translators solved that problem, as Payne and Leaf did, they were still faced with the difficulties of the *ghazal*'s inner nature. "Wonderful is the inconsecutiveness of the Persians," Emerson had said, referring to the apparent lack of unity of thought in the *ghazal*.[13] The nineteenth-century American Orientalist E. P. Evans, accepting the opinion of both Persians and Europeans that Hāfez was among the world's great poets, nevertheless despaired of rendering him in English. "The *ghazels* of Hafez," he wrote, "can never can be acclimatized and thoroughly naturalized in Western literature."[14]

The challenge has, of course, been irresistible to scholars in the twentieth century. The genius of the *ghazal* has been further probed, and more efforts have been made to capture it in translation. A. J. Arberry saw the *ghazal* as resembling the sonnet rather than the ode, although he was aware that the sonnet had a unity lacking in the *ghazal*. It seemed to him that the latter presented not the development of a single theme but a sort of theme and variations. He therefore sought contrapuntal musical effects, accepting two or more themes in one poem. The later Beethoven sonatas were his models rather than the more formally correct earlier ones.[15]

G. M. Wickens found the problem in the essentially different aesthetic principles of Persians and Westerners. For him, the *ghazal* was, like the courtyard in Persian architecture, inward-facing, rather than linear and dramatic as is most Western literature. Under another metaphor, he viewed the parts of the *ghazal* as spokes radiating from a hub or focal point. Thus each couplet was only indirectly related to those which preceded or followed it, rather than flowing out of or into them. Peter Avery continued this analysis by noting that the *ghazal* reflected the arabesque patterns of a Persian miniature and not the thematic Aristotelian structure of a Western ode.[16]

These and other attempts to explicate Hāfez for Western readers have been subjected to a close analysis by Michael C. Hillmann in a monograph on the problem of unity in the *ghazals* of Hāfez. Hillmann

[13]"Preface" to Sa'di's *The Gulistan or Rose-Garden,* tr. Francis Gladwin (Boston, 1865), xi.

[14]"Hafiz of Shiraz," *Atlantic Monthly* 53 (Jan. 1884): 107, and "Texts and Translations of Hafiz," ibid. (March 1884): 320.

[15]Examples of Arberry's translations may be found in his *Fifty Poems of Hafiz* (Cambridge, 1947), which also shows the variegated career of Hāfez in English translation.

[16]G. M. Wickens, "The Persian Conception of Artistic Unity in Poetry and Its Implications in Other Fields," *BSOAS* 14 (1952): 239–43; P. Avery and J. Heath-Stubbs, *Hafiz of Shiraz: Thirty Poems* (London, 1952).

does not himself offer literary translations, as did Arberry, being content with literal renditions that point up the inadequacies in the work of previous translators. Since, however, his book is addressed as much to English as to Persian readers, it occupies a significant place in this survey.[17] In summary, it cannot be said that all this scholarly activity on the subject of the *ghazals* of Hāfez has yet produced any translations that could bring him into the mainstream of Western literature, as FitzGerald's translation brought 'Omar Khayyām.

The amateurs have had somewhat better success—but with other poets, and in less orthodox ways. The British poet Basil Bunting—who says that he learned his craft as much from Manuchehri and Ferdowsi as from Dante and Wordsworth—prefers the word "overdraft" to "translation." Of his version of a poem of Rudaki, he confesses that "it would be gratuitous to assume that a mis-translation is unintentional." How much of the following is Rudaki and how much Bunting, then, becomes of little consequence; what matters is that it is a poem:

Came to me—
 Who?
She.
 When?
In the dawn, afraid.
 What of?
Anger.
 Whose?
Her father's.
 Confide!
I kissed her twice.
 Where?
On her moist mouth.
 Mouth?
No.
 What then?
Cornelian.
 How was it?
Sweet.[18]

[17]*Unity in the Ghazals of Hafez*, Studies in Middle Eastern Literatures no. 6 (Minneapolis and Chicago, 1976).

[18]Permission to quote from Basil Bunting's *Collected Poems* (London, 1968), 144, has been graciously granted by the Fulcrum Press.

To traditionalists, Omar Pound's version of a poem by Manuchehri must appear even more irresponsible, although his purpose is the legitimate one of doing for Persian poetry what his distinguished father did for Chinese, that is, naturalizing it in English. For Manuchehri's recall of famous lines of verse from the pre-Islamic classics, he substitutes the following English equivalents:

Whan that Aprille with his shoures soote . . .
Rough winds do shake the darling buds of May . . .
And did those feet . . .
Into the valley of . . .
Death be not proud . . .
Pull down thy vanity, I say, pull down. . . .

Then, to match the Persian poet's contempt for his rebeck-strumming rivals, Pound offers his own view of some of his contemporaries:

But now?
It's all Betjeman, Ginsberg, and Ogden Nash
guitars and Trinidaddy drums
metal drums, rhythm without song
hum-drumming poets out of town
and leaving none to honor men,
    events
    and verse. . . .[19]

Pound's clever version of 'Obayd-e Zākāni's *Mush o gorba* (Mouse and cat), under the title of "Gorby and the Rats," is even more autonomous as an English poem, down to the English pun in the closing lines:

Allah called,
our poet heard his name:
    OBEYD
and passed away.[20]

Such free adaptations of classical Persian poetry may very well be the

---

[19]These lines from Pound's translation are quoted from his *Arabic and Persian Poems in English* (New York, 1970), 56, by kind permission of New Directions Books and of the Fulcrum Press, British publishers of the book.
[20]Agenda Editions no. 2 (London, 1972).

inevitable consequence of the anti-historical bias of our time. Yet one wonders whether it has ever been otherwise. Did not Goethe and Emerson do the same with their Persian sources?

## The Modernists

Although the modern phase of Persian literature was launched in the aftermath of World War I—by Jamālzāda in prose and by Nimā Yushij in verse—it was not until after World War II that it made an impression upon the rest of the world. The introduction to English readers came in a special "Persian Writers" number of the British journal *Life and Letters*. The prose writers got the lion's share of the space by three pages to one. Moreover, they had the advantage of an enthusiastic advocate and translator in Henry G. D. Law, secretary of the Iran Society of London. He sought to acquaint English readers with the work of Hedāyat, Jalāl Āl-e Ahmad, and Chubak among others, and he at least told them about the trail-blazing work of Jamālzāda in the new fiction. Law further observed that "in the precious and well-beloved art of poetry," the Persians "do not easily tolerate any modernization, anything which savours of revolution." This was apparent in the poetic selections offered in this special issue by A. J. Arberry, who concentrated his attention not on the precursors of the future, but on those who (like Tavallali) sought to effect a transition from the classical past.[21]

Arberry did not even mention Nimā Yushij, with whom the poetic revolution had begun, and as late as 1953 a writer in the London *Times Literary Supplement* would speak of the classicists in Persian poetry as still holding the field. That this was widely thought to be the case is suggested by an article by G. M. Wickens on "Poetry in Modern Persia," published in 1959–60. It was based upon a 1954 Persian anthology from which some of the most prominent names of contemporary poets were missing.[22] A year after the death of Nimā Yushij, an Indian writer did indeed describe him as "the founder of the modernist school of Persian poetry,"[23] but it would be left to his disciples to erect the monument "founded" by Nimā Yushij. This lag was to be expected, for poetry was a more established Persian tradition than fiction. The short story was, for the most part, a new discovery traceable to French, Russian, English, and, later, American models.

[21]"Persian Writers," *Life and Letters and the London Mercury* 63/148 (December 1949).
[22]*University of Toronto Quarterly* 29 (1959–60), 262–81.
[23]M. Rahman, *Bulletin of the Institute of Islamic Studies* 4 (1960): 28–45.

The first and the most enduring world reputation to be established by a modern Persian author was that of Sādeq Hedāyat. His *Buf-e kur* was translated into French by Roger Lescot as *La Chouette Aveugle* in 1953 and into English by D. P. Costello as *The Blind Owl* in 1957. In Kamshad's important study of modern Persian prose (1966), Hedāyat was by far the largest figure, and that book, together with a paperback reissue of Costello's translation by Grove Press in 1969, may be said to account for the wide circulation of his name in the West. Still another English version of *Buf-e kur*, entitled "The Recluse," appeared in Iraj Bashiri's study, *Hedayat's Ivory Tower*, in 1974. It met criticism from Michael Beard, who thought Costello's more idiomatic in its English, and offered the wise counsel that ". . . a translator whose native tongue is not that 'target' language . . . should collaborate with a native speaker in a literary translation." The entire history of this important novella was surveyed in 1978 in Hillmann's *Hedayat's "The Blind Owl" Forty Years After*, which, in addition to sixteen articles by different hands on various aspects of the book, submitted translations of two short stories by Hedāyat.[24]

By now, Hedāyat's shorter stories have already begun to be translated and published, both in Iran and abroad. *Sadeq's Omnibus*, containing six stories translated by Siavosh Danesh, appeared in Tehran in the early 1970s. Others came out in American journals and anthologies, culminating in Ehsan Yarshater's *Sadeq Hedayat: An Anthology*, which included seventeen stories by various translators.[25] The last major work of Hedāyat, *Hāji Āqā*, was rendered in 1979 by G. M. Wickens, who had known the author personally. This model translation provides excellent annotation and the pagination of both the Persian text and a German translation by Werner Sundemann.[26] There was no doubt about Hedāyat's preeminence among modern Persian authors.

A chief contemporary and friend of Hedāyat, Bozurg 'Alavi, has had the benefit of Wickens's subtle translation of "The Lead Soldier,"

[24]Kamshad, *Mod. Prose; Hedāyat's "The Blind Owl" Forty Years After*, comp. and ed. M. C. Hillmann, Middle East Monographs 4 (Austin, Tex., 1978). Beard's review of Bashiri appears in *Iranian Studies* 9/1 (Winter 1976): 81.

[25]Modern Persian Literature Series no. 2 (Bibliotheca Persica, New York, 1979). The following have also appeared in the Series: Karimi-Hakák, *An Anthology of Modern Persian Poetry*, 1978; Āl-e Ahmad, *Plagued by the West*, tr. Paul Sprachman; Farrokhzād, *Bride of Acacias*, tr. J. Kessler and A. Banani; Jamālzāda, *Once Upon a Time*, tr. H. Moayyad and Paul Sprachman; Sholevar, *The Night's Journey and the Coming of the Messiah*, tr. by the author.

[26]*Hāji Āghā: Portrait of an Iranian Confidence Man*, Middle East Monographs no. 6 (Austin, Tex., 1979).

which offered the challenge of rendering colloquial Persian in an English that must avoid both cockney and American extremes.[27] 'Alavi's "The Man from Gilan" and "The Thresher" have also appeared, as have short stories by Chubak, Golestān, Golshiri, Sā'edi, and others. Permanent forums for translators have existed since the establishment, in 1968, of the journal *Iranian Studies* and, in 1976, of *Edebiyāt*. Full-dress surveys of contemporary Persian literature have been edited by Thomas M. Ricks and Michael C. Hillmann for *The Literary Review* and *Literature East and West,* respectively.[28]

Longer Persian fiction has been somewhat less successfully represented. Jalāl Āl-e Ahmad's *The School Principal* has had an independent publication in a translation by John K. Newton in the Bibliotheca Islamica (1974), and Golshiri's *Prince Ehtejāb,* an experimental short novel that attracted much attention in Iran, appeared in English dress in Hillmann's *Literature East and West* survey. The plot summaries of other novels in the same publication cannot be regarded as substitutes for translations. There is promise of more of the latter, however, from the Bibliotheca Persica.

Translation of modern literary essays in English is at least as old as M. K. Ostavar's version (however inept) of Hedāyat's preface to *Tarā-nahā-ye Khayyām*.[29] Samples by Jamālzāda and Āl-e Ahmad have appeared in the two surveys cited above, and the latter's seminal work on the Western mania among Persian intellectuals has now been translated by Paul Sprachman and Heshmat Mo'ayyad as *Plagued by the West*.[30]

A significant literary form that has been almost totally neglected is drama. A one-act play by Gowhar-e Morād (Gh. H. Sā'edi) translated by Eden Naby appears among the Persian selections in *New Writing from the Middle East.* Bizhan Mofid's *The Butterfly,* which the present writer has not seen, is listed by Hillmann as published by the Anchorage Press of Kentucky in 1974, in a translation by Don Laffoon.[31]

---

[27]In *New Writing from the Middle East,* ed. L. Hamalian and J. D. Yohannan (New York, 1978), 278–92.

[28]The Iran number of *The Literary Review* was 18/1 (Fall 1974); the *Literature East and West,* called "Major Voices in Contemporary Persian Literature," appeared in 20/1–4 (January–December 1976). The excellent bibliography appended to this number is perhaps more accessible than one provided by Hillmann for the Iranian Embassy on 21 March 1976 as "Twentieth Century Persian Literature in Translation: A Bibliography."

[29]Appended to *Rubaiyat of Omar Khayyam, the Second Edition 1868, Rendered into English Verse by Edward FitzGerald* (Tehran, 1964).

[30]Modern Persian Literature Series, 4; see n. 25.

[31]In Hillmann's Iranian Embassy "Bibliography."

An anthology of modern Persian plays by Gisèle Kapuscinski, based on her Ph.D. dissertation on modern Persian drama (Columbia University, 1982), has been announced by the Modern Persian Literature Series of Bibliotheca Persica.

For the earliest translations of contemporary Persian poetry credit must go to a Tehran publication, *Keyhan International,* which in the early sixties published English versions of Nimā Yushij, Shāmlu, Farrokhzād, and Akhavān-e Thāles (Omid). In 1968 the Geneva journal *Poèsie vivante* offered some samples of "Contemporary Iranian Poetry" that briefly represented the work of Yushij, Shāmlu, Hoquqi, Kasrā'i, and Farrokhzād, among others. The translators, Geoffrey Squires and Reza Nematollahi, conducted their discussion in both English and French but gave the translations in English only. They did not have a good opinion of the "new poetry," considering it sentimental, self-regarding and diffuse.

Subsequent presentations of contemporary Persian verse to English readers were perhaps more sympathetic to their subject but hardly more successful in enlarging its audience. The most hospitable American forum for keeping abreast of literary developments in Iran probably has been *Books Abroad* (now *World Literature Today*). Such bilingual Iranian scholars as Massud Farzan and Mannuchehr Āryanpur have submitted translations to it from the *she'r-e nov,* which added to already familiar names those of Sepehri and Nāderpour. A number of these poets have found their way into Middle Eastern anthologies and finally into a full-length *Anthology of Modern Persian Poetry* selected and translated by Ahmad Karimi-Hakkak for the Modern Persian Literature Series of Bibliotheca Persica.[32] It represents the culmination of English-language interest in the new Persian poetry.[33]

Even in excellent translation and with illuminating explication, the imagistic subtleties of Nimā Yushij and the moral ambiguities of Shāmlu could not be expected to command a large popular readership. That could only be accomplished by a young female poet with an attractive personality who in intensely personal verse challenged the moral code of the society into which she was born and died young and tragically in an automobile accident. Forugh Farrokhzād is by all odds the favorite modern Persian poet with English readers.

She had been first called to their attention in an Indian publication

---

[32]Delmar, N.Y., 1978.
[33]See the review by Hillmann which appears in *Literature East and West,* volume 20/ 1–4, 1976, survey edited by him, 314–18.

of 1964–65;[34] a little later, in a Parisian journal of 1967, Girdhari
Tikku described her as having a kinship with both her compatriot
Hāfez and the American poet Emily Dickinson.[35] When she died the
following year, Massud Farzan reviewed her tragic career and flatly
called her the best Persian woman poet since the year 1500. Probably
the surest explanation of her extraordinary appeal to readers across
the barriers of language and culture is offered by Rezā Barāheni, who
says that hers is a poetry of content, not of form or technique, and
moreover, that it is a poetry of feminine content.[36] She was thus a
natural candidate for inclusion in a book like *Middle Eastern Muslim
Women Speak*, to which Hillmann has contributed a brief biographical
sketch and translations of ten of her more defiant poems. Although
the translations are not exceptional, they have the merit of being accompanied by notes that describe the rhythmic and metrical forms of
the Persian originals.[37] Three of her poems served a similar purpose
in an anthology titled *The Other Voice: Twentieth Century Women's Poetry*.[38]

Two recent volumes of translations from Farrokhzād's work continue this emphasis on the biographical and feminist content. Hasan
Javadi and Susan Sallée draw upon transcripts of interviews, excerpts
from letters, and two critical articles on Farrokhzād's poetic method
to supplement their selections, which are from all four volumes published in her lifetime plus the posthumous work. The stress, however,
is on the volume from which their own takes its title, *Tavallodi digar*.[39]
Jascha Kessler and Amin Banani's *Bride of Acacias*,[40] in the Modern
Persian Literature Series of Bibliotheca Persica, represents the poet's
production similarly but somewhat more fully. Although there is less
critical apparatus, the personal note is struck in both Banani's "Introduction" and the terminal essay "Forugh Farrokhzād: a Feminist Perspective" by Farzaneh Milani.

It is impossible to view the comparatively large reputations earned
abroad by modern Persian authors like Hedāyat and Farrokhzād with
reference to the social and political circumstances out of which their

---

[34]M. Rahman, "Two Contemporary Poetesses of Iran," *Bulletin of the Institute of Islamic Studies* 8–9 (1965): 64–73.

[35]G. Tikku, "Furugh-i Farrukhzad: A New Direction in Persian Poetry," *Studia Islamica* 26 (1967): 149–73.

[36]Quoted by Hillmann in *Middle Eastern Muslim Women Speak*, ed. E. W. Fernea and B. Q. Bezirgan (Austin and London, 1977), 317.

[37]Ibid.

[38]Ed. J. Bankier, D. Lashgari, et al. (New York, 1976).

[39]*Another Birth: Selected Poems of Forugh Farrokhzād* (Emeryville, Cal., 1981).

[40]*Bride of Acacias: Selected Poems of Forugh Farrokhzād* (Delmar, N.Y., 1982).

work came. Hedāyat's is indeed a solid literary reputation, but his dramatic suicide no doubt added some notoriety to his fame. Farrokhzād will undoubtedly continue to be a cultural heroine of the worldwide women's liberation movement. Indeed, in translation these Persian authors today appear to belong more to the world than to their native land.

# 25. Select Bibliography of Translations from Persian Literature

## 1. CLASSICAL PERSIAN LITERATURE

Although substantial specimens of this literature have been rendered into the principal Western languages (as well as some minor ones) over the last two hundred years, this endeavor has tended to be largely unplanned, sporadic, and personal, with some Persian authors (deservedly or not) receiving more attention than others. Partly in line with the indigenous tradition, poetry is infinitely better represented in translation than is prose. Virtually all of these renderings have some merit, with few being utterly worthless. Some early versions, however, do suffer somewhat from the scholarly shortcomings of their time, and many are idiosyncratic or period-bound in taste and style. Most editions have been limited, and those published before 1920 or so are hard to come by, even in large or "learned" libraries. Recently, random items have begun to be reproduced as speculative publishing ventures, often being given the appearance and dating of completely new books. Considerable good material is "buried" in ephemeral or in specialized periodicals in "Oriental Studies," Comparative Literature, and so forth.

For all these reasons, the following list must be selective. Nevertheless, in view of the varying capacities of libraries, whether large or small, it has been thought advisable to err on the side of inclusion rather than exclusion. French and German translations have been merged with the English because they so often have had a bearing upon the English cultivation of Persian literature. The list is subdivided into Poetry, Prose, Mixed Genre, and Anthologies.

## A. Poetry

'Attār, Farid al-Din. *The Conference of the Birds.* Translated by Afkham Darbandi and Dick Davis. New York: Penguin, 1984. A modern verse translation of a mystical classic, *Manteq al-Tayr*, couched in allegorical form.

———. *A Bird's-Eye View of Farid-uddin Attar's Bird Parliament.* Translated by Edward FitzGerald. (Together with *Salaman and Absal, an Allegory*, ed. Nathan H. Dole.) Boston: Page and Co., 1899.

———. *The Conference of the Birds, a Sufi Allegory, Being an Abridged*

*Version of Farid-ud-din Attar's Mantiq ut-Tair.* Translated by R. P. Masani. London: Oxford, 1924.

———. *The Conference of the Birds.* Translated in prose "from the Literal and Complete French Translation of Garcin de Tassy" by C. S. Nott. Boulder, Col.: Shanbala, 1971 (first published in 1954).

———. *Le Livre Divin (Elahi-nameh).* French translation by Fuad Rouhani. Paris: Unesco Persian Series, 1961. A long religio-philosophical poem, with many illustrative stories.

———. *Ilahiname.* Translated by J. A. Boyle. Manchester: Manchester University Press (Persian Heritage Series no. 29), 1977. A reliable English version of *Le Livre Divin,* with some differences from the French rendering.

Ferdowsi. *The Shāhnāma of Firdausī.* Translated by A. G. and E. Warner. 9 vols. London: K. Paul, Trench, Trübner & Co., 1905–25. A passable verse rendering of the Iranian national epic ("The Book of the Kings," "The Epic of the Kings," etc.).

———. *The Epic of the Kings.* Translated by Reuben Levy. Chicago: University of Chicago Press (Persian Heritage Series no. 2), 1967. A prose version of the main episodes, interspersed with summaries of the less interesting passages. Useful for quick reference.

———. *The Shahnameh . . . translated and abridged,* by J. Atkinson. London: Oriental Translation Fund, 1832 (reprinted 1886). Example of early "amateur" effort at versification, often unsatisfactory as a "reproduction," and too heavily inspired by the taste of its own time.

———. *Le Livre des Rois.* French prose version by Jules Mohl, with Persian text (Paris, 1837–78) and separately (Paris, 1871–78). While it reads smoothly enough as a French narrative, it lacks the force and fire of the original and often glosses over difficulties. In places, its manuscript "base" differs somewhat from other versions in common use, so that comparison is not always easily practicable. (An excerpt from this edition was made by G. Lazard, together with an introduction and bridging passages, published under the same title.)

———. *Il Libro dei Rei,* a similar but versified rendering in Italian by Italo Pizzi. 8 vols. Turin, 1886–88. Again, this has been reissued in abridged form under the editorship of F. Gabrieli.

———. *Firdosi's Königsbuch.* Translated by Friedrich Rückert. Berlin, 1890–95. Of several German versions over the last one hundred years, most of them judiciously abridged, this rendering by a scholar-poet is perhaps the most successful.

————. *Suhrab and Rustam.* Translation of a famous episode from the Shāhnāma by James Atkinson. Delmar, N.Y.: Scholars' Facsimiles and Reprints, 1972. A reissue of Atkinson's *Soorab, a Poem Freely Translated from the Original Persian of Firdousee.* 1st ed., Calcutta, 1814; 2nd ed., Calcutta, 1828 (revised and enlarged).

————. *The Shah-Namah of Firdusi.* Translated from the original Persian by Alexander Rogers. London: Chapman and Hall, 1907. Various episodes rendered in heroic couplets and in prose paraphrase.

————. *Sketch of the Life and Writings of Ferdusi.* Translated by Samuel Robinson. London: Privately Printed, 1876. Forty pages of extracts from the *Shāhnāmah* in rhythmic prose, and the satire on Mahmud versified, by a scholarly amateur.

————. *The Epic of Kings: Stories Retold from Firdusi*, by Helen Zimmern. London: Fisher Unwin, 1882 and often reprinted. Based on the Mohl translation and in archaic English prose.

————. *Tales of Ancient Persia*, by Barbara Leonie Picard. London: Oxford University Press, 1972. Episodes from the first part of the *Shāhnāma* abridged and retold in prose (illustrated).

Gorgāni, Fakhr al-Din. *Vis and Ramin.* Translated by George Morrison. New York: Columbia University Press (Persian Heritage Series no. 14), 1972. An elegant prose version, lightly annotated, of a famous love story couched in the form of a romantic epic.

————. *Le Roman de Wîs et Râmîn.* French prose translation by Henri Massé. Paris: Paris Unesco Persian Series, 1959. Reliable, if somewhat less attractive than the English version.

Hāfez. *Der Diwan von Mohammed Schemseddin Hafiz.* 2 vols. Translated by Joseph von Hammer-Purgstall. Stuttgart and Tübingen (Cotta), 1812–13. First complete German translation and important as source of Goethe's and Emerson's interest in Hāfez.

————. *Der Diwan des Grossen Lyrischen Dichters Hafis.* An edition and German metrical translation by Vinzent Ritter von Rosenzweig-Schwannau. 3 vols. Vienna: 1856–64. Perhaps the most felicitous of all the major German versions.

————. *Diwan-i-Hafiz.* Translated by H. Wilberforce-Clarke. 2 vols. Calcutta, 1891. An idiosyncratic English version in literal and markedly artificial prose, with plentiful annotation. Based on German edition of Hermann Brockhaus (3 vols., Leipzig, 1854–56).

————. *The Poems of Shemseddin Mohammed Hafiz of Shiraz.* Translated by John Payne. 3 vols. London: The Villon Society, 1901. Second complete English rendering of the *Divan*, the *ghazals* in "isometric" form and often retaining the Persian wordplay.

———. *Hafiz of Shiraz, Selections from His Poems.* Translated by Herman Bicknell. London: Truebner & Co., 1875. About 150 poems in poetic, linear translation of high quality—a favorite with the Victorians.

———. *Poems from the Divan of Hafiz.* Translated by Gertrude M. L. Bell. London: William Heinemann, 1897 (reprinted 1928). This high-spirited aristocrat, traveler, and diplomat produced one of the finest renderings ever made of Hāfez.

———. *Versions from Hafiz, an Essay in Persian Metre.* Translated by Walter Leaf. London: G. Richards, 1898. Only twenty-eight *ghazals* rendered, but generally more successfully than Payne's.

———. *Fifty Poems of Hāfiz.* "Texts and translations collected and made, introduced and annotated" by Arthur J. Arberry. Cambridge: Cambridge University Press, 1947 (and reprinted with corrections). Though relatively small, this is by far the best all-round introduction to Hāfez and to the work of his main English translators. References are both comprehensive and accurate.

———. *Hafiz of Shiraz: Thirty Poems.* Translated by Peter Avery and John Heath-Stubbs. London: John Murray, 1952. Collaboration between scholar and poet, with a good discussion of the form of the *ghazal.*

———. *Unity in the Ghazals of Hafez,* by Michael C. Hillmann. Minneapolis and Chicago: Bibliotheca Islamica, 1976. Besides illustrating the problems of translating Hāfez (with some literal versions), this work brings Hāfez scholarship up to date over the thirty years since the publication of *Fifty Poems of Hāfiz.* Various articles have taken Hāfez studies still further over the ten years since this work appeared.

Jāmi. *FitzGerald's 'Salaman and Absal.'* Edited by A. J. Arberry. Cambridge: Cambridge University Press, 1956. A trilateral comparative exercise in translation (two by FitzGerald and one by Arberry, all in verse), together with a lengthy introduction. This work is both a romantic epic and a mystical-philosophical allegory.

———. *Analysis and Specimens of the Joseph and Zulaikha.* Translated by Samuel Robinson. London: Privately Printed, 1873. Some 150 pages, in prose paraphrase and linear translation, based on German version of Rosenzweig.

————. *Yusuf and Zulaikha.* Translated by Ralph T. H. Griffith. London: Truebner's, 1882. Nearly three-fourths of the poem in varied meters and with the excisions in an appendix. [See final work cited below]

————. *The Book of Joseph and Zuleikha, a Historical Romantic Persian Poem.* Translated by Alexander Rogers. London: David Nutt, 1892 (reprinted 1919). Almost the entire poem in rhymed couplets and with annotation. [See final work cited below]

————. An abridgement of Jāmi's poem based on the Griffith and Rogers translations is contained in *Joseph and Potiphar's Wife in World Literature* by John D. Yohannan. New York: New Directions, 1968, pp. 166–220.

Khayyām, 'Omar. *The Rubaiyat of Omar Khayyam.* Translation/adaptation/reworking by Edward FitzGerald. London, 1859 (and countless subsequent reprintings thereafter; among them, three varying editions during FitzGerald's own lifetime). This work, in one form or another, is always likely to be readily available. Several others have tried their hand on the same, or additional material, but virtually none of these—especially as a whole—approaches FitzGerald's "magic."

————. *The Quatrains of Omar Kheyyam of Nishapour.* Translated by John Payne. London: The Villon Society, 1898. Eight hundred and forty-five quatrains "in accordance with the original forms," but many of them undoubtedly spurious.

————. *The Sufistic Quatrains of Omar Khayyam.* Edited by Robert Arnot. New York and London: M. Walter Dunne, 1903. A very useful book that contains FitzGerald's first edition, Edward Heron-Allen's analysis of it, E. H. Whinfield's five hundred quatrains in verse, and J. B. Nicolas's Sufistic interpretation (of 1867) rendered in English prose.

————. *The Rubaiyat of Omar Khayyam.* Translated by Arthur J. Arberry. London: Emory Walker, 1949. Includes FitzGerald's first and fourth editions, Whinfield's translation, and Arberry's own version of a Chester Beatty ms. supposedly dated 1259–60.

————. *Omar Khayyam, a New Version Based upon Recent Discoveries.* Translated by Arthur J. Arberry. New Haven: Yale University Press, 1952. Serious doubt has been cast upon the authenticity of both of the above manuscripts.

————. *The Original Rubaiyyat of Omar Khayaam.* Translated by Robert Graves and Omar Ali-Shah. New York: Doubleday, 1968. A tendentious Sufistic interpretation based on a very questionable manuscript.

———. *In Search of Omar Khayyam,* by Ali Dashti (English translation and introduction by L. P. Elwell-Sutton). London: Allen and Unwin, 1971. This work offers a masterly and fascinating overview of Khayyam studies, putting in perspective several notorious controversies and dubious enterprises of the last thirty to forty years. It also contains much translated material, both fresh and comparative.

———. *Rubaiyat of Omar Khayyam.* Edited by Nathan H. Dole. Boston: Joseph Knight Co., 1896. English, French, and German translations, with FitzGerald's quatrains as focus.

———. *The Ruba'iyat of Omar Khayyam.* Translated by Peter Avery and John Heath-Stubbs. London: Allen Lane, 1979 (reprinted in Penguin Classics with an introduction and appendixes, 1981.) A close translation based on Forughi-Ghani and Hedāyat editions.

Nezāmi (of Ganja). *Haft Paikar (The Seven Beauties).* Translated by C. E. Wilson. 2 vols. London: Probsthain, 1924. A verse rendering of a romantic epic which may serve as an object lesson of Nezāmi's notorious difficulty and richness when offered in direct translation and unabridged. Useful commentary.

———. *Die Geschichten der sieben Prinzessinen.* German translation by R. Gelpke. Zurich: Manesse Verlag, 1959.

———. *Le sette principesse.* Italian translation by Alessandro Bausani. Rome: Leonardo da Vinci (Persian Heritage Series no. 6), 1967. An elegant "distilled" prose paraphrase of the *Haft Paikar.*

———. *Sikandar Nama E Bara, or the Book of Alexander the Great.* Translated by H. Wilberforce-Clarke. London: Allen, 1881. A prose version.

———. *Laili Majnun, a Poem from the Original Persian of Nizami.* Translated by James Atkinson. London: Oriental Translation Fund, 1836. 2nd ed. 1894, Indian reprint 1915. Over three thousand lines, mostly in rhymed couplets of four or five feet, but occasionally in stanzaic patterns.

———. *Lejla und Medshnun. Der berühmteste Liebesroman des Morgenlandes.* German version by R. Gelpke. Zurich: Manessa Bibliothek, 1963.

———. *The Story of Layla and Majnun.* Translated by R. Gelpke (with E. Mattin and G. Hill). Oxford: Cassirer, 1966. A prose condensation of the story, designed to meet the problems cited in the case of Wilson's translation of Haft Paikar.

———. *Le Roman des Chosroès et Chîrîn*. French translation by Henri Massé. Paris: Maisonneuve et Larose (Persian Heritage Series no. 2), 1970. Like preceding work cited, an attempt to "convey" a celebrated Persian romantic epic.

———. *Chosrou und Schirin*. German translation with an afterword and notes by Christopher Bürgel. Zurich: Manesse Verlag (Persian Heritage Series no. 36; Manesse Bibliothek der Weltliteratur), 1980. An elegant rendering in prose.

———. *The Treasury of Mysteries (Makhzan al Asrar)*. Translated by G. H. Darab. London: Probsthain, 1945. Linear prose version.

———. *Memoir of the Life and Writings of the Persian Poet Nizami*. Translated from the German of William Bacher by Samuel Robinson. London: Privately Printed, 1873. Robinson's renditions are in verse.

Rumi, Jalāl al-Din, Maulānā. *The Mathnawí of Jalálu'ddín Rúmí*. Edited, translated, and annotated by Reynold A. Nicholson. Leyden/London: Gibb Memorial Series (New Series IV), 1925–1940. Of the total of eight volumes, the translation, notes, and so forth are contained in Vols. 2, 4, 6–8. This English version of the supreme Persian mystical poem represents the most ambitious effort at translation ever made from that literature into a Western language. Despite its learning and insight, it does not display the translator's usual elegant skill to best advantage.

———. *Tales of Mystic Meaning, Being Selections from the Mathnawi of Jalal-ud-Din Rumi*. Translated by Reynold A. Nicholson. London: Chapman and Hall, 1931. Fifty-one stories, all but two in prose, intended for first readers.

———. *Tales from the Masnavi*. Translated by A. J. Arberry. London: Allen and Unwin, 1961. A "poetic-prose" retelling of one hundred anecdotes from the first work cited above, such anecdotes being important not only in themselves but for their illustration of the mystical thought as such.

———. *More Tales from the Masnavi*. Translated by A. J. Arberry. London: Allen and Unwin, 1963. Concludes the project initiated in *Tales from the Masnavi*.

———. *Masnavi i Ma'navi, the Spiritual Couplets of Maulana Jelal-ad-Din Muhammad i Rumi*. Translated and abridged by E. H. Whinfield. London: Kegan Paul, 1887. Some in prose, most in a kind of free verse. Annotated. Reissued as the *Teachings of Rumi: The Masnavi*. New York: E. P. Dutton & Co., 1975 (a Dutton Paperback).

————. *Selected Poems from the Divani Shamsi Tabriz.* Translated by Reynold A. Nicholson. Cambridge: Cambridge University Press, 1898. Generally successful English equivalents of Persian *ghazals.* Reprinted by Rainbow Bridge of San Francisco, 1973, with notes selected from the original edition.

————. *Mystical Poems of Rumi.* Translated by Arthur J. Arberry. Chicago: University of Chicago Press (Persian Heritage Series no. 3), 1968. Contains two hundred of Rumi's shorter poems.

————. *Mystical Poems of Rumi* (second selection). A continuation of preceding work, containing another two hundred poems of Rumi translated by A. J. Arberry, published posthumously. New York: Bibliotheca Persica (Persian Heritage Series no. 23), 1979.

————. *The Ruba'iyat of Jalal al-Din Rumi.* Translated by A. J. Arberry. London: Emery Walker, 1949. An interesting demonstration of the use of the *rubā'i* form by a poet other than 'Omar Khayyām.

————. *Unseen Rain: Quatrains of Rumi,* by John Moyne and Coleman Barks. Putney, Vt.: Threshold Books, 1986. Rendering of selected *rubā'i*s in free verse by a Persian scholar and an American poet.

————. *Night and Sleep.* Translation of selected poems by Coleman Barks. Cambridge, Mass.: Yellow Moon Press, 1981. With illustrations.

————. *Open Secret.* Translated in free verse by John Moyne and Coleman Barks. Putney, Vt.: Threshold Books, 1984. Translation of selections of Rumi's quatrains and odes, partially based on versions done by Arberry and Nicholson.

————. *The Triumphal Sun: A Study of the Works of Jalāloddin Rumi,* by Annemarie Schimmel. London/The Hague: East-West Publications (Persian Heritage Series no. 8), 1978. A full and informative work, strong on imagery and theological implications of the works of Rumi, with many illustrative quotations more or less freshly translated.

————. *Dschelaladdin Rumi, Aus dem Diwan.* Translated by Annemarie Schimmel. Stuttgart: 1964. A new German version (with introduction) of verses chosen from the collected lyrics.

————. *Licht und Reigen* "Gedichte aus dem Diwan des Größten Mystischen Dichters persicher Zunge." Selected, translated, and annotated by Johann Christopher Bürgel. Bern and Frankfurt: Herbert Lang (Persian Heritage Series no. 26), 1974.

Sa'di, Mosleh al-Din. *Morals Pointed and Tales Adorned: The Būstān of Sa'di.* Translated by G. M. Wickens. Toronto: University of Toronto Press (Persian Heritage Series no. 17), 1974 (reprinted 1978). A multistyle verse rendering of the most famous Persian didactic poem (over 4,100 double lines), containing moral and mystical counsel, illustrated by numerous anecdotes and pithy sayings. With annotation and commentary.

———. *The Bustan by Shaikh Muslih-ud-din Sa'di Shirazi.* Translated by H. Wilberforce-Clarke. London: Allen, 1879. Prose version, with notes and index.

———. *The Garden of Fragrance, Being a Complete Translation of the Bostan of Sadi,* by G. S. Davie. London: Kegan Paul, Trench, 1882. In rhymed couplets somewhat imitative of Sa'di's verse.

———. *Sa'di's Bostan.* Translated by Friedrich Rückert (under supervision of W. Pertsch). Leipzig, 1882. A posthumous German version, on the whole well-executed.

———. *Aus Sa'di's Diwan.* Translated by Friedrich Rückert (under supervision of E. A. Bayer). Berlin, 1893. A posthumous publication of German selections from Sa'di's collected shorter poems. Individual items are very successful; but like the preceding work, these versions are not equal to the poet's rendition of Ferdowsi (*Firdosi's Königsbuch*).

———. *Sa'di's Politische Gedichte.* Translated by Friedrich Rückert (under supervision of E. A. Bayer). Berlin, 1894. Another posthumous publication by the *doyen* of nineteenth-century German Orientalist translators. Here, Rückert, in his youth a celebrated patriotic poet in the anti-Napoleonic struggle, tries to recapture his early enthusiasm in another setting, that of thirteenth-century Iran. If the experiment is a little forced, its interest lies in its looking at Sa'di's poetry from an angle not hitherto regarded by others.

Shabestari, Mahmud. *Gulshan-i-Raz: the Mystic Rose Garden of S'ad ud din Mahmud Shabistari.* Translated by E. H. Whinfield. London: Truebner, 1880. Important discussion of Sufism.

———. *The Dialogue of the Gulshan-i-Raz or Mystical Garden of Roses . . . with Selections from the Rubaiyat of Omar Khayyam.* Translated by E. A. Johnson. London: Truebner, 1887 (reprinted 1898, 1908).

Tāher, Bābā. *The Lament of Baba Tahir. Being the Rubaiyat of Baba Tahir Hamadani (Uryan).*Translated by Edward Heron-Allen and Elizabeth A. C. Brenton. London: Quaritch, 1902. The ecstatic Sufi poet used as a foil for the agnostic Khayyam.

————. *Poems of a Persian Sufi.* Translated by Arthur J. Arberry. Cambridge: Heffer and Son, 1937.

Zākāni, 'Obaydallāh. *Gorby and the Rats: Mush-o-Gurbeh.* Translated by Omar S. Pound. London: Agenda Editions (no. 2), 1972. A free, spirited verse rendition full of wit and clever wordplay.

————. *The Ethics of the Aristocrats and Other Satirical Works.* Translation of *Akhlāq al-ashrāf, Ta'rifāt, Sadpand, Mush o gorbeh* ("Rats against Cats") by H. Javadi. Piedmont, Cal.: Jahan Book Co., 1985.

————. *Rats against Cats.* Translated by Mas'uud e Farzaad. London: Privately Printed, 1945.

————. Untitled translation in *Classical Persian Literature,* by A. J. Arberry. London: Allen and Unwin, 1958, pp. 291–96. Arberry's *Mush u Gurba* rendition is in unrhymed tetrameter lines.

## B. **Prose**

Anonymous. *Iskandarnamah: A Persian Medieval Alexander Romance.* Translated by Minoo S. Southgate. New York: Columbia University Press (Persian Heritage Series no. 31), 1978. A lesser-known example of a legend cycle that was even more important in Persian literature than in the medieval West. The romantic adventures and alleged wise sayings of Alexander are treated at length also by Ferdowsi, Nezāmi, and Jāmi. For a translation of Ferdowsi's treatment of the subject, see poetry section of this bibliography.

'Attār, Farid al-Din. *Muslim Saints and Mystics: Episodes from the Tadhkirat al-Auliyā.* Translated by Arthur J. Arberry (Persian Heritage Series no. 1). Chicago: University of Chicago Press, 1966; and London: Routledge and Kegan Paul, 1966 (reprinted, Routledge and Kegan Paul, 1973, 1976, paperback 1979, 1983). The original prose of this work is considered a masterpiece of elegance and simplicity, the poetic citations being incidental to the biographies (and by other hands than 'Attār's). Arberry provides a good introduction.

Bighami. *Love and War, Adventure from the Firuz Shah Nāma of Sheikh Bighami.* Translation of selected episodes with an introduction by William Hanaway Jr. Delmar, N.Y.: Scholars' Facsimile and Reprint (Persian Heritage Series no. 19), 1974.

Farāmarz-e Khodādād. *Samak-e Ayyār.* French translation by Frédérique Razavi. Paris: Unesco Persian Series (Persian Heritage Series no. 12), 1972. An early Persian prose romance *cum* picaresque novel. The present version, though far from complete, gives a good flavor of the whole.

Kai-Kā'us ebn-e Eskandar. *A Mirror for Princes.* Translated by Reuben Levy. London: E. P. Dutton, 1951. A classic of early medieval Persian prose, written by a ruler for his son. This work in fact gives counsels of "lifemanship" in all conceivable situations of prosperity and disaster, with (as usual) highly entertaining illustrative anecdotes.

Nezām al-Molk. *The Book of Government, or Rules for Kings.* Translated by Hubert S. Darke. London/New Haven: Routledge & Kegan Paul, 1960 (reprinted 1978 [as Persian Heritage Series no. 32]). A serious manual of instruction, but with illustrative anecdotes. The translation is smooth and elegant, and makes attractive reading.

Nezāmi 'Aruzi. *Chahār Maqāla: Four Discourses.* Translated by Edward G. Browne. London: Gibb Memorial Series XI/2, 1921. Four elegant essays on Civil Servants, Poets, Astrologers, and Physicians. The whole is illustrated with many famous anecdotes and citations. Excellent annotation.

———. *Les Quatre Discours.* French translation by Isabelle de Gastines. Paris: Unesco Persian Series (Persian Heritage Series no. 8), 1968. A good version, but owes much to preceding work cited.

Rumi, Jalāl al-Din. *Discourses of Rumi.* Translated by Arthur J. Arberry. London: G. Allen & Unwin, 1961. Samples of the great mystical poet's conversation and correspondence.

Tusi, Nasir al-Din. *The Nasirean Ethics.* Translated by G. M. Wickens. London: G. Allen & Unwin, 1964. A work which covers the whole moral and intellectual world-view of medieval Islamic culture. Renders in elegant and lucid English a work that is notoriously difficult and involved in the original. Ample annotation and commentary.

Varāvini, Sa'd al-Din. *The Tales of Marzuban.* Translated by Reuben Levy. Bloomington: Indiana University Press, 1959 (reprinted, Greenwood Press [as Persian Heritage Series no. 4], 1968). A famous old collection of instructive fables, many with animal characters, as well as sages, kings, and demons. The translation, as always with Levy, reads easily and attractively, despite the often difficult nature of the original.

Jovaini, 'Alā' al-Din 'Atā-Malek. *The History of the World Conqueror.* Translated from the text of Mirzā Mohammad Qazvini by John Andrew Boyle. 2 vols. Manchester: Manchester University Press (Unesco Persian Series), 1958. With an introduction, bibliography, and notes.

Rashid al-Din Fazl Allāh. *Rashid Al-Din's History of India: Collected Essays with Facsimiles and Indices,* by Karl Jahn. The Hague: Mouton and Co. (Central Asiatic Studies Series), 1965.
———. *The Successors of Genghis Khan.* Translated from the Persian by John Andrew Boyle. New York and London: Columbia University Press (Persian Heritage Series no. 10), 1971. Mongol, Turkish, and Il-Khan portions of preceding work cited.

## C. **Mixed Genre**

Jāmi. *Baharestan: Persian Wit and Humor.* Translated by C. E. Wilson. London: Chatto and Windus, 1883. The *Behārestān,* like Sa'di's *Golestān,* is a prose-cum-verse work of "entertainment together with some measure of edification."
———. *Beharistan (Abode of Spring).* [Translated by E. H. Rehatsek] "Benares," 1887. "Printed by the Kama Shastra Society for subscribers only." A literal and linear translation.
———. *Le Beharistan.* French translation by Henri Massé. Paris: P. Geuthner, 1925.
———. *Der Frühlingsgarten.* German translation by O. M. von Schlechta-Wssehrd. Vienna, 1846. This is a good translation, but virtually unobtainable.

Sa'di, Mosleh al-Din. *The Gulestan or Rose Garden of Sa'di.* Translated by Edward Rehatsek. London: Putnam, 1964; New York: Capricorn, 1966. A reissue of *The Gulistan or Rose-Garden of Sadi, Faithfully Translated into English,* Benares, Kama Shastra Society, 1888. The finest example in all Persian literature of the prose-and-verse entertainment, light but purportedly edifying. A long preface by W. G. Archer, and a comprehensive introduction by G. M. Wickens, serve to place the work (and Sa'di generally) in perspective.
———. *Tales from the Gulistân or Rose-Garden of the Sheikh Sa'di of Shirâz.* Translated by Sir Richard Burton and illustrated by J. Kettelwell.

London: Philip Allen & Co., 1928. This translation, attributed to Burton, is in fact by Rehatsek (possibly polished by Burton), and differs little from the above.

————. *The Rose Garden.* Translated with an introduction by Edward B. Eastwick. 2nd edition. London: Truebner, 1880 (reprinted, London: Octagon Press, 1975). A translation in prose and verse with annotations.

————. *Kings and Beggars.* Translated by A. J. Arberry. London: Luzac & Co., 1945. An excellent version of the first two chapters (never followed up), with a good introduction.

————. *Verse aus dem Gulistan.* Translated by Friedrich Rückert. ("Zeitschrift für vergleichende Literaturgeschichte," VII/X, 1895: under supervision of E. A. Bayer). Still another posthumous publication, this time in a German comparative-literature periodical. Well done, but not Rückert at his best.

## D. **Anthologies**

Arberry, Arthur John. *Classical Persian Literature.* London: Allen & Unwin, 1958. An excellent introduction to the classical period, tenth–fifteenth century A.D. Contains much translation, both borrowed and original, of poetry and prose.

————. *Persian Poems.* London/New York: Everyman 996, 1954. A miscellaneous collection of translations by the editor and many others. Good references to both original authors and translators. (A few of the items are postclassical.)

————. *Immortal Rose.* London: Luzac & Co., 1948. A collection of translations similar to the previous item, but less well-done and somewhat sentimental and archaic in tone. Concentrates on lyrical poetry.

Browne, Edward Granville. *A Literary History of Persia.* Cambridge: Cambridge University Press, 1902–24 (reprinted 1964). Though uneven, and now sometimes outdated, this remains the standard reference work. It contains many passages of translation, some of considerable length, of Persian literature in a broad sense. Of the four volumes, volumes II and III are concerned with the classical period (1000–1500 A.D.), volume I being a long introduction to Islamic history and culture generally.

Bowen, John C. E. *Poems from the Persian.* Oxford: Basil Blackwell,

1948. Fifty excerpts from about a dozen poets in verse translations.

von Hammer-Purgstall, Joseph. *Geschichte der schönen Redekünste Persiens.* Vienna, 1818. With an anthology of selections from two hundred poets. The source of Emerson's knowledge of Persian poetry.

Jackson, A. V. W. *Early Persian Poetry from the Beginnings down to the Time of Firdausi.* New York: Macmillan Co., 1920. Includes verse translations from, among others, Rudaki, Daqiqi, and Ferdowsi.

Levy, Reuben. *An Introduction to Persian Literature.* New York: Columbia University Press, 1969. A small work, but providing a good overview of "types." Contains considerable translated material.
———. *Stories from Sa'di's Bustan and Gulistan.* London: Chapman and Stall, 1928. A clever reworking of material from these two classics, the *Golestān* portions adapted from Gladwin's translation.

Massé, Henri, et al. *Anthologie Persane (XIᵉ–XIXᵉ siècles).* An anthology by Z. Safa, translated by G. Lazard, R. Lescot and H. Massé. Paris: Gallimard, 1950. Contains good French versions of material from 150 authors (some from the postclassical period).

Nicholson, Reynold A. *Translations of Eastern Poetry and Prose.* Cambridge: Cambridge University Press, 1922. A popular anthology of Arabic and Persian authors, both major and secondary.

Pound, Omar. *Arabic and Persian Poems in English.* The National Poetry Foundation, University of Maine at Orono and the Three Continents Press, Washington, D.C., 1986 (all published earlier in different publications). About a dozen selections from, among others, Rumi, Rudaki, and Manuchehri, as well as Zākāni's "Gorby and the Rats" (*Mush-o gorba*) all freely and ingeniously turned.

Robinson, Samuel. *Flowers Culled from Persian Gardens.* Manchester: Privately Printed, 1870. Tasteful linear translations from various poets. Much the same as *Persian Poetry for English Readers.* Glasgow: Privately Printed, 1883.

Schimmel, Annemarie. *Rückert 1788–1866: Übersetzungen persischer Poesie.* Wiesbaden: Harrassowitz, 1966. A short anthology of selections of translations by Rückert from Persian poetry into German "equivalents," with an introduction by the editor. The Persian texts are on facing pages. An enthusiastic tribute to Rückert.

———. *Orientalische Dichtung in der Übersetzung Fr. Rückerts.* Bremen: C. Schünemann, 1963. A more general and larger work than the previous one, with a lengthy introduction and covering translations from other literatures as well as Persian. However, the Persian section runs to some 150 pages and doubtless provides the primary focus of the editor's own interest.

Note: The Wisdom of the East Series, published by John Murray of London during the first half of the present century, included selections from Ansāri, Hāfez, Sa'di, and Shabestari, among others. Although some of the volumes leave much to be desired in scholarly apparatus, the series has supplied a popular need.

## 2. MODERNIST PERSIAN LITERATURE

Prose has played a more important role in Modernist Persian Literature than poetry; therefore, it has been assigned first place in the following list. Translations, however, have not always accurately reflected either the Persian reputations of authors or their critical significance in the history of Persian letters.

For instance, among the poets, Forugh Farrokhzād has had an enormous appeal to translators, while such equally important figures as Nimā Yushij and Shāmlu have been relatively neglected. Since some of these neglected authors, both in fiction and verse, have been taken notice of in periodicals, it has been thought advisable to admit a few journal entries among the anthologies. Two one-act plays by Sā'edi also are included.

### A. **Prose**

Āl-e Ahmad, Jalāl. *Plagued by the West (Gharbzadegi).* Translated by Paul Sprachman, with a foreword by E. Yarshater. Delmar, N.Y.: Caravan Books (Modern Persian Literature Series no. 4), 1982. Annotated.

———. *Gharbzadegi (Weststruckness).* Translated by John Green and Ahmad Alizadeh. Lexington, Ky.: Mazda, 1982. With an introduction on the Persian text and with notes.

———. *Occidentosis: a Plague from the West.* Translated by R. Campbell. Berkeley, Cal.: Mizan Press, 1984. With annotation, and with an introduction by Hamid Algar.

————. *The School Principal.* Translated by John K. Newton. Minneapolis: Bibliotheca Islamica, 1974. Includes an introduction to the works of Āl-e Ahmad and a translation of his short story "The China Flowerpot."

————. *Lost in the Crowd.* Translation of *Khasi dar Miqāt* by John Green, Ahmand Alizadeh, et al. Washington, D.C.: Three Continents Press, 1985. With an introduction by Michael Hillmann and a bibliography of Āl-e Ahmad, including all published translations.

————. *Iranian Society: an Anthology of Writings by Jalal Āl-e Ahmad.* Compiled and edited by Michael C. Hillmann. Lexington, Ky.: Mazda, 1982. This contains a bio-bibliographical preface by the editor, translations by several hands of both critical and fictional writings of Āl-e Ahmad.

'Alavi, Bozorg. *Scrap Papers from Prison. The Prison Papers of Bozorg Alavi: A Literary Odyssey.* Translated by Donné Raffat. Syracuse: Syracuse University Press, 1985, pp. 115–96. The odyssey referred to is the writing of this book, virtually an account of 'Alavi's career.

Behrangi, Samad. *The Little Black Fish and Other Modern Persian Stories.* Translated by Eric and Mary Hoogland, with a bibliographical-historical essay by Thomas Ricks. Washington, D.C.: Three Continents Press, 1976. Contains a translation of Sā'edi's memorial essay on Behrangi.

Golshiri, Hushang. *Prince Ehtejab.* Translated by Minoo R. Buffington and included in *Major Voices in Contemporary Persian Literature.* See **Anthologies and Periodicals.**

Hedāyat, Sadeq. *The Blind Owl.* Translated by D. P. Costello. New York: Evergreen, 1969. This remains the most readily available and accepted translation of Hedāyat's masterpiece.

————. *The Blind Owl and Other Hedayat Stories.* Compiled by Carol L. Sayers and edited by Russel P. Christenson. Minneapolis: Sorayya Publishers, 1984. Includes a revised version of a 1974 translation of *The Blind Owl* by Iraj Bashiri, and eleven short stories.

————. *Hedayat's 'The Blind Owl' Forty Years After.* Compiled and edited by Michael C. Hillmann. Austin, Tex.: University of Texas (Austin) Center for Middle Eastern Studies, 1978. This collection of critical essays also includes translations of "Buried Alive" by Carter Bryant and "Three Drops of Blood" by Guity Nashat and Marilyn R. Waldman.

———. *Haji Agha: Portrait of an Iranian Confidence Man.* Translated by
G. M. Wickens. Austin, Tex.: University of Texas (Austin) Center
for Middle Eastern Studies, 1979. This volume includes an introduction by Lois Beck, with bibliographical information and ex-
planatory notes by the translator.

———. *Hedayat: an Anthology.* Edited by Ehsan Yarshater. Delmar,
N.Y.: Caravan Books (Modern Persian Literature Series no. 2),
1979. To date, the most comprehensive collection of Hedayat's
short stories in English translation. It contains an introduction by
the editor and translations of seventeen short stories by, among
others, Brian Spooner, Gisele Kapuscinski, Ahmad Karimi-Hakkak, and Hubert Darke.

Jamālzādeh, Mohammad 'Ali. *Isfahan is Half the World: Memoirs of a
Persian Boyhood.* Translated by W. C. Heston. Princeton: Princeton
University Press, 1983 (paperback reprint, 1986). Some liberties
have been taken in the translation, but there are page references
to the Persian original.

———. *Once Upon a Time (Yeki Bud Yeki Nabud).* Translated by Heshmat
Moayyad and Paul Sprachman. Delmar, N.Y.: Caravan Books
(Modern Persian Literature Series no. 6), 1985. A complete trans-
lation of this well-known and pioneering modern classic.

Sā'edi, Gholām-Hoseyn. *Dandil: Stories from Iranian Life.* Translated by
Robert Campbell, Hassan Javadi, and Julie S. Meisami. New York:
Random House, 1981. Includes five short stories and an intro-
duction giving the political and cultural background.

———. *The Cow: a Screenplay.* Translated by Mohsen Ghadessy. *Iranian
Studies* XVIII (1985), pp. 257–323. The film of this play won
international awards.

———. *Fear and Trembling.* Translated by Minoo Southgate. Washington, D.C.: Three Continents Press, 1984. Includes a brief introduction on modern Iranian literature and Sā'edi's literary output,
as well as a (mostly Persian) bibliography of his work.

Sholevar, Bahman. *The Night's Journey* and *The Coming of the Messiah.*
Translated by the author. Philadelphia: Concourse Press (Modern
Persian Literature Series no. 7), 1984.

## B. Poetry

E'tesami, Parvin. *A Nightingale's Lament.* Translated by Moayyad Heshmat and A. Margaret Arent Madelung. Lexington, Ky.: Mazda, 1985. Eighty-two poems are prefaced by Moayyad's essay entitled "Parvin's Personality and Poetry" and followed by Madelung's "commentary."

Farrokhzād, Forugh. *Another Birth: Selected Poems of Forugh Farrokhzad.* Translated by Hasan Javadi and Susan Sallee. Emeryville, Cal.: Albany Press, 1981. This selection includes an introduction, thirty-four poems, three interviews with the poet, letters from the poet, two articles on Farrokhzād's work, and a selected bibliography.

―――. *Bride of Acacias.* Translated by Jascha Kessler and Amin Banani. Delmar, N.Y.: Caravan Books (Modern Persian Literature Series no. 5), 1982. This volume includes translations of the entire collection of *Another Birth* (1964), in addition to sixteen posthumous and early poems, through the collaboration of an American poet and a Persian scholar. An introduction by A. Banani and an afterword by Farzaneh Milani provide a background to the life and works of the poet. The most felicitous translation of Farrokhzad.

Nāderpur, Nāder. *False Dawn.* Translation of a selection of Nāderpur's poems by Michael C. Hillmann, with an introduction by the translator on the life and times of the poet and a critical essay on his poems as afterword by Leonard P. Alishan. *Literature East and West* 22 (1986), the University of Texas at Austin.

## C. Anthologies and Periodicals

*Life and Letters* 63, no. 148 (December 1949), "Persian Writers," pp. 196–270. Includes a selection of Persian poetry translated by Arthur J. Arberry and of prose fiction translated by D. G. Law, together with introductory essays by the translators.

"Contemporary Iranian Poetry," by Geoffrey Squires and Reza Nematollahi, in *Poesie Vivante* 28 (1968), pp. 3–17. A rather unfavorable view of the "new poetry" in a French and English discussion, but with translations in English only. Represented, among others, are Yushij, Shāmlu, Hoquqi, Kasra'i, and Farrokhzād.

*Modern Islamic Literature from 1800 to the Present.* Edited by James Kritzack. New York: Holt, Rinehart and Winston, 1970. Hardly an adequate selection of Modernist Persian literature, either in genre or in quality.

*The Literary Review* 18, no. 1 (Fall 1974), "Iran," edited by Thomas M. Ricks. Essays, poems, and short stories by, among others, Āl-e Ahmad, Chubak, Farrokhzād, Hedāyat, Yushij, and Shāmlu.

*An Anthology of Modern Persian Poetry.* Compiled and translated from the works of twenty-six poets by Ahmad Karimi-Hakkāk. New York: Westview Press (Modern Persian Literature Series no. 1), 1978. Includes a preface by E. Yarshater, an introduction by the translator, the greatest space being devoted to Farrokhzād, Shāmlu, Sepehri, Yushij, and Akhavān-e Sāles.

*New Writing from the Middle East.* Edited by Leo Hamalian and John D. Yohannan. New York: Mentor Books, 1978, "Persian Literature," pp. 271–400. This selection includes a brief background essay, translation of five short stories, the opening section from Reza Barāheni's unpublished 1972 novel titled *The Infernal Times of Āghā-ye Ayyāz,* twelve selections from the poetry of Forugh Farrokhzād, Sohrāb Sepehri, and Ahmad Shāmlu, and a one-act play by Gholām-Hoseyn Sā'edi.

*Major Voices in Contemporary Persian Literature.* Edited by Michael C. Hillmann, in *Literature East and West,* 20 (1976—actually published 1980). This volume includes thirteen short stories by Jalāl Āl-e Ahmad, Bozorg 'Alavi, Sādeq Chubak, Mohammad 'Ali Jamālzādeh, and Gholām Hoseyn Sā'edi, among others. It also has Hushang Golshiri's *Prince Ehtejab* (1969) and selections from the poetry of Mehdi Akhavān-e Sāles, Forugh Farrokhzād, Nāder Nāderpur, Nimā Yushij, and Ahmad Shāmlu. A brief bio-bibliographical note introduces each author. The partially annotated bibliography includes a list of modernist Persian writings in translation.

*Modern Persian Short Stories.* Edited and translated by Minoo Southgate. Washington, D.C.: Three Continents Press, 1980. The first volume in English is devoted to modern Persian short stories. It includes a short introduction and translations of one pre-World War II short story and fourteen stories from the 1960s and 1970s. Some of the authors represented are Āl-e Ahmad, Chubak, Golestān, Hedāyat, Nāder Ebrāhimi, Bahrām Sādeqi, Sā'edi, and Khosrow Shāhāni.

*Iranian Studies.* A quarterly published by the Iranian Studies Association since 1968. Includes translations from Āl-e Ahmad, Chubak,

Farrokhzād, Hedāyat, Sā'edi, Sepehri, and Shāmlu, among others. See particularly the following volumes: I (1968), III (1970), V (1973), VIII (1975), IX (1976), X (1977), XV (1982), XVIII (1985) (See Sā'edi, *The Cow: a Screenplay,* above.)

# Contributors

JES PETER ASMUSSEN, Professor of Iranian Studies at the University of Copenhagen, was born in 1928 in South Jutland and educated at the Theological Faculty in Copenhagen, after which he served for a time as a chaplain to the Royal Danish Navy. In 1960 he began teaching at the University of Copenhagen, succeeding the late Kay Barr as Professor of Iranian in 1967. He was elected a member of the Royal Danish Academy of Sciences in 1973, and made a Knight of Dannebrog in 1976. Among his books in English are *Manichaean Literature, Studies in Judeo-Persian Literature, Islam* and *Muhammad, Jesus, Abraham.* A festschrift was published in his honor in 1987.

AMIN BANANI, Professor of Persian and history at the University of California, Los Angeles, was born in Iran in 1926, received his B.A. (1947) and Ph.D. (1959) from Stanford University and his M.A. (1949) from Columbia University. He is the author of *The Modernization of Iran* and the editor and a contributing author of *Individualism and Conformity in Classical Islam,* and *State and Society in Iran.* He collaborated with Jascha Kessler in the verse translation of a collection of F. Farrokhzād's poems, *The Bride of Acacias.* He has contributed a number of chapters and articles on the history and culture of Iran to various publications, including *Iran Faces the Seventies* and *Nation and Ideology.* A former chairman of the Department of Near Eastern Languages and Cultures and a former acting director of the von Grunebaum Center for Near Eastern Studies at UCLA, Professor Banani has served on the Board of Directors of the Middle East Studies Association of North America, the Executive Council of the Society for Iranian Studies, and as Vice-President of the American Association of Iranian Studies.

MICHAEL BEARD is Associate Professor of English at the University of North Dakota, where he has been teaching since 1979. Born in 1944, he received his Ph.D. in Comparative Literature from Indiana University in 1974, and has taught at the American University in Cairo; he was the Mellon Fellow in Oriental Studies at the University of Pennsylvania in 1978–79. His study of the Arab poet Khalil Hawi in collaboration with Adnan Haydar was published in 1984.

DALE BISHOP is the Secretary for the Middle East, United Church Board for World Ministries in New York. He was born in 1946 in Canton, Ohio. He received his Ph.D. in Iranian Studies from Columbia University in 1974. He continued at Columbia as Assistant Professor of Middle East Languages and Cultures from 1974 to 1980, later becoming a Research Associate there. Specializing in Zoroastrian studies, his dissertation focused on the Vendidad, and he has published articles on both Avestan and Pahlavi literature. In 1979, Dr. Bishop was awarded a Fulbright Fellowship for the study of contemporary Zoroastrianism in India.

JOHANN CRISTOPH BÜRGEL is Professor Islamic Studies at the University of Bern, Switzerland. Born in 1931, he received his Ph.D. from the University of Göttingen in 1960, where he taught at the Seminar für Arabistik. He has translated classical poetry into German, including selections from the *divān*s of Rumi, Hāfez and Iqbāl, as well as Nezāmi's *Khosrow and Shirin*. He has published articles in Persian in *Rahnama-ye Ketab* and other journals; his articles in English include "The Pious Rogue" in *Edebiyat*, and "Love, Lust and Longing: Eroticism in Early Islam as Reflected in Literary Sources" in A. Lutfi al-Sayyid Marsot's *Society and the Sexes in Medieval Islam*.

PETER CHELKOWSKI was born in Poland in 1933, and earned degrees in Oriental Philology from Jagiello University in Poland, and in Persian Literature from Tehran University. He also pursued postgraduate studies in the History of the Islamic Near East at the School of Oriental and African Studies at the University of London. He is currently Professor of Near Eastern Studies at New York University. His publications include *Ta'ziyeh: Ritual and Drama in Iran* (ed. and contributor), *The Scholar and the Saint* (ed.), *Mirror of the Invisible World, Studies in Art and Literature of the Near East* (ed.), and *Iran: Continuity and Variety* (ed.).

JEROME W. CLINTON is Professor of Near Eastern Studies at Princeton University. Born in 1937, he studied English and American literature at Stanford University and the University of Pennsylvania before he directed his interest to Persian; he received his Ph.D. in Near Eastern Languages and Literatures in 1971 from the University of Michigan. He was director of the Tehran Center of the American Institute of Iranian Studies between 1972 and 1974. He was also on the executive board of the Society of Iranian Studies and an assistant editor of its journal, *Iranian Studies*; he is currently on the editorial board of *Edebiyat*. Professor Clinton has published *The Divān of Manuchehri Damghani, Spoken and Written Modern Persian*, and a number of articles on medieval Persian poetry as well as translations from both modern and medieval Persian poetry and prose.

L. P. ELWELL-SUTTON (1912–84) studied Arabic and Persian at the School of Oriental Studies, London University, and subsequently worked for the Anglo-Iranian Oil Company in Iran, the Eastern Services of the British Broadcasting Corporation, and the British Embassy in Tehran, where he was responsible for British wartime broadcasts in Persian and subsequently served as Press Attaché. From 1952 he lectured on Persian language, literature, and history at Edinburgh University where he was appointed a Personal Chair of Persian in 1976. His many publications include *Modern Iran, The Wonderful Sea-Horse and Other Persian Tales, Elementary Persian Grammar, The Persian Metres* and *The Horoscope of Asadullah Mirza*. He was General Editor of *Bibliographical Guide to Iran*. A Festschrift entitled *Qajar Iran*, edited by E. Bosworth and C. Hillenbrand (Edinburgh University Press, 1983), was presented to him shortly before his death.

MASSUD FARZAN is at present Visiting Professor in American Literature at Boston University. Born in Tabriz in 1936, he was educated in Iran and the United States, receiving his Ph.D. from the University of Michigan in 1964. He taught American literature, creative writing, and Persian and comparative literature in both countries, and has been affiliated with California State University, Columbia University, Dickinson College and Harvard University. He is the author of several books, including *The Tale of the Reed Pipe: Teachings of the Sufis* and *Kashan to Kalamazoo: Poems and Poems in Translation*. His fiction, poetry and essays have appeared in such journals as *Encounter, Prism International, London Magazine, Literary Review* and *Poetry*, as well as in various anthologies of prose and poetry.

ASHRAF GHANI was born in 1949, in Afghanistan, and from 1969 to 1973 he attended the American University of Beirut where he earned his B.A. and M.A. degrees in Political Science. He then returned to Kabul and taught Afghan Studies for four years at the College of Letters of the Kabul University. By 1982, he had completed a Ph.D. program in anthropology at Columbia University in New York. He has taught Anthropology at Aarhus University, Denmark, the University of California at Berkeley, and Johns Hopkins University where he is presently an Assistant Professor. Mr. Ghani is the author of *Production and Domination: Afghanistan 1747–1901*, a book to be published shortly by Columbia University Press.

M. R. GHANOONPARVAR received his B.A. from the University of Esfahan and his M.A. and Ph.D. from Eastern Michigan University. He has taught Persian language and literature courses at the University of Esfahan in Iran and the University of Virginia at Charlottesville and is currently teaching at the University of Texas at Austin. He is the author of *Prophets of Doom: Literature as a Socio-Political Phenomenon in Modern Iran* (University Press of America, 1984), *Persian for Beginners* (Mazda Publishers, 1985), and a number of articles on Persian Literature.

TALAT SAIT HALMAN (b. 1931) most recently served as the Ambassador for Cultural Affairs of the Turkish Republic. A poet, critic, translator and historian of literature, he has published some twenty-five books in English and Turkish, some of which have been translated into Persian, French and Urdu. His books include *Contemporary Turkish Literature, Yunus Emre and His Mystical Poetry*, and *Modern Turkish Drama*. He has taught Turkish language, literature and history of culture at Columbia University, New York University and Princeton University. His work on Rumi has appeared in various books and journals, including *The Nation, American Poetry Review, Chicago Review*, and *The Scholar and the Saint* edited by P. Chelkowski. With Metin And of Ankara University, he has written *Mevlana Celaleddin Rumi and the Whirling Dervishes* (1983). Mr. Halman was awarded the Thornton Wilder Prize in 1986 for his translations from American literature into Turkish.

WILLIAM L. HANAWAY, JR. is Associate Professor of Persian and has served as chairman of the Department of Oriental Studies at the University of Pennsylvania since 1981. Born in 1929, he spent a year in Iran (1967–68) before receiving his Ph.D. from Columbia University in 1970; since then, he has traveled to Iran numerous times. President of the American Institute of Iranian Studies 1979–1984, he is also the founder and editor of *Edebiyat,* a journal of Middle Eastern literatures. Among his published works are *Love and War: Adventures from the Firuz Shah-Nama of Sheikh Bighami, The Pre-Safavid Persian Inscriptions of Khurasan, I,* "Paradise on Earth: The Terrestrial Garden in Persian Literature" in *The Islamic Garden* and "The Iranian Epics" in F. Oinas's *Heroic Epic and Saga.*

MICHAEL CRAIG HILLMANN is Professor at the University of Texas in Austin. Born in 1940, he received his Ph.D. from the University of Chicago in 1974. He has spent upwards of seven years engaged in teaching and academic research in Iran, and is a leading American authority on post–World War II Persian literature. He has published numerous articles on related subjects and has edited four volumes of translations and essays on recent Persian literature. In addition he is the author of *Persian Carpets* (1984) and his translation of a selection of Nāderpour's poems has won the award of the Persian Heritage Foundation.

KEITH HITCHINS is professor of history at the University of Illinois at Urbana-Champaign. He received his Ph.D. from Harvard University in 1964. His areas of specialization are the intellectual and cultural history of Eastern Europe and the eastern Soviet republics. His recent publications include *Orthodoxy and Nationality* (Cambridge, Mass.: Harvard University Press, 1977), *Hungarica, 1961–74,* (*Historische Zeitschrift,* Sonderheft 9, Munich: Oldenburg, 1981), and articles on Azerbaijani, Kazakh, Tajik, and Kurdish literature. He is at present writing a *History of Rumania, 1774–1947* for the Oxford University Press's History of Modern Europe Series and a book about the Tajik novelist Sadr al-Din Aini.

GISELE KAPUSCINSKI is Assistant Professor of French at the State University of New York at Stony Brook. Born in Tehran in 1929, she received her baccalaureate from the University of Paris in 1951. She moved to the United States in 1960, continuing her studies at Hofstra University and Columbia University, where she received her Ph.D. in Persian Studies in 1982. Her doctoral dissertation dealt with modern Persian drama. Her publications include translations of "The Broken Mirror" and (with Mahin Hambly) "The Pilgrimage" and "The Benedictions" in *Sadeq Hedayat: An Anthology* published by the Modern Persian Literature Series, and the forthcoming *An Anthology of Modern Persian Drama.*

FARZANEH MILANI is Assistant Professor of Persian at the University of Virginia at Charlottesville. In addition to poems and articles in literary journals, she has also contributed to the following books: *Bride of Acacias, Women and Revolution in Iran, Women and the Family in the Middle East: New Voices of Change, A Rebirth, Women and the Family in Iran* (forthcoming).

HESHMAT MOAYYAD is Professor of Persian at the University of Chicago. Born in Hamadan, Iran, in 1927, he was educated at the University of Tehran and the University of Frankfurt A.M., from which he received his Ph.D. in 1958. His most recent publications include *Farā'ed-e Ghiāthi,* a collection of letters from the period 1100–1400 A.D. in two volumes, *Polyglotter Sprachführer für Persisch* (with K. J. Teubner), and the text of *Rawzat al-Rayāhin* by Darvish Ali Buzgani. He has published numerous articles and book reviews in such journals as *Sokhan, Oriens, Rahnemā-ye Ketāb* and *Annali dell' Instituto Orientale di Napoli* as well as the *Encyclopedia Iranica.* He has translated Sādeq Hedāyat's *Buf-e kur* into German, with Paul Sprachman has translated into English Jamālzāda's *Yeki bud yeki nabud,* (Once Upon A Time), and with Margaret Madelung, *A Nightingale's Lament: Selections from the Poems and Fables of Parvin 'Etesami (1907–41).*

ANNEMARIE SCHIMMEL (b. 1922) received her Ph.D. in Islamic studies from the University of Berlin in 1941; she has taught at the universities of Marburg, Ankara (Turkey) and Bonn, and since 1967 she has been Professor of Indo-Muslim Culture at Harvard University. She has received honorary degrees from the universities of Sind, Islamabad and Peshawar, as well as numerous literary awards and distinctions including the Order of Merit (First Class) from Germany. She is a member of the Royal Dutch Academy of Sciences, and is currently President of the International Association for the History of Religions. She has published widely in German and English, and has translated Persian, Arabic and Turkish works into German. Among her most recent publications are *Gabriel's Wing: A Study into the Religious Ideas of Sir Muhammad Iqbal, Islamic Calligraphy, Mystical Dimensions of Islam, As Through a Veil: Mystical Poetry in Islam,* and *The Triumphal Sun: A Study of the Works of Jalaloddin Rumi.*

PAUL SPRACHMAN (b. 1947) received his Ph.D. in Persian Literature in 1981 from the University of Chicago. A member of the Iranian Association of Teachers of Persian Language and Literature, his translation of Jalal Āl-e Ahmad's *Gharbzadegi* (Plagued by the West) was published by the Modern Persian Literature Series in 1982. His translation of M. A. Jamālzāda's *Yeki Bud Yeki Nabud* was published in the same series in 1985.

G. M. WICKENS is University Professor Emeritus, Department of Middle East and Islamic Studies, University of Toronto. He has served as lecturer in Arabic and Persian at the School of Oriental and African Studies, University of London, and at the University of Cambridge. Among his publications are translations of Tusi's *The Nasirean Ethics,* of Sa'di's *Morals Pointed and Tales Adorned: The "Bustān" of Sa'di,* and of Ṣādeq Hedāyat's *Hāji Āghā: Portrait of an Iranian Confidence Man.*

EHSAN YARSHATER is Hagop Kevorkian Professor of Iranian Studies at Columbia University and director of its Center for Iranian Studies. Born in Hamadan, Iran in 1920, he received his D.Lit. in Persian Literature from the University of Tehran in 1947 and a Ph.D. in Old and Middle Iranian from the University of London in 1960. He is the editor of the *Encyclopaedia Iranica* and of the Bibliotheca Persica, which includes the Persian Heritage Series, the Persian Studies Series and the Modern Persian Literature Series. His works pertaining to Persian literature include *Persian Poetry in the Fifteenth Century* (in Persian), "The Persian Modern Literary Idiom" in *Iran Faces the Seventies*, "Persian Literature in the Islamic Period" in *The Cambridge History of Islam*, vol. 2, "Affinities between Persian Poetry and Music" in *Art and Literature of the Near East: Studies in Honor of Richard Ettinghausen*, "Persian Poetry and Painting: Common Features," in A. U. Pope's *A Survey of Persian Art*, and "Timurid and Safavid Literature" in *The Cambridge History of Iran*, vol. 6. Most recently, he has edited *The Cambridge History of Iran*, vol. 3: Selucid, Parthian and Sasanian Periods.

JOHN D. YOHANNAN is Professor Emeritus of English and Comparative Literatures at The City College, C.U.N.Y. He was born in Iran in 1911 but was educated in the United States, receiving his Ph.D. from New York University in 1947. He was a Fulbright Lecturer in Greece from 1958 to 1960, and again in Japan in 1963–64. He is the author of *A Treasury of Asian Literature, Joseph and Potiphar's Wife in World Literature, Persian Poetry in England and America: A Two Hundred Year History*, and the co-editor of *New Writing from the Middle East*. He served for many years as a member of the advisory board of the journal *Literature East and West*, and edited a special Near East edition of it in 1967.

# Index

The index comprises proper names, technical terms, and titles of books and significant articles and poems. It also serves as a subject index. Names and book titles appearing in the footnotes have also been largely included. In the majority of cases the translation of Persian works and the year of their publication are given and the date of the writers have been indicated when they could be gleaned from the relevant chapters. Persian and Arabic terms have often been defined. The bibliographies and the bibliographical chapter have not, however, been taken into account in the index.

Diacritical marks have been added, where applicable, for the benefit of students and specialists. In the transcription scheme, the vowels *a, e, o,* are short and *ā, i, u* are long; *ż* has been generally rendered as *ż* as in Reżā.

# Index

"Affinities Between Persian Poetry and Music, The," 12 n. 11, 86 n. 12

*Afghān* (newspaper), 438

Afghan courts and their literary role in, 432–33; education in, 431–32

Afghani, M. A. (b. 1925): 310, 317; his work, *Showhar-e Āhu Khānom*, 17; discussion of his works, 307–08

Afghanistan, Persian literature in, 428ff; influence of Indian style in, 435; intellectuals' contributions to literary development, 438–41; literature of 1930–40s, 441–45; literature of 1950–63, 445–47; literature of 1963–78, 447–53; role of *Serāj al–Akhbār*, 433–35

*Afghanistan at the Beginning of the Twentieth Century*, 453

Aflāki, 207

Afrāsiyāb, 87, 93, 112, 115

*Afsāna*, 294

*Afsāna-ye āfarinesh* (by Hedāyat), 327

*Afsāna-ye bārān* (by Ebrāhimi), 306

*Afsānahā-ye Āzarbāyjān* (by Behrangi), 305

*Afsānahā-ye mardom*, 443 n. 19

Afshār, I., 453

Agamemnon, 118

*The Age of Alexander*, 381 n. 3

Agni, 53

Ahli of Shirāz (d. 1535), 270

Aḥmad, A., 487 n. 8

*Ahmad-e Donish*, 455 n. 2

Aḥmadi, Aḥmad Reżā (b. 1940), 344–47

Ahriman, 111; see also Angra Mainyu

*Āhu, Salander, Talhak o digarān* (by Āhu, Salander, Talhak and others), 392

*Āhu Khānom's husband* (by Afghāni), 17, 307

Ahuna Vairya prayer, 55, 56

Ahura Mazda: 5, 6, 7, 43, 46, 47, 53, 54, 55; role of, in *Vidēvdād*, 51

*Ā'in-e Akbari* (by Abu'l–Fażl 'Allāmi), 252 n. 14, 281

*Ā'ina* (newspaper), 457

*ā'in-e sharif*, see *samā*

*Ā'inahā tohist* (by M. Āzād), 338–39

Aini, Sadridden ('Ayni, Ṣadr al–Din, 1878–1954): 457–60, 463, 467–68; readings, 458; representative of the Jadids, 457; Soviet Tajik prose, pioneer of, 458

Ajax, 118

Akbar (Mughal emperor, 1556–1605), 14, 251, 281, 416

Akbarov, Iusuf, 473 n. 42

Akhavān-e Thāleth, see Omid

*Akhlāq al–ashrāf* (by 'Obayd-e Zākāni): discussion of, 227–30; objects of attack in, 229–30

*Akhlāq-e Nāṣeri*, 228 n. 12, 231–33

Ākhunzāda, 34–35, 383

Akvān, 100

Āl–e Aḥmad, Jalāl (1923–69): 34, 297, 298, 299, 303, 306, 307, 309, 310, 312 n. 42, 314, 315, 316, 332, 354, 494 n. 25; his opinion of Hedāyat, 326; his works discussed, 301–02

'Alavi, Bozorg (b. 1904): 297, 298, 299, 300, 301, 313; *Chashmhāyash*, discussion of, 34

*'Alaviyya Khānom* (by Hedāyat), 296, 320

*Alefbā* (literary magazine), 306

Alexander the Great, 189

*Alexander Romance* (by Pseudo-Callisthenes), 162

Algar, H., 383 n. 10

'Ali Shir Navā'i, 177, 270

Allahu Akbar (the pass), 220

Allberry, C. R. C., 62 n. 13

*alōpēx*, 68

*Amān-e Afghān*, 439, 440

Amānallāh, King (1919–29), 438

Amāni (11th cent. poet), 164

American objectivist poets, 343

Amesha Spentas, 47

Amin al–Dowla (governor of Isfahan), 287 n. 117

Amini, Y. (Maftun), 344

Amir 'Ali Shir, see 'Ali Shir

Amir Kabir, 308

Amir Khosrow of Delhi (d. 1325): 13, 140, 250, 251, 405, 407–12; epics of, 408–09; and Indian style, 408, 412; literary style of, 171; musical skills of, 174; mystical thought and, 176; Neẓāmi, compared to, 171; his works discussed, 170–71

528

# Index

# Index

Isolde, 165
*Istoriia persidsko–tadzhikskoi literatury,* 79 n. 6
Iusufov, K., 471 n. 36
*izads* (Zoroastrian deities), 8

Jabbāri, A., 311 n. 40
Jadidism, 457
Jāghori, Solaimān 'Ali, 446
Jahāngir, Mughal emperor (1605–1628), 14, 104, 251, 416
Jāḥeẓ, 12 n. 9
*jalāl* (majesjty), 223, 426
*Jalāl Ekrāmi,* 471 n. 37
Jalāli Era (Maleki), 150
*jamāl* (beauty), 223
Jamāli Kanboh, 411
Jamālzāda, Moḥammad 'Ali (b. 1892): 240–42, 245, 246, 294, 295, 299, 300, 301, 302, 307, 310, 312, 322, 328, 494 n. 25; his works discussed, 292–93; *Yeki bud, yeki nabud,* 33–34
Jāmi (d. 1492): 28, 144, 164, 175, 176, 191, 257, 277, 280, 282 n. 102, 411, 414, 482; his works discussed, 175–76
Jamshid, 47, 91, 94, 97, 104, 111, 114, 119, 154
*jānān* (beloved), 133
*Jāneshin* (The successor, 1970), see Sā'edi
Jannati 'Aṭā'i, 383 n. 11
Javādi, Ḥasan, 355 n. 8, 368 n. 5
*Jāvedāna Forugh Farrokhzād,* 367 n. 3
*Jāvid-nāma* (by Iqbal), 60 n. 9, 425–26
*Jawāme' al–ḥekāyāt* (Compendium of anecdotes, by 'Owfi), 407
*jenās* (homophony), 19, 269, 270
Jerusalem, 3
Jesus: 133; compared to Mani, 58; as *dāmād roshn,* 67; imagery for, 67–68; mentioned in Mani's *Epistles,* 64; relation to Mani's teachings, 60
*Jijak 'Ali Shāh,* 30, 242 n. 62
John XXIII, 191
Jonayd, 175
Jones, Sir William, 217, 225, 481, 483, 488 n. 10
*Jong-e Eṣfahān,* 306, 307
Joseph, 133

journalism: as instrument of social change, 33; role in development of contemporary language, 36
Jovayni, Shams al–Din, 216
Joyce, James, 328
"Juniper, The" (by Grimm), 330
*Jupiter Symphony,* 398, 401
*Juy o divār o teshna* (Stream and wall and thirst, 1967–68, by Golestān), 302–03

*Kabul,* 442
Kabul University, 442
"Kaddish" (Ginsberg), 347
Kaempfer, Engelbert, 216
Kafka, Franz, 322, 333, 399
*Kalāgh* (The Crow, by Bayżā'i), 392
*Kalamāt al–Sho'arā',* 260 n. 48
*Kalāta gol* (The flower hamlet, 1961), see Sā'edi
Kalidasa, 37
*Kalila and Demna,* 33
Kalim (d. 1651–1652), 28, 144, 259, 260, 262, 264, 267, 275, 415–16
Kamāl Kajkuli, 270
Kamāl al–Molk (d. 1938), 298
Kāmshād, Ḥasan, 226 n. 2, 291 n. 1, 294 n. 7, 295 n. 9, 318 n. 1, 325, 325 n. 8, 335, 383 n. 9, 494 n. 24
Kansaya Sea, 56
Kapuscinski, G., 320 n. 2
*karagöz* (Turkish plays), 382
Kāran, 164
Karbalā, 238, 279, 382
*kārgāh-e namāyesh* (theater workshop), 384
Karimi–Ḥakkāk, Aḥmad, 494 n. 25
Karim Khān Zand, 216
Kāshān, 239
*Kāshāna'i barāye shab* (A house for the night, by Ebrahimi), 306
Kāshāni, Sanjar, 257
Kāshghar, 215
Kasrā'i, 358
Kasravi, Aḥmad (1890–1946), 298
*Kāteb al–asrār,* 194
Kātebi (d. 1435), 270
Kathiawar, 215
Kāva, 119

542

# Index

# Index

## DATE DUE

| | |
|---|---|
| | |
| | |
| | |
| | |
| | |
| | |
| | |
| | |
| | |
| | |
| | |
| | |
| | |
| | |
| | |
| | |

The Library Store     #47-0106